THE OPEN LEARNING FOUNDATION

An Active Learning Approach

Business Functions

Blackwell Publishers

THE OPEN LEARNING FOUNDATION

An Active Learning Approach

BUSINESS FUNCTIONS

Lynne Butel, Tony Curtis,
Jacqueline McIntyre,
Jim Pearce, Stephen Rainbow,
David Smith,
Christine Swales

Blackwell Publishers

Editorial Offices:
108 Cowley Road, Oxford OX4 1JF, UK
Tel: +44 (0)1865 791100
Osney Mead, Oxford OX2 0EL, UK
Tel: +44 (0)1865 206206
Blackwell Publishing USA, 350 Main Street, Malden, MA 02148-5018, USA
Tel: +1 781 388 8250
Iowa State University Press, a Blackwell Publishing company, 2121 S. State Avenue, Ames, Iowa 50014-8300, USA
Tel: +1 515 292 0140
Blackwell Munksgaard, Nørre Søgade 35, PO Box 2148, Copenhagen, DK-1016, Denmark
Tel: +45 77 33 33 33
Blackwell Publishing Asia, 54 University Street, Carlton, Victoria 3053, Australia
Tel: +61 (0)3 9347 0300
Blackwell Verlag, Kurfürstendamm 57, 10707 Berlin, Germany
Tel: +49 (0)30 32 79 060
Blackwell Publishing, 10, rue Casimir Delavigne, 75006 Paris, France
Tel: +331 5310 3310

First published 1998 by Blackwell Publishers Ltd
Reprinted 1999 (twice), 2000 (twice), 2001, 2002

Library of Congress Cataloging-in-Publication Data has been applied for.

ISBN 0–631–20177–7

A catalogue record for this title is available from the British Library.

Set in 10 on 12pt Times New Roman
Printed and bound in Great Britain by MPG Books Ltd, Bodmin, Cornwall

For further information on
Blackwell Publishers visit our website:
www.blackwellpublishers.co.uk

Acknowledgements

For the Open Learning Foundation

Martin Gibson, *Series Editor*

Christine Swales, *Co-author and Editorial Adviser*

Maurice Benington, *Open Learning Editor*

Paul Stirner, (DSM Partnership), *Copy Editor*

John Naylor (Liverpool John Moores University), *Reviewer*

Leslie Mapp, *Director of Programmes*

Stephen Moulds, (DSM Partnership), *Production Manager*

Caroline Pelletier, *Publishing Manager*

Julia Peart, *Programmes Assistant*

The Open Learning Foundation wish to thank Tim Gutteridge for his assistance in publishing this title.

Copyright acknowledgements

Contents

GUIDE FOR STUDENTS

Course introduction

Welcome to Business Functions. The objectives of this guide are:

- to give you an outline of the subject of Business Functions
- to explain why it is important for you to study business functions as part of your degree
- to describe the nature of the material on which this workbook is based
- to outline the programme which you will be following
- to offer practical hints and advice on how to study business functions using the open learning approach
- to point out some of the advantages to you of studying business functions by the method used in this book.

What is included in Business Functions?

Business Functions presents an introductory over-view of the study of business organisations. It covers material one would normally expect to encounter in the first year of an undergraduate business studies degree.

We will be examining business organisations in terms of their missions and values, their structures and cultures and the key organisational processes which underpin business activity. Although organisations are essentially unique, they also share common features which are explored in detail. We also present a number of basic models for analysing business organisations and their performance. Business organisations can only be fully understood if we know how they interact with their environments and the text presents a number of ideas for analysing their interaction with their competitors, their markets and the wider set of prevailing circumstances which influence business performance.

The text considers some of the functional areas of business in particular depth and there are separate units devoted for instance to marketing, human resource management, logistics and operations management. Our aim in each case is to help you to understand their separate contribution to business performance but also to understand that ultimately business success depends on the integrated performance of all the functional areas of business. Finally we return to a more general analysis when in the final units we explore the importance of the planning and the strategy formation processes.

You will find that many of the ideas explored here are developed in greater detail in the other volumes in this series. For example there are separate modules on Marketing, Human Resource Management, and Strategic Management, corresponding more closely to the treatment one would encounter at levels 2 and 3 of an undergraduate business degree.

Why study Business Functions?

As we have already indicated, Business Functions provides an introduction to much of what will come later in your business studies and it lays the foundations for many of the theories, models, ideas, and concepts which will be developed in more depth in later modules. Business organisations increasingly require employees who are flexible and can make a contribution in many different aspects of the business, not just one. The days of the narrow specialist, concentrating on only one dimension of the business, are receding into the past. Line managers are increasingly having to take on some of the responsibilities of the human resource specialist, while managers in all functional areas need a working knowledge of effective marketing and need to be able to contribute to the process through their own specialist contributions. And increasingly, all business functions, whether it be design, training, production or whatever, need to be able to measure and justify their performance in terms of their contribution to the overall strategy of the business. In this respect, a broad understanding of the different functional areas and how they interact is a vital basis for an understanding of business and for building a business career.

What is in this workbook?

The workbook is divided into nine study units. These were written specifically for undergraduate business students by authors who are experienced in teaching such courses. Business Functions is designed as part of a series of interactive texts designed to cover the entire curriculum of an undergraduate Business Studies degree. It can be used by itself or in conjunction with other volumes in the series.

The units are particularly useful to students who may be following a course where an 'open learning' approach is being adopted. The features which make it particularly suitable for open learning include:

- Very careful sequencing of the materials so that there is a clear and logical progression;
- A step-by-step approach so that you will be able to understand each new point thoroughly before proceeding to the next one;
- A very clear layout with relatively short sections and paragraphs;
- Numerous short case studies and examples which help to illustrate the ideas and provide opportunities for analysis and developing understanding;
- Lots of opportunities for you to check that you understand what you have just read;
- Review activities for each unit which enable you to extend and apply your knowledge, as well as to test your understanding;
- Plenty of opportunities for you to test your progress through end-of-unit exercises to which solutions are provided.

Students on more conventional courses will also find that the workbook provides a useful supplement to other text books which they may have been recommended.

Although the workbook is designed to be complete in itself, your understanding of business subjects will be improved by wider reading. Each unit therefore has a list of recommended reading to guide you towards the more important and useful literature. In studying business functions in particular, you are encouraged to read the quality business newspapers and journals on a regular basis. This will enable you to seek out examples of the issues and ideas explored in this book, gain a wider and contemporary understanding of business in practice and consider for yourself the validity of the ideas presented here.

Using the workbook

You will probably find it most effective to work through the units in sequence. You should begin by noting the points which the unit outlines identify as the crucial aspects of the material. This will put the contents of the units into context and guide you through them.

Each unit is interspersed with a number of activities and review activities. All of these are intended to be attempted by you as they arise and should be completed before you move on. The suggested solutions to each activity or commentaries about them are given immediately following the activity. The solutions to the review activities are given at the end of the relevant unit.

The activities are intended to be a combination of a check that you are following the unit and understanding it on the one hand, and a way of making your learning a more active experience for you, on the other. By working through the activities, you can effectively divide your study time between that necessary for taking on new ideas and that which is necessary to reinforce those ideas. The review activities allow you to consider larger sections of material, testing and extending your understanding.

The self-assessment questions are intended to give you the opportunity to see whether you have really grasped the content of the unit. The additional exercises are intended to give you further practice and the opportunity to reinforce your knowledge and understanding. Avoid the temptation to skip through the exercises quickly. They are there to assist you in developing your knowledge and understanding and your confidence with the material.

Typically, the activities will only take you a few minutes to deal with. By contrast, the review activities may take considerably longer to complete. It is important that you discipline yourself to complete each activity, self-assessment question or exercise before you refer to the answer provided.

Avoid rote learning

You should avoid any attempt at rote learning the material in this workbook. You should aim to understand the underlying 'logic' in the ideas being presented by working through all the activities. Simply trying to learn the theories or remember the techniques is inappropriate and insufficient. Rather, you should attempt to understand the principles behind the theoretical ideas and models or understand the thinking behind the particular techniques presented.

Given the complexity of the subject matter which forms the focus of the study of business, it is rarely possible to present single solutions to problems. By working with the ideas, thinking about their implications and how they can be applied, you will develop a deeper understanding of them than if you simply attempt to commit them to memory.

Set aside time for your studies

At the start of the study period you will not know how long it will take to do the necessary work. It is sensible therefore, to make a start on the work at an early stage in the study period. Try to discipline yourself to set aside particular times in the week to study, though not necessarily the same times each week. Experiment with different ways of studying the material to find the one which suits you. Try skimming each unit to get a grasp of the ideas covered before you go through it in detail. Alternatively, try reading the unit objectives and the summaries before you settle down to study the unit in any depth. Try to find the most suitable time to study when your concentration is at its highest and interruptions are at a minimum. And do set aside sufficient time to complete all the activities - they are a crucial part of the learning process.

INTRODUCTION TO THE MODULE

This module serves as a basic introduction to organisations, their characteristic features and the fundamental functions that form part of their normal operations. In the first three units, we identify some key commonalities and differences between organisations which we put into context in their immediate competitive industrial environments and the wider business environment. We then look at the basic functions that every organisation performs in the following four units. In the final two units, we bring together all the functions and the overall objectives of the organisation in developing a business strategy, and in implementing this strategy through planning and the technique of project management. This module gives a very broad coverage of how an organisation operates in the business world, in other modules you will go on to study particular areas in more detail. Here, we simply highlight some key features and activities.

In the first unit, The Nature of Organisations, we start by answering some basic questions about an organisation – what it is and what it does. We examine the roles of the mission and organisational objectives and how they affect the organisation as a whole. We look at some legal structures and a number of organisational structures and structural changes that occur with growth. We use the transformation model with particular inputs and outputs and we use Porter's value chain to develop our ideas about what an organisation does. Using Porter's basic primary and support activities, we identify a number of functions that are common to all organisations. We extend these general comments into a detailed analysis in the rest of the module. We look briefly at the important roles that culture, information and communication play in an organisation.

Every organisation operates in a constantly changing business environment. This is our topic in Unit 2, The Business Environment. We identify the key aspects of the political, economic, social and technological environments and see how we can use this information in a technique for analysing the environment – PEST analysis. These environments are overlapping and interlinking and some environmental changes cannot be fitted neatly into one specific area. We need to understand an organisation's environment so we can react to and anticipate any changes that will affect success by providing a new opportunity or a threat to operation. Monitoring the environment is a time-consuming and complex activity; here we give you some ideas of the continuing demands on businesses as they are required to respond to anything from a European directive on staffing to a teenage fashion fad.

In the next unit, Competition and Change, we look at the environment closest to the organisation – the competitive or industrial environment. We can see overlapping areas between the organisation and the competitive environment. One key component is the organisation's stakeholders. These determine the direction the organisation takes, what it does and how it does it. We investigate this power and any conflicts that might arise between different parties.

Porter identifies five competitive forces within an industry and we use his model to detail changes and responses in the competitive environment. Using this model and the PEST analysis from Unit 2, we can conduct a full environmental analysis. We can investigate the organisational response to any changes in the environment and how this response is formulated into competitive strategies. The managing of change and dealing with resistance to change become important activities in an organisation's response to its environment and in achieving and maintaining competitive advantage. In the final section of this unit we summarise some key trends in business today.

In the next units, we look at some key functions – marketing, operations management, logistics and human resource management – in some detail. In Unit 4, Marketing we identify the customer as a key issue and marketing as a key primary activity in defining the product to meet the customer's needs in a particular market. We investigate the activities that marketing carries out to achieve competitive advantage through delivering to the customer the right product in the right place at the right time at the right price.

In Unit 5, Operations and Operations Management, we look at another primary activity. We extend operations to the slightly broader concept of all processes that concern how products are made and delivered to the customer. This concerns inbound and outbound logistics and procurement. This is obviously the core of the organisation, whether it is providing a service or a product. In Unit 6, Logistics, we look at some particular aspects of operations that concern managing the flow of materials through the organisation to the customer. It is an area of topical interest as the success of just-in-time supply, supply chain management and other innovations can be crucial in achieving competitive advantage. We look at logistics in action in a factory situation.

In Unit 7, Human Resource Management, we look at people as one of the key inputs to the business organisation and also as an element in all functional areas. An organisation's workforce can be regarded as its biggest asset. Work and education patterns have changed and there is a continuing requirement for a flexible, multiskilled workforce. We look at employee resourcing, training and development and employee relations.

We then bring all functions together in Unit 8, Business Strategy. We reconsider some of our earlier discussions about the organisation's mission and how this drives or is driven by organisational objectives. We investigate levels of strategy and how operational and functional strategies achieve corporate strategy. An organisation needs to respond to environmental changes, develop strategies and implement them. Implementing change requires careful management, especially because of the human aspects of any change. In Unit 9, Business Planning and Project Management, we look briefly at how strategy leads into business planning and at one technique, project management, that can be used both for implementing the business plan and in other functional areas, particularly operations. You develop a business plan for an organisation and practise its implementation through project management.

This module should give you an overall introduction to organisations in business. Through it, you should be able to see the individual contributions of each function and how they work together in achieving competitive advantage. Profit, quality and service become issues for each function and for the organisation as a whole.

UNIT 1
THE NATURE OF ORGANISATIONS

Introduction

In the developed world, the nature of business, the way we live and work depends on other people. Generally these other people and their activities are co-ordinated into organisations that affect every aspect of our daily life. The food we eat, the clothes we wear, the education we receive, the travel we undertake, the roads we drive on, the money we earn, the tax we pay, in fact everything that we do is underpinned by the work of organisations. These include governments, small street traders and large multi-nationals, employing many thousands of individuals. Every organisation is unique and operates in its own unique way. The way that an organisation operates varies with its type of business, the goods it produces and the services it provides, the raw materials it uses, its ownership, its environment, its size, its complexity, and its legal structure. There are many variable factors that affect how an organisation arranges its structure and operating systems, but there are also issues, problems and other characteristics common to all organisations.

In this first unit, we identify what organisations are and what they do and examine their key features. All organisations have a purpose – to meet the needs of their customers and clients in some way. They have to be aware of customers and clients and their needs and to work out how to deliver what the customers and clients want, at a price they are prepared to pay. In addition, an organisation has to meet the needs of all its interested parties or stakeholders, as well as society as a whole. We look first at what is common to all organisations and examine a model that helps us analyse the process of producing goods and services. This model looks at the whole process of transforming raw materials, or inputs, into goods and services, or outputs. This transformation model provides the basis for our further investigation of organisations.

We look at the changes that happen with the growth of an organisation. The organisational structure concerns the way in which the activities of the members are grouped together for the purposes of co-ordination. We study some of the factors that affect the choice of structure and some of the different ways of structuring an organisation. We look at some basic legal structures that organisations use. These provide a framework for their activities. We look at the business functions that form components of our transformation model, and we examine each function in detail in the rest of the module.

Every organisation has a unique culture. Within each body, members will have values, assumptions and attitudes, which result in a set of formal and informal rules, patterns of dress and language, ways of working and relating to other members of the organisation and other stakeholders. Various aspects of culture are derived from national cultural characteristics, other aspects from the main organisational stakeholders and from the organisation's purpose or mission. We will observe some of the factors that influence organisational culture, and see how culture influences the organisation.

Essential elements of organisation are information and communication. Information provides the basis for all decisions, from the amount and type of a product to produce and raw materials to buy, to the selection of employees and their development; it identifies the changes taking place in the business environment and possible adaptations the organisation should make. Managing this information is now a key factor in competing and succeeding. Communication enables management to set goals and to direct, control and co-ordinate activities.

In order to succeed in a competitive environment, an organisation needs to be effective and efficient. To be effective, an organisation must make the products or deliver the service that its customers or clients want, where and when they want it. To be efficient, an organisation's activities must be done well so that acceptable prices can be charged to make profits. How an organisation structures and co-ordinates its activities is important in achieving this success. The strategy of an organisation provides a blueprint for the way that it operates in order to achieve its objectives in an effective and efficient manner. The culture of an organisation and the roles that information and communication take enable strategy to be implemented and any changes managed.

In Units 2 and 3, we will place the organisation in the context of its environment. Unit 2 considers the general environment that affects all organisations. Unit 3 looks at the specific competitive industrial environment that an organisation experiences. To remain competitive, effective and efficient, an organisation has to adjust to these continually changing environments. It needs to take into account new competitors, new rules and regulations, a changing marketplace, changing workforce, and many other factors. We look at how the organisation takes the first step in making these adjustments by monitoring and analysing the environment. In the following units, we go on to look at the individual functions and areas that an organisation has to address, how they contribute to competitive advantage and how they need to be co-ordinated into the organisation as a whole.

Objectives

By the end of this unit, you will be able to:

- analyse and describe the basic features of organisations
- understand the fundamental role of the mission and organisational objectives
- evaluate the activity of an organisation in terms of an input–output system
- identify how changes in size affect an organisation
- identify the main organisational structures
- explain the legal structures that apply to organisations
- identify the main functional areas of an organisation
- identify the main features of organisational culture
- analyse the impact of national cultures on organisations
- describe the effects of culture in organisations

- explain the information needs of organisations and how organisations satisfy those needs
- identify the importance of information and communication.

SECTION 1

Organisations in Business

Introduction

As a starting point for our discussions about the individual business functions of organisations, we look at some overall features. What are organisations? Why do they exist? What do they do? Why and how do they grow? First, we define what is meant by 'an organisation', then we use a model in which inputs are transformed into outputs and each organisation is part of a value chain. Throughout this module, although we tend to talk about products, our discussions apply equally to services. You will find it helpful to try to identify the features and functions in a service organisation. We also tend to talk about 'business', however our comments can be applied to all organisations, including government and voluntary bodies. In some cases, for example with the change in ownership in the utility companies, previously publicly owned companies have taken on a business orientation and the distinctions have become blurred.

1.1 What is an organisation?

A good starting point is to look at a number of different organisations and see what they have in common and what makes them an organisation rather than any other form of social entity. Consider, for example, the common features of a supermarket, prison, nightclub, school, restaurant, charity, hospital, telephone company, manufacturer and church.

Organisations share several main features.

- **Clear boundaries** – We can identify who belongs to a particular organisation, which is not the case, for example, with a more fluid group of people attending a festival or attending a sporting event.
- **Stable structured relationships** – People collaborate with one another, and lines of communication are fairly well established through rules and procedures.
- **Defined and grouped tasks** – Individuals in organisations perform different tasks and have different roles.

- **Collective purpose** – The purpose of a school is to educate children; for a hospital, it is to heal the sick; for a motor manufacturing company, it is to make high-quality cars.

ACTIVITY 1

Think about your day. Spend five minutes writing down the organisations you have had interactions with – perhaps as a member, or as a customer.

Perhaps you started this morning by switching on the light, using electricity supplied by one organisation, and with a shower using water supplied by a water company. The shower equipment was manufactured by one organisation, your house or flat house was built by another, using many contractors and raw materials. You said 'Good morning' to a member of your family. You opened the post delivered by the Post Office, you received letters from your bank, the Inland Revenue and a business network, a flyer from a local restaurant and free films from a film processing lab. Then you dressed in clothes manufactured from a range of raw materials and bought either through mail order, direct from the manufacturer, or from a high street store. You ate your breakfast – tea from India, bread made from British grain, cornflakes made from American grain. You caught a bus to work. The list goes on and on.

You can identify many different types of organisation: state owned such as the Post Office, utilities such as electricity and water, now privately owned but state regulated, and commercial organisations of all types. You purchased many products – your home, food and clothes – from a number of sources. Here, you are acting as a consumer. At work or university, you are a member of an organisation. But what about your family? This is not an organisation, as you will see.

Organisations are doing something, adding value at their link in the chain of, say, the process that converts seed to grain to bread in the chain from farmer to miller to baker to supermarket. They produce something that the next link in the chain wants and is prepared to pay for. Organisations are prepared to pay for the **added value** produced by the preceding stage, rather than take in a rawer input and doing it themselves, but the product has to meet the needs of the customer all the way along the chain. The final customer, the 'consumer', buys and eats the bread. (It is worth noting that the final customer might not actually be the consumer; a parent, for example, will buy breakfast cereal for the child who is then the consumer.)

There are many ways of defining an organisation. Consider this definition:

> An organisation is a clearly bounded group of people who pursue separate co-ordinated and formally structured activities which together contribute to a common goal.

One essential element of an organisation is a common purpose to which the activities of all members are directed. A crowd on a beach are all there to enjoy the sun, but are they an organisation? No, people may be there to get a suntan, but this is an individual purpose in the company of others – we don't depend on anyone else to get the tan.

Another element of every organisation is the co-ordination of the activities of a number of people. So, a one-person business, a gardener, for example, is not an organisation since no co-ordination of people is needed. And this would be another reason why the crowd on a beach is not an organisation – their activities are not co-ordinated.

If you look at your list of daily activities, you can see that in our modern world most activities would be impossible to do on your own. Self-sufficiency might seem an ideological goal, but in reality is virtually impossible. Yes, you could collect water from a stream, if you lived in the mountains perhaps; but generally speaking you need the water company to supply water to your tap, you need the bus manufacturer and travel company to supply the bus to get you to work, and the cornflake manufacturer to supply cornflakes from the corn grown in the American farmer's fields to your breakfast table. Perhaps you could grow your own food in particular circumstances, however, in today's developed world, very few people are self-sufficient for food, energy and raw materials.

Imagine building a car or a house on your own, supplying all the raw materials and doing everything yourself. An individual does not have all the necessary skills, resources, physical energy and strength. So we need to work with other people in co-operative endeavour to achieve what would be impossible for people to do individually. This does not mean that in an organisation every single task has to be done within the organisation – the milk packager does not have to make the milk carton, it probably buys in the milk and the carton, for example, and may also contract out its cleaning or accounting. Consider the basic input as milk: this is transformed to output, cartons for sale to the customer via various marketing and distribution activities. At all stages, various activities are done within the organisation or are contracted out.

Most of your daily activities are undertaken as a consumer. But you might also be a member of a church, a professional organisation, college or social club. You might be an employee of an organisation, or perhaps you have become another type of stakeholder – a shareholder – following your building society's floatation on the stock exchange. Perhaps you work for a bank or a building society that lends money to other businesses. We examine the various different stakeholders involved in an organisation and their roles in Unit 3. A stakeholder is any party that has an interest in the organisation – as a member, a customer or a supplier, for example.

The range of organisations that you meet every day will encompass a range of legal and organisational structures. We look at these in more detail later in the unit. All organisations have to operate within a legal structure; the business world would break down without rules and regulations, and without the guidelines from professional associations, government bodies and regulators that regulate an organisation's behaviour.

There are many ways of structuring an organisation so that it carries out its basic transformation process efficiently and effectively. These affect and are dependent on procedures, staffing, management, communication, control, decision making and technology.

OBJECTIVES AND MISSION

An organisation exists to do something. Why does it exist? What does it exist for? What does it want to achieve? These are all part of an organisation's mission. The mission of an organisation is also likely to encapsulate its basic values and beliefs. In Unit 3, we look at an organisation's mission from the perspectives of the key stakeholders who drive it, its relationship with culture and with the approach that an organisation has to take towards changes in its environment. A company needs to identify what it is doing, how it wants to operate and why it is in business, before it can set a strategy, and then draw up and implement the business plan. We come back to this later in Unit 8, when we start to build an organisation's strategy. This strategy needs to include business objectives; it also needs a mission statement, which encapsulates the values of the organisation and its stakeholders.

A mission identifies what the company is in business to do and how it is going to do it. It is likely to include issues such as quality, value, service to customers, worldwide position, achieving a leading edge, being environmentally sensitive, and satisfying all stakeholders. It may be the vision of the owners. Bill Gates, for example, says about Microsoft: 'Microsoft was founded on my vision of a personal computer on every desk and in every home.' From the mission we can generate the business objectives. These are likely to be much more focused than the mission. They should be realistic and measurable in terms of the company's performance. They are likely to include things such as overall profit, market share, value added per employee, return on investment for shareholders, growth on turnover, and set targets to be achieved to a timescale. A statement of business objectives that includes this level of detail might not be released to shareholders and competitors; an open published statement is likely to be more vague and not so measurable. An organisation should fulfil its mission if it achieves its objectives in an ongoing manner.

You will find varying terminology used by organisations to describe the essence of what they do; it might be a formal mission, a vision as in that of Microsoft, a commitment or a goal. These might be anything from rather vague aspirations to very precise and measurable statements. Companies might identify their mission in a promise, as SmithKline Beecham does:

> '... healthcare is our purpose. Through our scientific excellence and commercial expertise we provide products and services throughout the world that promote health and well being. The source of our competitive advantage is the energy and ideas of our people. Our strength lies in what we value: customers, innovation, integrity, people, performance ... a 'simply better' healthcare company, as judged by all those we serve: customers, shareholders, employees and the global community'.

The missions of state services are more difficult to identify as they are restricted by funding and by law. Consider the following: 'The goal of the State of Jersey Police is to provide the best quality of policing to the community and to foster their active co-operation in the quest to enhance the quality of life in the Island.' There is nothing here that is measurable, but it presents how the police wish to appear to the public. Note here the word used is 'goal', meaning the overall goal of the organisation. There will be operational goals at different levels.

As you will see in Unit 8, we can view the mission as an internal means of communicating with staff, as an external means of communicating with the public in terms of PR and as a basis for measurable objectives in terms of organisational performance.

An organisation does not operate in isolation; it has a number of **stakeholders** – customers, employees, shareholders, pressure groups, government bodies – that all affect its operation at various levels and with varying power. It is dependent on a range of variables: other organisations for supplies, the workforce, the supply of money, the political and legal environment. An organisation operates in an environment that is continually changing; it has an immediate environment and it has a more general one – the industrial, national, international, geographical, social and political arena. We investigate these in Units 2 and 3. As its environment changes, so must the organisation if it is to be and remain successful. Change in the business world is a fact of life. We all change; our needs and wants change; nations change; the world changes and continually develops, offering new opportunities and taking away old ones. This means all kinds of change for the organisation: how it functions, how it is structured, the products, the markets, the inputs, the transformation process, the outputs, everything to do with what it does. An organisation achieves and maintains competitive advantage by keeping pace with change in its environment.

1.2 What do organisations do?

An organisation creates goods and services that are wanted by its customers. The customer may not be the end consumer of a particular product or service, but could be an organisation or individual at any of the different stages that go into the supply chain. Organisations create value that their customers want and are prepared to pay for, either directly or indirectly. They **add value** to all the inputs they use; if they did not add any value in what they were doing then there would not be any point in doing it and nobody would be prepared to buy the product or service. These inputs are raw materials, semi-finished goods, capital equipment, labour, land and property.

Figure 1 illustrates a basic input–output relationship for an organisation. It takes a number of inputs and adds value by processing the inputs and producing an output that is available for sale. This may then become the input to another organisation. The group of activities involved in getting from raw materials and other resources through to the final customer is called the **value system**, as each step or organisation in the system adds value to the product for which it receives the inputs of money necessary to fund all the other inputs. The set of activities carried out by a particular company within the value system form the **value chain** of that particular organisation. The collection of organisations involved in the activities required to produce a final product or service is known as the **supply chain**. The final product could be your new computer, or a sandwich you ate at lunch time, or the books you borrowed from your local library, or the money you took out of your bank account.

This final product is dependent on all the links in the supply chain, since any one organisation within that system will only be as good as the rest, so an organisation needs to look at all the links in its chain of suppliers and distributors as well as its internal operations. The shop where you bought your sandwich may be convenient, efficient and clean, but if the meat that made the sandwich was poor, or came from a supplier who did not keep the meat well, then the end result will be unsatisfactory. The shop has made the final stage possible, selling the product to the customer, but it is totally dependent on the other organisations in the chain for the quality of the product that it sells.

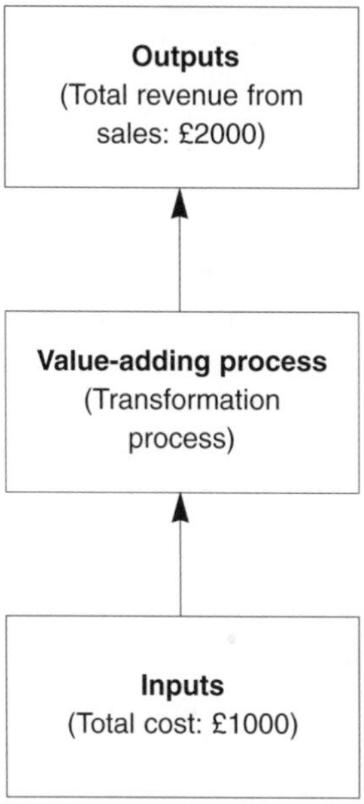

Figure 1: Inputs and outputs in the value-adding process

From Figure 1 you can see that the value of the output is more than the combination of the inputs, due to the value-adding process.

We need to provide some basic definitions of terms used in this model.

- **Costs** – the expense of producing a specified output. This includes the outlay for all the inputs: raw materials, energy costs, property costs and labour costs.
- **Price** – the sum of money asked for a specified commodity or service. If the organisation cannot get a price that is higher than the costs of

production, it will not make a profit. The total revenue from sales – the outputs – obviously depends on the price; the costs of the inputs depends on the prices charged by the previous supplier in the chain.

- **Value** – a subjective evaluation of **what something is worth.** This may be less than the price, it may even be less than the cost. Goods and services will only be purchased if the value is perceived by the potential customer, at the time of purchase, to be greater than or equal to the price asked. In purchasing a ready-made sandwich, you are balancing the value to you at a particular time with the price and the convenience. On one occasion, you might be very busy, say travelling to a meeting, and be prepared to pay for a sandwich purchased at a garage when you stop for petrol; on another occasion, you might be at home and have the time and ingredients to make a sandwich and you would not make any effort to go out and buy one.

An organisation takes inputs – raw materials, money, human resources and equipment – and makes outputs of goods and services that are then sold back to consumers: people are both producers and consumers. In the private sector, there is a circular flow of money as consumers spend money on products that they value, which goes into the organisations to create the product. People buy goods if the value to them is greater than the price.

Public sector organisations are funded by governments. They tend to provide outputs that the whole community collectively values, even those who do not use these products or services directly themselves. Through the UK tax system, for example, we pay for education, roads, hospitals, the police, the fire service, prisons, etc. You may not have to call out the fire brigade for a fire at your home – indeed, you hope that you never have to do so – but you are happy to have the service available to society. In this way, the value in publicly provided goods is estimated via the political process – the extent to which individuals support political parties and pressure groups that favour the provision of publicly provided goods and services. Some public services, such as road maintenance, are contracted out to private companies, but the funding still comes from the public purse. Other public sector organisations engage in joint ventures with the private sector, as is the case with quangos such as Training and Education Councils (TECs). Many previously public sector organisations, such as British Rail and British Gas, have now been privatised, so are subject to the competitive marketplace and also to regulation by government bodies that protect the consumer. This has meant that the boundaries between public and private sector organisations have become blurred.

ORGANISATIONAL PERFORMANCE

Organisational **effectiveness** is the extent to which organisational objectives have been met. If the business objectives have been poorly or inappropriately set, or badly measured, then the organisation will not be very effective. If it is producing the wrong output for its consumers' needs, then it will not meet those needs and it is ineffective. **Efficiency** is the extent to which the organisation is able to produce maximum outputs from the lowest level of inputs – people, raw materials, money, etc. It is usually measured by some kind of cash value being put on a unit production cost. Many organisations include efficiency in their target objectives. **Economy** is an even narrower measure and is the total value of the resources that an organisation uses. To be economical, an organisation must use fewer resources throughout its business; but, although an organisation could become more economical by reducing the cost of all its inputs, it may actually become *less* efficient if this leads to a drop in output, thus increasing the unit production cost.

These three measures need balancing. Effectiveness is the key measure, since it directs the organisation's activities to its outputs and hence its customers. No matter how efficient or economical a company is in producing something, if that something is wrong for its market in some way, whether, price, quality or function, then the organisation is not successful.

CASE STUDY

Jill's Jewellery

Jill went to art college and made jewellery, which she sold to her friends, from semi-precious stones that she bought cheaply while travelling in the Far East and India. When she left college, she worked from home, making highly individual pieces that she sold to a local gift shop. Gradually, her name became known as an interesting designer and she was able to sell her wares in a number of outlets. Eventually, she decided to put some money that her grandmother had left her into a small workshop and retail counter that she called Jill's Jewellery. She established the shop initially with just herself and part-time help, and then, as her business expanded, she hired two full-time staff, one to help on the sales side and one to help her on the assembly of the jewellery. She uses an accountant to do her books and a cleaner to clean the shop every day.

ACTIVITY 2

Identify and list the inputs, outputs and transformation process in the value chain of Jill's Jewellery. How would you measure effectiveness, efficiency and economy.

Jill's inputs are the raw materials of stones, settings, equipment, premises, labour, finance; the transformation process of cutting stones, mounting and soldering turns these inputs into jewellery products, which are the outputs that are sold to the end customer.

Jill can measure the effectiveness by the sales of individual items and lines; maybe the customers like her amethyst and silver brooches, but she can't sell her amethyst and gold earrings. Her efficiency is measured by the unit cost of production of each jewellery item; efficiency might be increased by careful use of raw materials, so minimising waste. Her economy is a measure of all her resources, including the inputs for the transformation process, her overheads and the costs of all aspects of her business. Measures of economy might be to hire a cleaner at a cheaper hourly rate to do the everyday cleaning rather than use her own time or that of a more expensive salesperson.

1.3 Organisations as systems

We can consider an organisation in terms of our simple model: input–transformation–output. An extension of this model focuses on the organisation as a system. A **system** is a collection of interacting parts, connected together in a significant way. Other features include **holism**, which means that the system as a whole behaves as more than the sum of its parts, and **hierarchy**, which means that systems are divided into parts that are also systems. Holism results from the nature and quality of interactions between the parts. In a sports team, for example, it could result from team spirit, shared understandings, and the level of anticipation between players that makes the team more than just a set of individuals.

Some examples of systems are the digestive system in the human body and the system of photosynthesis in plants. In each of these examples, different parts of the organism work together to transform inputs into products which are then 'exported' to other parts of the body or plant. A key feature of systems is the interaction between parts. If one part of the system malfunctions, the whole is upset. There is no value in making one part of the system work superbly if this is done at the expense of other parts, because it is the collaborative working that creates the desired outcome.

SUBSYSTEMS

The elements of a system are often themselves systems, and are called subsystems. There are many different ways of breaking down the organisation into subsystems, although all the functions still have to be carried out, regardless of the model used. Tayeb (1996) identifies the major subsystems in a typical organisation as:

- production subsystem – performs the main activity of the organisation, for example the manufacturing plant, the teaching staff in a school
- boundary spanning subsystem – handles interactions with the environment, for example the marketing department, the purchasing office
- maintenance subsystem – is responsible for the smooth operation of the organisation, for example the human resource department, employees' canteen
- adaptation subsystem – is responsible for helping the organisation to adapt to changes in the environment, for example the market research or planning department
- management subsystem – is responsible for directing and co-ordinating the other subsystems, for example the board of directors, chief executive.

The integration of the subsystems is vital, just as with a car – the engine is not much use unless it is matched by a good transmission system. In section 4, we shall use the value chain concepts of Porter (1985) to explore specific subsystems of a typical organisation and how these integrate to effect the transformation processes. These subsystems are the building blocks or functions of a business and all have a specific role to play in the organisation. In addition, they interact with each other and with the outside world.

The systems view is only one way of depicting and analysing organisations, although it is a common one that you will find used in other modules. Alternative approaches attempt to liken organisations to organisms, to brains, to political systems and to instruments of domination (Morgan, 1986). And we have already begun to consider organisations as 'cultures'. These other approaches recognise the human aspects of the organisation and consider that it is the social, cultural and people aspects that control and make the machine work. We can use Porter's systems approach as a basis, but we need to take into account the people of an organisation particularly through discussion of the stakeholders, human resources and culture.

The organisational structure is determined by how the transformation system is organised, and by its subsystems and supporting activities. This sets out the formal framework of activities and relationships within the organisation, the allocation of tasks, the grouping of tasks, the lines of communication and authority, and how co-ordination and control are achieved. This framework identifies who does what, how the jobs are grouped, who reports to whom, and who has authority over whom. We look at different organisational structures in the next section.

REVIEW ACTIVITY 1

Write a broad mission statement for Jill's Jewellery. Identify some business objectives that she could formulate.

Jill obviously doesn't work in isolation, she interacts with people and other organisations as part of her everyday business. Identify the main organisations and people that come into contact with her. We might call these her main stakeholders. Can you identify any effects that they have on her business?

Don't worry if you find this activity rather difficult. As you work through the unit and the module you will learn more about these issues.

Summary

In this section, we have examined the existence of organisations, what they are, and why they exist. We investigated a basic input–output model, which gives us a starting point to investigate more of the functions that occur in an organisation.

SECTION 2

Organisational Growth and Structure

Introduction

The business environment changes, and organisations grow and diversify. It is essential to structure an organisation in a way which effectively provides a secure framework for its ever-changing activities. If an organisation grows from a single shop to a multinational company, with manufacturing and distribution in many countries, then the organisational structures must obviously evolve as well. The key problem is that most organisations are structured for what they did rather than what they will need to do. A key strategic management task is to translate the changes in aims, objectives and the environment into effective working structures. These will reflect the phases in the growth of the organisation and its behaviour. In Unit 8 we look at this whole area of strategy – including the changes in organisational structure.

2.1 Growth

Organisations are continually changing in size and shape as they react to their environment and internal changes. They may grow or reduce in complexity and/or in size. They can grow by increasing the number of people employed, the amount of resources and inputs they are using and the outputs they produce. Or they can grow in complexity, undertaking different types of work, producing a greater range of products or services. An organisation might grow, for example, if it incorporates activities currently done by other organisations, such as when a company decides to do its own distribution or marketing that previously had been done through another company. Equally, a company might choose to restrict its activities, for example by contracting out parts of its business such as distribution or catering, so that it can concentrate on its production.

ORGANISATIONAL LIFE CYCLE

The idea of an organisational life cycle is linked to the concept of growth. As it changes, an organisation develops through a typical 'life cycle' that includes birth, growth, decline and death. Not every organisation will pass through each stage or at the same rate. As the organisation passes through the stages of the life cycle, its needs will change and various features of the organisation structure will need to change. Perhaps the owner of a delicatessen specialising in cheese and smoked meats decides to open another shop in a neighbouring village; an increase of inputs of all kinds will be required: manpower, money, raw materials, etc. A new shop manager will be required and, if the owner decides to take a more overall view of management and purchasing of the business, a manager for the first shop might also be needed.

ACTIVITY 3

The life cycle of Jill's Jewellery has shown a birth and a growth phase. Make a note of some of the differences between these two phases. What changes have happened to the organisational structure? What are the changing requirements for information, communication and control?

Jill went from the birth phase, when she just made the jewellery herself and sold it to other outlets, to the growth phase. The workshop and retail counter is running with two staff and Jill is aiming to increase her turnover by 30 per cent over the next two years. Her outputs will increase and her inputs of raw materials and staff will need to increase to support this growth. Her structure changes from a very simple one, where she does everything and makes all decisions, to a simple functional one where sales and marketing are separated from production. It may be that additional staff will be required in both areas.

She will need more supplies and raw materials, so she will need more information about materials and stocks as well as more information about her final products, the lines actually made, the amount of resources used and the packaging required to go with each product. She will need information about suppliers, information about sales, information about staff – such as hours worked and shifts for the staffing of the shop – and information on her overall income and overall expenses. Jill will need to control the resources used in production, to monitor quality, reliability, staff performance and to maintain records of staff details, inland revenue accounts, etc.

In Unit 8 we re-examine the phases of growth, and the links between organisational behaviour, structure and growth, when we look at business strategy.

2.2 Growth in today's business world

We now look at three types of growth: vertical integration, horizontal integration and conglomerate diversification. For most of the twentieth century, organisations have grown in size and complexity as activities, originally sourced externally, are included in the activities of the organisation. This form of growth is called **vertical integration**. Vertical integration can either develop backwards, into the suppliers of raw materials and semi-finished goods, or forwards, through the purchase of the distribution network or retail outlets, moving closer to the final consumer. For example, Jill started to sell direct to customers from her combined workshop and retail counter, rather than selling through jewellers and gift shops. When her business increases still further in size, she might decide to buy the supplier of gemstones that she uses for most of her raw materials.

Many of the big brewers in the brewing industry have integrated vertically by buying pubs and clubs. In this way, they are in a better position to control the way in which their beer is sold, the atmosphere of the pub, its decoration and other attractions. They could also vertically integrate backwards by taking over the suppliers of some of the main inputs into brewing – the suppliers of raw materials such as yeast, hops, malt and of semi-finished products such as bottles and barrels.

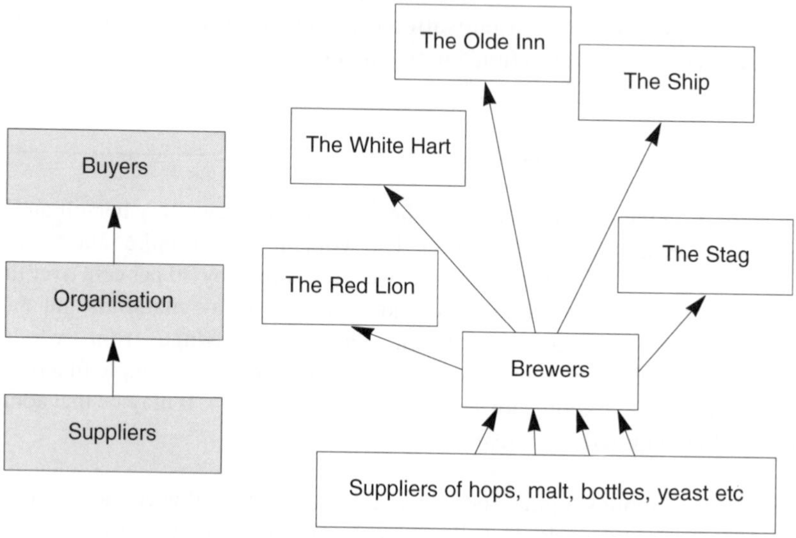

Figure 2: Vertical integration in the brewing industry

In the UK, the Monopolies and Mergers Commission (MMC) regulates the buying up of related businesses in the marketplace. It aims to protect consumer choice and acts if there is a danger of a monopoly being created. In 1989, the Monopolies and Mergers Commission examined vertical integration in the brewing industry. Breweries were buying up many of the pubs and there were very few free houses left. The MMC report concluded that this restricted the amount of choice available to such an extent that it resulted in breweries having a virtual monopoly of supply in some areas. Since then, breweries have sold off some of the pubs they owned and some pubs have been closed completely. In addition, in order to increase the choice available, those tied houses that remained in brewery ownership have offered 'guest' beers as well as beers brewed by their brewery owners. The situation in this industry is still changing; in 1995, the Office of Fair Trading launched an investigation into the prices for beer that brewers charged to their tied houses.

ACTIVITY 4

Spend five minutes listing the advantages and disadvantages of integration for breweries and for beer drinkers.

The MMC Beer Order in 1989 forced brewing firms to review their current aims and practices. This involved added cost. They were forced into changing their strategic focus by scaling down their retailing operations and concentrating on brewing. Small regional brewers and independent pub companies bought many of the pubs that were sold off. This tends to benefit beer drinkers: the brewery-owned pubs often offer a more limited range of beers and at higher prices as something of a monopoly is created.

Vertical integration has the advantage that it allows the organisation to have greater control over the quality, reliability and supply of its inputs and to oversee the way in which the product is sold to consumers. The main disadvantage is that the organisation can find its activities spread over a wide range of different goods and services, with quite different requirements. The skills required by the publican are not the same as those required by a brewer. However such integration is often justified on the grounds of the similarities of management skills and the organisation's greater access to capital markets that size confers.

Organisations also grow by increasing the size of the market for their products. This can be done gradually by winning new customers, either from competitors or by attracting those who have not used the product before. A quicker way for an organisation to increase its share of the market is to buy out competitors and absorb their market share. This is called **horizontal integration** – the take-over of other firms at the same stage of production: manufacturers buying other similar manufacturers, retailers buying retailers, etc. This is also regulated by the Monopolies and Mergers Commission.

The large profitable brewer is able to buy up smaller, perhaps less-profitable, brewers. In this way, the large brewery companies producing mass-produced beers almost squeezed out the smaller, more specialised, producers of real ale. Had it not been for the power of the consumers, embodied in the interest group the Campaign for Real Ale (CAMRA), many more small breweries would have been lost.

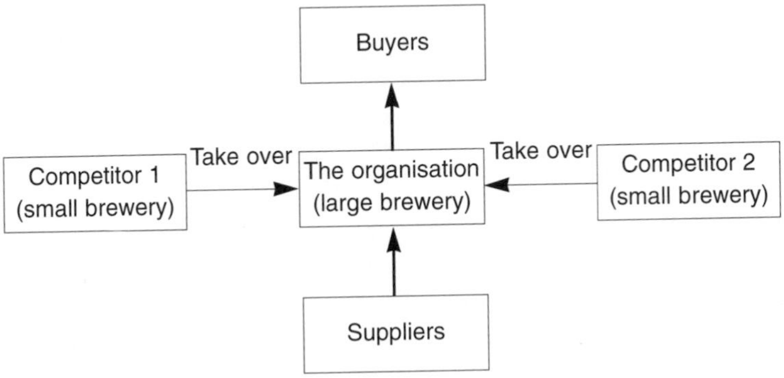

Figure 3: Horizontal integration in the brewing industry

The advantage of buying up the competition is that it reduces the influence of competitors on the organisation and, as an organisation increases the size of the market it serves, it can take advantage of **economies of scale**. This means that by buying in bulk, utilising plant and equipment cost-effectively, by minimising spare capacity and spreading overheads such as distribution costs and advertising over a larger output, the organisation can cut the average unit costs of production.

The third way in which organisations can grow is by expanding into what are apparently totally unrelated areas. The justification often given for this **conglomerate diversification** is that the managerial skills required are similar or that the businesses serve similar markets or customers. Thus, the brewery may diversify by buying a chain of opticians, a manufacturer of breakfast cereals or a newly privatised railway company.

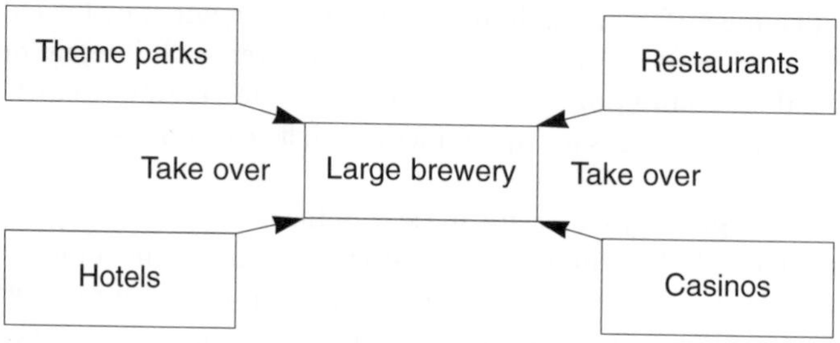

Figure 4: Conglomerate diversification or lateral integration

ACTIVITY 5

Read the Grand Metropolitan case study. Note down which of Grand Metropolitan's many acquisitions you would classify as horizontal, which vertical and which conglomerate diversification? List the advantages of being such a large diversified organisation? Can you think of any disadvantages?

CASE STUDY

Grand Metropolitan

The founder of Grand Metropolitan, Max Joseph, bought his first hotels in London, Monte Carlo, Madrid, Amsterdam, New York and Paris in 1947. Once established in the hotel business, GM began to purchase companies involved in drinks, food, catering and pubs, including Express Dairies and the Chef and Brewer pub-restaurants and off licences in the 1960s. A further development occurred in the 1970s, with the purchase of Mecca bingo and dance halls and casinos, and breweries such as Truman, Hanbury, Buxton and Watney Mann.

In an attempt to broaden its interests in the global market, GM acquired the Paddington Corporation, which had distributed its drinks and spirits in the US. This deal expanded GM's interests into cigarettes, soft drinks, bottling, fitness products and dog food. GM next acquired Intercontinental Hotels from Pan Am before taking over Children's World (retailers of children's clothing and other related goods), Pearle Optical (a chain of opticians) and Quality Care (a home healthcare company).

In the 1980s, GM acquired interests in a range of food manufacturers: Kaysens frozen gateau, Pilsbury (Green Giant, Haagen-Dazs, etc.) and Jus-rol frozen pastry. It also bought into Metaxa brandy, Mont La Salle Vineyards, Anglo Española de Distribución (sherry), Cinzano, as well as Vision Express and Eyelab. GM also decided to have a 'clear out' and disposed of many assets that did not easily fit into its portfolio.

GM's mission statement at this time was: 'Grand Met specialises in highly branded consumer businesses where its marketing and operational skills ensure it is a leading contender in every market in which it operates. The nature of these businesses is complementary, which adds to the value of the group as a whole.'

In 1997, Grand Metropolitan was considering a £24 billion merger with Guinness.

Sadler & Campbell (1994)

You might have arrived at the following classification of acquisitions: horizontal (hotels, catering, pubs); vertical (drinks, foods dairy, breweries); conglomerate (bingo halls, dance halls, casinos, Children's World, Eyelab, Pearle Optical). The advantages of being in such a large organisation include increased financial clout, and economies of scale. The disadvantages are on an operational level: the management structure is necessarily more complex, with different parts of the organisation having conflicting interests, and making conflicting demands on resources.

The growth of Grand Metropolitan in the 1960s, 1970s and early 1980s was typical of many successful organisations during the period. Its pattern of growth through integration and diversification is also typical. In the later 1980s and early 1990s, many large conglomerates began to see some disadvantages in their size and structure, as the business environment became more turbulent and competitive conditions became tougher. Downsizing and refocusing of activities, and the sale of many activities considered peripheral, became more common. For example, Hanson, the construction conglomerate, has sold off various companies, WH Smith has divested itself of Do It All, and Pepsico is selling its fast-food interest, including Taco Bell.

DOWNSIZING, SUBCONTRACTING AND ORGANISATIONAL FLEXIBILITY

The fiercer competitive climate of the late 1980s and early 1990s led many organisations to reassess their structures. Large conglomerates were considered too bureaucratic and inflexible for the rapidly changing business environment. They were not able to develop new products and services quickly enough in response to changing demands and competition. They were too committed to their old brands and were reluctant to invest in research and development for new products. Many organisations decided to **downsize** and to focus their business on **core activities** – those which were most profitable and had the best potential for market growth and long-term success. Organisations began to **subcontract** activities that they felt did not fit their overall portfolio and to sell off or close down departments or even whole businesses they no longer required. Many organisations chose to outsource activities to specialist organisations, contracting out functions like advertising, public relations, promotion, marketing, computer facilities – anything that might be done cheaper by an outside source. **Outsourcing** also extends to individuals, who may work for the organisation from home on a freelance basis. **Home working** saves the organisation in space, overheads and can also be of benefit to full-time or part-time employees.

Even some public sector bodies have been compelled by political pressure to concentrate on core activities and to subcontract other activities to organisations, that compete for the work through tenders. Hospitals have subcontracted catering, cleaning and other non-core activities; local councils have subcontracted out refuse collection and road cleaning. You only have to look around to see examples of this new approach to working. Perhaps you have friends that work on a freelance or consultancy basis or are subcontracted to a number of companies, or even work full-time for one organisation from home.

Organisations have to decide how much of their work they will do themselves and how much other organisations will do on their behalf. Do they subcontract someone to do a specific job for them or do they employ someone permanently within the organisation to be available to do that job as and when required? The decision is influenced by weighing the cost of employing someone permanently against the cost of subcontracting the work to an outside firm. Employing someone within the organisation runs the risk that there may be insufficient work for them to do on occasions; it might even be necessary to make the employee redundant. Consider Jill's position, for example, if she decides to extend her workshop and retail counter into a large display area. For reliability, she might decide to hire a full-time cleaner. Alternatively, she might contract a cleaning company that guarantees the cleaning and also insures their staff against any losses or breakages. This latter approach would ensure that the place always gets clean; if Jill employed a full-time cleaner, she would need to find some cover when the cleaner is off sick or on holiday.

The construction industry has traditionally consisted of large numbers of small firms with major projects managed by a co-ordinating firm. This structure is determined in part by the seasonal and cyclical nature of the industry. If a construction company employed all sorts of skilled building tradesmen and general labourers year round, it would have large numbers of idle employees during seasonal or cyclical downturns in the industry,

Other industries, with less cyclical patterns of demand, have tended to offer more secure employment, in larger companies. The need to recruit, train and keep employees has encouraged the development of large integrated organisations, offering employees the prospects of promotion and life-time employment. Recently, however, a turbulent business environment, including prolonged recession, rapid technological change and fierce international competition, has forced organisations in both the public and the private sector to consider whether it is more efficient to undertake certain activities in-house or to subcontract to outside agencies. In some creative industries, such as film, advertising, theatre and music, individuals are required only for a particular project or performance. In these industries most people are hired on a contract basis rather than offered full-time employment contracts.

Employees have also had to become more flexible. Secure life-time employment in a large organisation is no longer easily available. More people work in small organisations or for themselves, often working on projects subcontracted by the larger corporations. Many middle managers have been made redundant as organisations tried to become more efficient and more responsive to their customers. There has been a considerable rise in the number of part-time and temporary jobs available. However, some of the most successful organisations internationally continue to be giant conglomerates with vast hierarchies and bureaucratic organisational structures.

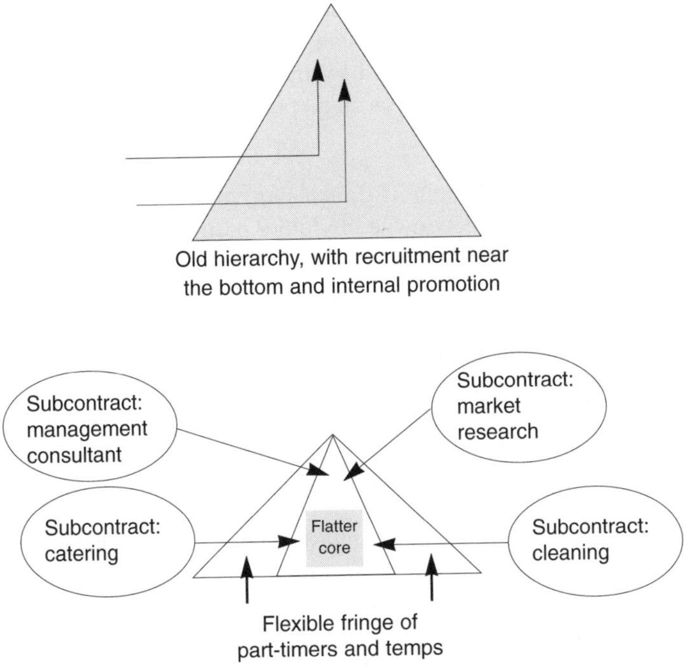

Figure 5: Bureaucratic hierarchy contrasted with a flatter, more flexible, corporate structure

As Figure 5 illustrates, by subcontracting activities previously done in-house, such as catering, cleaning, market research, designing and even strategic management, organisations have smaller structures with fewer core employees on permanent contracts. These organisations are designed to be more flexible to consumer requirements. Many organisations had, in the later 1980s and early 1990s, chosen to reverse the process of growth through diversification along the lines of Grand Metropolitan and have developed smaller, more flexible, organisational structures. By the late 1990s, however, many realised that they have probably gone too far along this road and organisations have begun to limit the subcontracting of activities.

JOINT VENTURES, CO-OPERATIVES, FRANCHISES, AGENCIES

There are a variety of looser arrangements that organisations can have with each other that are beneficial and continue the trend of flexibility. These include joint ventures, co-operatives, franchises and agencies.

In 1996, the sale of gas became deregulated in south-west England. Two companies had some interest in this market: Texaco has extensive gas fields; Calor has an extensive understanding of retail support of gas appliances. Their solution was to form a joint venture for that new part of their operations where they had a common interest.

A co-operative consists of a group of similar smaller businesses, such as farms or craftspeople, which come together to combine buying and/or selling. Each business carries on with its own operations, but marketing, distribution and/or purchasing might be collective. A co-operative can be a very precise form of business organisation that is effectively owned by individual members. Suppliers might also be members of the co-operative as might purchasers – the members in this case are also the customers.

An organisation can use a system of franchising, in which it gets its products to customers through retail outlets owned by other parties. These other parties (the franchisees) use the resources, name or operating system for a flat fee or a share of the profits. For example, although McDonald's owns some of its outlets in large cities where it can rationalise management costs, the company mainly operates through franchises. Its franchise contracts specify service and quality standards but allow some flexibility on decor within guidelines on the basic McDonald's colours and approach. Burger King, on the other hand, chooses to own and manage all its outlets. The Body Shop has 1,500 outlets in 46 countries; these are franchises that follow Body Shop criteria and only market Body Shop products.

An organisation can also use agencies and distributors to market and get its products to customers. Computers and cars are generally sold through a franchised dealer system, whereby the manufacturer has some control over the actual sales, but the dealerships are owned and managed by others. This is particularly relevant when a product needs technical guidance, both in support for the initial sale and for after-sales service. The bookselling industry uses a wholesaler system: a wholesaler stocks from publishers and distributes books to high street bookshops. This is not the whole story though, as many publishers do sell direct to some stores or direct to the customers.

2.3 Organisational structure

We have already considered some structural issues. Here we look at organisational structure in more depth. The structure of an organisation concerns the way in which different activities are co-ordinated. It indicates who is responsible for what and who communicates to whom about what, and how. Structure usually indicates a hierarchy of authority and control, and is the framework for the flow of information and communication within the organisation.

As well as the formal structure, there is often an **informal** structure reflecting how people link and interact; this depends on the culture of the organisation and we look at cultural issues later in this unit. Employees' working relationships are likely to be affected by factors such as membership of a trade union or professional association membership, the school and/or college they attended, whether they play for the company football team. The informal structure may be a powerful influence. If two employees from different departments live close to each other, they might meet socially or share a lift together to travel to work. They are likely to exchange information about what's happening at work much more quickly than through the formal channels; indeed, they may be able to resolve any work problems without ever going through the formal channels.

There are numerous ways in which activities may be **formally** grouped, however. Many organisations use the basic principles of one of the following:

- simple functional structure
- strategic business unit structure
- matrix organisation.

We will look at each of these in turn. In Unit 8, we look at how organisational structure is linked to strategy and organisational behaviour.

SIMPLE FUNCTIONAL STRUCTURE

The functional structure is a widely-used framework. The basic functions – such as logistics, operations, sales and marketing, field service, finance, human resource management, research and development, procurement and management information systems – are grouped together and report directly to the chief executive officer or managing director. An example of this type of structure is shown in Figure 6. It works well for smaller organisations. It also works well if an organisation's business environment is relatively stable. This structure is effective when an organisation's business interests are not too diverse and it does not operate in geographically dispersed locations.

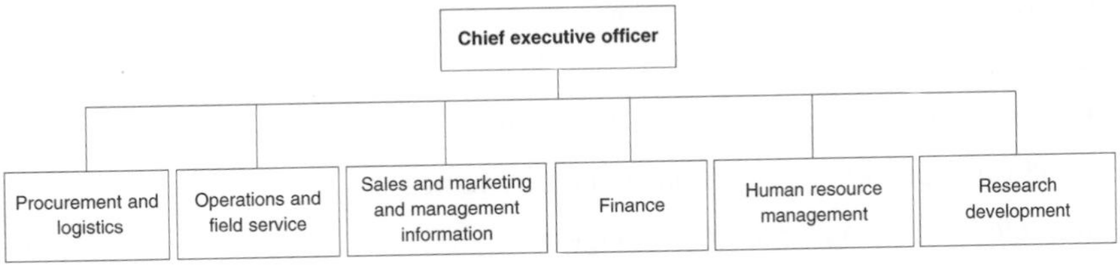

Figure 6: Functional structure

Appleby (1991) suggests that a functional structure has the advantage that:

- it is easy and logical to put together and usually effective in practice
- it follows the principle of specialisation and economies result.

However, he identifies a number of drawbacks.

- Functions may not be as important as other factors such as the geographical area covered by the organisation. If the company is split into different locations, or even across different countries, then each venue may have its own individual functional structure, giving an overall geographical structure.
- If a functional structure is applied rigidly, and if, for example, staff never have the opportunity to move between departments or take up short-term secondments, then functional specialists may develop very narrow perspectives on the business.

There are hidden problems. Co-ordination of activities may only take place at higher levels in the organisation, so it may require excessive amounts of senior management time to pursue new directions, such as new product development. Implementing change may be difficult as everything is viewed from a functional perspective. Enhanced communication and co-ordination, or a completely different structure, may be the best ways to achieve competitive advantage.

STRATEGIC BUSINESS UNIT STRUCTURE

As organisations become larger and their activities become more diverse, management becomes more difficult. A hitherto simple function such as production, for example, becomes less straightforward if a diverse range of products and services are produced for different markets. This requires different expertise, processes and raw materials. One solution is to structure the company into a number of operational units. These may be legal companies (wholly owned subsidiaries) or management structures within the company (strategic business units or SBUs). Unilever is a major multinational and owns companies across the world. Some of these are involved in the production of basic food products (such as edible oils and flavours), others are involved in the production and marketing of consumer products (ice cream and margarine). Within each strategic business unit, management can focus on one particular type of operation, and the structure of the unit can then be broken down into functional units themselves (Figure 7). This type of multi-divisional structure is also needed where parts of a company are geographically separated.

Lynch (1997) gives a number of advantages and disadvantages for the multi-divisional organisational structure. The advantages are that a multi-divisional structure:

- focuses on business areas
- eases functional co-ordination problems
- allows measurement of divisional performance
- provides training for future managers.

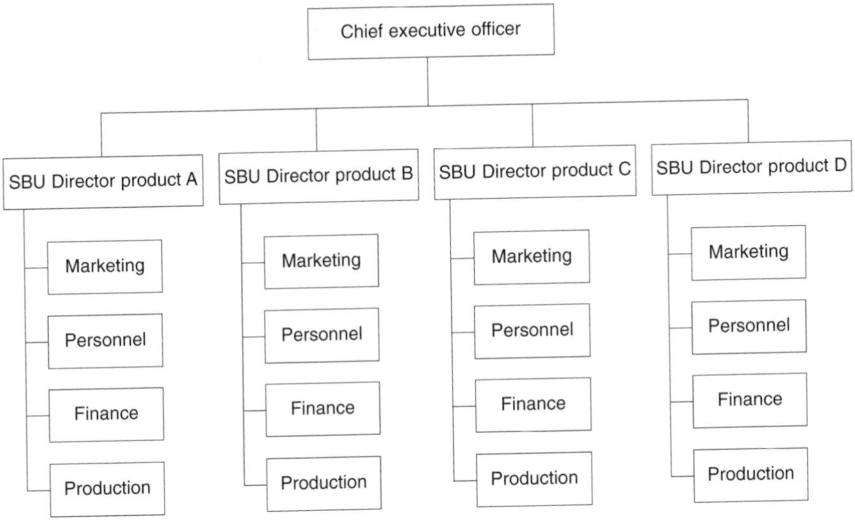

Figure 7: Multi-divisional structure

The disadvantages are:

- there is expensive duplication of functions
- divisions may compete against each other
- there is decreased interchange between functional specialists
- problems over relationships with central services.

Both functional and diversified structures operate through **line management**; managers having direct management roles over their function or facility. The operations manager manages production; the general manager or regional manager manages a strategic business unit. However, the production or general manager may need help to do his or her task, for example, by consulting the patents lawyer at head office. Patents lawyers are an example of personnel who do not manage anything; instead, they advise and support the managers who run the physical operations. This type of role is often described as a **staff role**. Head office staff are vital to large organisations as they provide expert services, such as legal, banking, taxation and training, that the individual parts of the company do not have the resources to provide.

MATRIX ORGANISATION

The simple functional structure is usually a traditional hierarchical structure in which the work of employees is co-ordinated by a manager and the manager's work is co-ordinated by a 'higher' manager, and so on. In this structure, one person is responsible for the work of each employee; the employee takes instructions from one manager.

A problem with this structure arises when managers are responsible for projects that involve specialists such as highly technical engineers. Although the managers can manage these projects by setting targets, moving resources to meet problems, checking on progress and so on, they are unable to give the specialists any technical guidance and support. A manager might be running a project within his or her department that uses a range of specialists; each specialist might be working in isolation and would lack the challenge, support and career opportunities of working with a group of similarly qualified colleagues.

The matrix organisation overcomes these problems. Consider an engineering company, split into electronics, mechanical, dynamics and materials departments. Each department is run by a manager who is a technical expert responsible for the department's work. The work of the engineering company consists of projects that require the services of more than one department; these projects are run by individual project managers. Each individual engineer is assigned temporarily to work on particular projects under the different project managers, so each individual has two managers – their project manager and their departmental manager. Figure 8 shows how staff A to M might be distributed among four projects. For example, project 4 employs staff drawn from both the mechanical and materials departments.

Technical Department Leader	Manager Project 1	Manager Project 2	Manager Project 3	Manager Project 4
Electronics	A, F	B, C		
Mechanical		E		I, J, K
Dynamics			G, H	
Materials				L, M

Figure 8: Matrix structure for an engineering company

A matrix structure is useful if a company is concerned with different production technologies (such as microelectronics and communications technologies), if it is marketing into different industry segments (such as offices, motor vehicle manufacture) and territories (such as the USA, Europe and Asia). An outline of a matrix structure is shown in Figure 9. A university might be structured on these lines, with, for example, three colleges of undergraduate, postgraduate and continuing education, each with its own head of college, but with lecturers also reporting to a head of department, such as of accounting and finance, engineering, and business studies. The university management would be brought together through a system of committees on which sit the representative heads of all colleges or departments, with an overall head or principal.

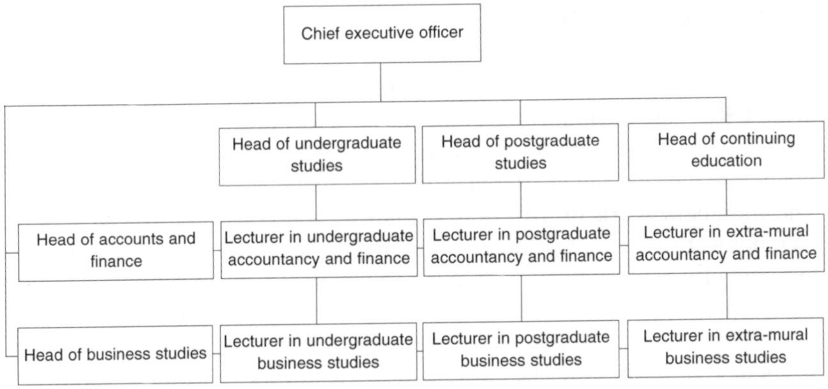

Figure 9: Matrix structure

In the multi-divisional structure, there may be expensive duplication of resources; but in the matrix structure such resources may be shared. In a university, for example, the general university facilities such as library, catering and student admissions – are shared by all colleges and departments Knight (1997). The matrix structure can aid control and accountability in the manner required by an organisation. For example, it allows accountability by say product range and by country. One of the major advantages of a matrix structure is adaptability. In situations of rapid environmental change and uncertainty, matrix structures recreate within large highly structured organisation some of the means of adaptation found in smaller organisations. The structure facilitates the fast exchange of information and feedback laterally between departments and different specialists, or between different colleges and departments within a university. For example, a change in requirements for accountants could be quickly fed through from the accountancy department into all the relevant programmes at undergraduate and postgraduate levels.

The advantages of a matrix structure, Lynch (1997) include:

- close co-ordination where decisions may conflict
- adaptable to specific strategic situations
- bureaucracy replaced by direct discussion
- increased managerial involvement.

The disadvantages of a matrix structure include:

- complex, slow decision-making – needs agreement of all participants
- unclear definition of responsibilities
- high tension between those involved if teamwork of some parts is poor.

REVIEW ACTIVITY 2

The Institution of Electrical Engineers (IEE) has just under 100,000 members in the UK. There are four types of members: student members (undergraduate students), young members (engineers in the first five years of their working life before they get full chartered status), full members, and retired members. The members work in different industries – defence, electrical power, communications and electronics – and may have different responsibilities – teaching, design, operations, marketing and management. In general, members are not prepared to travel a long distance for professional meetings.

In about 150 words, describe the structural framework you would propose for the IEE in order to ensure the co-ordination of its activities. Do not worry if you find this activity rather hard at this stage. Start by thinking about the physical location of the organisation, then the different types of members and then their interests.

Summary

In this section, we have looked at the main features of growth and organisational structure. We described some different types of growth and the major forms of structures used by organisations, and their advantages and disadvantages. The demands of the modern business world have meant that organisations have to be able to change their structure. The functional structure is the simplest, but when the business grows in size and diversity then the multi-divisional organisational structure is more appropriate. When a business has become more complex and the environment is fast changing, a more flexible type of structure is required to allow the organisation to adapt continually to circumstances. A matrix organisation allows the business to be managed more flexibly. Informal structures also exist within organisations.

SECTION 3

The Organisation as a Legal Entity

Introduction

The legal structure of an organisation defines the way it interacts with the outside world. This determines the way an organisation can interact with its markets, customers, employees, owners and other publics. In Unit 2, we look in some detail at the general external legal environment and how laws and regulations impinge on what an organisation does and how it does it. Here, we are concerned with the specific legal entities that organisations can adopt.

3.1 Sole traders

The sole trader is the simplest, and least structured, legal entity. A sole trader is an individual who owns, runs and is solely responsible for the organisation. There is, in effect, no distinction between the behaviour of the organisation and the behaviour of the individual. The sole trader is liable for the debts of the organisation and the organisation is liable for the sole trader's debt. There is no separate legal identity for the organisation other than that of its owner. Despite the name, the sole trader can still have employees and be an organisation according to our original definition. This is the most common type of business in Britain. It is the easiest to start and requires very little start-up capital. However, it is also the most likely to fail.

There are some advantages with this type of organisation. The owner has no constraints other than general law on his or her operation. He or she has no shareholders to constrain entrepreneurial activities. The sole trader is also likely to be very committed to his or her organisation – if the organisation loses money so does the sole trader – and can make all the decisions. Owners are likely to be close to their markets and customers, so they can respond quickly and can change faster than a cumbersome company. Also, accounts are not required to be published, ensuring the maximum privacy for the business.

There are some obvious disadvantages of the sole trader structure. The sole trader is often unwilling to take risks for fear of putting his or her personal assets at risk. The sole trader's access to capital is often more difficult than for other forms of organisation. The sole trader has either to rely on his or her own personal capital resources or to persuade a financial institution to lend him or her money, secured against his or her assets. Because of the lack of separate legal identity, the sole trader risks all of his or her assets on the success of the organisation.

3.2 Partnerships

A partnership is defined by the Partnership Act 1890 (s. 1(1)), as 'the relationship which exists between persons carrying on a business in common with a view to a profit'. A partnership exists where two or more individuals own an organisation. It is formed by a Deed of Partnership creating a legal relationship between the owners. Partnerships, like the sole trader, do not operate under company law and they are not required to file their accounts. Like the sole trader, the partners are liable – jointly and severally – for the debts of the partnership. What this means is that a creditor (or anyone else that has a claim for money from the partnership) can claim their money jointly from all partners or separately from just the one partner. Similarly, the partnership assets can be used as funds by a creditor to satisfy the debts of one of the partners. The legal relationship only effectively operates between the partners, not between the partnership itself and the people that do business with the partnership.

Except for groups of solicitors, accountants and stockbrokers, partnerships are limited to no more than 20 partners (Companies Act 1985 (s. 716)). In the case of solicitors and other professionals, where the partnerships become very large, it is not unusual to find groups of partnerships. An organisation such as Ernst Young, with 1,000 tax partners, would create a cumbersome and awkward senior decision-making body. Therefore, in each of the main countries in which it operates there are separate partnerships. Ernst Young International, a partnership whose partners are the national partnerships, guides overall worldwide activities.

The advantages of a partnership are very similar to the advantages of the sole trader but, by the fact that there is more than one individual putting funds into the partnership, there is potentially greater access to capital.

The disadvantages are again similar to the sole trader. However, the risk to the individual could be perceived to be both greater and reduced. Because the partnership is liable to the debts of the individual partners, the risk to partners increases; however, the fact that there is more than one individual involved in effect spreads that risk.

The Limited Partners Act 1907 created a form of limited liability for partners. It defined two types of partner: general partners and limited partners. The liability of limited partners is restricted to the capital that they invested in the partnership when it formed. However, limited partners can have no part in the management of the organisation. Any partner taking part in the management of a partnership automatically has the status of a general partner – and therefore becomes liable jointly and severally for all the partnership's debts. This way of restricting the liability of investors is not much used, as the incorporated company provides a much less cumbersome and restrictive method for protecting the interests of investors.

3.3 Incorporated companies

An incorporated company is an organisation with a legal identity – the body corporate – separate from that of its owners. This gives the company the right to own and sell property, to take legal action or have legal action taken against it independently of its owners. To quote Lord Macnagten rendering judgement: 'The company is at law a different person altogether from the subscribers of the memorandum' (Solomon v Solomon & Co [1987] AC 22).

Companies may be incorporated either as private or public companies. In practice, this makes little difference, except that:

- the minimum starting capital requirement for a public company is £50,000
- a private company cannot offer shares to the public, although it can to friends and family
- a public company must be limited by shares or guarantee.

Obviously, the demand for a starting capital of £50,000 may make a private company a more attractive option. However, the inability to raise capital by offering shares to the public, may restrict the growth of private companies. It is possible for a private company to re-register as a public company.

LIMITED LIABILITY

A company may be incorporated in one of three forms:

- limited by shares (Companies Act 1985 s. 1 (2) (a))
- limited by guarantee (Companies Act 1985 s. 1 (2) (b))
- unlimited (Companies Act 1985 s. 1 (2) (c)).

The owners of a company limited by shares are not responsible for the body corporate except to the amount unpaid on their shares. However, to protect shareholders, the public and creditors, the company must publish its accounts for its members and place a copy with the Registrar of Companies (Companies Act 1985 s. 241 (3)).

A company limited by guarantee is one where the liability of members and/or owners for the company's debts are limited to a fixed amount that the guarantors agree to contribute to the company in the event of it winding up. Like the limited company, a company limited by guarantee must publish accounts.

An unlimited company still has a separate legal identity from its owners, however its owners and members are liable for the debts of the company, should the company be wound up.

The Companies Act 1989 modified these rules a little, generally in respect of publication of accounts for small and medium-sized companies.

ACTIVITY 6

Look back again at the case study on Jill's Jewellery. In the light of our discussion on the legal structure of organisations, make notes on how Jill is likely to have started her business. How is it likely to have changed as she grows and develops? Why would these changes be advantageous?

Jill is likely to have started her business as a sole trader, or perhaps in partnership, with her father, say. With a large increase in size of turnover, more staff, and more responsibility to her various stakeholders, Jill is likely to form a company. With more turnover, there are VAT implications, and that will require more paperwork and accounting. Jill may need further capital to increase her turnover; this will be easier to raise with a limited company and it means that Jill's (and her father's) assets will not be at risk. With the increase in turnover and staffing, Jill will be able to bring additional skills and expertise into her business. Larger companies are likely to feel happier dealing with a company, and if she has it in mind eventually to sell the business, then it is easier for accountants and lawyers to cost and trade with a company structure.

FORMATION OF AN INCORPORATED COMPANY

To form a company, it is necessary to have a Memorandum of Association together with Articles of Association. (Articles may be omitted but then a standard form of regulations is applied, Company's Regulations SI 1985/805 Table A.) These must be accompanied by a document listing the directors and company secretary and a statement that the Companies Act has been complied with.

The Memorandum of Association is a document that defines the company's interaction with the outside world. It contains:

- the company's name
- the registered office (the company's official address)
- the object of the company
- a statement that the liability of the members is limited (if this is the case)
- the amount of share capital with which the company is to be registered and how that capital is divided into shares
- a statement that the subscribers want to form a company
- a list of the subscribers with their portion of the share capital.

Perhaps the most important part of the Memorandum of Association is the section about the object (or objects) of the company. This defines the purpose of the company. The reason it is so important is that the company is not legally able to act outside of its objects; when the company tries doing this it is said to be acting *ultra vires* or outside of its legal powers. Contracts made in this way are not legally enforceable. This concept was originally introduced to protect investors in companies from frivolous or foolhardy investments that early directors occasionally made. Unfortunately, English common law has enforced this principle to the extent that it has been used to protect companies from claims from creditors. A company's Memorandum of Association is a public document, and the law made the assumption that anyone dealing with the company should be fully aware of its objects and therefore has no redress should the courts decide that the contract was *ultra vires*. Recent legislation (Companies Act 1985 (s. 35) and European Economic Community Directive 68/151) offers more protection for people acting in good faith with the company. The Articles of Association regulate how the company will act but, unlike the Memorandum of Association, they are not a public document.

HOLDING COMPANY

A holding company is a company that owns other companies (Company's Act 1985 (s. 736)). This is generally done for two reasons.

The first reason is to allow a company to conduct activities in areas other than those covered by its Memorandum of Association. The company could set up a limited company that it wholly owns to conduct these new activities. It might also take over a competitor for similar reasons, and maintain that company's identity.

The second reason is to minimise risk. A company conducting various activities might chose to make each of these activities a subsidiary limited company, and set up a 'holding company' to own the subsidiaries. This means that if any of the activities conducted by one of the subsidiary companies should suffer large losses, the rest of the company is protected. As each company has a separate legal identity, including the holding company, the risk is minimised. It has the same effect as watertight doors on a ship – one area of the company may be badly damaged but the effect will be contained and the entire organisation will not necessarily 'go down' because of the losses of one subsidiary.

It is worth noting that an unlimited company cannot be a holding company or a subsidiary for a limited company.

3.4 Charities

A charity is an organisation which has a charitable purpose. Charities are exempt from English tax. There is no statutory definition of a charitable purpose but it is standard practice to rely upon the repealed definition in the Charitable Uses Act 1601. This Act defined charitable purposes as:

- relief of poverty and human suffering and distress
- advancement of education
- advancement of religion
- other purposes beneficial to the community.

Charities usually register with the Charities Commission. This is a body that ensures that charities do not abuse their privileges.

Charities are commonly trusts. A trust is defined by the Recognition of Trust Act 1987 (s. 1) as: 'The legal relationship created by a person, the settlor, when assets have been placed under the control of a trustee for the benefit of a beneficiary or for a specified person'.

A trust does not provide limited liability but does provide an extremely flexible way of creating organisations for charitable purposes; many clubs, societies, trade unions, etc. have been created in this way. Much law is devoted to the management of trusts and we will not deal with it any further here.

Other charities are formed as an incorporated company, often by guarantee, including professional organisations such as the Institute of Chartered Secretaries and Administrators (ICSA), while others, such as universities, are formed by charter.

REVIEW ACTIVITY 3

Consider the organisations listed below. Write down which legal structure you would recommend the organisations to use and explain your reasons.

(a) greengrocer's shop set up by an individual

(b) multinational frozen food producer

(c) playgroup set up by local parents

(d) private school

Summary

In this section, we have looked at the legal structures of organisations and the effect this has on the way in which they interact with the outside world. We examined the basic differences between a sole trader, a partnership and an incorporated company, and described the ways in which a company might be incorporated – limited by shares, limited by guarantee and unlimited. We looked at the steps it is necessary to take when setting up an incorporated company, and at the ways in which holding companies operate. Finally, we examined the legal status of charities.

SECTION 4

Business Functions

Introduction

Whatever an organisation's business, there are some fundamental activities that need to be done that relate to the basic process of inputs–transformation–outputs. We can regard these fundamental activities as building blocks or functions: In a small simple company, these functions are easily arranged and divided among a small number of people. In large complex organisations, there are many ways of dividing up and organising the separate functions.

In this section, we consider the functions required by most organisations. As you will see, an organisation works by the interaction of all its elements. Some functions are very tightly tied to others and may be grouped together in one company, or exist as separate departments in another. This grouping depends on the organisational structure, the business that the organisation is in, the culture and the mission.

Here, we take a general overview of these functions and look particularly at some current issues. We do not give an introduction to the theory and practice of each function, but rather provide a glimpse of certain areas that will enable you to get an overall perspective of how businesses run. Later in this module, we look at these functions in more detail and then you investigate them in depth in specialist modules.

We start by looking at a small company and then extend the ideas to larger, more complex situations, using Porter's value chain. This will give you an appreciation of the different functions, and shows also how interrelated and dependent they are on each other and on all the links in the complete value system. To be successful, an organisation has to address all these areas and linkages in its own value system. The more complex this is, the more complex will be the task of acquiring and maintaining competitive advantage.

4.1 Porter's value chain

Porter (1985) suggests that it is helpful to divide the activities of organisations into primary activities and support activities. The primary activities are what the organisation does as part of its fundamental value-adding transformation process. For example, a bakery bakes bread from raw ingredients. The support activities are required to keep the organisation running and include, for example, buying the raw materials, recruiting staff or keeping the accounts. He formulates this concept into a simple model called the **value chain**. This model gives us a framework in which to place the organisation. It is easiest to apply in manufacturing organisations that are producing a tangible product rather than a service. Publicly funded organisations are also harder to fit into the model, but we can apply the same concepts to many different circumstances, and you will have the chance to do this in some of the activities. As with all models, it does not precisely fit all situations. We can also link his ideas with our earlier discussion of management; generally speaking, in a functional structure line management concerns primary activities and staff management concerns secondary activities.

Porter divides the **primary activities** in the value chain into five areas.

- **Inbound logistics** – This is concerned with getting inputs to where the operations will take place and involves receiving, storing and internal distribution.
- **Operations** – This includes the actual transformation of the inputs into final products or services.
- **Outbound logistics** – This concerns transport and distribution of the final output to the customer.
- **Marketing and sales** – This identifies the market and the product to meet the customer's needs, makes the customer aware of the product or service and makes the final sale.
- **Service** – Added services can be provided that maintain or enhance the main product or service, for example through training, installation or repair.

He divides the **support activities** into four areas.

- **Infrastructure** – This includes the general management, organisational structure, control, co-ordination and financial controls that are necessary to support the whole chain.
- **Human resource management** – This concerns recruitment, training, remuneration and other people-related activities that are essential throughout the organisation.
- **Technology development** – Technology is used in all of the primary and support activities, whether in product design, processes used, service delivery, communication of information for decision-making; research and development is the centre of new technology, new innovations and new markets.
- **Procurement** – This concerns purchasing the inputs, whether they are raw materials, semi-finished goods, equipment or anything the organisation needs in its primary and support activities.

All these activities depend on each other, so not only are the activities themselves important but the linkages are also critical and need to be examined for effectiveness and efficiency at all levels. It is no good being very efficient in cutting production costs, if you are then inefficient at getting the product to the customer. And no matter how efficient you are, to be effective you need the right product to the right place at the right time. As we saw earlier, organisations can contract out activities, but then they are dependent on an outside source for that process in the value chain.

Let's consider Jill's Jewellery in terms of Porter's value chain. Jill is taking raw materials – semi-precious stones and settings – and making jewellery. She sells direct to the customer in the shop. She has to order the semi-precious stones from overseas, and she must ensure a high quality. She needs fittings from which she assembles the finished jewellery and which she has to hold in stock for her customers. She has a computer for her accounts, stock and pricing control, staff records, design specifications and database of customers; she has a phone, fax and e-mail facility to help her with overseas ordering. The shop has a till and credit card facilities. She has to keep the premises in good order, cleaned and safe for employees and customers. The property has to be approved for commercial use. She has to have insurance for the building and for her stock, and public liability insurance in case of an accident involving members of the public occurring on her premises. She will have to take precautions against theft by customers and staff as well as break-ins. Perhaps she has a direct alarm system with the police. Staff will need to be employed within legal guidelines.

ACTIVITY 7

Spend 20-30 minutes making notes on Jill's current business, using Porter's value chain headings to help you structure your thoughts.

Primary activities

- Inbound logistics
- Operations
- Outbound logistics
- Sales and marketing
- Service

Support activities

- Infrastructure
- Human Resource Management
- Technology Development
- Procurement

Inbound logistics concerns the receipt of inputs – the parts that Jill needs for jewellery manufacture such as stones, mountings, glue and solder. She will need to place orders with suppliers, monitor deliveries, check on quality, and monitor stocks. She needs to store all materials in an orderly way so that when she wants to make up a specific design she can quickly find what she needs. She will also have to store things for the shop, such as till rolls and packaging. The store needs to be dry and secure; although the items are not perishable, substantial investment will be tied up in gemstones waiting to be used.

Operations Jill is assembling and making her jewellery products from her raw materials. She will have some equipment for stone cutting and soldering, a work bench and tools, which will be laid out in a sensible way for her to work. Different pieces might be at different stages – stones being cut and mounted, some waiting for the finish to dry, others waiting for final polishing and packaging.

Outbound logistics concerns despatch of her finished stock to the customer. She might have display cabinets in the shop, and a secure area for the rest of the stock to be stored before it is moved into the shop for selling to the customer. Jill may, at a later date, consider selling by mail order, so she would also want to make provision to be able to pack up her jewellery for posting.

Jill's **sales** are through her shop, where customers can inspect and select items and then have them packed and, of course, pay for them. She needs to have a means of taking money and a credit card facility. She needs to maintain stock control through sales records. Her sales staff need to know her product lines and be trained in dealing with her particular type of customer. Her marketing efforts are currently through advertising in the local paper and through regional tourist brochures. She has prepared a small leaflet, featuring her continuing lines, and this she distributes to hotels and guest houses in the area. She is thinking of marketing on the Internet, having a web page where she can show particular designs; she will develop this idea when she has systems for direct mail order. She test markets particular designs before buying supplies in bulk. Her pricing in the early days was somewhat haphazard and generally on the basis of unit cost plus a percentage, but she has found that for some designs, and 'unusual' one-off ones, she can ask much higher prices.

Jill does not have a business where there is a lot of field **service**. However, she does provide a jewellery repair service for anything that falls apart, and she will replace worn stones, a lost earring, or restring pearls. She also needs to do insurance valuations. For her loyal and local customers whom she knows well, she will take a small collection around to their homes.

Jill's **infrastructure** includes the physical buildings, her financial structure – she might finance her business with a bank loan or might just have a bank overdraft – and her general administration of insurance, accounts, etc. She is taking money in every day, and will need to bank cash and cheques, and she will be paying suppliers. She will need to cost out her production for unit costing and subsequent pricing. She needs to do accounts for the Inland Revenue with help from her external accountant.

Her **human resources management** concerns the selection, motivation and training of her sales and production staff. She will need to set wages and schedule for shift work. Perhaps the sales staff have a commission-based element to their pay. Jill will need to work out national insurance contributions and tax and draw up work procedures and job descriptions.

Jill's **technology development** can be considered as her design work in producing new items and her investigations into new methods of production or new materials. Perhaps there is a new non-toxic glue she can try, or a new machine for stone cutting has been developed. Perhaps she can use CAD for working up new designs. She can use the Internet for marketing. She can use her database of customers for direct mailing and other promotions, and she can develop other mailing lists for direct ordering. As her stock enlarges, she will need to devise a better system of keeping track of supplies and stocks as items are purchased.

Procurement might involve ordering in bulk from overseas, but Jill will not want to tie up too much capital in her stock of raw materials, especially as fashions change and she is marketing an expensive luxury item. She will be concerned about quality and timely delivery from particular suppliers. She could cut out various stages by ordering direct from a supplier in India, rather than from a distributor. She will have other supplies to order for supporting the rest of the business – stationery, office supplies, computer facilities. Overall, she will need to balance orders against capital tied up in purchased and stored items.

Even with Jill's business we can gain an understanding of the value chain framework – its complexity and the enormous number of factors that need to be taken into account in running even a small business. Note the areas where effectiveness, efficiency and/or competitiveness can all be lost. As you work through this module, you will meet various ways of dealing with these factors and the linkages. Remember that the concepts can be applied to service organisations too, and in many industries manufacturing and service are closely linked.

4.2 Inbound and outbound logistics

There are two aspects to an organisation's logistics: the receipt of goods and their handling prior to manufacture, and the storage and dispatch of finished products to customers. In Porter's terms, these are the inbound and outbound logistics. In some cases, logistics includes the flow of raw materials and part finished goods throughout the organisation, and because the purchasing is tied in with the receipt of goods it can also include procurement. The dispatch of finished goods to the customer can involve transport and distribution.

Supplies received at the stores must be checked against the order and for quality. They need to be stored and stock controlled. As batches of a product are made, the right components must be taken out of the stores and delivered to the production assembly areas. Any inefficiency, such as not maintaining sufficient stock, will result in production hold-ups, so it is vital that there are good links with production and good forecasts of the production demands.

Increasingly, companies wish to reduce their costs by holding less stock and, instead, depend on a reliable service from their suppliers. Components can also be checked for quality by the supplier and not checked on delivery. Rather than being held in stores, incurring costs in storage and handling, the components can be delivered when the production line needs them. This method of working is known as 'just in time' (JIT), as the components are delivered only when they are required for production. This type of supply requires a high level of trust and communication between the supplier and the manufacturer and good internal communications on the level of production required to meet customers' orders.

When manufactured, the product must be packed and held in stores awaiting transport to the distribution network or to the customer. Sufficient stock must be held to meet customer needs. However, excess stock costs money. A special skill in delivery is route planning so that the required drops are effected in the minimum time and with the shortest distances being covered by the vehicles. Again, good sales planning is necessary as urgent, rush orders will disrupt the delivery routes and schedules, increasing costs.

We can view the basic flow through a manufacturing chain as:

supplier → stock of supplies → process → stock of products → customer.

Savings might be possible by removing the two stock-holding stages. In either case, this would demand good internal information and communication on requirements of supplies and products, and good communication with other members of the supply chain. In a service rather than a product situation, stock of supplies can be likened to queuing at a bank counter or booking with a doctor or hairdresser. Services which also run to a schedule, such as airlines and trains, have to be carefully planned for capacity. Other services operate on a 'do-it-yourself' approach, such as petrol service stations and fast-food restaurants.

ACTIVITY 8

Identify a service organisation of which you have had experience, such as a bank, hotel or hairdresser. Spend 10 minutes or so using Porter's model as a framework to make notes about its basic activities. Outline the inbound and outbound logistics in some detail.

Consider the hairdresser. You made a booking to avoid waiting. (Note you don't make a booking to buy a sandwich, for example.) You might have gone in for a quick trim, or for highlights with your favourite stylist. Perhaps, while a junior is washing your hair, your stylist is cutting someone else's and then is ready to cut yours while the other customer's hair is drying. Inward logistics include inputs: staff, stock of materials such as shampoo and colourings, equipment, salon and the customer. Outbound logistics include the stylist cutting your hair, his or her skill and experience, and direct interaction with client.

4.3 Operations (production)

Operations transforms the inputs into the final product or service. In manufacturing organisations, these activities might be grouped together into areas such as a workshop, shop or factory floor. The operations manager has to lay out the facilities to manufacture the products in the most effective and efficient way. Jill, for example, would lay out her production equipment in her workshop in the best manner for her way of working. To be effective, the right products must be made without defects at the time they are required. For the company to be profitable, this activity must be conducted in the most efficient way by using the minimum of raw materials and labour, with the minimum of wastage, and people should be kept working and not waiting for the delivery of parts and materials. Costs need to be tracked and controlled.

In a service organisation such as a hotel, operations might include the bedrooms, kitchen, restaurant, bar, reception, all providing part of the total service. You cannot identify just one activity as the core of the hotel. Although supply of bedrooms is a core activity, this is only part of the whole service. There are additional factors such as entertainment and catering. 'Occupancy' – of bedrooms, restaurant tables, bank counters, airline seats – is the key issue with service organisations, and efficiency is achieved by matching marketing to booking, staffing to occupancy and need requirements.

In a manufacturing situation, if a wide range of specialist products is to be assembled, a major consideration will be flexibility and the key need will be to keep track of the activity and costs associated with a diversity of products in production at the same time. In such a situation, the production may be arranged as a number of small work centres where one type of product is assembled by a small dedicated team. Where there are long runs of standard products, the operations manager will often arrange a dedicated line which increases the efficiency of production with some decrease in flexibility.

The ultimate in efficient, dedicated (specialised) production facilities can be seen in chemical manufacturing operations or automated car assembly lines. Here, labour costs are reduced to a minimum, with the use of automation and robots. However this efficiency is achieved at a cost, as such specialised lines may take a long time and a lot of money to change to a new product. It may, for example, require substantial investment to adapt an automated car assembly line to produce a new model. In addition, the efficiency may only be gained by large capital investment, so in these cases the production facility has to be run at full capacity to earn enough money to pay for the interest on the money used in its construction.

Although quality is the responsibility of all people in the organisation, in production poor training or poor alignment of the equipment will cause major quality problems. Quality control ensures that the processes are held within design limits. Increasingly, quality checks are not made on a finished product; if there are problems at this stage, it is too late. Quality measurement systems are built into the manufacturing lines so that the aim of zero defects can be achieved. Deviations from the ideal settings should be detected before defective products are manufactured. Systems may need to be fully working when they are installed, as the costs of rectifying defects during installation may eat up all the profits. You learn more about quality in Unit 5 on Operations and Operations Management.

The operations manager has two other major considerations – that of safety and environmental protection. Efficiency must not be achieved, for example, with any risk to staff or with damaging wastes being discharged into the environment. Some of these issues are covered by legislation, others by the organisation's own guidelines.

In a large organisation, there may be a department called production and another called quality control or quality assurance, and given the importance of safety and environmental issues there may also be a department called 'safety and environment'. Although quality and safety are very tightly linked to the production operations, their influence and work extend even further into areas such as marketing, since quality starts with the satisfaction of the customer and safety must include safety in the use of the product.

4.4 Sales and marketing

Sales reflect the final purchase by the customer – the product or service is exchanged for money. Marketing is the delivery to the customer of the right product, at the right place, at the right time, at the right price, to fulfil a need. Marketing is concerned with deciding what customers want through market research, providing it through production and new product development, and informing and persuading customers to buy the product through advertising and other forms of marketing communications such as public relations and publicity.

SALES

The sales function needs to make decisions about the basic selling process: how to sell efficiently and effectively to the customer, how payment is made, how information on stocks is made available and kept up to date, how to organise the sales force, and how to train and reward the sales force. 'Selling' occurs between organisations at each link of the supply chain, as well as at the point of supply to the final end customer. This has implications for stockholding and ordering throughout the supply chain. In the late 1990s, technology is a key issue in the selling process, making buying quick and easy for the customer. For the organisation, the sale becomes an important piece of information. We can see the use of technology in supermarkets and manufacturing operations that operate just-in-time systems for ordering and delivery. This system needs good computer links so that orders can be transmitted quickly and directly into the suppliers' systems without delay. Rapid communication with good sales forecasts is vital to ensure that appropriate stock levels are kept. If stocks are too high, money will be lost due to damage to the goods in stock and too much capital will be tied up in the stock itself. But running out of stock will mean that sales are lost to the competition.

In retailing particularly, effective and efficient sales systems are vital to competitive advantage. The laser checkout has become key. Electronic point of sales (EPOS) systems are linked with computers and networks into an electronic data interchange (EDI) system so that many aspects of the business can be managed effectively. As far as customers are concerned, the technology means that items are processed more quickly, payment can be made with cash or magnetic encoded cards (charge or credit cards) and they are provided with a full detailed bill. For the organisation, the technology means that it is able to have instant updating of stock levels and can track money received. The information gathered by point-of-sale technology can be used to tell if new advertising or store promotions are working. The analysis of customers' purchases can enable the retailer to obtain a better profile of its customers and to target special offers at specific groups of customers. The system also allows the store to monitor the performance of staff operating the checkouts.

For many sales, and for expensive consumer items, the customer needs to know much detail about the product. Personal contact may be necessary so that a full discussion can take place between the supplier and the customer to define what product will best meet the customer's needs. There may be some time between ordering and delivery for custom-made industrial or consumer products, so the sales staff must keep in contact with customers to keep them informed of progress. Success in this type of marketing often depends on the strength of the relationship built up between the sales staff and the customer. Complex industrial products, such as microchips, may require technical support for effective use of the product; complex consumer items such as computers also need field support. In the case of industrial buying, with just-in-time methods placing more demands on the supply chain, very close contact between organisations is needed to meet requirements.

MARKETING

Marketing determines what the organisation's customers want and ensures that the organisation can meet these needs. As other organisations will be competing, another role of marketing is to track the competition and to adapt the marketing efforts to maintain or extend market share.

To determine what the customer wants, the marketing function will research general trends; the number of people that own cars, for example, will indicate the size of the market for petrol. This use of published (secondary) data allows the organisation to build up a general view of the developments in the market, including tracking the competition and market shares. To better understand customers, the marketing group will do primary research through surveys or by test marketing ideas with selected groups of customers. The analysis of internal sales records also provides valuable information such as the response to a new product or a new advertising campaign.

Marketing determines the marketing mix, which includes four main components – product, price, place and promotion. Promotion includes all aspects of marketing communication – advertising, public relations, sponsorship, direct marketing. We look at marketing in detail in Unit 4. Obviously, it is at the heart of a successful company; without a product or a service that meets the needs of its customers, an organisation cannot be successful. No matter how good the staff, operations and logistics, they will not overcome poor positioning of the product with customers. As it is the link between customers and the organisation, the marketing department is vital to success.

ACTIVITY 9

Spend 10 minutes making notes on how Jill could improve the marketing of her business.

Jill could produce a brochure, do more promotions locally, hold functions and promotions in the shop, offer discounts for loyal customers, use her database for direct mailing to existing customers and potential new ones, do market research on her customers' tastes and buying habits, do secondary research on the characteristics and buying habits of her current customers, and use the information to develop future strategies. Perhaps she could develop a web site as a means of advertising. She would need to be able to accept and process all orders, including those from overseas, so payment is likely to be through credit card and prompt dispatch would be expected. She would need to respond to changes in the fashion world and design suitable accessories to match. Perhaps she could extend her market by developing a line for Harvey Nichols, the London and Leeds fashion store, or another major store on an exclusive basis.

4.5 Service

With the marketplace full of very similar products, it is often the service aspect that actually makes the sale. Service may include installation, training and repairs; with many high-price technical products, customers are more likely to buy if after-sales service is offered. You might be prepared to pay slightly more for a new computer system if the supplier will install it in your home or office. You might purchase a particular make of washing machine because either the manufacturer or the stockist has a very good repair system. You might buy a particular piece of software because there is an advice helpline. Organisations may buy from their suppliers for the same reasons.

4.6 Infrastructure

Porter (1985) identifies a number of activities, including general management, planning, finance, accounting, legal, government affairs and quality management, in his infrastructure support activity. In addition to these activities, other elements may be important for a particular organisation, such as physical infrastructure, information structure, demographic structure, organisation structure and culture, Curtis (1994).

These activities may be concentrated in a particular area or department, such as accounting and finance, but many activities, such as communication, management, control, and information technology, extend throughout the organisation. We look briefly at accounting and finance here to give you some ideas about its role, as we do not cover it later in the module.

ACCOUNTING AND FINANCE

Finance is one of the elements of infrastructure that spans the entire organisation. There are a number of activities in the accounting function, including those that are necessary for the legal record of the company (the formal accounts, the taxation records, etc.). The audit function checks that the organisation complies with financial regulations and that its records are true and accurate. Auditors check that expense claims are valid and stock has not been stolen, for example.

The day-to-day management of the company requires the collection of money (accounts receivable) and the payment of expenses (accounts payable and payroll). Businesses need money to pay the bills and stock needs to be purchased. The control of working capital and cash flow is vital to success. The source of this money is the customers, and if the organisation is paid after the goods or services have been provided, care has to be taken to check that customers can pay and on time; this is the function of credit control. For many small businesses, late payment from big customers and early demand for payment from big suppliers can cause cash-flow problems and force them out of business. In 1997, the government produced a green paper proposing that small businesses should have statutory interest on late payments. Any legislation could backfire, however, with large companies simply demanding new payment terms, say from 30 to 90 days. To qualify as a small business, an organisation has to meet two of three criteria: sales of no more than £2.8 million, a balance sheet total of no more than £1.4 million, and no more than 50 employees.

Longer-term strategic decisions have to be made about how to run the organisation in the future. Costing, budget preparation and financial management, such as investment appraisal, provide information to ensure future success. For example, one of Hewlett Packard's corporate objectives is to achieve sufficient profit to finance company growth and to provide the resources it needs to achieve other corporate objectives. The company reinvests most of its profits, so effective asset management is essential for this self-funding of growth. The company might use borrowed money as part of a prudent currency and tax management programme, but not to finance normal strategic growth.

4.7 Human resource management

Porter's value chain recognises that human resource management (HRM) is a key aspect of the transformation system. People are involved in all primary and support activities. An organisation needs to manage its workforce. People need to understand their roles and functions and their links with each other. Motivated staff will be more productive, they will have more job satisfaction, with less absenteeism and less staff turnover. Motivating people is a key part of achieving the overall mission of an organisation.

There are many legal requirements that cover the selection and employment of staff, for example equal opportunity legislation. All employment activities need to conform to the increasingly complex laws. Failure to do so may result in prosecution, substantial damages and a loss of reputation and credibility. In organisations with trade union agreements, extensive consultations and negotiations will be required. Mistakes can be expensive. British Airways lost around £80 million on the three-day cabin crew strike in June 1997; in 1996, it managed to avert a threatened strike by pilots but this still cost £15 million in lost profits. In 1997, BA announced a £94 million profit-sharing payout to staff and a fund to buy ten shares for each of its 48,000 staff in an effort to rebuild the management–staff relationship.

Human resource management involves both day-to-day and strategic issues. Staff have to be recruited. This may be a major issue in itself, requiring searches for suitable candidates, interviews and other selection procedures. Reward structures need to be formulated, involving appropriate levels of pay and non-pay elements, which may include company cars, health insurance, annual holiday entitlements, etc. Piece rates, bonuses and overtime payments need working out for production line and shift employees. Short-term measures may need to be taken to alleviate absenteeism and poor motivation problems. NHS staff, for example, have been offered various inducements to encourage attendance and performance.

On joining an organisation, people will need preliminary training and induction. Training, development and motivation are not once-a-year issues but activities that need to be considered and managed at all times. This is a partnership between functional managers and the human resources department. Operational staff, specialists and senior management require appropriate training, which must be agreed and co-ordinated into training programmes. Control systems need to measure staff performance, and appropriate appraisal reviews are required between staff and their immediate managers.

Human resource management can become part of the overall strategy of an organisation. Requirements and forward plans must be made to ensure that future skills needs are met through staff development strategies and succession planning. It should not be a surprise when someone retires or if particular skilled staff are required to carry out a new production process. The nature of employment is changing and, to maintain flexibility, many organisations are now not recruiting full-time staff on full employment contracts. Instead, increasing use is being made of short-term contracts, lasting perhaps one or two years. Additional flexibility is being created by the employment of contract staff. In many organisations more than half of the people operating on the site may be contract staff or on short-term contracts. This situation needs to be managed with care to ensure retention of key staff and to avoid any potential legal complications. In some areas, such as information technology and the building trade, there may be shortages of suitably skilled workers in the marketplace. Shortages are matched by wage increases, as staff can push for higher pay. Part of an organisation's strategic plan involves matching an organisation's resources, including its human resources, with its core values and mission and the business environment.

Consider Hewlett Packard's HRM policy. The company provides long-term employment and opportunities for personal growth and development; in return, employees are expected to perform to a certain standard, adjust to changes, be willing to learn new skills and to be flexible. The policy includes promotion from within where possible, which means that staff have to be trained from within to meet demands.

All organisations are required to adapt and change as environmental factors create different demands. Change cannot happen without the co-operation of the people within the organisation, so HRM is instrumental in the management of change. Changes in funding, in processes, in location, all require the co-operation of people to make them work.

The phases in an organisation's life cycle affect resource requirements and functions. The growth and any restructuring of an organisation involves hiring of staff, firing of staff, retraining of staff, maintaining morale with existing staff, change of working patterns through teams, different responsibilities, and different modes of decision-making. We've already talked about downsizing, subcontracting, flexible, flatter hierarchies; these developments all mean that there is a requirement for multi-skilled flexible staff. There is considerable divergence between remuneration of these multi-skilled staff between organisations, and heavy collective bargaining is generally restricted to the cash-strapped public sector. Unions, managers and shop-floor workers appreciate that an unsuccessful company cannot fund pay increases it cannot afford.

In the 1990s, organisations have accepted the crucial role of the customer in their strategy and operations. However, we can consider that the first step in satisfying the customer is to involve the employees and put them first. Company bosses talk about the workforce being their greatest asset, but they need to treat it as such. We can look at an extreme example: John Lewis department stores has a unique corporate structure without shareholders and it regards its 36,000 staff as partners with an entitlement to know what is going on, a responsibility to make the business successful and an entitlement to a share of the profits. This gives a three-fold dimension to the relationship between management and staff, of sharing knowledge, sharing power and sharing gain. The knowledge is shared through a weekly magazine that details the performance of stores, so that staff know exactly how well the company is doing, although it also means that competitors have immediate information too, which may have some negative effects. Power is shared through a branch council, with elected representatives from all departments and areas; a central council operates at national level. This may give a rather unwieldy structure that other companies could not manage. Sharing gain is through bonuses; in 1997, for example, John Lewis paid out £82 million – each employee, regardless of level, receiving the same percentage.

This attitude and approach to staff could still be applied within a more usual corporate structure. British Airways, for example, gives its employees the same information that it gives to the market and its shareholders and, in 1996, it distributed nearly £100 million to employees as part of its profit-share scheme, against £120 million to shareholders. At Microsoft, all full-time staff are offered share options that are probably worth around US$30 billion at 1997 prices. Many companies have developed variable bonuses and profit-linked pay, although these have undermined any notion of a national going rate for the job.

Human resource management is critical to the success of an organisation. A good working relationship is required with other functional management areas. Production workers gain most of their day-to-day training from supervisors and local managers rather than from training specialists. Much of the activity of human resource management is co-ordinating and developmental or strategic. As management of people is involved, so the people aspect of informal and formal relationships becomes clear, and the culture of the organisation becomes more important.

ACTIVITY 10

Jill is expanding her workforce by hiring two full-time sales personnel and a bookkeeper. List the HRM issues she will need to address.

The HRM issues include: legal requirements for employing staff, including recruitment and selection; terms and conditions of the job; means of recruitment and selection; details about the job tasks, and evaluation of appropriate staff with the right skills and qualifications; payment and rewards; induction and training; control and appraisal.

4.8 Research and development

Porter does not identify research and development (R&D) as a primary or a support activity as such. An organisation might place the R&D function in the technology or operations area through the development of new processes or products, or in the marketing area in the development of new products. Key concepts in innovation are 'time-to-market' (how long from the initial concept or idea to products on the shelf) and 'product life cycle' (how long the product exists in the market). For many organisations, the only way to remain successful is by a continuous process of innovation, Moore, Pessemier (1993, p11). All aspects of the product need to be researched: why customers use the product, how they use it, how it is manufactured, the materials of construction and how the product is marketed, Crawford (1991, pp 25–41).

Is innovation technology driven or customer led? In the marketplace, organisations have to find creative, effective and efficient ways to provide better benefits to customers, Curtis 1994, (pp 40–42). In the 1980s, there were two standards for VCRs: VHS and BETA. Many engineers, on specific technical grounds, considered the BETA format to provide better quality. However, the VHS format gained the larger market share as producers took care to ensure a full range of pre-recorded films. For research to be effective it needs good links with all parts of the company, including production and marketing. For some industries, such as pharmaceuticals, R&D has a crucial and never-ending role in new product development as drug patents expire. It is the same in the computer industry, where there is a continual requirement for technological developments. In mining and oil exploration, R&D also plays a big role.

In some organisations, innovation and creativity are encouraged in all staff. At Dyson, manufacturers of the bagless vacuum cleaner, staff are encouraged to dress creatively and think creatively. New ideas for operating, products and marketing are all welcomed, and the financial commitment to R&D is high. Apple computers welcomed individual creativity in the 1980s, but it was not able to harness this creativity into co-operation between R&D, marketing and manufacturing departments. In 1997, with the reappointment of one of its founders, Steve Jobs, Apple was seeking to re-establish entrepreneurialism and creativity.

Research may be long term: new technologies such as digital fibre optical communication highways to replace analogue copper wires may take a long time to be introduced. Research may be shorter term, geared to developing some modest product such as a new improved washing powder, or to process improvement such as Pilkington's revolutionary float glass process. Organisations that do not invest in the future, however, find that they have obsolete products that are over-expensive to produce. Increasingly, organisations are required to devote more effort to devising processes that are environmentally friendly, using resources that are recyclable, for example, and with environmentally friendly packaging. We look at this issue further in Unit 2.

The R&D team is at the centre of the new product development (NPD) process, but requires extensive links to other functions in the organisation, for example:

- finance, for costing and investment appraisal
- marketing, for consumer reaction and market-size analysis
- production, to discover if the product can be made economically and in large enough quantities
- human resource management, as new skills may be needed to manufacture, market and support the product in the field
- procurement, to decide what new raw materials and components are needed and where they can be sourced in sufficient quantities and quality.

The R&D function is the future of the organisation but it is only effective when linked into an organisation that directs and applies the advances in the marketplace.

ACTIVITY 11

The R&D department of a company that manufactures racing bikes has completed tests showing that the alloy frame could be replaced with a carbon fibre composite one. The experimental frame has been developed in collaboration with a university research group.

The experimental bike has been tested by the company's racing team on a test track and the product looks like a world beater. The organisation has no manufacturing experience of carbon fibre composites and no equipment suitable for fabricating the new high-performance frame. The company's racing team have had an indifferent year and the present machines appear to lack competitive edge over new imported ones. In the past, new breakthroughs have been launched onto the market with heavy promotion linked to the success of the racing team with the new cycles. Before suggesting the product change, what functional areas should the project manager talk to and what information is needed for a decision to be made?

Take about 15 minutes over this. Some issues you should consider include:

- should the company contract out a specialist to make the frame or develop the new manufacturing technology in-house?
- what would be the impact on production where the existing frame is made?
- would the marketing department need to be informed of the change?

There will be a long lead time for the company to use composites to make carbon fibre components so they could contract out the production. It would need to research suppliers through the university research department that developed these materials for the prototype. A specification for the supply of the frame would need to be drawn up. The marketing department would need to do market research on the customer base to discover any customer resistance and to consider what would be needed for the promotional launch with the racing team.

Finance would need to do costings and also to check the financial standing and stability of the intended contractors; if you have a supplier that goes out of business you may find your own production at a standstill until you can find a second source. Production would need to look at stocks and how the replacement frame might impact on its operations. Some people might lose their jobs. Specific information would be needed on the price and batch sizes given by the potential suppliers for the frame and on the length of time they would need for the initial order (they would have to make special moulds) and for subsequent orders (since they now would have the moulds this should take less time). Care would be needed in the change-over period to phase out the old model and introduce the new model. HRM would need to be involved, as there would be job changes and/or job losses.

R&D, and the new development process, tends to involve the whole organisation. Again, we see that success is not the result of the activity of a single person or function, but the co-ordination of the whole organisation's functions into an integrated team, Porter (1985, p164).

4.9 Procurement

Any organisation buys a large range of products and services, from the raw materials and components for manufacturing products to services such as telephones and cleaning. Purchasing is essential to the competitive advantage of the organisation. For every £1,000 that can be saved on purchasing, you might need to increase sales by £10,000, requiring additional resources, to get the same overall effect. Purchasing needs to be part of the strategy of the organisation. It involves sourcing materials and suppliers, matching supply and demand, controlling prices and costs, and maintaining quality of supply.

It is not just manufacturers that need to control purchasing, but service organisations. Midland Bank, for example, part of the HSBC group, spends £500 million each year on purchasing anything from pencils to cars and computers. It controls this budget through a 600-strong purchasing and administration group. Other service organisations may not have such centralised buying procedures, but still must address the same issues. Bankers Trust, a banking group based in New York, has a London-based purchasing team of 25, and saved £10.7 million on its worldwide telecommunications contracts over three years.

In the late 1990s, the role of suppliers has been under scrutiny. Porter considers that they should be seen as long-term partners and that strategic alliances are required to get the benefits of JIT, with no inspection of incoming goods, Porter, (1985, p. 50). Management of the supply system is just as important as the control of the internal operations; it involves the management of specifications, requisitioning, stock control, cost control, purchasing, receiving and payment. As you saw earlier, an organisation is only as good as all the links in the supply chain.

The motor industry uses five criteria for appraising a supplier's capability and potential, Payne, Chelsom, Reavill, (1996, p. 432):

- management ability and attitude
- quality performance
- delivery performance
- technical capability
- commercial performance.

These individual factors can be broken down into sub-factors. Ford, for example, scores quality performance under three headings with weightings for each:

- management attitude and commitment (20%)

- quality management system (30%)
- delivered quality performance (50%).

As with R&D, the performance of the buying function requires good co-operation and co-ordination with all other functions. Its effectiveness is dependent on the information acquired on supplies from other areas, so it is dependent on the organisational management information system (MIS). Cost, quality, and scheduling of resources, for example, affect other processes within the organisation. Logistics and procurement are tightly linked, as logistics is concerned with the inward flow of goods, or inputs to the transformation system, and procurement is concerned with the actual purchasing of this flow.

4.10 Management information systems

In Porter's model of an organisation no explicit element is devoted to information management. However there is a clear need to integrate all the organisation's functions and its links up and down the vertical integration of the industry. Here we briefly consider some of the management information system (MIS) issues that are needed to maintain and develop a company's competitive advantage.

To manage an individual function, staff need to know what they have to do; this sounds obvious but in practice management must give considerable thought to the way in which the right information gets to the right people at the right time. A production department needs to know how much of what product to make in any time period. There will be lots of data available: the present stock levels of components, part-assembled products, finished products and the sales forecasts for the period. Good management information systems will enable production to decide what and how much to make, stock control to know what is available, sales to know when delivery can be effected, and procurement to know what needs to be ordered, finance and accounts to know what inputs need paying for and what payment is received following delivery of the product. Sales and marketing need to know about its customers and their purchases. All functions and management needs to know what is happening in the outside world, both the immediate industrial, and the wider business, environments.

Information is needed for the day-to-day running of each function, for the integrated organisation and for strategic decision-making, planning and implementation. Internal databases hold information on customers, staff, competitors, suppliers, sales, stock of components, stock of finished products. This could be managed through the Intranet, an individual organisation's internal network of computers that shares information in a standard format. Employees have an increasing overload of information that needs to be managed effectively so that the right people deal with appropriate information. Managers access this information directly through their own computer terminals, not waiting any more for a sales or production report to arrive on their desks. The Internet supplies immediate information on the external environment, with anything from changes in share prices, news of interest rates, competitors' performances, details of current products in the global marketplace and their availability and prices, to political events and the latest developments in government. In 1997, 70 per cent of world wide web sites were corporate, compared with 20 per cent in 1996. All this knowledge needs to be managed for competitive advantage.

Certain key features must be kept in mind for maintaining an effective information system. It is essential that information should be captured as soon as possible and recorded in the system. If it takes two days to update the system, then management are attempting to run the operation as it was two days ago, not as it needs to be run today. If errors occur in sales forecasts or order entry, then production will make the wrong product and procurement will buy the wrong stocks. Information is the glue that holds the company together; without good information and rapid and accurate transmission the organisation can fall apart, Curtis (1994, p. 200). The various functions of an organisation will only add up to success if all functions are kept in gear doing the right things at the right time. Responsive and reliable information systems are essential for this.

ACTIVITY 12

Spend five or 10 minutes noting down Jill's information requirements.

Internally, Jill's information requirements include stock of lines, stock of supplies, product specifications, staff details and performance, customer details, supplier details, cash flow, accounts payable, accounts receivable.

Externally, information about the general and business environment is required, with particular information about competitors and suppliers. For example, political upheavals are affecting transport of supplies from Sri Lanka; the company that supplies earclips goes bankrupt and is bought out by a large group that will not give Jill any credit terms but wants minimum orders and payment up front. There might be changes in employment regulations, changes in the local environment or national trends to monitor.

REVIEW ACTIVITY 4

Over the last 20 years the concentration of the retail food sector has given the competitive advantage to the major supermarkets (Tesco, Sainsbury, etc.). As a result, suppliers including the food manufacturers (such as Heinz) and farmers (for fresh produce) have had their profit margins eroded. To respond to this competitive pressure from the major retailers, some producers of similar products such as wine have grouped into marketing associations or have formed full co-operative ventures. The case study below illustrates the type of situation that faces growers who wish to escape from this situation and claim more of the added value.

CASE STUDY

Helen Rice

Helen Rice owns a farm. Over the last few years, she has made less and less profit from the fruit and vegetables grown on the farm. A group of her neighbours have experienced the same problems and they have formed a co-operative to distribute and market their produce. The farms within the co-operative still operate in an individual way to produce their own outputs of produce. The co-operative is using this produce as its inputs.

There are two large barns, which are not used at the moment on the farm, with easy road access and hard standing. It is unlikely that planning permission to use these premises as a shop would be a problem. The group have decided to clean and pack their products to sell in a farm shop directly to the customer and to distribute to local retailers, restaurants and hotels.

What activities will be conducted by this co-operative and what functions need to be considered? Make notes, using Porter's value chain headings as a framework.

You will look at each of these elements in greater depth in later units but it is helpful to see first how all the parts fit together. Remember, in this small business you have to consider both packaging and bulk sales to restaurants and direct retail.

Summary

In this section, we have considered the contribution of the main functional areas to an organisation's success: inbound and outbound logistics, operations, sales and marketing, field service, infrastructure, human resource management, research and development and procurement. Throughout the module we look at some of these functions in more detail. One key component of the infrastructure is management information systems; without information there is no co-ordination, communication, or decision-making. We looked at logistics as the heart of the business – just how do we provide the goods and services? The business is of no value if we do not supply customers with what they want – the marketing and sales function determines what customers want, where and at what price and then inform and persuade them to purchase. People do not want a photocopier as a desirable piece of equipment, they want the service provided by the machine: clear, fast, cheap copies. For many types of products service is important for the customer, and this can be enhanced by training, installation and repair. Throughout an organisation, people are involved in everything and their performance is essential to the organisation's success, so managing an organisation's people is a very important activity.

SECTION 5

Organisational Culture

Introduction

Culture comprises the shared understandings, values, assumptions and aspirations that individuals learn and assume. These result in outlooks, codes of conduct, rituals, symbols and expectations that control and guide norms of behaviour. Culture was defined by Hofstede (1984) as: 'the collective programming of the mind which distinguishes the members of one human group from another. Culture, in this sense, includes systems of values, and values are amongst the building blocks of culture.' Depending on how established the culture is, the underlying values or the manifested behaviour may be the more powerful influence within the culture.

Differing groups have distinct cultures. Since an individual does not normally belong to a single group but to several groups, he or she may reflect many different cultural influences. In the same way, an organisation has a culture that is a total of all of its experiences and influences. If any of these is in conflict with any other, then obviously the organisation and its individual members will have a problem. Management needs to take differences into account to obtain the best individual and organisational performance.

Schneider and Barsoux (1997) view this cultural system as a set of interacting spheres of culture comprising the following elements:

- **national and regional** – geography, history, political and economic forces, climate, religion and language
- **professional** – education, training, selection, socialisation
- **industry** – resources, technology, product market, regulation, competitive advantage
- **company** – founder, leader, administrative heritage, nature of product and/or industry, stage of development
- **functional** – external environment, nature of task, time horizon.

Each sphere has its own set of values, beliefs and underlying assumptions. The influence that these cultural spheres have on any particular situation within an organisation will vary. We shall now examine some specific facets of culture affecting organisations.

5.1 National influences

An organisation is made up of people, so the cultural features of the national culture will form a basis for the organisational culture. Mead (1992) develops the theories researched by Hofstede (1983). His work compared attitudes held in 53 countries and he was able to analyse national cultures against four dimensions.

- **Power distance** – the distance between individuals at different levels of a hierarchy. In cultures with a greater 'power distance', authoritarian attitudes are easily accepted. In cultures with a low 'power distance', there are more non-elitist values and a more democratic style is acceptable.
- **Uncertainty avoidance** – more or less the need to avoid uncertainty about the future. In cultures with high 'uncertainty avoidance', people are prepared to take fewer risks and look to issues such as job security. In cultures of low 'uncertainty avoidance', there is more tolerance of conflict and competitiveness and less need for written rules.
- **Individualism versus collectivism** – the relations between the individual and his or her fellows. In individualistic cultures, the stress is on the individual's achievements and rights. In collectivist cultures, motivation is derived more from the individual's contribution to the group's achievement.
- **Masculinity versus femininity** – the division of roles and values in society. In masculine cultures, the gender roles are sharply differentiated. In feminine cultures, the gender roles are less differentiated.

The UK was found to have a low power distance and a weak uncertainty avoidance, whereas Japan was found to have high power distance relationships and strong uncertainty avoidance. This research would indicate that Japanese workers respond to hierarchical power, like to know exactly what they have to do and will take little risk, British workers respond less well to hierarchical power and will take more risk. We could argue that these factors are enduring values and are not accommodations to outside influences, so that an organisation would need to take these factors into account in a structure that promotes these cultural features. There is no single universal management approach that will fit all contexts. The international manager needs to adapt his or her style.

However, there is an interaction between the cultures of individuals acquired from the society they live in, and the culture of the organisation. In a healthy environment there will be a movement on both sides, as continual development takes place in cultural norms. This is evident where a major successful organisation moves operations into a new geographic location where the cultures are very different. Japanese operations have succeeded well in the UK, achieving levels of productivity that are among the best in the world, but this process has only been achieved by the adaptation of UK staff, and imagination and flexibility on the part of the Japanese management.

Companies have to reflect to some extent the values of the societies they operate within. The 'greening' of consumer products was not driven by legislation but by the demands of customers who demanded an environmentally responsible culture. Failure of an organisation to appreciate the culture of different markets is a frequent problem. Successful organisations appreciate the cultural differences in the market and ensure that their staff are appropriately trained and fit in with the culture of the new market.

5.2 What is organisational culture?

Lynch (1997) and Johnson (1992) have identified some cultural factors specific to the organisation. The history and ownership of an organisation influences culture, and may continue to do so for a considerable time. Consider the computing companies, IBM and Hewlett Packard. IBM has always been in office automation, HP was a science-based company making technical measurement equipment. These companies' routes into computing were along totally different paths, one from office mainframe (formal accounting systems), the other from science-based mini computers (real-time data acquisition from analytical instruments). Both organisations have a distinctive culture.

Technologies have their own cultures. Science-based and technology-based staff tend to come from a much less formal culture than some other professionals, such as accountants. This can cause tensions when an established organisation has to graft on new technologies. Growth influences culture. As a small firm increases in size there is a need for more formal structures and more defined roles and so larger organisations tend to have more formal cultures than smaller ones.

We can analyse the culture of an organisation through the framework of the **cultural web** that brings together a number of different components, Johnson, Scholes, (1997).

Organisational structure

Who reports to whom and what is the nature of the relationship? In a university there are a number of different functions, each with their own culture. In the area of new research (such as environmental science) cross-faculty teams will form under a framework of collaboration, and decisions about the research approach will be arrived at by discussion and by evolving a common view. Within a university, there are also day-to-day operational activities such as maintenance of the buildings and security. Here the situation is much more formal and the work activity much more controlled, with a hierarchical structure. Different structures and cultures can co-exist in the same organisation.

Symbols

These are means by which values and beliefs are made visible. They include logos, titles and language of address, for example. What are the symbols of office? These may be formal, such as academic robes at a university, a judge's wig in a law court or uniforms for supermarket staff, or informal, such as expensive designer suits and cigars for the chairman. Typical symbols are cost and type of company car. In a military establishment only certain higher officer ranks are permitted to have fully fitted carpets in their offices. EasyJet, the no-frills airline, dresses its staff in T-shirts and jeans rather than the smart uniforms of more traditional airlines, indicating to stakeholders that it is not wasting money on what it regards as unnecessary frills.

Routines

What are the normal ways of doing things? In an office, a simple note to the maintenance staff will get a defective light fitting repaired. In a safety critical environment, such as a chemical process plant, a very formal system of 'permit to work' would exist. Different routines and cultures develop under different conditions.

Stories

What do people talk about in the organisation? What matters in the organisation? These form the myths and folklore of the company and have the same importance as myths have on regional cultures. A particular company had a very long tradition of excellence in computer programming. In evening discussions after work, older programmers would tell younger programmers what it was like when 64K was a lot of memory and they held programs on paper tape. In a multinational with an international field salesforce, at the annual sales conference the talk would be about disastrous sales trips that ended up with the sales representative being stranded by floods or a revolution in some obscure part of the world and being rescued by an heroic chairman.

Rituals

Beyond the normal routine what does the organisation highlight? Some American-style companies have the ritual of 'dressing down' on Fridays to emphasise their informal culture. On the designated days, formal business dress is banned and staff are required to be 'casual'. The ritual can become quite precise, with unwritten rules which, for example, preclude jeans.

Power structures

Who makes the decisions and how are they influenced? In an organisation that has been created by an owner or founder you often find a very focused power structure with all important decisions made by the owner. In a small law or accountancy partnership, all the senior partners will be involved in key decisions, giving a devolved power or person culture.

Control systems

Is the control through bureaucracy and documentation or the reverse? For example, workers might be required to check in and out of work so that their hours are precisely timed, there might be designated coffee breaks, or workers might be just expected to 'do their job', and what time they get to work or leave, within reason, or what time they take off during the day is regarded as irrelevant. Is every process and procedure dictated by endless form filling?

Handy (1993) suggests that most organisations fall into four cultural styles:

- power culture
- role culture
- task culture
- person culture.

In a **power culture**, power flows from one dominant person or group. Decision making is fast. This situation is often found in entrepreneurial organisations built up by single-minded owners or founders, for example, Jill and her jewellery business, Richard Branson and the Virgin empire, Bill Gates and Microsoft. James Dyson, designer and maker of the UK market leader in vacuum cleaners, promotes his own culture in his organisation, encouraging his staff to follow him in being creative and pioneering. Memos are banned, e-mails are discouraged and face-to-face discussion is encouraged. He provides architect-designed premises and designer furniture and food for his staff.

In a **person culture**, the organisation exists for each individual's satisfaction, such as is the case with a doctor's or a lawyer's practice. In a **role culture** the system is run with rigid structures, rules and regulations, procedures and committees. This is a bureaucratic culture, and is likely to be found in the public sector or in insurance or banking. Change is difficult to manage.

In a **task culture**, the rules and procedures are much less important, and typically multidisciplinary teams adapt to the changing situations. This type of culture is likely to fit with a matrix organisational structure, as projects are managed individually. Here power rests with the team, as is the case, for example, in the advertising or film industries, where people are brought together for a particular project. Consider Imagination, a London design consultancy that specialises in architecture, lighting, graphics, and theatre projects. It promotes a culture of creativity through the design of its own premises, and imbues in the staff the importance of great design and individual designers. However, work has to be co-ordinated through team activity to deliver the product to the customer.

Human resource management plays a key role in hiring the right people to fit in with the culture of the organisation. If a manager likes to come to work in a suit, follow clear procedures where all instructions are confirmed in writing and there are guidelines for behaviour, then he or she will not fit into the casual innovative culture of Dyson, for example, no matter what experience or qualifications he or she has. Equally, if a manager is very flexible, enjoys a fast changing environment, likes to take the initiative and responds well to creative people and their ideas then perhaps he or she might fit in at Imagination, where Gary Withers, the chief executive officer, takes an active role in all recruitment.

The individual's beliefs and values have to reflect and accept those of the organisation. If you believe, for example, that animals should not be used for cosmetic testing, then just as you would not use a particular product so too you would not choose to work for an organisation that uses animals. Instead, you might choose to work for Body Shop, which does not test on animals and advocates a 'green' approach in the sourcing of its ingredients. As well as recruitment, HRM can also initiate and train new employees into the culture and the way that things are done.

ACTIVITY 13

In about 100 words evaluate which of the of the four culture types – power culture, role culture, task culture and person culture – you might expect to find in a law court. How would a barrister fit into this culture?

The objective of a court is to administer justice and evaluate evidence in a consistent way. People would be most concerned if the outcome of a trial depended on the day of the week, the location of the court or the law court personnel involved. You would find a role culture, with rules, regulations and procedures, that would ensure consistent administration of the law. Dress is very formal for all staff. A barrister would be required to adhere precisely to the operation of the court and to conform in terms of dress, although in fact he or she comes from chambers that have a person culture. Chambers is a collection of barristers, working individually, but with shared administrative and support activities. Any hierarchy within the chambers is as a result of the experience, expertise or success of the individuals.

5.3 Culture change

As organisations respond to environmental and internal pressures, this imposes a need for changes in the culture patterns. To change culture it is necessary not only to change behaviour but also to change the values and beliefs that underpin it.

Consider, for example, a large multinational organisation that is planning a strategic move from a production culture that responds to demands and policies set by senior management at head office, to an entrepreneur culture where the local regional management has total responsibility for its own direction. The organisation will stand or fall on the individual decisions of certain managers.

At the operational level, this change in emphasis will be reflected in the generation of a new culture, requiring more flexibility and adaptation. Given the greater uncertainty there will be a culture of judged risk taking and much less dependence on the formal rules which tend to exist in large organisations. As a result of this, not all staff will be happy with the changed corporate culture; some people may leave, and others may stay for financial reasons but be stressed under these new cultural conditions.

Many aspects of business development involve culture changes in their staff. At one time, the banks held a virtual monopoly of personal financial services. As such they could treat their customers as accounts and not people. As building societies, high street stores and supermarkets, such as Marks & Spencer and Sainsbury, began to offer financial services, banks have needed to become more customer friendly and marketing orientated. Some staff may prefer to deal with their customers as remote numbers; others may quickly adapt to dealing with customers in a friendly and competent way.

Two other areas where culture is considered essential to success are operational safety and total quality management. The structure and culture of safety and quality in the 1960s was by inspection with safety officers and quality control inspectors. Industry has moved to safety and quality being the individual responsibility of every member of the organisation. In many organisations now, there are no formal quality staff in the production areas; this is part of operations and the new operations culture.

As the organisation changes in response to revised objectives and in response to the external environment, so does power in the organisation. In a stable environment, many organisations were able to rely on a bureaucratic culture and power structure. In such a situation power flows from the top and work proceeds by a set of prescribed rules and regulations. Front-line staff are given little authority, discretion and freedom. Associated with this culture was a system of many intermediate layers of management, such as supervisors and departmental managers.

Given the context of the need for more organisational flexibility, this type of power culture has two key weaknesses. The operational rules are placed in an authoritative top-down approach and feedback from operations may be both slow and distorted. In this culture it is assumed that the top power base must have the answer, but in shifting situations answers may have to come from widely differing skill bases. Increasingly, organisations are having to move from positional power ('you do this because I am the boss and I have told you so') to expert power. The person who makes the decision is the person who has the best skills and knowledge. The result in this shift to more delegative styles of management is to cut out some layers of management, or de-layer, with an increase in the responsibility, authority and decision range of front-line staff.

REVIEW ACTIVITY 5

Take about 20 minutes to review an organisation of your own selection, such as a place in which you have worked or a club you belong to, and use the framework of the cultural web to explore its culture.

Make comments about your selected organisation under the headings:

- organisational structure
- symbols
- routines
- stories
- rituals
- power structures
- control systems.

Summary

Just as individuals have a culture so do organisations; management must manage both the organisational culture and the culture of the individuals within it. Organisations are not static and as they evolve the culture of the organisation must change, as must the culture of the individuals within the organisation. Culture change is not simple as it involves changing people's core values.

SECTION 6

Information

Introduction

To manage the future is to manage information. To make effective decisions at all levels of the organisation, decision makers need the right information at the right time. We first investigate the nature of information and how it differs from data. We look at the key features of information and, most importantly, the need for accuracy. Information from internal and external sources is needed for strategic decisions and for operational decisions within all the functional areas; not all areas require the same information in the same format. In today's information-rich world, information technology is vital to the management of information. The transmission of information requires the process of communication and channels of communication within the organisational structure.

6.1 Nature of information

We can define data as the raw material from which information is generated. Data are text, numbers, figures or any combination of these. Data itself is of little use; what is required for management action is information. Information is data processed and converted into a form that is useful to the decision maker (Gupta, 1996).

Gupta (1996) defines the main characteristics of information as:

- **subjectivity** – its value can be dependent on the attitudes of the recipient
- **relevance** – if you are running the purchasing department, you need stock and production figures, and sales figures may give you an idea of future requirements, but you don't need detailed sales figures based on responses to different promotions

- **timeliness** – stock control information is needed now, not next week
- **accuracy** – inaccurate information is worse than useless
- **format** – the information must be appropriate for the purpose and in a usable format
- **completeness** – if only part of the information is available then the decision maker either has further research to do or must make a risky decision based on incomplete information
- **accessibility** – it should be available where and when the manager needs it.

The problem in business is that there is too much data and not enough information. The process of converting data into information involves the initial collection, classification, sorting and other transformation processes, summarising, storing, retrieval and dissemination. Consider the amount of data that a company will have on a personnel record system. There will be the records of each employee's education, personal details that include address, next of kin, age, results of medical examinations, attendance record, pay records, training record, performance reviews, etc. These records will extend over the working life of the employee.

At the operational level, the payroll department just needs to have sufficient data to calculate next month's pay and tax, national insurance and pension deductions. At the strategic level, HRM may wish to know if there are people with particular qualifications, experience or training available in the organisation for a new position. In either case, the functional area needs information that is just part of the total amount of data available and in an easy-to-use form. The human resources manager does not want to be faced with 100 personnel files to go through to see if there is some member of staff who knows the company's product range, can speak Spanish and could be a suitable person for a new export sales position. The payroll clerk needs the number of normal hours worked, details of overtime and time off, not details of employees' education.

We can see two important points here. First, that in most cases, there is far too much data and selection of the relevant information is essential. Second, that access to data may often have to be restricted. Some of the information contained in company records will be highly confidential either from a personal or a commercial perspective. Thus, access to information should be restricted to those with legitimate reasons and authority.

The accuracy of the data for decisions depends on the nature of the decision. For example, for the calculation of pension rights, the precise dates that each individual joined the company are required. For a job selection exercise, it is sufficient to know that the person has more than five years' experience.

An organisation faced with the management of information has to make a number of key decisions.

- Who needs information?
- What data are needed to provide the information?

- How might this data be filtered, edited and presented to provide real information rather than data overload?
- How accurate does the data need to be?
- When and where is the information?
- What security, legal and ethical considerations are there in the collection, storage, transformation and access to data?
- Over what time-scales is it necessary to store the data? (The nature and time-scales for the future information needs of the organisation are impossible to predict; discarded data may be a valuable company resource.)

ACTIVITY 14

Many supermarkets have installed laser checkouts and many customers will use a loyalty or credit card with their purchase. Here is a list of some of the data which might be recorded from a single sales transaction:

- identity of the card used (with a profile of the user)
- identity of the operator
- date and time of the transaction
- list of products purchased
- pack size or amount
- price
- any promotional offers used.

Write down what information will be required by:

- checkout operator
- stock control management
- store personnel manager
- store security
- marketing department.

For the checkout operator, the information needed for the completion of the work is that the card identity is correct and valid (it is not a stolen card, for example), that each item has scanned correctly and the total sum to be collected.

The stock control management will not be concerned with the details of the individual transaction but will want to know at the end of the day what packs have been sold so that the stock can be re-ordered.

The store personnel manager will be concerned with the efficiency of the staff and will be concerned with the number of transactions completed and the number of errors made.

Store security will want to know if any suspect card is presented (out of credit limit, stolen, etc.). Security will also want the same information as the stock control. Only when the shelf stock is checked will it be possible to establish the level of theft (which is a significant loss of profit for some shops). The detailed breakdown will allow a check to be made if a suspicious person claims to have purchased goods.

The marketing department will need information about customers' individual purchases, so that consumer behaviour profiles can be built up for future promotions and as part of any market research. Personalised discount vouchers might be added to its mailings, and high-spending customers might be invited to special events such as wine tastings.

Each functional area only needs access to part of the available data in a usable format and the management information systems should have the capability of abstracting this desired information, thus making people more efficient.

6.2 Sources of information

There are two aspects to the sourcing of information: the collection of the data and its conversion into information. The most immediate source of data is within the company itself. One of the key reasons for the growth in competitive advantage of the high-street supermarkets is their ability to collect a vast amount of data about their customers' transactions and to convert it to timely information for the conduct of the business. This not only includes information about the transactions but other aspects of the business. For example, analysis of the data on customer complaints, not only allows defective goods to be identified, but often shows how better products can be created. Analysis of individual customer's spending patterns identifies trends and enables personalised promotions and product information to be directed to interested parties. Main selling lines can be selected for on-line purchase and delivery.

In general, a set of interacting sources is required for the organisation. Kotler (1997) lists the main elements as:

- internal information
- research information
- intelligence
- analytical systems.

We can illustrate these elements by looking at the process of the product development and launch of a new toothpaste by a major company. The **internal information**, for example, concerns sales of existing lines, production costs, equipment costs, etc.

Research is the systematic collection of data for a specific business or management need. A company would conduct **secondary research** from already published information. This might include the nature and occurrence of dental problems available from medical and industry sources over the Internet or in publications. The company would also conduct market research analysis to identify the target population, consumer buying patterns and competitors' products. Again, this information is from a secondary source. Secondary information costs less than primary research that requires the active collection and analysis of new data.

The organisation would then complete some **primary research** by questioning people to find out their views on oral hygiene through face-to-face surveys, telephone surveys or through postal questionnaires. It may be possible to include some appropriate questions in larger consumer surveys conducted by market research companies or consumer bodies. The information collected is **quantitative** (How often do you brush your teeth each day?) or **qualitative** (How do you feel after you have cleaned your teeth?). Both types of information are needed to make business decisions. The organisation would also need to know what toothpaste the consumer currently buys, from which outlet and why. Is the decision based on cost, flavour, additives, freshmint taste, plaque control, antibacterial mouthwash properties, colour, packaging, advertising, for example? Information about consumer attitudes to a whole range of product characteristics would be required. Does the consumer buy the same product for all members of the family? Does he or she buy several tubes at once? Does he or she respond to offers?

The combination of this primary and secondary research enables the company to formulate the new toothpaste. Large sums of money are spent in fundamental research into mechanisms of tooth decay, gum disease, tartar build-up and plaque and their control, for example, through fluoride and other additives. This is typical of most organisation's R&D and is a vital source of information. It is essential to direct the research, however, and the marketing research is a vital aspect of a sound R&D plan. It is no good the research department coming up with some wonderful new ingredient for toothpaste if it is too expensive to make or is unlikely to pass the health and safety regulations.

Intelligence is the specific collection of general information of business interest. Here it would be the activity of competitors. Trade literature might provide information about new marketing campaigns and product introductions and the Internet might carry information on new research projects and global product launches. The share prices of competitors and all those involved with the company's supply chain would be relevant. Samples of new products would be evaluated for performance in the laboratory, and chemical analysis would show how they had been formulated. Analysing a competitor's products can be a good way of improving your own product.

Sometimes the information is hidden or distorted. **Analytical systems** allow us to decode information. Consider the process used on a compact disc; the data is a series of binary codes, it takes an 'analytical' system to decode this and convert this to the 'information', the music. Such systems may be very complex mathematical models or very simple. For example, sales are often tracked on a month-by-month basis. Not all months have the same number of trading days, however; there are different numbers of days in the month, as well as bank holidays. So an apparent increase in sales of 10 per cent might just be the result of more working days in the month, for example. Or an increase in sales is likely to follow a special promotion, such as a 2-for-1 offer, which will lead people to stock up with a product, and then not buy any more for a while. This sales analysis is not just for the use of marketing but is vital to all parts of the organisation because operations, raw material purchases, etc. are sales driven. Poor sales forecasts will result in either stock-outs or excess stock – either event will damage the profitability of the organisation.

Information involves the collection and integration of data from a wide range of sources. The timely, effective and efficient sourcing of information provides critical competitive advantage. For example, supermarkets have found that significant revenue can be obtained by the sale of the marketing results from their laser point-of-sale computers to the manufacturers of leading branded products. There is some concern from consumer groups that information from loyalty cards, for example, can be sold on by the supermarkets to interested third parties. More stringent EU directives on consumer data control are likely. As you will see in Units 2 and 3 on the general and business environment, there is a vast amount of information available that concerns a business's activities. This has to be monitored selectively and then acted upon.

ACTIVITY 15

People have become more aware of problems associated with sugar, such as increased tooth decay and its contribution to weight problems. Confectionery companies are losing customers. One counter strategy is to produce sugar-free confectionery products.

You are the new product development manager of a confectionery company. You are considering the development of a sugar-free toffee to go alongside your usual toffee that is experiencing falling sales. Spend a few minutes jotting down what information you would need to help your decision making. Where and how could you collect it?

You would want to know, from internal sources, the current sales of toffee, with production costs, profit margins, etc. Externally, you need to research whether people would buy the new product. Do they buy toffee? For themselves or for other family or friends? Would they replace a purchase of the old toffee with the new one? Would they pay a premium price for it? Would they expect it to taste the same? Such information might be collected by a survey, perhaps linked to a prize draw on the wrapper of the existing toffee: fill in the questionnaire on sweet eating and return it for entry into the prize draw for an exotic holiday. Supermarket information on types of consumer, sales of related products, such as sugar-free chewing gum, would be helpful. Analysis of any competitor's products would be required.

General information on attitudes to sugar might be available from secondary sources. At a later stage, trial quantities of the product would have to be tested with a sample of potential customers to check for acceptability of the product.

You would need to make judgements about the effect of the new toffee. Will a new line take sales away from the existing lines, or recapture those customers that have recently been lost? Will it make the sales of existing lines fall even more? Will it need a new production line? Will it affect the production line of the existing toffee? Will it put the existing production into diseconomies of scale? What about advertising? Perhaps it would offer an opportunity to create a new health-conscious image for the company: 'You don't want your children to eat sugary toffee that damages their teeth. Try the new 'healthy' toffees from the company that cares!'

6.3 Accuracy of information

The accuracy of information is obviously most important for decision making. The two most common sources of error are **dispersion** and **bias**. Dispersion is random error. Bias occurs if there is a problem with the collection of data, such as when care is not taken with a survey to ensure that a cross section of the population is taken. A survey in a city centre shopping area during the day, for example, will miss a lot of working people who shop in the evening.

These two types of problem can be found in many business situations and, as data are collected, care should be taken to check for accuracy. **Accuracy** is not an absolute issue; data should be collected to the degree of accuracy needed for the decision in hand. An analytical chemist engaged in the analysis of sugar may need to know that the sample weight is 5.0236 grams. When we add sugar to a cup of coffee, we only need to know if one or two spoonfuls are required.

A final factor is that the information collected should be appropriate to the decision being made. For example, an organisation needs to know the cost of manufacture of a product. The actual costs of production for last month can be provided, but for the future cost of the product, estimated costs are needed that take into account possible increases in the cost of raw materials and labour, or variations in unit cost depending on the size of order. Historical information needs interpretation if it is to be used as an indicator of the future. Often there is a trade-off between accuracy and time. However, with increasing use of on-line real-time recording systems, it is becoming possible to obtain full and complete data without severe degradation in time scales. Data must be checked for dispersion (random error) and bias (systematic error), be appropriate in accuracy and in nature for the decision to be made, and be timely.

ACTIVITY16

You want to find out if using super rather than regular petrol will give you more miles to the litre. Briefly explain how you would collect the data for this comparison.

This is a typical example of how a simple question can be difficult to answer. The first problem is that the petrol consumption for any journey can be different – short distances in cold weather will give a higher than average consumption, for example. The fuel gauge on a car is not very accurate but the garage pumps are. You could run your car for a period of, say, two weeks with one grade, noting the petrol added to the tank and always filling to full capacity. Over this period you could note the miles travelled. You would have to have a few days without taking measurements while the tank contained mixed petrol and then run for another two weeks with the new grade. Given the size of the effect expected it may well be difficult to get accurate enough figures. You may have other suggestions. This type of problem is common in industry and this is why you will find statistics valuable when you get further into your studies.

6.4 Information flows and management

Information comes from the collection of various data and the subsequent integration of that information. A key figure for a company is the amount of stock it holds. This involves the collection from different parts of the organisation such as production and sales. Co-ordination is needed, since if the information is out of phase then errors will occur.

It is important that the flow of information is rapid and free from recording errors. The capture of information should involve the minimum of keying operations, direct-data capture should be considered wherever economic. The simple bar code systems use a check number, so a reading error will cause an invalid entry signal. Manual keying is much more prone to errors.

Information should be captured as close to the source as possible. Failure to do this tends to slow the process down and give increased possibilities for data loss and errors. Information is an asset as valuable as stock and so the responsibility for data should be clearly identified. The computer systems manager is not the information manager. The quality of sales data depends on the care with which information is entered.

Information technology embraces the collection of data and the storage and transmission of information and data. Gupta (1996) defines information technologies as: 'tools and techniques that support the design and development of information systems; these include hardware, software, databases, telecommunications (and other communication technologies) and client servers'. The capability of all of these tools and techniques has increased dramatically and will continue to do so. The impact of these technologies is such that it has created whole new ways of doing business. For example, direct marketing of products such as insurance just would not be possible without sophisticated application of both information and communication technologies. Many further developments in this area can be expected.

As computers have developed, the cost of data storage has dropped and vast amounts of information can now be held and accessed. Critical to the development of the hardware has been the development of the appropriate software. Almost every business person will be involved with four types of software: word processing, graphics, spreadsheets and database management. Word processing allows the management of text, graphics adds visual impact. Spreadsheets are packages which allow tables to be built up and financial analysis to be completed, for example, in the preparation of cash-flow projections. Databases are critical to the management of large amounts of information, allowing data to be abstracted and linked.

Information is valuable and should be freely available to the people who need to make decisions. However, information should be restricted to those who need to know. Open access may give a security problem where commercially sensitive information could become available to competitors.

The use of information is time dependent. It is of little use to get the Monday weather forecast on Tuesday. If company systems are not well devised it is quite possible for sales forecasts to be available too late for effective control of the systems and the result will be high stocks of the wrong products and stockouts for the right products.

6.5 Communication

Information needs to be transmitted to and understood by the intended recipients. This is **communication**. In making data available, it must be converted into an understandable form. Feedback may be significant and in allowing for this, communication becomes a two-way process. If communication is in one direction, without feedback, the communicator will not know whether the receiver has understood the information.

Figure 10 shows the key features of communication. First, the person sending the message must be clear about what they are seeking to transmit. This information must then be converted or encoded into the message. The message can get lost or distorted by 'noise'. How many times have you had a telephone message lost or not taken fully? At the receiving end, the message has to be decoded by the receiver. Feedback in a two-way situation checks that the message has been received, interpreted correctly and understood. Problems can arise at each stage of this process.

Communication in an organisation is a very human affair because the way people listen to and interpret communications is influenced by their educational, vocational and cultural backgrounds, and by the different problems and interests they have within the organisation. The responsibility of managers is two-fold: first, to speak in a language appropriate to their audiences, second, to match the message to the interests and concerns of the audience.

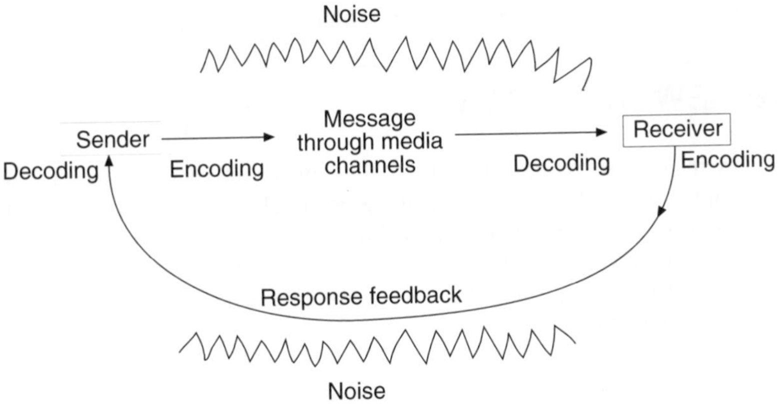

Figure 10: Model of communication

A major company entered into a large and expensive communication programme about its new marketing plan. This involved the managing director briefing all staff on all sites. The results were less than successful as the discussion was not modified sufficiently for the various audiences. The office staff were very concerned about the new export documentation, but the production operators were much more concerned with how much overtime working might be involved. A key problem in modern life is information overload, which can crowd out the communication. So to try to communicate too much can be just as bad as not communicating enough. With too much information, the recipient has a problem of sorting out what is relevant.

ACTIVITY 17

You have been asked to give two talks about the impact of ozone depletion to two groups:

- a group of university students
- a group of 9-year-old school children.

Spend five minutes making notes on how you would ensure effective communications in these two very different situations. How would you know if you were successful?

The key issue is that the amount of prior understanding would be very different between the two groups. For the student group, some detailed discussion of mechanisms with economic impact figures and tables might be appropriate. With the school group a broad-brush approach might be better, with simple diagrams and cartoons. To measure your success, you would ask a few key questions and for the school group possibly run a pictorial quiz to see if you had communicated the knowledge. The key tip is to start with the audience and then work out how you can get the message across. Different groups require different approaches.

REVIEW ACTIVITY 6

You are the club secretary for the football team at a university. You think that a computer would help you. You have been asked to explain why to the finance committee. In what ways would a system with word processing, graphics, spreadsheets and a database help you? What information would you store? What outputs would you have from the system over the full year of the club's operation?

Summary

Information is different from data. The information needs of managers require the timely collection of data of appropriate accuracy and its ordering, patterning and conversion into decision-making material – information. Information may already be available from company sources and external sources. The company needs systems to complete this type of analysis on a day-by-day basis. Competitor analysis and new product development, for example, will require specific information involving the collection of primary data, such as marketing research for business data and research and development for technical and production data.

Data needs to be appropriate for the decisions being made. It is important for the organisation to fully understand the flow of information and to have defined responsibilities for the maintenance of databases and for the dissemination of information.

Unit Review Activity

Jill's Jewellery has grown; she has extended her production and shop facilities to meet the demand that she has generated through direct mail orders, more sales through the shop, and a number of exclusive lines to Harvey Nichols. She now has ten staff in production, including a production manager and a designer, a full-time accountant, someone to help on the buying side, four staff in packaging and dispatch, and a shop manager and four staff in sales, plus many part-timers who help in all areas, and some freelance sales staff.

With this current and future business development, identify areas that Jill will need to address continually and possibly change, including the legal and organisational structure, physical resources, culture, functions and activities.

Unit Summary

In this unit you have been introduced to some of the main features of organisations and to why organisations exist. To understand complex organisations, it is useful to consider the basic building blocks that are common to organisations. We have seen how an organisation can be evaluated area by area: logistics, operations, sales and marketing, field service, infrastructure activities including finance and management information systems, human resources, R&D and procurement. We have seen that it is necessary not only to ensure that the separate functions perform but that these functions are integrated both to the other functions in the organisation and the various linkages that an organisation needs to the external environment for procurement, logistics and quality management.

We have examined some of the ways in which organisations can arrange their structures, the interrelationships between business functions and the threads of management control and the resulting management information needs.

Organisations are not machines; they involve people. We have reviewed the nature of organisational culture and its effects on the operation of an organisation.

This is the information age, and to manage the future is to be able to manage information. You have investigated the factors that differentiate data from information and the actions and structures needed to convert data to information.

References

Appleby, R (1991) *Modern Business Administration*, Pitman, 5th edn

Crawford, C (1991) *New Products Management*, Irwin, 3rd edn

Curtis, T (1994) *Business and Marketing for Engineers and Scientists*, McGraw-Hill

Goodstein, L and Pfeiffer, J (1985) *The 1985 Annual: Developing Human Resources*, Pfeiffer and Company

Gupta, U (1996) *Management Information Systems - a managerial perspective*, West Publishing Company

Handy, C (1993) *Understanding Organisations*, Penguin, 4th edn

Hofstede, G (1983) 'The cultural relativity of organisational practices and theories', *Journal of International Business Studies*, Fall

Hofstede, G (1984) *Hofstede Culture's Consequences*, Sage

Johnson, G (1992) 'Managing Strategic Change: Strategy, culture and action', *Long Range Planning*, 25

Johnson, G and Scholes, K (1997) *Exploring Corporate Strategy*, Prentice Hall, 4th edn

Knight, K (1997) *Matrix Management - A Cross-functional Approach to Organisation*, Gower Press

Kotler, P (1997) *Marketing Management: Analysis Planning Implementation and Control*, Prentice Hall, 9th edn

Lynch, R (1997) *Corporate Strategy*, Pitman Publishing

Mead, R (1992) *Cross-Cultural Management Communication*, Wiley

Morgan, G (1986) *Images of Organisation*, Sage

Moore, W and Pessemier, E (1993) *Product Planning and Management: designing and delivering value*, McGraw-Hill

Payne, A, Chelsom, J and Reavill, R (1996) *Management for Engineers*, Wiley

Porter, M (1985) *Competitive Advantage: Creating and sustaining superior performance,* Free Press

Sadler, D and Campbell, A (1994) Corporate Strategy at Grand Metropolitan, In DeWit and Meyer, *Strategy, Process and Context*, West

Schneider, S and Barsoux, J (1997) *Managing across Cultures*, Prentice Hall.

Tayeb, M (1996) *The Management of a Multicultural Workforce*, Wiley

Recommended Reading

Jennings, E (1996), 'Redistribution of power', *IEE Review*, Institution of Electrical Engineers Vol. 42.1

Kotler, P and Andreasen, A (1991), *Strategic Marketing for Nonprofit Organisations*, Prentice Hall, 4th edn

Mintzberg, H (1979) *The Structuring of Organisations,* Prentice Hall

Monopolies and Mergers Commission (1985) *The Brewing Industry*, London

Porter, M (1980) *Competitive Strategy: techniques for analysing industries and competitors*, Free Press.

Schein, E (1985) *Organisational Culture and Leadership: A Dynamic View*, San Francisco, Jossey-Bass

Thompson, J (1993) *Strategic Management: Awareness and Change*, Chapman & Hall, 2nd edn

Answers to Review Activities

Review Activity 1

Jill's Jewellery

Mission statement: to bring pleasure to people through fine jewellery made from natural materials.

Business objectives:

- to manufacture and sell existing range of jewellery to discerning customers in the one location
- to increase the business to two locations or something that is saleable within five years
- to increase turnover by 30% and reduce unit costs by 25% within two years.

Stakeholders

Jill herself is the main stakeholder and will be the most influential. She manages, directs, runs the company, and her design skills are key. But there are many other stakeholders from her customers to her accountant.

Customers: without these, it doesn't matter what Jill does; she won't achieve anything if she doesn't satisfy her customers' wants.

Staff: Jill needs the sales staff to help her sell and they won't be successful if they don't know the product, the customer, and the price; they need to be polite, helpful, etc. She needs the production staff to help her produce, and they need to use correct materials, in the right amount to the right design, quality and reliability. The product is no good if it falls apart, and all staff will need training and monitoring in some way. Jill will also need to take care of her legal obligations to staff.

Suppliers: for raw materials and stones from overseas; settings, glue, solder direct from source or distributors, and equipment, for production, as in soldering iron, computer, telephone system, utilities for shop.

Bank for loan to buy capital equipment, say, advice on original business plan, source of other legal and accounting advice.

Member of Association of Jewellery Manufacturers and Retailers: provides sources, customer help, marketing help, guidelines on quality, guideline on customer liability.

Federation of Small Businesses: for legal and other support.

Insurance: for premises, expensive raw materials and product, equipment, public liability insurance to protect her customers on the premises and for the use of the jewellery afterwards.

Accountant: accounting and legal advice.

Review Activity 2

This is a problem for many professional organisations. Start with a geographical breakdown. Given the high number of members it would not appear too difficult for the major areas to have branches so that members will not have to travel long distances to meetings. Then we have a number of other special variables. You might consider the key issues to be age (student, graduate and full, retired) and special interests (for example, power, communications). Thus, at national level the IEE has a head office with a range of special interest groups and these are reflected at local branch level. In each area there might be a young members' group, technical meetings for the various specialist areas, a management group and even a retired members' group. This effectively gives a multi-divisional structure.

Review Activity 3

(a) Like most business situations there are no definitive answers. The following are suggestions:

(i) Sole Trader – Simple to create; the added complexity of other organisation types may be inappropriate.

(ii) Private company limited by shares, with someone to purchase one or two shares. This would provide the owner with limited liability and tax advantages of a separate legal body.

(b) Generally you would expect this organisation to be in the form of a public company limited by shares. This gives the organisation the ability to spread the burden of its capital. Very few people have the finance to own a corporation like Unilever, for example. It also provides a limit to the liability of the investors.

(c) This would probably best be dealt with by creating a charitable trust. This provides a relatively informal and flexible organisation. If you were doing this, however, you would have to be careful regarding insurance, etc., as there is the potential for the trustees to be liable in the case of an accident.

(d) The legal structure would depend mainly on why you have started the school. If it is to make money you might consider a private limited company limited by shares or guarantee. If it is for philanthropic purposes you might consider a trust or a company limited by guarantee and you would certainly want to register the school as a charity.

Review Activity 4

Inbound logistics: The first operation is the grading, cleaning and packaging of the produce, which will have to be collected from the co-operative members' farms and delivered to the centre. To prevent damage and to provide ease of handling you could consider using standard plastic containers that would be light, rugged and easy to clean. You would also need an area to store the range of finished packaging you would need. The sales area would need good parking and exits for the customer. You would need easy access for the packed produce to move to the sales area. The products are seasonal and so you may buy in produce to cover when yours is not available (such as imported tomatoes in the winter).

Operations: Three linked areas would include firstly the cleaning of the produce, then the grading and finally the packaging. Since you will have different products you would need a very flexible line. In the shop area the needs are simple: keeping the shelves stacked but being careful to ensure strict stock rotation (first produce in is the first to be sold) and a procedure to eliminate products that are beyond their use-by date.

Outbound logistics: For the shop area this is not too much of a problem, however you do need to consider simple things like trolley return, which if not sorted out properly will cause difficulties for the customer. The bulk sales to restaurants needs more consideration. You will need a delivery vehicle(s), possibly with temperature control to keep the produce in good condition. There will be two issues that will need care: the 'picking' of the orders to the customers' requirements (a restaurant will ring, fax or e-mail a specific order, so each delivery drop is for a specific order), and the routing of the deliveries to ensure that orders are delivered with the minimum of lost time and mileage.

Marketing and sales: First, consider the sales system. The farm shop area should not be too much of a problem; all you need is some modest EPOS (electronic point of sale system) that will allow you to record what is sold, and with the ability to accept credit cards. The system for supplying restaurants need not be too complex. You need to be able to accept orders by post, telephone with an out-of-hours capability, fax and e-mail. These customer orders need to be converted to delivery notes, either hand-written, but for analysis later, or with the use of a simple computer system which could print out the delivery notes and monthly invoices for account holders.

Often small operations like this have a problem in that they know what they would like to sell but they need to know what the customers want to buy. There will be a lot more detail about this in the unit on marketing. You will need to get out and about to the local commercial customers (hotels and restaurants) to find out what they want and then to sell them the range when you are in operation. One big problem will be to match the needs of your customers with your production capability. The customers most likely will want a full range and you will only produce a restricted range. A restaurant owner will not want to make four telephone calls if it can be done with one call to the right supplier.

The members of the co-operative need to agree a growing plan to match what they think the demand will be for the items they can grow themselves and for those other items they will need to buy in to provide the full range. For your retail sales you will have to decide how to communicate with your customers through advertisements, publicity and promotional activities. You might take a view of other things you could do to attract customers – for example, children's play area, some working farm exhibits, see the cows milked, etc. You would have to think what the experience should be and how people would look; in effect you will have to create your own little brand image.

Service: Remember that in this context we are talking about added value services, such as maintenance to a photocopier. In this type of business there doesn't seem much you can do. Possibly you have thought of something? Perhaps you might provide recipe suggestions for some of the more unusual produce you sell.

Infrastructure: There are lots of things to consider here. You might consider setting up the co-operative as a limited company, with the members of the co-operative as shareholders. You would need to set up all the accounts and computer systems for the business. You would have to decide the physical lay-out of the buildings. To satisfy a customer, the organisation needs to focus various skills and functions. A key strategic skill in management is to decide what these functions should be, what resources they need and how they should be linked and co-ordinated. All functions are vital to the organisation – just as a car with a large engine is not much use without wheels. Success is as much about the integration of the functions as the correct operation of individual functions, so the overall control and management of the business will need addressing.

Human resource management: You will have to recruit staff. In terms of your organisation you will only need something simple with, say, three groups (functional areas): the packaging and commercial sales unit, the shop and an administration sales and marketing group. There are a lot of activities to cover and you will not be able to afford many staff so you will need people with a wide range of skills and flexibility. Note that you have safety and contract considerations, so you may need to use some specialist consultants to make certain you have appropriate contracts of service; as a small operation you will not be able to afford a dedicated specialist personnel manager.

Technology development: This may come as a surprise but even in this apparently simple business there are technology developments. These can include more efficient ways of cleaning the produce to minimise damage and increase shelf life. Environmental packaging and storage may be helpful. These are quite technical areas and the co-operative may well not have the specialist food technology type skills but may need to buy them in. Again you will not have the money for a full R&D team but still need to produce new products and innovations.

Procurement: A key issue is that the owners are the suppliers (the members of the co-operative) and you will need to decide how to regulate orders around the members. What do you do, for example, if one member does not produce to the required quality or does not deliver on time? You will also have to find suppliers for the lines you do not intend to produce yourself, and for the packaging. You also need a range of support services, such as maintenance for the vehicles, insurance and advertising space. Of course, when you set the business up you had large capital costs for the equipment and the building work. Good control of these costs will be essential.

Review Activity 5

Imagine that you work as a scientist in the R&D department developing new processes in an engineering company. This is what your company's cultural web might be like.

Organisational structure: The overall organisational structure is functional, with the R&D department reporting to the managing director. Head of the department is an R&D manager, with a number of group leaders reporting to him or her. Each group leader has several section leaders. Each section leader is responsible for a project and has a small number of technicians and scientists under his or her management control. There are two aspects to the relationship. A strict managerial relationship with accountability for budgets, etc., and a professional relationship in developing the technologies needed to advance the work. Thus, across the formal management structures would form informal frameworks of people with similar technical problems.

Symbols: In this environment perhaps there are obvious symbols of position. The managing director has a large suite of offices on the top floor. The R&D manager has an office which can only be entered through another office occupied by the departmental secretary. The group leaders have small offices and the section leaders have small cubicles off the laboratory area. The scientists have large desk areas in the laboratory area; the technicians have a shared desk area.

Routines: It is important to exchange findings between research groups and the rest of the functional managers; the informal Friday afternoon review meeting is critical to providing this forum.

Stories: The company is a leading innovator of technology, and stories would be told of the problems with the first large-scale implementations of the technology and the associated problems.

Rituals: A high premium is placed on not only the commercial implementation of the technologies but the academic rigor with which it is researched. The annual research conference is a ritual where presentations are made on a very esoteric academic level to other members of the research function based on other sites; other functional areas have similar conferences.

Power structures: The management structure is very authoritarian, with rigid controls on budgets, programmes of work and reports. Over this, in the R&D department, is an informal framework of technical interests based on expert power – the informal group is led by the person with the most experience and knowledge.

Control systems: The control system is very bureaucratic, with a rigid system of budgets, progress reports and project reports. The informal technical discussion groups have no formal record of their activities.

This organisation has evolved its cultural web. Through your analysis of your selected organisation you will have developed a greater insight into the cultural influences and norms that affect its operation and performance.

Review Activity 6

The word processing would allow you to produce fixture lists and letters and hold these on file. The graphics would allow you to make notices and letters more attractive and enhance the reputation of the club, possibly attracting new members. The spreadsheet would be of considerable value to keep the accounts and produce budgets. The database would be of value when you needed to mail members, as you could select the members you wanted and then merge with your word-processed document.

Over the full year of the club you would need to write letters to arrange fixtures and inform members of meetings, etc. You would have agendas for the meetings, followed by minutes of these meetings. At the start of the year you would produce a budget, and as the year went on you would keep track of the costs and income to produce accounts for the meetings. For the games you would produce selection lists and attractive notices to get other people along to see the games. You may well have thought of some other uses.

Answer to Unit Review Activity

Jill may wish to look at ways of raising capital for all this growth, and may want to change the legal structure to a public listed company and raise money through selling shares. She would then acquire additional stakeholders that would need attention.

The organisational structure has developed into a functional structure, with sales and marketing, and production her two main departments. Whereas previously a designer could come from the workshop into the shop itself and talk to a customer and sell a particular design, all employees' jobs are now clearly defined. However, if she decides to open outlets in other locations, she may end up with a multi-divisional structure. Perhaps she should consider franchising the outlets and concentrating on design and production. Physical resources will have to grow, perhaps moving production out of high-street facilities completely into, say, a cheaper industrial unit. This may cause a big problem with employees. New production facilities may be required with more automation; again craft employees will not be happy with this change in job function.

With the increase in turnover, Jill will have increased management, information and control needs. She will need to delegate management and control in some areas, say production and design; with this will come more procedures and more rules to be followed, as she has to designate exactly what everyone is doing. More information and communication will be required. Quality, service and efficiency are key issues. The customers are now more remote and the internal staff will not be able to identify with them, so they will need to be monitored carefully for changes in buying patterns and the success of particular lines. New products will need to be offered. Jill will need to continue to motivate the staff, even though she is not there, in striving to meet their needs and the customers' needs. HRM will need serious attention.

Jill is still involved as the main owner and entrepreneur so even though the business is larger, her personal approach will still have a big effect and it will effectively remain a power culture, as she is making the decisions. Jill is now involved much more on the buying side, spending large amounts of time overseas on sourcing new materials and buying stones, so is not managing the company on a day-to-day basis. This still has to be done, however, so she will need to appoint a manager to stand in for her. She is also involved in the marketing side, especially with Harvey Nichols, her big client. She should look carefully at how much she relies on one customer, and not become too dependent. If there are changes at Harvey Nichols or in the fashion world generally, then she may lose this business.

As you can see, as the business grows all primary and support activities will need careful monitoring and appropriate changes. Jill may decide that this is all too difficult and really she is not a businesswoman and wants to go back to just designing a few nice pieces for a known clientele. Her mission might not change, but her business objectives would.

UNIT 2
THE BUSINESS ENVIRONMENT

Introduction

All organisations, whatever their size and whether in the public or private sector, operate in a constantly changing environment. As it changes, this **business environment** offers organisations the **opportunities** they need to develop and grow. It may, for example, offer new markets to exploit, new technology to develop new products and new processes, ideas on how to manage operations better, new sources of raw materials or new ventures with new partners. The changes also, however, may present **threats** to organisations. These may be new competitors, changing fashions and tastes, new technology making existing products and processes obsolete, changing terms of trade making imported inputs expensive, and government policies changing the competitive or operating environment. As we discuss later in this unit, the legal implications of what organisations do are extensive and varied; effectively, the legal infrastructure constrains their activities.

All successful organisations continually monitor the environment in which they operate, both formally and informally, in order at least to react to the changes taking place through **reactive management**. At best, organisations seek to anticipate and take advantage of changes through **proactive management.** Any actions need to match an organisation's basic philosophy and its resources and abilities. We look at how an organisation does this later in the module, but the first step is recognising what is happening in the environment and evaluating its importance.

Of course not all business environments are identical, either in terms of the most influential factors shaping the environment or in the degree or speed of the changes taking place. Although some organisations continue to operate in relatively stable environments with limited, largely predictable, change, both the pace of environmental change and the magnitude of those changes have increased markedly in the last decade or so. Factors that have contributed to the increase in the pace of environmental change include privatisation and deregulation, internationalisation, and rapid technological change, particularly in information technology.

A complete and detailed analysis of all factors in the business environment capable of presenting a potential threat or an opportunity to any given organisation is impossible. However, a number of techniques of environmental analysis have been developed to simplify and codify this exercise.

Many successful organisations, particularly in the small- to medium-sized company sector (SMEs), have developed informal techniques of 'environmental scanning', through custom and practice, years of experience and common sense. In larger organisations, with more turbulent environments and more complex organisational structures, techniques of environmental scanning are applied more rigorously. British Airways, for example, carried out a very extensive scenario planning exercise in the mid 1990s. The company developed detailed scenarios of possible future environments and employees throughout British Airways were encouraged to participate in workshops to consider the implications of the scenarios for their particular section of the organisation.

In 1990 Shell had considerable success using similar techniques that identified two possible future scenarios, 'global mercantilism' and 'sustainable world'. The first scenario depicts instability in the world's economic and political systems, and an increased focus on regional pacts and bilateral agreements; competitiveness would be achieved through a free market approach, paying little attention to the natural environment. In the second scenario, the environment is regarded as the most significant factor; international powers are concerned with the marketplace, but place great emphasis on environmental regulations to reduce emissions and gain greater energy efficiency. In the late 1990s it would seem that the latter scenario has gained importance, with the 1997 Earth Summit high on the international political agenda, and moves in the developed world, including Britain, to reduce car usage and pollution and increase energy efficiency and recycling of materials.

Although the term **business environment** is used throughout this unit, the same methods of analysis can be applied to organisations operating in the public sector, such as local authorities, hospitals, schools and universities. In this unit, we look at the more general environment of an organisation and the key areas and factors in it. In the next unit, we consider the more specific and more immediate **competitive environment** within the industry sector. However, the distinction can be blurred. Some groups – consumer groups and pressure groups, for example – are effectively part of both environments, and the industry sector itself can be considered as the 'industry' or market of the competitive environment.

Objectives

By the end of this unit, you will be able to:

- monitor changes to the business environment and appreciate their significance for an organisation
- identify potential environmental opportunities and threats for particular organisations
- describe the components of a PEST or STEEP analysis
- detail the structure of the social and demographic environment
- detail the structure of the economic environment
- identify relevant factors in the industrial environment
- assess the implications of government policies for an organisation
- identify relevant factors in the political environment, including the law, society and international trade
- identify significant technological developments driving organisational and competitive change.

SECTION 1

Environmental Opportunities and Threats

Introduction

In this section, we look at the role that the environment plays in providing opportunities and threats to organisations. We identify and examine readily available sources of information on the business environment. We look at a representation of an organisation's business environment (Figure 1) and classify events as being political, economic, social or technological. We identify four stages of conducting an environmental analysis using readily available sources of information as a basis.

1.1 The organisation and its environment

All organisations, both in the public and the private sector, from multinationals to small local concerns, operate in an environment that, as it changes, offers both **opportunities** and **threats** to businesses.

Figure 1: The organisation in its environment

When doing environmental analysis, managers try to identify events which represent opportunities and threats to the organisation. For example, there may be opportunities to develop new products with new technology or to take advantage of changes in world trade agreements to expand into new markets. Appropriate actions and decisions by the organisation will allow it to take advantage of these opportunities. Threats could be presented to an organisation's way of operating by new EU legislation, for example. Threats could be to the supply of raw materials; for example, the impact of the BSE (bovine spongiform encephalopathy) crisis in the beef industry has affected the manufacturers of beef pies and pasties.

Figure 1 illustrates an organisation in its environment. Events occurring in the business environment are placed closer to the organisation if they are thought likely to have a direct impact, whether good or bad. Events are placed further away from the organisation if they are less likely to have a significant impact. All boundaries in this figure are blurred. The immediate environment is the **competitive environment**. We examine this in more detail in Unit 3. The broader business environment describes general events less directly associated with the organisation, but as it changes it is capable of offering significant opportunities and threats to the organisation. It is these events that need to be anticipated and prepared for, if at all possible.

The business environment is subdivided into four sections in Figure 1 for convenience and ease of use. We describe these sections as the **P**olitical, **E**conomic, **S**ocial, and **T**echnological environments in which all organisations operate at a national and international level. This allows us to conduct what is often called a **PEST** analysis, so called because PEST is an acronym of the four environments. You should note that there are many variants: some analysts include the green **E**nvironment, and form the acronym **STEEP**; some add an **O** for 'other', a catch-all category for events not easily classified under other headings, forming the acronym **PESTO**; others include **L**egal and **E**nvironmental and form **PESTLE**. The models can also be described as **DEPICTS** (**D**emographic, **E**conomic, **P**olitical, **I**nfrastructure, **C**ompetitive, **T**echnological and **S**ocio-legal) or **DEEPEST** (**D**emographic, **E**pidemiological, **E**thical and legal, **P**olitical, **E**conomic, **S**ocial and **T**echnological). All acronyms are effectively describing an environmental analysis, usually conducted for a specified organisation, ideally by the managers as an ongoing process, and the same basic issues are covered regardless of the particular acronym chosen. It is clear that many events do not fit neatly into specific categories. For example, unemployment is a political issue, but it is also an economic issue, a social one and a technological one. A legal requirement may be enforced through political or social pressure; environmental or green issues might be related to the use of technology or a particular European directive.

Examples of events occurring in the business environment can be found in the media. It may not be possible to identify all the organisations and industries likely to be affected by particular events. Sometimes, specific organisations might be named and others alluded to in articles. Some events may only be of direct relevance to one organisation. Newspapers, television and radio all carry business information these days. A manager can even access the news directly through a facility on a computer terminal that scrolls headlines across the top of the screen.

The news story can be accessed if the headline looks relevant to the business. Consider these 1997 news stories and their possible consequences.

Ionamin, used in the clinical treatment of obesity in America, may cause hypertension when used in conjunction with another treatment, fenfluramine. This has resulted in reduced sales and a drop in the share price of Medeva, the pharmaceutical group that produces Ionamin. While Medeva itself is directly involved, the story may also have effects on competitors with similar products, or on any links in Medeva's supply chain.

The new Labour government's foreign policy makes human rights a central issue. This is likely to affect the issuing of licences allowing British firms to export armoured vehicles and other weapons. The countries likely to be implicated are Indonesia, Saudi Arabia, China, Turkey, United Arab Emirates, Malaysia and Nigeria. Companies that may be affected included British Aerospace and Vickers.

In July 1997, the price of gold fell to its lowest level for 12 years. Some producers are suspending operations and postponing investment plans, gold mines have closed, and the pace of takeovers and mergers in the gold industry is picking up.

The government has cancelled the £73 million west London approach road scheme to upgrade stretches of the A40. Land had already been bought and properties demolished along the proposed route. Organisations operating in the area may be affected by continuing congestion along the existing road. Organisations hoping to be involved in the upgrading work will be disappointed. The government saves money but angers car users by not upgrading the road.

ACTIVITY 1

Consider which organisations may be affected by each of the following events occurring in Britain? Identify organisations for which the events provide an opportunity, and organisations for which they might pose a threat. You may be specific and name well-known organisations, or be more general and identify types of organisations.

Event:	**Opportunity for:**	**Threat to:**
A long hot summer		
Legislation requiring all buses to fit seat belts to be worn by passengers		
A significant increase in interest rates		
Massive investment in a new government-sponsored apprenticeship scheme		
A new superstore development on the edge of a small town		
The introduction of a minimum wage		

Of course, it is difficult with such limited information to identify clearly the opportunities and the threats. However, we can list some of the organisations that are affected by each of the events. For example, a long hot summer in Britain is likely to be an opportunity for ice cream manufacturers, UK hotels and holiday cottages, garden hose retailers, but a threat to umbrella manufacturers and indoor resort activities.

Similarly, UK legislation requiring all buses to fit seat belts for passengers is an opportunity for profitable bus companies that can afford to fit belts and for seat belt manufacturers but a threat for bus and coach companies that might struggle to finance the investment in new seat belts. A significant increase in interest rates is an opportunity for loan companies, debt collecting agencies, exporters as the exchange rate is likely to change and exports will be more attractive. It will pose a threat to businesses with loans and the building industry, since most buildings are purchased with loans.

A new government-sponsored apprenticeship scheme is an opportunity for companies recruiting unskilled labour but a threat to private training agencies. A new superstore development on the edge of a small town is an opportunity for property developers and estate agents, as more people are attracted to the area by the store, but a threat to the small shops in the town centre. The introduction of a minimum wage is an opportunity for companies already paying above the minimum who should face less intense competition from low-wage rivals, but poses a threat to companies currently paying below the minimum wage.

If you noted some of these kinds of organisations and identified the opportunities or threats, you are beginning to conduct an environmental analysis. Note that as well as the particular companies that are obviously directly affected, events can have an impact on all companies in the supply chain. So, for example, it is not only ice cream manufacturers that might benefit from a long hot summer but also the suppliers of ingredients and the retailers of ice cream to the consumer.

1.2 Environmental analysis

Newspapers and the news wires provide useful information on the ever-changing business environment. Monitoring the media is one of the most useful means of gaining information about the business environment. Each of the events considered in the previous activity could have been reported as an item of news by the press or other media. To complete the activity required making some assumptions about the events. With more information available, there is a greater chance of predicting which organisations will be affected and in what way events will affect them.

Researching the business environment is time-consuming and can be costly. Information can be unreliable, events unpredictable and the precise impact difficult to estimate. The challenge of environmental analysis is to keep investment in time and effort on such research as low as possible, while ensuring a reasonably reliable stream of appropriate information.

IDENTIFYING OPPORTUNITIES AND THREATS

The process of environmental analysis can be done in four stages as Figure 2 illustrates. It is first necessary to understand the basic components of the business environment. It is important to have some knowledge of the political process, the structure of the labour force and major technological advances that have implications for organisations and to understand how the economy functions and how industries and businesses are classified. We look at this process of monitoring the environment from two perspectives – from the organisation out and from the environment in – later in this section. Once we have a broad understanding of the nature of the business environment, we can move on to stage 2.

Stage 2 involves selecting **key drivers** of change from the broadly understood business environment appropriate to a specific organisation. Key drivers are those aspects of the environment known to have an important effect on the particular organisation. This effect might be from its customers, or the way it operates, or its raw materials, or its financing, or its staff. Remember the idea of the organisation as a transformation process from Unit 1. It may help to consider the various drivers that influence the inputs, the market for outputs or the processes themselves.

Stage 3 of the environmental audit is to monitor the movements of the key drivers. The purpose of this is to identify likely opportunities and threats for the specific organisation.

Stage 4 is the whole purpose of the exercise. Monitoring the key drivers really means watching what is going on. This can be done formally, in regular sessions during which managers present the movements of the key drivers to decision makers in the organisation. In many organisations, particularly small- to medium-sized enterprises (SMEs), monitoring tends to be done informally: decision makers have a reasonable idea of the key drivers and take into account what they believe to be their movements in deciding policies and strategies.

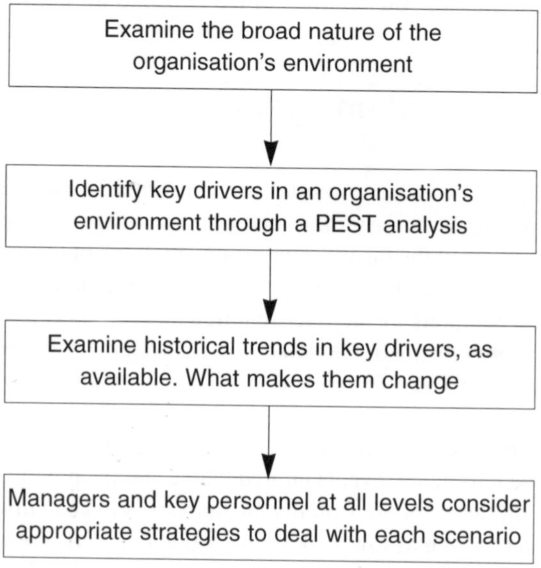

Figure 2: Stages of environmental analysis

ACTIVITY 2

A list of some key drivers and organisations is given below. Identify which key driver is most important for which organisation. Use arrows to indicate the connections.

Key Driver	Organisation
The age structure of the local population	A carpet manufacturer
The availability of land and planning permission	A wine importer
Long-range weather forecasts	A property developer
Household incomes	A travel agent
The number of new houses built and sold	A health centre
The strength of the pound against the franc, the peseta and the lire	A manufacturer of women's shoes

As we do not have details of these particular businesses, we can only identify a specific key driver in a rather obvious way.

The manufacturer of carpets knows that people are more likely to buy new carpets when they move house. Monitoring the number of new houses built and sold will give the company some idea of how many people are moving home. Although this is important, other factors also influence the demand for new carpets. A trend in recent years for harder floor coverings, such as wood, linoleum and tiles, has reduced the demand for fitted carpeting. We don't know enough about the inputs to identify a key driver here; perhaps a strong pound might help, by reducing the cost of some imported raw materials.

The health centre will need to monitor the age structure of the population as an indicator of likely demand, although other factors such as poverty and the gender of the population also influence patient needs. Demographic and economic factors are not the only indicators of need: a local factory may emit pollution that affects asthma sufferers or the town may attract holidaymakers who need additional medical help for minor ailments in the summer months.

A strong pound will mean cheaper wine imports. The property developer needs land with planning permission and is also affected by the number of houses built and sold. In a recession household incomes tend to be lower. As a result, women's shoe sales fall faster than the sales of children's or men's shoes. Predictions of a wet and cold summer send people into travel agents in search of sunshine.

In this exercise, we have simply isolated some key drivers; in each case, there may be others that we could only consider with more information and analysis.

Some key drivers in an organisation's environment can easily be monitored and even forecasted. Statistics produced by the Office for National Statistics on economic and social data are readily available. Private agencies, such as Incomes Data Services, provide data on industrial relations and human resource issues. Others, such as Mintel, provide information on markets and consumers. For a more detailed list see the end of this unit. Information about businesses can be gleaned from their annual reports, but many organisations are now using their web sites to publish very up-to-date information on their activities. Share prices, exchange rates and a wealth of information is available instantly on the Internet.

To start to build up a picture of events likely to have an impact on organisations, it is useful to be up to date in current world and business news. The media offers serious business and finance oriented newspapers and journals such as the *Financial Times, The Times*, the *Daily Telegraph* and *The Economist.* Television news and comment programmes such as *Panorama* and the *Money Programme* are also useful sources of information. Radio 4 provides an excellent coverage of news items in the morning and early evening. Regional and local press, television and radio stations are important vehicles for organisations scanning a more geographically limited area. They often act as a sifting point for general news, selecting those items they consider of most interest to local people and businesses.

Obviously, some events – such as legislation, tax issues, interest – apply directly to the business world, but also remember to monitor general news events that may impact on business. For example, political turmoil in an area that is a source of particular raw materials will impact on some manufacturers; James Goldsmith's death in 1997 will have far reaching effects on his vast business empire; deaths from the *E.coli* infection have resulted in changes to the regulations for catering establishments. Even the weather is important as it affects farmers' crops and all the organisations in the food supply chain. A chance event can trigger a whole series of changes that may affect your business.

Remember also to look at information about new products, technology and research, and to pay particular attention to your industry. Track shares on the stock market, monitor advertising and look out for PR announcements about new products, openings and closings of shops and factories, and staff movements and appointments. Consult trade and industry magazines which identify current trends. Review the science and technology pages of the national press; these may carry articles from *Nature, New Scientist, The Lancet, British Medical Journal*, for example, that you can follow up. The science correspondents cover events, innovations and research of general public interest, but stories may be of significant interest to the business world.

ACTIVITY 3

In July 1997, a hot-air balloon hit power lines near the Humber estuary and plunged to the ground, bursting into flames and killing one of its twelve passengers. List the various people and organisations involved (the stakeholders) and identify what opportunities and threats this chance accident might create for the ballooning company and other organisations and individuals.

The stakeholders in the hot-air ballooning company are likely to be affected in a number of ways.

- If the pilot suffered injuries, what is his future? Perhaps, the pilot will claim on the company insurance or sue for damages.
- The fatality is likely to lose the company business. This – and the accident itself – could have a serious effect on the morale of the staff, and some might need to be laid off.
- The boss would need to look at the effects of lost business, to replace equipment, and to re-evaluate the company's insurance cover for equipment, staff, against lost business, public liability insurance. The boss commented: "Any lessons that can be learnt will be. Standards are constantly being raised and we will continue to strive to make ballooning even safer".
- Investors or shareholders might be worried about their investment.
- Suppliers of ballooning equipment might be concerned about a down turn in business because of public wariness about the pastime. Although replacement of the original equipment would be required, makers of all components in the supply chain would be affected, and some may consider redirecting to another business area.
- Makers and innovators of safety equipment, especially fire blankets, could experience an upturn in business as a spin-off.
- Every year people give balloon rides as presents for birthdays and family birthday treats. The number of people going ballooning has doubled from 35,000 to 70,000 in the past eight years. Competitors running other leisure activities may be able to win some of this business by offering a 'safer treat'.
- All commercial hot-air balloon operators in Britain are licensed by the Civil Aviation Authority. In Britain, there are 250 operators and 1,200 balloons. The Civil Aviation Authority is likely to look at the need for stricter controls. The British Balloon and Airship Club helped the Air Accident Investigation Branch's inquiry into the crash.
- Solicitors and barristers may become involved if the family of the dead passenger sues the company or the pilot or seeks redress through the courts.
- Local emergency services were disappointed with their performance in handling the accident, they are revamping their procedures.

PEST ANALYSIS: MONITORING THE ENVIRONMENT

Monitoring the business environment in a formal or informal way is seen as an essential part of good business practice and constitutes stage 1 of our environmental analysis. In conducting a PEST analysis, an organisation steps back and considers in some detail the environment in which it operates. Most successful organisations are able to describe their immediate environment, their customers, their workers, their suppliers, etc. and – by working out from there – they are able to see the way in which events in the general business environment *could* influence them. This approach has the advantage that it is possible to focus on aspects of the environment known to have an impact on the organisation. The disadvantage is that major events may be ignored if they do not *currently* play a role. These events may suddenly move in and threaten the existence of the organisation. Who, for example, could have anticipated the decline in spending at funfairs and on pension schemes caused as a result of the massive interest in the national lottery? Obvious competitors such as premium bonds and the football pools would have identified the threat posed by the lottery, but funfairs offer another way of spending 'treat' money and saving for retirement seems unrelated to the lottery (although an irrelevant expenditure if you really believe you will win millions).

The alternative approach is to work from the general environment to the organisation-specific environment. Since all organisations operate in a section of the general business environment, an understanding of how that works and what is going on at the current time may be of interest. It makes it easier to anticipate new and otherwise unexpected opportunities the organisation may wish to exploit, and to foresee and avoid any likely threats. An understanding of the way in which the business environment is moving may allow an organisation to predict future patterns of consumer behaviour and needs. Since these threats and opportunities may come from quite unexpected quarters, starting by looking at the general environment and moving to the specific environment may allow the organisation to respond in anticipation of future likely trends rather than react to events as they occur.

ACTIVITY 4

Using a business magazine such as *The Economist* and newspapers such as the *Daily Telegraph*, *Sunday Times*, or *Financial Times* and a local paper as the source of environmental information, conduct a basic PEST analysis of the likely general environment for each of the following organisations: Shell, a general medical practice and a small grocery store. Read the main news sections (national and international) and the business section. Complete as many boxes in the table as possible, jotting down a few phrases that describe relevant events or circumstances.

Business	Shell	General medical practice	Grocery store
Political Economic Social Technological			

These three businesses are quite different both in scale – from multinational to SME – and in scope. Shell and the grocery store operate in the private sector, a general medical practice operates largely in the public sector. Shell is an Anglo-Dutch multinational, the grocery store has a small local market and the medical practice is part of a national network of health-care provision. The environments in which they operate are, in many aspects quite different, but all could be affected by, for example, a massive increase in unemployment, withdrawal of the UK from the European Union, or a long hot summer. And they are all affected by the environment at a local, national and international level. Here is our basic PEST analysis.

Shell. P: proposed environmental legislation, including recommendations from the Environmental Transport Association on reducing fuel consumption and pollution; at a local level, planning permission for a petrol station located on a new bypass. **E:** increase in duty on petrol in the UK budget; change in interest rates; strength of sterling. **T:** new process developed for oil refineries; new software developed for petrol station stock control.

General medical practice. P: new legislation on prescriptions; planning permission approved for new housing estate to be built on outskirts of town. **E:** public spending cuts in next budget. **S:** falling unemployment. **S:** new guidelines from British Medical Association on code of practice.

Grocery shop. E and **S**: Falling unemployment. **T:** a new EPOS system **P:** guidelines on the sale of alcopops; go ahead for new bypass; planning permission for out-of-town supermarket and new housing estate.

As you will have discovered many events do not fit neatly into any specific category.

Another way of considering the business environment is to pick a specific organisation or industry and see how changes in its environment have an impact on it. The pharmaceuticals industry involves a relatively small number of drug companies operating in a few countries around the world. In this review activity, you can see the complexity of the environment of these multinationals.

REVIEW ACTIVITY 1

Read the pharmaceuticals case study and identify the likely key drivers in the industry's environment. Can you classify these events as political, economic, social and technological? To what extent do they operate in national and international environments? Highlight and label each item as P, E, S, or T, as appropriate.

Pharmaceuticals

Britain's pharmaceuticals industry boomed in the early 1990s. Despite the recession, it continued to make a major contribution to the UK's exports. The success of the industry was due partly to a series of successful innovations developed through substantial investment in research and development. Top selling medicines such as Zantac, Ventolin, Zovirax, Tagamet, plus Tenormin and Augmentin, helped to cement the continued success of British companies.

At the start of the decade, five of the top fifty companies in the world were British: Glaxo-Wellcome, SmithKline Beecham, Zeneca, Boots and Fisons. However, fierce competition from American and Japanese companies threatened this pre-eminence. Governments around the world began to restrict the availability of drugs as the costs of health care rose rapidly. The cost of drugs exported from Britain became prohibitive for many other countries, and replacement products were rapidly developed.

With reduced profitability for the newly developed drugs, less money was available for research and development of new drugs. Scientists were recruited by foreign companies to work abroad and generally lower educational standards meant that there were fewer trained scientists available. The Japanese, who have had a consistent trade deficit in pharmaceutical products, began to buy European drug manufacturers.

The industry is tough: drug patents only last 15 years, allowing a company little time to charge high prices before rivals bring out new products as the patent expires. High prices are necessary to fund the incredibly large investment needed in research and development. For example, Glaxo was built on the success of Zantac. Used in the treatment of gastric ulcers, Zantac became the world's largest prescription drug with sales rising from £829 million in 1987 to a peak of £2.4 billion in 1994. However, the patent runs out in 1997, and it should be interesting to see whether the portfolio of products that the company has, especially through its purchase of Wellcome in 1994, survives. For example, new drugs like Serevent and Flixotide are likely to supplant older products such as Ventolin.

Summary

In this section, we have begun to build up a model or picture of the environment in which businesses operate. We have considered how a constantly changing environment might offer opportunities and threats to different organisations. In order to help us sort and classify information, we have looked at the way changing events can be described as Political, Economic, Social or Technological (PEST). In addition, we have placed these events in a national and an international context. We have learned about the four stages of environmental audit. We have used a PEST analysis to examine possible threats and opportunities to three very different businesses: from small owner-managed shops to major multinationals, from public to private ownership, the process remains the same.

SECTION 2

Social Environment

Introduction

In this section, we begin a more detailed analysis of many of the key changes taking place in the business environment. We start with the social environment, first looking at demographics, the study of population. This has considerable implications for organisations in terms of what they produce and how they produce it. We then look at social structures and behaviour patterns that affect what we buy and how we live.

We use statistics about the population, by age, sex and ethnicity, to describe patterns of work and patterns of consumption and to identify the opportunities and threats posed for different organisations. In addition, we explain how social structures are related to some aspects of consumer behaviour and describe some of the benefits and hazards of classifying consumers by social class.

2.1 Demographics and organisations

The demographic environment is fundamental to the monitoring of the business environment of any organisation. It comes under the social element of PEST. Demography describes the composition of the population by age and gender. It studies, among other things:

- the make-up of households – whether they consist of parents and children only, or include relations such as siblings, cousins or grandparents
- migration – the movement of people from one place to another
- economic activity – the percentage of the population working and the type of work carried out
- fertility and morbidity – birth and death rates which (together with migration and changes in longevity) determine population size
- change, and its causes, in population characteristics.

When combined with known spending patterns, a knowledge of the make-up of a population helps marketing managers to predict what people will buy, when and why. In other words, it helps to predict **consumer demand** for products and services. Demographic information is also useful to predict demand for educational provision, health care and infrastructure needs such as roads, hospitals and housing stock.

Demographics explains aspects of the size and shape of the **labour force**, which is a major contributor to the supply of goods and services. Most developed countries in the world have shown similar labour market trends. These include:

- decline of manufacturing and construction industries
- growth of the service industries
- decrease in full-time jobs, and increase in part-time and temporary contract jobs
- increase in female workforce
- increasing demand for skilled and flexible labour
- growth in long-term unemployed
- increase in the use of technology in production, communication and distribution, leading to a decrease in the people requirement in many different sectors
- effects of the 'unofficial' and black economy.

The cost of labour is probably the biggest cost that an organisation has to meet, and it needs to be carefully monitored. A balance between the requirements of the workforce in terms of pay and conditions and the requirements of the organisation in terms of productivity and costs has to be maintained. As organisations are always needing to change to respond to changes in their external and internal worlds, then the workforce also needs to change.

We look first at the economic activity of the UK. Because of the rapid growth of the service sector, there are shortages of skilled staff in some areas and in certain professional occupations. In addition, there is less need for manual labour as physical jobs are replaced by machines, but greater demand for non-manual labour with more desk jobs that require, for example, computer skills. As more technology is introduced, jobs change and staff need to be multiskilled. This offers both opportunities and threats for organisations. If you are in the service sector, you will be fighting for qualified staff in some areas of the country. There is a shortage of IT professionals and in some high-tech industries, employees can effectively state their terms.

ECONOMIC ACTIVITY

In Britain, roughly 25.5 million people produce the goods and services that we use. Of course, not all production is accounted for by people in employment and the self employed. There are numerous productive activities undertaken by people falling outside of these categories: this includes work in the house by 'housepersons' (such as cooking, cleaning, shopping and child care), do-it-yourself work, voluntary work and all activities in the black economy (work undertaken for payment but not accounted for by government). The official statistics only count those registered as employed, unemployed or self employed. Many other productive activities go unrecorded by these statistics.

Changes in household priorities – and the availability of paid work or a shortage of work – may shift activities into the marketplace, offering business opportunities for productive activity previously undertaken in the family. For example, the increase in nursing homes and sheltered housing for elderly people reflects two trends: first, the fact that people are living longer and, second, that they are less likely to be cared for by their close family. This may be because many women, the traditional carers in society, now choose or need to work outside the home. Similarly, the increasing number of paid child-minders and pre-school nurseries reflects a reduced reliance on the family as the provider of this service.

It is possible to divide the population according to their contribution to **economic activity** or their production of goods and services. It is reasonable to assume that all people in the UK are **consumers**, that is they buy and/or use goods and services produced by organisations in this country and abroad. However, not all of them are **producers**. Economic activity refers to the **official count** of the numbers of people contributing to the production of goods and services, with the provisos outlined above. The first thing we can do is divide the population up by age. The working ages are roughly from 16 to 60 or 65 (the minimum school leaving age to the official state retirement ages). Those too young to make a significant contribution to production are still at school or pre-school. Those above working age may, of course, still work – but most do not.

There are around 35 million people in Britain who are of working age (see Figure 3). Some, however, do not make a contribution to production. We call these **not economically active**. They may be continuing in education. They may be too ill to work. They may be housepersons. Finally, we arrive at the number counted as **economically active**. This includes the registered unemployed, who are not producing but are actively seeking work. The official figures show that around 25.5 million people actually contribute to the production of the goods and services we consume. This is less than half of the total population. Note that movements occur between categories all the time. Many who may be counted say as a houseperson are actually seeking work, many continuing in education would have preferred to get a job had one been available.

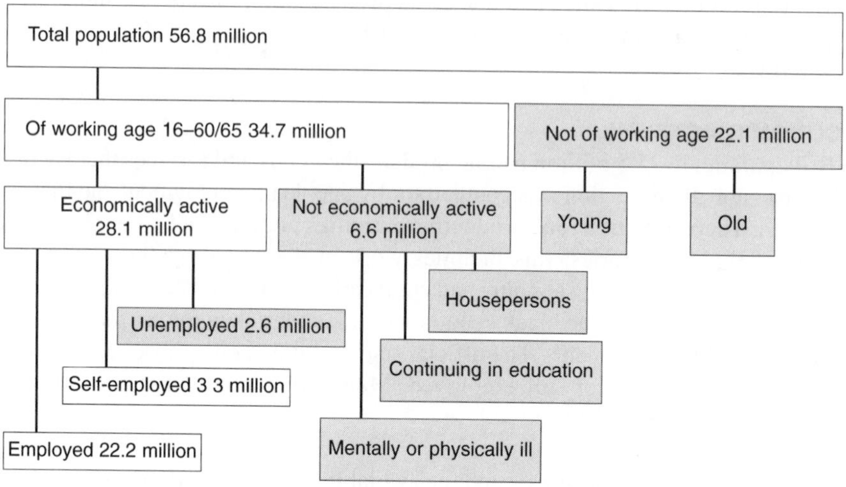

Figure 3: Structure of the British population by economic activity,1994
Source: Office of National Statistics

AGE STRUCTURE OF THE POPULATION

Figure 4 illustrates the age structure of the population in 1992 compared with projections for 2006. Of key interest for the business environment is the size and structure of population over the age of 15. These people represent the main consumers and the potential labour force. The labour force in 2006 is predicted to be older than the one in 1992, with a projected rise of 2.3 million 35–54 year olds and 0.7 million people over 55 years old. The number of people under the age of 35 are projected to fall by 1.4 million. Throughout the 1970s and 1980s the labour force increased nearly every year. This was mainly due to the growth of the female labour force: 94 per cent of the 3 million growth in the labour force during the 1970s and 1980s were women. The availability of more service sector employment and the decline of the traditionally male-dominated manufacturing sector partly explain this trend. Projections up to 2006 also predict an increased contribution by women.

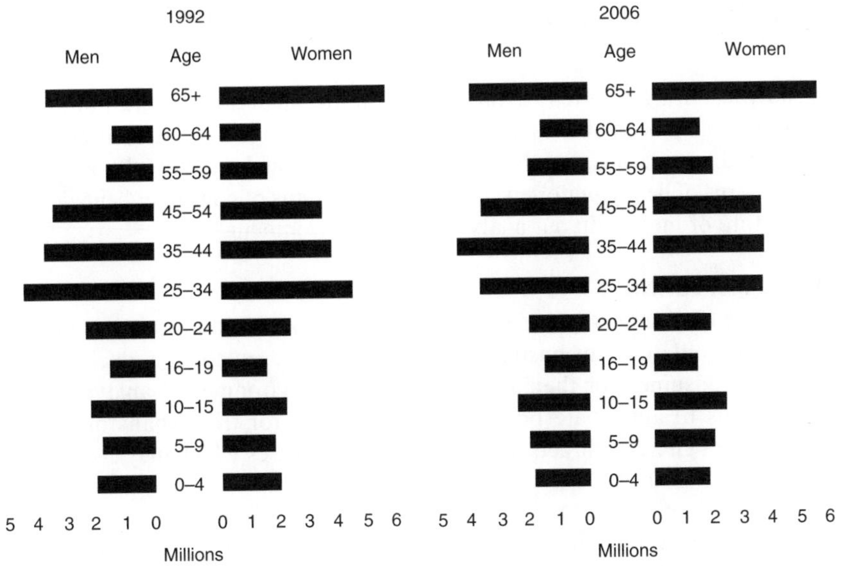

Figure 4: Structure of the population by age and sex, actual figures for 1992 and projections for 2006

Source: Labour force projections 1993–2006, *Employment Gazette* 1993

ETHNIC ORIGIN

The population of Britain includes a number of different ethnic groups, accounting for around 5 per cent of the total population but having a significant impact on the market and the supply of goods and services available. This influences the availability of ethnic restaurants, shops, cultural activities, and fashions in ethnic home furnishings and foods. In 1997, BT appointed its first ethnic marketing consultancy to improve communications with Britain's 3.3 million ethnic minority population, which accounts for £13 billion in consumer spending. BT is running adverts in Hindi and in Cantonese. There are many ethnic cable television stations, including African, Arabic, Indian and Chinese services, that could be used for wider advertising. Table 1 breaks down the labour force by ethnic group.

	White	Ethnic minority groups			
		All ethnic groups (%)	Black	Indian	Pakistani \Bangladeshi
All persons aged 16+ (thousands)					
All	41,980	2,110 (5.02)	550	700	430
Males	20,230	1,050 (5.19)	260	360	220
Females	21,760	1,060 (4.87)	290	340	210

Table 1: Structure of the British labour force by ethnic group

2.2 Social structures and behaviour patterns

Beyond the bare statistics of the demographic structure of the population, sociologists have been able to analyse the population by social structures such as families and households, and by behaviour patterns such as lifestyles and tastes. These patterns of behaviour often correspond to patterns of consumer behaviour and are therefore of interest in our analysis of the environment.

SOCIAL PATTERNS

The purpose of monitoring the business environment is first to identify threats to the organisation's current business that would be presented by a decline in the number of consumers or their incomes. Second, environmental analysis allows organisations to anticipate possible opportunities for the expansion of their operation through new markets, products and/or processes which may contribute to improved profitability.

The identification of groups within the population with similar **patterns of consumption** (both in terms of spending and using resources) allows organisations to predict the behaviour of large numbers of people on the basis of fairly limited information. Although these predictions cannot be right in every case, they are sufficiently accurate about large sections of the population to be useful.

One of the key structures in the social environment is the **household**. The General Household Survey, undertaken annually by the government, describes a household as a group of people who have the same address and share living accommodation and at least one meal a day. In the last 30 years, average household size has fallen from 3.1 to 2.5 persons, with 27 per cent of the population now living alone, compared with 14 per cent in 1961.

Social class provides another set of categories used to group people, allowing assumptions to be made about their behaviour and patterns of consumption and need. The main determinant of the categorisation by social class is the occupation of the main earner or breadwinner in a household. Factors such as the increase in the number of two-earner households, single-parent families and high male unemployment all undermine the value of classifying households on the basis of the occupation of the male breadwinner.

Social class has been categorised in different ways. Three are shown in Table 2: the Registrar General's classification, social grades and the verbal description of social status. Each of these classifications is matched against the others and with characteristic occupations. A simplification that is commonly used is a broad three-fold grouping corresponding to upper, middle and lower classes or A, B/C1 and C2/E.

Registrar General's social classes	**Social grades**	**Social status**	**Characteristics of occupation**
I	A	upper class, upper middle class	higher managerial and professional
II	B	middle class	intermediate managerial, administrative and professional
III (i) non-manual	C1	lower middle class	supervisory, clerical, junior managerial, administrative and professional
III (ii) manual	C2	skilled working class	skilled manual labour
IV	D	working class	semi-skilled manual labour
V	D	working class	unskilled manual labour
	E	lowest level of subsistence	state pensioners, widows, casual workers

Table 2: Categorising social class

Demographics concerns age, income, occupation, family size, dwelling, geography, city size, and stage in the life cycle; so, the social class may give an accurate impression of these factors or a totally misleading one.

There are many ways to break down the population further through various geo-demographic segmentation models. For example, the ACORN (A Classification of Residential Neighbourhoods) model uses census data to classify neighbourhoods into clusters according to demographic, lifestyle and consumption characteristics.

Social Trends, published annually by the government, provides a wealth of useful information about the lives that people lead. From this kind of information, it is possible to infer where possible threats and opportunities may lie. Newspaper comment on the findings of *Social Trends* provides businesses with useful information.

PSYCHOGRAPHICS

There are problems with broad categorising, and we need to look more closely at some important factors. In Unit 4, we address these issues more directly. Here, we just give you an idea of some of the factors involved. Some consumer behaviourists regard 'lifestyle' as a more useful indication of buying activity. Psychographics is used as a measure of lifestyle, and it includes **activities, interests** and **opinions.** The main dimensions that are used to measure lifestyles are:

- activities – work, social events, holidays, entertainment, club membership, community, shopping, sports
- interests – family, job, community, recreation, fashion, food, media, achievements
- opinions – about themselves, politics, business, economics, education, products, the future, culture

EDUCATION, MOBILITY AND SOCIAL CLASS

A far higher proportion of younger people going into further and higher education has contributed to the breakdown of some of the stereotypical differences in social classes. In addition, greater geographic mobility, as people travel further for work or for leisure, has tended to influence people's tastes. As a result of this and other social changes, groupings of people by tastes and spending patterns have become more fragmented and more difficult to infer. As a consequence, market researchers have developed more elaborate means of analysing consumer patterns, which we look at in Unit 4.

REVIEW ACTIVITY 2

Write in each box which characteristics of a population need to be incorporated into an environmental analysis for organisations providing the products or services listed in the first column of the table.

Product/service	**Demographic factors**	**Other environmental factors**
Nursing homes for elderly people		
Higher education qualifications		
Cook-chill, ready-made meals for one, available in Marks & Spencer and other stores		
Clothing retailing		
Grocery retailing		
Compact disc versions of 1960s hits		

Summary

We have analysed the population by economic activity and briefly considered the implications of changes in the population structure for business, both in terms of the demand for goods and services and the supply of labour. We can segment the population into age, sex and ethnic groups. Finally, we saw how it is possible to anticipate likely changes in the structure of the population over time, and to forecast future opportunities and threats to organisations.

Basic demographic information gives us a basis to identify consumer behaviour but there are many other factors, particularly lifestyle, that affect it. Grouping consumers on the basis of tastes and spending patterns is increasingly complex as traditional barriers of class, taste and consumer behaviour have been undermined by increased geographic and social mobility.

SECTION 3

Economic Environment

Introduction

The economic environment of an organisation, whether in the public or the private sector, includes the macroeconomy of the country and as well as the industrial sector environment of the organisation itself. We look at each of these areas and then at the effect of government policies on the total economic environment.

We need to know how the economy works as a whole. Macroeconomics tells us how all the different players in the business environment interact. It explains the role of households, and their saving and spending. It looks at the role of the government in taxing and spending. It explains the importance of exports and imports to the business environment. Governments find management of the macroeconomy difficult. Even in a well-managed economy, there will always be changing economic conditions. However, organisations must be able to observe the signs of the health of the macroeconomy and anticipate their likely consequence.

A full module on economics will provide you with far more detail than it is possible to cover here. In this section, we cover those aspects of the macroeconomic environment that are likely to be of most interest to a business organisation. We explain how households, governments and organisations interact as they produce and consume goods and services and we explain what is meant by the trade cycle, outlining some of its indicators.

In looking at the more immediate industrial environment, we describe how industries can be classified by the standard industrial classification system by sector and outline significant changes and trends in UK industrial structure and ownership during the last 20 years. We discuss the implications for individual businesses of changes in the industrial structure.

Governments have a number of ways to control the economy and face a number of difficulties in achieving their macroeconomic objectives. In the final part of this section, we look at how government policies affect the macroeconomy and the industrial environment.

3.1 Macroeconomy and governments

Governments must attempt to control the macroeconomy. To do this, they must measure important elements of the economy that are believed to be indicators of the economy's overall 'health'. Important indicators are unemployment, inflation, total output, interest rates, imports and exports, tax revenue and savings. It is reasonable to assume that the overriding priority of all governments is national economic growth, to produce more goods and services which will generate higher wages and salaries and may lead to more jobs, lower unemployment and more money to spend. However, governments also have other agendas: they want to achieve re-election, they may need to appease certain sections of society and they will have other political aspirations.

This means that governments seek to manipulate the main macroeconomic controls to achieve a range of political, social, economic and other goals. One of the key difficulties is that not all of their priorities are necessarily achievable simultaneously and governments are therefore forced to choose between priorities. The second difficulty is that the analysts disagree about the best method of measuring the key macroeconomic indicators such as 'money' and 'unemployment'. For example, economists who broadly agree about the importance of controlling the money supply, disagree strongly about the best method to measure (and thereby control) the money supply. So, in controlling and monitoring the macroeconomy, the **choice of measures** can be just as critical as the **choice of policy priority**.

To help us understand how the different economic elements interact, we can represent the economy diagrammatically. In Figure 5, the economy is presented as an engine with **money**, or spending power, as the oil that is constantly pumped around to ensure smooth running. Starting with the **income** received by households in payment for the use of their labour, land, raw materials, property, or capital, money moves around in the macroeconomy. Some of this income is immediately siphoned off by the government in **tax**. The money taken out of the system at this stage is not immediately spent by the government on the production of goods and services in the public sector – it may exceed or be less than the government spends at any one time. Some of the household income is **saved**. Not all households save, but some save a lot. These savings are placed in banks and building societies and other savings accounts, which are then available for others to **borrow**. These savings may not immediately be transferred into spending. Finally some household income is spent on foreign-produced goods and services (**imports**), so the spending does not directly generate spending on home-produced goods and services.

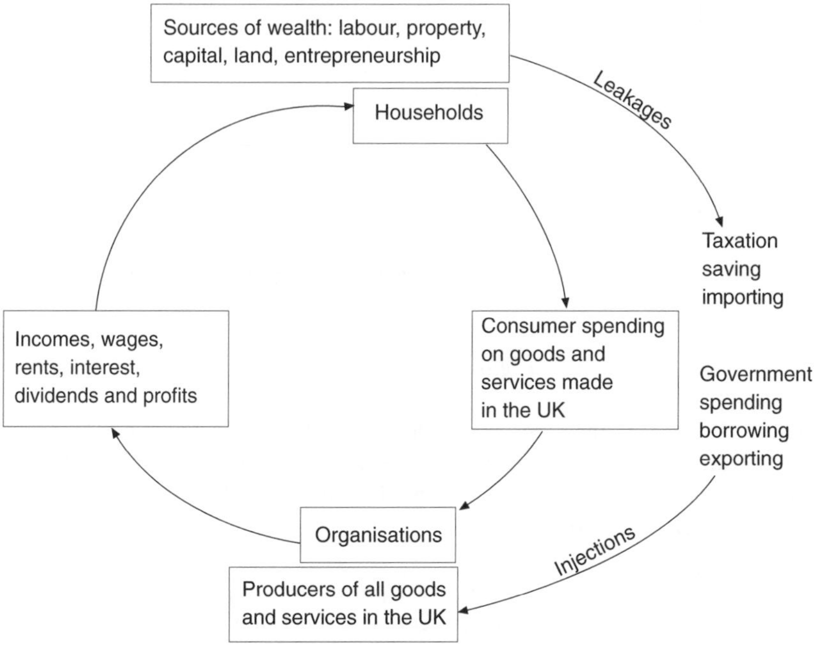

Figure 5: Modelling the macroeconomy – the circular flow of income

Tax revenue, savings and spending on imports are seen as **leakages** out of the circular flow, in that they do not immediately generate spending on home-produced goods and services. Any leakage of 'oil' from the engine will ultimately reduce the overall level going around the engine, with less to share out in terms of incomes in the next round. Government spending on goods and services such as hospitals, roads and universities, the spending of borrowed money and foreigners buying UK produced goods and services all count as **injections** of additional 'oil' into the engine. This increases the amount of money available to be distributed in income – rents, profits, wages and salaries, etc. In this way, it is possible to see that if withdrawals from the circular flow exceed injections, incomes will fall, living standards will decline and unemployment will increase. If injections exceed withdrawals, incomes will rise, unemployment will fall but inflationary pressure will increase.

As economies grow, the pattern of growth is rarely smooth with a constant annual percentage growth. Instead, economies go through a series of cycles called trade cycles (see Figure 6). The trade cycle follows a pattern of recovery, boom, recession and slump (or depression). In the recovery period, incomes are rising and unemployment falls. By the boom period, incomes are high and will probably continue to rise, companies have full order books, unemployment is low, but

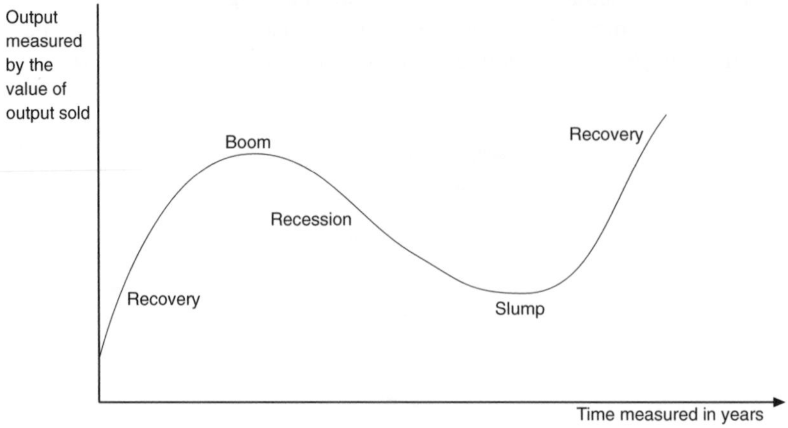

Figure 6: The trade cycle

inflation is rising. In the recession, orders begin to fall, incomes rise less quickly and may fall, and unemployment increases. In the slump, there is likely to be high unemployment, lower incomes and organisations may close down due to lack of orders, but inflation is low.

The length of the trade cycles and the depth of the slumps and the height of the booms varies from cycle to cycle. A very deep recession with a very high boom is more difficult for most organisations to cope with than one with more shallow cycles. In most of the post-war period, British governments of all political persuasions have sought to smooth out the worst excesses of the trade cycle to encourage business and to avoid the worst social effects of very high unemployment and very high inflation.

ACTIVITY 5

Study the following macroeconomic indicators.

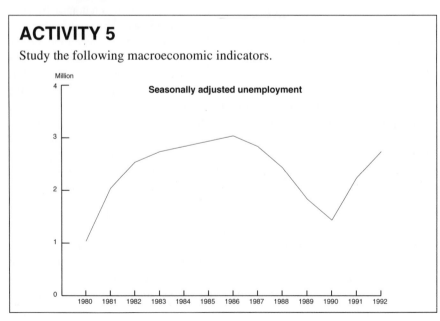

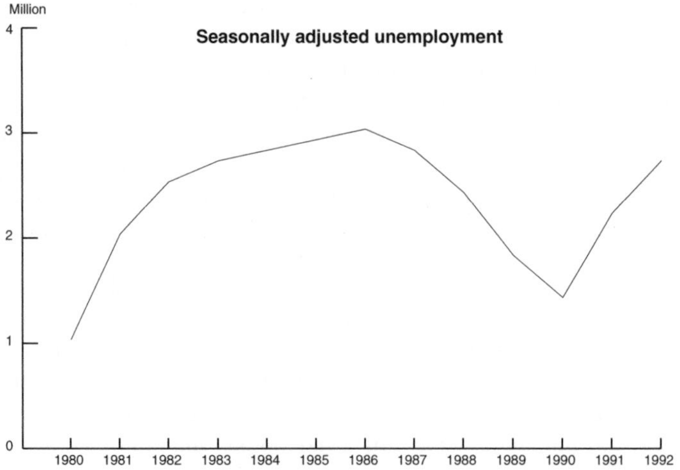

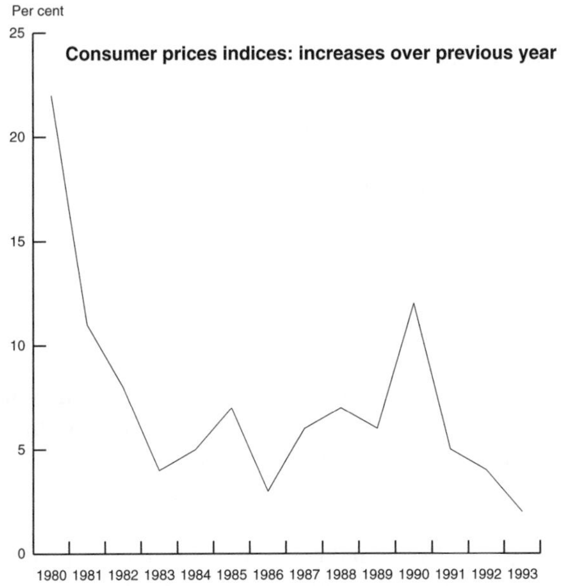
Per cent
Consumer prices indices: increases over previous year
25
20
15
10
5
0
1980 1981 1982 1983 1984 1985 1986 1987 1988 1989 1990 1991 1992 1993

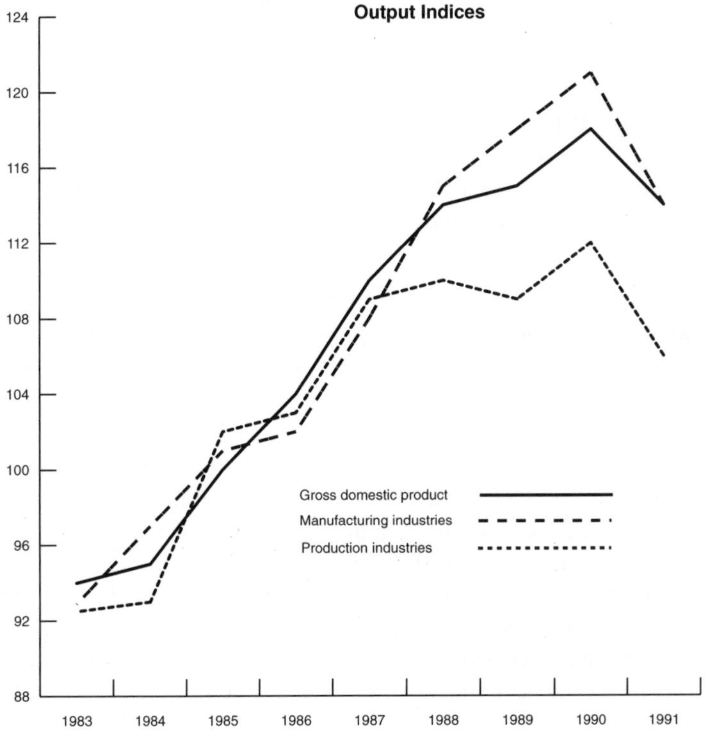
Output Indices
124
120
116
112
108
104
100
96
92
88
1983 1984 1985 1986 1987 1988 1989 1990 1991
Gross domestic product
Manufacturing industries
Production industries

At what stage of the trade cycle do you think the economy is at? What do these key indicators tell you about the economy in the last few years? If you are a business manager considering whether to invest in some new machinery for which you would have to take our a loan, would these macroeconomic indicators encourage or discourage you?

Make a note of your answers.

The key economic indicators presented in Activity 5 show an economy that is just recovering from a very severe and prolonged recession. **Unemployment** has begun to level off, having climbed from 1.5 million to nearly 3 million by 1993. (In July 1997, it stood at 1.6 million, or 5.7 per cent of the workforce and was gradually falling at a rate of around 30,000 per month.) **Inflation**, as shown by the consumer prices index, has fallen fairly steadily over the period shown, with a slight peak in 1990. Output, shown by the indices of **gross domestic product** (all industries), manufacturing industries and production industries (manufacturing and construction industries) had increased steadily from 1983 to 1990, when output began to decline. There is some evidence of a slight upturn in the output indices by mid 1992 but not sufficient to have any confidence in it continuing on an upward trend. On this evidence, if you were running an organisation and considering investing in some new machinery, you would have to think very carefully about the cost of the equipment, the cost of servicing the loan and your market.

MACROECONOMIC POLICIES

The health of the macroeconomy is capable of some control by governments. Economists are divided over the degree of control from the centre that is possible or even desirable. The tools of control at the disposal of the government are limited to:

- **fiscal policy**, which relates to both direct and indirect taxation
- **monetary policy**, which relates to the control of the supply of money in all its forms, from notes and coins to credit availability and interest rates
- **direct action**, as we outline later.

Central to the success of macroeconomic policy is the control of the level of **aggregate demand** in the economy. This is the demand of all consumers of UK goods and services and includes consumption by the general population, investment in plant and equipment by organisations, expenditure on goods and services by the government and spending on UK exports by other countries. Rising aggregate demand is usually associated with economic recovery and boom; falling aggregate demand with economic recession or slump. The government can affect the level of demand, and hence the general business trading conditions and employment opportunities, by adjusting the general level of taxation, the basic level of government expenditure and interest rates. Note that the level of interest rates also affects the foreign exchange rate.

In recent years, the emphasis of the British government's macroeconomic policy has shifted, with greater attention being paid to the less directly interventionist monetary policy. Greater involvement in European Monetary Union, with the emphasis on a move to a single European currency and a convergence of monetary and fiscal policies inevitably constrains the British government's ability to determine actions to suit Britain alone.

The goals of government macroeconomic policy are not easily achievable without some cost (as Table 3 illustrates). Policies like taxing the rich to create jobs for the unemployed or restricting imports with high-tariff barriers so that people are constrained to buy British goods and create more British jobs are no longer seen as efficient long-term solutions. With the emphasis on long-term efficiency, industry has been increasingly exposed to powerful international competition, removing complacency and forcing businesses to become more efficient to be able to compete on an international basis with high-tech countries such as Japan and low-wage countries such as China and Korea.

Priorities	**Reasoning**	**Associated problems**
Higher living standards	If people feel better off, they may want a continuation of the same government and its policies	Necessary to provide both the incentives and the opportunities for people to contribute to wealth creation
Low unemployment	High employment means that more people are earning money, more people are creating goods and services, and there are more people with a stake in society	Competition from low-wage Newly Industrialising Countries (NICs) together with technological advances has reduced the demand for unskilled labour in Europe
		High employment levels can result in incomes and spending power outstripping production, sucking in imports and boosting inflation.
Low inflation	Encourages confidence in the currency both at home, as people buy, sell and save, and abroad as they import and export.	Inflation can be caused by factors beyond the control of any one government, such as a substantial rise in the cost of key inputs like oil.

Priorities	Reasoning	Associated problems
	Encourages saving, and stops people on fixed incomes, for example, pensioners suffering from falling real incomes.	
Balance of international trade	Persistent trade deficits mean countries do not earn enough foreign currency to pay for their imports. Persistent surpluses probably mean other countries are running up deficits and may take retaliatory measures such as tariffs and other trade embargoes.	Growing economies often suck in imports of raw materials and foreign luxuries. Constraining imports of raw materials will limit growth. Tariffs and non-tariff barriers may cause retaliation by other countries.
Economic growth	If more is being produced and more being consumed, then living standards are rising, people feel happier.	Long-term economic growth is rarely achieved without substantial inflationary pressure building up in the economy.

Table 3: Macroeconomic priorities of governments

Using interest rates as a lever to control inflation affects the average individual with mortgage repayments or other debt. However, this has to be balanced against the impact of inflation on the overall health of the economy, unemployment, and the exchange rate. Individuals may immediately feel the direct effects of an interest rise but they may not appreciate that, without a rate rise, inflationary pressures will build up and the economy will suffer. This will impact on individuals in the longer term. The political agenda of the government will influence how they approach this balancing act.

In one of its first actions on taking office in 1997, the new Labour government gave control of the interest rates to the Bank of England. The government continues to set inflation targets but, under this new arrangement, the Bank of England acts to keep inflation within the targets by raising or lowering the interest rates. Events may upset the fine balance required. For example, in 1997 consumers received £35 billion in windfall payments as various building societies converted to banks and floated on the Stock Exchange. This money could lead to a growth in consumer spending, generating inflationary pressures. However, initial reports indicate that more than half of the recipients of shares are holding onto them, with a small percentage spending on holidays and home improvements, and the rest putting their windfall into other savings such as tax advantageous personal equity plans (PEPs).

3.2 Industrial environment

We now analyse the changing industrial environment. In analysing the environment of any organisation, one of the most important factors is the industrial sector that the organisation operates in. This applies to all organisations, whether publicly or privately owned.

STANDARD INDUSTRIAL CLASSIFICATION

All organisations are classified according to the Standard Industrial Classification (SIC). Last revised in 1980, the classification is designed to provide a consistent industrial breakdown in statistics on employment, unemployment, and production. The simplest level of classification is to describe the organisations as belonging to the

- **primary (extractive) sector**, which includes agriculture, energy and water supply, and mining
- **secondary or manufacturing sector**, which includes the construction industries
- **tertiary or service sector**, which includes education and, health care.

The Standard Industrial Classification provides a more detailed segmentation by defining ten divisions.

Division 0	Agriculture, forestry and fishing
Division 1	Energy, water supply industries
Division 2	Extraction of minerals and ores other than fuels; manufacture of metals, mineral products and chemicals
Division 3	Metal goods, engineering and vehicle industries
Division 4	Other manufacturing industries
Division 5	Construction
Division 6	Distribution, hotels and catering, repairs
Division 7	Transport and communication
Division 8	Insurance, banking, finance and business services
Division 9	Other services.

Within each division, further disaggregation allows more detail to be included. For example, Division 4, is broken down as follows:

41/42	Food, drink and tobacco
411/412	Meat and other meat products, organic oils, fats
413/424	All other food and drink manufacture
424/429	Alcoholic, soft drink and tobacco manufacture
43	Textiles
45	Footwear and clothing
46	Timber and wooden furniture
47	Paper, printing, publishing
471/2	Pulp, paper, board and derived products
475	Printing and publishing
48	Rubber and plastics
49	Other manufacture.

CHANGING STRUCTURE OF INDUSTRY

Over most of the twentieth century in the UK, there has been a steady decline in employment and production in the primary and secondary sectors. This trend has accelerated in the last twenty years. Much of the heavy and large-scale industrial production that was undertaken in the north of England, south Wales and the industrial belt of Scotland has disappeared as international competition has forced closure or relocation to low labour cost countries such as those in south-east Asia. However, the infrastructure (housing, schools, shopping facilities, etc.) in these areas – once decaying and under-utilised – has been upgraded with the help of government and EU grants. This has provided an incentive for foreign companies to locate in these areas and exploit the opportunities provided by a highly skilled and trained workforce, cheap land and industrial units.

Employment in the manufacturing and construction industries has shrunk continually since the 1970s. In contrast, employment in the services industries such as banking and insurance has increased but, even here, there were redundancies in the recession of the 1990s. This move from manufacturing to service industries can be termed **deindustrialisation**. The greatest decline in the UK has been in traditional industries such as textiles, shipbuilding and automobiles that succumbed to increasing competition from countries such as Japan, China, Malaysia and Taiwan. The growth in service industries is fuelled by rising national incomes. Consumers have more money to spend on leisure and other services and require banking and investment services to look after their savings. More widespread ownership of houses and cars requires insurance and legal services.

The face of the farming industry has changed through the effects of the EU's Common Agricultural Policy (CAP) and the use of technology that enables vast amounts of land to be cultivated with sophisticated machinery. Improved technology has enabled crop seeds and animals to be genetically developed for maximum yield, and fertilisers and pesticides have been developed for maximum effectiveness. The demands from consumers for a wide selection of 'perfect' cheap produce and the buying power of huge supermarkets has forced the closure of many small farms. Agricultural employment has fallen with the loss of small farms and the increased use of technology. It is expected that the changes proposed in 1997 for the reform of the Common Agricultural Policy CAP will continue this trend as subsidies are removed: the larger farmers with substantial resources will be the ones that survive, probably to the detriment of the countryside as yet more land is given over to large-scale farming. Proposed curbs on blood sports will also affect the countryside and threaten rural employment and, opponents claim, destroy the fabric of some farming environments.

Employment in the service sector has expanded. Some service sector jobs are poorly paid and require low-level skills, but the growth of service industry employment in the financial services, banking and insurance industries and the newer high technology industries such as microelectronics and bioengineering have provided employment opportunities for highly skilled and trained personnel. Much of the more skilled and better paid employment has developed in the south east of Britain, where considerable **agglomeration economies** exist as companies benefit from locating near to each other.

PRIVATISATION AND DEREGULATION

Another late twentieth century trend in the UK is the progressive selling of operations once controlled either directly or indirectly by the government. In a series of sales, collectively called **privatisation**, large-scale government-controlled operations from telecommunications to water and power supply have been converted into share capital and sold to individuals. The rationale for this policy is the belief that the market forces private sector companies to be more efficient and cost conscious than public sector organisations, that are automatically funded from the public purse. Privatisation sales raised billions of pounds for the government and effectively gave ownership of utilities to the people through shareholding.

This increased emphasis on private rather than public sector enterprise has provided many opportunities for new small businesses to establish themselves. Many small businesses now are contracted by public sector organisations like hospitals to undertake tasks such as cleaning, portering or catering. Companies have also been permitted to compete in what used to be state-controlled monopolies such as telecommunications, energy supply and transportation. The EU's policy of transport deregulation has allowed airlines to fly routes within Europe without obtaining permission of individual governments and has opened up the market to companies in the UK including Debonair and EasyJet.

To protect the consumer, the newly privatised industries however are still regulated by government bodies. For example, OFTEL regulates the telecommunications industry since the privatisation of British Telecom and OFWAT regulates the water supply industry. The biggest regulators though are the consumers themselves. For example, competition from companies like Mercury has forced BT to reduce prices and offer more services to keep their customers.

The government has tried to remove many regulations on business. The Deregulation and Contracting Out Act 1994 removed over 450 statutory regulations on business that limited competition in markets; these ranged from opening hours of shops, to the provision of bus services by private operators and the licensing of employment agencies.

Flexibility of the workforce

In the first half of the 1990s, many organisations began to de-integrate and downsize, subcontracting their peripheral activities to smaller, cheaper organisations. Costs have also been cut by relocating activities to areas where labour costs, energy costs, rents and raw materials are cheaper. The traditional workforce of full-time employees (who might have expected to stay with an organisation for many of their working years) has been replaced by a flexible workforce that is required to work part-time or on short-term contracts. Other workers are employed in a freelance capacity, being used as and when required by an organisation. This flexibility enables management to hire and fire easily and match their human resources more closely to their needs. Employees, however, have less job security and fewer opportunities for career progression. In addition, people on short-term contracts of less than two years can neither qualify for redundancy payments nor appeal against unfair dismissal. A 1997 EU directive aims to give part-time workers the same employment rights as full-time workers.

These changes mean that employees have to take more responsibility for their working life. There are no more 'jobs for life'; instead, workers need to be flexible and multiskilled so they can turn their hand to anything. Some organisations, such as HP, still aim to offer job security to their employees, however there is an expectation that the employees will offer something in return to their organisations by being flexible and becoming multiskilled.

Foreign businesses in Britain

In addition to British businesses established in the UK, overseas investment provides additional job opportunities and foreign expertise. However, foreign businesses also bring additional competitive forces as UK organisations may be forced to compete for skilled staff and to compete against additional competitively priced products in the marketplace. Inward investment brings different production, technological and management techniques and skills into the country that can be transferred to local businesses. The establishment of Japanese car manufacturing has increased the competitiveness of the UK automobile industry. London, New York and Tokyo are major attractors of foreign investment.

A study by KMPG Corporate Finance reported that the value of businesses and equity acquired by foreign companies rose 150 per cent in 1995 to £23.3 billion from £8.4 billion the previous year. Britain is second only to the USA as the most popular destination for global investment, according to the report. USA companies invested £8.6 billion in Britain in 1995, French companies £3.8 billion and German companies £2.9 billion. There was £4.5 billion invested in banking and finance, £2 billion in the utilities and £5 billion in pharmaceuticals. These are industrial sectors in which Britain has traditionally held expertise (banking, finance and pharmaceuticals), or where the purchasers believe there is considerable room for market development and expansion (utilities).

INDUSTRIAL CONCENTRATION

Some industries are dominated by a few very large companies. Others consist of many smaller companies all competing for market share. Concentration ratios are measures of the percentage of the market controlled by a specified number of companies. A **concentration ratio 4** (CR4) of 40 per cent shows that the top four organisations control 40 per cent of the market. The degree of industrial concentration gives some indication of the degree of competition in a particular market. A CR4 of 10 per cent is indicative of a market with lots of very small firms and, thus, suggests there are opportunities both for new business start-ups and for existing organisations to increase market share. A CR4 of 90 per cent is indicative of a market dominated by a few large firms which probably indicates that start-up costs are high and competition between the existing organisations is fierce. The concentration ratio does not give the additional information needed to understand all the details of the market. A CR4 market of 80 per cent could be an industry dominated by one very large organisation, with 80 per cent market share, or it could consist of five companies with roughly equal market share.

ACTIVITY 6

The table below gives concentration ratios of five US industries. Write down likely explanations for these levels of concentration.

Industry	**CR4**
Computers	65%
Cars	85%
Bread baking	12%
Flour mills	18%
Detergents	48%

Source: F M Scherer, Industrial Market Structure and Economic Performance. Quoted by Robert Grant (1995) *Contemporary Strategy Analysis*.

The size of an organisation in relation to its market depends upon the structure of the market and the likely **economies of scale**. It is relatively easy to establish a bakery, even on a very small scale with local customers. In contrast, the development costs required to produce new models of cars are so substantial that smaller car firms have been forced out of the market. In Europe there have been several mergers and strategic alliances in the car industry, with links established between Saab and General Motors, Jaguar and Ford, and Rover, Honda and BMW.

Similar scale economies exist in the aircraft industry which explains the high level of international collaboration. This also reflects the structure of the market. National airlines are more likely to buy aircraft that are, at least in part, sourced in the 'home' country.

In the detergent industry, the cost of advertising products means that it is difficult for small companies to gain a foothold in the market. Detergents are relatively inexpensive to produce, but they are difficult to sell without major expenditure on national advertising. Small companies cannot justify or afford the kind of spending on advertising required. Major sales come through the large supermarket chains which can dictate terms to suppliers. In addition, there is fierce competition from existing big groups.

The computer industry has high research and development costs on new product development. However, there are an increasingly large number of smaller companies that simply assemble 'clones' from off-the-shelf components of case, chips and operating systems. Therefore, although the concentration ratio is high, it is falling as less of the market is dominated by the few manufacturers developing and selling the most advanced models.

IMPLICATIONS OF INDUSTRIAL STRUCTURAL CHANGE

Changes in the structure of industry provide both opportunities and threats to all organisations. Some organisations relocate to take advantage of the availability of a plentiful supply of cheap labour, low rents and good communications. Labour must, however, increasingly be highly skilled to attract considerable inward movement of organisations from abroad. In recent years, Japanese car companies like Nissan and Toyota have set up plants in the European Union; in the electronics sector incoming Japanese and US companies include IBM and Motorola.

Towns that are successful in attracting and retaining good employers benefit from **local multiplier effects**, in which the income received by employees is mainly spent in local businesses thereby generating further income for the area. In towns in decline, the opposite effect occurs. Falling household incomes means there is less to spend; local businesses suffer from falling receipts and they may have to close. Even towns that are relatively close to each other may present different business opportunities. In one, perhaps, a major employer provides secure well-paid employment; money is spent in local businesses such as shops and restaurants and also on household maintenance and the revenue from council tax is higher. The town looks prosperous and well maintained. In the other, limited insecure, perhaps seasonal, employment and low incomes restricts the population's spending power. The better skilled and more able people tend to move to find employment. Those that remain are less skilled and therefore less employable. Both the households and the local authority has less to spend. The town is run down as a result.

It is possible, therefore, to identify both threats and opportunities as the structure of industry changes. These can have an impact on an organisation's operations. Organisations are likely to be attracted to areas that offer cheap labour, skilled labour, local firms providing suitable inputs, good communications networks and a pleasant environment to attract key employees to relocate. On the other hand, an area characterised by unskilled labour unused to regular employment, with few successful companies, poor communications with difficult access to airports, motorways and mainline stations, and an impoverished, run-down environment with limited cultural activities geared mainly to the indigenous population is not likely to attract organisations.

The impact of a region's prosperity and attractiveness can also affect an organisation's market or clients. A prosperous region is likely to attract more inward investment by organisations than a declining one, simply because there is more money which may be spent on the output of the incoming organisation.

3.3 Changing economic policies

It is possible to divide the economic policies of governments of interest in our analysis of the business environment into those which affect the **macroeconomic environment** of organisations and those which affect the **industrial environment**. We now examine how the political agenda has shaped the overall business environment.

In the past 20 years, both macroeconomic and microeconomic policies have moved to reduce the role of the state as the provider until, in some areas, it has become the provider of last resort. Macroeconomic policies have shifted from the Keynesian (where contentious decisions about taxation and government spending had to be made to keep employment levels high), towards an increased emphasis on the 'invisible hand' of the market. This means that it is the uncoordinated decisions of millions of spenders that determine the allocation of resources. The new role for government economic policies has been to **provide the enabling conditions** that promote the best possible utilisation of resources by the private sector. This has meant new opportunities but also new threats for businesses.

There have been three main policy changes of interest to businesses.

- **Competition policies**, which promote freer competition. The main thrust of competition policies has been the break up of the nationalised monopolies (through **privatisation**), the **deregulation** of industries previously controlled directly by central government and a greater emphasis on **regional** economic development policies.
- Support for **small-and medium-sized enterprises** (SMEs). SMEs are often the most innovative companies, but they frequently fail in their early

years due to a lack of understanding of some of the basic business methods. This has encouraged the government to support SMEs and to establish various schemes to aid their understanding of business and appropriate technology. The increased emphasis on the individual – and the freer market – has led to the promotion of entrepreneurialism, where innovation, risk taking and competitiveness are actively encouraged.

- **Life-long learning.** The rapidly changing business environment and the accelerating pace of technological change means that organisations can change products and methods of production more rapidly than they change personnel. The key requirement for employees today is that they are flexible and able to acquire new skills. As a consequence, human resources become the most important asset of many organisations, and training has become a major ongoing exercise and expense. The government has increasingly taken a major role in encouraging organisations to invest in life-long learning for their employees. Schools and universities increasingly teach practical vocational skills, in addition to pure education in its broadest sense.

COMPETITION POLICIES

Within the UK, the Office of Fair Trading (OFT) monitors competition. The Director General of Fair Trading has the legal power to refer any cases of anti-competitive behaviour to the Monopolies and Mergers Commission. A monopoly is judged to exist when a company controls 25 per cent or more of market share. Competition policy, however, has to attempt to balance the efficiency gains achievable through the economies of scale of large organisations with the possible abuse of market power. This has led to criticism in recent years that some mergers and acquisitions creating organisations capable of anti-competitive practices have gone unchecked in the interests of promoting large-scale organisations capable of competing in international markets. A highly concentrated industry, with considerable market share in the UK, may only be a small player in the international field. The OFT has also sought to promote competition through cost reduction, promoting the use of new technologies which increase international competitiveness without compromising competition policies at home.

Privatisation

From their election victory in 1979, successive Conservative governments progressively sold off the public sector utilities. The policy sought to promote competition and greater efficiency in these often over-manned and inflexible quasi-bureaucracies, but the government also obtained revenue with which to fund promised tax cuts and reductions in public sector borrowing. Some of the newly privatised industries have flourished in the private sector where their ability to fund further innovation and expansion is not constrained by the political process. The degree to which these organisations are genuinely facing competition is hotly debated. Many still have a virtual monopoly and their ability to exploit this position is only constrained by the political process not the marketplace. Efficiency gains have, in some cases, also resulted in a deterioration of service provision making pre- and post-privatisation comparisons difficult.

ACTIVITY 7

The organisation responsible for air traffic control in the UK has been made into a company wholly owned by the Civil Aviation Authority. The company needs substantial money to finance new investment in equipment and technology. The money is not available through the public purse. Explain in a few words what would be the key concern of raising capital through privatisation?

The key concern in this case is the maintenance of passenger safety with a private company. Some balance between money raised from shareholders and control through regulators could probably be reached. Privatisation used to be a political issue in the UK, a Conservative policy opposed by Labour. In 1997, the new Labour Government is not reversing any privatisations and is discussing further sell-offs, including with the Civil Aviation Authority.

Regional policies

There are wide economic disparities between areas in Britain. The government has made various attempts to level out these inequalities. For example, organisations have been encouraged to relocate to 'poorer' areas through grants and other assistance.

Since the early 1980s, there has been a fundamental change in Britain's regional policies, away from government-sponsored inward investment, towards the promotion of indigenous development, or 'development from within'. This places the responsibility on declining areas to regenerate themselves rather than rely on the action of central government. However, the government continues to offer substantial inducements to attract foreign-owned companies, particularly those who see investment in the UK as a means of gaining access to the whole EU market. These incentives have attracted Japanese car and electronics companies in particular. This not only produces much needed employment but has also led to the adoption of Japanese business practices in some British companies which, in some cases, has had a considerable impact on their international competitiveness. More recently, Korean firms have entered the UK. In 1997, Hyundai announced plans to invest £2.4 billion in microchip manufacture in Scotland, creating 2,000 jobs. And Samsung plans to establish a television factory in Newport, creating 6,000 jobs.

In the late 1990s, the Labour government is moving towards more regionalisation and, with devolution of power to Wales and Scotland from Westminster, the regional approach is reinforced. However, there are many issues still to be resolved that will affect businesses, particularly in Wales and Scotland. The extra tier of government might create added bureaucracy, increase uncertainty and cut investment. Any changes in Scottish income tax will affect both consumers and businesses. Traditionally, public spending per head of population has been higher in Wales and Scotland than in England; this is not likely to continue, which may affect the competitive nature of the regions.

PROMOTION OF SMEs

Both the British government and the European Union are keen to promote small businesses. The justification for this policy is that some small businesses will grow and become major competitors, and the more businesses that are encouraged to set up, the more chance there will be of some success. Small businesses are also employers and risk takers, and they are considered to be more flexible than the bureaucratic hierarchies of larger long-established companies. They are less likely to be unionised and their workers may be more willing to be flexible, to work longer hours if required, and to accept pay cuts if there is a downturn in trade in anticipation of bonuses if trade improves. In addition, small businesses are best able to exploit what can be very profitable niche markets.

The British government has provided various incentives for small businesses. These include the highest VAT threshold in Europe, the Business Expansion Scheme with generous tax advantages for those investing in small businesses and a simplified taxation scheme. The government has also sought to solve one of the most persistent problems facing small businesses that of late payments by customers. The availability of venture capital has been increased by schemes such as the Business Expansion Scheme.

The restructuring of many larger organisations, particularly through downsizing, means that small businesses pick up contracts as larger organisations concentrate on their core activities and sub-contract other work. This inevitably means that smaller organisations are the first to feel the pinch of recession; their contracts dry up as the larger organisations' orders decline. SMEs act as cushions to absorb the impact of recession for larger organisations. Many small businesses failed during the recession of the late 1980s and early 1990s.

LIFE-LONG LEARNING

Some people argue that international comparisons of training and education standards suggest that Britain's industrial decline can be attributed, in part at least, to a lack of commitment and investment in human resources. Training and Enterprise Councils (TECs) in England and Wales, and Local Enterprise Councils (LECs) in Scotland have been established to control a large government-funded training budget that pays for work-related education. They are managed by employer representatives. A number of Industry Training Organisations (ITOs) have been established in particular industry sectors to develop training programmes within these industries.

Youth Opportunities Programmes and Youth Training Schemes were introduced in the 1980s to combat unemployment and lack of training, but with the emphasis on cutting the unemployment count rather than developing genuine training, their success has been debatable. Employers often saw youth trainees as a source of cheap, easily replaceable labour rather than as potential life-time employees. More recently, the emphasis has been on encouraging the schools to develop more vocational education through initiatives such as the TVEI (Training and Vocational Education Initiative) and the development of National Vocational Qualifications through to university-level education.

The government has encouraged employers to regard training as an investment which will yield a future return. Investors in People is an initiative which encourages employers to consider the training need of all their employees and to provide the opportunity for all to update and upgrade their skills as appropriate. Companies with a comprehensive scheme are allowed to use the Investors in People label. A new Investors in People programme, announced in 1997, is directed at small businesses, and other new initiatives include the establishment of the University for Industry. The Investors in People scheme has been shown to reduce staff turnover and absenteeism and increase productivity. However, these effects may be attributed to more open-minded and ambitious management attitudes that provide better encouragement and rewards for staff. The scheme does give employees an indication that management 'cares' about them as individuals, even if it is just to improve productivity, and does give junior staff an opportunity to really ask questions about their jobs and about what the company is doing. Critics see the scheme as added bureaucracy, interference from an outside source that doesn't understand the business and an opportunity for bad management to 'just tick the boxes'.

In the 1997 budget, the new Labour government announced the welfare to work programme. This is designed to offer new work opportunities for young people and with all initiatives leading to qualifications. These opportunities will be linked to an individual's state benefits, which will be cut if the person does not take up one of the possible options. The options include a job with an employer, voluntary work, work with an environmental task force, or full-time education or training for those with no basic qualifications. In addition, employers will be offered a £75 per week subsidy to employ the long-term unemployed. One aim is to get 500,000 single parents off benefits, partly by training 50,000 as childcare workers. These new skilled workers should then enable thousands of other parents to work as they are currently not able to access or afford childcare facilities. Training is through an NVQ in childcare and education. The windfall tax levied on the privatised utilities, announced in the same budget, will contribute £4.8 billion to the welfare to work fund.

REVIEW ACTIVITY 3

What are your views about privatisation? Argue the case for and against privatisation. What effects have you experienced as a result of the sell-off of the public utilities?

Summary

In this section, we have seen how the main macroeconomic agents of households, governments and organisations interact. We have used some macroeconomic indicators to build up a picture of the business environment at a specific period in the trade cycle. In addition, we have begun to explore some of the controls that can be used to manipulate the macroeconomy.

We have seen how industries, the producers of goods and services, can be grouped under headings. We have used concentration ratios to provide simple but useful information about the competitive structure of industries and markets. We have identified some of the main trends in the industrial structure of Britain.

We have reviewed the interaction of political and economic pressures on the business environment. We have started to investigate the key trends in the political environment, including the government's competition policies, the encouragement of SMEs, regional and devolution policies and privatisation. These trends have created a businesses environment that has been welcomed by some businesses as creating conditions conducive to their growth and success. In the next unit, we look at some of these trends in relation to the more specific competitive environment.

SECTION 4

Political Environment

Introduction

The government shapes many determinants of a business's political environment through its policies on the economy, competition, regional development, devolution and employment. In this section, we look more closely at further aspects of the political environment of organisations in the UK. Every country provides a different environment for business companies. Businesses in the UK operate under local constraints, such as planning regulations, national constraints, European constraints and international constraints. They are constrained by legislation and directives from local and national government, from the European Union and from worldwide bodies such as the World Trade Organisation and World Health Organisation. The term 'political environment' covers influences on business from pressure groups, the media, trade unions and professional associations as well as influences from the legal and political arena. Monitoring this environment, and anticipating the pressures that may have an impact on an organisation, is a vital part of an environmental audit.

Later in this section, we examine some wider issues that concern international trade and production. We describe some of the international factors in the business environment. We identify the opportunities and threats presented to UK business by the international business environment. We conclude with a look at some environmental and ethical issues that have local and global significance.

4.1 Politics and power

An organisation is constrained by its legal environment. Laws govern how organisations conduct their business. They cover the types of legal structures that we looked at in Unit 1, customer and consumer rights, employee rights, health and safety, competitive practices, and pollution and the environment. In the UK, this legislation is set mainly through Acts of Parliament, although some common laws have been established through the judicial system of precedence over the centuries. Some European laws are binding in the UK, such as competition law through Articles 85 and 86 of the Treaty of Rome.

Parliament is made up of democratically elected members, and the political party with the most MPs forms the government. The party with the second largest number of MPs becomes the official opposition. The government, its politics and policies and the laws it passes are inextricably linked. The political agenda of the ruling government has a major impact on policies and legislation. The last Conservative government (1992–97) had a narrow majority, constraining its ability to get legislation on the statute books. The current Labour government (elected in 1997) has a large majority, so will be able to pass laws more easily.

Members of Parliament operate in constituencies, working on behalf of the whole electorate; in Parliament, they follow party guidelines. MPs are required to disclose their business interests, including directorships, shareholdings and consultancies, to avoid any conflicts of interest. The Standards and Privileges Committee oversees the conduct of MPs and disciplines any members breaching the rules.

ACTIVITY 8

Watch a television broadcast when Parliament is in session. Try and follow the reading of a particular bill or the debate of a particular issue that you think has some bearing on a business. Read the Parliament Today notices and the political commentaries in the newspaper. Note the questions asked. Who asked them? Note how the government and opposition debate issues. Are any companies or individuals mentioned by name?

The last activity should give you some idea of the way that Parliament and MPs operate and how the political process might affect the business community. Large companies, professional associations and other pressure groups can lobby politicians directly to take particular action and push for certain policies. Politicians can be very open to criticism if they are not seen to be campaigning for the interests for their constituents, perhaps fighting for a factory not to be closed or lobbying for a change in the law to deal with a nuclear waste problem in the area. Conflicts of interest can arise, for example, an MP may be a director of a company whose actions are being investigated by a Commons Select Committee on which he or she is sitting. We have seen these kinds of issues in the 'cash for questions' scandal, where a few MPs have received money for asking questions in Parliament.

As part of the European Union, Britain is also subject to European legislation and directives. The European Parliament, with elected representatives from the member countries, considers and amends proposals made by the European Commission, confirms membership of the Commission, determines EU membership and trade agreements with non-member states. We now look briefly at how the EU has developed and what it means for British business.

EUROPEAN UNION

From its early beginnings, in which members benefited from a strong external tariff and free trade within its borders, the EU has moved to extend its powers beyond the economic sphere. This is illustrated by changes of title – from the European Economic Community, the European Community to the European Union (see Figure 7). In this way, the political environment of the UK is increasingly being influenced by decision making in the EU.

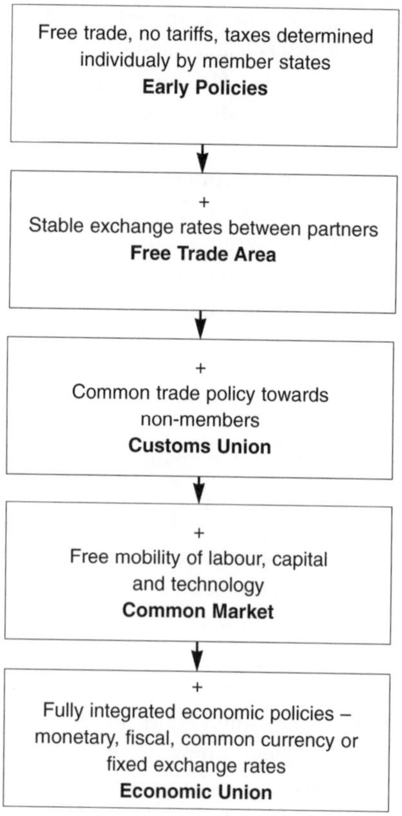

Figure 7: Stages of European economic integration

The **single European market** came into force on 1 January 1993. It covers issues concerning movement and free trade, including:

- checks at national borders
- reduction of importation bureaucracy
- common national product and safety standards
- common levels of indirect taxation.

Britain has found it more difficult to accept the extension of EU powers than some other countries. **Monetary Union** temporarily foundered as many countries did not adhere to the agreed principles of the Exchange Rate Mechanism. A common currency for all member states may ease the passage of international trade but it would remove powers from national governments to control their internal macroeconomic affairs through exchange rate controls, monetary policies and interest rates.

The **Social Chapter**, introducing European legislation regulating the length of the working week and guaranteeing rights of trade union representation, did not fit comfortably with the Conservative government's long-term aims of increasing the flexibility of the labour force. The Conservatives favoured fewer regulations and restrictions on terms and conditions of work. Accepting European social legislation would reduce the power of the British government. In 1997, the incoming Labour government indicated that it will behave differently in Europe as it has a different political agenda. Note how the politics of the government in power also impacts on our European standing, we are not just affected by government policy and law making actions within Britain.

The European Commission consists of commissioners who act independently of their national government, ensuring member states adhere to and implement agreed treaties. This Commission administers the European Regional Development Fund and the Cohesion Fund. The Council of Ministers is EU's decision-making body, comprising ministerial representatives from the governments of the member states governments.

The moves towards greater European integration have considerable implications for organisations within the UK. While many organisations will undoubtedly continue to benefit from easier access to large European markets, others have suffered at the hands of what they see as remote and relatively unaccountable legislators.

ACTIVITY 9

In July 1997, reforms in the EU Common Agricultural Policy (CAP) were announced. These reforms will probably have now been debated and formulated into policy. Through government or European Union sources in your library or through the Internet, identify the key features of the reforms and indicate how they will affect British farming. Comment on the small price reductions that are likely to be passed onto the consumer.

The reforms to the Common Agricultural Policy are aimed at making European farmers more efficient and they should lead to lower prices for consumers. The plans will cut production subsidies paid to farmers and guaranteed prices for crops, meat and milk. Direct subsidies, linked with measures to conserve wildlife and the countryside, will still be available. Ceilings will be put on direct aid paid to individual farmers. The reforms have been drawn up to prevent subsidised EU produce being blocked in world markets under World Trade Organisation agreements that promote fair international trade. The aim is to also to reduce surplus stocks in wine lakes and food mountains.

The price reduction passed on to the consumer will be very small after the produce has gone through the distribution chain. On average, Britain has the largest individual farms, largest flocks of sheep and largest herds of cattle, and limits that are put on maximum acreage and head of livestock will impact most on the largest farms. The reforms are expected to result in older farmers leaving the land as the industry becomes more competitive and many small farms may be bought up. As the proposals affect some crops, such as oilseed rape, the pattern of cultivation may change.

LOCAL GOVERNMENT

Local government is controlled through the democratic political system. District councils are directly elected and, at a lower level, parish councils are elected and function at a very detailed level of villages and town streets. The power of local authorities to raise revenues and to allocate them according to their own priorities has been curtailed in recent years as Conservative governments sought to constrain the powers of largely left-wing metropolitan authorities. Local authorities retain control over the provision of education, within the guidelines of the National Curriculum, libraries, town planning and refuse collection, and raise money through the council tax. All other activities are subject to indirect central government control through quangos or have been privatised. The ability of local authorities to act in the interests of businesses and the population of their area has been severely constrained.

Local authorities do have direct effects on businesses through planning regulations. They control the commercial use of premises through the Town Planning Act 1947, Town and Country Planning Act 1990 and the Planning (Consequential Provisions) Act 1990. Through this legislation, local authorities control land use and any development including building, engineering and mining works that change the nature of buildings or land. Businesses have to obtain permission through a development order, which may be very restricted if a conservation area or listed premises are involved. Procedures are streamlined in areas designated as a simplified planning zone or an enterprise zone.

Planning is also controlled through joint planning committees in London, the National Parks, enterprise zones, urban development areas, and housing action areas. Some developments can also involve compulsory purchase of land and premises, this requires appropriate compensation by law.

ACTIVITY 10

Look in your local paper for notices about planning permission. Think about how individuals and groups lobby planning authorities to deny permission and note down the implications for individual organisations and the area if permission is denied.

In looking for applications for planning permission, you may find some domestic applications such as for erecting a garage or conservatory but also a whole range of commercial applications, such as applications for the erection of new properties with access roads, change of usage of domestic properties to commercial offices, or from retail to catering use, for erection of sports facilities, and for the extraction of clay for construction work. Applications are required from all organisations; even the local authority must make an application if, for example, it wants to extend library facilities or build a new health centre. If an organisation has not sought and gained the right planning permission, it can be required to knock down the building and return everything to its former state. Any individual or organisation can contest permission, with reasons, and this will be taken into account before planning permission is granted or denied. Obviously, permission is more likely to be denied if there are a large number of contests.

QUANGOS AND REGULATORS

Despite the desire to reduce the role of government and to make its actions more open and accountable, the rapid growth of quangos (quasi-autonomous non-governmental organisations) has increased the influence of government. Quangos are funded largely by central government. They are set up to manage areas of government spending and to monitor and control the effectiveness of different aspects of government policies. Quangos include NHS Hospital Trusts, the BBC and the Monopolies and Mergers Commission. At best, these agencies can exert the necessary government control with the flexibility and efficiency of the private sector. At worst, they can be powerful organisations, with directors appointed on the basis of appropriate political connections rather than ability, that are unaccountable to the users of the service.

With the privatisation of the utilities, regulators have been established to make sure that there is no exploitation of the consumer and an appropriate service is supplied at a fair price. The regulators are OFTEL (telecommunications), OFGAS (gas), OFWAT (water), and OFFER (electricity). They are responsible for promoting competition and protecting the consumer. They can intervene in many areas of business, including investment, profits, prices, service and mergers. Regulators are also appointed for other operations such as the National Lottery. Even then, the government may not feel this is adequate control. In 1997, the government appointed an independent watchdog to oversee the National Lottery regulator, OFLOT, that oversees the existing operator Camelot. Despite concerns about excessive profits and over-generous bonuses for bosses, Camelot is likely to rebid for the franchise when the current contract ends in 2001. In the meantime, the government will be tightening the legislation through parliament to control any franchisee's operation. The independent watchdog will be monitoring the performance of OFLOT.

PRESSURE GROUPS

Pressure groups and interest groups are a legitimate part of the democratic process, seeking to influence decision makers in a wide variety of ways. Some groups are accepted insiders in the political process and are routinely consulted on matters likely to have an impact on their interests. The National Farmers' Union is consulted on matters relating to agricultural policies, the British Medical Association on medical concerns, and the Confederation of British Industry and Trades Union Congress on matters relating to business and industrial relations. Other pressure groups aim to have an impact on public opinion and, in this way, to influence the decision making process indirectly. Groups such as Friends of the Earth, the RSPCA and Greenpeace have well-established professional campaigners that seek to influence public opinion, government and the activities of individual organisations.

Some of these pressure groups, by influencing the government's economic and political decisions, impact on the business environment. For example, the anti-road lobby may influence the decisions on road construction and the routes of new roads, decisions that affects the infrastructure of a region. Individual organisations are affected, construction companies lose out if road building projects are cancelled, transport cafes and other businesses are affected if a new bypass diverts traffic from existing routes.

Organisations may make use of strong pressure groups by identifying with the principles the groups advocate. So a cosmetic firm could benefit from lobbies that advocate environmentalism, feminism, anti-corporate business, anti-vivisection, animal rights and health consciousness by promoting its products as untested on animals, enhancing health and vitality and selling them in recycled biodegradable packaging from franchises run by women. The Body Shop espouses most of these attributes, although in fact it relies on its own lobbying. However, it is obviously helped in its business by the increased awareness that is generated by other pressure groups.

Pressure groups carry out protests and directly lobby MPs and Parliament for action. They hope to build up public support through petitions and demonstrations. The media is always anxious to cover demonstrations, especially if they get out of hand and make newsworthy articles.

ACTIVITY 11

Huntingdon Life Sciences, a company specialising in extensive animal testing, was investigated by the Animals Inspectorate in 1997 following a Channel 4 documentary which showed staff ill treating animals. The Home Office has outlined some serious problems and demanded that they be addressed, otherwise the company's licence will be revoked.

Huntingdon Life Sciences is a large employer with around 1,400 employees. The Home Office initially suspended its Certificate of Designation which allows the company to experiment on animals. If the licence is permanently revoked, thousands of dogs, rabbits, baboons and rats could be slaughtered. In addition, animal studies will be affected and contracts with pharmaceutical companies to test drugs will obviously be terminated.

What are your views? Should the company be allowed to operate, provided it addresses the issues identified by the investigation? Is it enough to just have government control on sensitive business issues, even if the government is democratically elected? Do we need pressure groups to continually question the action of business? If we do, then consider the different actions of the pressure groups. Should police time be wasted on the protesters? Should the actions of activists from outside the area threaten the livelihoods of many within it? Is a petition more effective? Consider your own views on the nature of legitimate protest and the activities of pressure groups in a democratic society.

You should be able to develop your own views on this kind of situation. Your sympathies might lie with the animals that were cruelly treated, or the animals that are now threatened, with the drug companies that are testing new products, with the individual employees that might lose their jobs, with the shareholders, with the protesters, with the police, or you may have divided loyalties about it and may rely on the government to control these sensitive issues.

Consider the following events that surrounded this organisation. Protesters at the premises got somewhat out of hand as they attempted to stop employees leaving, even throwing bricks, and blamed the individuals for the problems of the company. Police riot vans and officers from throughout Cambridgeshire were called in to protect the protesters and the employees. Animal Aid, a group opposed to scientific research on animals, collected 30,000 signatures on a petition demanding that Huntingdon's Home Office licence be permanently revoked. Representatives presented this at the Houses of Parliament. Huntingdon Life Sciences shares were suspended on the Stock Exchange.

The chief executive of Huntingdon Life Sciences says that controls, training and procedures have been improved since the incidents of maltreatment occurred. Two staff have been charged under the 1911 Protection of Animals Act and a third has had his licence revoked. However, regardless of your ethical views, you might question the management of a company that has animal testing as its core activity and has allowed a situation to develop to the point where the company is in danger of losing its Home Office licence. We might think that its procedures, controls and human resource management practices for monitoring staff in such a sensitive area were extremely lax. In addition, perhaps the Home Office procedures were at fault and need reviewing as previous inspections had not revealed any mistreatment.

ROLE OF THE MEDIA

The media – radio, television, newspapers and journals – acts both as the main provider of information on the general environment and an interpreter of that information. Although reportage is mainly kept separate from the comment, the choice of news reports and the priority accorded to them within the newspaper or news bulletin influences our perception of their importance. The power of the media to shape opinions and influence political decision making is phenomenal. Ownership of the media has become increasingly concentrated in the hand of a few very wealthy individuals, causing political concern. External control is limited to the Press Complaints Commission.

Note that in Activity 11, the problem at Huntingdon Life Sciences was originally brought to light by a Channel 4 investigation. Perhaps there had been a tip-off by someone concerned within the company to start the interest.

The activity of MPs and other individuals in powerful positions, company bosses and other personnel in the public eye are coming under very close scrutiny by the media. This not only extends to their public lives but also into their private lives.

ACTIVITY 12

At a library, choose a news item and read the reporting in as many newspapers as you can. Notice the differences in emphasis and the different perspectives taken on the event, that must be based on same facts in all cases. If you have access, follow a news item direct from the news wires to the television the same day and into the newspapers the next day. Remember too that the information on the news wire is submitted by journalists in the field, so the information could still be subject to bias.

4.2 International business environment

As we have seen, a UK business operates in a local, national and European arena. In the 1990s, it also increasingly operates in a broader international arena. This affects its competition, its resources and its markets; national and European legislation and international trade agreements may control its actions. We need, therefore, to look at the wider international picture. As we know, the business environment consists of a changing complex interaction of the economy, social structures, technology and politics. All these effects operate at the global level not just at the domestic level. Improvements in transportation and communications have made it easy to process worldwide orders and ship raw materials, semi-finished products and completed goods throughout the world. Businesses of all sizes find themselves operating with substantial international competition and the UK needs to be able to compete at this level.

The ability of the UK to compete in international markets and to promote growth of national industry require sustained improvements in productivity, product quality and cost reduction. Indicators of the UK's changing competitiveness are:

- real gross domestic product
- UK share of world trade
- output per employee
- unit labour costs.

Gross domestic product (GDP) is a measure of the total value of all goods and services produced in a country over a certain period – GDP will rise with economic growth and with increase in prices. In the emerging markets of Latin America and south-east Asia real GDP is rising, whereas in the developed countries only just recovering from the 1990s recession, production has been cut back and real GDP has decreased. Despite growth in GDP in newly industrialised economies of China, Malaysia, Mexico and Brazil, these countries remain poor. They present the UK with an opportunity as an emerging market for British goods and services, but a threat as these countries are able to produce goods and services with low-cost labour and with increasing sophistication in technology and business expertise.

The UK is a net importer of physical commodities but manages to balance overseas payments through earnings from banking, insurance and finance, although London faces strong competition from other financial centres such as New York and Tokyo. However, there is an imbalance on manufactured goods as the UK imports more than it exports. Obviously, the sterling exchange rate has a very immediate effect on imports and exports of all descriptions; in 1997 for example, the strength on the pound was causing particular concern for the manufacturing industries.

Britain's output per employee (or productivity) has been increased by the use of technology in equipment and production processes, by the closure of inefficient factories and organisations, and by changes in working practices. Unit labour costs (the cost of labour per unit of output) in real terms have only marginally increased in the UK since the 1960s. Although the UK has improved over the past two or three decades compared with our main trading partners, there is still a differential in the main parameters of international competitiveness. Japanese companies continue to perform well: the value of output per employee is high and unit labour costs are relatively low, so Japanese manufacturing remains more profitable than its overseas competitors.

International trade functions on a number of levels. These include:

- obtaining part-finished goods from other countries, particularly the raw materials and components required in manufacturing
- obtaining foreign goods and services for direct consumption
- switching the locations of factories to take advantage of lower production costs
- trading in currencies to enable payment.

Some multinational enterprises (MNEs) have greater economic and political power than many national governments. They have the ability to relocate to take advantage of local resources and the best conditions for business anywhere in the world. Global trade is increasing the variety and reducing the price of goods available. However, thinking consumers are becoming concerned about the excessive exploitation of the world's resources, from deforestation in South America to pollution and over-fishing in British coastal waters. So, while the size and scope of the business environment grows as distances metaphorically shrink, the awareness of the vulnerability of the 'small lonely planet' to over exploitation increases.

The debates about the exploitation of the world by the developed capitalist countries revolve around issues such as the exploitation of child labour, poor working conditions for employees in developing countries, stripping out of natural resources, and sales of defence products to countries with poor civil rights. Others argue that the West is a force for good on the developing world: creating jobs, paying money for resources, bringing technology in the form of equipment and communications, and providing workforces with the skills and experience of western production and management methods.

TRADING BLOCS

Three groupings of nations contribute most to output and international trade on a global scale; they are the European Union, the United States and Japan. In the 1990s, this 'triad' controls 62 per cent of world manufacturing production, and 77 per cent of world exports. They are also the main providers and recipients of international investment.

These three great trading blocs are seeking to increase their strength and power through treaties and trading agreements. In western Europe, other countries are seeking to join the combined trading block of the European Union and the European Free Trade Area (EFTA). As a trading bloc, western Europe has massive purchasing power, with relatively high incomes and a high technology base. Moves to increase the links between the European Union and countries at the periphery such as Turkey have so far foundered because of conflicts of interests with existing member states. In the near future, the EU plans to allow in Poland and other countries from the ex-communist bloc in eastern Europe but still to keep Turkey out. The richer nations in Europe are concerned about subsidising the poorer ones.

The UK trade policy is defined in part by the EU's common competition policy. The EU operates within the General Agreement on Tariffs and Trade (GATT). There are 117 members of GATT. The last round of negotiations, which started in 1986 in Uruguay, concluded in 1993 with agreements to extend fair trade rules to agriculture, textiles, services, intellectual property and foreign investment. The World Trade Organisation (WTO) was established to oversee the implementation of these agreements and to promote open markets in international trade.

Within the EU, conflicting interests have meant that there is no common currency nor completely open borders. There is no common European language, unlike in the USA and Canada, to help unify the market. The Americans have sought to extend their market through the North American Free Trade Area (NAFTA), which includes Canada and Mexico. In Asia, the Association of South East Asian Nations (ASEAN), which includes Singapore, Thailand, Malaysia, the Philippines, Indonesia and Brunei, has been established. This includes nations whose rapid industrialisation and economic development are likely to pose a substantial threat to the more developed countries in the near future.

4.3 Environmentalism and social responsibility

As the world 'shrinks', and companies become larger and more powerful, some groups have sought to monitor and constrain the excesses of the economic exploitation. Once considered the province of idealistic cranks, **environmentalism** has moved to the top of the political agenda in many western countries. The increasing concern over the health of the planet has been heightened by major catastrophes such as the explosion at Chernobyl, and by scientific research showing the effects of chlorofluorocarbons (CFCs) on the ozone layer and of car exhaust fumes on pollution in cities.

The long-term implications of these and other environmental disasters have led to widespread recognition of the dangers of uncontrolled commercial activity. Environmental pressure groups have learned to use consumer power to influence the policies adopted by companies. Consumers are encouraged to only purchase goods and services from those companies that show signs of taking the environment seriously. This presents considerable threats to some companies and industries. The fur trade in Britain has almost disappeared as a result of environmental pressure and an increasingly violent campaign. Protesters continue to press for a ban on live animal exports and cosmetics tested on animals.

An organisation's activities are constrained by a number of laws that protect the environment. The Environmental Protection Act 1990 has meant that an organisation may have to reposition not just its products but its processes and whole way of doing business. In the UK, environmental protection is afforded to:

- water – following the privatisation of the water industry, the National Rivers Authority has responsibility to maintain water quality and control pollution
- air – local authorities can use various Acts to monitor and act on emissions into the atmosphere and, on a national level, Britain has agreed to phase out CFCs used in air conditioners, refrigerators and expanded polystyrene by 2000
- acid rain – Britain will act to reduce acid rain through phased reduction in emissions from power stations of sulphur dioxide by 2003 and of nitrogen oxides by 1998
- waste – controlled by local authorities through various Acts of Parliament
- dangerous substances such as pesticides and radioactive waste – various Acts control the use and disposal of these substances
- noise – local authorities monitor and control noise pollution.

In addition to products and services, processes can be made less environmentally threatening. Environmental audits of companies encourage them to develop processes and procedures that use less power, produce less waste and use renewable rather than finite resources. As we discussed in Unit 1, this will create a more efficient transformation process within the organisation. An environmental audit should appraise all environmental aspects of the business. Many organisations, such as those involved in the chemical and pharmaceutical industries, may never be totally environmentally friendly; however, all companies should do everything they can to minimise damage to the environment.

Everything is manufactured at some environmental cost, whether it is from the use of raw materials, non-sustainable energy resources or pollution. Products and processes can be changed to reduce environmental damage. So, Renault, Vauxhall and BMW have developed circulation systems allowing up to a quarter of car exhaust fumes to return to the engine. McDonald's no longer uses CFCs in its packaging; British Gas pulled out of oil exploration in Ecuador because of the destruction of rainforests by other unscrupulous operators. Varta, the German battery manufacturer markets mercury-free batteries. ICI advises farmers on the safe use of pesticides and agrochemicals. The Body Shop does not test its products on animals. However, on the negative side, we could identify cases of pollution through detergents and sewage in the waterways, through oil tanker disasters, through the destruction of the countryside to build roads, through quarrying and mining, over-fishing of coastal waters, killing of elephants for ivory, destruction of rainforests, and the overuse of pesticides.

As well as addressing environmental issues directly throughout their operations, some organisations make a direct contribution to the environment in spheres outside of their normal business activity. Tesco is supporting the skylark as part of the government's Biodiversity Challenge to save 116 species of British wildlife. ICI has sponsored action to save the endangered Large Blue and Pearl-bordered Fritillary butterflies, initially by donating £55,000 to reintroduce the Large Blue to 15 sites in the UK.

Society, governments and individual organisations have to guard against any abuse of the environment to the best of their abilities. However, there will be conflicting interests. For example, in 1997 the Department of Trade forecast that demand for flights from British airports will more than double over the next 18 years to 378 million passengers per year. This will mean further problems for the government in meeting its promise to reduce emissions of greenhouse gases by 20 per cent by 2015.

Consumer groups are important in helping governments to monitor the situation and in keeping some organisational strategies under control. For example, a consumer and environmental group in Dublin is fighting attempts to introduce genetically engineered crops into Ireland by the US agrochemical company Monsanto. Ethical, health and environmental concerns have been raised. The company has been conducting seed trials in the UK since 1995. In Germany, Unilever and Nestlé stopped producing genetically engineered soya because of consumer concern. Novartis's gene-modified maize has been banned in Austria, Italy and Luxembourg because of safety concerns. The European Commission is now working towards legislation that will force producers to label all seeds, animal feeds and consumer foods to indicate whether they contain genetically modified materials.

Many organisations have seen environmentalism as an opportunity, either to promote their particular range of products as being environmentally superior or to develop a range of appropriate products for which they can charge a premium price. Many products and marketing strategies – such as non-chlorine bleached paper, recycled packaging, fair trade with less developed countries, organic vegetables and traditionally reared meat – can be seen as a response to the increased interest in the environmental aspects of business. However, one of the problems for consumers is to determine the genuinely worthy and effective products from those that use environmentalism as a form of branding and packaging. For example, a shampoo manufacturer might advertise that it is against animal testing, but the shampoo might include formaldehyde and methylparaben which will have been tested on animals.

Consumers can now choose to invest in ethical businesses and still make a reasonable profit. Britain's first ethical fund was Friends Provident's Stewardship launched in 1984, it is worth in excess of £390 million and the group has £865 million under management in ethical funds. Funds take different approaches in classifying an acceptable company. Some only include those companies that are helping the environment; some exclude all companies that are involved in certain industries, such as military products, alcohol, tobacco, or those with records of high pollution or exploitation in the developing world.

The developed parts of the world have become more environmentally and socially aware, and governments have been pressured into increasing the regulation of industry. Many organisations are able to take advantage of the improvements in communications and transportation to relocate to parts of the world where the threat of extreme poverty and starvation are more immediately threatening than global warming or industrial injury.

There a number of ways that environmentalism can affect an organisation:

- through legislation and national, European and international policies
- through pressure from consumer groups and professional associations
- through the marketplace and the consumer's actions
- through other stakeholders, such as shareholders.

As with other threats and opportunities in the environment, the organisation needs to respond to these influences. It can:

- undertake an environmental audit to make operations more efficient
- develop new processes
- introduce new products and packaging for the green marketplace.

ACTIVITY 13

Through a media search or from your own knowledge and experience, make notes on a situation in which a company has been forced into an unexpected action through the legal system or through a pressure group lobbying on an environmental or conservation issue.

There are many examples that we could identify here, and you will have come up with your own situations. Consider this case. Hanson Land, a subsidiary of Hanson plc, received planning permission to build a new town on old brick fields near Peterborough in 1987. Previously worthless, the land rose in value to £200,000 per acre for the 2,500 acre site. However despite the planning permission, the development could not proceed as the area was the habitat of 30,000 very rare great crested newts that are protected under British and European legislation – Section 9 and Schedule 5 of the Wildlife and Countryside Act 1981, the Berne Convention Section 2 and the Habitat and Newts Directive (92/43/EEC). Other rare species of insects and vegetation were found in the self-contained world that had developed in the disused brickworks. Hanson had already invested £30 million, and the company spent the next 10 years experimenting with ways of moving the newts. Some 15,000 newts will now be moved to a new 276-acre nature reserve. It will cost around £1,000 to move each newt, and the entire conservation scheme is expected to cost around £1.5 million. However, in 1997, work can start on the building of houses, shops and schools.

ETHICS

Leading on from the environment, we can consider the whole area of an organisation's social and ethical responsibility. An organisation can take many stances on social and ethical issues. A tobacco company, for example, could argue that it is in business to make money and fulfil its obligations to its stakeholders, that an individual has the right to smoke and it is up to the government to legislate any constraints on its business activities. The tobacco company might also argue that it gives something back to society through sponsorship of the arts and sports; cynics would argue that they are only doing this for the publicity as the government considers even further controls on advertising. A road construction company could argue that it is operating within the law and to the best of its ability, and it is the government's problem to control its actions and, in any event, society benefits as a whole from new roads.

However, in today's world, when consumers are better educated and informed, it makes sense for every organisation to have a social conscience. We could also argue that the best way of making profits or operating within budgets is through socially and ethically responsible behaviour, producing products and services that meet consumers' needs, using a minimum of resource and treating staff in a fair and reasonable manner.

The first step in social and ethical responsibility is to have environmental responsibility as we have outlined above. Obviously, an organisation needs to make profits to stay in business, but it should not do this at the expense of social or ethical principles. An organisation needs to look at its products, and its marketing and advertising. Is the product or service meeting a real need of the consumer and not one that has been artificially created? Is the organisation giving incomplete or misleading information on the contents of products or the uses of products and services? Are products detrimental to the individual or society as a whole? Many of these issues are covered by legislation or by regulatory bodies such as the Advertising Standards Authority. However, not all concerns are covered by these bodies. For example, should the drinks industry have developed alcopops that may encourage underage drinking? The industry might argue that underage drinkers will drink cider and beer, and the product was designed for housewives anyway. You will have your own views.

An organisation also needs to look to its relationship with all its stakeholders. Is it fair and honest with all links in its supply chain; are all contracts and communications open and clear? Is it fair and honest to its staff? Do key personnel behave appropriately in their public life? You may or may not think that an organisation should also have concerns about the private life of key staff. Is it fair and honest with its shareholders, paying out appropriate dividends or paying its bosses large salaries? Again many of these issues are covered directly by legislation, but the organisation needs to address any 'grey' areas. Its actions will be governed by its culture and its underlying values and beliefs. These are also a reflection of the society in which it operates. For example, in some countries the giving and taking of bribes as part of a business contract is normal and expected; in other countries this practice is illegal or severely discouraged.

ACTIVITY 14

Select an advertisement that is currently running on television. Note down some comments on the product or the advertising from an ethical perspective.

You might have chosen an advertisement that promotes the 'healthy' qualities of breakfast cereal. Has it medically been shown to be healthy? What about beer advertisements showing young people having a good time? You might consider that much lifestyle advertising is close to the limit of acceptability. Is it right that cars are being developed to go at speeds much higher than the speed limit and are shown being driven at speed in advertisements? Is the use of very thin supermodels justifiable or does it promote anorexia in young girls? You will have your own views about these issues. It is useful to develop your own social and ethical responsibility through your reaction to events around you, but remember that each individual will have his or her own unique set of values and beliefs that guide his or her behaviour and society and organisations have to reach a balance with all these differing views.

REVIEW ACTIVITY 4

In the UK government's annual budget, the Chancellor of the Exchequer reviews the main trends in the UK economy and sets out a range of business and personal measures on tax and other issues such as public spending. Using the latest budget, identify the main features of the economic review and the main personal and business measures. Make brief comments on some likely responses from the business world to these measures. Note any 'green' or ethical issues.

Summary

In this section, we have looked at the basic political environment of UK organisations, including the national, EU and international guidelines and laws that governs their operations. The political environment extends beyond legislative and policy-making bodies to encompass the power and the interests of a very wide range of regulators, interest and pressure groups. Some of these groups have the power to influence the government's economic and political decisions which may change the business environment. Some may have an impact directly upon individual businesses.

We have considered the importance of international competitiveness and the UK's global position. Environmentalism is an international as well as a national issue, and there is far-reaching legislation to protect many aspects of the environment. In addition, organisations are now encouraged by government and professional bodies to adopt an environmentally friendly operation, and they are pushed by the demands of the consumer. This led into our final discussion about an organisation's social and ethical responsibilities to all its stakeholders, and to society in general. You will be able to develop your own views about these issues that will guide you in the types of products you buy, the way you live and the work you do, and the organisations that you choose to deal with.

SECTION 5

Technological Environment

Introduction

Technological change has probably been the most significant cause of recent environmental turbulence in the business environment. It affects all aspects of a business, from its products to processes, the way it makes them, to communication both within and beyond the organisation, to the degree of competition, and the degree of internationalisation. In this final section in Unit 2, we examine the role that technological change plays as the key driver of turbulence in the business environment. We look at the effect of incremental and generic technological changes on the economic cycle.

The pervasiveness of current technologies means that all organisations, whether public or private sector, large or small, have been influenced by the changing technological environment, for good or bad. Technological know-how is not, however, the key driver of change. It is the process whereby the technology is applied, adopted or utilised that creates the change. Technology can be seen as an enabling agent, one that makes it possible for businesses to make traditional products in new ways, such as irradiated food stuffs. We can make new products for traditional needs or we can make entirely new products or services, such as the Sony Walkman, that meet needs we did not know we had.

Once the extent of technology adoption has reached a critical size however, the technology itself becomes the key driver of change, since without the latest technology an organisation cannot compete. Those businesses without faxes, mobile phones, computers with modems, CD-ROM and Internet access are increasingly rare. Retailers increasingly must have EPOS and a stock control system. Many households have personal computers with modems and CD players. The availability of technology itself drives the organisation's changes, since the organisation is expected to have the latest technology if it is serious about competing.

Technology involves all the processes in the transformation of an organisation's inputs to outputs, and concerns all the primary and support activities in Porter's value chain. Developments in technology can affect one or all functional areas in some way and all links in the supply chain. Nothing escapes technology whether it is the mining of raw materials, the production of energy as inputs, the transformation process itself, or the type and nature of the outputs and their marketing and delivery to the customer. As you saw in Unit 1, people, information and communication are key elements in today's business world. These are all affected by technology and changes in it.

5.1 The new industrial revolution

Technological progress usually occurs continually in small **incremental** steps as slight improvements are made to existing processes and products. These small technological changes result in new or improved products and manufacturing processes, and the replacement of older ones. However, there are times when significant developments of technological know-how occur which have a radical effect on the current business environment. This development, called **generic change**, is substantial enough to result in entirely new processes and new products, services and systems, even new industries. Changes of this kind then stimulate clusters of both radical and incremental innovations so that all aspects of the social and economic environment are affected. As you can see from Figure 8, there have probably been four of these revolutions in the last 200 years. Each has shaken the stability of the business environment and created tremendous opportunities for some organisations, while causing the terminal decline of others.

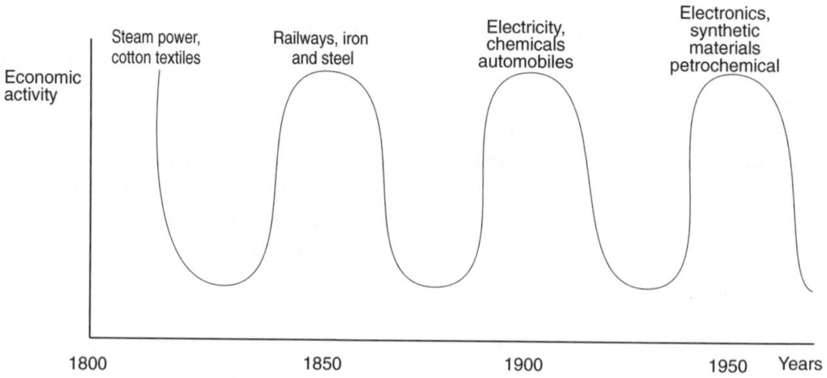

Figure 8: Industrial revolutions – Kondratiev's long waves

We could argue that the fifth Kondratiev cycle began in the late 1980s and is associated with information technology (IT). It represents the coming together of mechanical, electromechanical and early electronic technologies (typewriters, gramophones, cameras, radios and televisions) with microelectronic technology (computers, robots). By the early 1990s, computers and telecommunications were integrated into a single source of information processing and exchange.

The convergence of these technologies is probably the most important development in today's business environment and is likely to be in tomorrow's as well. These technologies have been described as **enabling technologies**. Transport and communication systems have created unprecedented mobility of raw materials, products, ideas and techniques. Transportation by jet and communication via optical fibres and satellites, by telephone and fax has reduced the apparent size of the world, making markets the other side of the world almost as accessible as domestic markets. The world's three major markets are now linked by a global digital network capable of carrying many thousands of messages simultaneously around the world. For businesses operating in international markets, the new communication technologies have become essential to their operations. The technology, which allows them to transmit information to all parts of their extensive operations simultaneously, improves organisational cohesiveness and strategic management. Decision making is improved by having the right information in the right place at the right time.

5.2 New products and processes

Manufacturing process can be divided into 3 major groups:

- unit and small batch production
- mass production
- continuous process production.

In all types of processes, advances in technology can change the process. This is obvious where machines are required to do most of the work in mass and continuous process production, but also applies in craft production where computer-aided design, for example, could help, or in vast one-off production projects such as building a road or an aircraft.

We can view the role of technology through its different contribution in the product's life cycle. We can identify the development of different methods of production from craft through to automation. We can identify the use of different technologies too, through analysis of the organisation's functions. Computer-aided design and manufacture (CAD/CAM) are used in design and engineering, databases for information, automation in operations, computers for mechanical tasks in accounting, databases for marketing, television and on-line shopping, and EPOS for sales and communication with electronic data interchange (EDI).

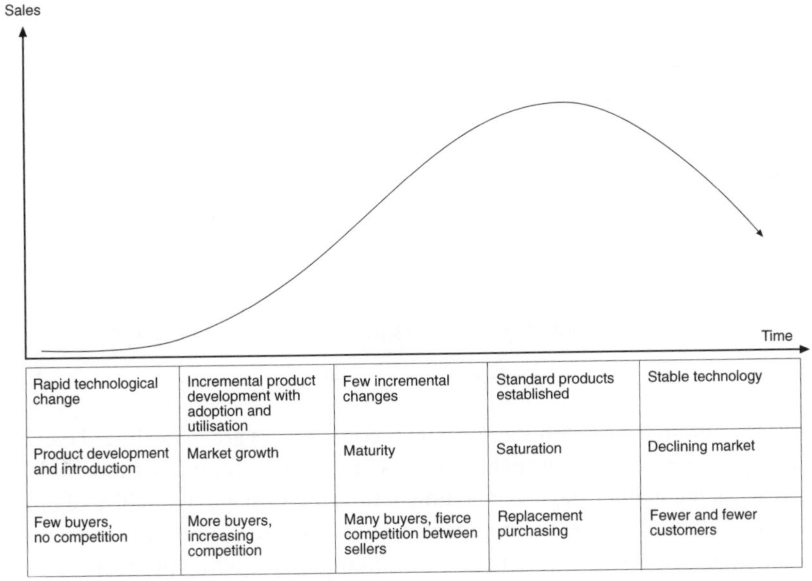

Rapid technological change	Incremental product development with adoption and utilisation	Few incremental changes	Standard products established	Stable technology
Product development and introduction	Market growth	Maturity	Saturation	Declining market
Few buyers, no competition	More buyers, increasing competition	Many buyers, fierce competition between sellers	Replacement purchasing	Fewer and fewer customers

Figure 9: Product life cycle and technological change

Most products move through a life cycle of five stages: introduction, growth, maturity, saturation and decline. At its **introduction** to the market, the product is new and untested by the customers. At this stage, it is likely that there is little direct competition for the product. The first customers might buy the product because they like to be one of the first people to have something new, or because it meets a particular need that they have and they can afford to pay a high price. The product is probably still developing as the manufacturer is making modifications to its design in the light of consumer experience. Technology is important in the initial design and the research and development phase through the use of computers, new innovations and new scientific developments.

Gradually as the product proves to be a success the market expands and more customers buy and use it. This is the **growth** phase. Volumes increase, so technology helps in the movement from craft production to automation. However, competitors also see the success of the product and try to copy it or to develop substitutes. The product is still being developed, but more slowly as the technology becomes established.

By the time the product gets to the **mature** stage, it is a well-established product and there are few changes to its design. Intense competition between the producers of this product means that it is now very cheap to buy. It can easily be mass produced and sold in very large numbers. In the **saturation** stage, sales reach a plateau and the market only consists of replacement purchasing. Finally, the product moves into **decline** as fewer and fewer people want to buy it and few organisations produce it in small quantities.

ACTIVITY 15

At what stage in its product life cycle has each of the following products reached.

- CD-ROMs
- record players
- televisions
- typewriters
- radios
- bar coding.

Name two or three products or services in their introduction stage.

CD-ROMs are in the growth stage, while record players are in decline. Televisions are in the mature stage or arguably in the saturation stage, typewriters in decline, radios are in the mature stage, bar coding in the growth stage. Examples of products in the introduction stage are compact digital cassettes, white noise emergency service sirens, Internet service providers and organic farming products.

The product life cycle describes the usual pattern of product introduction, growth, maturity, saturation and subsequent decline. Although these stages are, to all intents and purposes, inevitable, the exact length of each phase varies for different products. The 'natural' life cycle of a product may be extended by clever marketing, the fads of fashion or the chance coincidence of new technologies. For example radio, although clearly at the mature phase, has not gone through to decline as might have been predicted with the widespread adoption of television and video technology. The use of radios in cars, both for music and conversation and for road traffic information, has extended their use. The ability to use the radio while doing other things such as cooking, cleaning, building or even word-processing, has also extended its life cycle. Recent research has shown how inexpensive and effective advertising on the radio can be as audiences can be easily segmented by listening choice. All of these factors have extended the product life cycle of the radio.

Generally speaking, however, for most products the rapidly changing technological environment has diminished the time a product spends in the growth and mature phases. New products and new processes rapidly replace old ones. This discussion of product life cycle is developed in Unit 4 from the perspective of marketing.

The application of computers to production processes has resulted in a radical transformation of industry. After mass production, best exemplified by the Ford production lines of the first half of the twentieth century, computers have allowed industry not just to control production by automated systems within existing structures, but to generate more flexible systems of production. Henry Ford, remember, offered customers any colour as long as it was black. Mass production did not lend itself to the expression of individuality. Computers allow more sophisticated control over machines which permits the rapid switching from one part of a process to another. The Japanese have developed this to the extent that they are able to tailor production to the specific requirements of individual customers. The customer is not restricted to a range of colours, engine sizes and trim details, the car can be tailored to suit the driver in every respect, taking into account how tall he or she is, how heavy, whether he or she drives mostly on motorways or in towns, etc. Note the phrase 'mass customisation', where the best aspects of mass production – simplified production procedures, high economies of scale, mechanised production – can be combined with the best aspects of the craft-built product.

INFORMATION TECHNOLOGY

The impact of information technology on the way we do business is enormous. We use computers for communication within an organisation and with the outside world, for acquiring, managing, storing and presenting information. It has changed the way we do business, how we communicate and control, how we use information for decision making, how we perform tasks, how we market. It is a factor in all functions and has changed and continues to change the way that many functions and individuals operate. It includes some of the following areas:

- desktop publishing
- office automation
- database management systems

- networking
- electronic data interchange
- computer-aided design and manufacturing, and software engineering
- expert systems
- CD-ROM.

REVIEW ACTIVITY 5

With the developments in telecommunications, mobile phones, faxes, e-mails, direct computer links, video conferencing, you might expect that the marketplace for the Post Office in dealing with posted communication has changed. Analyse the effects of technology in the Post Office, both to its marketplace and its operations. You can get a lot of information from your mail itself and, from visiting a Post Office, you can research the rest or just use your imagination.

Summary

In this section, we have looked at the role technological change plays in offering opportunities and threats to organisations. We introduced some of the changes in processes and products, using the product life cycle concept. Technological change alters the way that an organisation operates and the products and services that it produces, thus it can provide a means of achieving competitive advantage.

Unit Review Activity

Using some of the sources identified in the Further Reading, conduct an environmental analysis using the PEST framework for an organisation of your choice, or do an imaginary one for Jill's Jewellery that you met in Unit 1. Identify some important features in either case and also identify issues of environmentalism and ethical and social responsibility.

Unit Summary

In this unit, we have looked at the broad business environment of an organisation using the PEST framework. We have investigated key features in each of these environments – political, economic, social and technological – that affect an organisation offering constraints, opportunities and threats. These areas are not distinct, as you saw, with political, economic and social issues being especially integrated. We viewed the organisation from a wider European and international perspective and looked at the pressures to become more environmentally friendly and socially responsible.

References

Dicken, P (1992) *Global Shift*, PCP

Employment Gazette April 1993, HMSO

Grant, R (1995) *Contemporary Strategy Analysis*, Blackwell

Recommended Reading

Clarke, R (1985) *Industrial Economics*, Blackwell

Green, F (1989) *The Restructuring of the UK Economy*, Harvester Wheatsheaf

Hay, D A and Morris, D J (1991) *Industrial Economics and Organisation*, Oxford

Nellis, J (1991) 'Demographic Changes and their Impact on Business', *Business Studies,* January

Westbrook, R and Williamson, P (1993) 'Mass Customisation', *European Management Journal*, March

The National Office for Statistics provides information on the UK national accounts, gross domestic product (output), income, expenditure, prices and the labour market. This information is contained in *Economic Trends*, published monthly.

The Economist Intelligence Unit provides information in the form of country reports on the business environment of 180 countries. This includes information on the political scene, economic policies. In addition, it publishes the *EIU Yearbook* with information on European trends relevant to environmental analysis.

The quality press has reliable business sections: the most detailed coverage is to be found in *The Times*, *The Daily Telegraph*, and their Sunday equivalents, and the *Financial Times*. The availability of newspapers on CD-ROM eases the search for relevant information. Current affairs programmes such as the *Money Programme* and *Panorama* are often sources of useful information.

NOMIS, the national on-line manpower information service, has information on employment. Mintel provides useful market reports and industry sector analyses. Other useful sources of information include the *UK Company Factfinder, FAME - Financial Analysis Made Easy and Euromonitor.*

The are several useful websites. Visit the Organisation for Economic Co-operation and Development's site at http://www.oecd.fr/. For regional and country specific information on the international business environment, visit http://ciber.bus.msu.edu/busres.htm.

Answers to Review Activities

Review Activity 1

The pharmaceuticals case study illustrates the multifaceted nature of the changing business environment. The industry is under threat from the actions of governments around the world seeking to reduce public spending on drugs (P&E); from countries seeking to reduce imports on pharmaceuticals from Britain (E); from lack of investment in research and development and in the training of scientists (T); from foreign competition and from Japanese buy-outs. These events can be classified as political, economic, social and technological. All were happening simultaneously during the period under review.

Note one very significant factor with new drugs is the 15-year patent (P); and the very high costs associated with the research and development required to develop new drugs (E). These two factors combined mean that to stay in business a pharmaceutical company must be continually investing in research and development. In addition, technology is required throughout the manufacturing process. Marketing is now geared towards advertising directly to the end user, the patient, so particular drugs are requested from their GPs by name. Changes in the NHS have made an internal competitive system of providers and receivers of care, and with the overall funding constraints, the budget for pharmaceuticals is tight and competition high (E).

We can conclude from this brief study of one industry that it is useful to know something about the historical trends in the business environment. It becomes easier to distinguish between one-off events which may prove to be isolated incidents and events which are part of a long-term trend. The expiry of a particular patent could be regarded as a one-off, the increasing competition from Japanese companies and the funding problems of the NHS might be regarded as part of a long-term trend.

Review Activity 2

There are many factors in the general business environment that will affect these types of businesses, but we can identify some demographic factors that will have a direct effect on the specific business activity. With nursing homes, for example, the number of old people is obvious, but the sex of them might be significant. Other environmental factors might be legislation, other sorts of provision of care in the community, there might even be a shift back in favour of social responsibilities towards parents.

Business	Demographic factors	Other environmental factors
Nursing homes for elderly people	Age structure, especially the number of old people	Existing health care provision, private insurance plans
Higher education qualifications	Age, sex	Government policy, industry's needs, employment opportunities
Cook-chill, ready-made meals for one, available in Marks & Spencer and other stores	Family structures, single -person households, dual-earner households	Town-centre employment, availability of microwaves, shopping patterns
Clothing retailing	Age, sex	Shopping patterns, fashions, income distribution
Grocery retailing	Family structures, ethnic origin	Shopping patterns, fashions, working patterns
Compact disc versions of 1960s hits	Age structure	Taste, income distribution

Review Activity 3

Arguments for privatisation

- The consumer was totally at the mercy of government to supply basic services, so public companies could simply raise prices and get away with poor service.
- Now private sector companies operate for profit efficiency has increased, there are lower prices and an improved quality of service, whereas previously the public sector could be inefficient.

- Privatisation raises government revenues without taxing individuals or corporations directly or indirectly.
- It gives ownership to the people, as shareholders they have some measure of control.

Arguments against privatisation

- Privatisation breaks up economies of scale. This could increase costs and prices.
- Public interest is no longer protected except through regulators. So, for example, rail services to remote parts of the country could be abolished if unprofitable. (However, there may be opportunities for private rail travel companies to offer niche services especially if the government creates incentives for rail companies to take the pressure off the road system and to reduce the use of cars.)
- Ownership is not with the people, the shares were bought mainly by financial institutions and overseas investors.
- Privatisation creates private sector monopolies that can force up prices.
- Salaries of the bosses are not controlled and become excessive.
- Customers are charged more so that companies can pay large dividends to shareholders.

Your arguments may be coloured by your personal experience. Perhaps you have experienced a better service or cheaper prices from BT, or a worse service from Yorkshire Water. Perhaps you have been inconvenienced by new booking systems with different rail bodies, or not known who to go to in the event of a gas leak. Or maybe you have made some money on National Power shares.

Review Activity 4

As an example, we show here the salient features of the 1997 budget. You will have your own answer based on the current budget.

Economic review

- Growth 3.25 per cent in 1997, 2.5 per cent in 1998. This forecast slowdown comes from the fall in Government consumption and a drop in exports as a result of the strong pound.
- Public Sector Borrowing Requirements (PSBR) is forecast to be £13.3 billion in 1997–98, £5.4 billion in 1998–99. Most of this reduction comes from existing plans for public spending control and the favourable effects of the cyclical upturn on tax revenues. PSBR projections show that a rough balance will be achieved by the end of the century, if the tough spending constraints are continued. However, £2 billion from the contingency reserves were allocated to health and education to help these areas.

- Inflation forecast to be 2.5 per cent by end 1997, 2.75 per cent by end 1998. The Bank of England is now charged with keeping the inflation rate within government targets, increasing interest rates as necessary.
- Current account deficit of £9 billion in 1998.
- Consumer spending growth forecast to be 4.5 per cent in 1997, 4 per cent in 1998. Little action proposed to curb spending.
- Main economic priorities are fiscal and monetary stability, a further shift towards green taxation particularly for motorists, promoting investment, research and development and welfare to work programmes, and a reduction of personal income tax to a starting rate of 10 per cent.

Personal measures

- Change to tax on dividends. For individual shareholders the overall effect is the same, but non taxpayers will not be able to claim tax credit, so after 5 April 1999 it will be more tax efficient to receive interest income than dividend income.
- Mortgage interest tax relief reduced from 15 per cent to 10 per cent with effect from 6 April 1998, the £30,000 limit remains the same; individuals will be affected but not by a large amount, although in total this measure will cost homeowners £900 million.
- New individual savings account announced for 1999, designed to encourage people – particularly those on low incomes – to save for the long term. The scheme will probably replace TESSAs and PEPs, making substantial changes throughout the financial services sector.
- Tax relief on private medical insurance for the over 60s abolished – changes in this sector will result.
- Stamp duty on property sales of over £250,000 increased to 1.5 per cent and on sales over £500,000 increased to 2.00 per cent. This will cost house buyers £125 million and will affect the top end of the property market.
- Welfare to work programme for young unemployed.
- Increase in duty on road fuels and aviation gasoline from 8.2 per cent to 9.3 per cent.
- Increase in duty on cigarettes, cigars, spirits, beer, cider, wine and alcopops.
- VAT cut on domestic fuel from 8 per cent to 5 per cent.

Business measures.

In the 1997 budget, the main source of revenue was from the business sector not individuals. The effect of raising revenue in this way will be seen throughout the economy in due course.

- Windfall tax aims to raise £5.2 billion from the main privatised utilities to fund the welfare to work programme. This tax is likely to affect the cash flow, accounting and dividends of the companies concerned and may have an additional impact on those owned by US companies as the tax is unlikely to be creditable for US tax purposes.

- Tax credits for dividends abolished for pension funds and UK companies. This may have a serious impact on pension funds, with employers and employees having to increase contributions by about 10 per cent to maintain the same value and pensioners getting reduced benefits.
- Corporation tax cut from 33 per cent to 31 per cent, and for small companies reduced from 23 per cent to 21 per cent. These rates are lower than in the USA, Japan and most EU countries and are obviously good for industry.
- First year capital allowances for machinery and plant for small and medium businesses reintroduced. This measure will give small businesses an incentive to invest.
- Review of tax avoidance, although a general anti-avoidance law is unlikely.
- Tightening of tax issues for foreign companies.
- Film production costs to be written off when a film is complete. This measure is designed to encourage production of films in the UK.
- VAT changes on capital goods and second-hand goods, and other anti-avoidance measures.

Review Activity 5

You might have thought that with new means of communication the usage of the Post Office and Royal Mail had gone down, but this is not the case. You can probably see this from the vast amounts of mail that you receive: social mail, perhaps a postcard from a friend on holiday, bank statements, credit card statements, direct mail promotion for insurance or a new credit card, utilities statements, customer services information from any number of organisations that you have contact with, direct shopping brochures and leaflets, shareholders statements – the list is endless. The use of new technologies in business life and individual's personal lives has generated vast amounts of new paperwork that still needs sending by mail. For example, a mobile phone account generates about 14 items of mail each year. The emphasis on the consumer means that there is more market research, with more surveys and questionnaires sent through the post.

There were 50 million letters sent a day in 1988, rising to 70 million in 1997. Social mail has reached a plateau, people use faxes and phone calls rather than letters to contact friends and family, but business use continues to increase.

Look at the post and the envelopes you receive. You will see signs of the use of technology: the post codes, franking of the postage, faint pink bar codes at the bottom right of most envelopes, various forms of direct mail with plastic envelopes, and delivery of flyers. Go into a Post Office and see what other services it offers other than mail.

Technology has helped the operations considerably.

- OCR scanners read postcodes, convert them into bar codes which are read and then sorted with sophisticated machines, manual labour is still required for unreadable or missing postcodes.
- Computer Post Box takes corporate letters and addresses on file and directly prints them, inserts them into bar-coded envelopes and puts them into the late stages of the sorting procedure, clients include Microsoft, insurance companies and banks.
- Benefits payments are facilitated through sophisticated computer networks.
- There is a system allowing the automated movement of mail, from sorting for loading onto lorries and the rail system.
- There is separate tube line for moving mail around London; it is computer controlled and driverless.
- The Railnet operation in north London is the biggest railway station to be built in Britain in the twentieth century; 16 new trains are designated mail trains.

Some features of mail delivery remain unchanged. Most personal mail is delivered by a postal worker on foot or on a bike. Technology has not yet come up with a better way of delivery and providing a personal service to each household.

Answer to Unit Review Activity

We will consider Jill's Jewellery as described in Unit 1 with one small outlet. Jill's Jewellery has to conform to UK legislation. This effects her company structure, her premises, her employment of staff, her accounts and tax returns, her dealings with customers, her products, etc. She must also work within any EU directives that might be appropriate. She would need to watch for any new legislation covering, for example, the rights of part-time staff, changes in taxation and National Insurance contributions for herself and her staff, changes in health and safety regulations for workers, and new rights for consumers. For example, if the government brings in new legislation on use of cars, and there is a very poor public transport system, customers will have problems getting to the shop. If planning permission was granted for a new car park, and parking close to her shop was stopped, her passing trade will be affected.

She is subject to UK economic trends. The level of interest rates will affect the cost of any borrowings she has either directly or through the loan on her premises. Interest rates will also affect her customers' spending power, as she is producing a luxury item. Luxuries are one of the first areas of economy for people in times of recession; perhaps she can use cheaper raw materials and reduce costs and still provide something affordable and suitable for gifts. Exchange rates will affect the cost of overseas supplies, particularly of her gemstones, silver and gold supplies – perhaps she buys in specialist equipment from the USA.

In the social environment, national demographics and social trends will not affect the business too much in the immediate future. However, these will give some indication of future customer requirements, especially with an exclusive fashion item that has an element of image attached and could quickly go out of date. The age and social structure of her local population will affect her business, as will general trends in shopping patterns. Perhaps in a few years we will do very little of our shopping in retail shops. And as the business is small, the availability of staff is not likely to be too much of a problem.

Technology is likely to be important in terms of new processes and better raw materials such as glues. Information technology will help in communication with suppliers, database management for customer details, CAD for design.

Jill might want to ensure that her processes are environmentally friendly, using the minimum of power and raw materials. She may wish to move away from stones such as amber that are very rare, but inevitably in all her products she is using a non-sustainable resource in the gemstones and metals such as silver and gold. If these are easily available, then their value is reduced, and their desirability from a customer point of view is also reduced. In many cases too, the mining of the stones may destroy countryside, and it may be carried out by exploited labour such as women and children in poor countries. So although, Jill may carry out her business in an environmentally, ethically and socially responsible way, what she is doing is taking materials from undeveloped countries and turning them into adornments for western women. Some people would consider that this was wrong on all counts. However, women (and men) will continue to wear jewellery. Perhaps Jill could investigate some renewable resource to use, cultured pearls maybe, or concentrate on the design aspect rather than the 'what kind of stone' aspect and even make a marketing feature out of it! Perhaps you can now begin to see some of the problems and conflicts that exist in the western business world.

UNIT 3
COMPETITION AND CHANGE

Introduction

The changing nature of the general business environment offers organisations both opportunities and threats. We can identify key drivers for specific organisations within this environment. We have seen that the monitoring of the environment is a key activity for all businesses. Here, we take the investigation a stage further by looking at the competition and what is happening in the competitive environment, the environment that is closest to the organisation and has the most immediate impact on it. Once we have analysed the competitive environment, we need to develop strategies, and then formulate and implement actions to put the strategy into practice. This will require change, so we look briefly at some of the factors concerned with successful change in an organisation.

In Unit 1, we briefly looked at the idea of stakeholders – these are the customers, suppliers, employees, owners, shareholders, pressure and consumer groups, regulators, professional organisations, competitors and any individual or organisation that has an interest in what an organisation does and how it does it. We have seen that some of these groups, such as consumer and pressure groups, are part of what we have termed the business environment. Some stakeholders such as employees are part of the organisation but, as customers, shareholders, members of pressure groups and members of professional organisations, they are also part of the competitive environment. So, not only are the boundaries between the business and competitive environment blurred, but these influential stakeholders also blur the boundaries between the organisation and the competitive environment. Therefore, before we look in depth at the competitive environment and how the organisation can respond to changes in it, we need to investigate stakeholders in more detail as they affect what the organisation is and what it does, and how it responds to the opportunities and threats in the business and the competitive environment.

We usually view the organisation as discrete and distinct from its environment. However, the precise boundaries of the organisation flex and change at the interface between the organisation and its environment. This occurs as the requirements of the organisation, the interests of the people of influence in the organisation and the shape of the environment changes. We use Porter's five forces model to analyse an organisation's immediate environment, its industry, and the activities of the organisation's competitors in the industry. We identify some responses the organisation can make.

We look at the sources of environmental information. We need to select and use appropriate information from the vast amounts of available data. We analyse an organisation's competitive and general environments, identify what we need to do with this information and see how the organisation responds to subsequent changes. This leads into an overall discussion of the nature of change in an organisation.

We bring the themes of Units 1, 2 and 3 together in the final section, when we look at the way that business has been changing over recent years and identify some current trends that may provide direction for the future. In today's competitive world, the concept of competitive advantage needs to become an integral part of the culture of an organisation; one that manifests itself in the structure and in all functions. Success is achieved by efficiency in all business functions, in good overall co-ordination within the organisation and by effectiveness in achieving the mission and corporate objectives.

Objectives

By the end of this unit, you will be able to:

- identify stakeholders, evaluate the impact of stakeholder power and identify areas of conflict
- analyse Porter's five competitive forces for an organisation in its industry
- identify sources of environmental information appropriate for a range of organisations
- conduct a full environmental analysis for any given organisation
- evaluate the environmental factors driving change
- appraise why organisations need to manage change
- describe some sources of resistance to change
- summarise the key trends in the business world and their implications for an organisation.

SECTION 1

Stakeholders

Introduction

In this section, we examine the environment as it encroaches directly upon the organisation. We investigate stakeholders and discuss what impact they can make on an organisation. Stakeholders determine much about an organisation, what it can do and the directions it can take in response to changes within its immediate competitive and more general environment. The implementation of any corporate strategy including competitive strategies is governed by stakeholder values, decisions and actions.

As we discussed briefly in Unit 1, the key stakeholders determine an organisation's mission and culture. Most organisations have a mission, whether implicitly included in the values and interests of the organisation or explicitly set out in a mission statement. A formal mission statement is drafted to present the *raison d'être* of the organisation and the interests of the main stakeholders. The statement may also outline the organisation's strategy, behaviour and practices. The culture, values and interests of the key stakeholders within the organisation determine the direction the organisation takes, the product range it offers, where its market is, where it sources its inputs and its key objectives, such as whether it is interested in growth or profits. We describe the roles and conflicting interests of the various stakeholders and how they exert power on the organisation.

1.1 Who and what are stakeholders?

Stakeholders are individuals or groups who have some form of interest in the organisation and some power to influence, to a greater or lesser extent, the organisation's decision making. These groups can be part of the organisation, and yet they are also part of the environment in which the organisation operates. Stakeholders are less likely to present the organisation with opportunities and threats in the conventional sense, but they are likely to influence the way the organisation responds to the opportunities and threats in its environment. If the organisation does not respond in the ways required by powerful stakeholders, then these stakeholders may exert their power in ways that may threaten the organisation.

External stakeholders include bankers, customers, suppliers, shareholders, trade unions, professional associations, consumer groups and governments. We could also consider society as a whole as a stakeholder in an organisation.

Internal stakeholders include all owners, employees and salaried managers. Employees in different departments and divisions, and at different stages in the hierarchy, may be influenced by or may seek to gain support from the external stakeholder groups, in support of their own interest within the organisation. Industrial action may be taken within the organisation supported by a trade union; professional standards may be changed as a result of a national campaign by a professional body; products may be amended in response to customer complaints or lobbying by a consumer group; expansion plans may be shelved in response to bankers' advice; the company chairman may appeal to shareholders for support. In all these examples, the outside environment encroaches on the organisation.

1.2 Conflicting interests

Although all stakeholders should have an interest in the continued success of the organisation, their specific interests depend upon who they are and what their connection is with the organisation. Often these specific interests conflict, and the interests of one group may need to be sacrificed to serve the interests of another.

Stakeholder	Interests	Possible conflicts
Shareholders	Dividends Share price growth	Expenditure on R&D Capital investment Wage increases
Owner managers	Profits Growth of organisation	Wage increases Other expenditure, for example, on R&D
Salaried managers	Growth of organisation Growth of department Pay and 'perks'	Profits Dividends Capital investment
Trade unions	Jobs Wages Conditions of work National political issues	Cost cutting Relocation to low-wage countries Job losses Downsizing High dividend pay-outs
Customers	Value for money Environment concerns Social concerns	All of the above
Government	Tax revenues Jobs Global competitiveness Legislation	Relocation to low-wage countries Job losses
Society	Pollution Use of non-sustainable resources Animal right issues Human rights issues	Production methods R&D methods Product usage
Marketing department	Output available on demand Quality Inexpensive products	Finance and operations
Finance department	Low level of stocks Low wastage Stability	Marketing and operations
Operations department	Regular orders Some organisational slack	Marketing and finance

Table 1: Stakeholder interests and conflicts

Individuals who may belong to more than one stakeholder group, under ethical business practice and, in some cases, by professional guidelines or legislation, are required to make clear their interests. For example, MPs are required to declare their shareholdings and directorships. Most employment contracts require individuals to declare any consultancy work done for competitors. Table 1 maps out some of the possible stakeholder interests and conflicts.

ACTIVITY 1

Study Table 1. Note down those stakeholders who you think might be likely to promote greater investment in the organisation at the expense of shareholders' dividends and those who you think might prefer higher dividends.

We cannot state with certainty that one type of stakeholder will certainly advocate one action rather than another in any particular organisation. There is a danger of oversimplifying the issues as there are so many factors involved, but we can make some general assumptions about behaviour.

Many shareholders might prefer higher dividends in preference to greater investment. On the other hand, owner managers might advocate greater investment because they want the organisation to become more prosperous and strong. However owner mangers are also likely to be shareholders too, so they may want a more immediate return in dividend payments.

Many organisations make special arrangements for staff at all levels to own shares. These may be awarded as free shares or as share options. Depending on their personal circumstances, staff who are shareholders might want to see the success of the organisation reflected in their wages, in profit-sharing bonuses or in the dividends.

Governments might wish to encourage the strengthening of the industrial base by greater investment. Pension fund managers and other investment managers who are institutional shareholders need dividends to pay pensions and to reward individual investors – they are under pressure to show good performance, so they are likely to favour higher dividends.

Trade unions might want higher wages or even higher dividends in preference to more investment in new technology which might threaten jobs. But they have to balance the desire for higher wages in the short term against the long-term job security of the remaining workers if the investment is made in new technology.

Customers would like to see reductions in prices rather than higher dividend pay-outs, unless they happen to be shareholders as well.

1.3 Stakeholder power

What do we mean by the word, power? What about the terms, influence and authority – do they mean the same? It is important to have some understanding of these terms; it will put into context the position that stakeholders can hold.

The terms power, influence and authority each have something in common. Each implies that holders (of power, influence and authority) are more likely to get their way, and are more able to change or guide the behaviour of other people. But the terms do have different meanings.

- **Power** is the ability to compel others to act in a certain way. A compulsion that may be based on the ability to reward or punish, or to physically coerce.
- **Influence** is the ability to get others to act in a desired way even in the absence of power or authority.
- **Authority** confers the right to be obeyed, even if no one does so! You can have power but no authority, as when thugs demand money for protection. And you can have authority with no power, as when a single policeman tries to stop a violent mob from attacking a suspect, for example.

The ability of different groups to pursue their interests within the organisation depends upon their power relative to other stakeholders. In this way, the need to placate the unions to win a large order may take immediate priority over the longer-term aim of reducing the size of the labour force and introducing more capital intensive methods of production. On another occasion, or in another organisation, a weaker union, stable order books and unambitious salaried managers may permit larger dividend pay-outs to happy shareholders.

The source of stakeholder power within the organisation depends upon two main issues. First, power comes from the position of the stakeholder group within the organisation's hierarchy. This is the formal aspect of power; individuals higher up the hierarchy are more important and usually have the authority to match their power.

Second, power comes more informally through personal relationships. This means that many people within organisations are more powerful than their position within the hierarchy would suggest. This power may be due to personal relationships that develop through, for example, membership of a body outside the company to which other members of the hierarchy also belong. Additional power might also be conferred by membership of a particular church group, by being active in a particular political party or by being from a particular school or university. Some individuals might join these groups purely to network and deliberately display their membership.

Some achieve informal power within an organisation through dedication and availability. For example, you will gain influence if you are always prepared to take on extra work, if you work hard at building networks of useful contacts across the organisation, and you are known to be reliable. This influence may be held by someone who is socially adept, perhaps a very charismatic person who is readily liked by those above and below in the hierarchy, and also by people who are known to do a good job.

ACTIVITY 2

You can think of a university or college as having stakeholders. Each group has special interests and tries to affect decision making by using their power or influence.

Write down three or four stakeholders in your current (or previous) university or college. Identify their main interests. Briefly describe how each one may try to influence decisions.

A university or college is just like any other business in that it has 'customers', suppliers, employees and interested parties in the outside world. With students, the customers, now being required to pay tuition fees at certain levels, education may develop like any other marketplace, and universities will need to compete for the most valued customers. Table 2 summarises the main stakeholders in higher education, and their interests and methods of exerting influence.

EXERTION OF POWER

The direction and scope of an organisation through its mission and culture is dictated by the exertion of power of the key stakeholders. Within the organisation, control of the main decision-making body – whether the board of directors or an executive management team – creates the power to direct the organisation. Depending on the organisational structure and culture, individual managers and directors may have more or less power.

All stakeholders have some sort of power. The workforce as a whole has power, both within the organisation and outside. If it does not perform well, then the organisation will not be successful. If individuals do not want to work for the organisation for whatever reason, it will not have staff. Particularly brilliant or creative individuals may be able to dictate their own terms and affect the direction of the organisation. All links in the supply chain can hold power. If suppliers are not happy (by being not paid, for example), they can withhold supplies or, if they are a sole supplier, they can dictate their own terms. The government, regulators and watchdog committees can directly affect the operation of some organisations as we discussed in Unit 2.

The customer is a key stakeholder. Without a customer to buy its products, the organisation can do nothing. It is important for an organisation to gather as much information as possible about its customers, their needs and how it can satisfy these needs in the best possible way. If it does not meet these needs and make sales, then it matters little how efficient or effective is the rest of its business.

Stakeholders	Interests	Methods of influence
Lecturers	Appropriate employment Research facilities Adequate pay Good conditions	Staff committees Professional associations Political lobbying
Students	Qualifications with value Fees Study conditions Sport facilities Teaching standards	Course committees Students' union Rallies, strikes
Government	A well-qualified workforce Reduction in unemployment	Legislation Charging student fees Controlling funding
Employers	Qualified graduates High-quality research Consultancy Reputation of the institutions (as part of their environment)	On consultative committees Influence through Chamber of Commerce, TECs, MPs Consultancy fees Grants to support research
Parents	Care of students Value of qualifications Teaching standards Costs	Personal contact with course tutors and governors Influence through MPs, councillors or the press
Local authority	Maintain reputation of institution to attract students to their area	Through Board of Governors Direct contact with Principal

Table 2: Stakeholders in higher education

The customer can exert direct influence by simply not buying. This may have devastating effects. For example, the BSE scare in the 1990s had an immediate effect not just on farmers but on abattoirs, cattle auctions, butchers and retailers, and manufacturers that used beef products, as consumers stopped buying beef and avoided eating beef in restaurants. Customers may respond to political or environmental concerns. In the early 1990s, many people boycotted products from France in protest at the nuclear testing in the south Pacific; some French restaurants were forced to claim that all their produce came from Britain but the food was prepared according to traditional French recipes. Customers can also have an influence through consumer groups. Consumer groups such as the Consumers' Association or other pressure groups can have a very substantial influence on organisations.

Professional associations can support and create power within organisations. For example, membership of the British Medical Association, the Institute of Chartered

Accountants or the Royal Institute of Chartered Surveyors confers a licence to do certain jobs, provides guidelines for behaviour and provides some professional back-up if required.

The influence of shareholders and bankers varies. If shareholders are a widely dispersed group of individuals with little interest or knowledge in the day-to-day operation of the business, satisfied with earning a reasonable income from their shares, they will be less demanding at shareholders' meetings and less likely to sell shares at the first hint of a reduced dividend because of a policy decision or a poor performance. If most shares are owned by institutional groups such as pension funds, managed by professionals with great knowledge and interest in the operation of the organisation, then these shareholders can express their views forcefully. Their knowledge of business confers authority – they should be listened to. Their voting rights confers power – the ability to impose their will on the organisation. Shell, for example, has been forced by large institutional investors into publicly disclosing its performance against internal targets rather than its previous practice of announcing company forecasts.

The control of banks over organisations depends to a large extent upon how dependent an individual organisation is upon the bank, or vice versa. Many SMEs have blamed their failure upon banks. They have complained that banks give them poor advice, allow them to borrow beyond their ability to repay, or fail to provide support at critical times by withdrawing overdraft facilities. However, large corporations can have some influence over the banks. If you owe the bank £10,000, then it is your problem if you cannot pay the debt – it is a small sum for the bank but not for you. However, if you owe the bank £1 million, then it becomes the bank's problem if you cannot repay the debt.

POWER THROUGH ORGANISATIONAL CULTURE

We introduced the concept of culture in Unit 1. Culture is the characteristic way of living in a society. It includes the language, dress, taboos, technology, rites and religion and all other aspects of living that differentiate one society from another. Organisational culture is experienced by the organisation's members and consists of shared values and attitudes and their expression in terms of conventions, dress and practices. It develops through the interaction of the main stakeholders and the society in which the organisation exists. However, organisations within the same industry, with employees from similar backgrounds and similar experiences, can have quite different cultures as you saw with IBM and Hewlett Packard.

The culture of the organisation embodies its values and ethics. It is determined by the interaction of the interests of the main stakeholders. Values dictate the way that the organisation behaves, and identify the issues that it gives priority to and regards as important. So, for example, an organisation's culture will dictate whether it will supply countries that have a poor human rights record, produce organic foodstuffs, be environmentally friendly, be a good employer, provide the best possible return on shareholders' invested funds or provide the best possible service to the community.

SYMBOLS OF POWER

Within organisations, holders of power may display their status through the size of their office, the number of secretaries, the size of their desk, and so on. The chairman is likely to wear expensive suits, have a large office and a chauffeur-driven car. Bosses in the public sector are particularly open to criticism if they are seen to be wasting money or being overly grand. In 1997, the new Labour government has taken a more casual approach dropping formal attire at specific functions, and removing some of the formality from the House of Commons. However Tony Blair, the Prime Minister, flew by Concorde to the USA for the Earth Summit in 1997, not the cheapest way to go.

In entrepreneurial cultures, symbols of power tend to reflect the owner or entrepreneur's personal style and may not follow traditional ideas. James Dyson dresses very casually at Dyson, as does Bill Gates at Microsoft. However, Bill Gates is spending a lot of money on building a very grand house. Richard Branson may dress casually, but international hot-air ballooning is hardly a sport taken up by many of his employees.

There are many more subtle ways of displaying power. So, for example, people give impressions of being indispensable, staying late and arriving early, having an enormous work load, always being available by mobile phone even when on holiday. These individuals display how important they are to the organisation.

POWER THROUGH ORGANISATIONAL MISSION

Just as the power of the main stakeholders shapes an organisation's culture, so it also shapes its mission. We discussed organisational missions and business objectives in Unit 1. Mission statements, popularised in the 1980s as a means of focusing the attention of managers on core activities and capabilities, are now widely used. A mission should be a genuine expression of the interests and concerns of the organisation. The activity of drawing up a mission can be a useful one as you see in Unit 8, when you look at it as a starting point for strategy. Mission statements may summarise a thorough evaluation of the resources and capabilities of the organisation. They may anticipate the utilisation of these resources and capabilities in the medium term. They may also contain, often implicitly, the key values of the organisation.

ACTIVITY 3

Examine these extracts from the mission statements of two British universities. They are quite different. Identify the priorities of each organisation to their stakeholders.

> '... to encourage and enable individuals to develop their full potential by providing a high quality and stimulating learning environment encompassing a wide range of relevant educational activities.'

'... to be a leading teaching and research institution, providing education of the highest possible quality which is relevant to the individual, the region, the nation and the international community.'

Each mission statement contains reference to different stakeholders of the organisations but reflects different priorities in the provision of services to what many might consider the main stakeholder, the student. The first statement identifies its stakeholders as individuals, the second identifies its stakeholders as the individual, the region, the nation and the international community. The former statement focuses on developing the potential of **individuals** and emphasises the whole learning and educational experience in **providing a learning environment**. In this, we might assume that the individual is the student but it might be anyone, including the staff. The latter has the clear aim of **providing an education** to the **individual**, but with wider **regional, national** and **international** requirements for the community, and the institution sees itself as a teaching and research body. On examination, especially if you are a student yourself, you might find both of these mission statements rather irritating as they are not clear enough in their intentions towards students. They are however only extracts, the full mission statements are likely to be more complete expressions of an organisation's values, culture and objectives.

REVIEW ACTIVITY 1

Select two or three companies that are listed on the Stock Exchange and are included in the FTSE-100 index. Monitor the on-line news or published articles for news about the company that would concern any of its stakeholders – directors, competitors, shareholders, the government, employees, consumer groups, professional associations. To give you a broader picture of the company, follow the share prices for a month. Check share prices every few days, and monitor them closely if something unexpected happens in the business environment of your companies or to any of their stakeholders, such as a disaster of some sort or an increase in interest rates or the ousting of a chief executive officer. Also, monitor the exchange rate of sterling, other world markets and the FTSE-100 index itself so you can put the activities of your organisations into context. Is it following trends or is it experiencing something unique to its own operations?

Summary

In this section, we have examined the role of stakeholders in an organisation and the kinds of power and influence they may exert. They are all important and an organisation has to take into account its owners, shareholders, customers, suppliers, workforce, bankers, professional and consumer groups. In the next section, we look at the industry and competitor effects. The key stakeholders affect the culture and values of an organisation. The basic mission of an organisation is also determined by the key stakeholders.

SECTION 2

Market Forces

Introduction

In this section, we analyse the competitive environment of an organisation using Porter's model to look at competitors in a particular industry. However, we first look at factors that concern an industry as a whole, as this obviously affects all competitors within it.

2.1 Industry life cycle

We can analyse the key trends in an industry through the concept of an industry life cycle. Sales in all markets and industries tend to follow a similar pattern of growth which we can formulate into the industry life cycle. This bears some relation to the product life cycle that we discussed in Unit 2. We can identify three main phases in this cycle: **emerging** or **growing**, **maturing** and **declining**. As with all models, industries do not necessarily fit neatly into this model, they will pass through at a different speed or some will miss out phases. For example, industries such as housing or clothing will never decline; some such as computers will have short life cycles, so companies have to innovate to generate a new market with new emerging technologies.

The emerging or growing industry is characterised by many different forms of competition, haphazard information about customers and their needs, uncertainty about costs and technologies, many new entrants and small companies, and a shortage of supplies, such as raw materials and staff.

The maturing industry is characterised by rules for competition, with defined patterns of organisational behaviour, and dominated by fewer larger organisations. In a maturing industry, there tends to be a slowdown in customer demand so there is intense competitive rivalry through price cutting, for example. There is lots of knowledge about customers and the marketplace. New entrants can challenge the existing ways of doing business, the range of products offered, and the relationships in the supply chain by analysing the activities in the value chain in the light of this knowledge and experience. We would put grocery retailing into this category.

The declining industry is characterised by withdrawal of companies, declining demand, and a consequent cutting back in production. Maintenance of unit costs is difficult with reduced production, but there is still intense rivalry within the remaining market. Eventually, a product and the organisations that make and supply the product are forced out of the market, by:

- changes in technology – for example, calculators have been replaced by computers, compact disc players are replacing record players
- changes in needs and tastes – for example, consumers are preferring healthier foods to red meat and high-fat products
- changes in industrial requirements – for example, causing the decline of coal mining as cheaper fuels become available
- democratic shifts – such as declining birth rates, an ageing population.

In addition to examining the industry life cycle, we can look at other general characteristics of the industrial environment, such as its stability and its complexity. This will give us more information about the influences on the organisations operating within the industry.

DIFFERENT TYPES OF INDUSTRIAL ENVIRONMENT

The industrial environment provides the opportunities and threats that allow new entrants to challenge existing organisations with established competitive advantages. New entrants aim to gain the competitive edge themselves and push existing organisations out of the market. The industrial environment provides both the incentives and the opportunities for continuous improvement of technology, products, processes and services. It determines the size, structure, form and type of all organisations that exist within the industry.

An organisation needs to understand the level of uncertainty and unpredictability in its environment. Uncertainty may be due to the varied nature of the environment (complexity), due to its instability and susceptibility to rapid and major changes (dynamism), or due to the availability of its resources (richness).

- **Complexity** concerns the numbers of and the diversity of the elements involved in the industrial environment, its operation and its relationships with the outside world. For example, the grocery retailing industry is dependent on hundreds of factors in the PEST environment and in the competitive environment. Complexity increases as an industry becomes larger and more diverse. In a **simple** industrial environment, an organisation would carry out a small number of operations in a limited market with limited interactions with the outside world. It is hard to think of any examples of a truly simple industrial environment, although perhaps funeral services operate in a simple environment. The industry will always have customers, easily tracked from population statistics, and the requirements have remained fairly static over the years even with the decrease in the numbers of actual burials.

- **Dynamism** concerns the extent and speed of changes in an industry. Examples of dynamic industries include the software industry in which the technology is continually changing, and the music, fashion and advertising industries in which consumer tastes are continually changing. A **stable** environment might exist where there are no new entrants, technology has limited impact, and there are few government restrictions. Stable environments require no major changes in policies and little effort is needed to forecast of future trends. Religious bodies, for example, tend to operate in relatively stable environments; however, even the Church of England has used advertising to generate interest in the light of falling attendance, and the Roman Catholic Church has been harried on its attitudes towards celibacy for priests and towards women, so no organisation is exempt from change.
- **Richness** concerns the availability of resources, such as skilled labour, money, and raw materials. The gold and silver mining industries producing precious metals operate in a resource **poor** environment. A resource **rich** environment would provide all the skilled labour, money and raw materials that organisations need.

After looking at the wider industrial context, we can then start to look at some of the forces operating within the industry. Here we regard the industry as a group of organisations producing similar products or services for the same market. The term industry is also used to describe industry sectors. The two different usages may be coincident in some cases, but you should note that organisations often operate in several markets with very different characteristics.

2.2 Porter's five forces

The most useful model for examining the immediate interface between an organisation and its environment is one developed by Michael Porter (1970). Developing the models of inputs, outputs and horizontal, vertical and lateral integration you met in Unit 1, Porter shows how each facet of the organisation that is exposed to external forces is a potential target for competitive threats. He identifies five major forces that drive industry competition:

- competition from existing rivals
- threat of new entrants
- threat of substitutes
- bargaining power of buyers
- bargaining power of suppliers.

We can use Porter's model at different levels: for the industry as a whole or in segmented markets. For any individual organisation, the strengths or weaknesses of the forces in any analysis will indicate where competitive advantage might be gained by taking opportunities or by avoiding or dealing with threats through different competitive strategies.

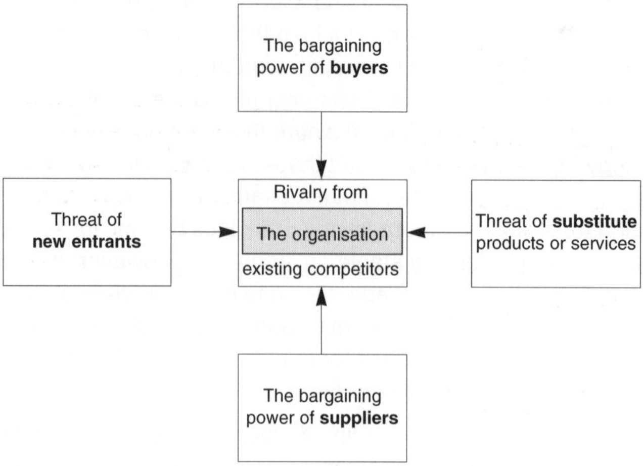

Figure 1: Porter's forces driving industry competition (Porter, 1980)

Analysis of the environment can be a useful exercise in itself as it involves understanding an organisation's markets and its customers and competitors. However, we need to use this information for developing competitive advantage through different strategies. In Unit 8, we look at how competitive strategies fit in with the overall strategy of the organisation and how they can help in meeting corporate objectives. Here, we take a broad overview, giving you some idea of the factors involved.

RIVALRY BETWEEN EXISTING COMPETITORS

The most immediately obvious form of competitive threat is rivalry between an organisation's existing competitors within its industry. Six main determinants explain the extent of rivalry.

- The **number of and size of competitors** and the balance of **market power** between them. Concentration ratios can be used to assess the strength of the main players in a market. We explained this measure in Unit 2. The concentration of market power in the hands of a few large organisations can result in intense competitive rivalry. In grocery retailing, for example, the big supermarket chains like Safeway, Sainsbury, Tesco and a number of smaller companies battle for market share. In the quality newspaper market, *The Times* and *The Daily Telegraph* have been competing against each other with price reductions and special deals.
- The **rate of growth of demand** for the products or services. This tends to follow the industry life cycle of emerging, maturing and declining phases. New growing markets with a small number of smaller competitive organisations may allow the competitors the opportunity to grow and to distinguish themselves in some way as they develop within the industry. In a market where demand is in decline and which is oversupplied with products, companies will have to sell products by discounting, special offers and special sales promotions. Mature markets with slow growth, such as grocery retailing, provide few opportunities for

organisations to develop a distinct identity from the competition. So grocery retailers have adopted a variety of strategies to win customers, such as loyalty cards and additional products like financial services, as well as maintaining competitive prices. In many mature markets, with large numbers of producers offering almost identical products, price is the main form of competition. However in a buoyant market, competition is more likely to take the form of non-price competition. This is where innovative products, new designs and clever marketing encourage the customer to differentiate between competitors, Customers want the best design, the most interesting, the most novel, or the best after-sales service, not necessarily the cheapest product. In these markets, companies can charge a price premium for products.

- **The extent of product differentiation**. This depends on the product and the market. For example, many consumer items such as washing powder are differentiated by brand names and advertising. Commodities – oil, grain, raw materials, etc. – are so similar that any differentiation is difficult and competition will be on price. Differentiation can be **actual,** such as Rolls-Royce's excellence in design and manufacturing of cars or **perceived**, through the use of advertising to create a strong brand image, such as Coca-Cola.
- The **structure of costs** in the industry. If unit costs are high, continual sales need to be generated: flying a plane costs the same whether its full or empty, so airlines have a complicated fare structure to get 'people on seats'. However, a few business class or full-fare economy seats will generate the same revenue as many discounted economy fares, so airlines have to be careful on how they discount fares.
- The **height of exit barriers**. If it is difficult for an organisation to leave the industry, then it may have to stay. A shipyard, for example, cannot be moved and used for a different purpose, aircraft can only be used for transport of people or freight. Shipbuilders and airlines cannot easily switch into other industries, they must stay and compete in their core businesses and this increases the competition within their industries.
- **Excess capacity**. If changing consumer requirements have reduced demand for the end product, then the final manufacturer and its suppliers will have excess capacity. There is excess capacity, for example, in the steel and petrochemicals industries. Similarly, there is excess capacity in shipbuilding, exacerbated by high exit barriers. In these markets, competition is then likely to be based on price.

ACTIVITY 4

Analyse the grocery retailing industry and the competitors in the industry. Identify some strategies that the main competitors are undertaking to compete for market share.

Grocery retailing is in a mature phase. There are some big chains such as Tesco, Sainsbury, Safeway, and smaller ones including Waitrose, Kwik Save, Asda, Rainbow and Somerfield. The smaller chains tend to offer slightly different services. For example, Waitrose is aimed more at the higher end of the market, Kwik Save at the budget end. In addition, the stores tend to be smaller, and can be sustained by a smaller population, so they can exist in smaller towns. There tends to be a geographical split, with some chains concentrating in particular areas. Waitrose is mainly in the South of England, for example. The main chains are competing fiercely through price cutting, national advertising, continually upgrading and establishing out-of-town stores, offering additional products and services such as petrol and banking, loyalty cards, and use of technology. Because the major chains are such large buyers, they are able to control their suppliers on price and service.

THREAT OF NEW ENTRANTS

In some industries, it is very difficult for new entrants to become established in the market place. In others it is relatively easy. The height of the **barriers to the entry** of new competitors in a market determine the extent to which this represents a threat to existing organisations. In some industries, there are natural barriers to entry that prevent all but the most persistent rival gaining a foothold. The difficulty of gaining access to all the appropriate **inputs** is a key deterrent.

The high cost of **capital equipment**, plant and machinery, appropriate property or land, access to key personnel and the basic **raw materials** all deter entrants to industries such as oil exploration, nuclear power and international banking. The high R&D investment required deters new entrants to the pharmaceutical industry. If the initial investment is high, small optimistic companies may not be able to raise the necessary initial capital even if the prospects are good. On the output side, the difficulty of gaining access to appropriate **distribution channels**, breaking existing customer loyalties and, in international markets, the difficulty of breaking through trade barriers, all deter would-be entrants. In the airline industry, in addition to the cost of buying aircraft and setting up the systems to run an airline, one of the key barriers to entry is restricted access to landing slots at appropriate times.

Where such barriers do not exist naturally, organisations have attempted to create artificial entry barriers to their markets. These barriers can be blatant attempts to restrict free trade and act against the interests of customers. For example, Harley Davidson, the US motorbike manufacturer managed to get tariffs placed on imported Japanese bikes, pushing up their prices in the US markets, allowing Harley Davidson time to reorganise and regain its competitiveness. On the other hand, these artificial barriers can be the natural consequence of other forms of competitive activity. For example, the high advertising spending on building brand awareness and loyalty by the manufacturers of shampoos can be spread thinly over the high output sold by Proctor & Gamble and Unilever, the companies that make many of the shampoos we see advertised in magazines and on television. A small company attempting to get a foothold in a market, where production is relatively inexpensive, cannot afford to spend anything like enough on marketing to establish its presence. It does not have a sufficient level of output to spread the costs of advertising thinly.

Complicated legislation may affect new entrants. For example, a Home Office licence is required for testing on animals, planning permission is required for building premises. Even a sole trader opening up a small snack kiosk must meet fire and health and safety regulations.

The absolute cost advantages of large organisations operating in established markets also acts as a deterrent to newer firms. These cost advantages are gained from economies of scale in production processes, low input costs due to bulk buying and the increased power of the purchaser and the spreading of overhead costs. In addition to these direct costs, there is also an experience curve – as an organisation gains experience in production and distribution, then unit production costs fall. In general, the more complex and capital intensive the operation, the more benefits there are to be gained with experience. This effect is not so pronounced in service industries, but experience can have some bearing in all aspects of the organisation including management.

Government policies, once designed to protect what were considered 'natural monopolies' in industries such as telecommunications and energy supply, now encourage competition. Deregulation, privatisation and the promotion of competition has opened up whole industries. This has provided a host of opportunities for new entrants and very considerable threats to existing organisations.

CASE STUDY

The British gas industry

Competition to supply gas to households in Devon and Cornwall commenced in April 1996. British Gas, previously a state-owned monopoly has relinquished some of its market share to new entrants. There were originally ten new companies offering to supply domestic gas to households: SWEBGAS, Calortex, Amerada Hess, Eastern, Total, Norweb, BFG, Eastern, Southern and Phillips Gas, and Northern Electric. The Gas Consumers Council reported in January 1997, after almost a full year of competition, that the switch to the new providers had been slower than was originally hoped. The Council believed that consumers were switching largely on the basis of the price of the supplied gas, with little reference to the other services offered such as annual contracts for the servicing of boilers and appliances.

British Gas was locked into expensive long-term contracts to source gas from fields in the North Sea. It was finally forced to reduce its prices in March 1997 as competition spread to Dorset, and new competitors gained a licence to supply gas to the domestic market. Many of the competitors had experience, and a reputation, in the supply of other energy sources. Some are electricity companies and the suppliers of bottled gas. Others have experience of oil and gas exploration and access to the gas fields of the North Sea. Companies without a well-known name spent heavily on promoting themselves on television, through mail-shots and on advertising hoardings. Transco, the pipeline company, continues to own the gas pipelines and most of the meters. By April 1997, British Gas was feeling the effect of competition. It introduced substantial discounts for customers paying by direct debit and its advertising heavily stressed British Gas' reliability and authenticity.

ACTIVITY 5

Read the case study about the British gas industry.

- How are the new entrants trying to build market share?
- What barriers to entry exist in this market?
- How have the new competitors overcome these barriers?

The new entrants are competing by offering lower prices than British Gas. British Gas could not cut its own prices because it was tied to expensive long-term contracts for the purchase of the gas and it wanted to maintain the prices it is continuing to charge its domestic customers in the rest of the UK, where it is still a monopoly supplier in the domestic market. The new entrants have to get a licence to be able to supply gas and they have to have access to supplies of gas from the gas fields. Most of the competitors have an existing reputation for supplying other utilities such as electricity, water or bottled gas. Companies that have not got such a reputation in the UK have spent considerable sums on advertising themselves. People may be reluctant to purchase gas from a unknown company.

THREAT OF SUBSTITUTES

When we talk about the allocation of spending, we are assuming that ultimately all products, goods and services are substitutes for each other. Households probably consider how to allocate their spending by weighing up the benefits and costs of a whole range of possible products. Many choices would not be considered substitutes in the conventional sense. So, a family may decide to go on holiday this year rather than have a new kitchen or to visit the garden centre and buy a few plants rather than to go to a theme park, or to have more leisure time by working less rather than earning more money. In 1997, the windfalls from building society share offers have been spent on home improvements, such as new kitchens and conservatories, some will have been spent on holidays and some will have been saved for pensions. These diverse products and services at first glance do not appear to be substitutes for each other.

The degree of substitutability of products depends on the benefits the purchaser gets from the products, rather than the precise use to which the products are put. Our ability to estimate the extent to which products are substitutes depends upon our understanding of the bundle of attributes that goes to make up a product in the perception of the customer. In other words, it depends on market knowledge. In consumer markets, these bundles of characteristics may be complex and changing. In industrial markets, they are probably more straightforward. Goods and services are needed by organisations to do specific jobs. The organisation will assess these inputs on the basis of factors such as price, availability, quality and suitability. The threat of substitutes may be more predictable.

The significance of any threat posed by substitutes depends upon the ease with which existing customers can find substitutes and change their allegiance. In consumer markets, it is likely to be more difficult to assess this threat than in industrial markets. The greater the number of substitutes and the ease with which the customer can change products affects the price (or the price elasticity of demand) of the product, and the extent to which pricing can be used as a competitive strategy. There are a number of factors that help to determine the threat posed by substitute products.

- **The cross elasticity of demand**. If products are directly substitutable, then they have a **positive** cross elasticity of demand; for example, if the price of tea goes up then the demand for coffee goes up.
- **Complementarity**. Complementary goods have a **negative cross elasticity of demand**, if the price of one goes up and overall demand falls then demand for the other falls, too. For example, there is joint demand for cars and car tyres.
- **Switching costs**. These are costs of switching from one supplier to another. High switching costs obviously limits substitutability. For example, if you want to use software designed specifically for Apple Macintosh, you obviously need an Apple Macintosh computer. If you have an IBM-compatible PC, you are only likely to buy PC software. The need for a new range of kitchen equipment is a disincentive to convert from electricity to gas as a source of energy.
- **Time factor**. The long-term effects of changing supplier affect substitutability. If, for example, you found that you continually wanted to use Apple software you might eventually change your computer, or if the pricing of gas as a substitute energy source was such that gas central heating was going to be cheaper over three years despite the installation of new equipment, you may decide to make the change.

ACTIVITY 6

You have been asked to give general advice to a small business catering for a large student population near a university. The business currently prepares sandwiches and baguettes for the lunch-time takeaway trade. The owner is thinking of opening in the evenings and offering takeaway pizzas, pasta meals, burgers and other snacks.

- Prepare a list of likely competitors, such as Chinese takeaways, fish and chip shops.
- Prepare a list of likely substitute activities, such as going to the pubs or going to the cinema.
- List the factors that the sandwich bar would need to take into account to analyse this possible strategy, for example, staff, additional cooking facilities, additional storage facilities.

There are many direct competitors such as self-catering, Indian takeaways, pizza places, McDonald's, the Students' Union and the university canteen. As well as the direct rivals for supply of food, there are many substitutes that place demands on a student's time in the evening: sport, socialising in pubs, nightclubs or coffee bars, Student Union activities, political, church or club activities, hobbies, television – even studying.

There are a number of factors to take into account when considering a new product strategy.

- The competition. What is the proximity, convenience, price, image and availability of directly competing products for the evening trade?
- The potential difficulties. Are there new health and safety regulations on preparing hot food? What is the availability of suitably qualified evening staff? Do staff need special training to make the new products? What are the overheads for operating in the evening? What is the availability and price of supplies for different products such as pizza and pastas? Does the business need any additional equipment, a pizza oven or a larger refrigerator for storage, for example? What new packaging do you need for hot food? What are the local regulations on opening hours? Are the current premises in the right location for evening trade? Are you located near a hall of residence that already supplies students' evening meals (if the hall does not supply lunch, this would explain your lunch-time customers)? How do you get your current trade? What happens to your business out of term time? What are local residents' attitudes to takeaways? Where are the students actually going to take the takeaways to eat them? Should you consider a delivery service? What about the capital required for the new investment? Will a bank lend to this business?
- The business objectives. Perhaps, the owner just has an idea about expanding, but maybe there is too much competition in this area. The business might do better to target a more consistent population or to trade during vacations, rather than expand into evening trade for the same market.

POWER OF BUYERS AND SUPPLIERS

The power and influence a buyer has over the supplier depends upon its relative size and the availability of substitutes both in supply and in demand. In highly concentrated industries, where a large proportion of market share is controlled by a few companies, the suppliers will have more power than the buyers. In this way, the supermarket chains have considerable market power.

However, the village shop offering bread and a range of fresh products, in an area where public transport is limited and where people would need to drive to a supermarket, also has supplier power. In a large shopping centre, customers have a wide choice of easily accessible supplies and, as collective buyers, have the power to make demands upon the sellers.

Integration, whether partial, through long-term contracts or full, through direct ownership, locks suppliers and buyers into a relationship that, in restricting choice, reduces the incentive to improve the quality of the supply. De-integration and the opening of contracts to bidders on a regular basis can provide the competitive edge necessary to improve the quality of products and services.

By the mid 1990s, however, some organisations have begun to reintegrate, and they are no longer subcontracting so many of their activities to other companies. For example, IBM found that it was over-reliant on external providers to provide key activities, and the process was difficult to manage both in terms of quality control and timing of supplies. The need to manage efficient just-in-time schemes, where inputs are brought to the producers just when they are needed rather than held as stock, has meant that buyers have sought to build up strong links with their key suppliers.

The power of the supplier is likely to be greater when:

- there are a few suppliers and many buyers – for example, a few breweries supply many pubs
- the industry, or buyer, is not an important or main customer of the supplier
- the product being supplied is essential, say a part in a process
- there are no substitutes, or the product has been so heavily differentiated to make it impossible to substitute
- switching costs are high
- forward integration is possible, with suppliers entering the buyer's market.

The power of the buyer is likely to be greater when:

- there are few buyers and many suppliers
- purchase is important to the seller
- purchase is not important to the buyer
- there are close substitutes with little product differentiation
- switching costs are low
- backward integration is possible, with buyers entering the supplier's market

CASE STUDY

Benetton

In the late 1980s, Benetton was a large vertically de-integrated company. Manufacturing, styling and design, distribution and sales were all undertaken by companies outside Benetton. The company employed a number of outside stylists whose designs were then developed by Giulianna Benetton. More than 80 per cent of Benetton's manufacturing was done outside the company by about 350 subcontractors employing about 10,000 people. The remaining 20 per cent of production was mainly dyeing and was performed in-house by

700 to 800 workers. Logistics and distribution activities were also undertaken by subcontracted firms. As you can see, much of its value chain was undertaken by subcontractors, with Benetton only undertaking dyeing and management itself.

An external sales organisation of some 80 agents managed a retailing system of 4,000 shops spread all over the world. Fewer than ten shops were operated by Benetton; those in key cities such as Milan, Rome, New York and Dusseldorf. The remainder were set up by independent entrepreneurs. This was not strictly a franchise arrangement in that they did not pay a fee for the use of the name nor a royalty on a percentage of sales. However, shop managers had to meet detailed requirements to ensure a standard layout, image and pricing structure.

Information drawn from Jose-Carlos Jarillo and Jon Martinez's 1988 study of Benetton SpA, Mintzberg *et al* (1998).

REVIEW ACTIVITY 2

Read the Benetton case study. Identify the activities which are done by subcontractors and those which are conducted in-house. What are the advantages to Benetton of subcontracting its production to large numbers of small textile and clothing producers? Why does Benetton use a form of franchising as a means of selling its products to consumers? Given what you know about the changeable nature of the fashion business, explain why Benetton retained some activities in the value adding process. What are the disadvantages of this way of operating?

Summary

In this section, we have looked at the interface between the organisation and its immediate environment and examined the impact the industry has on the nature of competition. Porter's model identifies five competitive forces. We identified the barriers that exist to entering markets. We analysed the relationship that exists between suppliers and buyers, close links promoting quality and reliability.

SECTION 3

Conducting an Environmental Analysis

Introduction

From an environmental analysis we can find out what is happening in the environment in which an organisation operates and the effects that this has on the organisation. From this analysis of the current situation, we hope to be able to get some idea of what might happen in the future. Conducting a survey of the environment for a specific organisation is a complex and demanding task. It involves understanding how each aspect of the general environment works. It also requires some understanding of the stakeholders and their power and it requires the ability to place all this background knowledge in the context of developments in the very specific contemporary environment of the organisation, as and when they occur.

We need to look at the overall PEST environment, at what is happening in the industry and then at the organisation's competitors. What are the objectives of rivals? Are they trying to increase market share or profit? How are they doing this – through new products, cost cutting or by expanding into new markets? Are they achieving their objectives? We need to analyse the strengths and weaknesses of the competition in terms of finance, workforce, product range, management and overall strategy. How will the competition react to anything that you do?

3.1 Monitoring the environment

Monitoring the business environment for any organisation involves researching vast quantities of information. When we know what has happened in the past, and try to understand why it happened, then we can make some estimates for the future.

As you know from Unit 2, readily available sources of environmental information include the quality daily press, and journals like *The Economist*. However, note that this information is not 'raw', but it is selected and interpreted by journalists. Raw environmental information may be harder to find but some is available on-line from government sources, from research bodies and from organisations themselves. The Internet has made a lot of information readily and instantly available.

Organisations have access to information available through the professional associations and bodies associated with their industry. These bodies will provide an initial screening of relevant information about developments, competitors and outside environmental influences. Information will be disseminated through newsletters, conferences, exhibitions and seminars.

AURAL INFORMATION

Much information can be gained by listening. This informal acquisition of environmental information from both within and beyond the boundaries of the organisation can be used productively. Listening to customers, listening to competitors, listening to the workforce all contribute to the understanding of the organisation's environment. Are the customers happy? Are they likely to go elsewhere? Is the workforce content? Are they likely to take industrial action? What are the competitors likely to do to gain competitive advantage?

Information can be obtained by attending meetings and by monitoring customer satisfaction more formally through surveys and analysis of sales and customer complaints. The media, including radio and television, provides useful information on trends in the general business environment. Organisations must also listen to their suppliers, their bankers, shareholders, business and professional associations, regulators, watchdog committees, consultants and government or academic advisers. A large number of contacts surveyed on a regular basis is an effective form of scanning.

PUBLISHED INFORMATION

As you know, newspapers, trade journals and industry newsletters publish information on the general business environment. With newspapers now available in CD-ROM versions and on the Internet, there is less need for a clippings service to gather appropriate information from the papers. Key word searches easily identify relevant articles. It is possible to subcontract this activity to outside agencies. The *Financial Times*, for example will do a company survey for a fee, but it may be of more value if the company conducts the search itself on an ongoing basis.

On-line information is directly available from news wires and from the Internet. News items, share prices, foreign exchange rates, consumer reports, government and company information can all be instantly accessed. There is so much information available that to find what you are looking for or to monitor competitors in your particular industry is difficult, and you may need first to go to a research company. For example, the UK Company Research Centre provides selected directory and financial information on UK businesses. You can access the information directly from worldwide databases such as *Dun and Bradstreet's Market Identifiers* which lists details of 1.2 million major UK public and private companies, which is updated quarterly with weekly updates of financial datasheets. Other databases (which are all updated weekly) include *ICC British Company Directory* and *Financial Datasheets, Jordan's Registered Companies*, which includes a listing of the most recent documents that have been filed by companies, and *FT Analysis Reports*, which give financial information on selected UK public companies, with a business summary, profit and loss account, five-year balance sheet and capital structure.

The formalisation of information gathering into a full management information system (MIS), is increasingly used by organisations with a fully integrated computer network. However, it is difficult to set up systems that are sufficiently flexible to select and combine appropriate information, particularly that coming from unexpected quarters.

ACTIVITY 7

Select one of the companies that you identified in Review Activity 1. Find out more about the company and its industry using the information sources mentioned above.

You should already have an idea about the company's performance and some of the other factors in its business environment – exchange rates, interest rates, stakeholder activities, for example. To complete the activity, you need to look more closely at the competitive environment including the industry. On-line services and the Internet will give you more information about company performance. Public libraries have easily accessible information contained on CD-ROMs and, possibly, Internet access. Perhaps there is an Internet cafe in your town that offers public access to the Internet. If you are a student at a university or college, then you will probably be able to use student or library computing facilities that have access to on-line databases and the Internet. If you work for an organisation in some capacity, again you may be able to use their computing and library facilities.

The company probably has a web page. Using this as a starting point, you can begin to build a picture of your company in its environment. Does it have a mission statement? What is the company structure? Who runs the company? How many employees does it have? Does it have worldwide connections? What industries is it operating in? Is it operating in diverse industries? Or at many stages in the supply chain or in just one?

More traditional sources of information such as the press, trade and scientific journals, consumer reports, government papers and market research reports are often available in public libraries. These will give you more information about the particular industry you are investigating. Find out more about the main industry associations or related associations, they too might have a web page which will give you other points of contact and sources of information. As you find out more about the company and the industries that it operates in, you will see how much information there is available, how many factors are involved and how complicated it is to make a complete analysis. Here you are just making a start, but the exercise should give you some ideas of how this might be done as part of an organisation's normal practice.

3.2 Using environmental information

The purpose of environmental analysis is to find out what is happening and what is likely to happen in the environment in which an organisation operates. Once a clear picture of the environment has been established, it becomes easier to make decisions within the organisation. It also allows the organisation to be **proactive** rather than **reactive**, and to make decisions in anticipation of a changing environment rather than just in response to it. As we have seen, there are innumerable factors affecting the business and the competitive environment. How can we possibly use all the information we have collected and make any sense of it for the future? Forecasting trends is always going to be difficult, and almost impossible in some environments. This is why it is so important for organisations operating in a turbulent environment to be flexible so that they can easily adapt to change.

FORECASTING

Forecasting is normally done by the organisation's planners once the key drivers, or most important influences, in the organisation's environment have been identified and monitored over a period of time.

Consider, as an example, a business that produces Artex finishings on ceilings. The core activity is supplying Artex ceilings in new houses. The company is involved in the redevelopment, restoration and repair work, but this is not its main income. You will want to follow the trends in the construction business carefully. By monitoring what is happening in the construction industry, you should be able to forecast upturns and downturns in the company's business.

The construction industry is strongly pro-cyclical, as its trade cycle is ahead of the general business cycle. Many other industries, such as home furnishings, wallpapers, paints, furniture and carpets, garden plants and furnishings, removal firms, brick and tile manufacturers, concrete and tarmac producers, and the government itself, also monitor the construction industry. In addition, the construction and related industries are major employers, so it provides a good indicator of the general health of the economy which can be a useful forecasting tool.

For other organisations, the forecasting method may be more specific. Weather forecasts may encourage certain types of activity and subsequent expenditure. The Meteorological Office has made extensive surveys to see how consumer spending patterns fluctuate as the weather changes. It forecasts that soft drinks sales take off when the temperature reaches 16°C, but above 24°C sales of expensive brands drop off. The Meteorological Office is selling this service to supermarkets to help with their stock control and shelf-stocking strategies. There are more predictable influences of an organisation's environment, for example the change of population structures over time will directly affect the demand for healthcare and provision for the elderly.

ENVIRONMENTAL APPRAISAL

We can conduct a rather more formal appraisal by making a thorough analysis of the PEST environment to indicate trends in the competitive environment. If the PEST analysis is viewing some of the key drivers for a particular organisation, then the information may be even more valuable. However, there is a tendency to view the organisation as it currently exists in its environment not how it would or could exist in the future. Changes to key drivers can be assessed in relation to Porter's five forces and a matrix formulated as a framework for future developments. If the organisation operates in different markets, then there will be different key drivers to monitor and a different matrix to formulate. These matrices can map out the basic route of likely industry or market development, indicate where the organisation fits in the industry or market and suggest what strategies might be developed to stay competitive.

The next stage of an environmental appraisal is to ask a number of crucial questions.

- **What is likely to happen to demand?** Will there be new buyers in the market? Will existing buyers change their pattern of buying? Will their needs change? Will new needs emerge?
- **Are there likely to be changes in competitive behaviour?** Will there be new entrants to the industry with different ways of competing? Will there be new ways of marketing, for example?
- **What are likely to be the changes in industry structure?** Where is the industry in its life cycle? What new processes or products are there likely to be? How can uncertainty in the industry be reduced?

Answers to these questions are required for the development of strategies. These must fit in with the organisation's mission, its strengths and weaknesses and meet its objectives. Strategies are developed at all levels of the organisation and need to fulfil the overall corporate strategy. This analysis of the competitive and general environment will provide the information necessary for developing competitive strategies. There are many models that take this information further and attempt to ensure a fit with what the organisation wants to do and what it is capable of doing in a particular market. Many approaches have been developed that analyse particular criteria in the environment for a particular organisation. These include:

- **EVR congruence** – matches the demands of the environment with the values and resources of the organisation (we look at this approach further in Unit 8)
- **SWOT analysis** – matches an organisation's strengths and weaknesses with the environment's opportunities and threats (you use this technique in Unit 8)
- **Boston Consulting Group matrix** – balances products with product lines (or SBUs) within the organisation through analysis of the relative market share and the market growth rate
- **McKinsey/General Electric matrix** – uses market attractiveness through a number of PEST and industry criteria and the competitive position of the organisation through a number of organisational criteria
- **business profile matrix** –based on the dimensions of market position and industry maturity
- **directional policy matrix** – based on prospects for sector profitability and the organisation's competitive capabilities (we look at the Shell directional policy matrix which compares the attractiveness of the product or market with the competitive position in Unit 8).

We look at the overall concept of strategy in Unit 8. You will meet many sophisticated models and techniques in further strategy modules. Here we simply give you an idea of the factors involved and the use to which you can put some of the information gathered. Scenario planning is a technique that may bring a rather more human element to this theoretical view of the environment.

SCENARIO PLANNING

Using our environmental information, we can carry out an exercise which attempts to model future scenarios and allows managers to develop strategies to respond to the opportunities and threats these scenarios may present. This encourages managers to consider all the aspects of the organisation's environment that we have covered in Units 2 and 3, and to systematically work through appropriate organisational responses.

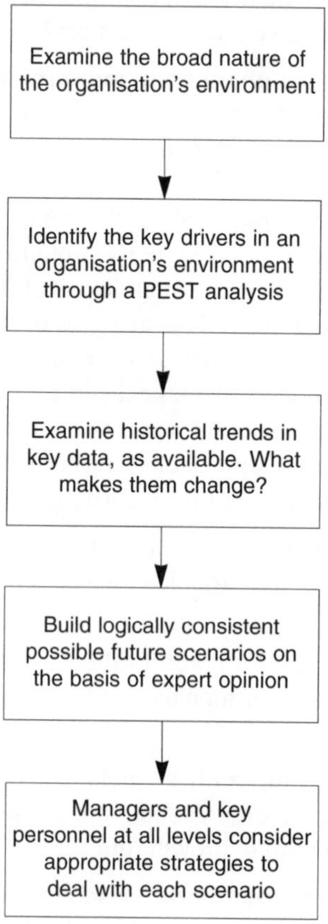

Figure 2: Scenario planning

The advantages of scenario building are that it encourages managers and key personnel throughout the organisation to take a longer-term view, rather than to base all operational decisions on short-term considerations. In involving key staff throughout the organisation in the planning process, it ensures that the operational implications of any chosen strategies or plans are thought through. Scenario planning exercises ensure that all participants have a better understanding of the organisational implications of the complex changing environment. As you will see in Unit 8, this activity can be tied in with the overall strategic approach of the organisation.

REVIEW ACTIVITY 3

The Internet allows people to access information and communicate on a worldwide basis. Hopefully, you have used it in completing Activity 7. Information that can be accessed includes text, pictures, sound and computer programs. Through e-mail, you can send large amounts of information very cheaply around the world. Various organisations are providing services such as banking and 'virtual' shopping over the Internet. To service this market, a large number of Internet access provider companies have been set up. These firms charge a modest monthly charge to allow the individual access to the full Internet via connection over a local telephone line. Using the PEST structure identify key factors in each category that a manager of an Internet access firm might wish to consider as possibly creating a business opportunity or presenting a threat to the service that it offers now. This investigation would form the first step in an environmental analysis.

Summary

An organisation needs to know about its general business environment and the specific industrial environment in which it operates. This involves a vast amount of information about the business world in general and about detail such as the specific action of competitors. An organisation needs to monitor the changes that are occurring so it can respond by developing the appropriate strategies and then implementing these strategies through the change process.

SECTION 4

Change and Competitive Advantage

Introduction

Understanding and monitoring an organisation's business and competitive environments provides a basis for progress and continuing success. However, the organisation has to respond to this information and this involves formulating a strategy, decision making, planning and then implementing the necessary changes. Change has always been a factor of business activity. The pace of change has increased (Moore and Pessemier, 1993). Change may come both from within the organisation as staff or structures change and from the PEST and competitive environment. The rule of business is adaptation or extinction; you do not have to change, but if you don't you will go out of business!

Various models of change have been proposed and these enable managers to identify the roles and stages needed for the effective conduct of change processes. A key issue is the identification of the sources and nature of resistance to change in managing the change process. The management of change is a discipline in its own right, here we just look at some overall features. You will meet further analysis in your strategy modules.

4.1 Responding to the PEST environment

We looked at the PEST environment in some detail in Unit 2. You have just investigated a particular PEST environment for the Internet access industry in Review Activity 3. Here we review the major areas again. Any changes might have industry-wide implication, so they will affect all of an organisation's competitors, or they may be very specific. They can affect all elements of the value chain and all the primary or support activities. As you investigate the business functions in the rest of the module, bear in mind the changes that might have to be implemented in individual functions as well as in the organisation as a whole. Competitive advantage is something to be achieved throughout the organisation.

POLITICAL AND LEGAL ISSUES

The law, and the degree to which it is applied and the ways in which it is enforced, has a dramatic effect on businesses. The law affects every aspect of the business: how goods are procured (contract law), how they are manufactured (health and safety law), how they are distributed (transport regulations), how they may be marketed and sold (sale of goods laws), finance (tax laws), human resources (equal opportunity laws) and research and development (patent law). Any legal changes require instant compliance by an organisation, whether it is a UK tax regulation, a new health and safety regulation, or an EU directive.

ECONOMIC ISSUES

Changes in the economic situation can dramatically affect a business. For example, a lowering of interest rates could stimulate the building of houses affecting not only the construction industry but also related industries. Industries as diverse as domestic white goods (refrigerators, freezers and cookers), furnishings and DIY decorating goods are all affected.

SOCIAL ISSUES

Social attitudes and structures have changed all aspects of our lives. The population is changing in structure. People are tending to leave home earlier and marry later.

There is a much higher rate of divorce leading to many more single-parent families. When people are old they tend not to live in an extended family but on their own. The impact of social changes is very extensive and a simple change may have unexpected effects. Shopping patterns are changing.

TECHNOLOGICAL ISSUES

Technology might affect any aspects of an organisation's activities including its products, processes, functions, information and communication. We look at one example here. In the 1960s, advances in chemistry made it possible to determine the structures of proteins and to apply this knowledge to genetics. In the 1970s and early 1980s, this understanding made it possible to determine and affect how plants and organisms behaved. The science and technology of molecular biology and genetic engineering had fully arrived. In 1996, genetically modified tomatoes (designed to stay fresh longer) become available in the UK and genetically modified animals started to be used to produce products for the pharmaceutical industry. The cost of this research runs into many millions of pounds. It was one of the major influences in the global mergers forced on the pharmaceutical giants in the 1990s.

4.2 Responding to the competitive environment

An organisation can respond to a particular environment by basically just getting out of the market. More constructively, it can choose to reduce its environmental uncertainty by strategies that include:

- monitoring and analysing the environment and competitors so it can take avoiding action
- moving to a more favourable environment
- contingency planning, protecting itself through ensuring its supplies and training its staff
- physical relocation to take advantage of local resources
- reducing risk through relationships with other organisations
- lobbying government on regulations
- investing in R&D and technology.

It can also choose to gain competitive advantage in its industry or competitive environment by developing a number of competitive strategies. Porter identifies three generic strategies.

- **Producing the product at a lower cost** than competitors, through cost reduction in inputs and all elements of the transformation process and high-volume production. Skoda aims to do this in the car industry and supermarkets take this approach in the no-frills approach of their own-brand products. The airline EasyJet also offers a no-frills service.
- **Differentiating the product** so that customers are prepared to pay a premium price for superior technology, product reliability, design, image, availability, exclusivity, service and performance. For example, designer

clothes, Rolex watches, Mercedes cars, golf club membership are all products that are well differentiated from the competition and for which premium prices can be charged.

- **Targeting the product** into a narrower segment of the market and then competing either through cost leadership or differentiation. The market segment might be defined by geography, age, lifestyle, sex, product usage or any of the factors that marketers can use to target their customers. For example, car manufacturers produce a range of cars to appeal to different market segments: families, women, company fleets, etc.

Using our environmental information, we can formulate more detailed strategies for different industrial contexts, for emerging, maturing and declining markets. We can formulate detailed strategies for organisations in different market position contexts, for market leaders, market followers and weak competitors.

Strategies can cover a range of activities that include:

- inventing a new product
- building or holding market share
- developing market segments
- becoming market leader
- reorganising distribution channels
- locking in suppliers
- identifying target competitors
- rationalising operations
- creating efficiency in the value chain
- rejuvenating the product
- diversifying
- backward or forward vertical integration
- globalisation.

Organisations must track competition and respond with changes in possibly all functional areas (finance, production, logistics, marketing), service, organisational structure, product range, pricing structure, marketing communication and distribution.

We can examine the three generic strategies in conjunction with Porter's five forces of competition and identify the sorts of strategies and change that the organisation will need to implement. Our discussion of Porter's model here is limited to considering the implications in the context of organisational change.

Direct competition

How does the organisation respond if a competitor produces a more advanced product or introduces a more efficient and lower-cost manufacturing process? The deregulation of airlines in the EU has opened up the market for new carriers that provide no-frills services at significantly lower costs than the established national airlines. The established airlines are being forced to meet this competition with new products, including low-cost fares that they will have to cover through a reduction in their operating costs to continue to make profits. Thus, they are having to follow a cost leadership strategy. Although, for example, Air UK may be competing with EasyJet on particular routes and has reduced fares, it has not done so on other routes, and it has not changed its overall marketing strategy retaining its lucrative and high-priced business class services.

Substitute competition

Technical advances may allow a new product or service which can sharply change the nature of the competition. In the early 1950s, travel between North America and Europe was by sea in large ocean liners. With technological advances, the jet passenger aircraft was introduced and passengers moved to air travel. The liner fleet was finished as a means of transatlantic travel, and operators switched to holiday cruising. Companies had to move from transportation to a leisure business. Although retaining the ships and links with the sea as a means of travel, this move affected their entire operation.

In the late 1990s, Air UK, for example, competes on its Paris route with the direct rail services that are run by Eurostar, a result of the technology that built the Channel tunnel. On its Edinburgh route, Air UK is not only competing with other 'traditional' airlines, but with EasyJet, and against the discounted rail fares brought in by the privatised rail companies. It is responding by special fare deals and it is having to cut costs affecting functions throughout the company.

New entrants

Thirty years ago, personal financial services were provided exclusively by banks. The banks were happy to remain closed on Saturdays as there was no other competition. As building societies and even high street shops began to offer financial services, the banks had to change and provide a more customer-orientated service. Now many branches in the high street are open on Saturdays.

Foreign companies have moved into international markets. In the 1960s, car manufacture was dominated by US and European companies. Japan built up a substantial industry and provided dangerous competition to both the US and European car manufacturers in their own domestic markets. Domestic manufacturers faced substantial losses and have had to restructure to provide better products with higher quality manufactured at lower costs. They have been able to do this through various corporate alliances, improved technology in manufacturing, reduction in costs from different ways of working in teams and just-in-time deals with suppliers. They have segmented the market, with specialisation into niche markets, and have become more efficient and effective in particular sectors.

Supplier power

Microsoft does not make computers but it is one of the most profitable companies in the computer sector. As the added value in computing moved from the hardware to the software, so the power moved from the manufacturers of computers to the suppliers of the software. Computer manufacturers have restructured to be able to provide both hardware and software. For example, the purchase of Lotus by IBM has enabled it to gain a significant share of the office PC software market.

Buyer power

The major supermarkets have a high proportion of the market. Food manufacturers find that this gives the supermarket chains a very powerful bargaining position, forcing margins down and even driving manufacturers of branded products to also produce own-label products for the major supermarkets. At the front end of the production chain, farmers have found that they have almost zero bargaining power. With no real negotiating position, many farmers found themselves in a simple 'take it or leave it' situation. The power comes from the relative sizes of the organisations in the product market. So when a co-operative was formed to sell milk (Milk Marque), a high percentage of the supply was in producers' hands, and they were able to force up the price of milk and increase their profit margins. They had restructured and changed to recover a competitive position.

ACTIVITY 8

Gravesend is a small town on the north Kent coast. It is close to London and near to one of the new Channel link international railway stations. For a number of years, the town centre was in a state of decline. However, a town centre manager has been appointed and the centre is slowly regenerating. Moreover, a systematic exploitation of the local history and proximity of the Channel tunnel link has resulted in a significant and increasing number of tourists to the town.

James Kingsley is a master baker with a shop in the town centre. Previously owned by his father, James now owns the freehold of the shop which is increasing in value as a result of the regeneration of the town centre. However, sales and profits are declining as a result of competition from out-of-town supermarkets and the high costs of labour to work overnight to bake products for the morning.

James craft bakes his products using fresh ingredients. In contrast, most supermarkets have their own bakeries that use raw frozen ingredients in new specialised computer-operated ovens needing little labour and a short baking period - called bake off. The supermarkets also bring in chilled and fresh products that are baked in a central bakery and delivered on a daily basis.

James has a good relationship with his bank. It has indicated that it will lend him the money to redevelop the business if he can come up with a plan to restructure and reposition the business to meet the competitive influences on his company. He has asked you as a business consultant to advise him on what he should do. He is thinking of changing the business into a sandwich bar with a small eating-in area, still baking bread but supplying sandwiches for the takeaway trade. How would you advise him to analyse his problems and start his decision-making process?

First he should review the PEST environment for the new type of business that he proposes.

There are several political and legal issues factors to take into account. Is planning permission required for any changes to the building? What fire and hygiene regulations apply to the new operations? What toilet facilities will be required by law? What planning requirements will be needed for this? Economic factors mainly concern interest rates. If James intends to borrow a substantial sum from the bank, he will need to monitor interest rates carefully, and structure his pricing to take this into account. Social factors are chiefly a demographic consideration. James would want to get a feel for the numbers of visitors and office workers in his locality and what numbers of customers that he might be able to attract if he changed the business. Note also the changes in people's expectations of eating out in terms of higher standards and frequency of use. The technological issues concern the new technologies in cooking and baking that will allow you to serve more people in a restricted area. Have a look at the operations in a fast-food outlet such as McDonald's.

You should check for any direct competition in terms of other eating out establishments and evaluate indirect competition such as Boots who sell sandwiches. Many small business have located in the city centre but do not have canteens and staff go out at lunch time to sandwich bars for takeaway meals. Tourists are looking for value-for-money simple meals with a coffee or tea in an informal setting.

The present bakery and storage facilities are large and extensive. The installation of new computer-operated ovens would allow significant floor space to be freed for redevelopment. There would appear to be no major structural or planning problems in adapting this space for any reasonable use.

Your recommendations on modifying the shop to cater for eating in and to providing a takeaway service would depend on your analysis. James is changing his product and his service, and his customers. Does he have the necessary expertise to do this? What about his old customers? Perhaps he could develop a different strategy in providing more products for his existing customers, such as specialist pies and cakes that they could not buy from the supermarket, and extend this range through buying in delicatessen type products. Perhaps he could provide a delivery service or a home catering service. Many different strategies could be formulated using sophisticated matrices and techniques that you will learn about in further modules. Scenario planning could also be used to investigate the ideas further.

4.3 Implementing change

Consider that, through a process of environmental analysis, appraisal and investigation of some scenarios, a new competitive strategy has been formulated. What happens next? This will require formulation into a series of actions and those actions will need to be implemented. This will require change. Change management is a field in its own right, all we can do in this short section is give you some ideas about implementation and the types of problems that are encountered. The ease of introducing change will depend on many factors including:

- the culture of the organisation
- the structure of the organisation
- the extent and type of changes
- the amount of involvement of the organisation in the initial decisions.

There is a tendency for the organisation to want to maintain the status quo and for individuals within it to continue doing things the way they always have. This is compounded by the fact that the structures and processes of the organisation provide the framework for these routines. It is hard to change the routines without changing the structures, and as these are dependent on the culture, it may be necessary to change the underlying culture. If the organisation has a functional structure, then any changes will tend to be implemented through the functional areas but this process may miss more overall organisational activities that are actually achieving competitive advantage. These organisational activities may need to work with the functional areas to help them to achieve performance, and organisations may need to consider a matrix type structure. For example, a strategy will need to be addressed across the organisation if it is concerned with issues such as:

- achieving lowest delivered cost against use of resources, thus increasing profit
- attracting and retaining employees who are motivated, flexible or multiskilled
- achieving new product innovations
- upgrading quality and service.

This effectively means that quality, service, profits and competitive advantage become a common theme for all functions within the organisation. Remember this concept as we work through the individual functions in the rest of the module and analyse how these themes could be enhanced throughout the organisation. To achieve this type of strategic change, we can use a number of processes that include management through:

- small teams working with different functions
- a project management approach (we look at this in Unit 9)
- cross-functional teams
- reorganisation.

MODELS FOR THE CHANGE PROCESS

There are a number of models that break down the process of change into a number of steps. Steps in the change process include:

- recognising a problem and the need to change, or an enforced disturbance
- deciding to act

- defining the problem
- finding a solution
- implementing the solution
- allowing and responding to feedback.

Drawing on the work of Kurt Lewin, Thompson (1993) discusses a simple model where the process is seen as moving from one stable state through a transition or change state to a new steady state. He identifies this as:

- unfreezing the old state
- change
- refreezing the new state.

However, change is a continuous process. Organisations need to consider change not as an occasional one-off event but a continual way of existing in the present business context.

The definition of the problem is not a mechanical process, it requires insight and originality. Alternative definitions of the problem may well take the organisation in completely different directions. Earlier, we noted the switch of transatlantic passengers from liners to aircraft. There could be many alternative ways of defining the problem facing the liner operators. Depending on the definition, the organisation would develop a completely different competitive strategy. For example, we could look at the liner problem from the perspective of the product or from the market.

Product definition of the problem

We can define the problem from the perspective of our current market and customer. We have ships which are expensive and are difficult to sell, we have lost our customers and we cannot compete with airlines on cost and speed. Technology will never make ships go as fast as planes. What can we do with our basic product to make it attractive again? Can we change our product to meet another market need? The answer is yes, we can offer luxury travel where the customer need is not 'getting there', but 'having a good time while travelling'. Travel itself becomes the *raison d'être* not transport from one place to another.

Market definition of the problem

Our customers need a fast way of transport, therefore if we want to compete for this custom we need to move into the airline business. Thus, we change our industry and competitive environment.

One feature is common to the two definitions, the organisation needs to search for solutions which are outside of its present skill base. If these provide the answer, then the company will need to recruit new staff or employ consultants to provide the new skills and knowledge. By staying in the ship industry, there will be a better match of resources in that operators already have ships and people who are used to working on ships. However, the luxury liner business requires a different service and quality approach to passengers, who expect leisure and entertainment, and this will require a major change in employees. If the alternative move into the airline business is taken, then major investment would be needed to buy aircraft. This is a already a very competitive marketplace as it had many new entrants in the early days, it is subject to government regulation and, importantly, the current skills and interests of the employees learnt on ships will be of little value in the new business. Everything will need to change and start again.

No solution is of any value unless it can be applied with skill and made to be both effective and efficient. New business directions require new structures, new ways of working, new styles and even new values in the organisation. In our transatlantic liner example, it requires a change of direction from 'we are in transport' to 'we are in entertainment and leisure'. Built into any new structure and operation, measures of performance will be required so that the process of adaptation can be continuous. If an organisation makes an effective competitive change, then the competition is likely to make some response. Long-term success comes from continual tracking of changes in the environment and successive development of market-sensitive responses. For example, by establishing a cruise line business, the liner operators now face direct competition from other companies in the luxury holiday travel business.

EMPLOYEE RESISTANCE TO CHANGE

Organisational change affects all stakeholders, but it is likely to have an immediate and profound impact on employees. This may be either desirable or undesirable from their perspective. For example, they may be given:

- better working conditions
- higher pay and more interesting work
- greater opportunities for self-development and career progression.

These changes would be willingly accepted. However, organisations are likely to encounter some employee resistance if change involves:

- a new organisational structure with different lines of communication, control and authority
- retraining and learning new skills for new working methods
- taking on new tasks and new methods, with a new remuneration structure
- moving to a new location
- increased stress and uncertainty over the future
- taking a pay cut or having reduced benefits
- working longer hours
- being forced to take a lower-level job, early retirement or redundancy
- new corporate values that now are not in accordance with employees' own values
- new ownership or management that removes charismatic individuals that employee were prepared to follow – perhaps a family-run company is bought out by a large corporation
- new relationships with other stakeholders, customers, suppliers.

When employees have worked in a particular way, it is unreasonable to expect them to impassively accept a change which has significant consequences for their everyday work. A new challenge may generate some excitement, but there is more likely to be resentment and anxiety about the changes. This will be exacerbated if it is unclear whether the changes will work, there is doubt about how well they have been planned, there has been little consultation, and if people do not know why they are being implemented. As far as employees are concerned, they may have everything to lose, including their job or career at worst, or everyday satisfaction with their work. People affected by change may resist it, and if they do so, they can make implementation very difficult. They may even sabotage it altogether.

Any major internal changes in the organisation will probably affect:

- pay and benefits
- security
- group and personal relationships
- status
- personal values
- personal and group power
- personal and group skills.

The ease with which change can be implemented in an organisation often depends upon its culture and structure. Staff are more likely to accept change as part of their normal working life in an innovative flexible company with a flatter organisational structure working in a very competitive industry such as software or advertising. However, in a traditional hierarchical organisation such as the Inland Revenue, employees are less likely to react well. In an entrepreneurial culture employees are more prepared to follow the vision of their leader, and change can be implemented more easily. In all organisations, human resource management has a key role to play in the implementation process. Given the increasing pace of change, the process of change management has become as important to success as the initial analysis and decision making.

Note how one organisation deals with change. In 1997, Steve Jobs, the original founder of Apple, returned to help get the company on its feet again. He wrote to Apple's employees to tell them about some belt-tightening measures: 'Today we are taking a few more steps which will begin to take Apple back to its roots as a more egalitarian, entrepreneurial company.' The measures included no more paid sabbaticals, travelling economy on Apple business, and share options instead of cash bonuses. How do you think the employees reacted? Probably well, as they appreciate that the company has to take steps to cut costs and tighten business operations, and would have faith in the original founder to achieve success. Other stakeholders, such as the shareholders, would also be pleased. Apple's share prices rose by 64 per cent in a month following the announcement of a big investment and alliance deal with Microsoft. Note also that Jobs 'talked' to the staff through an internal electronic memo.

4.4 Future trends

As we have discussed throughout these first units, the general and competitive environment can force change in a number of ways. Here we summarise some of the key trends mainly through examples and look at some possibilities for the future. Each organisation is unique, so it will respond to change and develop in its own way of devising a complete range of scenarios for the future. We can be sure that some events will happen: change will continue, technology will continue to be a key driving force and a means of competitive advantage, and the world will continue to become increasingly competitive. We can summarise the main trends in today's business world under these headings:

- change in size
- change in concept
- change in working patterns
- change in marketplace
- change in ownership.

We review each of these areas from the perspective of what is happening within the organisation, although some areas are obviously linked and we need to look at the complete organisation. Note also that technology is involved in all these areas and can cut across the organisation to enable new processes, new products, new ways of working, new markets, better information and communication to become established.

CHANGE IN SIZE

As you have seen, organisations buy up and sell suppliers, customers and competitors as part of their competitive strategy. Each organisation responds to changes in its external environments in its own unique way. There may be trends for smaller company structures through downsizing, subcontracting and break-ups of conglomerations, but others see that their strength is in size. WPP, the world's largest marketing services group, including J Walter Thompson, Ogilvy and Mather, Hill and Knowlton, Ogilvy, Adams and Rhinehart, estimates that US$60 million of extra revenue is generated from referrals within the group. In 1996, the media buying operations of J Walter Thompson and Ogilvy and Mather were merged, giving more economies of scale and power in the marketplace.

On the other hand, Hanson is selling off Hanson Electrical, Grove Cranes and Australian interests in gold companies from its vast conglomerate that it accumulated through large acquisitions in the 1980s and 1990s. Hanson is now concentrating on its core activities of aggregates and road and building construction.

CHANGE IN CONCEPT

Many organisations are **outsourcing** parts of the business such as distribution and information technology to outside providers. This may result in an overall reduction of staff and cause job losses. Individuals may face the possibility of pay cuts and redundancy. Subcontractors undertake a range of tasks throughout organisations; remember how Benetton operates in Review Activity 2.

The dependency of links in the supply chain means that **supply chain management** is now a critical factor for organisations. Petersen Spring, a West Midlands spring manufacturer, supplies the motor trade. Its customers include Lucas, Rover and Ford. The company was under intense pressure from its customers to reduce prices. Meanwhile, a main competitor in Spain was buying raw materials cheaper. This led to a complete change of strategy in purchasing, with the focus on total price including delivery costs and quality. Petersen Spring reduced the number of suppliers, and entered into partnership sourcing agreements with them. Since its remaining suppliers were being given larger orders, they could become more efficient in supply and delivery. Petersen Spring used electronic data interchange (EDI) to help information flow. This new approach has reduced paperwork and reduced prices, reduced the numbers of deliveries and increased productivity.

CHANGE IN WORKING PATTERNS

Because change is an inevitable part of organisational success, the requirements in the future are likely to be for a multiskilled flexible workforce with more emphasis on team working. External to the organisation, outsourcing and subcontracting mean that patterns of working are changing. There is more home working and freelancing, and part-time jobs are replacing traditional in-house job functions. The traditional office week – from 9 a.m. to 5 p.m., Monday to Friday – is changing. Many businesses are required to provide much more to meet customer service needs, and this means that it has to be supplied through more demands on a flexible workforce. An international marketplace means that the business world operates round the clock, an organisation might have offices that are closed in London but operating in Vancouver. If you want to speak to a colleague there, you will have to do it out of traditional office hours.

Technology also means that jobs are done in a different way and can be done in a different location – mobile phones, laptops, on-line access to head office, worldwide telecommunications, video-conferencing provide the means for many activities to be carried out at distance from the office. Technology has obviously had a vast effect on many aspects of how people work within the organisation.

- Changes in **information technology** may mean a change in status. Many jobs in financial services such as loan decisions are now largely system based. Thus, the high level of independence of a high street bank manager is changed. The manager is now mainly an administrator of an outlet rather than the centre of decision making. Even if the individual suffers no loss in rewards, there may be perceived loss of self esteem and interest as the job has been deskilled.
- Consider **process technology** in the newspaper industry. Hot metal printing required high-level skills and was done in major centralised locations; printers and unions had considerable power and could command high pay. However, now journalists work directly on computers, and final printing is done using sophisticated presses in dispersed locations. The need for the skills and the power of the group have been eroded by the implementation of the new technology. The skilled printer had to be retrained as did the journalist who had to work in a different way.

In the UK, there are increasing numbers of people with qualifications – more have good grades at GCSE and A levels, more go on to further and higher education than ever before. One in three school-leavers go on to university instead of 1 in 20 a few decades ago. Thus, the workforce of tomorrow will have different skills and abilities and different expectations from previous generations. These expectations will be reflected in lifestyles and ways of living, in attitudes in the workplace and towards the government for provision of healthcare and pensions. Individuals are likely to take more responsibility for their wellbeing rather than rely on the state for help in unemployment, ill-health and old age. They are likely to make more individual demands on employers for rewards rather than through union action, and they are likely to demand continual upgrades of skills and knowledge through training and development.

CHANGE IN MARKETPLACE

We look at the change in the marketplace from three different perspectives: globalisation, technology and consumerism. Worldwide markets are possible with the developments of communication and transport networks, and international manufacturing and retailing. We think nothing of being able to buy Spanish tomatoes, South African melons and Australian wine at our local supermarket, or a CD player manufactured in the UK but with Japanese components, or a jacket manufactured in China. Just as the global market provides opportunities for foreign businesses in the UK, it provides a wealth of opportunities for British organisations to market in other areas.

Globalisation

British brewers, Boddington's, Bass, Newcastle Brown and McEwans are finally making inroads into the Australian beer market using widget cans, English-style pubs and witty advertising slogans; Newcastle Brown is promoted as 'pommy holy water'. They are competing against the enormous market for ice-cold lagers from Fosters and other breweries, and they only have about 1 per cent of the market. However, they can charge a premium price, about double the price of local beers.

In 1997, Tottenham Hotspur announced that it has taken a stake in Shanghai Shenua, China's leading team. In return, Tottenham will offer technical advice on stadium management, merchandising, sponsorship and groundsmanship. Football is the fastest-growing sport in China. In 1996, 3.2 million watched Chinese football matches paying about £2.50, a large percentage of an average £60 monthly Shanghai salary. In addition, many Chinese are avid British football fans; television stations in Beijing and Shanghai are each estimated to pay US$400,000 a season to broadcast a live Premiership match every Saturday. Shanghai Shenua has future plans to list on the stock exchange. This will give Spurs an enormous potential for growth away from the highly developed UK market.

Technology

The effects of technology fall into two main areas:

- marketing developments that are possible through enabling technologies, for example, on-line ordering through computer networks

- new products themselves, which may stem from an innovation or a new approach to marketing.

Waterstone's, the UK bookseller, is planning a web site to market 1.4 million titles; and Dillons has an autumn 1997 launch of a virtual bookstore with 1.2 million titles. These on-line facilities will enable British book buyers to buy books from UK suppliers, as well as through the existing large web sites of US companies Amazon and Noble. This will mean that British publishers will have to compete more on price as the American groups offer better discounts. It will also probably mean changes in the timing of releases of new publications on both sides of the Atlantic, as US editions are normally available months before the UK release. The globalisation of the book market would eventually have highlighted these issues of pricing and timing, but on-line bookselling will speed up the process.

On-line banking is still in its infancy in the late 1990s. However, there will be continuing improvements and home banking is probably part of our future. It will give you complete and up-to-date information about your accounts, and you can get access without having to go through a bank employee. Nationwide provides a web-based service for customers to access their accounts and use an on-line bill payment system. Barclays has tied its system in with Microsoft Money; this enables transactions to be set up off-line and then transmitted. However, all systems currently expect the customer to pay for the service, and this policy may have to be modified in the future to encourage more use.

You can now make travel bookings on-line and even buy your groceries; Tesco, for example, offers a restricted on-line ordering facility with home delivery. Perhaps the technology of the future will enable commodity items to be delivered directly to your home when they run out, supplied by information that comes directly from your kitchen to the supplier.

In the watch industry, Switzerland was, historically, the centre of world excellence. With microelectronics and quartz oscillators, the skill in watch-making moved from miniature mechanical engineering to mass consumer electronics. The Swiss redefined a watch as personal adornment that told the time and invented the Swatch. This has been consistently successful in innovative design. However, note that the competitive advantage Swatch enjoys comes not from the microelectronics technology but in the design of the case and marketing the watch as a fashion item.

Consumerism

Consumer awareness about what they eat, breathe, drink, drive, and wear, and about society and the global environment, is increased through more education and more information. The media and political pressure groups also play a part in raising consumer awareness. Organisations need to take into account the protection offered to the consumer by consumer groups and by legislation. For example, organisations are required by law to list the ingredients of food products and indicate a sell-by date; they are required to reduce the release of emissions into the atmosphere from processes and from use of their products; they are encouraged to use recycled materials and sustainable energy sources; they are encouraged to operate in a societally and ethically sound way in terms of processes, products, marketing and advertising.

ACTIVITY 9

In the late 1990s, there is continuing anxiety about the role of the car in our society. There are concerns about the pollution of emissions, town and city centre traffic jams, and the use of natural resources in car manufacture and car use. Car manufacturers are being encouraged to cut down on pollutants from car emissions and to use recyclable and sustainable resources. Car users are being encouraged to cut down on unnecessary journeys, share vehicles and use public transport. Use your own experiences and imagination to identify how technology could help in getting people to leave their car at home and use public transport.

The major problem in persuading people to leave their cars is that public transport does not offer an attractive and in some cases even a viable alternative. In country areas it is unlikely that people will be persuaded to leave their cars at home, in some areas the only alternative to the car is walking or cycling. The use of buses and trains makes many routes unviable unless there are massive government subsidies. However, in the towns and cities it is a different matter. Many people within London, for example, automatically travel by tube and bus because its much faster, and there is nowhere to park the car. In cities and towns generally, public transport could be made more attractive by improving reliability. Efficient timetabling would help. Perhaps dedicated bus lanes could have priority at junctions, with special sensors allowing buses through on traffic lights. (If there were less cars, then the traffic would not get so clogged up anyway.) Does the bus go where you want it to? Surveys and computer mapping technology could ensure that bus and train schedules correspond to the journeys that people actually want to make. The 73 bus route in London, for example, still goes along the same route through the West End that it did 30 years ago. If you stand at a bus stop, you don't know how long you've got to wait – indicators could show when the next bus is due to arrive.

If you're doing a journey by bus and by train, often you can't get the right information and the right connections. In Ipswich, for example, a trial scheme is displaying train information in buses to the railway station. Technology could provide integrated information from door-to-door. Smart cards could be used for the complete journey, bus, train, tube and taxi, the technology exists to charge different amounts depending on the time of day and the type of passenger. For example, now you can buy a tube pass with your rail ticket. In Holland, a scheme called Treintaxi allows rail passengers to pay for the taxi from the station to their final destination as part of their rail ticket. However, the government would need to intervene to facilitate seamless travel using different modes as so many different operators are involved.

By charging road users to use certain roads, or to enter city centres, or by placing a prohibitive charge on city centre carparks will also deter motorists. Leicester has trialed a dashboard-mounted smart card system that charges motorists to enter the city centre and with a higher charge at rush hour. This card can also be used to pay for the park and ride scheme which works out much cheaper than taking the car into the city centre.

Large employers can work out their own measures. In Plymouth, Derriford Hospital has an innovative scheme to reduce the 3 million car journeys its 5,000 staff make each year. Some bus routes, unchanged from the 1950s, were remapped using computers. Staff can travel to work using a subsidised smart card for £1 per day. Staff who drive are charged to use the hospital car park unless they bring another staff member with them, and then parking is free.

You might have come up with some other interesting ideas, but it is likely that many measures have now been brought in to deter the car user and promote public transport.

CHANGE IN OWNERSHIP

As you saw in Unit 2, changes in government policies towards state-run monopolies has meant that many organisations, from British Airways to British Gas, have been privatised. This privatisation has forced large changes in organisational and individual values. Profits as well as service have become an essential part of the new culture. Control is not through direct state intervention but through the marketplace and government regulators.

Twenty years ago, utility operations – gas, water, electricity, rail and public road transport – may have been described as public services; privatisation has vastly affected the structure and delivery of these services. The restructuring of these industries has been driven by the desire to achieve greater efficiency and service by introducing competition. In the case of electricity. three distinct aspects of the supply of electricity were identified:

- generation of electricity
- distribution of electricity
- sale of electricity.

There have been further developments in the formation of local utility companies. South Western Electricity, for example, supplies domestic consumers with gas, electricity, water and even telephone services. Such regional organisations can generate savings by cost reductions in reading meters and billing their customers.The case study below illustrates the way in which the structure of the domestic gas supply industry has changed significantly.

CASE STUDY

Domestic gas supply

The UK's gas comes from a variety of oil companies that have exploited the North Sea. They not only produce gas but oil to be refined into petrol. They sell this gas into the distribution network. The national distribution of gas in the UK is by Transco, a national company solely responsible for gas distribution. Gas can be sold to consumers by licensed operators who buy the gas from the suppliers, and use the national gas distribution system.

This arrangement has allowed many new organisations to enter the gas market such as South West Electricity. Calor gas is a company that supplies bottled gas to campers, caravaners and to remote cottages. To exploit the changes, Calor linked with a North Sea oil company to form Calortex, enabling Calor to supply gas to mains consumers for the first time.

Gas is dangerous and gas sales organisations are not able to provide the necessary safety cover. Emergency services for gas leaks is the responsibility of Transco. The supply of consumer services such as the sale, installation and maintenance of appliances may be done by the sellers of gas or independent firms. Calor has a range of agents and distributors for its bottled gas and for the sale of appliances. This provides Calor with a structure of complementary customer support.

Note the structure of the industry: the source of the gas, who distributes gas to domestic customers, who sells gas to domestic consumers, who provides emergency service (leaks) and who provides domestic service (supply and maintenance of gas appliances). Previously, this whole area came under the state-owned British Gas. Now many companies are involved, and the consumer expects to get a better service with keener pricing as they now have a choice.

In the 1990s, many building societies have changed from a membership arrangement to open market shareholdings, giving many individuals their first experience of being a different type of stakeholder with different returns, different risks and different expectations. Not all have viewed this as a positive step and, in 1997, Nationwide members voted against converting into a bank and floating on the Stock Exchange.

REVIEW ACTIVITY 4

Over a long period of time, town councils in the UK have built up substantial amounts of council property. It requires a big housing department to manage these properties, responsibilities include collection of rents, maintenance, repairs and renovation. However, in many areas the council property has been sold to individual tenants or sold to housing associations. The association has taken over the tasks of the housing department and takes responsibility for administration, maintenance and renovation.

Suggest some concerns that might be generated about this change of ownership of the housing stock from the state to the private or voluntary sector. Consider, separately, the views of:

- tenants
- maintenance staff.

What would be the best way to implement the changes with the tenants?

Unit Review Activitiy

Langstone Charts

Langstone Charts is a small family company that has been established for over fifty years. It supplies charts and navigational instruments to leisure and sporting sailors. It is located on the waterside of a marina in south-east England. The business moved to its present location in 1990 when the marina was built. However over the last few years, sales of charts and traditional navigational instruments have started to decline. Last year, a new company opened up just a few hundred yards away called Blue Sky Windows. This company specialised in the new generation of electronic instruments including GPS, auto pilots and electronic charts.

GPS (Global Positioning Systems) was introduced by the USA military to provide accurate navigation for ships, aircraft and guided missiles. The system relies on a set of satellites which provide positioning signals. Ten years ago, these systems cost in excess of £10,000; now, a hand-held GPS system can be purchased for less than £300. This technology linked to autopilots – that can steer a boat without manual intervention – and digitised charts on a computer screen are rendering traditional charts and navigational instruments obsolete.

Jean Fleming has just taken over Langstone Charts from her father who has retired. She has recognised that either the company changes and adapts to the new situation in some way or it will gradually go out of business. The present shop has a staff of four who understand traditional instrumentation well and are worried about the future.

Jean visited the London boat show and noted that the competition are not just selling the new equipment but offering a fitting service, training and a mail order service. The sales people appeared more computer-orientated than boat-orientated and are well versed in the new technology.

Jean has discussed her business problem with you and she has concluded that she needs to take her company into sales of the electronic equipment, with the provision of facilities for mail order and installation. She has asked you to prepare a report for her, examining some of the issues which this would raise. She is concerned about the organisational issues, environmental influences, cultural and change issues that need to be managed. Structure your short report under the headings: organisational issues, environmental influences (PEST), competition issues, information needs and change issues.

Unit Summary

The forces in the environment provide drivers requiring organisations to adapt. Any of the PEST factors and competition may, singly or in conjunction, force a change onto an organisation. Failure to adapt will involve loss of competitive position and possibly force the organisation out of business.

The simple model of change suggests that the change process consists of a number of steps, from recognition of a disturbance followed by a decision that the disturbance is significant resulting in a decision that some action may be necessary. The next steps are very creative in that the problem must be defined in appropriate terms and innovative potential solutions searched for and an appropriate one selected. The final stages are to consolidate and apply the solution and to provide control systems to continue to adapt the solution. Change is not a 'once and for all' activity but a way of commercial life.

Threats to pay, security, relationships, status, values, power and skills are all possibilities perceived by the individual or a work group. These forces must be managed. Even if the change requires downsizing the organisation and causes redundancy, this must be well managed not only for the staff that have to leave but for the staff that remain. If the changes are not well managed, staff may just consider it will be their turn next and become demotivated.

References

Mintzberg, H, James, BQ, and Ghoshal, S (1998) *The Strategy Process*, Revised European edn, pp 233 – 252,

Moore, W and Pessemier, E (1993) *Product Planning and Management: Designing and Delivering Value*, McGraw-Hill

Porter, M (1980) *Competitive Strategy*, Macmillan

Thompson, J (1993) *Strategic Management: Awareness and Change*, Chapman and Hall 2nd edn

Recommended Reading

Dun and Bradstreet's Market Identifiers

ICC British Company Directory and Financial Datasheets

Jordan's Registered Companies

Johnson, G (1992) Managing strategic change: strategy, culture and action, *Long Range Planning*, 25

Lewin, K (1952) *Field Theory in Social Science,* London: Tavistock

Porter, M (1985) *Competitive Advantage: Creating and Sustaining Superior Performance,* Free Press

FT analysis reports

See also recommended reading in Unit 2 for environmental analysis sources.

Answers to Review Activities

Review Activity 1

You may have chosen a very stable time or very stable companies. For example, you might have chosen BP, British Airways, Marks and Spencer, Reuters, Commercial Union, Schroders, Cable and Wireless, Abbey National, Burmah Oil, Scottish Power. These are a wide range of different types of company and from varied industries. You might have taken an easy option and just checked very popular companies that a newspaper might report on regularly. You may have picked up an array of developments about the company that concern stakeholders in some manner including:

- staff movements
- industrial action by staff
- award of bonuses to bosses or staff
- scandal about a director with conflicting interests
- mergers, demergers, alliances with competitors, suppliers and buyers
- major purchases or sales of competitors, suppliers and buyers
- takeovers or restructuring of a major competitor
- bankruptcy of a supplier or buyer
- dividend payouts to shareholders
- advertisements or notices to shareholders
- suspending of shares
- major selling of shares by individual or institutional investors
- questions asked about company or individual's activities in Parliament
- lobbying of professional or consumer groups
- activities of government, regulator or watchdog committees
- announcements about new products or new technology
- price increase on products or services
- advertisements to customer.

You are likely to have picked up a whole range of fluctuations in the share prices. Can you see any linkages with any of the above events? At this level of analysis, it is unlikely that you will be able to tell very much but it will give you an idea of what you need to track in a real situation. Note any movements in your shares, and also the overall movements in London and in other world stock markets. Are your companies following general trends, perhaps caused by a change in interest rates, exchange rates or world events, or are they reacting to events in their own competitive environment? Can you identify the roles taken by stakeholders, and any of their effects? Can you identify conflicts between any of the different stakeholder groups? For example, perhaps you can identify conflicts of interest between management and staff, shareholders and employees, customers and management.

Review Activity 2

Benetton is in the designing, manufacturing and fashion retailing business. Its value chain consists of taking raw materials, and making and then selling fashion items. The company must keep up with trends and tastes worldwide and there is seasonal demand in each geographical market.

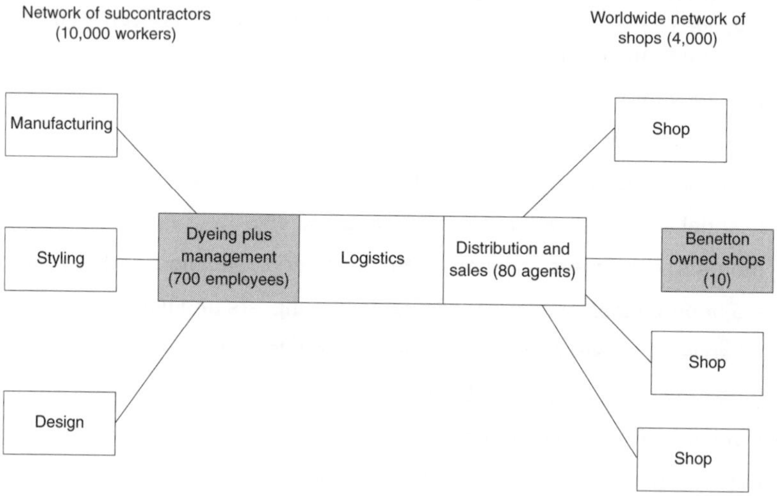

Figure 3: Benetton's value chain and supply chain

We can break down its activities (Figure 3). The company owns those areas shaded in grey. All other activities, including styling, design, manufacturing, logistics, distribution and retailing, are subcontracted to other organisations. As you can see, the company has a very small core activity. Subcontracting has the advantages of flexibility and low cost labour for manufacturing. Sales through franchise-type arrangements allows the company to avoid heavy investment in retail outlets. Benetton has developed a large and influential network of retail outlets supplied with its identical products all over the world. This allows the company to retain flexibility in an industry notorious for its volatility. Ownership of ten shops, in key locations, means it can continue to keep an eye on the marketplace.

Co-ordination and management of all activities, including marketing, are high value-added, core activities, and are undertaken by Benetton. It is essential that it keeps central control over the company's diversified activities. It has some control over its suppliers and buyers through tight contracts, size of orders and family shareholdings. This vast de-integrated network of subcontractors means that suppliers and buyers are always being put under pressure to perform. Benetton did, however, find the management of such a large and complex set of subcontracting relationships hard. By the late 1980s, it sought to restrict the number of subcontracted production units and members of the Benetton family bought shares in the largest subcontractor companies thus giving them more control with this flexible set-up.

Review Activity 3

There are a considerable number of factors and your selection may be different. In this business situation, the manager would have to consider the full range of factors carefully as this is such a fast developing sector. The industry life cycle will be short and the environment is complex and unstable.

Political and legal. Copyright is a difficult area as users have access to information provided by any other user. This may give rise to unauthorised distribution of copyright material. Given the open access, governments will find it difficult to control information directly and they may attempt to do this through the access providers.

Economic. Any organisation is subject to changes in the interest rates and the general health of the economy

Social. A key issue is the rate of growth of Internet connections. The new services are expected to lead to rapid growth in associated infrastructure and equipment. The manager will need to estimate the rate of the growth to provide sufficient capacity. In the early stages, growth was so rapid that providers could not keep up and access times became seriously degraded. The medium will provide the capability to provide material such as computer programs, so the manager will need to evaluate the potential of this market and opportunities for profitable exploitation. The open access allows the dissemination of material that may be regarded as offensive and parents may well be concerned about their children's access to such material. Shopping patterns may gradually change with more on-line access, so more and more people want to use the Internet for leisure purposes not just information.

Technological. Convergence of computer, communication and television technologies will allow increases in the provision of services such as CD and video on demand and the downloading of computer programs. The system allows open access, so it provides a channel for the distribution of computer viruses; providers may need to provide up to date virus checkers to protect their users.

Other significant factors are low entry barriers and the fact that there is little that can be done to distinguish services from competitors, so competition will be through price. One that seems to be successful is Virgin Net which, in 1997, claimed 50,000 subscribers and was growing at the rate of 10,000 new subscribers each month, Virgin expects 150,000 to 200,000 subscribers by 1998. One distinguishing feature of this service is an e-mail from Richard Branson welcoming each new subscriber. The service is developing a web site as part of on-line services aimed at non-technical customers including young people and parents of young children and as a means for selling CDs from Virgin Megastores, booking theatre tickets and selling books.

Review Activity 4

The tenants are in a difficult position as there is not much they can really do about any changes if they want to continue to live in the properties. The major concern is probably financial in that they may have concerns about rent increases. Previously, rents were controlled by the council. How is the housing association to work? Who has control over it? Is somebody going to make money out of them? Do tenants have any different rights? Who will they call when they have a plumbing problem? What happens if they get into arrears? What has happened to their friend in the council office that always handled things for them? The tenants knew the system and what to do if anything went wrong, they knew that their rents were controlled and repairs would be fixed.

To handle the change, tenants need to be informed well in advance about what will happen and when, to be allowed to participate as much as possible, and they need to be reassured that rents will be monitored carefully and repairs carried out promptly and efficiently. It is important to communicate procedures in the changeover and to identify the responsibilities of all parties. With the housing association, tenants may be able to participate in the running of their properties, they may have and they will expect better service and repairs as a commercial organisation is now controlling the operation.

For the maintenance staff, the major concern is the potential threat of job losses. If they worked full-time for the council, either as an employee or as a subcontractor, then their job with the council is obviously under threat. The housing association can still hire them, again as employer or as a subcontractor, but they will now need to compete with other suppliers. They are likely to have to perform a better service and be more competitive on price to get the housing association business.

Answer to Unit Review Activity

Organisational issues

Though the charts and instruments are in decline, there is still a significant business so for the present operation could be maintained in some reduced form. Perhaps this side of the business could be built up by positioning charts and traditional navigational equipment as suitable for decorative purposes, or to position them as products to be used in addition to the new gadgets. From our discussion with Jill, it would appear that we need to devote the greater part of the sales area to the new electronics, develop a mail order section and retain the services of experts who can install the new equipment and support users. This will represent both a significant change and increase in the scope of the firm's activity.

PEST

Political and legal. This is taking the company into new areas of electronics with different standards for installation and safety. There are also issues about warranty and after-sales service which again do not occur with the sale of charts.

Economic. The major factor in the economic environment will be the general health of the economy. Sales of equipment will be linked to the sale of middle-range boats in this marina and others nearby – a market affected very dramatically by inflation, interest rates, etc.

Social. The new technology provides an element of 'trendiness', so it could appeal to young sailors who need the latest equipment, and efforts will be needed to persuade older sailors that are used to using traditional ways that the new technology is not just a new-fangled gadget that they won't be able to use. Langstone Charts needs to look at the demographics of boat owners and its current customer base, and to pitch the new business appropriately.

Technological. The whole field of electronics is fast moving and Langstone will need to monitor new product developments carefully. There will be a continual training need to keep staff knowledgeable about the latest developments and new products to market. Stock will need to be watched carefully, obsolescence could be a problem. A key issue could be price. GPS systems previously costing £10,000 are now available for just a few hundred pounds; in a few years they could cost even less. This will again change the marketplace.

Competition

Following Porter's model, direct competition is the most significant threat. Langstone Charts has a competitor on its doorstep. If it cannot compete on price and service with the same product then perhaps there is no future in this market anyway. Obviously Blue Sky Windows will respond to the competition, so Langstone have to look ahead and be really sure about what they are offering the customer. Perhaps they are sure that sailors will buy from a shop that has long experience in the traditional way of sailing, rather than from a computer expert. However, the customer will still want Langstone to at least match the price and the service that Blue Sky offers. The company will need to make substantial investment in stock and training – so will it be able to price accordingly?

The establishment of Blue Sky Windows might indicate that other computer-based companies could come into the sector. The sourcing of equipment may be an issue as the company will need to arrange agency terms with selected suppliers. In terms of buyers, there is likely to be little brand loyalty and we can anticipate a very competitive market. The organisation will have to become much more responsive and active with promotions than it has in the past with the relatively stable market in the sale of charts. There does not appear to be much problem with substitute products.

Information issues

Again, the firm will need to be much more responsive. There will be a need to find out potential sources of the new equipment so that it can make the right approaches for agency relationships. There will be a need to profile the companies that

Langstone wishes to work with, for example it would not want to become agents to a company that goes out of business because its lacks financial stability. It will need a close relationship with the supplier, so it only makes the minimum of investment in stock, but it will need to guarantee quality and delivery to its customers. Langstone will need to track market and technology developments so it can sell the products in a convincing way. With the increased marketing activity there will be a need to check out which approaches are working and which are not. For the mail order business, there will be a need to work with databases. Overall the company will need to go into an area where much more information will be required and the information sources will be fast changing. This is a significant change issue.

Change issues

The existing staff know much about an area which is of decreasing importance to the firm. There will be a need to train them in the new technologies and to recruit new staff. Some redundancies may have to be made. There may be some fear and resistance to change on the part of the existing staff. Job functions will change and, with new ways of selling through mail order, they will lose contact with customers and their customers will change. The whole selling process will change and become much more dependent on a competitive price and the installation and training services offered. A chart sale was easy and often based on a very personal relationship with a well-known customer. Langstone needs to use this relationship in its new business, but it won't be quite so 'cosy' with a piece of technical equipment. There will be the need to establish a new culture in the organisation to meet the challenge of the more turbulent environment that is based on technology and sailing, not just sailing. Staff who are just interested in 'the sea' and do not like technology will find the new organisation hard to adjust to and will probably leave despite any training given to them.

UNIT 4
MARKETING

Introduction

Organisations exist to 'do something', taking inputs and transforming them into outputs with added value. These outputs, either products or services, need to meet the customer's needs otherwise they will not be bought. Through the income that is generated by sales, the organisation is able to fund the whole process and hopefully make a profit. Marketing is a crucial function within the organisation and is one of Porter's primary activities as it defines the market, the product and the customer. In this unit, we look at key features of these three elements and show how marketing brings them together for competitive advantage.

In a commercial situation, organisations need people to buy their products and services. Income is usually measured as units of money and buying is the transfer of money from buyer to seller. However, this does not always have to be the case. Fire services need income, for example, but they do not directly sell their services to the general public. Nevertheless, they must persuade the funding bodies to provide the income they need – they must persuade them to 'buy' their services. During this unit, we will mostly refer to the conventional commercial situation in which a product or service is 'bought' for money. However, throughout this unit you should continue to think about buyers and sellers in the widest possible way.

In this unit, we examine the role of marketing in the organisation and the key characteristics of the function. In other marketing modules, you will take this preliminary investigation further.

Objectives

At the end of this unit, you will be able to:

- distinguish between marketing as a functional activity and as a business philosophy
- explain the importance of the consumer to the organisation
- evaluate the applicability of different business orientations
- describe the marketing concept
- identify the main elements of a marketing plan
- explain how markets are segmented and targets selected
- identify the role of marketing research
- describe the main stages of the market research process
- describe how primary data is collected
- discuss the nature of and describe the elements of the marketing mix.

SECTION 1

Introduction to Marketing

Introduction

Although the basic ideas that comprise marketing are relatively straightforward, marketing often means different things to different people. Many people think that marketing is just another word for selling, but it is very much more than that. In this section, we examine why marketing is so important in modern business. We look at the primary tasks of marketing managers and the extent to which different types of organisation are able to use marketing. You will become familiar with the words and phrases used in marketing.

We investigate the difference between marketing as a function and as a business philosophy and recognise that there are different business orientations.

1.1 What is marketing?

The term 'marketing' is a relatively recent addition to the business dictionary, but the fundamental ideas behind marketing are very much older; Thorelli (1983, p. 5), for example, argues that marketing began with Adam and Eve! The first written work that many academics recognise as containing the seeds of modern marketing thought was published by Adam Smith in 1776. He wrote: 'Consumption is the sole end and purpose of all production; the interests of the producer ought to be attended to only as far as it may be necessary for promoting that of the consumer'.

Modern marketing, however, is largely a twentieth century phenomenon. It dates from around the very end of the nineteenth century in the USA and developed particularly from the late 1920s when the ability of the American economy to produce began to exceed demand (Stanton, 1971, p. 5). The great development in marketing took place in the period following the Second World War, in particular in companies like General Electric, Proctor and Gamble and General Motors. Michael Baker (1995) argues that the approach to marketing recognised and practised today dates from the publication of *Marketing Myopia*, the seminal work of Theodore Levitt (1960, pp. 24–47). Baker goes on to assert that marketing only really became an accepted function within business outside of the USA from this time.

ACTIVITY 1

In not more than 50 words, write down what you think marketing is. When you have completed this activity keep it ready to use a little later in this section.

The word marketing is derived from the Latin word *mercatus*, meaning marketplace, a meeting place for the purpose of trade. Trade is the process of exchange and so a marketplace is a place where exchange occurs. An exchange is the 'transfer of goods, services or ideas in return for something of value', Dibb, Simpkin, Pride and Ferrell (1994, p. 4). Marketing is therefore the facilitation of exchange relationships and a market is 'a collection of people sharing a common want or need and who are motivated to enter into exchange processes to satisfy that need or want', Proctor (1996, p. 3). When marketers use the term 'market' they normally talk in terms of size (by total value or by volume of units demanded) and of the characteristics of the consumers within the market.

The notion of exchange is at the very heart of marketing. If human beings could exist without needing to become involved in an exchange process, then marketing would not itself exist. In the typical marketing situation, the exchange occurs between buyer and seller, where the seller exchanges goods, services or ideas with the buyer, for something the seller wants. This is typically, but not necessarily, money. Successful exchanges require three conditions:

- parties to the exchange must be able to offer to each other something of value that each wants
- communication must exist between the parties
- the exchange must be satisfying to both parties – each party must feel that it has gained more than it has given up.

Marketing is a term that is often misused and misunderstood. It can mean very different things to different people. If you asked 100 people at random the question 'what is marketing?', you would probably get 100 different responses. The responses would range from the very *specific* such as 'marketing is selling', 'another word for advertising', 'all about packaging'; through to the very *general*, for example 'marketing is everything an organisation does'. It would also no doubt include responses from people that view marketing as some form of exploitation perpetrated by organisations upon the unsuspecting public.

The specific responses would show the very wide-ranging nature of marketing and would include suggestions that it is concerned with advertising, setting prices, selling, launching new products, conducting market research, public relations, retailing and many, many more activities. There would be many more examples of the specific than of the general. This is not so surprising, since it is the specific activities of marketing that are the most visible to people, both as employees and consumers. Most people believe that marketing is about these specific activities. However, as we shall see, although marketing does include such activities it is a much more wide-ranging term than is at first obvious.

Peter Drucker, a well-known writer on management, states: 'Marketing is not only much broader than selling ... it encompasses the entire business. It is the whole business seen from the point of view of its final result, that is, from the customer's point of view. Concern and responsibility for marketing must, therefore, permeate all areas of the enterprise', Drucker (1968, p. 56). Drucker suggests that marketing is a general and total approach to business, an approach that can be used to give direction to all of the activities of an organisation. It is a philosophy of business, a basis upon which to operate the whole organisation.

Thus marketing can have these two apparently separate meanings: it can be used to describe a set of activities and it can represent a general approach to business. We will examine both meanings, but first we consider some definitions of marketing.

DEFINITIONS OF MARKETING

Definitions try to provide a succinct summary of a topic. However, there is no single universally accepted definition of marketing; indeed, there have been many advanced by writers and speakers and these have tended to change over time. Lancaster and Massingham (1993, p. 2) describe marketing as 'a chameleon word, apt to mean whatever the user wants it to mean'. In Lamb's view (1965, p. 43):

> [Marketing] has been described by one person or another as a business activity; as a group of related business activities; as a trade phenomenon; as a frame of mind; as a co-ordinative, integrative function in policy making; as a sense of business purpose; as an economic process; as a structure of institutions; as the process of exchanging or transferring ownership of products; ... and as many other things.

Given the very wide-ranging nature of marketing and the way that it is both a set of specific activities and a business philosophy, it is perhaps not surprising that there have been so many attempts at providing a succinct definition. Some writers, McCarthy and Perreault (1993, pp. 8–10) have drawn a distinction between definitions of micro-marketing and of macro-marketing. Micro-marketing is defined around a set of activities carried out by an individual organisation. Macro-marketing concentrates on the processes which allows suppliers and consumers to interact across a whole society. Others, Proctor (1996, p. 2) have pointed out that attempts at definition have always reflected the era within which they were written and were appropriate at that time, but have subsequently been superseded. This indicates the dynamic nature of exchange relationships. The problem in defining marketing is that incorporating all facets of the discipline into a short statement is very difficult.

Definitions which are appropriate and usable share four basic characteristics:

- a certainty that satisfying the customer is the key to success – the consumer therefore stands at the centre of organisational activity
- an acceptance that organisations are value driven – there is a need for organisations to make profits
- a belief that both parties in a transaction must gain if there is to be a long-term relationship
- a recognition that marketing operates in a dynamic environment – that change is inevitable and therefore marketing must be proactive.

The main professional body for marketing in the United Kingdom, the Chartered Institute of Marketing, defines marketing as:

> ... the management process responsible for identifying, anticipating and satisfying consumers' requirements efficiently and profitably.

The American Marketing Association defines marketing as:

> ... the process of planning and executing the conception, pricing, promotion and distribution of ideas, goods and services to create exchanges that will satisfy individual and organisational objectives.

MARKETING AS A FUNCTIONAL ACTIVITY

The commonest way of viewing marketing is probably as a functional activity. Increasingly, organisations tend to have a department called marketing or some area within which the term marketing is used. In this department, various specialists will come together to use a whole range of tools and techniques to meet some defined set of objectives. The activities performed will include advertising, sales, merchandising, setting prices, market research, distribution, customer services, public relations, new product development among others. It is the marketing department that interfaces with customers, and it usually has some role in terms of customer liaison before, during and after the sale. Marketing as a function, therefore, brings together the different activity areas that we previously identified. It is the 'doing' part of marketing, Cameron, Rushton and Carson, (1988, p. 20).

As a functional activity, marketing:

- decides on the organisation's customers
- arranges for the necessary exchange processes to occur
- facilitates their successful conclusion.

The wide range of interrelated and interdependent activities that marketing managers can use to achieve these two latter objectives for the organisation are often referred to as the controllable variables of marketing, McCarthy, and Perreault (1993, p. 44). The selection and manipulation of the appropriate controllable variables by marketing managers is known as the creation of a marketing mix. The elements of the marketing mix include product, price, promotion and place. We consider the marketing mix in more detail later.

Those who view marketing as primarily a functional area of business activity may see it as an equal, inferior or superior partner of the other business functions such as production and human resource management.

MARKETING AS A BUSINESS PHILOSOPHY

The functional activities of marketing have been practised in organisations for many years. The way in which the activities are applied has, however, varied greatly and indeed still does. The particular way depends upon the organisation's basic business orientation. This approach guides its overall activities and directs its decision making.

Kotler (1997, p. 17) suggests that there are five basic business orientations. They are often considered as historical, developmental and sequential as organisations have tended to progress through the orientations as time passed and as they, and the economy in which they operated, have developed. However, organisations do not change their business orientation just as a result of the passage of time. Today, both newly formed and older organisations may be using any of the five orientations.

Kotler's five business orientations are:

- production
- product
- sales
- marketing
- societal marketing.

Production orientation

In the nineteenth century and the early part of the twentieth century, the biggest problem faced by the manufacturing sectors of the economy was to satisfy demand. Demand outstripped supply and the main problem for individual organisations was to make as much as possible. Organisations tended to concentrate upon the production process, using mass production techniques to produce an extremely limited range of basic products, thereby increasing output and bringing down costs. As costs fall so the price charged by the organisation can fall thereby allowing more people to be able to buy the product. It was thought that profit was generated through manufacturing volume. Henry Ford's statement about the Model T motor car produced by his Ford Motor Company, 'you can have any colour you want as long as it's black', is an example of a production orientation. In organisations using the production concept, the production and finance functions will be the main functional areas.

Such an approach was appropriate to the circumstances of the time, but as the ability to supply began to overtake the demand for goods and services so a changed approach was needed. Today this production orientation is still used in it's original form by some service providers; for example, doctors, hospitals and some dentists operate on a production line basis in order to see as many patients as possible. A production orientation is also used in a modified form by some manufacturers. It is not uncommon for newly formed small businesses to attempt to use a production orientation.

Product orientation

The product orientation is a modified form of the production orientation – the organisation still focuses on producing what it is good at, however here the concentration is not on using the production process to produce the cheapest possible product but on the product or service itself, and the driving orientation is to produce products that have more quality, features, styles and performance. The organisation believes that building what it sees as a better product is the way to greater sales and, therefore, success. It concentrates on producing what it believes to be the right product, rather than finding out what the consumer thinks is the right product.

Sales orientation

Once it became apparent that supply exceeded demand, organisations realised that it was no longer sufficient for goods to be merely produced; consumers had a choice and could choose to buy or not to buy an individual organisation's offerings. Organisations responded to this by concentrating on selling. Operating with a sales orientation means making the heart of organisational activity the sales effort. The sales orientation is based on a belief that consumers have a natural aversion to purchasing and that this can only be overcome by the use of aggressive selling techniques and vigorous promotion.

Practitioners of this approach believe that the consumer can always be persuaded to buy more if the right sales techniques are used. Advertising, sales promotions and other techniques used in modern marketing are all practised in the sales orientation, but the emphasis in their use is always on aggressive selling. Profit, it is suggested, is obtained through sales volume.

A sales orientation is likely to be effective only in the short term, since it does not concern itself with generating customer loyalty; a sale to a particular customer is seen as being a one-off event. Fitted kitchens, double glazing and encyclopaedias are often quoted as examples of products where a sales orientation is often practised Lancaster and Massingham (1993, pp. 12–13). Hill and O'Sullivan (1996, p. 16) argue that 'election campaigns are characterised by similar approaches; promises may be made that prove impossible to fulfil, but once elected a candidate need not worry about getting votes for another five years'.

Organisations using a sales orientation will usually give a sales department equal status to the finance, production and human resource departments.

Marketing orientation

The marketing orientation approaches business from the opposite direction. The production, product and sales orientations are all inward looking, concentrating on the organisation. The marketing orientation, on the other hand, concentrates on the consumer; it looks out from the organisation. The marketing orientation holds that an organisation will survive and prosper in the long term if it produces the goods and services that people want. To do this, it is necessary to decide which customers the organisation wishes to serve, to discover their needs and wants and then to produce the appropriate goods and services to satisfy these needs and wants. The primary objective is to have satisfied customers, because satisfied customers return and bring their friends with them!

Theodore Levitt (1960, pp. 24–47) explained the difference between the sales and marketing orientations: 'Selling focuses on the needs of the seller; marketing on the needs of the buyer. Selling is preoccupied with the seller's need to convert his product into cash; marketing with the idea of satisfying the needs of the consumer by means of the product and the whole cluster of things associated with creating, delivering and finally consuming it.'

To those organisations operating with a genuine marketing orientation, the consumer is always the key and is always the centre of organisational activity. Peter

Drucker (1973, pp. 64–65) argues that the true objective of a marketing orientation is to produce products and services that so satisfy the consumer, they make selling superfluous! He accepts, however, that this will rarely happen in practice. Figure 1 illustrates the selling and marketing orientations.

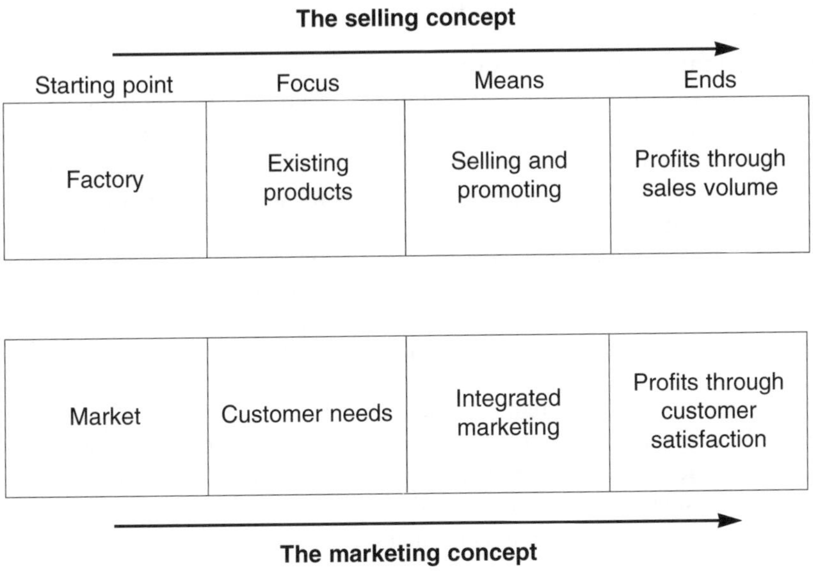

The selling concept
Starting point
Focus
Means
Ends
Factory
Existing products
Selling and promoting
Profits through sales volume
Market
Customer needs
Integrated marketing
Profits through customer satisfaction
The marketing concept

Figure 1: Selling and marketing concepts

ACTIVITY 2

Supra Company manufactures a range of dishwashers. It receives a letter from a customer asking if it can make and sell a totally silent dishwasher. Although this is technically impossible at present, describe the reaction the letter might provoke in:

- an organisation with a sales orientation
- an organisation with a marketing orientation.

Write a short paragraph of the likely reaction for each orientation.

An organisation with a sales orientation would accept that a totally silent dishwasher could not be manufactured at present but would attempt to sell the customer a model from the existing range. If it was unsuccessful, it would examine its sales techniques to try to ensure that it did not fail to sell a dishwasher the next time.

An organisation with a marketing orientation would use the letter as an indication of a potential customer need and would seek further information. It would seek to find out whether there was sufficient customer demand for a silent dishwasher to make its manufacture a viable proposition for the Supra Company. At the same time, it would try to discover why the customer wanted a silent dishwasher and whether the particular need could be satisfied in some other way, perhaps by offering additional benefits with an existing product. If there was sufficient demand and a real need for a truly silent dishwasher, the organisation would then seek to develop the necessary new technology.

Societal marketing orientation

The four previous orientations have all been concerned with supplying goods and services to individual consumers and have ignored the needs of society. However, it is possible that in satisfying customers in the short term, society may be damaged in the longer term. For example, the desire of western consumers for hardwood mahogany products has led to the gradual destruction of large tracts of the world's rainforests which in turn causes detrimental effects to a very wide range of people; the growing demand for disposable plastic products causes serious waste management problems; the demand for cheap beef products led to the use of cheaper foodstuffs for cattle and ultimately caused BSE in British beef cattle.

The societal marketing orientation suggests that organisations should seek to balance the needs of the individual consumer with those of society as a whole. They should produce and offer products and services which are to the long-term advantage of society as a whole, even though this may mean failing to satisfy the short-term desires of individual consumers; in other words, organisations should become socially responsible.

The main difficulty with this latest business orientation is that opinions on what is social responsibility lie with individuals and their own ethical positions. Many of the decisions are not easy. For example, should organisations manufacture and market cigarettes knowing the health dangers? Increasingly, customers are becoming more socially aware and more willing to boycott companies that do not meet the social standards they would want. But should business be the decider of what is right for society? Or is that more properly the role of elected representatives?

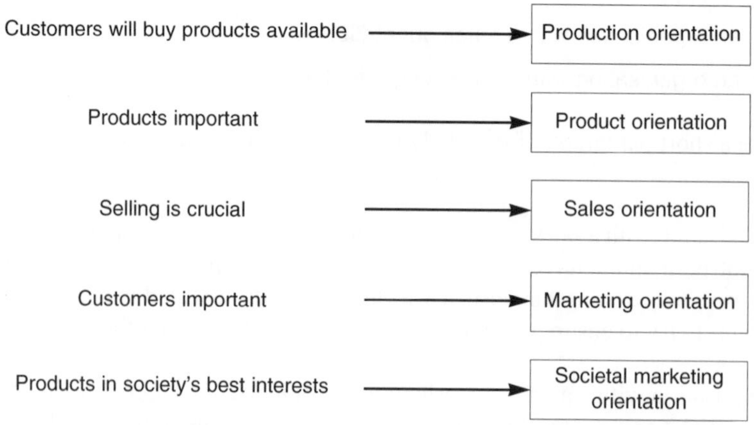

Figure 2: Business orientations

ACTIVITY 3

The following table contains a series of quotes from the owners of various businesses. For each quote, indicate which business orientation you think they are practising.

Quote	**Business orientation**				
	Production	Product	Sales	Marketing	Societal
We must add some extra nutrition to this cola drink					
Our products are the best on the market and they sell themselves					
We have the finest sales force and the biggest discounts in the industry, that is why we sell so many widgets					
This year we will open extra hours for the convenience of our shoppers					
We must as a priority continue to seek economies in the manufacture of our clothes and reduce the production time per garment					
This company exists only because consumers allow it to exist					
There will always be a need for clothes that are well made and durable					

A business practising a production orientation might say 'we must as a priority continue to seek economies in the manufacture of our clothes and reduce the production time per garment'. These next two quotes are evidence of a product orientation: 'our products are the best made on the market and sell themselves' and 'there will always be a need for clothes that are well made and durable'. A sales orientation is shown by 'we have the finest sales force and the biggest discounts in the industry that's why we sell so many widgets'. These two quotes are evidence of a marketing orientation: 'this year we will open extra hours for the convenience of our shoppers' and 'this company exists only because consumers allow it to exist'. A business with a societal marketing orientation might say 'we must add some extra nutrition to this cola drink'.

PHILOSOPHY OR FUNCTION?

We noted earlier that different writers give different responses to the question 'what is marketing?' The main confusion often arises because they want marketing to be either a philosophy or a function and many writers seem to suggest it must be one or the other. It is both!

As we have seen, it is an orientation that drives the business, but an orientation needs to be implemented and part of the practice requires the application of a set of management tools and techniques in order that the end objectives are achieved. Part of the function of marketing, therefore, is to identify the needs and wants of groups of consumers so that the whole organisation can act upon this knowledge. It is at the same time a philosophy and a function – the function enables the philosophy to be implemented.

ACTIVITY 4

Look at your answer to Activity 1. Have you changed your mind at all? If so, how would you rewrite your answer now?

Perhaps you have studied marketing before and so your answer to Activity 1 fits with your study of this unit so far. If you have not studied marketing before, however, it is likely that your first answer concentrated upon functional activities and, in particular, upon advertising and selling. In this case, your new answer should now emphasise marketing as a way of doing business based upon the customer. As a final stage to this activity compare both your original and latest answers to the definitions given earlier.

1.2 The marketing concept

An organisation which is using a marketing orientation is said to have adopted the **marketing concept**. The marketing concept is a way of thinking, a management philosophy that can be used to guide an organisation's overall activities. Organisations which apply the marketing concept will demonstrate acceptance of three key considerations:

- customer centrality
- co-ordinated effort
- goal orientation.

We consider each of these aspects in turn.

Customer centrality

The customer is the pivotal point of all organisational activity and all decisions within the organisation should be driven by the desire to satisfy the customer. There are many implications of customer centrality for an organisation, but the crucial ones for you to understand at this point are:

- there will be a substantial need for information – about consumers, about competitors, about suppliers and about the macro-environments
- this requirement is continuous – constant monitoring is needed
- the organisation will need to decide exactly which group(s) of customers it is trying to serve
- a matching of the needs of this defined group of consumers with the resources of the organisation is required.

An acceptance of the need to be customer centred will be reflected in the way an organisation defines the particular market within which it is operating. This definition needs to be based on consumers and not on the organisation or its products. Definitions based on the organisation or its products tend to be far too narrow and ultimately restricting to the organisation. To illustrate the difference between these two definitional approaches, consider the example of rail transport in Britain. In the nineteenth and the early part of the twentieth centuries, when the railways were doing very well, there seemed to be no problem with a market defined as 'the market for rail travel'. This was a definition based upon the product itself – the train. However, the advent of the motor car and of aircraft meant that the railways lost large parts of their markets and eventually many railway companies went out of business. Had they defined their market in terms of customers, perhaps as 'the market for the transportation of people and goods' they may well still be in business today. In Canada, Canadian Pacific railways moved into various other forms of transportation (airlines, haulage, etc.), as well as continuing in rail. It then moved into telecommunications to become one of the largest businesses involved in transportation.

ACTIVITY 5

Complete the table, providing customer-based descriptions of the business of a number of organisations. The first entry is completed as an example.

Organisation	Product-based description of business	Customer-based description of business
South West Trains	Rail travel	Transportation of people and goods
BT	Telephone calls	
Shell	Petroleum	
Swallow Hotels	Overnight accommodation and food	
Sainsbury	Retail of grocery products	
A college or university	Courses for students	

We have come up with these customer-based descriptions for the organisations in the table: provision of communication services (BT), provision of energy (Shell), leisure business (Swallow Hotels), provision of retail services to customers (Sainsbury), lifetime education for society (a college or university).

CO-ORDINATED EFFORT

The idea that the customer is the centre of all organisational effort leads naturally to the notion that all parts of the organisation should work together to ensure that the aim of customer satisfaction is achieved. Traditionally, most organisations are departmentalised. Each department tends to work in isolation, often considering itself the core of the company, and works to optimise it's own operations. The marketing concept requires that the organisation works as a total system, with the individual departments coming together to satisfy the customer, rather than as a collection of separate parts. As you saw in Unit 3, all primary and secondary activities of the organisation have a part to play in service, quality, profit and competitive advantage, and essentially this is the marketing approach. The function might operate as individual departments but they work together to achieve the goal of customer satisfaction. No single function is more important than any other, they all make an equal and vital contribution. Figure 3 shows the essential difference between the traditional departmentalised structure and the total system view.

GOAL ORIENTATION

In order to survive, organisations need to set and achieve objectives. In most commercial organisations, the need to generate profit will be one of the foremost objectives since it is profit that allows a commercial organisation to survive over the long term. But profit is only one objective that organisations set, and some organisations, such as the Fire Service, do not aim to generate financial profit at all. The important point is that clear objectives are set, whether they are economic or social. It is not enough that customer satisfaction is obtained; this is easy to achieveby giving away free products! The aim is to achieve customer satisfaction through the setting and achieving of organisational objectives.

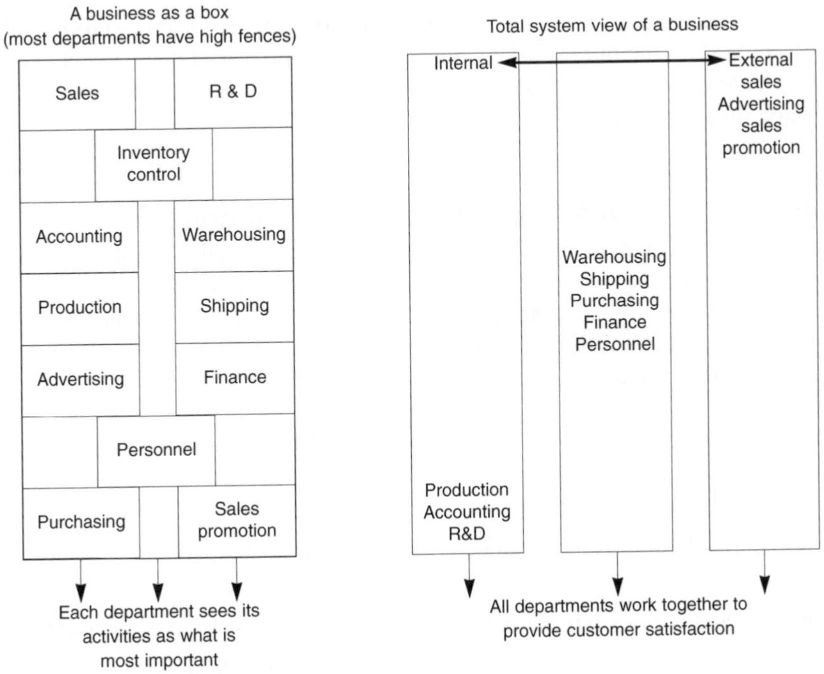

Figure 3: Departmentalised functional structure and total system view

Of course, it is perfectly possible for an organisation to claim to be marketing oriented. Many organisations claim that they are customer led, that they have embraced and adopted the marketing concept. Unfortunately, it is all too often the case that this claim is more honoured in the breach than in fact. Why should this be so? After all the essential nature of the marketing concept is simple, logical and attractive. The primary reason is that, in reality, the apparent simplicity of the marketing concept masks the difficulty faced by organisations when they attempt its implementation. What looks elegant and desirable in theory can be fraught with problems when it is translated into the reality of the working day. In addition, not only is it difficult to implement the marketing concept, but it is very easy (and tempting) to slip back into a production orientation. After all, who wants to open the shop during the evenings and at weekends? Wouldn't it be nice to stage the plays we enjoy rather than those the audience likes to watch but we don't like to perform? Many organisations find the marketing concept attractive, but the implementation very difficult.

ACTIVITY 6

Consider an organisation that you know something about – it might be where you work, or where you study, or where you go socially, a sports centre or a restaurant perhaps, or where you go shopping. Is it marketing orientated? Or does it just say that it is? If you are a customer, are your needs more important than those of the organisation? If you are an employee, are your customers' needs more important than those of the organisation? Can you see indications of the organisation working as a whole? Can you identify clear organisational objectives? Using our three key considerations, make brief notes to help you to decide your answers. List some ways the organisation could become more marketing orientated.

CRITICISM OF MARKETING AND THE MARKETING CONCEPT

One criticism frequently aimed at marketing is that it persuades people to buy what they do not need or want and in some way, therefore, causes damage to the individual. Marketing supporters reply that this criticism invokes the idea of the defenceless consumer; that the average consumer has little perceptive power and even less intelligence, and that they are simply gullible.

Some commentators have developed the example of the individual consumer a stage further and argued that the marketing concept has failed and that the whole of society has suffered as a result. They claim as evidence of this failure:

- the growth of the consumerist market shows that customers' needs are not being satisfied
- products are being produced which are clearly against the public interest
- consumer knowledge has led to dubious practices – for example, health insurance is sold using the 'fear factor' in its advertising
- the despoliation of parts of the world for the benefit of consumers in other parts
- the advent of conspicuous and excess consumption
- the waste of resources, for example, in packaging.

Although some of these examples are very persuasive, it is more probable that the concept has not failed, but that it has often been poorly implemented. Many organisations do not use a marketing orientation at all and others have applied it in name only, but not in spirit. Even in those organisations which have implemented the marketing concept, mistakes have, of course, been made, some intentionally but many quite unintentionally. Critics will always identify the mistakes! There are also, as in all areas of human activity, a small minority of dishonest and unscrupulous individuals prepared to advance their own objectives to the detriment of others and who will give their profession a bad name. Organisations will always face difficult external decisions, rarely are situations completely black and white; often, satisfying one set of consumers will infuriate another.

For an excellent discussion of whether marketing is unethical see Christopher and McDonald (1995, pp. 14–23).

SCOPE OF MARKETING AND THE MARKETING CONCEPT

Many people think that marketing only concerns fast-moving consumer goods produced by large companies in advanced western economies. While it is true that marketing has perhaps been most widely adopted by large private sector organisations operating in the consumer goods industries, the basic principles of marketing apply to a vast number of activities and gradually the marketing concept is being adopted by a wide range of organisations.

As we have seen, marketing is primarily about exchange. Organisations provide something that has value to the customer, who in turn provides something of value to the organisation. Often the something of value that is provided by the purchaser is money; but it does not have to be money. If you believe that all exchange involves money then you might also believe that marketing can only be of use to large, private, consumer goods companies.

ACTIVITY 7

Identify some exchange activities that do not involve direct transfer of money in exchange for a product or service? One example might be the act of voting for a political party.

There are many examples of situations where consumers 'buy' something but do not necessarily pay with money at the time of obtaining the product or service, although there may be some indirect payment at another time. Examples include:

- choosing a school, college or university, though now university students will possibly need to pay some tuition fees
- selecting a doctor or dentist through the NHS
- using the road system
- going to a church or other place of worship
- visiting a museum or art gallery
- using services provided by local government agencies or charities
- making a charitable donation
- borrowing books from a library
- calling an emergency service
- phoning a helpline.

Marketing came of age with the very large manufacturers of fast moving consumer goods, but its utility has now been recognised by just about every sector of activity in the advanced economies and by many areas in the emerging economies. In fact, marketing philosophies and practices can be used by any organisation or individual involved in an exchange process. Even the socialist economies used elements of the philosophy. Marketing is increasingly being used by a very wide range of organisations including:

- those involved in the production and sale of consumer goods
- those involved in the provision of consumer services
- those involved in business-to-business transactions
- public sector organisations, such as schools and colleges
- not-for-profit organisations, such as Oxfam
- small organisations.

ACTIVITY 8

In less than 50 words, explain why small businesses can use the marketing concept just as readily as large organisations.

Small businesses just like large businesses have customers, need to make profits and usually operate in competitive markets. In fact, it should be easier for a small business to obtain a clear customer focus since the owners of small businesses are normally in much more regular and direct contact with their customers and, as such, are in a very good position to be able to identify and respond to customer needs.

It is perhaps worth remembering that you can adopt the marketing concept for yourself. What is it that the people who 'buy' your activities (that is, your superiors, peers, tutors, etc.) want? How will they decide if you are giving them good value? Once you know this, then you can tailor your offering to ensure success. You can become customer centred in just the same way as an organisation can. You can adopt the marketing concept for yourself!

1.3 Marketing management

Marketing is the link between the organisation and its customers. Responsibility for ensuring the establishment and maintenance of a successful interlinking of organisation and customers lies with marketing management. Marketing managers are involved with:

- planning
- organisation
- control of marketing activity.

PLANNING

Marketing management can take part in planning at two distinct levels within the business. First, marketing has a major role to play in the planning of activities for the organisation as a whole. It should help to decide what business the organisation should be in, what markets it should serve and what products and services it should offer. Second, marketing management must take responsibility for the detailed planning of the activities of the marketing function, such as what advertising to carry out, how much to charge for the product, and the development of the organisation's sales force.

ORGANISATION

Marketing management must, as must all functional management, ensure the cost-effective operation of those activities for which it has responsibility. It must organise operations within the functional area of marketing in such a way as to ensure that targets are met.

In addition, marketing management must organise its relationships with the other functional areas of the organisation to ensure that the importance of the customer is at all times clear and that the whole organisation is sensitive to the market(s) it serves.

CONTROL

In order to ensure that plans are being implemented in such a way that targets and objectives are being met, marketing management must establish control systems. These are mechanisms which allow the level of performance to be assessed at any one time so that any deviations from the plans can be corrected. Control is a constant and continuous process that links not just with implementation, but with the planning stage itself. The feedback from control processes can often lead to changes being made to the plans, or indeed to new plans being produced. We can summarise these points with a very simple schematic of marketing management (Figure 4).

It is very important to note the continuous nature of the process. As the needs of the market change, so the ability of the organisation to satisfy these needs changes. It is vital that the organisation constantly adapts to changing market situations such that its resources and abilities are constantly in balance with the requirements of the marketplace.

Let's look a little more closely at how the marketing manager helps the organisation to achieve its objectives. What steps does he or she need to go through in order to be able to plan, implement and control marketing activities?

MARKETING IN PRACTICE

At the simplest level, marketing management has two basic tasks:

- selecting a group of consumers, that is, a target market
- developing a marketing mix to satisfy this target market.

Figure 4: Marketing management

Continual monitoring of the market is needed to ensure that both the target and the marketing mix are constantly appropriate to the satisfaction of the organisational objects.

The combination of choosing a target market and developing a marketing mix for that target is known as **marketing strategy.** Most organisations have more than one product which they offer to a market. Sometimes the products that an organisation offers may be similar – for example, Vauxhall's products include the different car models, the Corsa, Astra, Vectra, Omega, etc. – or they may be quite different – for example, Boots' products include soaps, throat lozenges, cosmetics, nappies and electric razors. A marketing strategy will be needed for each product market that an organisation wishes to operate in.

The marketing strategy provides a broad view of what the organisation intends to do in a specific market. The implementation of a strategy requires a plan. A **marketing plan** is a written document which explains in detail the target market, the marketing mix, the resources that will be needed to achieve the desired objectives, such as the money that will need to be spent and the human resources that will be needed, and the measures that will be used to assess the progress towards the objectives. These measures can be thought of as milestones along a path and could include sales targets, the extent of market penetration and the number of customers who have tried the product.

A **marketing programme** blends together the marketing plans of all an organisation's products into one coherent whole (Figure 5).

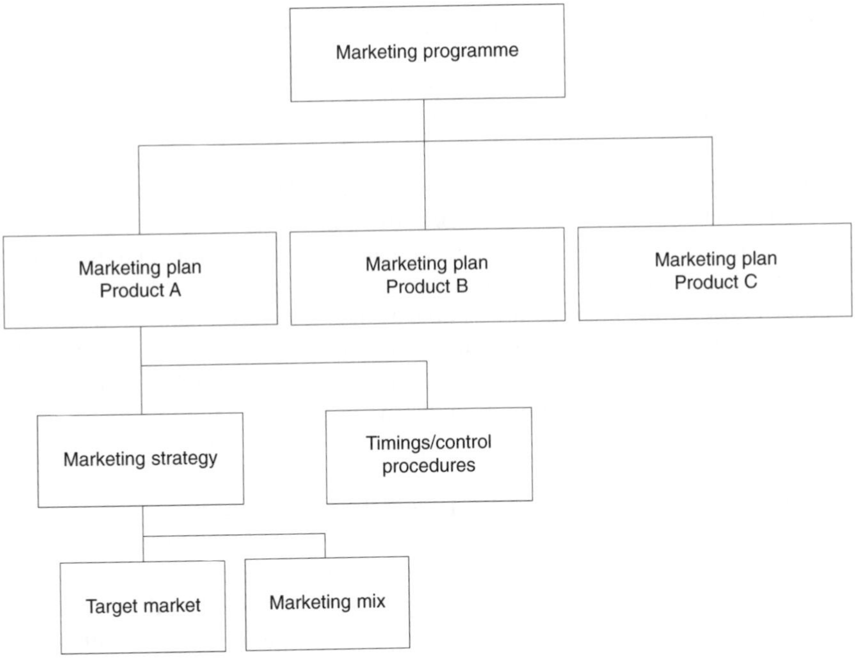

Figure 5: The marketing programme

REVIEW ACTIVITY 1

Read this scenario and then answer the questions that follow.

'It's good to talk!'

The board of Jimcrack plc is in session. All directors are present. Jimcrack is a manufacturing company that produces a range of domestic appliances in very competitive domestic markets. The current range comprises radios, enthusiast 'ham' radio equipment, complete MIDI hi-fi systems, portable radio-cassette units, headphones, electric kettles, electric toasters, electric carving knives, yoghurt makers, electric mixers and electric can openers. From its inception, the company has marketed a wide range of ancillary equipment including portable aerials, domestic signal boosters, hi-fi cleaning equipment, microphones, cables and carry cases of various sorts.

As the meeting moves towards the end of its published agenda, Mr Reynolds, the managing director, is talking: 'Just before we arrived today I was having a quick chat with Jeff and I think you should hear what he said to me. Jeff, over to you.' Jeff Watkins rises to his feet.

'Thank you Paul. Travelling home from Euston station the other week I found myself asking the question: "What is the one electrical product that causes the most annoyance to the most number of people?" Answer: the portable phone. Musing on this for a while, I realised that the reason for this is that there are so many of them around and the number is growing all the time. According to my research, the household penetration of these little devils is now some 5 per cent and that's with the digital network still in its infancy. And they change in shape, size, facilities and technologies regularly. This is a product to be in on. Essentially, these are radio transmitters and receivers and the technology needed to construct them should be both available and reasonably well known to us. We would buy in subassemblies which will be brought together in final assembly. The skills of the existing workforce are expected to be sufficient for this task. Much as I dislike the idea, these things are the future and we need to move with the times.'

'Wretched little things', booms a deep, rich voice. Almost as one the board looks towards the owner of the voice, the president of the company, Josiah Woodwedge. 'But I suppose we can't stop the so-called march of progress!' A large, flamboyant man, Josiah fixes each member of the board in turn with a friendly but determined stare, as if he is daring them to disagree with what he is about to say.

'This company was founded on a set of principles, and we should not leave them now.' Josiah pauses dramatically for effect. 'Quality, reliability, solidity, that's what we are, always have been. It is what made Britain what it was and it is still as applicable today. Quality and reliability, that is what we are and that is what any new range should be. Doesn't matter whether it is phones, televisions or simple test equipment. No flashing lights, no bells and whistles. No multicoloured cases and boxes. Just rock solid, dependable products. That is what the Bulldog name is all about and it gives the sales boys something to get their teeth into.'

Paul Reynolds looks thoughtful. He explains that he is not so sure about the whole idea. 'It seems a good market to be in', he muses, 'but, well ...'.

'A good market, and simple.' Josiah hits the table with his fist. 'We can design and manufacture with little problem. It is just a bit of plastic that you can make a telephone call with. What else is there to know? This is a chance to draw upon our roots and show the foreign competition a thing or two about quality British products.'

Mr Reynolds hesitates and then seems to wake from his contemplation. 'At a practical level, we need to consider finance and space. As you know, the factory is using all of its space. If we are to take on this idea we would have to stop production of one or two of our existing lines or, of course, acquire extra factory space. The latter is not difficult, but it might be more expensive than we can afford. To fund the initial development we would have to raise finance in some way. So, what do you think? Where do we go from here?'

Discussion carries on for some time. The meeting ends with the agreement of the board to begin developments of a range of mobile phones and to create production capacity by dropping some existing product lines.

1 Which business orientation do you think that Jimcrack plc uses? In about 100 words, explain the reasons for your answer.

2 Is this an appropriate orientation for the company? In about 50 words, explain your answer.

Summary

Marketing is primarily concerned with arranging and facilitating mutually satisfying exchange relationships. It has been defined in many ways, but at the core of all definitions is the need for the organisation to focus upon customers and their needs and wants. Marketing is both a management function and a business philosophy. As a business philosophy, marketing is concerned in directing the efforts and decisions of the organisation towards achieving long-term consumer satisfaction. It is a philosophy which requires the organisation to be outward looking. In contrast, the production, product and sales orientations are all centred upon the organisation itself and tend to be inward looking.

As a management function, marketing has the responsibility for selecting target groups of customers and then designing and implementing marketing mix(es) that will be aimed at each target market. Marketing is a dynamic discipline requiring constant monitoring of the environment and the markets which the organisation seeks to serve.

SECTION 2

Markets and Customers

Introduction

The most fundamental part of marketing is also the most obvious – to stay in business a company has to make a profit, and to make a profit it has to persuade others, people or organisations, to buy its product or service for more than it costs it to provide.

We can put this another way: if the company can find enough customers that want its products or services and are willing and able to pay for them at a price which more than covers its costs, then it may have a business. In the long term, the only way an organisation can generate money is from selling to customers. Of course, if it does not generate money then it goes out of business.

Customers are the market. Other businesses will also be operating within the market trying to sell to customers. If an organisation is to succeed in business, then it will have to compete – but competition will not welcome it with open arms. Quite the reverse! They will do whatever they can to ensure that they succeed and their competitors do not . To defeat or avoid the competition, it is necessary to understand the market, to monitor changes in its activities and to plan carefully all organisational efforts. The key to achieving the knowledge needed to allow an organisation to compete effectively is information and that **information** is provided by **marketing research**.

In this section, you should appreciate the central importance of the customer to an organisation. You will come to understand the stages of selecting target markets and you will recognise the importance of information in marketing decision making.

2.1 Customers

Customers are the sole reason for any business organisation's existence. Without customers, it has no reason for, nor means of, existence. You have seen that the importance of tailoring the market offering to a particular group of customers is at the very heart of marketing activity. To do this effectively, it is necessary to know as much about these customers as possible. There is a great deal of information that organisations can gather on customers. This can be grouped in a number of different ways but one easy way of starting to think about this is to ask this question:

Who buys **what**, **where**, **when**, **how** and **why?**

The most difficult part of the question to answer is the **'why'**. Why do people buy certain products and services? Why, when confronted with a wide variety of potential buying opportunities, do they decide to buy one offering instead of another? Why Coca-Cola and not Pepsi, for instance? What process did they go through to arrive at that decision? Trying to understand why people make the purchases they do is the process of buyer behaviour.

2.2 Competition

We know that the marketplace is competitive. It always will be. In western societies, there is nearly always more supply capacity than there is demand. In other words, there is not enough room in the market for every business that would like to be there. Unless a business is very lucky, it will be fighting for its share of a very finite cake and the objective of its competitors will be to see that it goes hungry. 'Know thine enemy' is an apposite saying. After all, if you don't know who your enemies are and how they fight, how can you expect to beat them? In order to be able to compete, an organisation needs to know as much about its competition as it possibly can.

ACTIVITY 9

Tom Smith has long wanted to run his own business. Recently, circumstances have made his long-term dream a reality. Tom has set up a business making and selling copper artefacts. He has been able to raise the finance to enable him to get started and his industrial background as an engineer means that the technical skills needed for the business are not new to him. His business background is, however, very limited. What information would Tom need to have about his competitors?

Tom needs to know who he is competing against, where competitors are located, what their target market is, what they have to offer, how much they charge, how they promote their businesses, how they distribute their products and how the market views them. Tom will need to list the strengths and weaknesses of the competition and compare them with his own strengths and weaknesses. He will have to consider how he might exploit the competitors' weaknesses while minimising the impact of the competitors' strengths on his own business. Ultimately, he will have to consider what is so special about his market offering that consumers will buy it in preference to that of the competition? And, of course, all the time he is watching his competitors, they are watching him and planning to compete even more fiercely.

Remember that there is not only direct competition but often indirect competition as well. People only have a finite sum of money to spend. If they spend it on one product they may not be able to afford another. Restaurants not only compete with other restaurants but with all the other businesses with which consumers can spend their leisure money. Does the consumer go out for a meal, go to a sports fixture, buy a new book, or go to the cinema?

As we saw in Units 2 and 3, there are a vast number of factors that will impinge on Tom's business activity. He needs to look at these as well as finding out about the direct competition. He needs to analyse the Porter's five forces that are operating in his marketplace.

2.3 Market segmentation

The basic idea of a marketing orientation is that the organisation produces products and services that satisfy the needs and wants of the market. Implementing this idea requires that an organisation starts by examining the needs and wants of the market and not with a particular product or service that the organisation would like to offer. If we can understand what it is that the market wants, then it is possible to build a product or offer a service that will meet those needs.

This raises the question: to what extent is it possible to design a product or service which will satisfy the needs and wants of every customer? Can a product or service be 'all things to all people'? The obvious answer to this question is that usually it is not possible to be all things to all people, and very often this is the correct answer. It would only be possible to offer such products or services if three conditions apply:

- everybody seeking to buy the product or service has exactly the same needs and wants
- there is no other organisation competing in the market for this product or service
- there are no substitute products or services.

In fact, in modern societies production capacity and ability usually outstrips demand and as a result competition ensures that products and services need to be different from each other if they are to be competitive. Once you have different products and services available, then the possibility of one product being 'all things to all people' becomes remote. Theoretically, there are situations where virtually all consumers want the same thing; this can be the case for staple products, for example. There will also be situations in which there is only one product or service available; in this case, if consumers wish to have such a product or service then they will have to purchase it, even if it does not quite match their exact needs.

So, although people may have a basic need in common, it does not follow that they will all want the same product. We all have a basic need to cover our feet with some form of shoe, but within this basic need there are many different requirements: shoes that are for walking, shoes that are for dressy occasions, shoes that are for sports, shoes that are cool, shoes that are warm, shoes that are for use in dangerous situations, shoes that are waterproof, shoes of different colours, shoes for medical conditions.

There is, then, a market for shoes, but clearly it consists of lots of different subgroups of need. These subgroups are referred to as **segments** of the market. A segment of the market is a grouping of people who are homogeneous with respect to each other; they share similar behaviour patterns which are different to the behaviour patterns of other segments.

Market segmentation is defined as 'a process by which a market is divided into distinct customer subsets of people with similar needs and characteristics that lead them to respond in similar ways to a particular product or service offering', Boyd, Walker and Larreche (1995, p. 180).

In theory, the number of segments in a market can vary from a maximum, where each consumer is a separate segment, to a minimum, where there is only one segment which consists of all consumers. Both of these extremes are unlikely though not impossible. Segments can exist at different levels. For example, within the total market for cars there are segments for large cars and for small cars, for sports cars and for family cars, for luxury cars and for estate cars. Within the estate car segment, there are segments for sports estates, luxury estates, four-wheel drive estates, diesel estates, and so on.

It is most unlikely that one company would be able to produce products or services to compete in all the segments of an individual market. The cost alone would probably be prohibitive. It is much more likely that it would wish to choose certain market segment(s) at which to aim its products. By choosing to produce market offerings for specific segments, organisations are adopting a strategy that is known as **target marketing**. The opposite approach is **mass marketing** where an organisation offers only one product to the whole market. An organisation wishing to operate a strategy of target marketing will go through a number of stages. These are shown in Figure 6. Now, let's look at each of these three stages in turn.

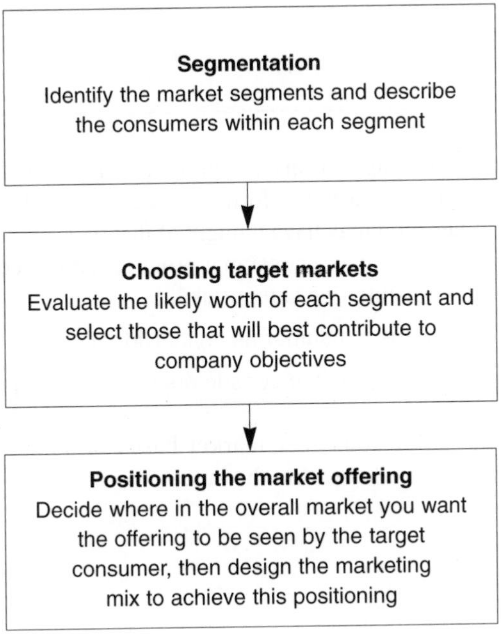

Figure 6: Target marketing

SEGMENTATION

The objective of this stage of the process is to divide the total market into a number of segments. Each segment should exhibit unique characteristics and a profile can be drawn up of consumers within each segment. A profile is simply a description of the typical consumer within the segment. Note, again, that the emphasis here is on the consumers and their behaviour and not on the products that they buy.

There is no formal way of segmenting a market. Successful segmentation relies on the skill of the marketing manager. There are many different ways in which markets can be segmented and many different variables that can be used to assist in splitting a market into segments. These variables are referred to as **bases**. The bases used will vary from market to market, but those used should be the ones that are best at predicting consumer behaviour within the particular market being segmented.

There are likely to be different variables used in the consumer and organisational markets. Consumer markets can be defined as those markets that provide goods and services that are primarily bought by individual consumers using their own money. Organisational markets, on the other hand, are those markets that provide goods and services which are bought by other organisations, usually for use in the production of products and services which they will then offer to a market.

ACTIVITY 10

Depstores operates a number of department stores. These sell clothing as well as furniture, cosmetics, toys, sports equipment and other items. What bases might it use to segment the market for clothes?

There are many different suggestions that you might have made. You might have suggested sex, age, income, casual or formal, price, fashionable or traditional, but there are so many others you may have thought of that they cannot all be listed here. Clothes are usually thought of as a consumer product and it is convenient to divide the commonly used bases into two categories:

- those that relate to the consumer as an individual
- those that relate to the way the consumers behave in the marketplace.

Table 1 shows the major consumer market bases in common use with some examples of the variables used within the base.

Consumer characteristics		Consumer behaviour	
Base	**Examples of variables used**	**Base**	**Examples of variables used**
Geography	Country, region, town, population density, climate	Buying habits	Amount purchased, shops used, buying frequency, media habits
Demographics	Age, gender, education, occupation, family size, religion, race, income, physical characteristics	Consumption habits	Frequency of use, degree of brand loyalty, time of use, way of use, heavy or light user
Psychographics	Activities, interests, opinions, personality, life style, social class	Product variables	Benefits sought, product knowledge, associated product ownership, response to marketing variables

Table 1: Some bases and variables used for market segmentation

It would be very rare for only one base to be used in segmenting a market. The usual approach would be to use a combination of bases. For example, one very widely used method, originally developed in 1971 by Richard Webber, is in itself a combination of several of the variables listed in the Table 1. This is the ACORN (A Classification Of Residential Neighbourhoods) system, which is based on the proposition that residential neighbourhoods have similar types of housing and the occupants of that housing exhibit similar demographic and social characteristics. It uses over 40 different variables taken from the census (a government population study undertaken every ten years), for example, number of people in household, cars per household, occupation, ethnic background, type and size of dwelling. The system takes each of the 125,000 census enumeration districts in the United Kingdom and places them into 36 different categories of residential neighbourhoods. Using this basic information, ACORN can then divide the households of the United Kingdom into six basic types (see Table 2).

Type	Description	Percentage of UK population
A	Thriving	19.8
B	Expanding	11.6
C	Rising	7.5
D	Settling	24.1
E	Aspiring	13.7
F	Striving	22.8
	Unclassified	0.5

Table 2: ACORN classification of UK residential households

Each of the ACORN categories can be broken down into a small number of groups, and each group into a number of residential types. Table 3 shows this breakdown for category B, expanding households.

Groups	%age in population	Types	%age in population
Affluent executives, family areas	3.8	Affluent working families with mortgages	2.1
		Affluent working couples with mortgages, new homes	1.3
		Transient workforces living at their place of work	0.4
Well-off workers, family areas	7.8	Home-owning families	2.6
		Home-owning families, older children	3.0
		Families with mortgages, younger children	2.2

Table 3: Residential types within ACORN category B households
Source: CACI Ltd, 1993

All of these types can be identified by postcode. The information can be used by marketing managers in a large number of different ways. For example, it can be used for directing mailshots or for deciding upon the location for a particular type of shop.

The most frequently used bases in the organisational market are shown in Table 4.

Base	Examples of variables used
Geography	Country, region, location, town
Organisation size	Turnover, capital employed, number of employees
Usage	Products made, rate of usage, order size
Standard Industrial Classification	Type of industry, purchasing process, technology used

Table 4: Organisational bases

Once the market has been segmented, then the marketing manager must build up a profile for the typical consumer within each of the segments identified. A profile is a detailed description; for example, in the consumer market it would include demographic, geographic and pyschographic variables as well as information on brand preferences, product usage, media habits and many other descriptors.

CHOOSING TARGET MARKETS

Once the company has segmented the market and drawn up customer profiles, the next step is to decide upon which segment or segments it will attempt to serve. This decision will be a function of a number of variables but essentially will depend on the potential profitability of each segment.

ACTIVITY 11

The potential profitability of a segment is influenced by a number of factors, such as the number of customers within a particular segment. The marketing manager of Fancy Shoes wants to estimate which segments of the shoe market are likely to be the most profitable. Two characteristics that he or she should consider when trying to judge the profitability of different segments are the number of consumers in each segment and their income, and the costs of advertising. List at least ten more factors that should be taken into account when judging the costs and potential revenues.

The profit that can be derived from any segment will depend upon two groups of factors:

- total value of sales that Fancy Shoes can make
- costs associated with making those sales.

The total sales value will depend upon the number of people within the segment, the amount of money they have to spend on the goods and services in question, and the number and strengths of competitors. As well as the number of people within the segment and their level of income, you may well, therefore, have suggested factors such as their willingness to spend on shoes, the number of competitors, and the strength of competition, both direct and indirect.

The costs of making the sales will be a function of the costs of producing and marketing the shoes. Production and marketing costs will include the materials used, the style, design and quality of the product, the manufacturing process, levels of indirect taxation, distribution costs, advertising costs, and the packaging. In addition, each product makes a contribution to the organisation's total overheads such as premises, staffing, administration, etc.

An organisation will need to consider its resources, its objectives and the potential of each segment before it is able to choose which segments it wishes to serve. It rarely follows that the biggest segment is the best to target; the one with the most potential will often not be the biggest, since competition in the biggest segment will almost always tend to push up the cost of operating in that segment and therefore reduce revenue.

POSITIONING THE MARKET OFFERING

Having defined the segment(s) that the company wishes to target, the next thing to consider is positioning. Within a segment there can be a lot of competition, and organisations need to differentiate their offering from that of competition. They need to position their offering so that it is seen as being different from that of the competition. The difference might be real or implied. It is how the consumer perceives the market offering relative to that of the competition that is important.

Each consumer in a segment has a mental map of the products or services in the market positioned against the criteria that they (the consumers) use to help decide which offering they wish to purchase. In reality, there are many criteria that consumers use to evaluate market offerings and the 'map' will, therefore, exist in multidimensional space. However, it is possible to illustrate this idea by using just two dimensions and a simple two-dimensional map.

ACTIVITY 12

Consider the market for wristwatches. In not more than 50 words, describe the criteria that consumers might use to evaluate this product.

There are many criteria that you may have listed: price, extent to which the watch is waterproof, the features and functions of the watch (divers, chronograph, alarm, calculator), the material of the casing (gold, silver, steel, plastic, etc.), styling, degree to which the watch is fashionable, quality, availability of parts and ease of servicing, size, exclusivity, strength, movement (quartz, solar, automatic, self winding).

If two of these dimensions are chosen, say fashion and purchase price, then a positioning map for one segment of the market might look like Figure 7.

The position labelled 'new brand?' would be a possible position that a company could seek to take up if research showed enough potential customers.

Once the desired position has been agreed then the next stage is to develop a marketing mix which allows the organisation to achieve the desired position. We consider the marketing mix in section three of this unit.

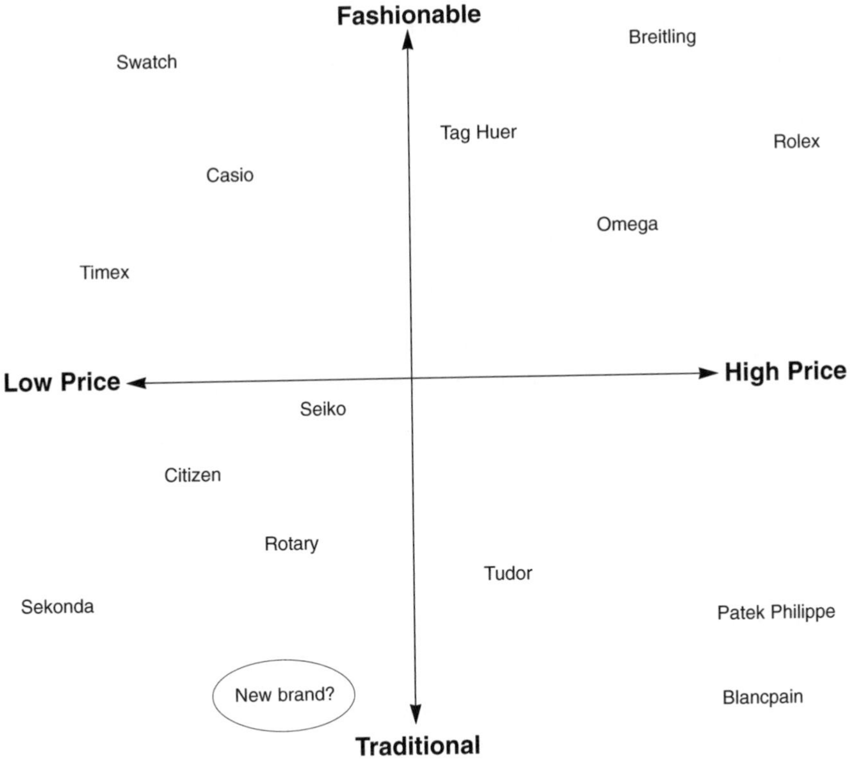

Figure 7: Market positioning for wristwatches

2.4 Marketing research

This section has concentrated so far on customers and markets. Throughout our discussion, we have stressed the need to understand consumers and competitors. Understanding and knowledge comes from information. Information is an essential prerequisite to successful marketing. Without it, there is little chance of a company competing in the marketplace effectively over any time period other than the very short term. Where will all the information a company needs come from? The answer is from **marketing research**.

Marketing research is the link between a company and the markets in which it operates. It is the way in which companies seek to understand the consumers in the markets in which they operate, the competitors they face and the way in which the activities of the company itself are evaluated by the consumers. It is a vital activity, and one that can never be considered optional. However, it must also be remembered that marketing research is not an end in itself. Rather, it is a tool to aid decision making within a company. It is not a replacement for decision making merely an aid to it.

Marketing research is defined as: 'The systematic ... collection, interpretation and reporting of information to help marketers solve specific marketing problems or take advantage of marketing opportunities', Dibb, Simpkin, Pride and Ferrell (1994, p. 157). Marketing research can be used to provide information across the whole range of marketing activities. Table 5 outlines the main types of marketing research that are carried out and gives examples of each type.

Type	Examples of research activity
Market research	Value and volume of sales; trends, competitors' activities
Sales research	Sales forecasting; evaluating sales techniques, establishing sales territories and sales quotas
Customer research	Examining buying behaviour; attitudes to products; image research; service and care perceptions
Product research	New product research; product performance; features and benefits; quality perceptions; packaging types
Promotion research	Advertising effectiveness; which media for which market?; merchandising methods; copy testing
Pricing research	Sales volumes and price; price/value relationships; psychological pricing; added benefit values
Distribution research	Number, type and location of retail outlets; transport methods; warehouse locations; service levels

Table 5: Types of marketing research

Although many people use the terms interchangeably, Table 5 shows that **market research** is one part of **marketing research**. Market research is the investigation of the size and nature of markets, but marketing research includes investigations into all areas of an organisation's marketing activity.

Organisations can undertake their own marketing research and many large organisations have a specialist market research department. There are also many specialist companies that provide research services for a fee. Some of these specialist companies provide general marketing research services, while some concentrate in certain areas of marketing activity, for example packaging research or retail research. Organisations that have their own marketing research departments will often also use the services of marketing research companies for specialist tasks.

Examples of specialist research companies include Nielsen, known for grocery consumer panels, J D Power, known for its car reliability surveys, and Mintel, the producers of research reports on selected markets. Euromonitor publishes annual

European statistics for a variety of markets and activities and also journals, such as *Monthly Research Europe*. The Target Group Index (TGI), an annual survey of brands and consumer characteristics, has been in operation since 1969; it covers over 5,000 brands and is based on 45,000 interviews. Mercer (1996, p106) claims that a profile of an individual brand can be purchased annually for about £20,000 and that 'a third of organisations purchase such data'.

INFORMATION VALUE

All information has a value but it also has a cost associated with its collection. It is pointless to commission research that will cost more than the contribution the collected information can make to profitability. Assume you have laid a bet with a friend on the outcome of a particular cricket match. You stand to win £5 if you can predict the outcome of the match. How much would you be prepared to pay for information on the outcome before you place your bet? The answer is of course any sum of money that is less than the amount you stand to win. In this case, you would be prepared to pay up to £5. Any more than this and you would lose more than you would gain. This simple example holds true for all marketing research.

2.5 Marketing research process

The collection of data is not normally especially difficult; the skill is to collect information that marketing management can use to assist in making effective decisions and to do so at a cost that is less than the value of the information collected. To ensure that marketing research is carried out as effectively and systematically as possible, there is a sequential process that can be applied every time information is required (see Figure 8).

The starting point in any marketing research must be a careful definition of the problem that is to be studied. The quality and utility of the final information will depend on how well the problem is defined. The greatest danger in any marketing research is that it is based on attempting to find solutions to the symptoms of a problem and not on finding solutions to the problem itself. Falling sales is not a problem, it is a symptom of a problem. The problem might be that the pricing is wrong, the service is poor, the quality of the product is wrong, the benefits of the offering are not being communicated to the target consumers, or many other possibilities. Once the problem is understood, it is possible to specify the particular objectives that will need to be met if the problem is to be solved and to list the information that will be needed to meet these objectives. Armed with this list, the search for the information can then begin.

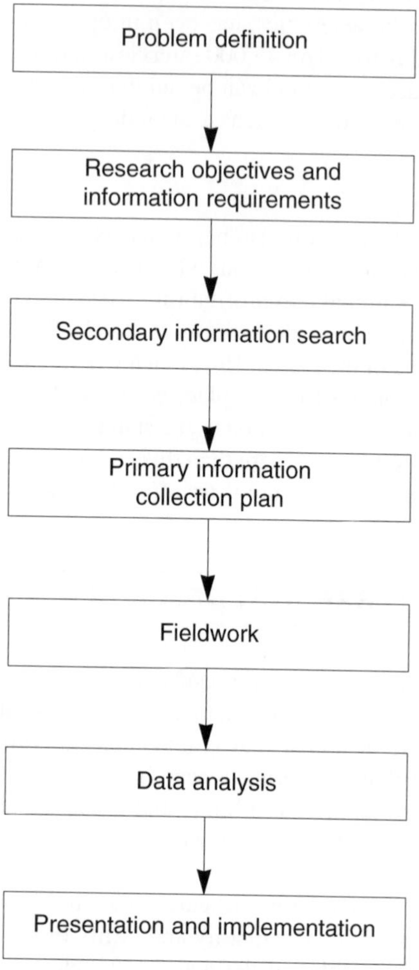

Figure 8: The marketing research process

TYPES OF MARKETING INFORMATION

There are two distinct forms of information: primary and secondary. **Secondary data** is information which already exists, which has been collected previously for some other purpose and is now recorded and stored somewhere. **Primary data** is information which has never previously been collected. If it is needed, it will have to be collected for the first time.

The collection of secondary information is often called **desk research** because it requires the researcher to identify where the information is kept and then to abstract the parts that are relevant to the new study. The collection of primary information is often referred to as **field research** since it requires the researcher to go out and collect information that is needed for the first time.

ACTIVITY 13

Would you begin a marketing research exercise with primary or secondary sources? Why?

You should begin any search with a study of secondary information sources since secondary information is generally quicker, cheaper and easier to find. Only after exhausting secondary sources would you investigate primary sources.

There are five main sources of secondary information available in the UK:

- internal sources
- government statistics
- published reports
- trade press
- other sources.

Internal sources

These are data which are already recorded within the company but which might not perhaps be in the form required. Sales invoices, for example, can be used to split down a company's existing market by customer, by volume sold, by region, or by salesperson.

Government statistics

The government collects a wide range of information across many industries and topics. All of this information is made available to the public very cheaply. For examples of the sort of information that is available from the government visit a public library and ask the librarian for the appropriate section. Look, for example, at the Family Expenditure Survey to see the detailed nature of information available from government sources.

Published reports

There are many organisations which publish reports on topics which they have researched. These include various commercial research companies, educational institutions and trade bodies. All of these organisations sell the results of their studies, sometimes reasonably cheaply and sometimes for rather large sums; the price reflects the value of the information.

Trade press

There are over 3,000 specialist trade publications in the UK. These are journals, magazines, newspapers and newsletters which are devoted to an industry or area of activity. Most of these carry articles on particular markets.

Other sources

These include radio and television programmes, newspaper articles, newsletters from competitors and company reports. During your next visit to your public or college library ask the librarian for details of the abstraction services held within the library. These are designed to allow speedy access to newspaper and journal reports. One particularly useful abstraction service is the Research Index.

Increasingly, new technology is making the collection of secondary data much quicker and often more effective through the use of on-line databases, as you saw in Unit 3.

If the information required cannot be obtained from secondary sources then **primary research** will need to be carried out. There are four major approaches to the collection of primary information:

- survey
- observation
- experimentation
- qualitative techniques.

Survey

If you want information from somebody the easiest way of getting it is to ask them for it. This can be done through personal interviews, postal questionnaires or telephone interviews. For example, Birmingham Midshires Building Society makes regular postal surveys of its investors and borrowers to investigate opportunities for improving customer service.

Observation

There are occasions where people are unwilling or unable to answer questions. In these circumstances, it might be possible to obtain the information needed by observing activity. This can be done by the use of the human eye or ear or using mechanical recording devices. Many retailers use 'mystery' shoppers to observe the quality of customer service delivered in their shops. Through the use of video cameras, information about, for example, patterns of movement within a store, ways of making purchase, time spent in the shop can be recorded. This provides valuable information especially when tied in with actual purchases identified at the check-out tills and analysis of regular purchases made through a supermarket loyalty card.

Experimentation

There are two basic forms of experimentation. One approach tests in the market place; perhaps trying two different packages to see which generates more sales from a target group. The other is laboratory experimentation where the reactions of consumers to particular stimuli can be monitored and measured. An example of the latter would be the testing of proposed television advertisements on consumers in a laboratory situation. Companies hire students, for example, and measure their reactions to different advertisements.

Qualitative techniques

Qualitative techniques try to discover the underlying desires, motives and drives of a group of consumers. They usually involve group or individual discussion between a researcher and a sample of the market under study, or in the interpretation of tests undertaken by a sample of the market.

The type of approach depends on the particular information requirements, the cost of each method, the level of accuracy needed and the availability of the people who need to be investigated.

COLLECTING PRIMARY DATA

In collecting primary data, we first need to decide who will be researched in order to provide the required information. A survey of all the members of the market under study is called a **census**. Where the total number of individuals in the study area is small, then a census could be used for the collection of data. However, most populations studied in marketing research are large and conducting a census would be too expensive and too time consuming. In such situations it is usual to use a **sample**. A sample is 'simply a portion, or subset, of a larger population', Zikmund and d'Amico (1994, p. 110). Properly constructed, a sample will be representative of the total population. There are many ways of taking a sample, but they can be categorised as either probability or non-probability sampling.

- **Random (or probability) sampling** is a method of sampling in which every member of the population under study has an equal chance of being selected for the sample. Random number tables are usually used to select who will be interviewed. This approach allows great statistical confidence in the analysis and output but does require that a list of every member of the population under study exists.
- **Non-probability sampling** includes all approaches which do not use completely random processes. In this approach, respondents are selected by the researcher on the basis of predetermined population characteristics in such a way that the sample will reflect the population. For example, if the population under study is 60 per cent men and 40 per cent women, then the researcher would select men and women in these proportions in the sample taken.

Quota sampling is a widely used variant of non-probability sampling that requires researchers to recruit respondents to a set of quotas. For example, a survey into breakfast cereal purchase may require an individual researcher to select to the following quotas:

- 10 men aged 36–44
- 30 women aged 26–35
- 10 either age or sex
- 40 to be married
- 30 to have children below the age of 18 living at home.

Stratified sampling is often used as a sampling method. Here, the population being studied is broken down into strata (or groups) and then set proportions of the total sample are taken from each strata. For example, if the sales of a supplier of industrial cleaning equipment comes from three different types of industry in the proportions 45:35:20 then a sample would be drawn from each of the industries in those proportions. The actual respondents within each strata could be selected using either random or non-random techniques.

As in many areas of market research, the choice of which approach to use is often a compromise between cost and accuracy. In general, random approaches, although statistically much more reliable, are more expensive and often logistically difficult; non-random approaches are often quicker, cheaper and easier to use and, as such, are far more commonly used in marketing research. The larger the sample the more likely it will be to represent the population, although again in practice the size of the sample will usually be a compromise between cost and required accuracy. The important point is that the sample should be large enough to provide a representation of the population being studied. In fact, sample sizes are often not as large as might be thought: many European-wide surveys of consumer buying habits have samples of about 2,000 people. A sample of 300 organisations would be quite common in UK industrial markets and most political opinion polls are based on approximately 500-1,000 interviews.

Many marketing research projects use questionnaires to elicit the information needed. Designing a questionnaire is actually rather more difficult than most people would believe. There are essentially three different types of question that can be asked. **Dichotomous questions** have only two possible answers, both of which are known by the researcher in advance of asking the question. **Multiple-choice questions** are similar but have more than two possible answers. **Open-ended questions** are those that have an infinite number of possible responses. The distinction is important since all data that has been collected has to be analysed. The analysis of dichotomous and multiple-choice questions is relatively easy but the analysis of open-ended questions is much more difficult. Questionnaires should contain as few open-ended questions as possible. Examples of the three question types are shown in Figure 9.

Example of a dichotomous question

1.4 Is the vehicle still covered by a warranty?

Yes	
No	

Example of an open-ended question

4.4 Why do you think you have had problems recruiting part time staff in the last two years

____

____

____

____

Examples of multiple-choice questions

Tick

1.1 What is the registration letter of your vehicle?

N reg.		J reg.	
M reg.		H reg.	
L reg.		G reg. or earlier	
K reg.			

Checklist

5.3 What do you feel has been the main reasons these particular vacancies have been difficult to fill?
Please tick as many reasons as apply to you.

Few applicants	
Skills missing	
Wage expectations	
Transport problems	
Applicants overqualified	
Applicants underqualified	
Hours of work	

Rating

3.10 I am going to read to you a number of different statements. Would you please indicate the extent to which you agree with each statement using the following scales:-

Always	Usually	Occasionally	Rarely	I cannot judge
1	2	3	4	5

The quality of workmanship is high ☐
The charges made appear to be reasonable ☐
They make promised telephone calls ☐
They keep me informed of what is happening ☐
They keep to promised deadlines ☐
They explain what has been done in a non-technical way ☐
The receptionists are efficient and effective ☐
There is a friendly welcome ☐

Ranking

2.14 Place the criteria below in the order of importance to you when you selected a University at which to study. Place a 1 against the factor that was most important to you, a 2 against the second most important factor and so on.

Distance from home ☐
Availability of accommodation ☐
Sports facilities ☐
Teaching reputation ☐
Research record ☐
School recommendation ☐
Cost of living ☐
There was a friendly welcome at interview ☐

Figure 9: Examples of marketing research question types

Once the data collection is complete, the task is to analyse the information and present it to marketing managers in such a way that assists in decision making. Usually, a report is written which notes the research objectives, explains the methodology that has been used, lays out the information collected and then explains the findings of the research in as clear a form as possible. The analysis of quantitative research findings is today largely carried out using statistical computer programmes. Indeed, increasingly there are packages which integrate questionnaire design, data collation, verification and data analysis.

REVIEW ACTIVITY 2

'I have been running this company for the last ten years, I must know by now just about everything there is to know about this market and my business. I read the papers, I watch the television, I talk to my customers. What use would marketing research be to me? What can it do for me?'

1 In no more than two paragraphs, explain how you would respond to this speaker.

2 Write a short paragraph explaining what marketing research does not do.

Summary

The most important part of any organisation is its customers. It is through its customers that an organisation is able to realise its objectives. It is vital that an organisation understands the buying behaviour of the markets within which it operates. Most organisations have competitors and competition can be direct or indirect.

It is most unlikely that any organisation will be offering a product or service which appeals to everybody within a market. It is more likely that it will choose to serve only certain segments of the market. These segments will be chosen to enable the organisation to meet its objectives.

Understanding and targeting customers requires information to aid in decision making. Marketing research is the tool which is used to provide this information. All information has a cost and a value. Secondary data is cheaper and quicker to obtain, but primary data is likely to be needed for many situations.

SECTION 3

The Marketing Mix

Introduction

Once a company has decided on its target market(s), the process of putting together the offering to attack these targets can begin. Once again note that the company puts together its market offering (its products and services) after it has been decided which market(s) it is going to try to serve. As we saw earlier, the set of controllable marketing variables that the organisation can use to create its market offering is called the marketing mix. In this section, we look in more detail at the concept of the marketing mix and then move on to look at each of the mix variables in turn and consider how they are put together into the mix. We identify the central role of the product and its relationship to the life of the company. We consider the different approaches to setting a price and identify a range of different types of distribution channel. Finally, we describe the ways in which organisations can communicate with their customers.

3.1 What is the marketing mix?

The process of formulating the market offering is known as building the marketing mix. The term 'marketing mix' was coined in 1965 by an American academic, Neil Borden. He suggested that the organisation had a wide range of variables that it mixed together to form its market offering. Another American, Jerome McCarthy, suggested that this wide range of variables could be classified into the four basic areas of **product, price, promotion** and **place**. He referred to these as the **four Ps**, a term that has been widely used ever since. Place might more correctly be referred to as distribution. The marketing mix includes everything that a company can do to try and generate sales for its products.

We can also add another three Ps to this basic concept; they are **physical evidence**, that is all aspects of the physical environment that concern the product, **participants**, the people involved in the transaction, and **process**, the ease with which the transaction can take place. These three Ps have largely arisen because of more awareness of the service approach required even to sell a product, and the whole bundle of benefits that a consumer wants and expects from the product.

Boyd, Walker and Larreche (1995, p. 19) define the marketing mix as 'the combination of controllable marketing variables that a manager uses to carry out a marketing strategy in pursuit of the firm's objectives in a given target market'.

Within each of the four major elements of the marketing mix (the four Ps), there are a number of subelements about which decisions have to be made. Table 6 shows some of the subelements within each of the four main areas. Here, we concentrate on these four Ps but you should keep in mind the service approach in delivery of any product.

Product	Price	Promotion	Place
Quality	List price	Advertising	Number and type of distributors
Style	Discounts	Personal selling	
Features	Trade prices	Public relations	Tasks of the distributors
Packaging	Credit terms	Sales promotions	
Brand name	Payment periods	Exhibitions	Locations
Sizes	Extras	Point-of-sale material	Transport
Guarantees	Special offers	Media choice	Inventory levels
Service	Quality/value	Timing	Service levels

Table 6: Subelements within the four Ps

Although the company makes decisions in each of the four main areas, it is the total offering which is seen by the market. Potential customers do not see each subelement separately, rather they see the sum of these elements; they see only the whole. It is very important that the elements chosen for any mix blend together harmoniously. Rolex watches are sold as a high-quality item. They are advertised in quality magazines, have a high price and are only available through a limited number of exclusive jewellers. Each element blends together and the result is a successful product. Would they be so successful if, instead of being only available through a small number of exclusive jewellers, Rolex were sold in every jeweller, department store, chain store and mail-order catalogue in the UK?

There is rarely, if ever, one marketing mix for any given situation. There will usually be many possibilities. There is a high degree of substitutability between the variables, for example instead of reducing price to try and improve sales, the company could choose to increase advertising, or increase the quantity of product offered, or provide special gifts, or increase the number of outlets in which the product is available. The list is almost endless.

The ability to manipulate the variables will be constrained to some extent by factors which are largely outside of the company's control. A company developing a major new convenience food product, for example, will be forced to spend fairly large sums of money on major media advertising. The reason for this is that to sell such a product it will be necessary to obtain shelf space in the major supermarket chains, and they are unlikely to take the product unless it is backed by major advertising. Similarly, there are various legal regulations which act to constrain the manipulation of the four elements of the marketing mix.

Managing the marketing mix is the task which will take up the vast majority of the time of many marketing managers. For many, it is their day-to-day responsibility. It is not only the case that there are many possible marketing mixes that a manager might develop in response to a given target market, it is also the case that the most appropriate mix will change over time and hence the management task is one of continuous monitoring and manipulation of the four variables. As you saw in Units 2 and 3, environmental adaptation is important in achieving and maintaining competitive advantage.

3.2 Products, services and benefits

Most commercial organisations have as their primary objective some form of survival. This is almost inevitably tied in with the need to generate income. Income is generated from the sale of **products and services**. At first sight this would seem to suggest that the product (or service) is at the centre of the marketing mix; sell enough product – generate enough profit – stay in business. However correct this may appear at first sight, concentrating heavily on the product is today likely to be an inappropriate approach to business. (If it is not clear to you why this is likely to be an inappropriate approach to business, return to section 1 and look again at the idea of marketing as business philosophy.)

In considering the product, we also need to note that for the consumer a service is a product; the difference lies only in the tangibility of the offering. A product can be touched since it has tangibility, whereas a service cannot since it is intangible. Both, however, are bought to satisfy needs; to be successful both need to be matched to the desires of consumers. We consider products and services together in this section. There are differences in the way products and services are ultimately managed but we consider the basic concepts together.

It is too easy for organisations and their employees to become tied down with the product itself, to become enmeshed with problems of design, manufacture or modification, to concentrate on manipulating the smallest detail. The reasons are often understandable, sometimes even laudable. However, all members of an organisation must accept that products in a business sense, are simply tools. They are the means of helping to satisfy corporate objectives and no more.

BENEFITS

The most important initial lesson to learn is that what people buy is usually very different from what is sold. This is because people buy **benefit**; they buy not what the product is, but rather what it can do for them. 'Customers don't buy products....they seek to acquire benefit', Mercer, (1996, p. 38).

Three examples will help to highlight this difference.

First, consider a washing machine. Compare how it might be seen by an engineer and a housewife. To the engineer, a washing machine is an amalgam of mechanical and electronic subassemblies. It actually is some metal, some wiring, some tubing, some plastic, even on occasions some concrete. No customer would pay up to £400 for that, however! What the customer buys is the ability to clean clothes quickly, easily, safely and reliably. The customer really doesn't care how it works, just as long as it does.

Perhaps the favourite example of many marketing commentators is that of the drill. Customers do not buy a 10 mm drill, they buy a 10 mm hole! How it is created is incidental.

Charles Revson, the founder of the Revlon Cosmetics empire is alleged to have once said, in a rather sexist comment, that he owned factories in which he produced cosmetics but owned shops in which he sold hope!

ACTIVITY 14

Consider further the difference between what a washing machine is and why customers buy it.

A washing machine is:	**A washing machine is bought to:**
Five sheets of metal	Clean clothes effectively
A stainless steel drum	Save time
Some rubber tubing	Save hard work
A circuit board	Prevent clothes from being damaged in washing
Some plastic castors	Look attractive
A lot of wiring	Make a statement
Some metal springs	Satisfy engineering desires
A weight (sometimes concrete!)	
A series of push buttons	

Now consider perfume. When you pay up to £100 for a small bottle of perfume, you get alcohol, chemicals, essential oils, lavender, a glass bottle, advertising, paper, packaging.

Make a list of the reasons why people actually buy perfume.

There are many different reasons that you might have noted down. You might have included the following: to create an image, please other people, hide smells considered less pleasant, show love or affection when bought as a gift, make a statement, demonstrate wealth, generate passion, revive memories, or be fashionable.

Benefit accrues to customers not just from the product or service that they purchase, but from the totality of the 'offering' made by the company. This total offering is what the potential customer considers, gives a value to and uses in the ultimate decision about whether to purchase or not. This total offering includes contributions from the other three elements of the marketing mix. It is only when this total offering is right that potential customers are turned into actual customers. For example, the ultimate success or failure of so-called designer clothes over the last few years has often depended on the label or logo attached to the clothes, not on the cloth, its cut or its colour.

The two key points to always remember are that the customer buys benefits, therefore the company must sell benefits and not features and that ultimately the product is what the customer thinks it is, not what the organisation knows it is!

WHAT IS A PRODUCT?

All products can be thought of as having three distinct levels or layers:

- core product
- formal product
- augmented product.

The **core product** is the essential benefit that comes from the product. In our example of the washing machine, this core benefit would be the ability to clean clothes. For aircraft, it is speed of travel. All products in the class would normally offer the same core benefit.

The **formal product** is that which is offered to the market; the form in which the customer is allowed to purchase the product. This will include the packaging, name, branding, product quality, style, etc. It is at this level that organisations have traditionally sought to compete with one another. There is no difference in the core benefit offered by the Ford Escort and the Volkswagen Golf, but yet there are many differences and intense competition at the level of the formal product.

The **augmented product** is the area in which, increasingly, organisations are seeking to gain competitive advantage. At this level is added a whole range of additional benefits that enhance the product and its use. They are central to the product which can function very well without them but they are strong competitive weapons. The core of the personal computer is the ability to process large amounts of information quickly. The formal product, as offered to the market, comprises certain configurations of memory and storage, screens and keyboards, in different shapes and sizes and colours and prices. Competition at this level is intense, and the products seen by the consumer are essentially very similar. The augmented product offers installation, training, software, phone helplines, maintenance agreements, trade-in agreements, guaranteed updates, etc.

ACTIVITY 15

Electrical goods such as televisions, washing machines and hi-fi equipment are all the same or very similar at the core and formal levels. Note down a few examples of how retailers could compete at the augmented level.

You might have included some of the following ideas:

- special facilities to see, hear and test the products on offer
- facilities to test certain types of products in your own home
- seven-day exchange offers
- full servicing facilities on site
- special purchasing deals
- special finance deals
- type of guarantee
- free delivery and set up where appropriate
- provision of more product information
- user clubs, newsletters, information lines
- in-store entertainment or special events
- a cafe in which customers can consider their choice.

3.3 Product classification

Different types of product require different types of marketing activity and management strategies. It is possible to produce a classification system for products that can be used to guide the development of an appropriate marketing mix. There are two broad classes of products. **Consumer goods** are those that are purchased and consumed within the domestic market. **Industrial goods** are those that are purchased by organisations for use in the production of other products. It is quite possible for a product to be in both classes; for example, envelopes are used by both domestic consumers and by organisations. Within these two broad classes, there are a number of subclassifications.

Let's look first at consumer products. These can be classified as:

- convenience products
- shopping products
- speciality products
- unsought products.

Convenience products

Convenience products are bought frequently and with very little shopping effort on the part of the consumer. They are usually inexpensive. They can be split into staple products, for example, bread, milk, most packaged goods; impulse products which are bought as an unplanned purchase, such as a cold drink bought from a street seller on a hot day; and emergency products, such as products needed in a hurry – an umbrella in a rain storm or a forgotten bottle of wine before a dinner party.

ACTIVITY 16

Write down the four main elements of the marketing mix and the names of four convenience staple products. State which element of the marketing mix you think needs to be emphasised to maximise the sales of impulse convenience products.

The main elements of the marketing mix are product, promotion, price and distribution. There are very many convenience staple products that you might have included: many types of fruit and vegetables, bread, milk, sugar, soap, toilet paper, washing powder, various tinned products, etc.

The most important element of the marketing mix for impulse items is distribution. Purchase of these products is not planned and, as such, sales will only be made if they are brought to the attention of the consumer at the right time. This means having wide distribution of the products and using high visibility spots in shops (known as hot spots), placing chocolate at the check-out in supermarkets for example, and catching the consumer at exactly the right time, such as selling holiday and travel insurance at airports. The important thing to note about these products is that the classification is based upon the way the consumer thinks about them and not on the basis of any features of the products themselves.

Shopping products

These are products that are bought fairly infrequently and are usually higher value items. As such, the consumer is willing to spend some time and effort in the decision process and will compare products, their benefits and their prices. Certain types of shopping product will be bought on the basis of price alone because the consumer feels that they are all essentially similar, other types will have price as a secondary consideration.

Speciality products

Speciality products have very special features or such a strong brand name that the consumer is prepared to put a lot of shopping effort into obtaining them, or at least they are prepared to put a lot of effort in should it prove necessary. Little if any comparison is carried out by the consumer. These items are often, but not always, expensive. Examples of expensive speciality goods include Porsche cars and Hasselbad photographic equipment. Examples of less expensive speciality services and products include a particular dentist, a particular cheese from a delicatessen, a hairdresser that a consumer is prepared to travel to or wait for an appointment.

Unsought products

These are products that the consumer either is unaware of, perhaps because they are new to the market, or is aware of but never normally thinks about, for example, life insurance. The nature of these goods requires that they are brought to the attention of potential buyers in a way that minimises the opportunity for the consumer to ignore the message. This usually means extensive promotional activities often centred around personal selling and direct mail techniques. There is a danger with this group of products of too much (or too heavy-handed) promotion which can have subsequent detrimental effects on the product's image. So, for example, the image of time-share holiday apartments has been tarnished.

In the same way that consumer products can be split down into four major types, so industrial products can be classified under six headings:

- installations
- accessories
- supplies
- professional services
- raw materials
- components.

Installations

Installations are major capital items like plant, buildings and land. These are central to the organisation, without them the organisation effectively does not have a business. They are the most important assets a company will buy and as such the buying decision is likely to be protracted, require lots of information input and it is unlikely to view price as the major decision criterion.

Accessories

Accessories are at the other end of the capital scale. They are items that will normally have a shorter life and be much lower in price. Examples of this category of product include office equipment such as copiers and desks, and small items of plant such as bench drills and catering ranges.

Supplies

Supplies are the small usually inexpensive products that are used to allow the company to function and produce output. They do not form part of the product that is being produced but they are consumed very regularly. Examples range from paint and light bulbs through lubricating oils, grinding pastes, paper and envelopes, to products like filters and bearings that wear out in the course of using capital items in the installation and accessories categories.

Professional services

Professional services are those services which the company buys in rather than provides itself. These are services where it is possible through specialisation for supplying companies to provide a cheaper and better service than the company could supply itself. Examples include cleaning services, training, catering and advertising.

Raw materials and components

All the four previous industrial product categories are based around products and services that go to help produce output but are not in themselves part of the finished product. Raw materials and components are two categories of industrial products that become part of the finished product.

The type of product, whether it is consumer or industrial, will help to give direction to the type of marketing mix that will be needed. Product classification however, is not the only idea that can be used to help guide the development of a marketing mix. Along with the type of product, the idea that products have lives can be used. This idea has been refined into what is known as the **product life cycle**. You met this idea in Unit 2 in relation to the implications of technology in the organisation.

3.4 Product life cycle

A product can be said to have a life in the same way that humans have lives; both are born, grow up, reach old age and eventually die. The similarity can be taken further since, just as some humans lives are cut short and they never reach maturity, so it is with some products. It is possible to take this idea of the life of a product a stage further and break a product's life up into stages; and each stage represents a different challenge to marketing managers. The product life cycle is normally shown as a diagram which illustrates a typical life-time sales picture (Figure 10).

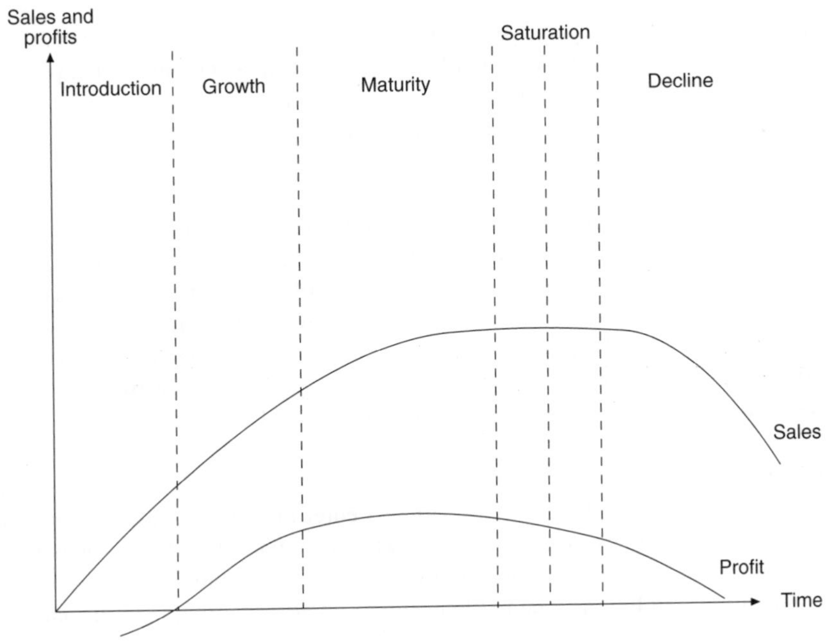

Figure 10: Product life cycle

Figure 10 shows a typical life cycle and associated profit curve. It is important to realise that we are considering here a 'typical' product. In reality, every product will have a shape that is unique to that product. Similarly, the time axis will vary greatly from product to product. Neither the shape nor the time for any given product will be known with any certainty in advance.

The area under the curve can be split up into a number of 'stages' and each stage requires a different marketing approach. The five stages are:

- introduction
- growth
- maturity
- saturation
- decline.

Introduction

Introduction is the stage at which the product is first released onto the market.

ACTIVITY 17

What do you think will be the most important task for marketing management at the introduction stage in the product life cycle?

At this point in the life cycle, very few people are aware of the existence of the product and so the major task for marketing is to create awareness of the product amongst the target market and to encourage customers to try the product. Sales growth will inevitably be slow and profits negative.

Growth

Growth is characterised by an acceleration of sales as more buyers enter the market and also by an increase in competition as more sellers enter the market. As the product moves through the growth stage, so it is likely that the emphasis of the marketing mix will change from stimulating demand for the product idea to stimulating demand for the particular offering or brand of the company. Profits usually become positive at about this stage. The growth in the overall market means that all companies operating in the market can also grow.

Maturity

Over time, as fewer and fewer new customers enter the market, sales growth will inevitably begin to slow down. This stage is known as maturity. Sales growth is still possible for some companies but it will no longer be possible for all to grow and so competition will hot up. The battle becomes one of retaining market share. As the level of competition increases, so the profits earned by companies will start to decline.

Saturation

Once the market consists only of replacement purchasing, saturation is said to have been reached. Sales here have reached a plateau and companies can only grow by taking market share from their competitors.

Decline

Profits will inevitably decline. Eventually, sales will begin to decline as the product is no longer required by consumers as better products become available. If organisations take no action, product sales will eventually fall to zero. However, profits will have become negative long before this point is reached, so most products will be 'retired' before the zero sales position is reached.

ACTIVITY 18

At which stage do you think the following products and services are in the product life cycles.

- cigarettes
- coffee
- suntan lotions
- manual typewriters
- 'all-in-one' home exercise machines
- personal bank accounts
- all-inclusive holidays
- digital video cameras
- small family cars.

There is likely to always be some argument as to exactly where a product or service is in the product life cycle. You will probably find a discussion of this answer with a friend or colleague useful. Here are our suggestions.

Digital video cameras are in the introduction stage. In growth, 'all-in-one' home exercise machines and all-inclusive holidays. Suntan lotions are probably somewhere between growth and maturity. Other products in maturity are personal bank accounts and small family cars. In decline, cigarettes and manual typewriters.

There are two major learning points to take from the concept of the product life cycle. The first comes from the shape of the life cycle and the way in which it eventually returns to zero sales. Any company which offers only one product to the market has a life cycle that is exactly the same in shape and time as that of the product life cycle itself. In other words, to survive in the long term a company has to at least introduce a new product to replace an existing one that has entered the decline stage. Indeed, in order to be successful, it must have several products at different stages in their life cycles.

The second observation develops this idea one stage further by considering profits. We can see that because of competition the profit curve associated with a product is likely to peak before its sales peak. In addition, profits are negative in the early stages of the life cycle. If a company is to at least maintain profits levels over time then it needs to have a balanced range of products where the profit curves of each are complementary, that is, the negative profits of one product are at least balanced by the positive profits of another.

So far we have been talking about the product life cycle. In fact, life cycles exist at different levels. It is possible to define at least three different levels of product life cycle, two relate to an industry as a whole and one to the offering of an individual company. It is perhaps easiest to explain this idea by way of an example.

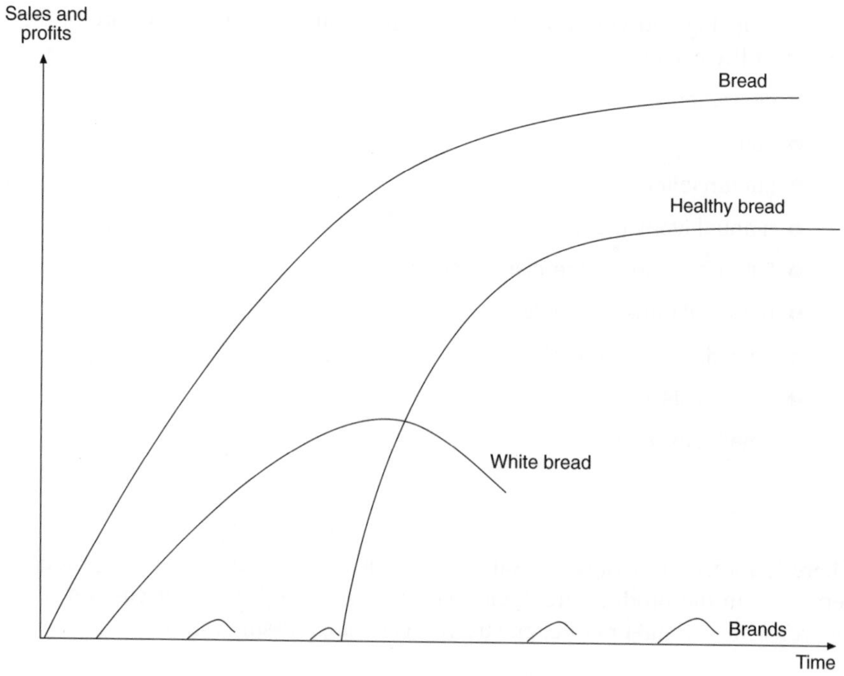

Figure 11: Product life cycle for bread

Bread has been available for many hundreds of years. However, different types of bread have enjoyed, and are enjoying, varying degrees of popularity. In recent years, white sliced bread has become less popular. Instead, there is greater demand for what we might call more 'healthy bread'. Both types of bread have life cycles at the industry level. Within these two product areas, there are many individual products and brands, each of which has an associated life cycle. In the case of these, some will have lived long lives and then died, some will have had very short lives, some will have only just been born, some will be into their maturity. This notion of life cycles at different levels is important since it helps to demonstrate to management what is happening to individual products. If an individual brand moves into decline but the product type, for example, white bread, is still strong then management can seek to extend the life cycle of that brand or introduce a new version of it. If, however, the product type is moving into decline then so will all the individual brands. The same argument holds true for product types within the generic product, in this case bread.

The length of the product life cycle will vary depending on the particular product and its level in the hierarchy shown above. In general, life cycles are getting shorter; approximately a half of the profits of UK companies today comes from products that were not on the market ten years ago. One reason for this is the increasing pace of technological development which, in certain markets, can render products obsolete in very short periods of time. For example, the development of colour television rapidly caused the decline in demand for black and white sets; and fax machines killed off the demand for telex. Similarly, changing fashions and tastes can rapidly reduce life cycle lengths.

Another of the main reasons for shortening life cycles is the degree of competition. This operates in two ways. First, new developments are very rapidly copied. Second, with very intense competition for market share, many companies see the best way of gaining share is through the introduction of constantly updated products. So, for example, the car market has annual model updates. The main implication of the ever shortening life cycles of many products is that companies find themselves needing to develop new products all the time.

3.5 Product mix

Most businesses have more than one product that they offer to the market. The collection of all the products offered by an organisation is known as its product mix. (Product assortment is also sometimes used to describe the product mix.) Products are usually grouped into collections of similar items, and such a grouping is known as a product line. For example, a manufacturer of clothing might group its products into three lines – shirts, trousers and sweaters. A further breakdown could be used splitting shirts into two lines – dress and leisure. As you might imagine, some companies have many different lines with a multitude of products within each line; others only have a very few lines, each with as few as one or two products. The total product mix of any company can be described using four variables.

- **Width** is the number of different product lines in the total product mix. In our clothing manufacturer example, the width is three – men's shirts, trousers and sweaters.
- **Depth** is the number of individual products in a specific product line. In our example, men's shirts might have a depth of three – casual shirts, office working shirts, evening dress shirts.

- **Length** is the total number of products in the product mix. The clothing manufacturer might make 25 different types of shirts, trousers and sweaters, and then there will be different sizes, styles and colours within each product.
- **Consistency** concerns the degree of relationship between the various product lines. The clothing manufacturer has a very high degree of consistency between the lines. However, if the company adds two new lines – radios and soap powder – then the degree of consistency would clearly be greatly reduced.

Any company can consider future development in terms of its product mix. It can add new lines, increase the depth of existing lines or change its consistency.

3.6 Setting prices

Until comparatively recently, price was considered to be the most important variable in deciding the level of sales. Many managers thought that price was the mechanism of competition. Today, this is no longer considered to be the case, and price is just one form of competition. Indeed, some suggest that price alone is perhaps not a very good form of competition, Dibb, Simpkin, Pride and Ferrell, (1994, pp. 480–482).

ACTIVITY 19

Explain briefly why you think that price alone is not a very good form of competition.

There are two interlinked reasons why price has fallen from favour as a primary means of competition. The first is that as a competitive weapon it suffers from ease of copying. What company A does today in terms of setting a price, company B can copy almost immediately. This is particularly true if the two companies have products which are essentially homogeneous. The second reason lies with the nature of price competition. In almost every case, to compete on price means to lower price. As one company follows another so a downward price spiral ensues: this is very good news in the short term for the consumer, but very bad news for the companies and perhaps ultimately for the consumer. Why should it be bad news for the consumer and the company? The answer lies in two of the most basic business equations.

$$\text{profit} = \text{sales} - \text{costs}$$

$$\text{sales} = \text{items sold} \times \text{price charged}$$

As price falls, so the level of the sales value relative to costs falls. In turn, this means that profits fall. However, organisations only survive in the long term if they make regular profits at a level acceptable to the providers of their funds. Driving down price can result in an organisation failing to produce enough profit and consequently ceasing to trade. If two organisations, A and B, are supplying products to a particular market and, as a result of price competition, company A is forced to stop trading, it could mean that not only would the consumer lose choice but company B might also be able to charge high prices as there is no longer competition.

Many companies have, therefore, moved away from pure price competition and into non-price mechanisms. Pricing, however, is still seen as a crucial element, simply because it is the only element of the marketing mix that produces revenue directly; all other elements of the marketing mix are costs.

In some markets, price is still emphasised by sellers. These are normally markets for commodity products or a market segment which is both price sensitive and in which a seller has some sort of cost advantage over its competition. Proton cars, for example, are sold in the UK on the basis of price; its promotion stresses the price advantage that Protons have over similarly sized vehicles. The company is able to offer low prices as it has low costs of manufacture derived from using superseded technology with relatively cheap labour.

Pricing objectives

Before it can be decided exactly what price to charge for a product, it is necessary to know what the organisation is seeking to achieve with its prices. Each organisation will have particular objectives. However, there are objectives which are common to most organisations. Almost all organisations have survival as a primary business objective, and this has implications for the prices they must charge over the longer term; although, in the short term, they may be prepared to charge prices which create losses in order to ensure long-term survival. Examples of objectives that affect the prices an organisation sets include:

- to make a profit
- to achieve a specified return on investment
- to boost cash flow
- to recover development costs as quickly as possible
- to project an image of high quality
- to maintain market share.

PRICING METHODS

The price that a company decides to charge for a product or service can be based upon three variables: cost; competition; customers.

Cost-plus pricing

The simplest way of setting a price is to add a fixed percentage to the total cost of producing a product. This is known as cost-plus pricing. In certain situations, this is actually a good way of establishing a price. Government has often awarded contracts on the basis of cost plus; many small tradespeople add a fixed percentage to materials they use in the jobs they carry out; most retailers use standard mark-ups; many restaurants use cost plus to set their meal prices.

In the vast majority of cases, however, cost-plus pricing is not particularly appropriate and Mercer (1996, p. 265) suggests that over 70 per cent of organisations use other approaches. The main problem with cost-plus pricing is that it is price setting from the viewpoint of the manufacturer not the customer. The customer is not interested in the costs of production but in the benefits that will accrue if they use the product. Furthermore, they will decide on the acceptability of price by not only valuing the benefits that they will receive, but also by comparing the price and the benefits to those of competitors. Using a cost-plus pricing system means that a single price is set for a product irrespective of the willingness of the customer to pay.

An alternative approach to setting a price, therefore, is to base the decision not upon the organisation, but on either the customer, or the competition, or both.

Demand-based pricing

Prices based upon the customer are usually referred to as demand-based pricing (or value-based pricing). In this approach to pricing, the costs of production are only relevant to the extent that they provide a base below which price must not fall. The actual price charged reflects the price the organisation believes the customer will pay to obtain the benefits that ownership of the product confers. The customer may derive benefit from the quality of the product, or from particular features of the product, or perhaps from some psychological element such as rarity or prestige. Rolex watches are priced against customer perceptions of quality and status; Hermes silk scarves are priced as a prestige item; Heinz baked beans are priced on quality. All three products have direct competition but are examples in which the price actually charged for the product reflects what the customer will pay to obtain the benefits they perceive as coming with the product, rather than the cost of production.

Customer-based pricing also allows for flexibility of price. Some products exhibit high demand at one time and somewhat lower demand at other times. In this situation, the price can be adjusted accordingly. So, for example, hotels in holiday locations charge higher prices in the summer when demand is high and less in the off-season when demand is very much lower; hotels in business centres charge more during the week and reduce their rates at weekends when business use is very light. UK railway companies use this approach to price setting, charging customers different fares depending upon the time of day and day of the week they want to travel. At periods of peak demand, very much higher prices are charged than at periods of low demand.

Competitor-based pricing

Competitor-based pricing (sometimes called going-rate pricing) requires the company to set its price on the basis of what other companies are charging. This does not mean that prices are set identical to those of competition but that some sort of relationship is established and maintained, such as 25p more or 10 per cent less.

The second level petrol companies, such as Jet, often charge 2–3p less per litre than the major companies.

ACTIVITY 20

Whatever method is used to generate a price, if the product or service is to be successful in the long term, the price charged must satisfy three basic criteria. What do you think these three criteria are? Remember that in a successful exchange transaction all parties must satisfy their own objectives.

Prices must:

- cover the costs of the seller
- produce the required level of profit for the seller
- be acceptable to the purchaser and be at a level that the purchaser is able to pay.

PSYCHOLOGY OF PRICE

Customer perceptions of price are very rarely totally rational; they are likely to be at least, in part, emotionally based. Price is often seen as a guide to quality; Stella Artois lager is advertised with the line 'reassuringly expensive'. Indeed, in the absence of any other knowledge, price is likely to be the only way customers will believe that they can judge quality.

There are, however, many other ways in which marketing can use knowledge of the psychology of price. One of the best-known examples of using psychology in setting a price is the use of 'odd' and 'even' pricing. In 'odd' pricing, a product would not be priced at £10 but at £9.99, or perhaps £9.95, with the objective of making the product appear to be less expensive and better value. Conversely, 'even' prices are claimed to give a product a more up-market feel and to cause the customer to perceive the product as being a premium item. There is little evidence to support the belief that either approach increases sales, Zikmund and d'Amico, (1994, p. 519), although it is more usual to see 'odd' prices charged.

Certain products have expected prices. This is the amount the customer expects to pay for the product. It is becoming less common today as prices are much less stable but, for many products, there is still a band within which consumers expect to find the price. So, customers have an expectation about the price of chocolate countlines like Mars, Crunchie and Flake. In similar vein, there are certain purchasing situations in which customers will not expect to spend more than a certain figure, such as the purchase of a child's gift. In these situations, manufacturers will attempt to ensure that the final retail price meets these expectations.

NEW PRODUCT PRICING

In the pricing of a new innovative product companies have a choice of two basic approaches – **market skimming** and **market penetration**. The two approaches are at opposite ends of the price spectrum; one approach sets a high price, the other sets a low price.

Market skimming

Market skimming involves setting a high price. The logic is that the product will be offered to that segment of the market which responds to exclusivity, likes to own innovative products and will be relatively insensitive to price. Once this segment of the market has been exhausted, the price can be brought down slightly and offered to a segment which is slightly more price sensitive, perhaps by offering a less well-specified version. This process can continue until all the market has been offered the product. Such an approach works well where there are barriers to competition and where the product has real differential advantage. Many new electronic products fall into this category, such as calculators, personal computers, digital watches and CD players. Gradually reducing the price is not always necessary; in some cases skimming can continue throughout the life of the product, as for example with Rolex watches or Joy perfume.

Market penetration

The opposite strategy is market penetration. Here, a low price is set with a view to obtaining a high market share as rapidly as possible. It is a mass market strategy aimed at retaining a large market share in the later stages of the product life cycle when competition will be fierce. It is particularly appropriate when there are no barriers to competition and when patents and production processes require high volume output to be efficient. Setting a low price can sometimes act as a barrier to entry to other companies; they might feel that profits will be difficult to achieve or take too many years and, as a result, choose not to enter the market.

Penetration pricing can also be used to gain entry to a particular market segment. Once established, the company can raise prices. The Co-operative Bank used this approach with its Gold credit card which it introduced with no annual fee and offered a low rate of interest on outstanding credit balances.

A variant of penetration pricing can sometimes be used to achieve profit over time. For example, a car manufacturer might set the new price of the car fairly low and then seek to make profits through pricing spares rather more highly than other manufacturers. Aircraft engine manufacturers often price at very little more than breakeven in order to achieve sales, since they know that once an engine is installed in an aircraft there will be a constant demand for service and replacement parts. In any situation where replacements are required, consideration can be given to seeking to make profits not from the initial purchase but from subsequent purchases. A manufacturer of men's razors might establish a very low price for the razor and seek to make long-term profits through the sale of the razor blades that fit the razor. An extreme example might be to sell the product at cost or even give it away. Soap powder manufacturers, for example, give away the detergent containers that go inside the washing machine in order to capture customers and their future purchases.

ACTIVITY 21

You are about to launch these new products.

- A wheat-based breakfast cereal
- A new (patented) drug for the relief of arthritic conditions
- A micro-sized digital video camera

Explain briefly for each product the pricing strategy you would you use – penetration or skimming – and why.

The breakfast cereal market is both very competitive and saturated with products. Walk along the appropriate aisle of your nearest superstore and you will probably be able to count at least fifty different types of breakfast cereal. Most of the products are priced very similarly and it is unlikely that a newcomer would be able to command a significantly different price unless it offered some novel benefit to the consumer. In addition, for any new product of this type, the major task will be to induce trial, that is, to persuade the consumer to make a first purchase. In this set of circumstances, a penetration strategy is more likely to be successful than a skimming strategy.

With patent protection, if the drug is genuinely effective then a skimming strategy is likely to appear at first sight as the most appropriate, particularly as there are estimated to be 20 million arthritis sufferers in the UK alone. However, remember that the vast majority of prescribed drugs are obtained by sufferers through the National Health Service and if the price is set too high then health authorities may be reluctant to allow it to be prescribed. This happened with Riluzole, a drug used in the treatment of motor neurone disease.

A micro-sized digital video camera is a classic example of a consumer product made possible through technological developments and which will probably have a high initial status value. As a new introduction to the market, skimming should be possible with the price gradually coming down as competition develops and those consumers prepared to pay a high price for status are saturated. Polaroid cameras, the ball-point pen and pocket calculators are all examples of products that have followed this route. At the time of writing, JVC have just introduced a micro-sized digital video camera onto the market. It is selling for approximately £2,000. What price is it now?

3.7 Role of distribution

In marketing, distribution is about making goods and services available to customers. Rarely will it be the case that producers and suppliers are together in the same place; the task of distribution is to overcome the 'gaps' that separate the products and services from those who create them and those who wish to use them. Put very simply, distribution is the process used by an organisation to ensure that the **right product** is made available in the **right quantities** at the **right time** at the **right place**. If the organisation can ensure that these four 'rights' are met then the process of exchange can take place.

There are many thousands of organisations and individuals that exist to assist in the process of overcoming the 'gap'. Each of these organisations or individuals is known as a **marketing intermediary**. A **marketing channel** or **channel of distribution** consists of the producer of a product or the provider of a service, the customer and the collection of intermediaries that are used to link these two and allow the product or service to move from the producer to the customer.

The method of distribution that a company employs is a key variable in its marketing mix and recently has come to be seen by some managers and writers as an important means of achieving competitive advantage, Christopher and McDonald (1995, p. 249), through using the distribution process to improve the total bundle of benefits received by the customer. However, as Baker (1992, p. 386) observes 'despite its obvious importance, distribution remains a largely neglected topic in marketing'.

Marketing managers have to make decisions in two separate but interlinked areas.

- They must build and manage the channel(s) of distribution. This entails deciding on the type and length of marketing channel to use; the number, type and selection of intermediaries; the management of the channel.
- They must ensure that the product is physically available to the consumer. Physical distribution management will usually encompass the activities of stock storage and control, the handling of materials, order processing, and transportation.

It is quite possible to undertake the first of these two tasks and not the second. For example, the manufacturer of tinned beans might have decided to use retailers to help make their product available to consumers and they might have selected the exact shops, provided appropriate in-store promotional material and agreed the terms of business with the retailers. However, if the product is then not physically delivered to the shops no exchange can take place.

Why use intermediaries?

At first sight, it might appear that each time an intermediary is involved in the distribution process the producer gives up some level of control and profit to that intermediary. Why then does a producer wish to use intermediaries at all? The answer lies in the way in which intermediaries increase the efficiency of the distribution of products and thereby increase sales and reduce costs for the producer. Consider the problem faced by the Wrigley Company. If there are no intermediaries, the Wrigley Company would have to visit every potential user of chewing gum regularly in order to sell its product. With millions of potential customers using the product every day, this would be an enormous and potentially very expensive process. Intermediaries increase the efficiency of the distribution process by reducing the number of contacts between manufacturer and customer. In Figure 12, the top diagram shows the situation for four manufacturers of chewing gum each needing to contact six customers. As you can see, 24 contacts are needed for all potential exchanges to take place. The bottom diagram shows what happens if one intermediary is placed between the manufacturers and the customers. The number of contacts is now reduced to ten.

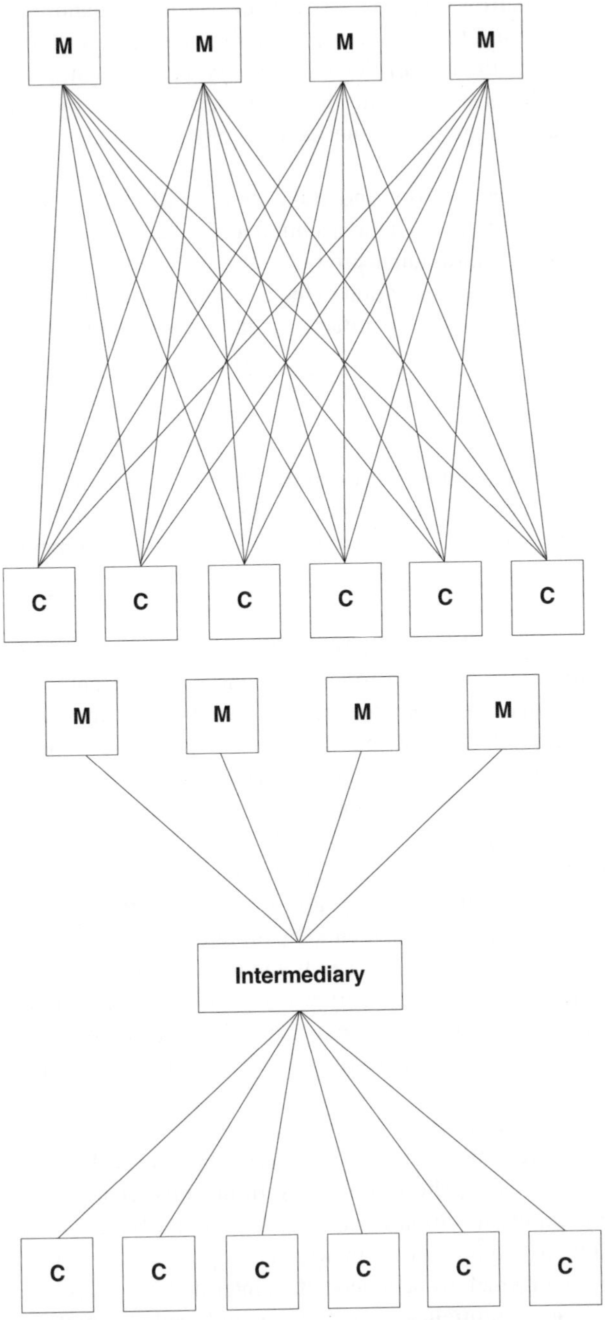

Figure 12: Use of intermediaries

Reducing the number of contacts reduces the costs involved in the distributive process. If we increase the number of manufacturers in Figure 12 to many thousands and the customers to many millions the total potential savings are very substantial. These savings are then able to be passed on to the consumer.

Intermediaries not only reduce the final cost to the customer, they also play a major role in helping to bring together and match supply and demand. Producers tend to make fairly narrow ranges of products in very large quantities, but customers want wide ranges of products available in small quantities. Kotler and Armstrong (1994, p. 350) define the role of the intermediary as 'to transform the assortment of products made by producers into the assortments wanted by consumers'. This constitutes the value chain of the intermediary organisation.

To fulfil this role, intermediaries undertake some or all of the following activities: the provision of variety through the accumulation of a wide variety of goods; the packaging and sale of individual products; the provision of delivery and credit services; the provision of information to the customer; repair services; the provision of customer knowledge to the manufacturer; the provision of storage facilities.

ACTIVITY 22

It might appear that universities and colleges do not need to consider distribution when developing their marketing mix. Can you think of ways in which distribution can be important to educational establishments?

Most universities and colleges have fixed buildings, sometimes grouped together, sometimes spread throughout a town or county. A dominant feature of these establishments is that the customer (student) visits them in order to be able to obtain the offered product. Many potential customers for education, however, are not able to visit the providers, perhaps because they work full time, look after children, are carers, or live in remote areas, and so they need the providers to come to them. The Open University is the prime example of an educational institution catering for this customer need. Many colleges and universities are now using distribution strategies by allowing other providers to deliver their courses through franchise arrangements, by producing open and distance learning materials, by running courses at weekends and in towns and cities remote from the institution itself, by delivering education via satellite and telephone links, and by developing interactive multimedia materials. They are practising marketing by providing the product or service when and where the customer wants.

DISTRIBUTION CHANNELS

We saw that there are many thousands of intermediaries involved in the process of distribution. As a result, there are many thousands of possible channels of distribution that an organisation might select. Essentially, the available channels break down into two types: those in which the producer contacts the customer directly and those in which some independent intermediary is involved. The former are known as **direct channels** and the latter as **indirect channels**.

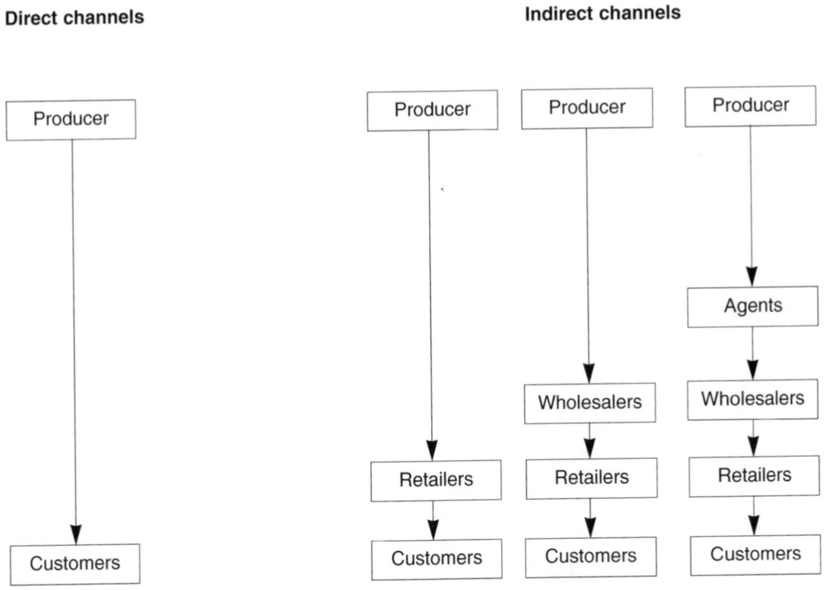

Figure 13: Distribution channels

Direct channels include the use of mail-order catalogues, for example many horticultural growers distribute their bulbs, seeds and plants through mail order catalogues; producer-owned and controlled sales forces, such as Avon Cosmetics, Everest double-glazing; factory shops where the manufacturer sells directly to the public through a shop on the factory premises; manufacturer-owned retailers, for example Boots. The latest direct channel which is being explored by many producers is the use of the Internet.

There are two important points to note. First, it does not follow that the shortest channel will be the cheapest or the most effective. Second, producers will use as many channels of distribution as are needed to ensure that they reach all the segments of the market that they have targeted. Many manufacturers of packaged food products, for example, will sell directly to retailers as well as through wholesalers. The number and type of intermediaries and channels will depend to a large extent on the decision the organisation makes about the extent of market coverage that it wishes for its products. There are three coverage strategies.

- **Intensive** distribution requires that the product is made available in as many ways and in as many places as possible.
- **Exclusive** distribution makes the product available from only one place in any given geographical area.
- **Selective** distribution limits the number of ways and places in which the product is made available to the customer.

ACTIVITY 23

For each of the three distribution strategies – intensive, selective and exclusive – state what sort of products would best be served by using this strategy. Give two examples of specific products best served by each strategy.

Exclusive distribution is best suited to those products that are bought infrequently, need high levels of service both pre- and post-sale and have a limited potential market. They are usually products for which the customer is prepared to travel to purchase. Examples include Rolls-Royce and other exclusive and usually expensive motor cars; certain brands of designer clothing, for example, Gucci; and, some brands of audio equipment, for example Bose.

Intensive distribution is used for convenience products such as bread, milk, confectionery, tobacco, newspapers and, indeed, most packaged consumer items. These products require very little service and because they are replaced frequently the customer is not prepared to put other than the minimum amount of time into purchasing these items. The intermediary is required to do little other than make the product available. Obtaining intensive distribution will require the producer to use a wide variety of channels.

Selective distribution is particularly suited to shopping products. These are products where customers are prepared to devote some time and energy to finding the correct product that meets their needs. Some level of pre- and post-sale service will be required, and the producer will usually choose the intermediaries that will be able to provide the support that maintains the good name of the manufacturer. Many durable products are offered in this way, such as Sony audio equipment, Hoover washing machines, middle-range watches such as Rotary and Seiko, shoes such as Church's and other clothing brands like Barbour coats and jackets.

3.8 Promotion

Promotion is probably the most visible aspect of marketing activity and as such it is often seen to be the essence of marketing. Section 1 of this unit should have dispelled this myth; should you still believe that marketing is essentially about promotion, and in particular about advertising, please reread section 1 now.

ACTIVITY 24

Ralph Waldo Emerson said: 'If a man ... make a better mouse trap ... though he builds his home in the woods, the world will beat a path to his door.' Write a short paragraph explaining why Emerson was wrong.

Before the world will beat a path to the door of the inventor of a better mousetrap, several conditions have to be met:

- there must be a need for a mousetrap
- people with this need must know of the existence of this mousetrap
- they need to know where the mousetrap can be obtained
- they must be able to travel to the place of exchange
- they need to know what makes this mousetrap better
- they need to know how much the mousetrap will cost
- they must believe that the new mousetrap is worth the asking price.

In summary, the potential buyers will need a considerable amount of information before they would be prepared to consider buying the new mousetrap. In order to provide this information, the inventor of the new mousetrap will have to communicate with those who have a need for a mousetrap. It is this information that potential customers will use to assist them in deciding whether to buy or not.

Marketing communication refers to the provision of information that will assist in the establishment, operation and completion of the exchange process. The term **promotion** refers to the range of techniques that organisations use to carry out the communication tasks. Promotion is, therefore, applied marketing communication. Zikmund and d'Amico (1994, p. 392) say that promotion is 'communication with a purpose'.

Promotion should be viewed as the totality of all communications sent out by an organisation, whether intentional or not. The sum total of all the marketing communications associated with an organisation – often referred to as the **communications mix** – has to complement the positioning of the product in the marketplace. Promotion, like all other parts of the marketing mix, cannot be treated in isolation but must be employed as an integral component of a total marketing effort.

PROMOTIONAL OBJECTIVES

Promotion is used to 'communicate with individuals, groups or organisations with the aim of directly or indirectly facilitating exchanges by informing and persuading...' Dibb, Simpkin, Pride and Ferrell (1994, p. 376).

Marketing communications can be viewed as a means of indicating that what the company has on offer matches with what the customer is seeking to find. In terms of the marketing mix, promotion usually is designed to achieve three basic objectives.

- **Informing**. It is important to provide information relating to the organisation and its products or services. This is the most basic function of promotion since prospective customers must know of the existence of a product before they can even begin to consider buying it. Information also covers essential knowledge about the product: where it may be obtained, its price and some consideration of the benefits that will accrue to purchasers.

- **Persuading**. In competitive markets, simply telling consumers of the existence of a product is unlikely to be enough. It will be necessary to also persuade potential customers to buy one product in preference to another, often by demonstrating that the benefits of the product will provide a better match with customer requirements than will those of other products.
- **Reminding**. All organisations in a competitive market will be aiming persuasive messages at customers in an attempt to gain their business. The organisation that presently has that business will seek to retain it by reminding its customers of the reasons why they should continue to buy the product.

METHODS OF PROMOTION

There are four traditional elements of promotion. These are advertising, personal selling, publicity and sales promotion. Two new elements have recently become increasingly important: direct mail and sponsorship. We shall briefly overview each of these six element in turn. You will investigate them in much more detail in later marketing modules.

Advertising

Advertising is a form of mass communication. It is a form of non-personal presentation of products, services or ideas. An advertisement will have an identified sponsor who will have paid for the advertisement and the organisation or products of the sponsor will be identified in some way. It includes the use of television, newspapers, magazines, radio, cinema, posters, bus sides, etc. Advertising is able to communicate with a large number of people at a time, at reasonably low cost per person, and will deliver the message in a standard form with great frequency.

Personal selling

Personal selling can be carried out over the telephone or face to face. It is a direct interaction between a member of an organisation and an individual potential customer, usually with a view to persuade the potential customer to become an actual customer. It is very flexible, allowing the communication to be adapted as the interchange takes place. It is a two-way form of promotion. It can however be a very expensive form of promotion.

Publicity

Sometimes, an organisation and/or its products will be newsworthy in some way and will be featured in one or more of the mass media. **Publicity** is very similar to advertising in that it uses some of the same non-personal mass media to carry a message about an organisation and its offerings. The difference is that publicity is not directly paid for by the organisation and the exact nature of the message is determined by a third party, usually an employee of the media that has decided to publicise the organisation and its offerings. **Public relations** is the systematic attempt to manage the nature of the publicity that an organisation receives so that a positive image of the organisation is projected by the media.

Sales promotion

Sales promotion is the term given to specific short-term activities that are designed to increase sales of a product. These activities are not routine events and have a specified life. Examples of sales promotions include temporary price reductions, coupons, free gifts, samples, competitions, bonus deals, extra value packs, display items for retail use, and demonstrations. This is a rapidly growing area and 'expenditure on sales promotion in the UK now exceeds that spent on advertising' Palmer and Worthington, (1992, p. 28).

Direct mail

Direct mail is the use of individually targeted letters and other promotional material sent through the postal system. It is non-personal and has an identified sponsor who will have paid for the communication. This is the fastest growing form of promotion with expenditure estimated to be growing at some 30 per cent annually in the UK (Randall, 1993, p.162). Many non-commercial organisations are making increasing use of direct mail; charities, in particular, are major users of direct-mail approaches.

Sponsorship

Sponsorship attempts to associate an organisation with various activities that the organisation's target markets may see to be worthy. By appearing to be freely supporting these activities, organisations are attempting to enhance their public image. Sponsorship can be defined as 'the financial or material support of an event, activity, person or product by an unrelated organisation or donor' Dibb, Simpkin, Pride and Ferrell, (1994, p. 431). In return for the sponsorship, the sponsor's name and products receive exposure. The use of sponsorship has grown in popularity and there are now many forms of sponsorship in the UK.

Sporting sponsorship is particularly widespread. It is difficult to think of a sport that is now not in receipt of some sponsor's funds. In many sports, it is not just the sport as a whole that receives sponsorship. In football, for example, Carling sponsors the English Premier League but organisations also sponsor individual teams –the electronics company Sharp sponsors Manchester United, for example. The arts is another field of endeavour that attracts a significant amount of support in this way, as do charities and other 'good causes'.

Promotional mix

Each of the six elements of promotion has strengths and weaknesses. The particular elements an organisation uses and the decisions made within an element, will depend upon the complexity of its products and services, its target markets, the objectives set for promotion and the particular message that needs to be conveyed. The particular combination of promotional elements chosen by an organisation is known as the **promotional mix**.

Although promotional activities directed at the final customer are the ones that are visible to most people, in fact these are only half of the story. When an organisation decides to use channels of distribution that include marketing intermediaries, the promotional mix must also have elements that are designed to assist in persuading the intermediaries to help to move the products through the channel. Promoting to the intermediaries is known as a **push strategy** and promoting to the final customer is called a **pull strategy**.

Push promotions are designed to get the intermediaries to stock products. Thus, organisations will use techniques to 'push' their merchandise into the channel to wholesalers and other distributors and retailers. The aim is to have the intermediaries with stocks of the product, so that they will then push the product right through the channel to the final consumer.

Pull promotions are designed to get final consumers to ask for the product. So, organisations employ methods to encourage a 'pull' effect from customers, that is, to develop sufficient interest in the product for potential consumers to go and request the product or information about the product's availability from intermediaries, hence pulling it through the channel.

In practice, organisations will usually use a blend of push and pull to try to ensure maximum availability of, and demand for, the products and services that it has to offer.

ACTIVITY 25

The management of Heinz are considering promotional activities. Provide four examples of activities that could be used as part of a push strategy and four that could be used as part of a pull strategy.

Marketing is an art and not a science. The examples that you have suggested will be a result of your individual creativity. The main promotional element emphasised in push strategies is personal selling. This is often backed up with direct mail and advertising in the trade journals. Sales promotional activities are usually directed at improving the short-term profits of the intermediary, for example cash discounts and special deals, free product, special volume discounts. Here are a few examples that you might have considered:

- extra sales visits from sales personnel
- discounts for larger orders
- competitions for intermediary staff
- advertisements in trade journals
- attendance at trade fairs and exhibitions
- provision of free product, such as 'buy one pack, get one pack free'
- provision of special sales fixtures
- offers to design in-store product space allocation.

Pull strategies utilise advertising, publicity, sales promotion and direct mail. Direct mail is becoming increasingly important, particularly in the use of coupons and special offers. Here are a few examples that you might have considered:

- advertising campaigns in newspapers, magazines, television, radio
- sponsorship of events and activities important to the target market
- special offers, such as larger size for same price, 'buy two get one free'
- poster campaigns
- coupons for money-off or special deal.
- product placement, for example, Omega watches in the James Bond films
- giving free samples to famous personalities or organisations
- sponsoring charities
- joint promotions with complimentary products, for example, eggs with bacon or pasta with pasta sauce.

REVIEW ACTIVITY 3

Read the Mosaic Tile Floor Company case study. Identify three target markets and develop a profile of each market. Which of these target segments should Eric and Annabel seek to reach through advertising, and which would they be better using other forms of promotion? Why?

Mosaic Tile Floor Company

Eric and Annabel met at art college some ten years ago. On leaving college, they both obtained jobs that used their art and design training. They very soon tired of the regular hours and fixed nature of their employment and decided to spend some years travelling. To fund this lifestyle, they have worked in a variety of jobs all over the world. Returning home, they decided that they wanted to be able to work together in a situation where they could use their art and design training, while living in a 'nice part of the country'. They eventually decided to rent a house in Plymouth.

After a lot of thought, they came up with what they considered would be a good idea for a business of their own. They decided to start a company that designs and lays mosaic tile floors. These floors would be totally individual, each floor being designed in shapes, textures and colours specifically for each customer. No two floors need ever be the same. They could work together and use all their design ability and training. While travelling they had seen just the type of tiles they would need being manufactured in Portugal and, after a little research, they discovered that these tiles were imported through a London-based wholesaler. They obtained an account with this wholesaler, and enthusiastically set up in business.

Two years on, and things have not been going well. They are back working in odd jobs. They have obtained almost no work but, although despondent, Eric and Annabel are still convinced that they have a good idea. They have come to accept that their total lack of any business knowledge is much more of a problem than they originally assumed that it would be, but they are hoping to get some real help from Eric's youngest sister. Katie is presently in the placement year of a business studies degree and has agreed to come down to Plymouth with a view to combining a holiday with giving some advice on how they might resurrect their business idea. After spending time listening to the ideas they have, and what they have done so far, Katie delivers her initial thoughts.

'I don't want to be rude, but you really haven't got a clue! The basic idea might well be sound but the way you have tackled the problem of establishing your business has been far too messy and much too haphazard. You only have to look around this house to see that you have real design talent, but that will not be nearly enough to bring you success in business. You need to develop a very structured approach to defining and building your business and that means deciding upon your target market and building a marketing mix to reach it. I think that the first thing we need to do is to be very clear about exactly what this business is to be involved in; what it is that we are talking about.' With that Katie produced paper, pens and a laptop. It was going to be a long hard night.

By the following morning, they had built up a clear picture of the basics of the idea. They used a series of simple headings and put notes against these headings. As a working name they had decided upon 'The Mosaic Tile Floor Company'. Katie typed up their findings.

Product outline

What – individually designed mosaic tile floor. Designed and laid to the customer's requirements from design ideas supplied and adapted by the company.

Where – suitable for internal use only. Domestic applications only. Anywhere a hard-wearing attractive domestic floor is needed. Kitchen, bathroom, conservatory, porch, entrance hall.

When – whenever a 'new' floor is desired. Usually on three occasions:

- when a kitchen or bathroom is being refurbished or refitted
- when a new house is being built
- when an existing property is being completely rebuilt or converted, for example, barn conversions.

How – can only be laid on solid floors. Not suitable for use on suspended wooden flooring. Thus, can only be laid in ground-floor bathrooms or in buildings with solid upper floors, such as warehouse conversions, flats.

Why – people will buy because it offers the only way to get a totally unique floor. Two will never be the same. Possible to fit perfectly with any situation. Offers a 'talking' point. Recreates Roman and Greek flooring. Reminiscent of Mediterranean holidays. Is handmade and exclusively designed.

What else – floors need to be fairly large if the full effect of design possibilities is to be achieved. If the cost of design time is to be recovered, it needs to be spread over a reasonable floor area so that the cost per square yard is not prohibitive. It will not blend well with the cheapest kitchen or bathroom units. Best results are achieved in kitchens when set against natural materials such as wooden kitchen units; it will make good units look like the most expensive. It will be expensive – on average over £50 a square yard; and considerably more for intricate designs. Eric and Annabel do not want to work more than 30 miles from their home. At first, they will have to lay the tiles themselves.

The three review the initial product outline and agree that it is a good reflection of the current position. Eric and Annabel look pleased with themselves; the hard work was over and now they could become designers again. Katie smiled knowingly: 'OK, now we can start! The first thing that we need to do is to try and get some idea of the target market for this product.'

Summary

The marketing mix is the combination of the marketing tools used by marketing management. The objective of an organisation is to create a marketing mix that will satisfy the needs of the target market while generating sufficient sales to ensure an acceptable level of profit for the organisation. The four main ingredients of the marketing mix are product, price, promotion and distribution. The product or service is fundamental to an organisation because it is usually the sole means the organisation has of generating income. The most important point to remember about the product is that what people buy is the benefits that they obtain from having the product. Prices should be a reflection of the willingness of the market to pay, and not simply a mark up on the cost of production. Rarely will producers and suppliers be together in the same place; so distribution is about making goods and services available to customers when and where they need them. The primary role of promotion is to communicate with individuals, groups and organisations in order to provide information and encourage the purchase of the goods and services of the organisation.

Unit Review Activitiy
Case study

Drake Chemicals

Drake Chemicals is a medium-sized company in north-east England. For nearly sixty years, it has been manufacturing a range of household cleansing products. The current product mix consists of floor polishes, oven cleaners, starch, scouring powders and washing soda, all of which are marketed under the Drake brand and nationally advertised.

The company distributes the products nationally through a number of wholesalers, and they each have exclusive territories. Drake places no restrictions on the wholesalers; they may distribute the products as they see fit. In addition, Drake deals directly with two large supermarket groups. All products are priced by Drake on a sliding scale, based on volume per order with a rebate scheme based on annual purchases (for details, see Table 7).

Quantity discount on all household goods (case size 96 units)

Order (cases)	0–10	11–20	21–30	31–40	41–50	51–100	100+
Discount	0%	1.5%	2%	2.5%	3%	5%	7.5%

Annual rebate

Cases	100–500	501–1,000	1,001–2,000	2,001–5,000	5,001+
Rebate	0%	0.5%	1%	1.5%	2.5%

Table 7: Drake's discount policy

The company has a sales force of six, who have responsibility for sales of all the products throughout the UK. Each has a geographically defined territory, for which he has total responsibility. They operate at the retail level, working in conjunction with the wholesalers, and they also have some merchandising. Remuneration is by way of basic salary plus commission on sales over target. They sell both direct to retailers and to wholesalers. Current earnings average £21,500 plus the usual benefits package of company car, life insurance, expenses, profit-related bonus. The sales force (all male) have been with the company for a long time and two are due to retire within the next three months. Drake has been finding it increasingly difficult to maintain distribution of the products and in recent years it has seen its retail customer base gradually shrink to the point where at least one of the territories is now no longer really viable. The company's sales picture has been relatively stable over the last decade although a downward trend appears to be developing (see Table 8).

Year	**Sales** (£000)
1986	20,462
1987	20,542
1988	20,483
1989	20,467
1990	20,448
1991	20,394
1992	20,298
1993	20,301
1994	20,297
1995	20,199
1996	20,154
1997	20,106

Table 8: Drake's sales

Tim Bryant, who ran the firm since 1945, has recently died at the age of 84. Drake had been Tim's life; he had never married and had no family to succeed him. Always a family firm, the ownership of the company has now passed to his great niece Jane Perkold. Jane is a 28-year-old history graduate who has spent the years since graduation working overseas as a voluntary aid worker.

Promotional activity is mainly centred around trade journals and the provision of point-of-sale material. There is no real promotional strategy other than a continuation of what has always been done. Occasionally, Tim was persuaded by an advertising representative to place some local newspaper, radio or television advertisements but this was always on an *ad hoc* basis. The one constant has been Drake's attendance at three annual trade fairs – one for household products, one for small north-eastern manufacturing businesses and one run by the Newcastle Chamber of Commerce. Tim always enjoyed these events enormously although just how much business they produced was open to question.

As a result of a meeting at one of these fairs, Tim had been considering starting a new line for Drake. He was giving serious consideration to an idea offered to him by a local inventor. Essentially, the idea consists of a high-pressure lance which, when combined with a special cleanser, cleans industrial equipment more quickly and efficiently. Tim considered that the lance had wide application in industry, particularly where it is necessary to clean machinery in confined spaces such as on an assembly line or a packaging line.

Drake has developed a special type of industrial cleansing agent for the lance, and Tim was sure that the company has the necessary technical know-how and could raise the finance to produce the cleanser. Seacroft Engineering, a small local engineering firm, has agreed to produce the lance. It is believed that Seacroft will be able to produce the lance at sufficient levels of quantity and quality. If Drake markets the lance, fixed costs are likely to be £175,000 (including a payment to Seacroft and the inventor). Seacroft would charge Drake £12.50 per lance and the inventor requires a royalty payment of £1.50 per lance. The cleanser itself would be relatively expensive to manufacture and the board estimates that it will have to sell at approximately twice the price of traditional cleansing agents.

After spending a short time being introduced to the company and its operations, Jane decides she must undertake a programme of change designed to ensure the continued health of the company. She is greatly troubled by her lack of a commercial or industrial background. Should she go ahead with the lance idea? Should she replace the retiring salesmen? Surely television advertising is the thing to do? What about the forthcoming trade fair? So much to think about, and so little help readily available. Unsure of what to do next, Jane turns to her younger sister Kate, who is in the first year of her undergraduate business course. She asks Kate to help her to understand what she should do, what decisions need to be made and what those decisions should be, what information she needs and how market research might help.

What advice should Kate give to her sister? Write notes that Kate might use to deliver her advice to Jane using the three headings below. You should write no more than 250 words for each heading.

- An analysis of the situation with the existing products
- An analysis of the new idea
- What actions should be taken

This activity is designed to demonstrate how the elements of marketing fit together in a realistic situation. The objective is for you to arrive at concrete statements of what you would do. It is no good making very general statements or quoting concepts; you need to apply what you have been learning.

Unit Summary

In this unit, we have examined the area of business activity known as marketing. Marketing is both a functional area of business activity and a management philosophy which guides the whole approach of an organisation towards doing business. The marketing orientation holds that organisations will survive and prosper in the long term if they produce the goods and services that people want. To do this, it is necessary to decide which customers the organisations wishes to serve, to discover their needs and wants and then to produce the appropriate goods and services to satisfy these needs and wants. This means placing the customer at the centre of all organisational activities and requires that organisations obtain as much knowledge as possible about customers. Marketing research is the key to obtaining this understanding. An organisation which is using a marketing orientation is said to have adopted the marketing concept. Marketing is not only of use to very large organisations but can be practised by all organisations whatever their size, product range or profit orientation.

The primary tasks of marketing management are the selection of a group of consumers at whom the product or service will be aimed and the development of the market offering for these consumers. The combination of choosing a target market and developing a market offering for that target is known as marketing strategy.

The selection of a target market requires that the total marketplace is split into subsets of consumers known as segments and the process of splitting the market in this way is known as segmentation. The purpose of segmentation is to allow organisations to choose those segment or segments which will allow them to meet their corporate objectives. The set of controllable marketing variables that the organisation can use to create its market offering is called the marketing mix.

The elements of the marketing mix can be placed into the four main categories of product, price, promotion and place. Although decisions are made in each of the four areas separately, it is the total offering which is seen by the market and the key to developing a successful marketing mix is the blending together into a complete whole.

References

American Marketing Association (1988) *Marketing Definitions: A Glossary of Marketing Terms*

Baker, M (1991) *The Marketing Book*, Heinemann

Baker, M (1992) *Marketing Strategy and Management*, Macmillan, 2nd edn

Baker, M (1995) *The Marketing Mix in Action*, TV Choice Ltd 1995

Boyd, H, Walker, O and Larreche, J (1995) *Marketing Management*, Irwin, 2nd edn

Cameron, M, Rushton, A and Carson, D (1988) *Marketing*, Penguin

Chartered Institute of Marketing (1990) *Marketing Definitions*

Christopher, M and McDonald, M (1995) *Marketing: An Introductory Text*, Macmillan

Dibb, S, Simpkin, L, Pride, W and Ferrell, O (1994) *Marketing: Concepts and Strategies,* Houghton Mifflin, 2nd edn

Drucker, P (1964) *The Practice of Management*, Pan Books

Drucker, P (1973) *Management: Tasks, Responsibilities, Practices*, Harper and Row

Hill, E and O'Sullivan, T (1996) *Marketing*, Longman

Kotler, P and Armstrong, G (1994) *Principles of Marketing* Prentice Hall, 4th edn

Kotler, P (1996) *Marketing Management* Prentice Hall, 9th edn

Lamb, J (ed) (1963) 'A statement of marketing philosophy' in *Journal of Marketing,* January

Lancaster, G and Massingham, L (1993) *Essentials of Marketing*, McGraw Hill, 2nd edn

Lancaster, G and Massingham, L (1993) *Marketing Management*, McGraw Hill

Levitt, T (1960) 'Marketing Myopia' in *Harvard Business Review Vol 38,* July

McCarthy, E and Perreault, W (1993) *Basic Marketing: a Managerial Approach*, Irwin, 11th edn

Mercer, D (1996) *Marketing*, Blackwell, 2nd edn

Palmer, A and Worthington, I (1992) *The Business and Marketing Environment*, McGraw Hill

Proctor, T (1996) *Marketing Management* International Thompson Business Press

Randall, G (1993) *Principles of Marketing*, Routledge

Smith, A (1937) *The Wealth of Nations*, Random House

Stanton, W J (1971) *Fundamentals of Marketing*, McGraw Hill, 3rd edn

Thorelli, H B in Varadarayan, P (ed) (1983) *The Marketing Concept; perspectives and viewpoints* A & M University

Zikmund, G and d'Amico, M (1994) *Effective Marketing*, West

Recommended Reading

Chee, H and Harris, R (1993) *Marketing; A Global Perspective*, Pitman

Christopher, M and McDonald, M (1995) *Marketing: An Introductory Text*, Macmillan

Dibb, S, Simpkin, L, Pride, W and Ferrell, O (1994) *Marketing: Concepts and Strategies*, Houghton Mifflin, 2nd edn

Hill, E and O'Sullivan, T (1996) *Marketing*, Longman

Kotler, P, Armstrong, G, Sanders, J and Won, V (1996) *Principles of Marketing* Prentice Hall, 5th edn

Lancaster, G and Massingham, L (1993) *Essentials of Marketing*, McGraw Hill, 2nd edn

McCarthy, E and Perreault, W (1993) *Basic Marketing: a Managerial Approach*, Irwin, 11th edn

Mercer, D (1996) Marketing, Blackwell, 2nd edn

Palmer, A and Worthington, I (1992) *The Business and Marketing Environment*, McGraw Hill

Proctor, T (1996) *Marketing Management International,* Thompson Business Press

Randall, G (1993) *Principles of Marketing*, Routledge

Zikmund, G and d'Amico, M (1994) *Effective Marketing*, West

Answers to Review Activities

Review Activity 1

1 Jimcrack is typical of many organisations in that it exhibits some elements of several business philosophies. However, it is mainly operating with a product orientation. It concentrates on producing what it believes to be the right product, rather than finding out what the consumer wants and needs in the product. Although it has identified a market which appears to have growth potential and within which products are being produced that reflect customer needs, Jimcrack intends to produce its view of what the market wants. This view does not appear to be based upon discovering what the customer actually wants and will buy, nor has there been any systematic attempt to monitor the environments and markets within which Jimcrack operates. If it had been undertaking such monitoring, it would have been aware of the potential of the product much earlier and would understand the current state of the market, where in fact there is very intense competition over the wide range of features that the phones support – a fact which Jeff Watkins points out.

2 Jimcrack currently operates in markets where the ability to supply exceeds demand by a comfortable margin. In such markets, there will be intense competition, constantly evolving products and, usually, careful targeting of customer groups with specific product offers. As such, it is unlikely that a product orientation will be appropriate. Such an approach will not provide the first hand knowledge of customers and their changing needs and product perceptions that will be necessary for an organisation to compete effectively.

3 A marketing orientation would be the most appropriate orientation for Jimcrack. The marketing orientation concentrates on the consumer, causing the organisation to discover the needs and wants of customers and then to produce the appropriate goods and services to satisfy these needs and wants. By concentrating their efforts on the customer and by monitoring the markets within which the organisation operates, Jimcrack will be able to change its product offer as the needs of the market change. A marketing orientation will allow a matching of the needs of the defined group(s) of consumers with the resources of the organisation.

Review Activity 2

1 Any organisation which is marketing orientated needs to have accurate information on a regular basis. This information is used by managers as an input to their decision making. Correctly structured, marketing research provides reliable information that can help to ensure that an organisation is as close to its customers and competitors as is possible and as such can be used as an input to the planning process. Marketing research can help to monitor marketing operations and evaluate the results of marketing activities. If the speaker is certain that he has complete knowledge on his markets, competitors and customers; that he is constantly monitoring these three elements and attempting to see how movements in the environment will affect his organisation; that he checks the results of all his marketing activities and ensures that he has unbiased information on the views of his customers, then marketing research may indeed have limited utility to him. However, it is unlikely that simply having been a part of an industry for a long time, reading the newspapers and watching the television, will give him the information that he needs to run his organisation effectively.

2 Marketing research does not claim to give answers to marketing problems; it is an input to decision making and not a replacement for managerial judgement. It can not tell the manager what to do, merely assist in the decisions that have to be made. One very famous advertising executive, David Ogilvy, is alleged to have said that too many managers use marketing research rather like a drunk uses a lamp post: more for support than for illumination!

Review Activity 3

There are several market segments for this product. Here we identify three and develop a profile of the customers.

The home market

Home-owners either with no children or aged over 35 with children; living in properties with kitchens in excess of 20 square metres in size. Property values probably in excess of £120,000. Mainly older properties but probably not over 300 years old. Likely to buy fitted kitchens from up-market suppliers. Probably have two bathrooms. Hallways, porches could be feature in Victorian houses. Usually take continental holidays. Probably professional or self employed. Annual income likely to be in excess of £30,000. Probably entertain at home regularly. Male and female make joint decisions but female plays major role. Would like to think that they have some design flair. Home is an important possession to them.

The building market

Builders converting large old houses, commercial properties or old agricultural buildings. Some new blocks of flats, for example converted mill or marina developments. Possibly new speculative individual houses. Unit values in excess of £150,000. Kitchens in excess of 20 square metres.

Builders wishing to offer unusual features. Those fitting high quality kitchens or bathrooms or leaving choice to purchaser. Perhaps those finding sales difficult. Good for show properties.

With the exception of flats unlikely to appeal to those building more than eight units at any one site. Unlikely to be swayed by anything but 'added value'. Unlikely to want to participate in the design work.

The conservatory market

Home-owners adding conservatories in excess of 20 square metres in internal dimension or in excess of £15,000 in cost. Similar profile to the home market, although properties will be both new and old. As totally new sub floors will be laid when the conservatory is built there will be no age limit on the properties but again a solid floor is required. Properties likely to be detached or larger semi-detached. Will be an important 'show' possession. Lifestyle likely to be important to potential purchasers – probably will be extensively used in the summer months for entertaining, perhaps associated with barbecues. Will often have bought from suppliers' brochures and may have bought a whole package including flooring.

Using these three segments we can make some suggestions about the promotional tools, where we could use their advantages and avoid their disadvantages. One suggestion might be:

- home – advertising and leaflets
- building – personal selling
- conservatory – mixture of advertising and personal selling, with personal selling to sellers and builders of conservatories.

The main advantage of advertising is that it enables you to reach a large number of people very quickly and relatively cheaply. It is most useful when you have a low unit value product or where you cannot detail potential customers by name and address. Eric and Annabel know who is likely to buy their product in the home market but not by name and address. People who are likely to buy will be actively looking for flooring. Advertising will probably be the cheapest way of reaching these people.

Buyers in the building market, on the other hand, is likely to be relatively small in number, not too difficult to identify and more likely to be persuaded by personal selling than by advertisements. Any advertisement placed for the domestic market may, of course, spill over into the builders' market.

For both markets, some sales literature, probably a colour leaflet, will be necessary. Such literature can be left with builders, with clients responding to advertisements and can also be left at appropriate locations, where, for example, Eric and Annabel see a property which meets the specification being developed.

Answer to Unit Review Activity

The existing situation

1 Things are far worse than they at first seem. If you allow the effects of inflation, then the volume of sales being made is declining very substantially.

2 The primary reason for this is to be found in the concept of the product life cycle. The products are clearly reaching the end of their life cycles, and sales are falling as expected. If the company understood the product life cycle concept, it would have seen the need to introduce new products several years ago.

3 Why has the company allowed the sales fall to happen? Quite simply, it has not been monitoring its market. Which customers are Drake aiming at? Has it regularly researched this market? Answers to both questions are clearly no. This is an organisation that is not practising the marketing concept.

4 Drake's distributive policy is hopeless. Less then 10 per cent of its product category is sold through independent stores – which are supplied by wholesalers. Drake only sells to two of the major supermarket groups, which is where most of the market is today. It is quite simply not able to reach the vast bulk of the population even if its products are good.

5 The wholesalers will not be pushing the product – not surprisingly. If Drake was tied in with the major supermarkets, it would have discovered by now the ageing nature of the products.

6 The pricing structure is geared to the old retail situation where most sales were made through small cornershops. It is wholly inappropriate to the modern day retail scene. Most of the large supermarket groups have well over 150 branches and so would order more than 600 cases each week.

7 Promotion is a key variable in this market, with the emphasis being on pulling the products through. Most of Drake's are based upon a push strategy. The attendance at trade fairs is unlikely to have produced business – would the major supermarket buyers be likely to be there?

The new idea

1 Drake has no previous experience in this market. It is not known by any of the buyers or sellers in the market. It has never manufactured industrial products before. It has no real knowledge of this market.

2 The distributive set up in this market is very different from that of the domestic market. Distribution is primarily through engineering supply houses – Drake has no contact with these people.

3 The existing sales force has no experience or contacts in this market.

4 Production of the lance would be outside of Drake's control – both in terms of quality and quantity.

5 Is there any evidence that there is a market for the idea? What research did Tim carry out? Did he talk to companies that might use the lance? What is the size of the market? What is the competition?

6 The real profit would come from the sales of the cleanser. What is to stop Drake from being undercut here? A patent is highly unlikely and probably easily circumvented.

7 How many lances would need to be sold and at what price?

Action

1 Drake must adopt the marketing concept for the cleansing market and concentrate upon trying to understand who buys what, where, how, and why. It needs to have a system that monitors and regularly provides information on its markets. Who is it aiming at? What do these people want? What are the competition providing?

2 Drake must be in a precarious position – in real terms, sales volume and hence cash has been falling dramatically. There will be a short-term need to at least ensure that revenues stay stable. Drake should examine how it might take its existing products into other markets. This would mean marketing institutional packs to hospitals, schools, residential homes, etc., where the products are still used. This could be done fairly quickly.

3 Existing products are no longer of any major use in the domestic market. New cleaning products are needed here. This requires a careful analysis of the domestic cleaning market, looking for niches in the market which Drake might fill. Also, in the meantime, it should seek to discover who is still using the existing products and concentrate a little effort here.

4 Drake must review its distributive, promotional and pricing policies. Does it need the existing sales force? Could it achieve similar sales with a slimmed down and restructured version?

5 The new idea is very risky. The best idea would be to try to sell the idea to one of the major engineering supply houses and then make the cleanser as an own brand.

6 Drake's real skill appears to be in manufacturing and packaging cleansing agents. Perhaps it should investigate the market for producing own brands for the major retail multiples

UNIT 5
OPERATIONS AND OPERATIONS MANAGEMENT

Introduction

Businesses survive by selling products. These products may be goods, like food or washing machines, or services, like banking. Producing these is what the business does to make money. As you saw in Unit 1, Porter identifies **operations** as a primary activity that produces these products and services. It is a key element in the transformation model of organisations in which inputs are transformed into outputs with added value.

We take a slightly broader view here and define **operations management** as 'concerning all the processes of how products are made and delivered to the customer' such that it may involve part of Porter's other primary activities of inbound and outbound logistics and procurement. It involves all the parts of the business which produce and deliver the goods or services – a very wide spread. From buying raw materials to transporting the products to the customer and all that happens between, the operations system involves a wealth of different activities which are focused on delivering to the customers what they require.

For a washing machine manufacturer, it involves buying, making and storing parts, ensuring the right parts are available, assembling them into a finished machine and delivering that machine to the right customer. In a bank, it would involve the cashiers' work – exchanging payment, cashing cheques, answering queries – carrying out the transactions, managing accounts and sending statements and letters to customers.

In this unit, you will gain some insight into the scope and challenges of operations for a range of businesses and an overview of some recent developments in the field.

Objectives

At the end of this unit, you will be able to:

- outline the scope of operations using different definitions
- apply the transformational model of operations to a range of service and manufacturing industries
- apply the concept of adding value to operations
- describe the different activities within operations and the interaction between them
- explain the five key features of operations
- describe some design features in operations
- define what quality means from a business perspective.

SECTION 1

What are Operations?

Introduction

'Operations ... constitute the primary function of virtually every organisation' (Meredith, 1992, p.10). Operations are the activities involved in producing and delivering goods and services to the customer. This overlaps with some of the areas of marketing you investigated in Unit 4, such as satisfying consumers requirements and the distribution of ideas, goods and services. There will also be links with the human resources function, since many of an organisation's personnel will be involved in the production and delivery of the product. There is no clear boundary between operations and the other functions of the organisation, and some writers seek to incorporate most of the organisation in 'operations'. 'A very broad definition of operations would include all activities which had any connection with the production of goods and services – in practice every activity with the exception of the core marketing, selling and accounting, and finance activities' (Slack, Chambers, Harland, Harrison and Johnston, 1996, p. 9).

1.1 Definitions

The boundary of 'operations' within the company is blurred, with some authors incorporating almost all of the organisation and some limiting it to a production function (Porter, 1985). Although the links with other functions are vital for a successful company and will be discussed later in the unit, here we use a more manageable and limited definition of operations management. 'Operations management is concerned with the design and the operation of systems for manufacture, transport, supply or service' (Wild, 1995).

This definition brings up again the apparent difference between organisations which supply goods and those which supply services. At first sight, the two seem very different and would require very different approaches. Most products are in fact a mix of product and service. When you buy a bag of sugar from a supermarket, it may appear that you are simply buying a physical product. There are, however, several services linked to the bag of sugar: there might be a recipe on the packaging suggesting how you can use the sugar, the supermarket may offer to pack the sugar with your other shopping and even deliver it to your car. Most importantly, you can be confident that if the sugar is faulty (if it is lumpy, has dirt in it or the packet is half full), the supermarket will replace it. Taking another example, when companies buy computers, one of the key factors they considered is the back up service: what happens if a computer goes wrong, who will train people to use the system?

In this unit, therefore, although examples use particular 'goods' or 'service' products, there will be no clear distinction made between goods and services.

In order to clarify our perspective on operations, it may be worth looking at a very simple example. Consider the case of Jack, a self-employed plumber that works on his own. Using Wild's definition of operations management, what are his operations? Here is a possible list.

- *Order processing* – He needs to take 'orders' for work, say a customer asks him to fit a new hot water boiler.
- *Estimating* – He will need to assess the time it will take and what materials are needed. In this case, he may need to order the boiler. He needs to submit a quotation to the customer before ordering the boiler.
- *Purchasing* – He needs to contact suppliers for the best price and buy the materials before starting the work.
- *Scheduling 1* – He needs to decide when he can do the work, fitting it around both any other work he has arranged and his customer's needs.
- *Stock management* – He will need to keep a stock of pipes, fittings, tools and materials to cover day-to-day working and emergencies. Stock management ensures that the stock is secure and safe, and that he keeps an economic quantity of materials and parts.
- *Delivery* – He, and the materials, need to arrive on site at the agreed time, despite illness, a broken-down van or problems with suppliers.
- *Scheduling 2* – How will he do the work? Will he take out the old boiler first, or reroute the piping?
- *Production* – He has to carry out the work, as quickly and as well as possible. Shoddy work could be dangerous for the customer and expensive for him.
- *Testing* – Does everything work as intended? Is some more work needed?
- *Training* – The customer will need to understand how the new boiler works.
- *Back-up service* – If the boiler breaks down, or the plumbing springs a leak, the plumber will need to make a repair. Perhaps he offers some kind of guarantee, based maybe on the guarantee offered by his boiler supplier.

Note what is excluded from the list. There is no mention of marketing (how does he get work and how does he know what services people want?) and finance (keeping accounts, making sure people pay for his work, negotiating prices). Jack is a one-man business so the human resources element is missing and we have not mentioned technology, though he will need to keep up-to-date with product developments and new equipment. These activities are linked to, but are not directly part of, operations management. We can break down all the activities into Porter's primary and secondary activities that you met in Unit 1 and we can match them to the individual tasks that he has to perform.

Even for a very small business, note that operations involves a wide variety of tasks, interlinked with marketing, accounting and finance, and technology. Failure in any task will affect the customer and there are many outside influences (suppliers, illness) which could throw work off course.

ACTIVITY 1

Consider a large supermarket. Take 20 minutes to draw up a list of operations issues similar to the one we produced for the plumber. You may find it useful to use the generalised descriptions given as a starting point, and describe how they apply to the supermarket.

Here is our list of a supermarket's operations.

- *Order processing* – The supermarket collects 'orders' from the customer at the checkout.
- *Estimating* – The supermarket has to estimate its costs of buying, storing, displaying and selling goods. (These are taken into account when deciding what price to charge.)
- *Scheduling* – This is less of a problem, as customers can come and go as they like. However, the question of opening hours needs to be considered. When do customers want to shop? What are the legal restrictions? What are the requirements for staffing, cleaning and shelf stocking activities at different times.
- *Purchasing* – The supermarket needs to buy in the right products, of the right quality, and at the right price.
- *Stock management* – The goods are kept in the back room of the supermarket until required for the shelves. Stock management ensures the security of the stock, low deterioration and that stock levels are just enough to meet customer demands.
- *Delivery* – We are not talking here about delivery of goods to the supermarket but to the customer. The plumber has to work out how he can he get to his customers; here, the problem is how the customers can get to the supermarket. There are issues of access, parking, trolleys, and so on.
- *Production* – The supermarket provides a service in making the products available for purchase on the shelves.
- *Testing* – The 'product' will need to be tested in different ways. The goods on sale need to be tested: this may be a visual check to see the fruit is still fresh or it may be more extensive testing of a new delivery. In addition, the service needs to be up to the required standard; the service at the checkout needs to be quick and courteous, for example.
- *Training* – The customer will need to understand how to 'use' new foods, but more importantly the staff will need to be trained in their function and role in the organisation.

- *Back-up service* – Part of the back-up service will be how the supermarket deals with complaints and replacement of faulty items. This may be vital for the image of the shop.

Operations, then, involves a wide variety of activities and issues. There will be differences, both in content and emphasis, between organisations. There are, however, a lot of similarities between even very different organisations.

1.2 Transformation for the customer

We can define operations in terms of the transformation process. Operations within an organisation involves inputs – raw materials, staff, energy, buildings, etc. – and transforms them in some way into outputs for the customer.

There are various forms of transformation. In oil refining, there is a physical change – the nature of the crude oil is changed. Similarly, in manufacturing industries the transformation process involves making a physical change to the inputs. However, the transformation process need not be physical. A lending library transforms (or transfers) the possession (but not the ownership) of books. A building society transforms (transfers) the right to use money from lenders to borrowers. The transformation involved in a delivery service concerns transportation.

It is relatively easy to see what a supermarket or a plumber does; what their operations involve. Some organisations are more difficult to define. What does a university do, for example? Single activities can be identified – lectures or research – but the bigger picture is more confused. However, the transformation model allows us to compare different organisations and gain a better understanding of what the 'operations' are.

TRANSFORMATION MODEL

The first stage of the transformation model involves three parts: inputs, some form of transformation process and outputs. All organisations must have some form of input, and some form of output.

Inputs include the materials, energy, etc. which will be **transformed** into the products, but also the people who work in the company, the buildings they work in, and so on. As we showed above, the transformation process varies from business to business, but there is one common feature: **it must add value for the customer**. The outputs are not only the goods or services sold to customers but also waste, such as scrap materials, wasted energy and time.

This transformation process needs to be controlled, to see whether it is going well or badly and to allow improvements to be made where necessary. One other element is needed, therefore: performance information needs to be fed back from the outputs. This is the second stage of the model (see Figure 1). Examples of this information could be the number of products sold, customer complaints and the amount of waste. This information would be used to plan future operations, and to direct changes to the transformation process or inputs.

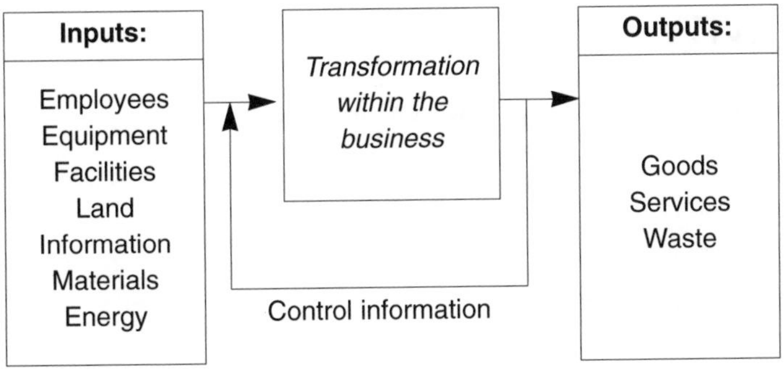

Figure 1: The transformation model of operations with feedback

To get a clear grasp of the different inputs, outputs, transformation processes and performance information used by organisations, study Table 1. This shows the transformation model applied to five different organisations. You may find it useful to try and suggest the outputs and control information for the other organisations listed in the left-hand column after studying the rest of the table.

Inputs	Transformation Process	Outputs	Control Information
TV Manufacturer Parts: screens, cases, electronic components Production workers, factories	Physical assembly: from parts to consumer product	Televisions, scrap parts, effluent from production processes	Number of each model sold. Which models are breaking down and how
Doctor's surgery (GP) The surgery building, receptionists, nurses, physiotherapists, instruments pharmaceuticals, patients	Physically changing the patient: treating illness or injury	Healthy patients, used medical equipment	Death rate, recovery rate, complaints from patients, number of patients joining or leaving the practice
Post office Letters, parcels, vans, sorting machines, trains, postal workers	Changing location: the letters are moved	Delivered post	Number of stamps sold, number of letters delivered on time
University Students, lecturers, books, buildings, paper, equipment	Creation of knowledge, changing ownership of knowledge	Informed and well rounded students	Number of applications, government reports and league tables, inspectors reports, research reports
Supermarket Goods to be sold, shelf fillers, checkout workers, trucks, stores	Changing ownership of the goods: from the producer or wholesaler to the customer, by transporting them, displaying them with other goods and selling them	Shopping	Number of goods sold, number of customers, customer complaints, health inspectors

Table 1: Transformation processes

As you can see the type of transformation differs enormously for different businesses. The operations system will have to reflect these differences.

ACTIVITY 2

Study Table 1 closely. Apply the same model to:

- a farm
- a prison
- a travel agent
- a holiday tour operator.

For each organisation, list the inputs, transformation processes and outputs. Describe in a few words which inputs have been transformed into specific outputs. Describe different types of control information which might be fed back to control the transformation process.

There are no exact answers for this activity. For example, because of different circumstances, a prison in one country may use very different control information from one in another country. However, we can suggest some possible answers.

Probably the easiest organisation to consider is the farm. The inputs are mostly tangible: seed, animals for fattening, breeding, or milking, fertilisers, land, labour, and so on. The outputs are animals for slaughter, milk, grain, and other types of food. There is a physical change as, for example, crops are grown and harvested. The feedback information includes the prices paid for the animals at market and information from customers. Wholesalers or supermarket chains will complain when there are problems with the produce; they might even give praise when the products are good. In addition, there are more immediate sources of feedback: for example, the yield of grain – that is, how many tonnes are grown per hectare.

The prison's main inputs and outputs could be convicted criminals and reformed criminals. For this organisation, the feedback takes different forms as it is a public organisation. Output figures such as how many ex-prisoners reoffend may play a part, but the prison will be inspected by a controlling authority and the reports from these inspections will be very influential.

The service based organisations are a little more difficult to categorise. The travel agent and tour operator look similar but in fact carry out very different transformations. The travel agent is really just a shop, selling holidays (and a few related services); the transformation is changing ownership. Any other activity such as providing flight information is of little value unless it is related to the main transformation process. Control information is mainly financial: such as how much money has been paid for holidays and how many holidays of which type have been sold.

The tour operator provides the products the travel agent sells. The main input is the customer, perhaps worn down by a year of hard work, while the main output should be a satisfied customer, refreshed and relaxed by the holiday. As a business, financial data will be an important source of control information, but the tour operator can also get immediate feedback by interviewing a sample of holidaymakers or by giving them a questionnaire.

1.3 Value added

Operations need to add value in the transformation process. Businesses can improve efficiency and effectiveness by concentrating on the aspects of operations which add value. This idea of adding value for the customer was introduced in Unit 1. This is an important concept, particularly for commercial organisations, and one where the link between operations and marketing occurs again. In order to add value for the customer, the company must know what the customer values. Recall Porter's value chain from Unit 1 and compare the five 'primary activities' with our discussions of operations. Notice that four of the five primary activities would come within our definition of operations (see Section 1.1 above).

How does a supermarket add value to the bags of sugar it sells? When the consumer carries it out of the supermarket, the bag of sugar is the same as when it left the factory where it was produced (or at least it should be). Yet the customer pays up to 100 per cent more for the product than the supermarket does. Looking a little more closely at the transformation process, there are several ways the value is added:

- the goods are nearer the customer's home
- the factory will probably only sell in volume (hundreds of bags), the supermarket breaks this down into single items
- the goods are placed next to a range of other goods, adding convenience – customers can get all their shopping in one store
- the guarantee that the goods are not faulty adds value
- the image of the store may add value in itself.

There are, in addition, a lot of activities which add no value to the customer, such as storing goods and moving them around the store. These activities need to be minimised or eliminated. The concentration on the activities which add value should be balanced with a similar effort to eliminate 'non value-adding' activities. Porter's concept goes even further, suggesting that the approach of 'adding' value limits the perception of value within the organisation, incorrectly distinguishing raw materials from other inputs. The core concept of value should perhaps be that the transformation process takes a range of inputs and transforms them into outputs of goods, services and waste: the value of the goods and services to the customer should be maximised and the waste minimised.

REVIEW ACTIVITY 1

Match the list of value-adding activities of the supermarket (given above) with Porter's primary activities. Are there any primary activities not included? Suggest what they might be.

Summary

Operations include a wide variety of the organisation's activities. Most definitions centre around the activities concerned with the design and operation of systems for manufacture, transport, supply or service. A convenient way of looking at operations is how it transforms the inputs of an organisation into outputs, and how that is controlled. There are many different transformation processes, but all need to add value for the customer.

SECTION 2

Running Operations

Introduction

In Section 1 we introduced the concepts of operations, transformation and value. We now use these concepts to look at the issues of running operations. What needs to be considered? Where do the problems come from? Where are the opportunities for improvement? In Section 3 we look at how both products and systems are designed for the smooth running of operations, but it is worth looking at how things work before looking at how they should be designed.

In industries as diverse as car production and grocery retailing, the last 30 years have brought dramatic changes in the way operations are carried out. For example, within the UK, the nature of retailing, particularly food retailing, has changed radically through national competition. First supermarkets and then superstores have taken over from small independent shops. Now, almost two thirds of all retail business is held by large multiples. In the drive to compete and offer a better service to the customer, operations has been a significant weapon, from quality improvements gained by selecting and developing suppliers to the use of information technology both at the checkout and to develop customer profiles through loyalty cards.

In the car industry, the change has been global. In 1964, almost half the world's cars were made in North America. Europe made almost 40 per cent. By 1990, both Europe and North America had a smaller share of the market, each producing around 30 per cent of the world's cars, while Japanese car production – just 8 per cent of the market in 1964 – was almost at the same level as North America. This dramatic growth in the Japanese car industry has been attributed almost entirely to vastly superior operations. A typical German car manufacturer spends more time correcting faults on cars it has just made than a Japanese manufacturer will spend making the car from start to finish. Japanese manufacturers have striven to improve quality, eliminating problems as they arise, and to eliminate unnecessary costs (Womack *et al.*, 1990, p. 44 and p. 91).

As competition in both retailing and car manufacture has developed, the demands on operations to deliver have increased. The operations systems of these companies have had to find methods of making radical improvements. Consider stock handling. A large superstore or a car manufacturer now holds almost no stock which is not being used: either on the shelf in front of the customer or being assembled into a car. This saves space, risk of damage and money. Suppliers have responded by being able to deliver within hours and with near perfect reliability. Quality is measured in failures per million products. Three or four decades ago, delivery times were measured in months and failures in 10–20 products per hundred. These advances have put pressure on operations systems around the world.

2.1 The operations challenge

Why is it difficult to deliver quickly and on time? Why shouldn't it be possible to make products without errors? If Ford, for example, have been making cars for almost 90 years, cars which use the same basic technology, why are there still problems? There are, of course, a number of reasons. These may be called the five key aspects of operations and they present challenges to all organisations. They are:

- complexity
- flexibility
- cost
- quality
- delivery.

COMPLEXITY

A high street bank carries out hundreds of thousands of transactions each working day, involving thousands of other accounts and hundreds of other banks. Making a car involves assembling 6,000 individual parts from up to 1,000 different suppliers and using the skills of perhaps 4,000 employees. Every one of those parts must fit and work correctly and be on the production line at the right place at the right time. This requires considerable co-ordination – the task of operations management – and is, of course, very complex.

To illustrate the potential complexity, consider the problem of scheduling work in a bank office that processes mortgage applications. Assume that here are four people working in the office and four different mortgages arrive. They must be processed urgently, each one needs to be checked, calculated, credit checked and entered into the database. These can happen in any order, but each takes a different length of time. A schedule is needed to decide which activities will be carried out on which mortgages by which employees first. The schedule wanted is the one that will take the minimum time.

If you look at this problem in simple terms, one way to find the quickest schedule is to compare all the possible schedules. This requires two steps:

- find out the length of time each of the 16 activities will take
- look at the different possible schedules for processing the four different mortgages and pick the shortest.

If this sort of work is carried out frequently, this first step is relatively simple. If not, some measuring or estimating is needed. The second step is more time consuming. For this example, there are 414 different schedules (331,776). To find the quickest, most or all of them will need to be compared.

Most companies have more than four people to do the work. With five people, five operations and five different products, the number of possible schedules is almost 25 billion. Beyond that, it's not worth counting. This is before considering any problems of slow work, wrongly estimating the times, tea breaks, and all the other variables of people at work.

This means that operations management needs to have methods for dealing with complex real problems in simple ways. The first challenge is to cope with this complexity. It is vital that the system used to co-ordinate operations helps to minimise management effort and leads to **simplicity of operation.**

FLEXIBILITY

We need to consider two aspects of flexibility:

- flexibility of production
- flexibility of capacity.

Flexibility of production

At the same time as the pressure for reduced cost, improved quality and better delivery has developed, the demand for a range of different products and new products has increased. If a company can bring out a new product faster than its competitors, it gains a competitive advantage. In some markets, such as fashion design and computers, failure to keep up with the introduction of new products by other companies will drag a company down very quickly.

Flexibility of capacity

The issue of developing new products is looked at in the next section, but even for a business which does not need to develop new products very frequently, there is still one aspect of change which needs to be addressed: the change in demand.

Demand goes up and down year by year, month by month and day by day.

Each business has a certain **capacity**: the number of products it can produce each hour, day or week. This may be determined, among other factors, by:

- space – a university lecture theatre will only hold so many students
- machinery – a supermarket has a limited number of tills
- people – there may only be a limited number of trained staff.

What happens if a business has the wrong capacity? If it has too little capacity, it will not be able to cope with increased demand, delivery times may rise and customers may be lost. If it has too much capacity, a fall in demand will cost money, in some cases a lot of money. It may not cost a supermarket much to have a till standing idle, but to have a lot of trained staff and expensive machinery not producing in a factory can be extremely expensive.

As an example, consider the electricity generating industry. Power stations are expensive to build, costing millions or billions of pounds, and they take years to construct. For safety reasons, there must be enough generating capacity to meet the peak demand, but that demand changes very rapidly and quite substantially. In the middle of winter, in the early evening, as a popular television programme finishes, millions of people across the country go to their kitchens, switch on the lights and put the kettle on for a cup of tea. The demand for power will surge dramatically in a few seconds.

With such a difficult problem, generating companies have developed a range of ways of varying capacity. Nuclear power stations are slow to start and stop, so they are left running, with variations made as the weather forecast changes. Coal- or gas-powered stations can be fired up within hours to cope with a predicted surge. The huge surge as kettles are switched on may be covered by hydroelectric stations which can be turned on very quickly.

This need for flexibility is the second challenge in operations management. The flexibility to produce new products, or to change to different products, or just to produce more of the same very rapidly, is important in gaining an advantage or just keeping up with the competition. There are many other forms of flexibility – such as adapting to new technology – but flexibility for innovation and capacity are the uppermost challenges.

COST, QUALITY AND DELIVERY

Aside from the need for flexibility and complexity inherent in operations, there is one more source of problems. To illustrate these issues, consider the transformation process from the different perspectives of the employee and the customer.

The employee's perspective

For those people working within the business, attention naturally focuses on the inputs: the people around them, the factory itself, or the transformation process – how the machines work, transaction processing in a bank. If attention falls on the outputs, this has traditionally been either because of a problem, for example the product is faulty, or because output is used as a measure of performance and may be related to pay.

The customer's perspective

Customers see things differently. They have very little interest in the inputs or the transformation process. Few people care exactly how their cheques are processed or who works in the company, they want to know how soon the cheque will clear, they want to be sure the amount of money in their account is correct. Customers concentrate on the **outputs**.

This difference in perspective can lead to problems and partly explains why some companies decline. If too much attention is focused inside the company and the outputs suffer, this will result in loss of customer satisfaction and, ultimately, loss of customers. In order for the organisation to perform well, all those involved in operations should be well aware of the customer's perception of the outputs.

Fortunately, customers generally take a relatively simple view of the outputs. For simplicity, in this section we ignore the elements of the product determined by design (range of products, features, and so on). Macbeth (1989, p. 14) argues that for a manufacturing business we are left with three 'deliverables' from the customer's perspective – the most important features of the outputs are cost, quality and delivery. In fact, the customer is interested in the price not the cost of producing the outputs. However, as cost is determined by the operations system while the price can be set independently, here we concentrate on cost. Macbeth also highlights the 'overarching requirement' of quality. By looking at the outputs in terms of cost, quality and delivery, we have a simple framework for assessing the running of operations.

- **Cost:** – How much do the products cost to make? Reducing costs allows a company to reduce prices, which will increase customer satisfaction and sales in some markets. Even if the price is kept high, for example to maintain an image of exclusivity in the perfume market, lower costs mean more profit. This is a benefit for the company.
- **Quality:** – The product should do what the customer wants. If it is a bank account, the balance must be correct, the chequebook must have the right name on it, the ATM machine must give out the money in the account. A car should not break down, the paint work should be of a high standard, there should be no rips in the upholstery, and so on.
- **Delivery:** – There are two aspects to this: whether it is on time (punctuality) and how long it takes (lead time). If a cheque is paid into a bank account, the customer wants to know not just how long it will take to clear but to be sure it will be cleared on the right day. It may be better for the customer to be completely certain that the cheque will clear in three days, than 80 per cent certain it will clear in one day. In this case being on time is more important than a short lead time.

ACTIVITY 3

Consider these businesses:

- high street film processing shop
- personal computer manufacturer
- hairdresser.

In terms of cost quality and delivery, describe the levels of performance that you, as a potential consumer, would expect. For example, what lead time would you expect from a hairdresser? What would you expect to pay for film processing? Ignore other ways of competing such as offering new products.

If these businesses wanted to gain advantage over their competitors, which aspect would you recommend they try to improve and by how much? Would a hairdresser gain an advantage by reducing its lead time by 50 per cent, for example, or should it improve quality? Suggest a way of gaining advantage for each business.

Obviously, you would expect to pay a 'going rate' that compares with other shops and a certain level of performance in all three fields.

For the film processing shop, the price (hence the cost) must be competitive and quality must be of a very high standard – if the shop loses a customer's wedding or holiday photos, it will almost certainly lose the customer. Worse than this, the customer will probably tell all his or her friends and relations. Most shops offer a one-day service plus a one- or two-hour service for which they charge a premium. For both services, delivery must be on time – that is the film must be ready, as this is what the customer expects. If the film processing shop could offer a 10-minute service at the price normally charged for a one-day service, it would probably gain a great competitive advantage, but the quality would have to remain at the same standard.

Computers are expensive items, customers shop around for a good value purchase so cost will be very important in allowing a company to sell a computer at a low price. Consumers will also expect a fairly short lead time – days rather than weeks or months – but will probably put up with it being a little late or even early. A computer which does not work at all will be very unpopular, but most people seem to accept it will not work immediately 'out of the box', that they will have to spend a little time setting it up and fiddling with it. Customers also accept small problems with their computers, finding ways around those problems rather than complaining about every fault. The best way to competitive advantage here, then seems to be in cutting costs or offering an installation service so people do not have to set it up themselves.

Reducing the lead time of a hairdresser may even lose competitive advantage. If customers phone for appointments and find they have to wait a few days, they may feel this shows that the hairdresser is popular and in demand. If the appointment is instant, it may seem that the hairdresser is short of work because of poor quality. Even being on time may not be that important, some customers may be happy to wait for 10 or 15 minutes, reading magazines or chatting. For others, speed of service might be an issue, and you certainly do not want to be kept waiting a long time. Cost is a factor, but similar services can vary in price enormously. The vital factor here is quality, the work must be good enough: customers will be angry if their hair is dyed the wrong colour or responds badly to some chemicals used. The overall experience for the customer must be pleasurable, relaxing and of high quality. The hairdresser may upgrade the facilities, offer free tea or coffee, and provide a range of up-to-date magazines for competitive advantage.

It is obvious that different businesses compete on different factors. Improving the operations system in ways which offer no competitive advantage are not particularly valuable. Spending a lot of effort in improving the quality of a computer (beyond the level of the competition) may be effort wasted. That effort could be spent in reducing cost. Reducing costs in the hairdresser's may help improve profits, but concentrating on the quality could offer far greater advantage. Reducing quality at the expense of cost may be disastrous.

We now have a framework for looking at running operations, with five key aspects:

- *inside the organisation* – concentrate on **flexibility** and **simplicity** of operation
- *for outputs* – concentrate on **cost, quality** and **delivery**.

2.2 Activities within operations

With a simple framework for assessing operations, you are in a position to look at the activities involved in operations and what will be expected from them. Figure 2 divides the activities within operations into three parts or stages. This takes a much simpler approach than Porter's value chain as we are not considering sales, marketing and service here. We are looking at operations as production and inventory management that include all the activities which provide the goods and services the customer pays for. In the next unit on logistics, we examine more closely the flow of materials through an organisation to the customer, so this also covers some of the functions of operations management.

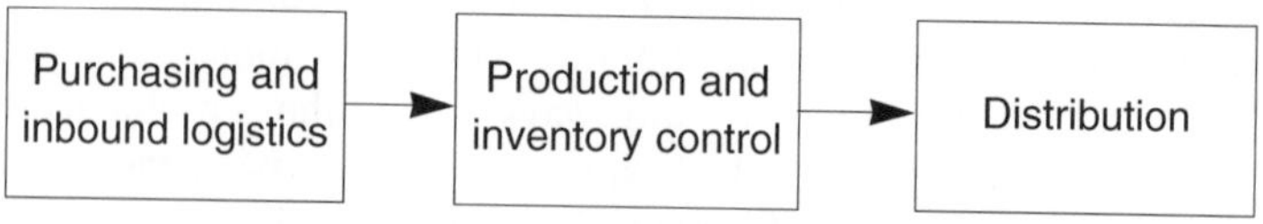

Figure 2: Activities within the operations system

PURCHASING AND INBOUND LOGISTICS

The activities involved in getting the inputs into the company are at the beginning of the operations process. Obviously, this involves buying the inputs, but it also involves transporting them to where they will be needed and at the right time. There is some confusion over terms here. For many companies and authors, 'purchasing' means the activity of getting the materials into the company, and therefore includes inbound logistics. Others call this 'procurement' and confine 'purchasing' to the specific activity of buying the items (Waters, 1996). This unit will use 'purchasing' and 'inbound logistics' to refer to the two activities. Again note the links with Porter's chain and procurement in Unit 1 and logistics in Unit 6.

In the long term, **capital** items will be needed such as the factory or offices, the machines involved in production, computers, etc. In the shorter term, **production** items will be needed such as parts and raw materials, heat, light and water, packaging, and so on. In addition, there are items which are necessary for the running of the company such as telephone, security services and postage; we call these **support** purchases.

Capital, production and support purchases each have a different set of requirements and challenges. All of them impact on the five key aspects or features of operations. The costs of purchasing directly affect the costs of the outputs; if the cost of raw materials increases, either profits go down, prices go up, or savings must be found elsewhere in the organisation. The quality of raw materials or parts will affect the quality of the final product. If the supply of parts is unreliable, the output of products will often be unreliable too. Inflexible unreliable suppliers will reduce the simplicity of operation and prevent the operations system offering flexibility to their customers.

Support purchases

Telephone services, security services, postage and so on are generally bought on an ongoing basis. As such, their primary impact is on **cost**. The challenge for the procurement function is to obtain a reliable service while minimising total cost.

Production purchases

Cost is also a big factor here. In a car manufacturing company, for example, 70 per cent of all the company's costs can be spent on production purchases, small increases can have very large effects. The cost of parts in these circumstances is very carefully controlled and measured in 10 millionths of a pound.

Cost is not the only consideration, of course. It is useless to buy in cheaper parts which are not of the required quality. **Quality** is vital: one faulty bolt could cause a car to crash in use, potentially costing millions of pounds in law suits.

Delivery (timing, reliability and quantity) is also crucial. At a modern car plant, each part will be delivered up to five times a day, timed to within 15 minutes after a journey of perhaps hundreds of miles. If the delivery of one part is late, the parts will run out in a few hours, production will stop and the deliveries of the other 6,000 parts will pile up, filling the factory while the company loses perhaps £3,000 each minute. It is vital that deliveries are reliable and on time.

Orders for the goods can change suddenly, the supplier needs to be able to rapidly increase or decrease deliveries, **flexibility** both in the ordering system and from suppliers is critical.

Finally, if there are difficulties in maintaining quality, delivery cost or flexibility, the operation will become more complex – the **simplicity of operation** will decline.

Capital purchases

Buying machinery or buildings are activities which involve large amounts of money and have long-term effects on the company, so it is vital to make the right decisions. However, capital purchases are less frequent than the support or production purchases.

Consider a high street bank investing in a new computer system. The initial cost will probably be high, and the bank will get a range of prices from different suppliers. The longer-term costs may well be far larger, however. There is an array of questions that will need to be considered before purchase is made, each impacting on different aspects of that framework. These include:

- how many people will be needed to support the system (cost)
- how long will data entry take (cost, delivery)
- how long will it take to process transactions (delivery)
- what is the possibility of computer errors (quality)
- how will the system adapt to new products (flexibility)
- how much time will be needed on control and co-ordination (simplicity of operation).

PRODUCTION AND INVENTORY CONTROL

Production and inventory control is concerned with what happens in the company: transforming inputs into outputs, changing the purchases into finished goods. Some aspects of design that relate to this activity will be covered in the next section. Here, our objective is to explain what is involved.

Production processes

Production processes need to be designed, tested and linked to one another. What happens to a cheque once it is passed over the counter of the bank? Who should it be passed to? What does the bank need to do with it? How long will that take? How does the bank ensure it ends up in the right account? How does it ensure that the cheque is not lost or stolen? The process needs to be planned, then the people involved need to be trained and the process needs to be monitored to make sure it's working correctly.

Scheduling

When all the production processes for any one product have been planned out, one of the most difficult problems of production must be addressed: scheduling. This has many different factors, some are given here, but more extensive treatments can be found in Slack (1996), Wild (1995) and in detail in Krajewski and Ritzman (1996).

- *Uncertainty of demand* – The demand from customers can be uncertain, even in the near future, as highlighted earlier by the example of the electricity generating industry.
- *Uncertainty of supply* – The materials or parts needed for the process may not be available when you need them: they may be late, lost or faulty.
- *Process uncertainty* – The process itself may fail, a machine may jam, documents may be lost or misread. The process may take a longer or shorter time than expected. In addition, there are some products which need certain resources, requiring, for example, an employee who has particular expertise.
- *Potential for optimisation* – Processes may be more efficient in a certain sequence. For example, spray painting equipment takes some time to clean, so starting with a light colour and moving to darker can save a lot of time. It may be more efficient to spray in one colour, reducing the time spent setting up, but this will delay jobs of other colours. People are more efficient at different times of day; a complex task may suffer if scheduled for just after lunch when the employee is sleepy.
- *Differences of demand* – Different products may have different priorities. Scheduling work is easier if the time involved is known from the order. For example, the time to make a television in mass production is fairly standard. (This is called *dependent* demand.) If, two years later, a repair shop receives that same television for repair, the time needed could vary from minutes to hours (*independent* demand).

With all these different factors, it is not possible to set simple guidelines for finding the perfect schedule for every situation, but there are many ways of addressing the problem. To look at how scheduling can be tackled, let's consider an example from the simpler end of the scale: a doctor carrying out a session examining patients.

The resource that needs scheduling is the doctor's time. A little prior planning is carried out dividing the working time into appointments of perhaps five or ten minutes. These will be scheduled to allow the doctor time for other activities, such as follow-up paperwork or home visits. Demand from patients can vary. This is dealt with by historical analysis; demand is generally higher on a Monday morning, for example. Fluctuations in demand can also be managed to some extent by making demand (patients) fit in with the process; so if appointments are full for the day, patients are asked to come another day. The demand is independent: each consultation may take more or less than the allotted time. Patients may also not turn up. This is generally managed by keeping a queue of patients in a waiting room and running appointments slightly late. This way the doctor is not be kept waiting. There is flexibility in the system for problems: a patient may turn up needing immediate attention. In this case, the schedule is simply delayed. The records for a patient may be missing (supply uncertainty), again delaying the schedule.

Inventory

Inventory is stock or stores of raw materials, half-finished parts or finished goods. The level of inventory must be carefully controlled and balanced against the needs of production.

High stocks mean the business is protected from sudden problems. If there is a sudden large order, a large stock of goods will allow the business to fulfil the order immediately. If one machine breaks down, and there is a stock of parts which that machine has completed, the rest of the company can carry on working. It helps to prevent the company from running out and having to stop production.

There are several major problems with high inventory, however.

- *Stock costs money.* All stock costs money to buy, which is money wasted if the stock is not used. Storing stock costs money. Many companies devote 25 per cent of their space to stock; if the stock is removed, companies could use buildings 25 per cent smaller, offering savings in rent, rates, heating and lighting, etc.
- *Stock deteriorates.* Fresh food deteriorates rapidly, of course, so a large stock can be lost for example in a heat wave. The same problem occurs with more durable items, steel rusts, electronic components corrode. More importantly, if a new product replaces an existing item, the value of existing stock can plummet. Computers lose up to 10 per cent of their value every month.
- *Stock reduces flexibility.* A large stock of parts will need to be used up before a new product can be made requiring different components.
- *A large stock makes quality problems more expensive.* Suppose a large stock of computers is built up before the launch of a new model. Once the model is launched, it is found there is a problem, after three days' use the computer's power unit fails. All the computers in stock will need to be thrown away or repaired. With fewer computers in stock, the quality problem would be smaller and cheaper to rectify.

Distribution

Distribution is covered in detail in Unit 6, so it only receives a brief mention here. Whatever the product, however well made, cheap and desirable, it is useless unless it reaches the customer when it is wanted. Many companies insist that deliveries are made within 15 minutes of the scheduled time, if deliveries are late, they are rejected; this might be after a journey of hundreds of miles from the supplier's premises. The potential for damage or just adding cost by transporting products around the countryside is enormous; organisations can minimise this risk by reducing carriage and handling.

REVIEW ACTIVITY 2

Kurdenwey is a small dairy producing milk, cream, ice cream, hard and soft cheese, yoghurt and other dairy products. It has 70 employees and 112 customers, including one big supermarket chain which buys 30 per cent of its production.

1 In what ways will Kurdenwey need to be flexible? Describe two forms of flexibility and suggest some changes which will require flexibility in these forms.

2 How and why is there a difference between the employees' and customers' perspectives of operations?

3 What will make the management of operations complex? Suggest at least three different factors.

4 List three problems Kurdenwey will face in its operations system that a toy manufacturer would not face and explain why.

Summary

This section has looked at what is involved in running operations, we look at design issues in the next section. There have been some radical changes in organisations and markets around the world forming a 'challenge' for operations.

Within the organisation, there is a need for:

- flexibility – to new developments and, in this context particularly, to variations in demand
- simplicity of operation – to cope with the complexity of operations.

In terms of the outputs, the focus is on:

- cost – controlling or reducing cost allows the organisation to make more profit, to reduce prices or to spend more money elsewhere
- quality – the customer is very often interested in quality, it is an overarching issue
- delivery – delivering on time and rapidly are factors which, once again, have an impact on the customer.

This framework of five key aspects or features of operations can be used to look at the activities within operations. Those activities are:

- purchasing and inbound logistics – bringing the (inanimate) inputs into the organisation
- production – transforming those inputs into the products
- distribution – getting those products to the customer.

SECTION 3

Design within Operations

Introduction

We have looked at many of the factors which are involved in the running of operations. In this section, we investigate some of the design processes and considerations of operations management. The first area that we cover is product design and development, then we examine system design.

We can split design into three parts:

- designing (and developing) products
- designing the operations system and processes
- quality and quality management.

These parts combine to dictate many of the outputs of operations: the goods and services for the customer.

3.1 Product design and development

Getting the design of the products right will dictate whether or not a company is successful. There are many steps in developing an individual product and the process will involve all the functions of the organisation. The range, quality, cost and customer appeal of products will be set in this process. Figure 3 shows the interaction with the operations functions previously identified. The thick arrows are the flow of products, the thinner double-headed arrows denote information flows.

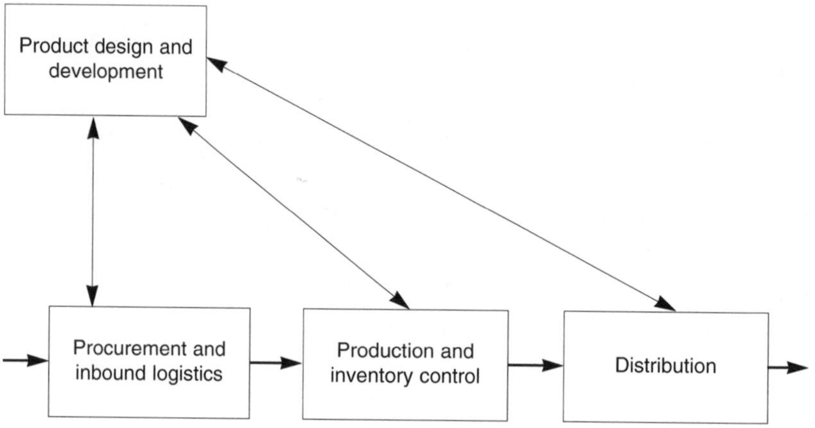

Figure 3: The link between product design and operations

There are many ways that new products reach the market. Curtis (1994, p. 271) offers an extensive look at an ideal new product development process. Slack (1995, p. 102) emphasises the strategic nature of product development and the long-term impact on the company. The orientation of a company can impact on the product development process.

In practice, the process varies hugely from company to company. In some companies, the research and development team will come up with a product, production will be told to make it, and the marketing function will be told to sell it. Other companies have a strong marketing function; these organisations will ask customers what they want, accommodate all the customers' requirements, fix a price, take an order then instruct the rest of the company to make it. Some companies survive for a long time on one idea; some develop products because senior managers think they are a good idea; some produce copies of competitors' products; some pick up a technological development and rush it onto the market.

With companies succeeding (and failing) with a variety of new product development processes, there can be no right or wrong way. Here, we describe a generalised process, not the process every company does or should follow, but one that involves most aspects of getting a product to market successfully. The factors involved apply similarly to products which are mostly goods and products which are biased towards services. Figure 4 shows a generalised process. It starts at the top and works downwards. Each stage is explained below, so refer back to the figure as you read about the process.

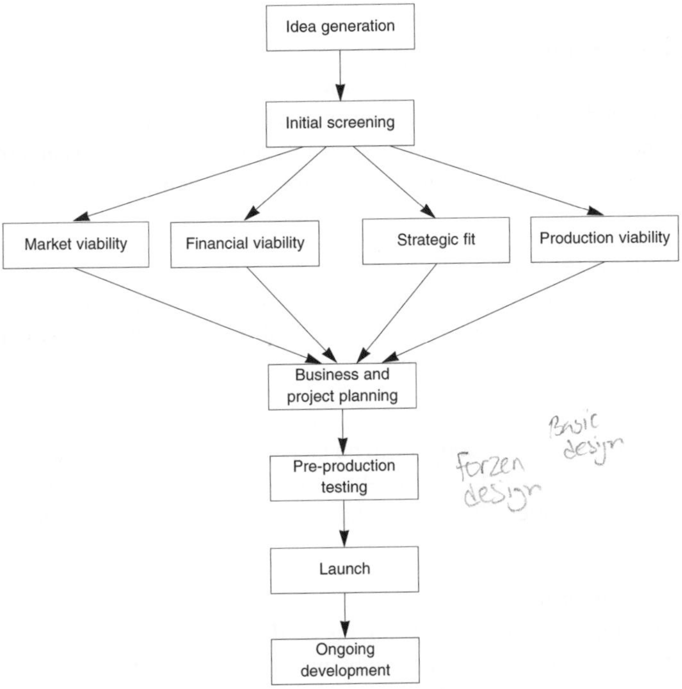

Figure 4: A generalised new product development process

Idea generation
This is the start of the process. A broad range of ideas for a new product should be developed, some very similar, some radical, some mundane. Sometimes, however, a single significant idea might be the starting point for the whole process. The idea for a new product can come from any number of sources: developing an old product, a spark of inspiration from an employee, an identified market need, a new technological development. No source of ideas is necessarily better than the others, different businesses and different products have different sources of new ideas.

Initial screening
The first stage is to reduce the number of ideas to a manageable level and to sift out the ideas which are almost certain not to work. This is often carried out with little investigation, and should involve as little time as possible.

Viability and fit
Any idea should pass the next four hurdles in no particular order. There is one general 'rule of thumb': the more radical the product, the greater the long-term potential from it but the greater the risk of failure.

- **Market viability** – Will it sell in large enough numbers? For how much and how long?
- **Financial viability** – Can the business afford it? Will it make a profit?
- **Strategic fit** – It may be a good idea, but does it fit in with the rest of the business and where the business is going?
- **Production viability** – Can it be made at the right price and in sufficient volume?

Business and project planning
If the idea is considered viable, the production, launch, advertising, supply, delivery and financial needs must be mapped out in detail. Exactly how much money will be needed, and when? When will the first prototypes be ready, when can production start, how long will it take to build up stock for the launch? When is the best time for the launch?

Pre-production testing
Samples are made and tested, first to see if they work correctly 'in the laboratory', then to see if they work correctly in service, and finally with the customer to see whether it is what the customer wants.

Launch
Once testing is finished, the product can be launched. Production needs to be set up for the launch and the sales that will follow. Potential customers need to be made aware of the new product. Supply of parts for production and distribution of the product needs to be considered.

Ongoing development
This is often neglected. Once the product is on the market, there may be problems which need solving. Improvements can be made to the operations system to drive down cost or increase quality and reliability. Customers' needs change, the product should change with them.

At each stage of the idealised new product development process, several different functions within the business are involved. In order to give products and therefore the business the best chance for success, the different functions must collaborate, co-ordinate and communicate effectively. Figure 5 shows some of these functions. You will be familiar with three of them from the previous section, but there are others which need to have involvement in the development process.

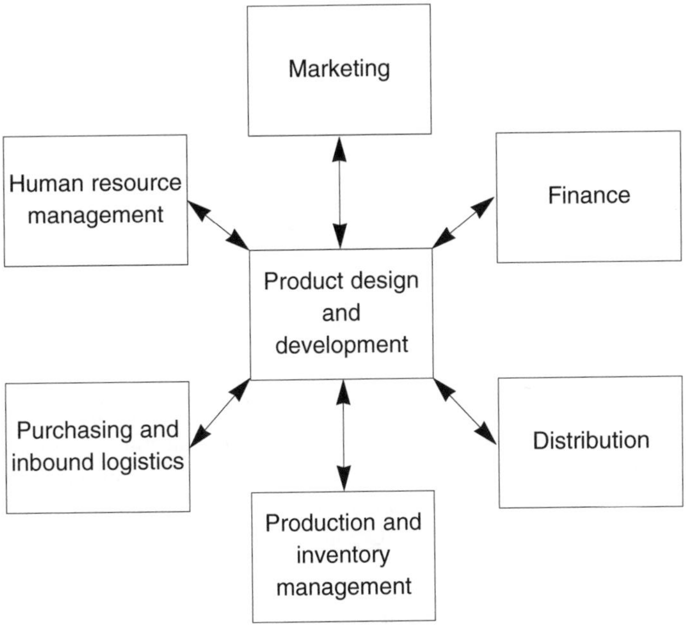

Figure 5: Co-ordination within the business

ACTIVITY 4

Take the functions of finance, marketing and purchasing and inbound logistics and consider these stages in the new product development process:

- financial viability testing
- pre-production testing
- product launch.

Suggest one or two ways the functions will need to be involved in each stage of the product development process by completing the following table.

Functions / Stages	Marketing	Purchasing and inbound logistics	Finance
Financial viability testing			
Pre-production testing			
Product launch			

Here are our suggested answers. For financial viability, the marketing function will provide information on potential sales and pricing; purchasing and inbound logistics will determining the funds required for buying and storing materials and necessary equipment; finance will collate and examine the information and co-ordinate this stage. Finance will have the overall responsibility for judging the financial viability of the project.

For pre-production testing, marketing could provide ideas about what the consumer will want from the product and how they will use it; purchasing and inbound logistics will obtain the materials for the test products and perhaps organise outside testing facilities; the finance function will find the money to fund the testing.

For the product launch, marketing will advise on promotion and the potential for sales at launch, so indicating the production capability needed; purchasing and inbound logistics will obtain the new materials needed to support production; the finance function will find the funds for the launch and, just as importantly, control the money generated by sales.

It is vital that the goods and services produced by the business meet the needs and requirements of the customers and consumers. This is only part of the challenge, however. The products must fit with the operations system of a company. No matter how successful a proposed product is with customers, if it cannot be produced by the company to the necessary cost, quality and delivery specifications, it will fail. Success here involves the co-ordination of all aspects of the business.

3.2 System and process design

The whole of operations needs to be co-ordinated and the various different activities controlled. Every company is different, even companies with very similar products aimed at the same customers will have very different operations management systems. In many companies the operations system evolves as the company grows and changes, this often leads to wasted effort and conflict between different parts of the company. The planning of the operations system is critical to its effectiveness. Here we look at the design of the operations system itself, we follow with a discussion about the particular processes involved. These two areas are specifically linked through the layout of the people and equipment involved in operations.

SYSTEM DESIGN

Decisions made at the design stage of an operations system will affect the working of the company dramatically. Waters (1996, p. 294) suggests that as much as 85 per cent of the productivity of employees is fixed by the system they work in, only 15 per cent can be determined by the individuals themselves.

Setting up the operations system well in the first place and maintaining it, is vital for efficiency. Perhaps the best place to start is with an overview of the whole operations system. We know what the system does: it transforms inputs into outputs, to provide what the customer wants or will buy. And we know some of the demands and problems of running the system. What forms this system, though? How would you create or plan one?

Most systems, in fact, evolve as the organisation grows and develops. Due to conflicting requirements, most companies have systems which are good in some areas of operations and weaker in others. Studies have attempted to find out what sort of organisation is more effective at innovation – developing new products – but without any clear results. This is because developing new products has two parts and two requirements. It involves generating and accepting new ideas (the first two stages in the new product process), and this is often carried out well in companies with non-rigid structures and personal autonomy. The remaining stages (see figure 4) are carried out more successfully by companies which have more rigid structures and clearly delineated responsibilities. This has led some to suggest that a truly innovative company will need to have both types of system in place (Peters and Waterman, 1982).

Without prescribing what system is better, then, it will be useful to look at different aspects and decisions which need to be addressed in developing the operations system. Some of these issues you met earlier, here we consider them from the perspective of operations.

Plant size, focus and location

Larger organisations frequently have many sites carrying out different operations. As the environment changes, decisions must be made about relocating, merging or expanding these sites. Two recent trends illustrate this issue.

- Some Japanese companies are relocating their factories to other countries, attracted by low wages (among other things). Similarly, US companies are opening plants in Mexico. Supermarkets in Britain have relocated to out-of-town locations to allow larger sites, with lower land prices and better road communications.

- Some large companies have felt that their size makes them unwieldy and slow to change. They have separated their operations into smaller business units of perhaps 100-200 employees, creating effectively mini companies.

Vertical integration

You met the concept of vertical integration in Unit 1. This is also linked to plant size and focus. A company which is highly vertically integrated will develop a product from raw material to the finished article for the consumer. For example, a highly vertically integrated oil company might be involved in extracting oil from the ground, through transportation, refining, to selling its products direct to consumers. Low vertical integration is when an organisation only carries out a small part of the transformation from raw material to delivered product. High integration allows the company to control its 'suppliers'; they are part of the company and it generates more income for each product sold. Low integration allows companies to concentrate on what they are good at. Car manufacturers, for example, have recently moved towards less vertical integration. Led by the Japanese, companies are becoming assemblers of parts made by other companies. Capacity can be altered by varying integration: when there is excess capacity, companies can make more of the product themselves, when there is too much work, parts can be bought in.

Information flows and control

With parts of the business on different sites or even different continents, communication and control is essential for success. If there is too little information or control, different parts of the business will drift away from each other, and no longer co-ordinate their efforts; in fact, they may end up hampering or competing with one another. Too much information will prevent the company understanding and acting on all of it. Excess control will stifle development, innovation and entrepreneurship.

The reasons some large businesses have restructured into smaller 100-200 employee units is to encourage flexibility and entrepreneurship and in recognition of the impossibility of closely controlling thousands of employees. It has been suggested that this size of unit offers the best balance between good internal communications and the economies of scale of a large business.

PROCESS DESIGN

The processes used in any company will reflect many factors, from historical accident, through expertise and understanding, and the demand for flexibility, to the particular transformation process involved. Rather than attempting to cover all the many facets of process design, it may be more useful to look at one common feature, layout, which links process and system design.

Layout, in simple terms, is the location and arrangement of the people and machines in the operations system. Two of the main influencing factors on layout, and much of process design, are product volume and variety. How many of each product will be sold? How similar are the different products the business produces? The layout and process for producing high volumes of similar products will be substantially different from that used to produce a small number of customised products.

There is a continuum between the production of a unique one-off product and continuous production in huge volume. This continuum can be divided into five broad types or forms of process (Waters, 1996, p.193; Slack et al., 1995, p. 240).

- *Projects* – At one end of the continuum there are activities which are 'one -offs'. These are generally large in terms of size, cost or time involved and require a lot of new technology or activity. This size and novelty leads to uncertainty, so the management of projects has developed into a distinct discipline. Examples are building a new motorway, running a space exploration programme or an election campaign.
- *Individual production (job shop)* – Most individual products involve specialist expertise but are based on previous products. A boat yard, for example, will tailor each boat to the customer, but will use the same principles, techniques and even parts for each boat. A doctor will treat each patient individually, but the ailments will often be similar, requiring the same treatment. The ordering of special inputs will increase the cost and complexity. This form of production, with individual products but similar processes, is known as 'jobbing' or 'job shop'. Examples are bespoke tailoring and hairdressing.
- *Batch production* – Beyond job shops, for larger volumes there is the potential for batch production. Either there is a fairly steady but small demand, so it is cheaper to produce in a large batch and hold stock for future demand, or the product is ordered in batches of similar products. Much of manufacturing production has traditionally fallen into this category. Examples are printing books or magazines. A cinema is an example of 'batch production' in a service industry.
- *Mass production* – It is cheapest to produce high volume and low variety, that is to produce a large number of very similar products. Much effort can be spent planning the cheapest way to produce and deliver the product; machines can be dedicated to one product allowing automation, inputs can be purchased in bulk offering economies of scale. This form of production typically involves a production line with products passing (flowing) from one stage to the next until they reach the end of the line. Examples are manufacturing washing machines, tourists visiting a monument or stately home.
- *Continuous production* – At the end of the continuum with least volume and variety lies continuous production. This deals with products like oil and chemicals which are not discrete items. In order to process large volumes, facilities are built and managed to run up to 24 hours a day with minimal changes. Although continuous production techniques are well developed in manufacturing (partly due to the huge investments required) parallels in services are limited. Manufacturing examples include oil refining, chemical production, and some information processing operations.

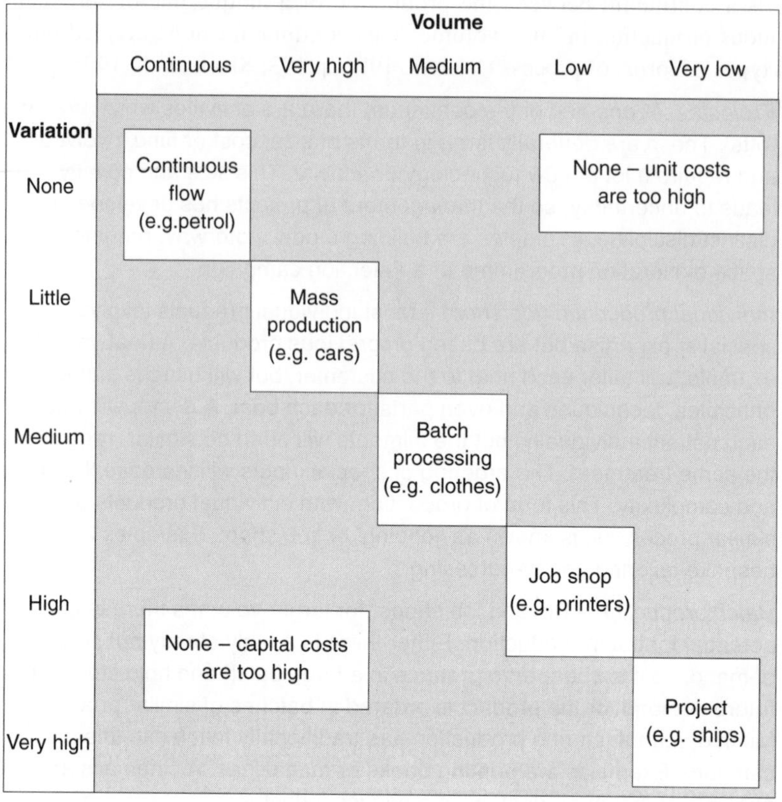

Figure 6: Relationship between variation and volume of products and types of production (Waters, 1996, p.198)

Each of these five types needs different systems, staff and equipment to work efficiently. One-off production requires skill and flexibility, working on a flow production line will tend to be more repetitive. Machines must similarly be more flexible for batch or jobbing production. Most importantly, the control methods required to run a flow or mass production line are completely different from those involved in one-off production. It is often easier to move into a different business altogether than to move from one-off to mass production. This relationship between volume and variety is demonstrated in Figure 6.

DIFFERENT TYPES OF LAYOUT

Slack et al. (1995, p. 240), among others, identifies four 'basic layout types'. These are shown in Figure 7.

Product layout

For continuous or mass production, activities must be grouped according to the requirements of the **product**. On a production line, the product moves from one machine or person to the next, often on a conveyor. In a canteen, the customers move along a line 'assembling' their meals.

Manufacturing process types	Basic layout types
Project process	Fixed position layout
Jobbing processes	Process layout
Batch processes	Cell layout
Mass processes	Product layout
Continuous processes	

Figure 7: Basic layout types and manufacturing process types

Process layout

Organising activities around the product works well with similar products, but for a job shop, the difference in products may mean there is no standard sequence for activities, or even standard activities. A second option is to organise activities around the **process**. Here, similar activities will be grouped together; for example, hospitals are frequently grouped around the process of treating a sick patient with oncology in one area, radiology in another, operating theatres in another, wards in another, and so on. This allows pools of expertise, so that all the X-ray specialists and operating theatre nurses will work in specific areas. As there is no fixed path, in theory flexibility is high; any product can take any path between activities. For example, a patient can be sent from oncology to radiology to the ward and back again for treatment or diagnosis.

Cell layout

While process layout offers flexibility in theory, it has a number of problems. Product movement is complex, leading to wasted time and lost items, and there is increased complexity in control. One aerospace manufacturer found that the core parts of a missile travelled 10 times further around the factory than the missile would ever do in the air. These problems have led to the development of cell layouts, which try to offer some of the benefits of mass production to lower volume, higher variety production. Products or parts or elements are grouped into 'families' around a similarity. This similarity may be similar activities involved in production, size or one common process they all need. All the activities, people and machines needed for that family are grouped together in a cell. The complexity of control, movement, time taken to control quality problems and so on are all addressed. While some theoretical flexibility is lost, few companies produce entirely individual products, so many have benefited from this approach.

Fixed position layout

The type of layout is again dictated by the product. When building ships or large bridges, the product cannot be moved around very much. They are built in situ, or in 'fixed position'. Large parts can be built away from the site and just assembled on site. With the construction of large bridges, for example, segments of the bridge weighing hundreds of tonnes are made at a production site and moved into position. This layout is also used in restaurants. Customers stay in one place and have meals brought to them. However, other types of restaurant layout are possible with a self-service line or a buffet-style system. Figure 8 shows different layout types that could be used by a restaurant business.

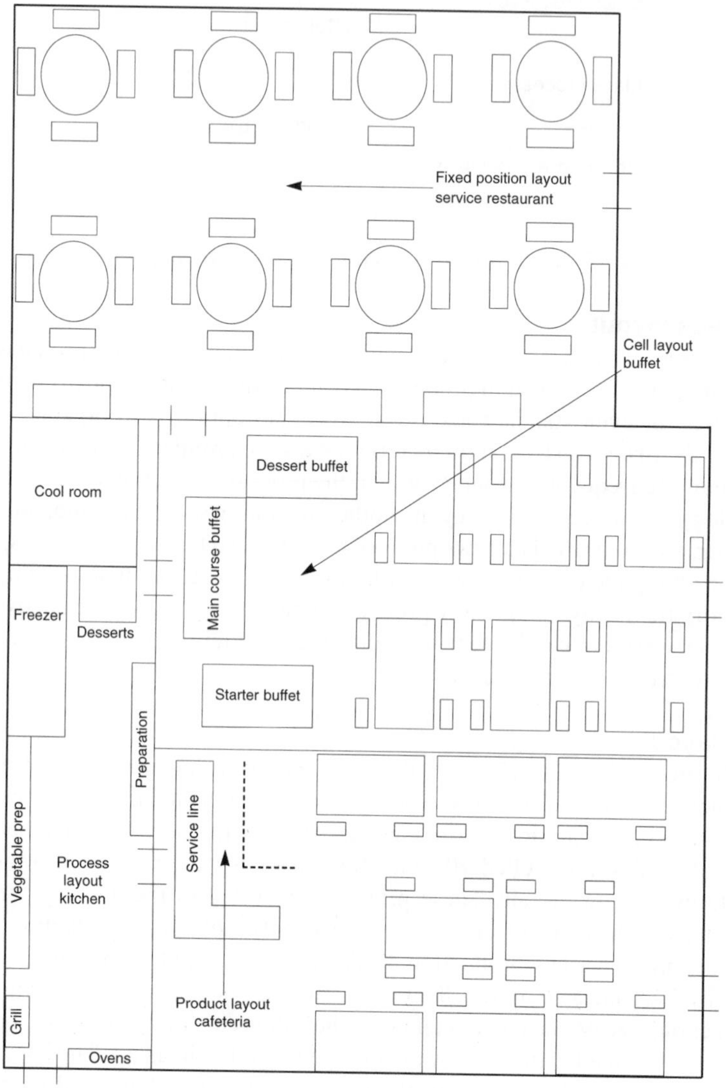

Figure 8: A restaurant complex with all four basic layout types (Slack, 1995, p. 251)

The relationship between designing the layout and the volume and variety is not entirely deterministic, but frequently follows the pattern shown in Figures 6 and 7.

As the volume increases and variety decreases, layout moves from fixed position, through process and cell to product. If you consider this for a while, you may be able to think of examples which do not follow the pattern. The restaurant is not truly a project organisation, yet uses a fixed position layout. Writing a book could be described as a project, yet in the editing process it does not stay in one place, but it is sent to editors and reviewers.

Choosing a layout reflects some of the common elements of process design:

- it will affect future operations, for better or worse
- the starting point is the product, particularly the volume of production and variety
- there is a general rule of thumb that follows the relationship shown in Figure 7
- other factors may need to be considered that complicate the decision.

3.3 Quality and quality management

Surrounding and infused through the design and running of operations is the issue of quality and quality management. Following rapid changes in a vast range of markets and industries, some central ideas have emerged.

- Quality can be considered as **conformance to requirements**, rather than any abstract concepts of 'good' or 'high quality'.
- Quality is at the mercy of, and is the responsibility of, everyone in the organisation, with each employee being responsible for his or her work.
- Improving quality not only improves the value to the customer, but it can reduce cost.

We can view operations as a system (see Figure 9). Running operations involves the activities which transform the inputs to outputs. Linked to these is the activity of designing and developing products. As a background to all these activities is the design of the system and processes involved, while throughout, quality remains a constant presence.

Thirty years ago, it was accepted in many markets that some products would fail, and a percentage of the goods supplied to the customer would be below the required standard. This was formalised in 'acceptable quality levels': the percentage of failed parts which was considered to be acceptable. It was generally accepted that it cost more money to achieve higher quality and fewer failures. Quality control departments existed in companies to inspect the products on a sample basis and highlight any problems. As such they were responsible for maintaining quality. Quality itself was generally defined as **conformance to specification**. Provided the specification fitted the customer's requirements, there was no problem. However there was no direct link between the specification and changing customer requirements. In summary, the customer was often supplied with a poor product.

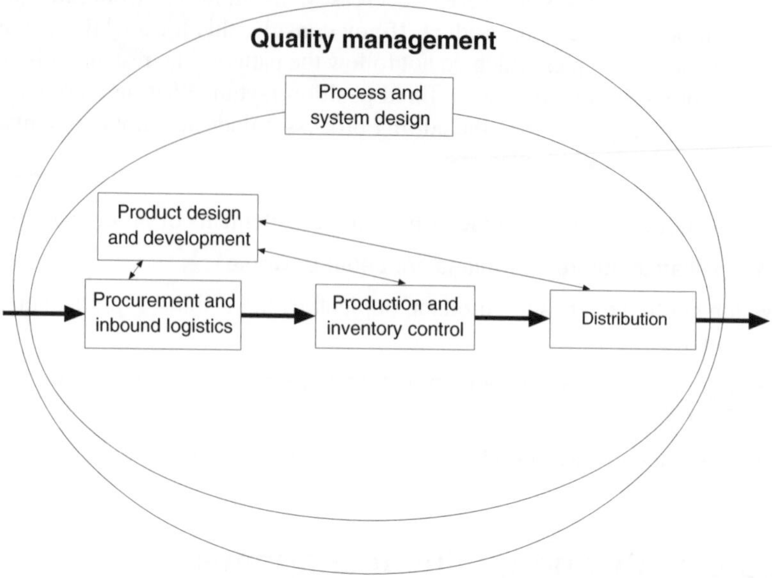

Figure 9: The operations system as a whole

Since then, there has been something of a revolution. Quality is currently one of the hottest issues in business, with companies changing radically to adopt new quality regimes. Much has been written about it.

The first part of this revolution is the realisation that making 5-10 per cent faulty products does not, in fact, reduce costs. The cost of repairing or replacing faulty goods and the loss of sales resulting from dissatisfied customers can be immense, up to 30 per cent of all the company's costs (Crosby, 1980).

The second part of that revolution was a change in the definition of quality to put the focus back on the customer and consider quality as **conformance to requirements** (Crosby 1980). Exact definitions vary slightly, but the basis is the same: if a product does what the customer requires, it is the right quality. To illustrate this, try the next activity.

ACTIVITY 5

Consider two chairs:

- an antique Chippendale, value £9,000
- a second-hand revolving office chair, value £20.

Which do you consider to be of higher quality? List the features of each chair which show the 'quality'.

People have different views on quality and what they think of as 'high quality' goods, but many people would naturally choose the Chippendale chair as being of high quality. It is worth more money, it is probably better made and more attractive and it has already lasted many years, so it will probably go on working for a while longer.

However, quality in this sense is hard to define. If we use the definition of quality as 'conformance to requirements', the situation becomes much clearer. If you are furnishing a room in a stately home, the Chippendale is almost certainly better. If, however, you want something to sit on in an office, the Chippendale is less useful, it is probably less comfortable for using at a desk, there would be a constant problem of accidental damage, it is probably far too expensive and would put up the office insurance premiums. By similarly applying this definition to other products, we can see that quality is not 'the best' according to abstract measures but 'the best for the job'.

Companies which went back to customers to find out their requirements, then worked to make sure that their products meet these needs every time, gained a competitive advantage. The products were more attractive, customer satisfaction led to more orders, the cost of repairs and replacement dwindled and not having to scrap the 5-10 per cent of products that were faulty saved money. As Crosby (1990) suggests, 'quality is not just free, it pays'.

Linked to this drive for quality is the requirement to find out what the customers want. This does not necessarily mean employing people to carry out marketing research; instead, many companies have tried to bring more people in the company 'closer' to the customer. By developing contacts between designers, engineers, managers, production workers and customers, and by making visits from one company to another, provides the opportunity for much better communication and closer customer-supplier relationships. It is vital to use this information in the development of new and existing products and to sell the customer the right product in the first place.

It follows that from a customer's perspective quality will include everyone in the organisation, from the receptionist, who often gives the first impression of the company, to the people actually producing the product. If everyone has some impact on the output of the company, everyone's efforts will go towards achieving customer satisfaction or dissatisfaction.

REVIEW ACTIVITY 3

Ouvretup Ltd is a national company specialising in office cleaning. It has 1,680 employees and 2,000 customers, ranging from a solicitor's office to a government department. It is thinking of expanding by offering new products (services). Answer the following questions, use your imagination and think about some of the answers in broad terms.

1 Describe some new products (services) that it could offer.

2 Take one of these product ideas and describe in your own words the steps that should be completed before Ouvretup put it on the market. Why is initial screening important in new product development? What would be the last stage in the new product process and why is it important?

3 Look back at the review activity at the end of Section 2. This discussed Kurdenwey dairy. Explain whether Ouvretup's or Kurdenwey's products are more *time sensitive*.

4 What form of layout would Ouvretup use for its normal cleaning activities? Why? What type of cleaning (cleaning any object, not just offices) could use product layout? How would this work?

5 List some ways in which Ouvretup could measure its product quality. Who do you think should be responsible for quality?

Summary

We have looked at product design, and system and process design. Neither can be prescribed, as they involve many different factors, but we have suggested some generalised guidelines. There are various stages involved in product development, although organisations will approach those stages differently. One of the most important features is the collaboration of all parts of the organisation.

Unit Review Activity

Case study

Aertec

Aertec is a manufacturing company with around 200 employees. It specialises in pneumatic and hydraulic products. Four years ago, the development workshop came up with the idea of a compact wall-mounted hose reel. It consists of a 10 metre hose, coiled on a reel fixed to the wall, permanently connected and ready to use, that could be pulled out when needed. When the hose was no longer required, a spring would coil the hose back up, similar in principle to a tape measure.

One of the development engineers made a prototype from the parts available in the workshop and showed it to the technical manager and the sales manager. The technical manager felt it was an excellent invention, the sales manager thought it was a reasonable idea and orders were given for a batch of 20 to be made for the sales force. The prototype was given to production to show them what to do.

The sales force found that the hoses were a little expensive, but sold well to garages. One large order was taken from a bus company with garages all over Europe. The bus company wanted 200 reels for urgent delivery to be fixed to garage roofs.

In trying to fulfil this large order, production problems started cropping up. The prototype, built from odds and ends, used eight different sizes of bolt and needed a lot of machining. This made it expensive to reproduce and involved a lot of time ordering different parts. One part that caused particular problems was a simple rubber ball with a hole in it, this was threaded onto the hose to protect it. The prototype was made by drilling a hole in a squash ball. Unfortunately, rubber is too soft for easy drilling, so each ball had to be frozen before the hole was cut. However, because this was how the prototype was made, this process was used for production. Aertec wasted a lot of time because some balls thawed out while waiting to be drilled; this had to be scrapped. It took a good deal of time to overcome all the production problems, causing a backlog of other products waiting to use the machines.

The first batch were finally finished and delivered a month late to the bus company. By the time the bus company order was complete, problems were showing up in use. The springs were too weak and they stopped working after a short time – they were not strong enough to counter the weight of hose hanging down from the roof. The hoses started leaking as seals broke down.

Development engineers were flown around Europe to repair the reels, but quality and production problems persisted and finally the product was withdrawn. Around £400,000 of parts were in stock in the factory and became obsolete overnight.

There were obviously some failures in Aertec's operations. Consider the failures by answering these questions.

1 In terms of *running* operations, identify as many problems as you can. Look back at the unit and identify the different parts of the operations system. Compare an ideal operations systems with what happened at Aertec. You may find it useful to consider the five key features of operations and the transformation model.

2 Now consider design issues. Write down the separate failures in product design, process and system design, and quality management. Look back at

our discussion of the development of new products and compare the process with Aertec's. Then consider process design: is there any evidence of failure here? There may be some problems with quality, consider what they might be. Look at the product from a customer's point of view: what would a customer expect in terms of quality?

3 Suggest what could be done to reduce the chance of this type of failure. If you cannot suggest any improvements, go back to question 1 and consider how these problems arose. Consider the different perspectives of customers and employees. Look at the new development process, the system and process design, and suggest some improvements.

Unit Summary

In this unit we have looked at operations and operations management. Operations is at the heart of what an organisation does; if we consider the transformation model, an organisation takes inputs, transforms them through some kind of process and delivers the outputs with value added to the customer. We consider five key features of operations: flexibility, simplicity, cost, quality and delivery.

The design of the system and the process are fundamental, and we investigated some different processes and how they might be laid out. Finally, we considered quality as an issue that applies throughout operations and throughout the organisation. Quality is conformance to requirements not specification.

References

Crosby, P B (1980) *Quality is Free: The Art of Making Quality Certain*, McGraw-Hill

Curtis, T (1994) *Business and Marketing for Engineers and Scientists,* McGraw-Hill

Krajewski, L J and Ritzman, L P (1996) *Operations Management, Strategy and Analysis*, Addison Wesley

Macbeth, D K (1989) *Advanced Manufacturing Strategy and Management,* IFS

Meredith, J R (1992) *The Management of Operations: A Conceptual Emphasis*, John Wiley and Sons

Peters, T J and Waterman, R H (1982) *In Search of Excellence*, Harper and Row

Porter, M E (1985) *Competitive Advantage*, Macmillan

Slack, N, Chambers, S, Harland, C, Harrison, A, and Johnston, R (1996) *Operations Management*, Pitman

Waters, D (1996) *Operations Management*, Addison Wesley

Wild, R (1995) *Production and Operations Management*, Cassell Educational

Womack, J P et al. (1990) *The Machine That Changed the World*, Macmillan

Recommended Reading

There is much literature on operations management. We have listed here a few of the broader texts which cover some of the subjects in this unit in more depth. In addition, for current detailed work one of the best journals is the *International Journal of Operations and Production Management* (MCB University Press).

Burman, R (1995) *Manufacturing Management Principles and Systems*, McGraw-Hill

Chase, R B and Aquilano, N J (1995) *Production and Operations Management: Manufacturing and Services*, Irwin

Dilworth, J B (1992) *Operations Management: Design Planning and Control for Manufacturing and Services*, McGraw-Hill

Flaherty, M T (1996) *Global Operations Management*, McGraw-Hill

Krajewski, L J and Ritzman, L P (1996) *Operations Management, Strategy and Analysis*, Addison Wesley

Muhlemann, AP, Oakland, JS and Lockyer, KG (1992) *Production and Operations Management,* Pitman

Slack, N, Chambers, S, Harland, C, Harrison, A, and Johnston, R (1996) *Operations Management*, Pitman

Waters, D (1996) *Operations Management*, Addison Wesley

Wild, R (1995) *Production and Operations Management*, Cassell Educational

Answers to Review Activities

Review Activity 1

'The goods are nearer the customer's home' – this is **inbound logistics**.

'The factory will probably only sell in volume' and *'the goods are placed next to a range of other goods, adding convenience'*. This is really what a supermarket does for **operations**, transforming the product from bulk lots of single items to a range of goods which can fill the customer's shopping basket.

'The guarantee that the goods are not faulty adds value' – this is **service**.

'The image of the store may add value in itself' – this is **marketing and sales**.

This leaves **outbound logistics**. What form does this take? The customer has to take the goods out of the store, so one vital area is getting the customer to and from the shop. The customer gets added **value** if it is easy to get to the shop, and easy to get through the checkout with the shopping and home.

Review Activity 2

1 The first way Kurdenwey needs to be flexible is in increasing or decreasing production: ice cream sales can fluctuate wildly with the weather, for example. It is no good ordering ingredients in fixed quantities months or even weeks in advance; when demand changes, there will either be too much or too little in stock. Supermarket chains often want large orders delivered at 12 hours' notice, and this requires a lot of flexibility.

In the longer term, consumer tastes change. In the past few years, ice cream has become far more popular as a year-round indulgence in Britain. Any manufacturer still focused on the summer trade is ignoring a big and potentially profitable new market. This links to the second form of flexibility: bringing in new products. New more luxurious flavours of ice cream are popular, while low fat and vegetarian cheeses are gaining ground against more established products. Kurdenwey will suffer if it cannot respond to this new demand.

2 Employees (naturally) tend to focus on what is closest to them, which in this case includes the work they are doing or the materials they are using; that is, they focus on the transformation process. Consider an employee cleaning out a large machine after it has been used to make yoghurt. The job is boring, back-breaking and very messy, so he or she will want to get it over with quickly. The employee will probably not be meditating upon the quality of the product or the customer's potential enjoyment. Customers, on the other hand, are interested in the yoghurt

itself. They are not concerned about what effort went into making it or how it was made, but they are very concerned with its texture, flavour and purity. They get angry if it's too sloppy, if it tastes wrong or if there is a hair in it. The different perspectives of employees and customers clearly relate to their interest in the operation. One is more concerned with the transformation, the other with the product.

3 The range of products, the number of employees and processes, difficulties of working with dairy and fruit farms, problems of disease and fluctuating production, and varying customer demand are just a few of the factors here.

4 There are a number of problems and issues that Kurdenwey must address. These include:

- dairy supplies and products go bad quickly, so inbound and outbound logistics have to be in refrigerated transport and delivered to a tight schedule
- sales fluctuate rapidly with the weather
- hygiene is a major issue
- health scares
- storage is refrigerated and hence very expensive
- the price and quality of raw materials fluctuates with the growing conditions – in 1996 soft fruit prices shot up and many manufacturers had to buy very expensive fruit for their yoghurts to fulfil orders.

Review Activity 3

1 We don't know exactly what products Ouvretup offers at the moment, but there will almost certainly be room for new services. Here are some suggestions:

- a complete cleaning and preparation service for new offices or houses, this is often necessary once builders have finished
- a domestic cleaning service, perhaps a team could spring clean a house in a couple of hours, or just offer cleaning services on a weekly or monthly basis
- expand into decorating – this could also include carpet supply
- a complete service, including window cleaning, for high-rise buildings.

The company could also develop products which keep up with business trends. For example, it could look out for organisations which are going through a restructuring process with changes in hierarchies and redundancies and offer a redecorating service for its offices.

2 Let's concentrate on the decorating idea. The idea generation stage has already been completed. The next stage is initial screening. The point here is to eliminate any ideas which will not succeed as early on as possible. You may feel that the

service decorating the offices of people made redundant or changed in hierarchy should be screened out. If Ouvretup leaves this step out of the development process, it will be spending a lot of time developing useless ideas. Initial screening is important for two reasons. The company will be able to cope with only a few of the new ideas, selecting the best at an early stage is important in order to allow the others to develop. Rather like growing trees, more seeds are planted than will grow to fruition, the seedlings are thinned out at an early stage to allow the others to grow. The second reason is that it is very expensive in time, resources and money to develop a product towards sale. If bad original ideas are developed, time, money and resources will be wasted.

There will be a need to check viability and fit. There will need to be a market for the service. Ouvretup could talk to its existing customers to find out whether they would buy the service. It would also need to find out about competition. It may not cost Ouvretup much to set up a new service, in terms of equipment and training, but financial viability must be examined. In terms of strategy, is decorating what Ouvretup wants to do, or will it be over stretching or fragmenting the company? Finally, can Ouvretup do it? Is the production viable? How much training is needed? How many new staff? What new equipment? Will it clash with the other products?

If the decorating idea survives this analysis, then **business and project planning** will need to be carried out. Who will do what and when, when will money be needed and when will there be a return in terms of sales? This will also link into the launch, when the service will be announced or advertised. How will it be presented to the customers? Perhaps, the company could use its cleaners to identify customers who could benefit from the service.

There should be **pre-production testing** to iron out any problems with the service. Where will the product be tried out – on a willing customer, perhaps in the Ouvretup offices or in some empty offices? But, just as importantly, the other elements of the service need testing. For example, the initial contact with the customer will be very important: taking the order, preparing a quote, arranging a schedule for work. If the company slips up in these areas it will be potentially very expensive and embarrassing. A 'dry run' exercise which involves the whole process would help to reduce the chance of failure.

The product will need to be **launched**. You may have seen some of the publicity associated with the launch of, say, a new airline or a new fast-food chain. While Ouvretup may not be going to those lengths or expense, it will need some form of publicity and will have planned how the launch will happen. Perhaps a few selected customers will be targeted, and the product will start 'small' and grow. Perhaps Ouvretup will go for a big launch, communicating with as many existing and potential customers as possible.

The final stage is, of course, **ongoing development**. The company needs to monitor how well the service is received, who buys it, what they want, how it can be improved, expanded or even discontinued, if necessary. It is possible that the product has been launched without any problems, but this is unusual. Any problems will need to be reduced or eliminated. If it is a radical product, competitors may be launching their own products, perhaps driving the price down, in which case there may be a need for cost reduction. Even if these factors do not apply, customers' needs are often changing, another reason for ongoing development.

3 Kurdenwey's products go off quickly: milk has a short shelf life and customers will notice very quickly if they don't get their delivery on time. So it may appear, at a first glance, that the dairy's products are more time sensitive. Ouvretup has different time pressures, however. Most office cleaning is carried out when the office is 'closed' – at night, in the early morning and at weekends. The office staff will complain quite soon if the cleaning work over runs and their work becomes disrupted. The time sensitivity and demands of the products for each company, then, are different, but both rely on on-time delivery.

4 The layout has to be **fixed position**. Offices cannot be moved to a location more convenient for cleaning.

In order to be suitable for a **product layout**, the object cleaned would generally have to be high volume, low variety. Laundries that clean sheets and overalls for hospitals often use a product layout, for example. Ouvretup could use a product layout for anything that could be taken away from the offices in reasonable numbers and cleaned elsewhere such as office chairs. It could offer an overnight chair cleaning service, taking the chair away and running it along a cleaning 'production' line. Obviously, the company would need to assess the demand for such a service.

5 One way to identify means of measuring product quality is to look at how the product performs for the customer. The company can use this information to find ways to ensure the standard of quality. Possible measures include:

- monitoring customer complaints – although, when a customer complains, it's a bit late
- surveying customer satisfaction
- discussing performance and means of improvement with a range of customers
- random inspections of cleaned offices
- persuading operators to check each other's work
- most importantly, monitoring how many customers are being lost or won.

Who should be responsible for quality? The people who do the work: that is, everyone in the company.

Answer to Unit Review Activity

1 What were the problems? Almost everything in the operations system was a long way from ideal. From the time the reel was put forward as an idea, the company has stumbled from crisis to crisis. Your answer may have identified a whole

range of points, but you should have noticed that there were problems with all five features of cost, quality, delivery complexity and flexibility.

Looking at **purchasing and inbound logistics**, there is no information on problems of late delivery of parts, but there are a lot of different parts which seems to cause a problem in purchasing. The problems in **production** are substantial. The processes are complex and wasteful. In addition, there are scheduling and capacity problems, with other products suffering because of problems with the hose reel. In terms of distribution, there is a problem with late deliveries, but this may well be caused by problems elsewhere. This is at least one area where failures cannot positively be identified.

We can use the five point framework to identify other problems. **Cost** problems are explicit. The product is 'a little expensive', deriving from the variety of parts – stock, time spent on ordering and control – and the production problems. Rushing parts out late can also be expensive. The wasted parts are a **quality** problem, and the products fail in use, though this seems to be derived from design problems. **Delivery** seems to be caused by problems in production but, again, is explicitly identified. **Flexibility** in terms of **adopting** new products seems to be less of a problem than coping with the changes in production. The product was accepted rapidly, but then the problems began. **Simplicity** of operation is a problem. The complexity of the product, the difficulty of integrating production with other products, the purchasing problems, all indicate that complexity is having an unfortunate impact.

2 You may have noticed particular problems with the new product development process. There was very little **viability and fit assessment** and even less **business and project planning**. The product had to be withdrawn because it kept breaking down, so **testing** was obviously lacking. However, the product sold to customers, so if it had been developed to be cheaper and more reliable, even after its disastrous launch, it may well have been successful.

In terms of **process design**, the prototype was not designed for production leading to problems. These problems would be likely to interfere with the rest of production, and they did. This would interfere with **production and inventory control**.

In terms of production and inventory control, why was there £400,000 worth of parts in stock? If there was less stock, the company would have lost less money.

3 There are no right or wrong answers here. It is better to concentrate on solving basic causes, however, and on solutions which are easy to implement.

The new product development process needs improvement, of course, but the one thing that would have helped most is if the different business functions had been involved. Production involvement in the design would have made it easier (and cheaper) to manufacture the reel, while integrating production itself more effectively with existing products. Marketing involvement could have directed the design and testing to how the reel would be used as well as addressing pricing and likely production problems.

The employees have been concentrating on the transformation process rather than the outputs; on the machines and the product rather than how the customer sees things. As a result, the five key aspects – cost, quality, delivery, flexibility and management effort – have suffered. The product is expensive, doesn't work, it's late, and the company cannot produce enough quickly enough or to the quality that meets the customer's requirements. The management effort being poured into this product will be starving better products of attention.

Quality management is definitely an issue. The product is not 'fit' for its purpose, partly as a result of lack of communication between functions, but also due to poor quality work throughout. The design was unfit for production, for example.

Every activity within operations needs improvement, with the exception of distribution. You may have come up with solutions for the some of the problems mentioned.

- Rather than flying engineers around Europe to try to patch up the reels, it may have been better to recall all the products and refund the purchase cost to the customers, allowing a relaunch when the product works.
- Simple things such as the frozen squash ball should be cured: moving the freezer next to the drilling machine (better layout) would help, but the product should use a different part or process. Buy a rubber part with a hole in it already, for example. There is room here for some improvement in purchasing by finding a product which does the job of the squash ball with no machining.
- In terms of layout, it may have been possible to set up a 'cell' for production of this product, reducing interference with other products and adding some simplicity.

In summary, although you should have identified solutions for individual problems, perhaps more importantly, you should address the problem of new product design and development, system or process design issues and the management of quality.

UNIT 6
LOGISTICS

Introduction

In this unit we examine **logistics**. Logistics is concerned with managing the flow of materials through an organisation to the customer. It is concerned with making things happen. It organises inputs (receipts from suppliers), supplies the transformation process (work in progress) and is finally responsible for delivering the output (finished goods) to the customer. As you can see, it is heavily linked to the operations management process that we discussed in Unit 5.

Increasingly, organisations are looking at their products or services as part of a chain or network. They are looking at what they produce and trying to optimise the value of all the inputs from all sources – that is, all the suppliers in the chain of supply. This is called **supply chain management**. This closer linking between customer and supplier organisations obviously needs much closer integration, and organisations are sharing much more information to achieve this. This involves utilising information technology for sharing data about stock levels, demand and trends. These initiatives use technology such as EPOS (electronic point of sale equipment), EDI (electronic data interchange), scanning and bar-coding.

Objectives

By the end of this unit, you should be able to:

- define logistics
- explain how logistics works in a factory, from goods in to distribution out
- identify the problems involved in stock holding and control
- understand just-in-time (JIT) approaches
- understand the role played by distribution
- identify key performance measures and the role of benchmarking in logistics
- appreciate that logistics strategy is linked to an organisation's corporate strategy.

SECTION 1

What is Logistics?

Introduction

In this section, we introduce the military origins of the word logistics, and outline why it has become such an important function. We use the problem of supplying an army in the field to understand the issues that are addressed by logistics and the skills it requires. We then define logistics in business. We discuss the impact of the different types of material movement, covering materials coming into the organisation, work that is moved within the organisation and finished goods that are moved out of the organisation. We identify the problems caused by 'double handling' and describe techniques for avoiding this situation. Having established that different logistics skills are used in different stages, we see why organisations come to unique decisions about how to organise their logistics.

Finally, we link logistics to the overall goal, or strategy, of an organisation and the increasing use of computer technology to both provide better service to customers (wherever they are in the supply chain) and to gain competitive advantage over rivals.

1.1 Origins of logistics

The modern use of the word 'logistics' comes from the armed services. The military developed logistics units for the very purpose of supplying armies in the field, often having to cope with the practicalities of supplying an army thousands of miles from base. Modern armies work on the principle that it takes more soldiers to 'support' an army in the field than it does to fight the battle. The ratio of support to fighting soldiers can be as high as thirteen to one. This is the critical role the logistics function plays, controlling the flow of men, materials and information. Logistics, therefore, concerns flow.

Perhaps forces are being sent into a trouble spot. How is the military going to organise the expedition? How is it going to feed the army when it is thousands of miles away? How is it going to bring back any injured? What transport should it use? What would influence the choices about methods of transport – the climate, the distance involved, what is being moved? These are all logistical issues. In the following activity, concentrate on how supplies would be moved.

ACTIVITY 1

1 Make a list of about 20 items an army of soldiers would need in a field situation. Think of everyday things we all use, as well as weapons and ammunitions. What else would be needed if the war zone is extremely hot or extremely cold?

2 List some activities that an army would need to arrange so that it could be effective. For example, it would need to arrange for:

- transportation and security of supplies
- inoculation of combatants and the disinfestation of tents
- post and medical services.

Write down six more services that would have to be provided.

3 Your list of required necessary items might have included a radio transmitter, fuel for tanks, and perishable foodstuffs for the troops. You are going to have to transport these and many other items to the forward troops. What do you need to know before you begin to supply them?

You probably found that the more you thought about this activity, the more questions you needed to answer. How many soldiers? For how long? How would supplies be shipped – by air, land or sea? You may have thought of weapons, essential medical supplies, soap and water, even toilet paper. An army in the field needs a lot of people in 'support roles' to bring them all the supplies they need. Some supplies, such as food, will have to be supplied over and over again; there will be a 'cycle', a time within which rations must be resupplied. What do you need to know before you begin to supply the materials? Here are some suggestions.

- About your resources – what (working) transport and manpower you can command, and what is their current deployment.
- About the army – how far the army is from a port, railhead, roads and an airport under its control; is transport available at the front (it is time-wasting to deliver container loads of materials if they have to be split up into jeep-sized parcels on arrival).
- About the environment – what is the terrain, sand, swamp, mountain; what weather is expected, monsoons, hurricanes, blizzards etc.
- About the military situation – are transport routes under enemy fire; is there an active 'underground' movement.
- About the cargoes – the weight and bulk of each item; whether it can be dropped by parachute or is it fragile; the quantities of each item; the special conditions under which items must be carried (radio isotopes, fresh foods and ammunition all require different handling).

You can use this framework to come up with your own specific answers to the questions.

In this activity, the army is operating like a business which uses its logistics function to bring in more raw materials and distribute them to customers in the form of finished goods. For example, if you are in the international transport business, you need to know much of the same information if, say, you are asked to transport unspecified materials across Asia to the middle of China. Even sending goods to Middlesex needs most of the information but, because it is already known (you don't expect brigands, typhoons and sandstorms in Middlesex), you do not always recognise that you need the information.

You should also note that this logistics function requires a great variety of expertise. A logistics function in business is concerned with buying materials and securing their efficient flow into, through, and out of the factory to the customers. Still using the perspective of supplying an army, try the following activity.

ACTIVITY 2

Within the logistics function, people are needed with skills in:

- forecasting or predicting
- stock or inventory control
- purchasing
- warehousing
- transportation expertise
- using and maintaining reliable and up-to-date information systems.

Write down (in four or five line answers) why these skills would be needed in a logistics function.

Logistics needs some form of forecasting to judge or estimate how quickly supplies like food and water will be used up. This determines how often will they need to be resupplied. In manufacturing, the sales forecast will indicate to production the quantities of raw materials that must be purchased and supplied to make the products.

This leads directly into stock control – we need reliable information about how much has been delivered to the factory, how much has been used, and what is left. Without accurate records mistakes will be inevitable.

Why is purchasing critical to logistics? Well, if you go shopping, you can usually guarantee that the local grocery store will have a can of beans. However, if you are obtaining supplies for an army, could you go to a supermarket and buy 10,000 tins of beans? Logistics needs skills to control purchasing on cost, quality and delivery.

Warehousing skills are necessary because a vast collection and storage operation would be needed to supply such a large force, requiring huge storage or warehouse facilities, both at the home base and overseas.

How is this tremendous flow of materials and supplies to be shifted? Some items might need to be air-freighted, some would be too bulky and may need to be shipped by sea.

Why does the logistics function need information systems and skills? There is simply so much going on, with so many records and information required between the separate activities that need control and management. Modern logistics is at the forefront of utilising computing power for business. The rise of logistics since the 1960s has been in part because of the growth of powerful and cheap computing that can 'crunch' or calculate all the data that a complex logistics system generates and needs to manage.

In summary, logistics is about flow, maintaining a flow of materials and to maintain this flow requires purchasing, forecasting, stock control, warehousing, transport skills and of course – information systems.

1.2 Defining logistics

We have seen that from a military perspective logistics involves integrating and co-ordinating information and tangible items to maintain a flow, and this is true of its use in business. Waters (1996) offers a simple definition: 'Logistics is responsible for the physical movement of all materials through an organisation.'

We can break logistics into three functional areas concerned with the movement of materials:

- movement of raw materials into an organisation
- movement of materials through the organisation
- movement of finished goods out to the customer.

MOVEMENTS OF RAW MATERIALS

Any process, as you saw in Unit 5, has to take inputs to transform them into outputs. This means supplies have to be moved into the organisation from suppliers. A saw mill needs wood as its inputs or raw material, a book shop needs books as its inputs. 'Raw material' is the input for that stage of the process.

The variety of raw materials means that the logistics function needs very specific skills and experience of:

- purchasing, ensuring the right quality, price and delivery time
- receiving, checking that what is coming in is what is required
- warehousing, so that stocks either can be used immediately or easily be accessed when they are required.

MOVEMENT OF WORK IN PROGRESS

In many operations, a product will move many times within the organisation. These **internal** movements from one process to another are moving work that is in progress – literally work that is not yet a finished product. In a saw mill, raw timber would go through many stages internally, being first stripped of its bark, and then dried out and cut into more manageable lengths before being cut into planks. At each stage, there would be work in progress. Logistics needs skills in material handling, in moving and storing items around the various stages in production. This means understanding the best method of transporting goods and the most appropriate containers to move them in.

With the growth of environmental awareness, businesses have become more conscious of generating waste. This has led to two developments that involve logistics: reducing packaging wherever possible, and the introduction of reusable containers.

Consider this example. The office supplies company, Office World, has several ranges where the goods can be displayed in the 'transit' packaging. An example is photocopy paper. A large consignment of paper will arrive on a wooden pallet with slats in the base wide enough to fit the forks of a forklift truck. Office World's forklift truck operator can then pick the consignment off the lorry and transport it directly to where it will be sold in the shop, leaving it on the pallet. This saves the time involved in opening a carton, unpacking it, placing it into a store and then moving it to the display shelf. Logistics professionals would say Office World is avoiding 'double handling' – this is literally avoiding handling the material more than necessary.

Why do you think logistics workers always try and avoid 'double handling'? What problems could double handling cause? We look at this issue later in the unit.

MOVEMENT OF FINISHED GOODS

Once again in logistics we see this sense of a chain or flow emerging. Raw materials have been brought in, work in progress has been moved around internally, then we complete the chain with the stage that ships finished goods out to the customer. Remember, just as raw materials refers only to inputs to that step, not 'rawness', so finished goods means the outputs from that operation. It does not necessarily mean they are finished and ready to be sold to the final customer. In shipping material to customers, logistics workers need skills in how goods are packaged, matching customer's orders to stock and managing warehouses and transportation. They would also have to schedule and meet delivery dates.

In this section, we have broken logistics down by the type of operation it is performing, and we have seen that while logistics covers a range of skills, different types of physical movements are more likely to emphasise some skills than others.

ACTIVITY 3

Consider these activities:

- packaging and packing
- knowing how much stock has been **sold**
- maintaining a warehouse fleet of forklift trucks
- checking that goods from suppliers have been received and are sound and the correct quantity.

In terms of managing the logistics function, which one of the three types of physical material movement would be most concerned with each one of these activities. Support your answer with a few lines explaining your choice for each activity.

In trying to decide which area would have most to do with packaging, you could approach it from the perspective of which movement has most to do with the final customer? This would lead you to the movement of finished goods, as these obviously have to be packaged in a manner that protects them. If you instead selected raw materials movement, well that is not the right answer, but you are thinking along the right lines. Accepting materials into a work place often deals indirectly with packaging too, particularly if incoming material has to be opened and split down further.

The emphasis on 'sold' stock was the clue in the second part of the activity. Again the answer is movement of finished goods. Every part of logistics needs to know something about stock levels, but sold stock is stock that has been passed to the customer, this is not as immediately relevant for say raw materials logistics. Finished goods would want to be the first to know sales figures, but these would be ultimately relevant to the other areas. Stock that has been sold needs to be replaced, and that means ordering the relevant raw materials and having the correct balance of work in progress.

Who would be most concerned with forklift trucks? Again, each area of logistics will have some form of equipment for moving materials, finished goods might have lorries, raw materials conveyor belts, all three might have forklift trucks. But the largest number, and responsibility for looking after them, is likely to be within the operation – it is, therefore, the concern of movement of work in progress.

The final part of the question again could be answered by saying that all three areas need to check what they receive, but the stress in the question on 'from suppliers' suggests that it will be the area that receives supplies; checking material from suppliers is a function of raw materials movements.

We have subdivided logistics into three areas – movement of raw materials, movement of work in progress, movement of finished goods – but it is important to note that the skills and expertise required tend to overlap. Let's take stock control as an example. Stock control will be important in all parts of logistics, each element of the logistics function needs to know what is happening with stock, what the fast moving (fastest selling) lines are (to plan to produce more), what is not selling (to plan how to reduce production).

There are other conceptions of logistics. For example, we could also subdivide logistics into two parts:

- **materials management** – responsible for the movement of materials into and within the organisation
- **physical distribution** – responsible for movement of finished goods out to the customer.

In logistics, many different terms are used and, similarly, organisations view logistics differently. We can put these into an overall picture of logistics (see Figure 1).

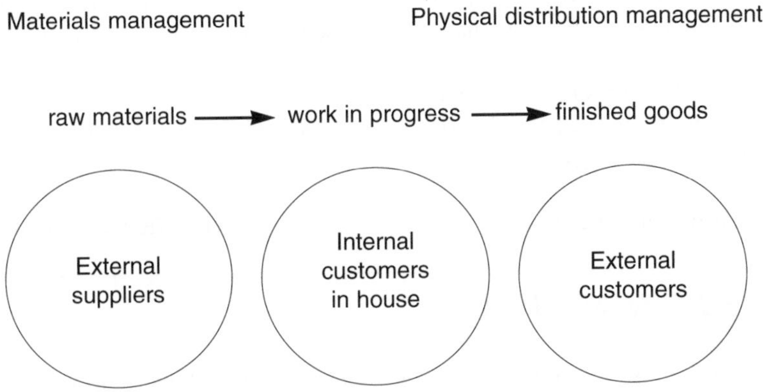

Figure 1: Conceptions of logistics

If all three elements of logistics – raw materials, work in progress, finished goods – are combined, then the resulting function is often called **integrated materials management.** The most important issue in an integrated approach is information. Accurate, up-to-date information is vital, and computers are very important in providing that information. In a fast-moving logistics environment like a supermarket chain, information is essential for planning and co-ordination. Recently a new term has been coined, **supply chain management**. This describes a situation in which the whole area of external supply is integrated into one process, from suppliers to final customers. This involves co-ordinating all the suppliers or intermediaries involved in the chain of supply. However, supply chain management has even wider implications and we will discuss these in detail in Section 4.

1.3 Logistics strategy and information technology

Information technology (IT) is one of the major reasons logistics has grown in prominence. Modern computing power enables a logistics function to add value to an organisation. In the 1990s, customers will usually not wait for goods to arrive, they expect to be served immediately or they will go elsewhere. Logistics helps a business by ensuring customer demand can be met. Some commentators have identified the rise of 'time-based competition', that is, business sectors where to be successful it is essential to be 'fast'. Later we look at two 'direct mail' businesses that work in environments where they have to be fast to win customers. Being fast is a keystone of their respective business strategies, and logistics has a vital role to play in creating the organisational capacity to respond quickly.

The integration of information (about stock levels, about what customers are buying or not buying, etc.) is a logistical function vital to a successful business. Increasingly, companies are sharing this information with suppliers. Co-ordinated and integrated logistics, made possible by computer systems stretching from suppliers to the point of sale, has been seen as the best organisational response to customer pressure for top quality, delivery and service. The role of logistics in supporting business strategy has been defined by Bowersox and Closs (1996):

'Logistical management includes the design and administration of systems to control the flow of material, work in process, and finished inventory to support business unit strategy.'

The definition brings together three key words – **systems, flow** and **strategy**.

REVIEW ACTIVITY 1

You have just been placed in charge of a large regional distribution centre for a major supermarket chain. The distribution centre receives deliveries from the supermarket's suppliers, stores them, and then ships them out to individual stores in its region.

As the manager of a distribution centre, you are responsible for shipping stock out to the supermarkets efficiently and cost effectively. You have staff and a fleet of vehicles at your disposal. The stores you supply vary in size, and their stock requirements will vary daily. You want to use as few lorries as possible to serve as many stores as possible, with no rearranging of products inside the lorries.

Suppose you are planning the delivery for Thursday next week. Identify some information that you will require and the role that information technology plays.

Summary

In this section, we have moved from a simple definition of logistics, as being all about flow, to a more refined definition that highlights the other issues necessary to control the flow – systems and strategy. Flow includes information as well as materials, so that we need systems to control the information as well as the material. So our definition has expanded to include flow of materials and information. We have seen that there are three task elements to logistics – moving raw materials in, work in progress, and moving raw materials out. Planning and co-ordinating the flow is a means of supporting the business unit's strategy. This is the last jigsaw piece of our definition: logistics is about the flow of materials and information in such a way that supports the wider strategic direction of the company. In the next section, we look at logistics in action and investigate what actually happens in a factory environment.

SECTION 2

Logistics in Practice: A Factory Visit

Introduction

In this section, we look in more detail at the specific activities within logistics by seeing how it works in practice. We follow a shipment from a supplier through an organisation and out to the customer. We look at all the individual jobs that go to make up the logistics function. We visit a factory and actually see each job or role in action. In order to follow all the roles or steps in logistics, we will follow the progress of an order through all the stages of production, step by step.

By tracking the physical progress of material received through an organisation, we list the key jobs within logistics – procurement, stores management, receiving, warehousing, materials handling and containerisation – and outline their contribution. We can also identify areas where computers can increase efficiency.

2.1 Factory tour

We visit Pump Co., a medium-sized company manufacturing pumps that are used in construction. Pump Co. does not sell directly to the public, it supplies wholesalers, and occasionally delivers very large orders to individual customers. Like most manufacturers, Pump Co. does not make the entire pump, it 'buys in' certain components where it feels that is more efficient. We look at the buying in of a valve system, and trace its movements.

PROCUREMENT

Procurement (or purchasing) is the first of the key jobs. It is the activity that is concerned with understanding and meeting the organisation's material and services needs. It selects the suppliers, agrees terms and places orders. Sometimes it is referred to as 'buying'.

Purchasing orders may be 'open' - which is an agreement that the supplier will deliver agreed quantities until told not to, or 'closed' – where the order is for a fixed, predetermined quantity and (usually) value.

In our case, Pump Co. has an open order with Valve Ltd to supply a particular valve identified by the part number AB1234. This means that Pump Co.'s purchasing function has agreed a price and a delivery schedule with Valve Ltd. A delivery schedule is simply a plan or forecast of what goods or services are required.

	Thursday 26th	Thursday 3rd	Thursday 10th	Thursday 17th
Valve AB1234	18	18	36	18

Table 1: Supplier schedule for Valve AB1234

The schedule in Table 1 tells Valve Ltd. to deliver 18 valves a week, on Thursdays (except on the 10th when double quantity is required), and might well include a delivery time – say, 10 a.m. Schedules are usually issued once a month, this gives the supplier time to plan production and delivery.

ACTIVITY 4

Imagine you are the purchasing officer at Pump Co.

1 What information would you need in order to issue a supplier schedule?

2 What would a supplier use a schedule for?

3 Imagine a schedule has been issued with the wrong quantities on it – actually double what is required. What problems would that cause?

4 What problems would it cause if a schedule orders too little material – say half what is really required?

5 Companies can purchase items without issuing schedules. What kind of purchases do you think would be made without using a schedule?

In order to 'raise' a schedule on a supplier, as the Pump Co. buyer, you need to know how many of the items containing part AB1234 production plans to build the following week. Remember that not all the pumps that Pump Co. manufactures use this particular valve. You also need to know how many AB1234s are in stock; if you already have a large number then it may not be necessary to purchase more valves that week.

Suppliers need information in order to plan their own production. Valve Ltd probably has suppliers that make parts which go in to AB1234, and it may need to keep its suppliers informed of changing requirements.

If you issued a schedule asking for 36 AB1234s a week when you actually require 18 valves, then there would be a build up of stock at Pump Co. as production will use less than you have received. This would mean money was tied up in buying stock before it was needed. For very bulky items, this might cause real storage problems. This is unlikely to be the case with a valve but imagine if you over-ordered a supply of aircraft wings. It might cause Valve Ltd problems to supply such a big rise in demand. Hopefully, Valve Ltd might query the schedule, as such a rise over a month might disrupt its production planning. Valve Ltd might have to work overtime (paying employees a premium rate for working longer than normal hours) to meet the schedule or it may find that its suppliers have problems supplying the extra components to meet the increased demand AB1234s. If the schedule orders insufficient material, Pump Co. would find that it could not produce that pump because it does not have enough of the right valves – it would have a 'shortage'.

When you purchase something, you do not raise a schedule; you just go to a shop and buy it. However, schedules are a way of simple and easy repeat buying. Usually Pump Co. buys AB1234 every week, so it would be a nonsense to go through supplier selection and delivery and price agreements every week. Instead, for these 'routine' repeat purchases, a schedule is ideal. It would not be used for 'one-off' purchases such as a major new tooling machine or a new photocopier. These one-off or unique purchases would be dealt with one at a time without a schedule. A few other items such as stationery might also not merit a schedule.

Purchasing raises schedules for suppliers, to inform them what will be required over the coming period. Now we look at stores management, beginning with receiving – the function within Pump Co. that actually physically receives the valves.

STORES MANAGEMENT

The stores management function has responsibility for:

- receiving materials
- updating stores records
- storing materials away
- internal movement of materials to where they will be used when they are required – that is, handling the work in progress
- transporting work to the finished goods store – from where physical distribution will be responsible.

Receiving

Once the material has been ordered using a schedule, it will arrive on the day the buyer specified – and, in many businesses, at the time the buyer specified. The receiving stores unloads the lorry, reads the attached paper work, inspects the goods if necessary to confirm that they match the paperwork, books the new material into the company's stock record system, and moves them to the main store area, where they will be put into a location.

At Pump Co., the receiving stores reads Valve Ltd's advice note. An advice note always accompanies material, it literally advises the receiving company what has been shipped (part number AB1234) and in what quantity (18). This is perhaps the most important stores document. The supplier, Valve Ltd, will invoice (that is ask to be paid for) for whatever quantities are on the advice note. A copy will go to Pump Co.'s accounts department. When it receives an invoice from Valve Ltd for

18 AB1234 valves delivered on the 26th, it will match this invoice against the delivery note. This matching confirms everything is in order and that the invoice can be paid; it is an accurate record of what Pump Co. has purchased.

Having used the advice note to confirm the goods are correct, receiving stores has to ensure that the material is booked in, that is that the new stock has been added to the quantity already in the factory. This may be a paper-based system, a simple stores record card. However, it is more likely to be a computerised system. A computer system may well record the exact delivery note so that if there was any problem with the parts there would be 'trace-ability' – literally the ability to track down which batch was faulty so that the supplier can discover exactly what went wrong.

Warehousing

Finally, receiving stores would be responsible for storing the material. A computerised system might suggest a location, usually such locations are rows of racks, identified by row and the level. This is how Pump Co.'s stores operates (see Figure 2).

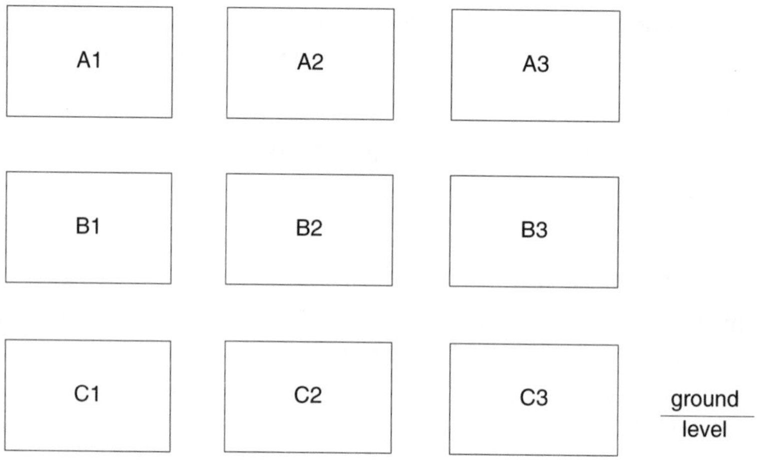

Figure 2: Scheme of Pump Co.'s stores racking

Bins or stock pallets are arranged in rows, each row is three storage bins high. Our delivery has been placed in bin B1, stored in the second row in the first column of the racking.

The material has now been stored where it can found, and the stock records have been amended to take account of the new delivery. The material is waiting to be used. At some point, production will need further supplies of AB1234 in order to produce more pumps. Whether by computer or manually, a message will come through to the stores requesting more AB1234s. The materials handling function will respond and **issue** the stock to production. A computer-generated list of stores issues will be a useful document for recording what is being built and establishing that there will still be sufficient stock for the next period's production. The recording of 'issues' to production tells the system (and inventory control) that that pallet is no longer in the stores and is being used by production.

MATERIALS HANDLING

Materials handling is responsible for moving stocks from the stores to the production area, and sometimes for movements within the production area. Materials handling can be described as three movements:

- selecting materials from where they are being stored (in our example rack B1)
- moving the materials from their storage spot to their destination (in our case the valve assembly area)
- placing the materials exactly where they are required.

A number of issues have to be taken into account in designing a materials handling system including the type of materials, their characteristics, and the resources available to fund the system. Table 2 shows how some materials would be handled.

Method of packaging	Method of handling
Sacks and bags	Conveyor system
Bulk liquids	Pipelines and tankers
Small light items	Manual handling

Table 2: Different methods of material handling and packaging

We noted earlier the problem of handling the materials more times than is needed, or **double handling**. The task for the materials manager here is to find the methods, the routes or work flows, the layouts and the containers needed to minimise double handling. Double handling does not add value, it raises costs in terms of fuel, maintenance, risk of accidents and the possibility of stock damage.

In many organisations, **materials flow** has been given a low priority. Layouts and store locations have developed both by accident and by what was convenient in the past; such situations need review. If goods are stored in a poor location, they will have to be moved again later. If the wrong form of internal transport is used, this could result in double handling. Think about moving a container load of cement bags with a wheelbarrow – many journeys would be required. Poor communication can result in too little or too much material being delivered to the factory floor.

The example of moving sacks of cement highlights two key areas of responsibility for materials handling: **internal transportation equipment** and **containerisation**. Materials handling functions often have fleets of forklift trucks, smaller manual trucks called reach pallet stackers for loads which do not move far above ground level, and (possibly) racked storage bays with electric reach trucks able to retrieve materials that are stored many metres high; these electric reach trucks may be computer controlled.

Think about a trip to the supermarket. You can use two transportation forms, a small shopping basket you carry around or a larger shopping trolley with wheels. The choice of which one to use is similar to decisions a material handling manager faces. How much, of what weight and what size, are you trying to move?

Containerisation

Earlier we mentioned the greater environmental concern about waste which places greater emphasis on recycling. Increasingly, businesses are trying to make the container that they use function as both the transit protection packaging and the container the customer uses. This saves handling and packaging waste. Often, when a supplier delivers such a container it will collect empty containers back from the customer so that they can be reused. This is more environmentally friendly than disposable containers. Increasingly, material handling is involved in investigating the best form of containerisation. Businesses want containers that avoid double handling, that are reusable and that minimise environmental damage by avoiding unnecessary packaging. Can you identify a product that you buy in which the container you use the product in is the same as the one the product was delivered in?

ACTIVITY 5

Using our tour of Pump Co. to help you track materials into, through and out of the factory, identify six key activities within logistics. Write down briefly what each activity does.

Here is our list of the six key activities within logistics.

- Procurement (or purchasing) – identifies the expected production over the next period and obtains supplies for manufacture.
- Stores management – accepts materials from suppliers, stores them, delivers the material to the shop floor, moves it (now called work in progress) as it is worked on in the factory, and then stores the products in the finished goods store. And, importantly, keeps accurate records of all goods and their locations.
- Receiving – unloads lorries, checks that goods ordered have arrived, checks for damage, checks invoices against advice notes. Moves materials into store. Books the new material into the stock record system.
- Warehousing – once the materials have been placed in store, warehousing takes responsibility for a system of efficient retrieval and security.
- Materials handling – selects required materials from the warehouse, and moves them to where needed. It aims to use the most efficient form of packaging and transport.

- Containerisation – packaging for transport. Materials handling will advise on how to achieve efficient methods of protecting goods, reducing cost and meeting environmental concerns about waste.

2.2 Stock control systems

Think about the food you have at home in the kitchen cupboards, refrigerator and freezer. You would know broadly what you have, and you could look in the kitchen and make a precise list of what provisions you might need for everyday or special use. For a complex business, this kind of stock management using eyesight and memory is not possible. Computers are used to maintain and track **inventory**, that is stock record information. Stock or inventory control is so important it exists as a separate function, the **inventory control function**.

INVENTORY CONTROL FUNCTION

The overall responsibility of inventory control can be summarised as keeping production going with the minimum of inventory. This involves ensuring that:

- the right bill of materials (BOM) is available – the BOM contains the ingredients or parts lists which indicate the amount and type of materials required for manufacture, (for example, a BOM for a McDonald's burger would be itemised as a sesame bun, lettuce, beefburger, dill and sauce)
- stock records are accurate
- liaison with suppliers dealing with problems such as stock that is not being used or is not being rotated.

Although the principles and techniques of logistics apply to all businesses, companies choose different organisational structures and titles for the various functions that perform the logistics role. With Pump Co., we are looking at the physical movement of inventory through a particular factory and functions would literally 'touch' the physical stock. Some organisations would include inventory control within material handling, others see it more as a planning discipline and keep it separate, some even attach it to finance as large sums of money may be involved.

Materials handling has responsibility for storing parts where they can be accessed, and for ensuring that they are used in the correct rotation, this is normally on the principle of 'first in, first out' (FIFO). The first ones that came in are the first to be used; this ensures that the stock is rotated. An alternative used in some industries is 'last in, first out' (LIFO); here the newest arrivals are the first ones to be shipped out.

The inventory control team will keep a close eye on stock rotation, using computer-generated reports. Modern stores computer systems record what date material is received and are capable of generating reports of 'ageing or slow-moving stock'. Armed with this information, inventory control can consult material handling to see if there is a problem or to ward off a potential problem.

STOCK RECORDS AND STOCKTAKING

We have seen that responsibility for stock levels lies with inventory control, which is dependent on the accuracy of the stock records system. With modern bar-code reading equipment and computer-controlled systems, stock records are becoming increasingly accurate. However, they follow the rule for all records: 'garbage in, garbage out'. If an entry is incorrectly made into the system, the information output from the system will be wrong.

Inventory control uses stocktaking to ensure stock records are accurate; it means physically counting the stock. As so much of a company's money is locked up in stock and work in progress, in many countries it is a legal or statutory requirement to 'verify' once a year that stock records are accurate. This is the **annual stock take**. However, inventory control is likely to run its own programme of counts throughout the year, usually by requesting materials handling to do a count.

The final part of our factory tour takes us to the finished goods warehouse. We have seen that materials handling has been involved in moving new stocks and work in progress through the factory. Physical distribution deals with sending finished products out to the final customer.

2.3 Physical distribution

We have been tracing a component purchased from a supplier through the factory. The AB1234 valves have been received, booked in, allocated a stores location and finally issued to production. Pump Co.'s production unit has now assembled a batch of pumps, using up the delivery of AB1234s in the process. Remember that logistics is all about flow. Having received and 'used up' the AB1234s, more supplies will be needed. A new schedule will be issued and a further delivery will be made from Valve Ltd. Supplies come in, they are used, and shipped out, this is the flow of logistics. Now we look at the last element of the flow, the flow of finished goods out to the customer. This is **physical distribution.**

Physical distribution has been described as the task of ensuring that the goods and services produced by the organisation are transported from the place of production to the point of consumption, as efficiently as possible and as economically as possible (Carter and Price, 1993).

Physical distribution is responsible for:

- despatch
- packaging
- transportation – a company may run its own fleet of vehicles or it may hire or contract in a third party haulier to do all the transport (this is becoming increasingly common as organisations focus on a few core skills or competencies and leave other areas, like transportation, to hired professionals)

- route scheduling
- loading lorries so that they are economical – trying to avoid, for example, transporting 'fresh air' in a half-empty lorry
- supply to intermediaries or the end user – if the company is large enough, it may choose to have its own regional warehouses, and physical distribution would supply to these warehouses
- sales order processing – recording what is available, when it can be delivered, and the most efficient way of taking it there.

Pump Co. does not supply direct to the final customer. Instead, it supplies intermediaries, warehouses and distributors, which supply the user (these are Pump Co.'s **channels**). If these warehouses and distributors find that they are running down their stocks of this particular pump, they would order more. A distributor might ask for a large delivery of say 72 pumps. This order could be by mail or telephone, but increasingly companies are introducing electronic data interchange (EDI), so that they can share information with suppliers.

Pump Co. has EDI with its largest customer, Big Distribution Co. This means that Pump Co.'s physical distribution department can see from the EDI system what stock Big Distribution has in its warehouse. If Big Distribution has an agreed stock-level holding for the part with Pump Co. (as it would have for a fast-selling product, much as Pump Co. has an open schedule with suppliers of fast-moving parts), all Pump Co. needs to do is consult the system to ensure it 'tops it up' at the right time.

To fulfil the order for 72 pumps, Pump Co. needs to deliver four boxes (the pumps are packed in boxes of 18). What will delivering four boxes involve? We have already commented that it is expensive to transport 'air', so one task will be to ensure delivery vehicles are as full as possible. There are a number of warehouses that Pump Co. supplies, located in different areas of the country. Pump Co.'s physical distribution department will need to plan the routes of its vehicles to ensure that they are travelling the minimum distance while supplying the maximum number of pumps. Delivery and fleet maintenance are expensive and the physical distribution section will certainly be required to provide forecasts and estimates of how much delivery will cost per budget period, and then it will have to explain any under- or over-estimate. Large companies will use complex route planning and scheduling software. Smaller companies rely on the abilities of the transport manager.

RETURNS

Physical distribution will be involved if there is a **return**. Following a return through the system will demonstrate how closely all the functions of logistics work together and remind us of the role each plays.

Suppose one of Pump Co's pumps is found to be faulty. The customer would return it to the warehouse or distributor and either get money back or a new pump. The distributor would then return the pump to Pump Co. through physical distribution when it made its next delivery. Earlier, we stressed the role of computer stock records in ensuring 'trace-ability'. A faulty product is a very serious matter and the company would want to find out what went wrong in case there was a batch of faulty products.

Physical distribution would collect the faulty part, and return it to the factory where it would be booked in, and then its part number tracked back to the batch of production. The faulty part could then be examined, the cause identified and any flaw in the production process could be rectified. If the faulty pump could be repaired, it will be returned to stock, from where it could be reissued and sold again.

CASE STUDY

Honda UK

Honda has a plant at Swindon in England, where it produces cars for the European market. The plant has been built on a 'greenfield' site. As a new facility, it has the advantage of being built to suit the flow of materials into the plant. (Older factories have to adapt and make do.)

The assembly plant part has been built basically as a rectangle, with many loading bays at the sides (see Figure 3). This means that lorries can deliver the material not just to the building but virtually to the precise location that materials are required in the assembly operation. This reduces the need for material handling and double handling.

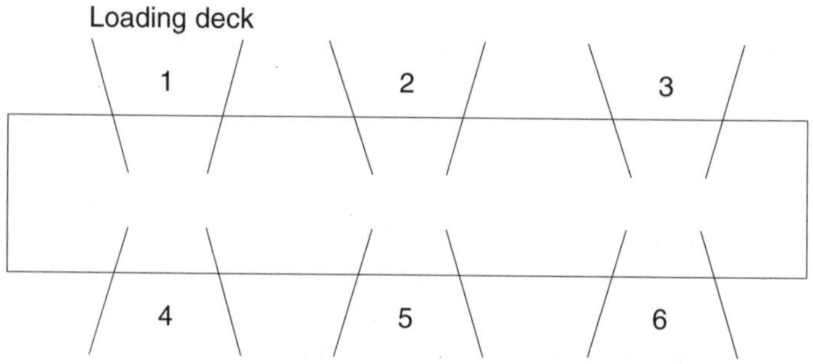

Figure 3: Representation of the layout of Honda's assembly plant.

However Honda has gone even further in its material handling operation. Every car has what is called a headliner, literally the cloth roof to the car. This comes supplied complete, with various hooks and handles; Honda does not have to do anything to the component, it can be fitted straight to the car. Not all headliners are identical, some have grey plastic handles to match grey trim in the rest of the car, some have other colours to match different trims. Honda informs the supplier exactly which car is being built in what order, and the supplier then delivers the headliners in precise sequence needed to ensure that the handles match the colour of the trim. The headliners do not need to be taken out and sorted by Honda, they are delivered to the production line correctly sequenced.

Another step Honda has taken is to require the supplier to deliver in special trolleys that can be simply wheeled from the lorry to the production area – and the empties wheeled back. It uses reusable containers and does not need to wait for a forklift truck to be available. The goods can be delivered and the empty pallets taken back very quickly.

Honda has refined the materials receiving process and abolished manual receipt of the materials. Because the supplier has been informed exactly what to deliver at a specific time, and in an exact sequence (for example, three grey headliners followed by two beige, then four grey and then four beige), Honda knows precisely what is on delivery lorries. A video camera records the lorry driving up and wheeling out the trolleys. This video record is taken as proof of delivery; no paper work is stamped, indeed there is no paper work. Honda's systems generate automatic payment without an invoice having been received.

REVIEW ACTIVITY 2

Honda's system works in a high-volume environment. Consider suppliers to smaller-scale organisations, say a local newsagent. Why are the morning newspapers not delivered to a newsagent in the order the customers come in and buy them?

Work back through the material in this section and record all the manual activities that Honda's system has eliminated.

What does such a system tell us about relationships between Honda and its suppliers that use this system?

Summary

In this section, we have traced material coming in from a supplier, the procedure for booking it in and adding it to the stock records. We saw that materials handling has responsibility for ensuring that production have materials when they need them, which involves both knowing the best place to store inputs, how to store them, and how to deliver them to production.

Physical distribution has responsibility for delivering to the customer (or warehouse) at the right time in the quantity required. You should realise the critical importance of stock recording and, therefore, the role inventory control plays in ensuring that everything can run smoothly. All this information can best be handled by computers and you have some concepts of how computers can speed up and improve logistics systems.

In the next section, we look at how companies plan and control their materials requirements.

SECTION 3

Controlling Supply: Materials Planning and Control

Introduction

Information is vital to logistics managers. It is needed on a daily, weekly and monthly basis, and into the future through forecasting, as managers try to match what customers will buy (demand) to what is needed to supply that demand. Much of the day-to-day work of logistics is concerned with developing plans and mechanisms to ensure that, as far as possible, products and services are available at the time required by the customer.

We focus here on this vital role of planning and controlling materials. We outline the purpose of materials control and identify the constraints on materials planning and control. We identify the problems involved in holding stock. We make a simple schedule forecast and explain why it may vary, period to period. Materials ordering systems are needed, and we investigate the principles behind one example, economic order quantity (EOQ). Finally, we look at what is meant by just in time (JIT) and how it differs from traditional logistics practice.

3.1 Scope and purpose of materials control

We are all familiar with the basic principles of materials control and planning from everyday life. Remember the last time you prepared to go food shopping in preparation for a big party, or for your holidays. Why did you go? Because you needed something. Did you need it immediately? Probably not, it could have waited another day perhaps. Without specifically acting out the role of materials planners in our daily lives, we plan our requirements. We are able to think about what we will need to buy before we actually need it. Also, we know that some foods don't last, so we know to buy fresh fish on the day we want to use it. We know that a weekend may be the only time we can get to certain shops, so we plan ahead. Generally speaking though, we would expect to find all our general food requirements met by products on the supermarket's shelves. A particular favourite brand might be unavailable, but even this is fairly unlikely. In a business context, the processes of planning and co-ordinating are more complex as the next case study demonstrates.

CASE STUDY

Toshiba

The Japanese company, Toshiba, has a factory at Plymouth in England that manufactures televisions. Like many electronics companies, Toshiba buys most components in from suppliers. In fact, around 85 per cent of the value of a Toshiba television is made up of parts from suppliers. This means only 15 per cent of the television is supplied directly by Toshiba. This may surprise you, but it is very common when a product is as complex as a television. In many automobile companies, the 'bought in' content of a car is approaching 75 per cent.

Buying in such a high proportion of the content means Toshiba has to co-ordinate between 150 and 200 suppliers. Most of the electronic components it requires are only made in the Far East. Toshiba actually faces a 90-day wait for many key components while they are shipped over to Europe. The company cannot walk into a shop and buy components off the shelf like you could with your shopping. In business, the time it takes for a supplier to deliver a product is known as the 'lead time'. Here, Toshiba is facing a lead time of 90 days. From the day it orders a component from Singapore, it will take 90 days to be manufactured and delivered to the factory in Swindon.

Imagine what this means in terms of ensuring that all the parts that go to make up a television, supplied from all these suppliers, are available at the right time. The situation becomes even more complex when you realise that Toshiba does not build one type of television, it produces a small basic model, a mid-range model and a high-tech giant screen top-of-the-range model. Within these three basic categories there are several options; for example, televisions can be supplied with or without certain features like a remote control.

The co-ordination of the demand for televisions (from customers like us) with the supply of televisions (which means assembling all the components at the right time) is the part played by material controls and planning. It is essentially a balancing act, trying to balance supply with demand.

ACTIVITY 6

You are going to buy margarine. Note down your answers to the following questions.

1 What prompts you to buy margarine? How do you know when to buy it?

2 What does a packet of margarine cost, roughly. What would be the cost of buying a year's supply? (You will have to estimate how long one packet will last and multiply that by the cost.)

3 Now calculate the amount of space you would need to keep a year's supply at home.

4 How long does margarine last? (A packet should have a use-by date on it.)

The aim of this activity is to get you thinking about the constraints involved in 'stock'. You probably buy margarine when you 'forecast' that you are going to run out, or you might even wait until you had run out. You should have calculated that it is a fair sum of money to spend on a year's supply, and to tie up in 'stocks' of margarine. In any event, your refrigerator almost certainly couldn't hold a year's supply. The final constraint here is, of course, that margarine 'spoils', after a certain time it is no use. Many businesses face such issues, and not just in the food industry. Think of the fashion industry and the market for seasonal clothes; it is no good a shop receiving winter coats at the beginning of summer, or last season's designs for this season.

3.2 Constraints on materials planning and control

You saw in the last activity that even for a simple purchase like margarine there are constraints, literally borders or features that we have to work within. Businesses face these constraints all the time, and the function of materials control and planning is to:

- recognise constraints
- work within these constraints.

Let's now look at constraints in a business context, and at the tools materials planners have to tackle them. We can break them down into:

- constraints of time (forecasting)
- constraints on stock holding.

TIME AND FORECASTING

Many of the goods we buy can be obtained immediately in a shop. This is not true for businesses, particularly for businesses which assemble parts from many suppliers. We have seen that electronics businesses can face lead times measured in months not days. Because a business faces these lead times, it must buy ahead. This means it has to forecast what it will require days, even years, ahead. For example, aircraft manufacturers have lead times measured in years.

How does a complex business make a forecast about the supplies it will need? A business has to forecast first what its customers will want to buy, and then calculate what parts and services it will need to purchase to meet that demand. All businesses make **sales forecasts**. A newsagent selling daily papers will make a forecast of how many papers will be sold the next day and, from that forecast, adjust how many it will have to order; a baker will forecast how much bread it will sell, and from that how much dough it will need.

Let's look at a simplified sales forecast that a newsagent might prepare (Table 3).

	Mon	**Tues**	**Wed**	**Thurs**	**Fri**	**Sat**	**Sun**
Sales forecast	100	90	85	85	90	70	120

Table 3: Weekly sales forecast for newspaper sales

ACTIVITY 7

Explain why the newsagent thinks that more papers will be sold on some days than others?

Can you think of any problems that would come from having highs and lows of demand.

Let's say one paper has a special offer in Thursday's edition – a free entry for a holiday competition say with every copy – what would that mean for the shop?

What 'special events' could affect newspaper sales?

There might be many different reasons for the variations in sales. The newsagent has tried to forecast demand for the week. The vendor seems to think sales will dip during the week from a peak on Monday and then rise as the weekend approaches – but dip again on Saturday. There could be many reasons for this pattern of sales; many people work during the week and use Saturday for shopping and odd jobs, perhaps they don't have time to read a paper, or they might normally read a paper when they get to work, so don't actually buy one on Saturday. In a different location, there might be lots of passing trade and a Monday market that brings more people to the town centre, or people might be buying a paper on the way to a train station.

The problem for the newsagent is that demand varies. If we assume that it takes one salesperson to handle 50 newspaper sales, then on Monday the shop would require two people. But from Tuesday to Saturday the sales staff would have time on their hands, demand would not meet capacity. However, on Sunday two people would be over-stretched, and the newsagent would need to employ a third person.

If one paper had a really good special offer, then that paper might sell out very quickly – perhaps customers who normally buy it would turn up to find it sold out, and then go elsewhere or not buy a paper at all. Similarly, some events attract so much interest that newspapers are bought in greater quantities as everybody wants to know what is going on. During an election or a popular sporting event, newspaper sales increase and if the newsagent's forecasts underestimate demand, the business would have lost a lot of potential sales. Even terrible weather can affect sales.

This activity has encouraged you to think about the problems with forecasting demand and how hard it is to get right; there are so many 'variables' that can affect the forecast. Nevertheless, businesses have to forecast demand in order to begin the process of estimating what they will need to meet that demand. All materials planning and control will reflect the sales forecast. So far, we have used as an example a product that sells the day it is produced, and there is little point in keeping stocks of yesterday's newspapers; but other businesses do keep stock. We now look at the constraints of holding stocks.

STOCKHOLDING

We can look at the problems with holding stock under four headings:

- cost
- space
- stock loss
- obsolescence.

Cost

It obviously costs money to buy stock in the first place. Once that money has been spent on purchasing stock, it cannot be used in other parts of the business. This may mean that a new marketing campaign cannot be launched due to lack of funds, or an opportunity has to be missed – even the option of buying the same stock at a new lower price due to a special offer. The cash tied up in holding stock could be used more profitably in other activities, so there is an opportunity cost associated with carrying stock.

Any business that ties up a lot of its money in stock runs a considerable risk. Many materials and components deteriorate over time. This means that a lot of stock 'depreciates', it is worth less than was originally paid for it. Some stock, such as dangerous chemicals, have serious safety requirements. Logistics has a responsibility to ensure the safety of the company's employees, and this can be costly. In some businesses, it is important that components are relatively new – would you want ice cream from a manufacturer that uses one-year-old cream? Many businesses are compelled to keep fresh stocks, so they cannot buy too far ahead.

Some businesses work on the basis that holding stock costs a proportion of the value of the stock held; this can be as high as 30 per cent.

Space

Very few businesses are so fortunate that they have unlimited space and, generally, the more space a business occupies the more it pays in rent, local government taxes and utilities charges. Some stocks take up a tremendous amount of space. Imagine the space a manufacturer of prefabricated homes would require to hold a year's stock. Think of how much it would cost to rent this space each year.

In manufacturing businesses, particularly, space tends to be very limited in production areas – there is no room for large stocks. If these are kept farther away in a remote store, then there would be 'double handling' which we know is poor logistics. Some forms of stock require dedicated space. Liquids require drums or a tank, a dangerous chemical might need to be stored in specific conditions at particular temperatures.

Space is a constraint as it is often fixed, to occupy more costs more, and using space for storing stock lowers flexibility as you cannot use the space for something else.

Stock loss

All businesses experience stock loss, it is literally stock that goes missing. In some cases, this may be due to theft and pilferage. There may also be damage, a forklift truck can accidentally collide with a rack of stock, some can be dropped or damaged, rain can seep in from poorly maintained buildings. All kinds of circumstances conspire to 'lose' stock.

Obsolescence

Obsolescence is when a product becomes redundant, it is no longer useful for the job it was intended for. This might not be a problem for an antiques dealer, who lives by buying and selling aged but valuable household articles, but for a computer manufacturer it is critical. In recent years, one major computer manufacturer badly miscalculated and suffered the consequence of obsolescence. Because lead times are very long on computer microprocessors, the manufacturer signed contracts with various suppliers buying up 286 microprocessors. It built up a huge stock of 286 processors. The organisation did not see how quickly consumers would abandon buying 286 machines in favour of computers powered by 386 processors. It found itself left with large numbers of components for which there was little demand. In a short space of time, the processors were obsolete. They could be reused or even sold as 286s but not at the prices this company had anticipated; hence the company did not survive.

Not all business sectors are as fast moving as computers, but one of the themes of the 1990s has been shorter product life cycles as you saw in Unit 2. Products are withdrawn and replaced by new ones faster than ever before, so that components are changed more frequently. This increases the gamble of holding stock. If you make washing machines and you know your new line will be in production for only two years before it is replaced by a new improved line, you will not want to hold excessive quantities of stock.

3.3 Reordering stock

Most businesses have to carry some stock and stock ordering has to be based on estimated forecasts not hard facts. Yet, there are numerous risks and costs associated with carrying stock. This presents managers with the problem of trying to meet two conflicting aims. Materials control and planning sections need to juggle conflicting requirements. We now explain how materials controllers and planners use stock control systems to manage the conflict.

Earlier we examined how a schedule is set up with a supplier. This schedule is normally calculated by a computer, linked to the stock records system that can take into account current stock levels. The buyer may have indicated that the company would buy approximately 10,000 units of a component in a year, an average of about 200 a week. But the schedule is unlikely to require a constant 200 units each week because machines break down or have to be allocated to other jobs, or sales are lower than expected, or one of many other variables.

The weekly schedule will be adjusted for stock in plant. There are various models for calculating the reorder quantity for stock which takes into account various practical issues. For example, a manufacturer of screws would not be prepared to deliver one or even a handful of screws, the transportation costs would make it impractical. Similarly, there is a physical limits to how much can be transported in one lorry, and ordering a quantity that would require an additional lorry would dramatically affect the economics of the order.

Another issue is that it is very difficult to precisely identify the 'transaction' costs of reordering. How much does it cost a company to reorder? It is obviously difficult to separate out the time and effort each buyer spends on one order.

The problem is to balance the advantages of ordering large quantities infrequently and buying small quantities frequently. While we have stressed the disadvantages to a business of holding too much stock (buying large quantities infrequently), a business cannot afford to tie up key personnel in daily reordering. And, of course, if parts are not available, the business runs the risk of losing sales because it does not have products available when demanded. There has to be a balance between the two objectives.

One method to balance the two objectives is to use a calculation known as the **economic order quantity** (EOQ). This method takes into account the cost per order, the cost of each item of inventory, a carrying cost per year as a fraction of inventory value, demand during the year and an order quantity. This method obviously involves collecting a great deal of data, and making a number of assumptions or estimates. Computers are ideal for calculating such models and some large companies such as DEC have developed their own in-house variants of economic order quantity systems.

However, many companies are turning away from EOQ as being too cumbersome to administer in the fast-changing modern business world. EOQ and related systems are techniques, 'tools' for doing the job of reordering. Next, we look at another system which originated in Japan that takes a different approach to the reordering problem. It is known as just in time (JIT).

ACTIVITY 8

If a product has a long lead time, why will a business have to forecast its demand if it wants to ensure it always has the product in stock?

Identify some ways in which businesses can lose stock.

If a product has a long lead time, it means that it either takes a long time to make or that some of its components have a long delivery time. In either case, estimates will need to be made about future demand. For example, because there is a long lead time on some television components, Toshiba will have to make forecasts of sales of televisions.

Businesses can lose stock through damage or obsolescence by, for example, damage in warehousing, spoiling of fresh ingredients, stockpiling components for products no longer in demand such as manual typewriters.

3.4 Just in time

Japanese companies have achieved dominance in leading manufacturing industries, especially in the car and consumer electronics sectors. This success has been attributed to many reasons. Common to most suggestions has been that leading Japanese companies have concentrated on eliminating waste and making continuous improvements. Two general management philosophies underpin these efforts – **just-in-time** and **total quality management**. These are called philosophies rather than techniques because Japanese managers think organisations ought to make a commitment to these ideas as part of the way they are managed.

Just in time (JIT) is more than a logistical or inventory control technique, it is actually a manufacturing control philosophy. It has had a significant impact on the logistics function, which may seem to imply that JIT has features that can be adopted without taking on board the whole 'spirit' or philosophy of JIT. In fact, the JIT philosophy has major ramifications for the whole manufacturing process, and it requires a dramatic change from traditional relationships with suppliers. Here, we are only dealing with the issues relating to logistics. We are examining the implications of arranging for the delivery of goods and services 'just in time' to internal and external customers.

We can take the meaning of JIT at face value: it literally means producing goods exactly when they are needed – not before they are needed so that goods wait as inventory, nor after they are needed so that customers have to wait for goods. But this only looks at the time-based element of JIT. As an approach, JIT has more to offer. It seeks to eliminate all waste – in double handling, transportation, inspection and inventory.

The best way of understanding how a JIT approach differs from more traditional approaches to manufacturing control is to contrast two simplified manufacturing systems (see Figure 4).

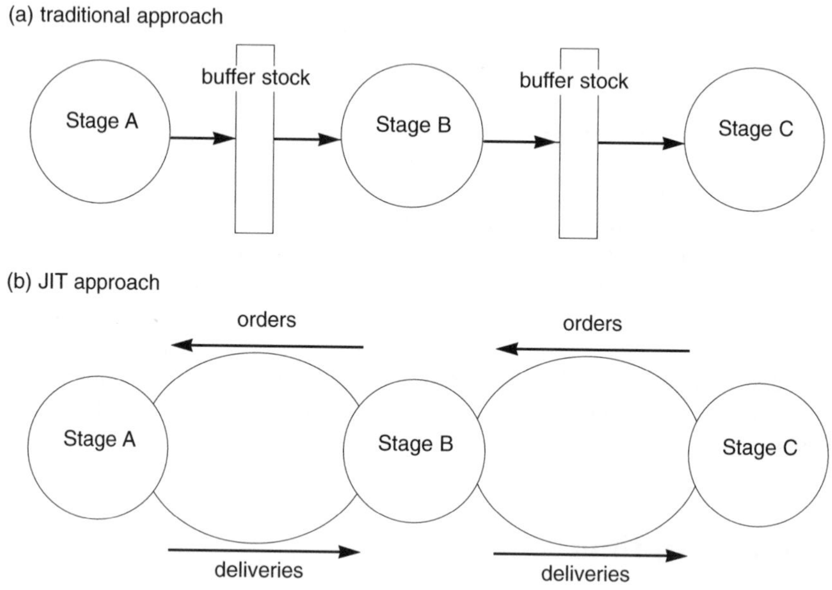

Figures 4: Traditional and JIT approaches

In the traditional system, inventory is held as a buffer between each stage of the manufacturing system, literally as insurance for when things go wrong. The advantage this gives is that the system can keep working even without fresh deliveries from the previous stage, it can use up its buffer stocks. However, this leads to high inventory costs, slower response to customer orders, loss of space, loss of control and, most critically, any problems are hidden.

In the JIT system, parts are produced and then passed directly to the next stage 'just in time' for them to be processed. Deliveries are only made when requested. Problems at any stage have a very different impact on this system. If stage A has a problem, stages B and C will immediately be affected, there is no buffer stock for them to continue work until the problem is resolved. One result of this is that a problem with one stage becomes everyone's problem – which increases the chances of the problem being solved as it is now affecting the whole work area.

By stopping inventory accumulating between stages, the operation has increased the chances of the plant becoming more effective. In JIT, a problem can stop all production; in traditional Western manufacturing systems, short-term 'remedies' would be put into place before the buffer stocks ran out, so that production would resume – until the same problem reoccurred. Two examples of problems that stop production are poor supplier quality and unreliable machinery.

JIT sees stock as a 'blanket of obscurity' which lies over the production system and prevents problems being noticed. This concept of inventory as obscuring problems is often presented metaphorically as a ship (the organisation) sailing over hidden rocks (the problems) protected by the sea (inventory) (Figure 5). Yet, even though the rocks cannot be seen, they slow the progress of the sea's flow and cause turbulence. Gradually reducing the depth of the water (inventory) exposes the worst of the problems which can then be resolved, after which more inventory is taken out, new rocks or problems emerge and are tackled.

Figure 5: 'Stock provides a blanket of obscurity'

IMPLICATIONS OF JIT FOR LOGISTICS

JIT is a **pull system** that is, products are only pulled to the next link, machine or process by a specific demand. A contrasting system, which we don't cover in detail here, is material requirement planning (MRP), **a push system** whereby each link, machine or process pushes its products towards the next stage whether it is needed immediately or not.

What does this mean in practice? In a push system such as MRP, a stores person would deliver the output of stage A to stage B as soon as stage A had finished it. This allows the build up of the buffer stock in the traditional system. In a JIT system, nothing would be produced that is not required, so that the stores person would only deliver stock when stage B requested it. In JIT systems, these requests are called **kanbans**; the word is the name of the card used to indicate the request in Japanese. This system has the advantage of being very simple and easy to understand, coloured cards are often used.

As with all the features of JIT, its very simplicity is an asset as control is possible with eyesight instead of complicated (and expensive) computer software. There is a price to pay though, because JIT emphasises reducing waste and delivering just in time, it means that lots of deliveries of small quantities replace a few deliveries of large quantities.

This has implications for the logistics teams. For a large factory that has its suppliers delivering JIT, it means that the operation of receiving goods has to be very efficient, capable of turning around a delivery very quickly. As many more lorries will be received than under traditional methods, lorries are given 'time slots' which help reduce the level of inventory held to hours not days. Full-scale implementation of JIT sometimes requires suppliers to relocate their operations to be near to the customer company. This is very much the approach taken in Japan, where suppliers tend to locate in a cluster around a large manufacturing company. JIT operations, therefore, place enormous importance on material handling and packaging so that efforts can be minimised.

REVIEW ACTIVITY 3

At the end of Section 2 we looked at a case study about Honda's Swindon factory. Do you remember the shape of the site? Go back to Figure 3 and remind yourself of Honda's basic assembly plant layout. Honda, we know, practices JIT. Now, why do you think Honda wanted a rectangular shape for the main assembly area? Why has it got many delivery decks? Traditional delivery systems have one receiving deck. What advantages could there be for a JIT system in having lots of delivery decks? Describe how Honda is using just-in-time approaches and contrast this with how a traditional company would operate. (In other words, contrast JIT and more traditional techniques.)

Summary

Organisations face constraints in what material they can hold (supply) and in how accurately they can forecast what customers will buy (demand). Some face very long lead times and forecasting becomes critical. Materials planning and control perform this balancing act between trying to have enough, but not too much, stock. Computers are commonly used for materials requirement planning, and we have met briefly three systems, EOQ, MRP and JIT.

JIT is a philosophy which believes that activities that add no value are waste. It is a 'pull' not a 'push' system, inventory only being supplied when it is requested ('pulled') from the next step in the production process. This is in contrast to traditional systems which rely on buffer stock to overcome rather than solve problems. JIT highlights problems, involves much closer co-ordination and requires far closer relationships with suppliers.

Suppliers are depended on to a far larger extent by companies operating JIT, and as they have no buffer stock to protect them from supplier errors, they rely on timely deliveries. In the past, suppliers were accustomed to delivering as much as they could; JIT requires them to make smaller but more frequent deliveries. We deal with the changing relationship between customers and suppliers in the next section.

SECTION 4

Supply Chain Management and Distribution Systems

Introduction

In this section, we look at how companies are moving from concentrating logistical effort on just the internal flow of material and information to taking a much wider view in managing the flow from raw materials to the final customer. This means closer ties and information sharing between organisations, and is called **supply chain management**. This involves moving from suspicion and distrust to much closer relationships, and partnership or sole source agreements. Supply base management encourages organisations to have **preferred suppliers** that have long-term agreements with customer organisations and in return offer enhanced service and quality levels.

We look briefly at the 'globalisation' of logistics; as the world becomes smaller, logistics will increasingly involve movements of goods between nations and continents. We investigate the various methods that can be used for this global distribution – road, rail, water, air and pipeline. We also look at the role of warehouses.

4.1 What is supply chain management?

Supply chain management, the new trend in logistics, is an approach which seeks competitive advantage by attempting to organise all suppliers in a chain. Traditionally, companies have organised their logistics around their own flows, without attempting to influence the logistics of the chain beyond their own organisation's boundaries. Supply chain management is 'boundary spanning' in that it is about the co-ordination and optimisation of flows between companies. Through supply chain management, an organisation believes that only by all the parties in a supply chain talking to each other and co-operating can the best offer be made to a customer.

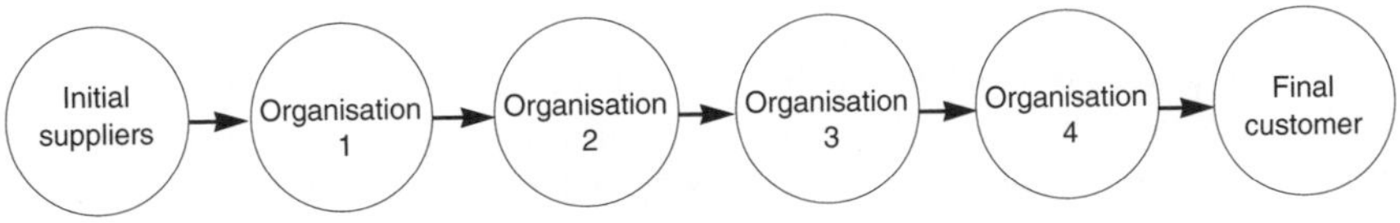

Figure 6: Elements in a supply chain

As we saw with Toshiba, companies now assemble products with parts that come from all over the world; one car model may have components from Europe, North America, South America and the Far East. The German vehicle manufacturer BMW is building a new car in England but with engines made in Brazil.

Imagine the complexity of the supply chain. Increasingly, logistics is becoming a global not a national business and logistics professionals have to understand international logistical and transportation issues.

4.2 Relationships in supply chains and partnership sourcing

Part of the JIT philosophy is to involve suppliers much more and to form much closer relationships between an organisation and its suppliers. Traditionally, Western companies both in Europe and North America have tried to buy supplies at the cheapest price. If another supplier, or competitor, offered a lower price the organisation would switch to the new supplier.

We all have experienced how the apparently cheapest deal does not always work out for the best. There are other elements to getting a good deal on a purchase than just the price. How long does the product last? What was the delivery like? How good is the after-sales service? Will the supplier be helpful if there is a problem?

SUPPLY BASE MANAGEMENT

No company can afford close relations with a lot of suppliers. The trend is to develop a partnership with one supplier for each item, or if it is possible, one supplier for each class or 'family' of items. The objective is to reduce the number of suppliers and have a small number of preferred suppliers. This is termed **supply base management**.

Minimising the number of suppliers in the organisation's supplier database saves money; there are less transaction costs. Each additional supplier involves more expense in:

- purchasing – selecting and reviewing suppliers
- finance – extra invoices and queries to deal with
- logistics – extra deliveries, extra paperwork
- general administration.

Organisations are discovering it is better to look at the 'total cost' of using many suppliers (even if they are all offering a cheap price) against the much reduced administration and transaction costs of using only one 'preferred' or partnership supplier. However, and just as importantly, giving a supplier a longer-term contract can improve service and quality levels as the preferred supplier sees the relationship as more valuable and will work harder at pleasing the customer.

Let's consider an example. A manufacturing organisation had a very old fleet of forklift trucks that were in poor condition. Only the dedication and experience of the company's drivers managed to keep them going. One day, they were told by management that there would be a new tyre supplier for the forklift trucks. The new supplier was cheaper than the old. Forklift truck tyres take a lot of wear and tear, and the drivers soon found that the new tyres were wearing out in about six weeks. The old ones lasted about four months. The drivers asked if they could go back to the old supplier. 'No,' they were told, 'the new supplier is cheaper'.

This kind of purchasing policy wasted the company's money and upset the drivers, nobody benefited. In the 1990s, companies have become more conscious that buying on price alone is not always the best policy. Take a complex machine that an organisation would be unable to repair. It would be silly to buy it for the cheapest price if the supplier skimped on after-sales service and the organisation ended up paying someone else (probably one of the slightly more expensive suppliers) to come in and fix it.

We are not arguing here for paying a high price! What companies are increasingly doing is looking at the 'whole transaction cost' of dealing with suppliers. This includes how easy they are to deal with, how reliable they are, what levels of service they offer. Companies are now going for the company that offers the best overall deal or 'package' of benefits, not just the cheapest price.

PARTNERSHIP SOURCING

The movement away from making purchasing decisions based solely on price has led to the development of what are called partnership sourcing agreements. The two parties to the agreement decide that they are going to trade more as partners than as companies always looking to win an advantage over each other. A typical partnership agreement simplifies arrangements for both companies, often it includes a **sole source agreement** that means that in return for a very high standard of service including help with how the customer can save money (even if that means fewer sales for the supplier), the customer agrees to buy (source) only (solely) from that supplier.

Consider, as an example, the requirements of a very large military dockyard for electrical supplies. The dockyard is spread over a huge site and is divided into areas occupied by many different departments. There are thousands of electrical sockets, bulbs, batteries, strip lights, etc. As often happens on large sprawling sites, co-ordinating activities is difficult. Buildings have different lighting systems, sections used a range of equipment requiring different batteries. The purchasing department is faced with a real problem, it needs to buy spares for the new equipment as well as for old equipment that still functions. Purchasing has dealt with many suppliers, often for a very small annual 'spend' with an individual supplier. The purchasing department keeps records on how much the dockyard spends with individual suppliers and, if it has a high 'spend' with one, it will have a good chance of negotiating a discount. This arrangement costs a lot of money in tying up buyers' time in chasing very small orders of spares.

ACTIVITY 9

The dockyard has now negotiated a 'partnership' agreement with a small local electrical supplier. Identify what advantages partnership sourcing offered each party.

We can summarise the benefits of this partnership agreement in Table 4.

Features	**Benefits for the dockyard**	**Benefits for the electrical supplier**
Sole sourcing	Only one organisation to deal with, saves buyers time and saves on administration	Guarantees the supplier a huge amount of business, in return it can invest in dedicated equipment
Set but guaranteed profit	Knows that they are not being taken for a ride	Knows that the company will make a profit
Simplifies stock handling	No longer has the costs of holding lots of small stock items, saves money and space	Can build up expertise and slowly 'standardise' spares, volume gives supplier 'buying power'
Long-term agreement	Gives purchasing more time to consider the procurement of really strategic and important items	Can concentrate on doing an excellent job and on 'continuous improvement' knowing that it has won the business

Table 4: Advantages of partnership sourcing

By changing its purchasing arrangements, the dockyard has a streamlined service – there is one point of contact for everybody, odd queries about spares for things that are very specialised or very old are now dealt with by professionals (buyers are professional buyers not electricians). The supplier is delighted to have a guaranteed annual rate of return, and the dockyard has started saving money.

The electrical supplier is able to use its experience to begin the task of standardising components wherever possible, and it is using its purchasing power to buy at discounts. For example, the electrical supplier has been able to identify that the yard was buying a more expensive type of battery than it needed for a high-volume job. The supplier convinced the dockyard to switch to a cheaper, less powerful battery. Tests showed that this made no difference to the quality of the work. In the past, this would not have happened; the supplier of the powerful (but more expensive) batteries would not have told the dockyard that it could have used a cheaper alternative for fear of losing sales. But by allowing a supplier to use all its skills and knowledge, companies can gain real benefits.

At the same dockyard, thousands of uniforms and overalls are supplied and washed each week by a number of laundry companies. How has this happened? In the original bids, one company was cheapest for washing white canteen coats, one company was cheapest for oily overalls that had been worn by maintenance workers, and so on. Some workers have complained that they have to deal with two different laundry companies and there are often problems with things getting lost, mixed up or delayed.

Although each individual deal had been struck at the best price, the dockyard has found it hard to deal with so many different suppliers. It is an expensive arrangement in terms of 'transaction' costs, and no individual supplier has any incentive to come up with ideas for improvements as that could jeopardise its small weekly business. Again, a single supplier (sole sourcing) should be able to come up with economies and service improvements for the dockyard.

The electrical supplier that entered the dockyard partnership agreement is not a manufacturer but a distributor, that is to say the supplier receives stock from manufacturers and sells it on to its customers. Next, we look at the role distributors play in logistics.

DISTRIBUTORS

Distributors are responsible for receiving parts or finished goods, storing them until they are required, and then delivering them to the customer. Distribution skills include warehouse management and transport management. The main modes of transport available are road, rail, water, air and pipeline.

Each mode of transport has advantages and disadvantages depending on the type of material that needs to be distributed. For example, air transport is fast but expensive and has limited space (the size of the aircraft). Transporting by water (shipping) is slow but cheap for bulky items, pipelines obviously suit high-volume liquids and gases. A decision has to be made about the form of transport to be used, and sometimes it will be a mix of types. European companies might usually import from the Far East by sea, but if they have a urgent shortage of a part they may arrange to have it air-freighted in. The television manufacturer Toshiba imports from the Far East mainly by ship and you may be familiar with the fact that many UK florists get their stock of fresh flowers air freighted from North America and Africa.

WAREHOUSES AND DISTRIBUTION

Distributors 'consolidate' loads from suppliers, that is they collect together and store parts and goods. Sometimes organisations own their own distribution network – a collection of large warehouses from which they supply their customers. Planning the location of these warehouses is critical; transport in and out is very important, so they are usually sited near major road networks. An example of a distribution system for a clothing manufacturer is shown in Figure 7. This simple system allows two warehouses to serve the whole country, the north is supplied by the north area warehouse, the south of the country by the southern warehouse.

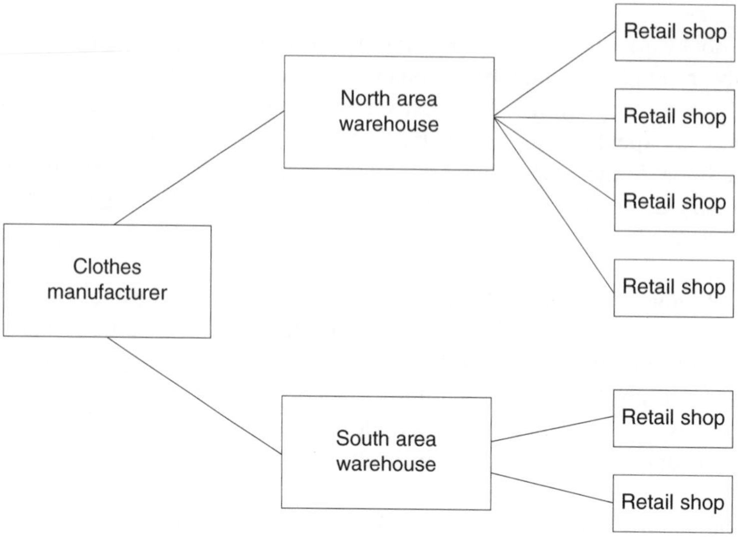

Figure 7: A clothing manufacturer's distribution system

ACTIVITY 10

Consider the case of the clothing manufacturer that uses the distribution system illustrated in Figure 7. Explain:

- why it is not operating with the minimum of stock
- why it would choose to make this decision.

Do you think it would be better if the company had only one warehouse that covered the whole country? List the advantages and potential cost savings and disadvantages and potential cost increases of having only one warehouse.

The clothing manufacturer has stock in the factory and in its two warehouses. It has taken a strategic decision in this respect. It is more concerned with having availability and the capacity to meet demand than stock minimisation. This suits the fashion industry as there are seasonal variations in demand for items.

With one warehouse, the company would reduce the stock it has to hold and save the costs of running an extra warehouse. However, the costs of transport would rise with longer journeys, and it may not serve the needs of its customers at the opposite end of the country so flexibly.

REVIEW ACTIVITY 4

Consider the supply chain for a packet of crisps:

raw potatoes in fields on a farm

↓

harvested by farmer, stored and washed

↓

transported to huge warehouse owned by potato wholesalers

↓

bought and collected by crisp company

↓

delivered to crisp factory on to huge conveyor belt

↓

washed (again) and sliced into wafers (crisps)

↓

cooked in oil, left to cool and salted

↓

sorted into little bags on another conveyor

↓

individual crisp bags fed into cardboard boxes

↓

third-party hired haulier delivers cartons to shop

↓

shop unpacks carton and puts crisp packet on shelf

↓

you buy a packet!

There are several organisations involved in this chain. Write a list of all the suppliers that would have to be involved to produce a pallet containing 24 cartons of packets of cheese and onion flavoured crisps.

What other actions are being performed? (Think about other suppliers.) Draw the supply chain as a series of companies (including the ones you identified above). You need only draw a circle for each company involved, but link them with arrows where they connect. For example, there would be an arrow from the farmer to the agricultural warehouse. You should find that most arrows are heading towards the crisp factory, since it co-ordinates most of the inputs from suppliers.

Now concentrate on the arrows, the links between the businesses, these should represent the physical transfer of ingredients. Let's take the link between the farmer and the agricultural warehouse. In what 'logistical' ways can the farmer and the warehouse co-operate to 'smooth the flow' of materials using containers?

Think back over what you have learned about material handling and inventory control. It would be a good idea to review these sections.

Summary

The new trend in logistics – trying to manage as one process the total flow from the beginning of the raw materials to the final customer – is supply chain management. Partnership or preferred supplier agreements can reduce costs for the customer and give the supplier incentives for improving. We have considered how the chosen method of distribution must reflect the nature of the materials or finished goods involved. We have seen the increasing 'globalisation' of logistics.

SECTION 5

Strategy, Performance and Key Measures

Introduction

In this section, we outline how the logistics strategy supports the overall strategy and plans of an organisation. Essentially, logistics performance must be measured to ensure that such plans are being met. Measurement is also necessary to allocate resources effectively. We go on to highlight the key measures used in logistics, discussing the trend towards measures that consider the total cost of fulfilling a customer order. This is a new development in the 1990s, as companies have traditionally used measures that divide a company's operations into a series of functions rather than measuring the whole process and the overall outcomes. We describe the use of benchmarking. Finally, we look at the impact on logistics of the latest advances in new technology.

5.1 Logistics strategy, fit and performance

All companies need to know what business they are in, what market they are serving, and which customers they are after. The answers to these questions will reflect the strengths and weaknesses of the company. The process of deciding where the company is heading and how it is going to get there is called strategy formation and the end product, usually in the form of a written document, is the strategic direction of the organisation. Few organisations are successful without a clear strategic direction. We investigate the key features and the formulation of corporate strategy in Unit 8.

However, strategic planning documents are a statement of goals rather than a set of instructions on how to run a business. The strategy for the organisation is 'operationalised' by senior managers who break the overall strategy down into plans and targets for their section of the business. In this section, we are only dealing with logistics strategy, but it is important to realise that the logistics strategy is designed to support the wider strategic direction of the company; there must be a 'fit'.

Let's consider a specific example. A mail-order company has set up in business to retail ethnic hair-care products. The company sees a business opportunity: ethnic products are not readily available in the high street, people have to travel to obtain the products from specialist shops, and this involves expense, time and effort for the customer. The company reasons that there is a market for a significantly faster but more expensive, direct mail-order business. Its business strategy depends on serving these customers quickly.

To support this business strategy, the company needs a logistics strategy that offers speed. It has negotiated an agreement with a third-party courier that can guarantee next-day delivery. This is an example of the logistics strategy fitting the wider strategic goal of the company.

PERFORMANCE MEASURES

Companies develop logistics strategies that support their overall corporate plan or strategy. These are operationalised by logistics. In developing a logistics strategy, a company should simultaneously develop measures to find out how well or how poorly this strategy is performing. These measures should be recorded and passed on to senior management which will use them to understand how the strategy is working, where resources need to be increased; they might even show which employees are performing their jobs well.

Computers can generate many forms of performance reports without someone losing valuable working time by having to key in specific data such as receipts, stock levels, fast-moving items, slow-moving items and delivery times. All this information can be pulled off advanced systems from data already captured by bar-code readers, and EPOS and EDI systems. However, with all performance measures there is one golden rule, do not make the measurement unless you are going to do something with the resulting information! Setting formal targets or objectives also acts as motivation for employees who know what the company expects of them.

Three types of measures are used in evaluating logistics performance measurement systems:

- **monitoring** measures track past performance for reporting to management and customers
- **controlling** measures track ongoing performance and are designed to highlight problems
- **directing** measures are designed to motivate personnel, for example, drivers might be rewarded for being consistently on time.

An example of a controlling measure would be to record how often products are damaged in transportation. This might highlight that an investigation is needed, there might be a problem with the packaging or the loading or unloading process.

INTERNAL PERFORMANCE MEASUREMENTS

Here we look at internal measures which focus on comparing the achievement levels of current activities and processes to previous operations. For example, we might compare the achievement levels of customer service in giving despatch the right part numbers and address details, compared to last period's actual performance, as well as to the target for this period.

Internal measures are used widely because management understands where the information came from and because data are cheap and easy to collect. The three most common logistics performance measures are:

- cost
- customer service
- productivity measures.

Cost is the most easily understood logistics measure. How much did it cost to perform a specific task such as deliver an order? Costs are usually measured against a budget or estimate of what costs would be incurred in a period. It is useful to remember that logistics costs rise and fall in proportion to the business's activity, this is not so clear cut in other functions like marketing or finance.

Cost measures vary in importance depending on the logistics activity covered. Four typical cost measures would be:

- inbound freight
- outbound freight
- warehouse costs
- comparison of actual against budget costs.

Customer service measures examine an organisation's relative ability to satisfy customers, for example:

- running out of stock, 'stockouts'
- customer feedback

- shipping errors
- on-time delivery.

The third common set of measures are **staff productivity** measures such as:

- units shipped per employee
- orders per salesperson
- units shipped per labour cost unit.

ACTIVITY 11

We have described the three major types of performance measures used in logistics. Perhaps some are unfamiliar to you. Write one line explaining why an organisation would wish to use each of these types of measures.

Cost measures are obvious in term's of an organisation's efficiency and profits. Customer services are important in terms of the customer, an organisation is nothing if it does not meet customer requirements. Staff productivity again has implications for efficiency and profit.

EXTERNAL PERFORMANCE MEASURES

Internal performance measures capture what is going on inside an organisation, but they are less good at measuring external perspectives. They do not see the company as customers and competitors see the company. External measures of performance in logistics are called **benchmarking**.

Leading logistical firms increasingly organise measurement of their customer's perception of them. It does not matter how good you think you are, what will make or break the business is how good customers think you are.

5.2 Benchmarking

In the 1990s, more and more companies started to use a technique known as benchmarking to compare their operations with competitors and leading companies that perform similar operations (although they could be in completely different industries).

A benchmarking exercise focuses on and collects data about the measures, practices and processes of a comparable organisation. Benchmarking, literally comparing how well you do something with a competitor or 'best practice' leading company, helps introduce new ideas, improve performance measures and open people's eyes to new ways of doing things.

For example, a computer company like Zebra that sells direct could benchmark itself with another leading computer company to see what a rival company does better. An alternative would be to decide which organisation is the best in the country at direct supply logistics and to benchmark against that organisation. Let's say that company turned out to be a mail-order book club. Some might say the two industries have nothing in common, books are certainly a simpler product to handle than computers. But both have logistical systems designed to serve customers quickly, and in collecting performance data, companies can learn from looking at what other companies in other fields do to achieve best practice. Xerox is credited with popularising benchmarking.

CASE STUDY

Xerox

Some companies are so renowned for their product that the company's name is given to the whole family of the product. Xerox was like that, its photocopiers made it the leading name in the field.

However, by 1979 it found itself facing a crisis, it was 'leaking' market share – down from 49 per cent to 22 per cent. Lower-priced Japanese copiers were taking the market. At first, Xerox directors could not believe what was happening. Finally, they discovered that the sale price of a copier from a leading Japanese company was lower than the cost of making a Xerox copier before it left the factory. Yet, the Japanese company was importing its copier, making a profit and producing a profit for the dealer and all the other links in the chain.

Stunned, Xerox directors ordered a number of initiatives, one of which developed into benchmarking. The manager of benchmarking quality and customer satisfaction at Xerox Corporation in New York formally defines benchmarking as 'the continuous process of measuring our products, services, and practices against those of our toughest competitors or companies renowned as leaders'. However his unofficial definition is even better, capturing the power (and simplicity) of the concept 'finding and implementing the best business practice – it needn't be any more complicated than that'.

REVIEW ACTIVITY 5

Sweep Limited supplies vacuum cleaners and spare parts for vacuum cleaners. This company has the long-term aim or strategic goal of being a 'one-stop shop' for spares of all vacuum cleaners, both old and new makes. Sweep's rivals only stock the vacuum cleaners and spares for one manufacturer. Customers will be able to find a Sweep outlet 'in all major shopping centres'. It has the stated goal of telling customers that if it has not got the part in stock it will get it within 24 hours or they will get their money back.

What logistical skills will Sweep Limited need to support this strategy – that is to have thousands of spare parts readily available? List your answers under the headings warehousing, transport and IT.

Summary

An organisation's logistics strategy is linked to its overall business strategy. Three major types of internal performance measures are cost, customer service and productivity. We outlined specific internal measures that can be recorded and compared to target or budget figures. However, you should note the pitfalls in using only internal measures of logistical performance; external benchmarking can be introduced as a complementary but not a replacement measure. Both internal and external performance measures are used by today's leading logistical firms which want to remain tomorrow's leaders, too.

Unit Review Activity

Toyota has been the international benchmark in the car industry, The Toyota Production System (TPS) was the basis of the lean-production revolution in worldwide car manufacturing, this included JIT, total quality management and continuous improvement. The company has taken this a stage further in the layout of the factory with workers grouped into areas to do particular tasks on the cars as they come through the factory; workers are aided by machines but not taken over by them. It has achieved high efficiency over conventional more automated systems that have more maintenance problems. It also allows for continuous improvement and total quality management to operate effectively. In developing new products, Toyota is using as many components from other ranges as it can. How will other manufacturers respond to this competition?

Unit Summary

In this unit, we have investigated the role that logistics plays in an organisation. This involves purchasing and procurement, warehousing and stock control, and operations management. The logistics function provides inputs that supply the transformation process and is finally responsible for delivering the output to the customer. Achieving efficiency in this process is crucial to the success of the organisation and can be a major factor in achieving competitive advantage. In supplying the inputs to the transformation process, companies traditionally have held supplies of stock; however, we looked at some new ways of operating through a JIT approach where no stock is held and organisations rely heavily on suppliers to deliver direct into the production process. This approach and the realisation of the importance of links in the supply chain has changed the basis of relationships with suppliers and led to a whole new area of supply chain management. An organisation needs to monitor, control and direct performance of logistics through internal and external measures.

References

Bowersox, D J and Closs, D J (1996) *Logistical Management*, McGraw-Hill

Carter, R J and Price, P M (1993) *Integrated Materials Management*, Pitman

Waters, D (1996) *Operations Management*, Addison Wesley

Recommended Reading

Attwood, P and Attwood, N (1992) *Logistics of a Distribution System*, Gower

Ballou, R H (1992) *Business Logistics Management*, Prentice Hall

Bowersox, D J and Closs, D J (1996) *Logistical Management*, McGraw-Hill

Carter, R J and Price, P M (1993) *Integrated Materials Management*, Pitman

Christopher, M (1992) *Logistics: The strategic issues*, Chapman and Hall

Christopher, M (1994) *The Strategy of Distribution Management*, Butterworth Heinemann

Codling, S (1992) *Best Practice Benchmarking,* Gower

Cooper, J (ed) (1993) *Strategy Planning In Logistics and Transportation*, Kogan Page

Cooper, J (ed) (1996) *Logistics and Distribution Planning*, Kogan Page

Fawcett, P, McLeish, R and Ogden, I (1996) *Logistics Management*, M&E Books

Jessop, D and Morrison, A (1986) *Storage and Supply of Materials*, Pitman

Kelly, J (1993) *Purchasing for Profit*, Pitman, NatWest

Lysons, K (1996) *Purchasing*, Pitman

Martin, C (1989) *The Strategy of Distribution Management*, Heinemann Professional Publishing

Martin, C (1990) *Logistics and Supply Chain Management*, Pitman

Naylor, J (1996) *Operations Management*, Pitman

Slack, N, Chambers, S, Harland, C, Harrison, A and Johnston, R, (1996) *Operations Management*, Pitman

Waters, D (1996) *Operations Management*, Addison Wesley

Answers to Review Activities

Review Activity 1

As the manager of a distribution centre, you are responsible for shipping stock out to the supermarkets. You will be very involved in transport decisions. You would need to know the number and capacity of your fleet of vehicles. You would need knowledge of route planning and relevant legislation. You will not just have to ensure the vehicles carry full loads, you will have to 'load' the vehicles so that they can be unloaded easily and in the right sequence. There are complex computer modelling software packages that can assist these decisions for a distribution manager. However, the manager is very involved in setting up the model and the data – lorry dimensions, distances between stores, ease of unloading etc. – that the model uses.

Supermarkets with their high turnover and need for fresh, daily deliveries are some of the biggest users of EDI (electronic data interchange) and EPOS (electronic point of sale) equipment. EPOS can be used by having hand readers or scanners that can be held over bar codes to 'read in' the information stored on the bar code as a series of numbers. This might be used in a supermarket at the check out; linked to a computer the scanner would record all the stock sold that day. Once all the sales have been collected from the computer, the store can calculated what will need to be restocked.

Review Activity 2

Honda knows exactly what car is being built next. Not all businesses are so lucky. The order that newspapers are sold will be completely random and unsequenced, so stock will need to be checked in as it comes from the supplier and returns sent back.

The manual activities Honda has eliminated concern goods receiving. Honda is working in 'synchronisation' with its suppliers, and this would be very difficult without close co-operation. The ordering of supplies is linked directly to what is happening on the production line and delivery is in the required place in the required sequence at the required time directly to it. This means that it is following a just-in-time system, where no stock is held, but inputs are delivered from suppliers when they are needed, that is 'just in time for production'. Full trolleys are wheeled from the lorry into the production area and empties returned back. There is no checking of deliveries and no delivery advice notes, the order is expected to be received as specified and the delivery is recorded by video. Automatic payment is made on the basis of this video record and the supply schedule.

Such an advanced and 'lean' system is only possible by use of computer communications, EDI, and very close and honest working relationships between Honda and some of its suppliers.

Review Activity 3

A JIT approach requires lots of deliveries, but of small quantities, just when they are needed. The layout of Honda's plant facilitates deliveries to the exact point where they will be used in the factory. This minimises double handling. Traffic jams or congestion are avoided by the number of delivery points. In traditional sites, there would be chaos if many lorries turned up at the same time. The synchronisation of deliveries and production would break down.

With JIT no buffer stock is held, orders are delivered and then immediately used. With a traditional approach, a buffer stock is held. The holding of stock has implications for warehousing and stock control. Efficient receipt of many small orders is required with the minimum of checking and 'pieces of paper'. Honda relies on the supplier to supply in a sequence, at the required time and in the required place. A traditional approach would have deliveries shipped into the warehouse and then the internal distribution system would get the right components to the right place at the right time. Honda has to have a very close relationship with its suppliers as it is totally dependent on them. Honda avoids a lot of paperwork by videoing the deliveries and automatically implementing payment without needing delivery notes to be checked and invoices to be raised. The traditional approach has money tied up in stock.

Review Activity 4

Suppliers would provide the crisp bags, the cartons, the oil, the salt, flavours. Perhaps you have identified even more. We want to see a smooth flow of material (potatoes) from beginning to end. How can we help smooth that flow? Sharing information is a key method – information about sales, about stock levels – but what about containers? The raw material is perishable and can be damaged, it undergoes a lot of handling, if the parties co-operate they can design transit protection that helps them all.

Perhaps the farmer delivered the potatoes to a wholesaler in boxes too large for their pallet racks. Immediately they would have to be repackaged (or as a logistics person would call it 'decanted' into smaller containers). This would be double handling and also risk damage. Imagine the time and effort wasted. But if they arrange it together, say the farmer buys a machine that puts the potatoes in bags of the same weight that suit the wholesaler, and then puts them on pallets that the wholesaler's goods receiving can lift off the lorry with a forklift truck, the material can flow efficiently through the system or 'supply chain'.

Similarly if all parties co-ordinate, the crisp manufacturer can purchase a machine that can strip the tie from the sack as the potatoes come in – and return the original bag to the farmer via the wholesaler. Imagine what savings could be made if they agreed between them on a simple bar-coding system.

Review Activity 5

Land for shops is more expensive than land for **warehouses**, it would not be possible to hold all the stock ranges in high street shops as the costs of storage would be prohibitive. Instead Sweep could perform some analysis to identify the most popular spares and stock those in carefully laid out racking. Less frequently requested spares could then be stored in warehouses.

Transport and route planning would be critical skills, ensuring that warehouses delivered daily to every shop. EDI from the shop to the warehouse would allow instant 'picking' of the parts required. Integrated EDI across the company would mean the company could minimise holdings of very rarely requested items but still have up-to-date information on where in the system they are.

Sweep Limited developed fast response, internal logistics, warehousing, and distribution united by advanced **IT**.

Answer to Unit Review Activity

Competitors will need to look at their logistics function, that is delivering the inputs to the process, managing the flow through the process and then delivering to the customer. Toyota has used a JIT approach which must be combined with a close relationship with its suppliers to deliver components into the production line. The production line itself has been redesigned so that workers now do some of the jobs previously done by robots, they are aided by robots but automation has been reduced and the maintenance problems that are normally encountered are reduced. Competitors will need to evaluate this way of working and the ease with which a new factory layout could be created. Employees would have new job functions which would need implementing.

The use of the same components in several products means that the design to production process is cut down in terms of time and research, development of the production process itself will be easier and the relationship with suppliers already exists. This obviously can save a lot of time and money. Competitors will need to look at this area.

The delivery of the product to the customer will need addressing, in an international context, perhaps factories should be set up in each major market region.

UNIT 7

HUMAN RESOURCE MANAGEMENT

Introduction

As you saw in Unit 1, human resource management (HRM) is regarded by Porter as one of the primary activities in an organisation. It is responsible for one of the key inputs of the transformation process and it is also involved in all other functions and activities as they all have a human element. HRM is concerned with all aspects of people management in organisations, from the initial contact through to termination of employment (and beyond in some cases). The management of people in organisations is becoming more widely recognised as a factor critical to organisational success (Storey, 1992, p. 46). The workforce can be regarded as an organisation's greatest asset and is crucial in achieving and sustaining competitive advantage.

In this unit, we consider the background to and philosophy of HRM and will concentrate on some of the tasks carried out that can influence the effectiveness of people within the work environment.

Objectives

By the end of this unit, you will be able to:

- distinguish between the concepts of personnel management and HRM
- explain how the function has developed and the influences upon it
- outline the range of tasks carried out within people management
- describe the factors which impact on manpower and human resource planning
- outline recruitment and selection processes and methods
- describe the stages in the training cycle
- explain the role of assessment and appraisal
- define appraisal methods and their usage
- outline the main factors in employer/employee relations and the role of unions
- identify the value of HRM procedures that are grounded in a legislative framework.

SECTION 1

Nature of Human Resource Management and its Function

Introduction

As with many other issues in the business world, HRM has different meanings for different people. Bratton and Gold (1994, p. 5) suggest that it is 'that part of the management process that specialises in the management of people in work organisations. HRM emphasises that employees are the primary resource for gaining sustainable competitive advantage, that human resource activities need to be integrated with the corporate strategy, and that the human resource specialists help organisational controllers to meet both efficiency and equity objectives.'

HRM is concerned with management of people and all aspects of their employment in organisations. The term HRM is often used interchangeably with the term **personnel management**. In applying for a job, for example, you might have been asked to address your application to the human resource manager or the personnel manager. In this section, you consider some opinions on the differences and similarities between human resource management and personnel management. To help you to put these approaches into context, you will study a brief history of the background to HRM. Finally, you will consider some of the roles within people management in organisations. You will be able to recognise why effective people management is important to organisational success.

1.1 Historical aspects

The way in which people have been managed in organisations has developed during the last 70 years. As the needs of organisations and employees have changed markedly, so the role of people management in organisations has changed. Its roots are in welfare. In the UK, welfare officers were appointed by organisations such as Rowntree and Cadbury during the first world war. They were also frequently employed by traditionally paternalistic retail companies such as Woolworth and Marks and Spencer. Welfare officers were responsible for the provision of benefits to employees. These organisations were advanced for their time; they had developed staff benefits packages with, for example, sickness benefits and subsidised housing. One reason for giving benefits was the belief that employees deserved them, but an additional reason was also the belief that the employer should provide them in a rather paternalistic way. In the cases of Cadbury and Rowntree, the decision to provide employee benefits was largely based on Quaker principles.

HRM still encompasses welfare management, but this has taken on a variety of different forms over the years. The provision of childcare facilities for employees, for example, is a 'benefit' currently provided by some employers in the light of emphasis on the 'family friendly' organisation and bringing women back into the workplace. Creches and nurseries, childcare costs and provision of a career structure with breaks for childcare are included in HRM strategies in the 1990s.

People management, however, is not simply concerned with the welfare and wellbeing of the workforce. Over the years, it has expanded into a much wider and more complex role, as a result of change both within and outside of the organisation. Its development has been influenced by UK and European legislation, societal changes in attitudes and behaviours, beliefs about the way that people should be managed and the changing economic situation. The effect of these factors can be shown by tracing the history of the role of people management from those welfare origins to the present day.

The years between the two world wars brought about the introduction of administrative support to managers 'in the form of recruitment, training and record keeping' (Armstrong, 1991, p. 28). During this time, the way in which employees were managed was initially influenced by Taylorism and the application of scientific methods to production, when the employee was simply viewed as an extension to a machine. The work of Elton Mayo, in what became known as the Hawthorne experiments, was to further influence the way that people were managed, when, as the instigator of the Human Relations movement, he suggested that more emphasis should be placed on the individual in the workplace. It was Mayo who first suggested greater integration of staff into the organisation.

Following the second world war and into the 1950s, the range of personnel services increased. This was at a tactical level however, with no strategic involvement for personnel specialists. Full employment and the increase in trade union membership resulted in the acquisition of bargaining expertise by personnel managers.

During the 1960s and 1970s, the range of personnel management involvement was extended still further. The role began to take on more strategic importance as directors of personnel were appointed. There was a move away from dealing with employees on behalf of the management towards dealing with the whole activity as a management integrated process. In this period, the activity of negotiation increased as trade unions increased their involvement in personnel activities. The increase in employment legislation also brought about a management focus on employment protection, particularly in the area of unfair dismissal, due to concern about industrial tribunals.

In the 1980s, the personnel function moved towards the integration of business and personnel strategies and the HRM concept emerged. Personnel management and its associated job titles survived until the mid-1980s when the terminology began to change to HRM.

In addition, the notion that the workforce is of vital importance to each organisation and hence to its industry (and, by extension, to the country) has prompted a number of government initiatives to train and develop the workforce. We discussed some of these in Unit 2. The aim is to make Britain's workforce skilled and trained for international as well as national competitiveness. This further extended the tasks of personnel management into strategic human resources. Initiatives include the Investors in People scheme run within organisations which was updated in 1997 for small businesses and the establishment of employer-led Training and Enterprise Councils in England and Wales and Local Enterprise Councils in Scotland. These bodies are government funded and promote training and development in the private sector, particularly youth training and training for the unemployed. Reforms in 1997 are likely to emphasise more employee training.

1.2 Human resource management (HRM) or personnel management?

During the last ten years, people management has sparked interest and debate, particularly concerning the differences between personnel management (PM) and human resource management (HRM). Are they the same? Are there any differences between the two? What do we mean by people management?

Some organisations may simply rename a jaded personnel department as human resources to reflect modern thinking, or may use it as a way of describing a 'good' personnel department. However, strategic HRM needs to consider how the human resource fits into the organisation, how it is managed, and how all the individual tasks within the people management role fit 'into a coherent whole' for competitive advantage throughout all functions. The key issue is that HRM has a strategic role in the organisation and effectively encompasses all personnel management tasks.

For the HRM concept to work, an organisation needs:

- corporate leadership providing support from the top and reflecting HRM values
- strategic vision embedded in the organisational culture – a view which is shared by all
- technological and production feasibility whereby the methods used within the organisation can enable the HRM concept to be put into practice
- an industrial relations environment which enables the development of the human resource
- capable personnel managers to put HRM policies into practice and to manage change.

Some writers draw distinct differences between personnel management and human resource management. Personnel management is **workforce centred**, for example, concerned with employee needs, whereas human resource management is **resource centred** and, as such, is concerned with management needs for human resources (Torrington and Hall, 1995). Personnel management can be seen as acting at the interface between the employee and the organisation, and balancing differing requirements; HRM sees the employee as a key stakeholder within the organisation, with each individual contributing to the success of the organisation and the organisation responding to each individual.

The task of problem solving in HRM tends to be carried out with individual's line managers rather than with employees or their representatives. HRM is based upon the premise that the human resource is no different to any other resource at the manager's disposal, and effectiveness can only be obtained through management and mutual trust and respect between all parties. Personnel management has long been criticised for lack of strategic planning. HRM has a more strategic role that is tied in with the overall business strategy.

We can divide the differences between personnel management and HRM into four key areas:

- beliefs and assumptions
- strategic concepts
- line management
- key levers (Storey, 1992).

The link between managing human resources, integrating policies and practices, and business strategy emerges; and HRM is seen as a key management role. Traditionally, personnel departments have created policies and procedures to deal with human resource issues. However, unless these policies form part of the overall business strategy, have the support of line managers and top management and are integrated with the organisational culture, they will not be very successful. When they do, they form part of the HRM strategy.

Developments both within and outside organisations have influenced management of the human resource. Personnel duties are increasingly being devolved to line managers (Hutchinson, 1995). Greater flexibility is being demanded by organisations and by employees and there is a growing need for all functions of a business to be accountable. Staff are one of the last sources of competitive advantage that remains in many highly competitive industries such as the retail industry, and that advantage can only be achieved by getting the most out of employees. HRM is a key issue in managing change, and change is now part of every organisation's environment. We have seen the changing nature of organisations and their environments. This impacts on people, and HRM is instrumental in achieving competitive advantage throughout the value chain, whether we call it HRM or personnel management.

To summarise, the debate regarding HRM and personnel management is still ongoing. There are a range of approaches from the purist view that the two are fundamentally different, to the other extreme where HRM is seen as simply a fashionable term to describe personnel management.

ACTIVITY 1

Identify the main features of HRM and personnel management.

Those who emphasise the differences between the two approaches does so by identifying distinct features of personnel management and human resource management. Personnel management concerns:

- obtaining, developing and motivating the people required by the organisation
- developing policies and procedures for implementing human resource issues
- making the best use of the skills and capacities of those employed in the organisation
- ensuring that the organisation meets its social and legal responsibilities towards its employees.

Human resource management concerns:

- developing and implementing human resource strategies as part of the overall corporate strategy
- developing the culture, values and structure of the organisation and the employees together
- ensuring quality, motivation and commitment of employees throughout the organisation.

HRM, it is claimed, takes a broader more integrated view of the personnel function, ensuring that it is built into the fabric of the business, linking it firmly to the attainment of the long-term strategies of the organisation, and ensuring that personnel people provide the guidance and expert support needed to accomplish these strategies (Armstrong, 1989).

Both HRM and personnel management encompass a range of tasks involved with the management of people in organisations. The way that these tasks are fulfilled by the personnel management/HRM specialist will not just be determined by the job or department title, but also by the values, aims, philosophy and management style of the organisation. Its structure and stage in its life cycle will also impact on the style of people management.

1.3 The function

The way that HRM operates and the size and extent of any HR department will differ from one organisation to another. The department can consist of any number of employees, depending upon the organisation's structure, philosophy, culture, strategy, aims and objectives. The stage that the organisation is in its life cycle will also be an influencing factor, particularly for organisations in their infancy, where it is unlikely that an HR specialist will be employed at all, since the costs involved could not be justified for small numbers of employees. In this case, the role will probably be carried out either by the owner or manager who has overall responsibility for the organisation or by line managers. The way that people are managed in organisations will influence their long-term success and their achievement of competitive advantage. People cannot be treated just like all other inputs, they have to be managed with care. People management, therefore, takes on a vital role in organisational success. But what does it actually involve?

We can identify five functional areas of HRM in the UK in the 1990s:

- staffing
- rewards
- employee development
- employee maintenance
- employee and industrial relations.

The range of tasks within each area will be individual to the organisation. As with other functions in an organisation such as marketing and finance, the HRM function cannot work in isolation. One of the criticisms that may be levelled at it is that it is too removed from line management and the day-to-day operation of the business, and the personnel involved in HRM need an understanding of business and strategic approaches. This point was taken on board by the Institute of Personnel and Development in the UK. In 1996, it restructured and redesigned its professional qualifications. These new standards for professional membership of the Institute of Personnel and Development have been designed to ensure that all graduates demonstrate an overall business knowledge as a criterion for qualification.

REVIEW ACTIVITY 1

Freestyle produces and retails leisure wear and has been in business for four years. It was set up by a young couple, Ian and Amy Green, who identified a gap in the market for children's leisure wear which is reasonably priced and versatile, lightweight, washable and quick drying, while retaining its waterproofing. The jackets and tops could fold into themselves and be carried in their own bags. The idea was quickly taken up by the market and the company has expanded rapidly and currently employs 100 people.

Freestyle has already set up a retail outlet at the factory, has five other retail outlets in nearby towns, each employing on average five staff including the manager, and has plans to expand still further during the next two years.

Ian and Amy know all their staff personally and have been involved with their recruitment, but both of them think that the expansion of the business, both in size and geographically, will make it impossible for them to continue to take responsibility for all human resource matters. They are aware of the function's role in recruitment and selection, but what other tasks do you think could ultimately be included in the HRM function in Freestyle?

Summary

HRM is concerned with all aspects of employees' working lives. Employees are one of the sources of competitive advantage and, as such, need to be managed effectively for organisational success. The human resource function works in conjunction with other functional managers to assist in effective workforce management.

HRM has developed from a welfare role to a wide-reaching and diverse role which involves resourcing the organisation, employee development and employee relations. We consider each of these areas in this unit. Debate continues about the terminology (personnel management or human resource management) used to describe the practice of people management, but in reality the terms are often blurred and used interchangeably in organisations. In some cases, human resource managers carry out what are ostensibly personnel tasks only and in other cases a personnel manager is involved in strategic decision making and implementation of a human resource strategy. For many managers involved in people management, the job is a mixture of both.

SECTION 2

Employee Resourcing

Introduction

We have considered some of the factors which have influenced the development of HRM, and you have become aware of some of the debates concerning the terms personnel management and human resource management. In this section, you meet some practical tasks which are carried out within HRM and fall under the heading of **employee resourcing**. Here, we are concerned with the day-to-day responsibility of ensuring that the right people are recruited at the right times and location to meet organisational objectives and that they are rewarded in an appropriate way.

We investigate the concepts of human resource planning and manpower planning and describe factors which influence the planning process. We outline the recruitment and selection process. You need to be aware of the different methods of reward that can be used and the rationale behind each method.

2.1 What is human resource planning?

There are arguably two ends to the spectrum of **human resource planning** (HRP). At one end are the 'hard facts' of the current workforce, usually provided in numerical form and covering data such as number of employees, structure of the workforce by age, gender, etc., job groupings, labour turnover and absentee rates. This information is needed for what is known as **manpower planning**.

At the other end is what many writers see as the 'softer' elements of human resource planning including activities which affect the way that people behave in the organisation and features of its culture. Examples include trying to establish why absenteeism is at its current levels, or what can be done to reduce the level of staff turnover, or why the staff in a particular area are demotivated.

Human resource planning also has implications in the strategic approach of HRM and we look at this later in the section.

MANPOWER PLANNING

Manpower planning is concerned with ensuring that there are adequate levels of the 'right' staff to achieve organisational objectives. The creation of the manpower plan involves forecasting the likely demand for labour of all kinds and then making plans to attract and train new staff and to redeploy and/or dismiss existing staff. Organisations use statistical information on performance such as sales per employee and productivity rates per employee, to help determine numbers of staff required.

We can develop a manpower plan by:

- analysing existing organisational manpower resources
- reviewing labour utilisation
- forecasting the demand for labour
- forecasting the supply of labour
- developing a manpower plan.

Analysing existing organisational manpower resources

Before we can make any decisions about the future requirements in the manpower plan, we obviously need to have a clear picture about what we currently have in terms of human resources, together with information about any current problems and ideas about how we could utilise staff more effectively. We need to build an overall picture of the existing staff situation, with information about the total number of employees and all their details including payments, absenteeism and turnover, and training and development activities. This analysis must involve an investigation of all aspects of the current staffing. We consider this further in the next activity.

ACTIVITY 2

We introduced the Freestyle organisation in the review activity at the end of Section 1. The company has now decided to expand. A new range of clothing for adults has been designed. This development, together with the increased demand for the company's existing ranges, will require an increase in staffing of approximately 30 full-time equivalent employees. (Assuming that a full-time employee normally works 39 hours a week, Freestyle needs to find an additional 1,170 staff hours each week – 1,170 being 39 multiplied by 30.)

The new staff might be a mix of full-time and part-time employees and might include some seasonal workers to cope with increased demand at certain times of the year. The expansion will obviously create some supervisory and/or management posts. The planned expansion has given Ian and Amy the opportunity to assess their existing workforce. Note down the kind of information about the workforce that would be useful to Ian and Amy.

The aim is to find out as much as possible about the workforce: its skills, experience and future capability. You might have included:

- total pay-roll costs
- staff numbers – by skills, gender, age, experience, qualifications
- absenteeism
- labour turnover – the rate at which staff leave per annum
- analysis of the type of person who joins the organisation
- training and development programmes.

The age range of the workforce is useful information for planning. One international organisation, which successfully set up in the UK some thirty years ago, has boasted a very low labour turnover rate and has a policy of developing its own staff. It currently is in the unfortunate position of losing a large number of its workforce through retirement! Planning ahead for such a situation is essential.

Actual costs, that is, not simply the salaries, but additional costs to the organisation, such as holiday and sickness pay and national insurance and pension contributions, is vital information for the planning process.

All this information is used when forecasting for the future. It is possible, for example, to predict the number of staff leaving the company in the coming year. It is also possible to study the reasons why people leave, noting other information such as their length of service and background, and use this information to develop a strategy to reduce labour turnover in the coming year. There are some reasons given by leavers which it might not be appropriate to change, some people might simply be unsuitable, but the selection process can be improved to select employees who are suited to particular circumstances, for example, those who like customer contact. There are other reasons for leaving the organisation which might prove to be an immediate concern to the employer, such as the lack of competitiveness of pay rates and conditions. This will strongly influence the ability to attract and retain suitably qualified and skilled staff. Leaver analysis is a source of information on the workplace which can be used to predict trends and also to identify problems.

Reviewing labour utilisation

As the next part of drawing up the manpower plan, we need to review the existing utilisation of staff and any areas of overstaffing or understaffing. We need to identify any areas that are appropriate for change and any staff with the potential for promotion through training and development. Begin with the next activity.

ACTIVITY 3

Consider the following scenario. Some years ago, a multiple retail organisation became aware that although the overall store labour turnover figure was 28 per cent, the turnover for staff employed on the main checkouts was much higher. Further analysis revealed that the turnover was highest for full-time staff in the 16–20 age group. (Full-time employees worked Tuesday to Saturday, with a late night Thursday or Friday.) Additionally, the highest levels of absenteeism were recorded for this group.

Discussion with the staff highlighted the following issues:

- young people applied for the posts because pay was higher and checkout staff were perceived as 'better' than sales floor staff
- the job was perceived as more highly skilled
- the hours had changed – with the increase in opening hours to include Friday night, the heaviest trading period of the week, staff rarely left the store before 9.30 p.m.
- the job itself was highly pressured at certain times, with staff bearing the brunt of customer frustration.

What would you suggest that management could do to deal with the problems identified?

There are a number of extreme methods that could be used. Managers could accept that this particular group had a higher turnover but the benefits of employing young people outweigh the costs and management could plan for absenteeism accordingly. This, however, is not only costly, as greater numbers of staff would need to be employed, but is unrealistic for effective people management. Managers could interview all staff and consider the absenteeism problem a disciplinary issue and warn staff about attendance and time-keeping. This would not resolve the problem as it does not attempt to identify why the problem continues.

Management could train the staff for alternative jobs in administration and related jobs in the cash office. This was an attractive option as it was clear from an assessment of their skills and qualifications that the talents of the young staff were not being fully utilised. As vacancies arose as a result of these moves and because additional sales generated an increase in the salaries budget, part-time rotas were created which ensured that staff were not on the checkouts for longer than an eight-hour shift excluding breaks.

Although there might be a need in this case to reduce staff turnover to an acceptable level, it is unlikely that an organisation would wish to reduce turnover to nil. The employment of new staff can bring in new ideas, skills and expertise to the organisation. Reduction in the demand for a product or service often results in overstaffing. Natural wastage through labour turnover can enable the organisation to reduce its staffing levels without creating redundancies.

Analysis of existing staff utilisation can enable the creation of a succession plan, whereby staff can be identified as suitable for promotion and can be trained and developed accordingly.

Forecasting labour demand

Organisations have to predict staffing requirements. It is not sufficient, for example, for Freestyle to simply state that the planned expansion will require 30 new employees. It will need to predict production levels and decide what staffing levels will be needed. This will include consideration of the type and level of staff – how many supervisors, for example – and the times they would be required. These decisions would be influenced by a number of factors.

- **Competition** – consider the impact on the Body Shop when other companies started to sell the same kind of products. If sales drop as a result of competition, staffing levels have to be changed accordingly.
- **Changes** in product or in production methods might result in the need for different numbers and types of staff and/or the need to retrain existing staff. Examples of this kind of change has occurred in the high street banks. The move by banks to sell insurance and other financial products and provide stockbroker and other services (new products) has meant that bank clerks require new skills and new training. However, the extensive introduction of cash dispensers (a new 'production' technique) has meant that fewer counter clerks are needed for cash dispensing and this has led to a reduction in the numbers of staff employed.
- The buoyancy of the **economy** will influence spending power and, therefore, staffing levels will need to be adjusted if all sales opportunities are to be taken.

- **Organisational policy** impacts on staffing decisions. If the organisation decides to focus on customer care, it will have to review not only numbers of staff, but also will need to identify what skills are required to meet the strategic objectives and train existing staff or recruit new staff to meet the demands of the new strategy. It will, perhaps, need to review numbers of staff employed and in what jobs. For example, Tesco's 'one-in-front' queue reduction initiative required greater staff flexibility in order that staff could be called from other areas of the store to increase the checkout staffing levels as needed.

Forecasting labour supply

To expand its production capability, an organisation might decide to set up a division in a different area of the country. It would require information on the labour supply such as:

- legislative restrictions or requirements for particular tasks
- information on the job market
- local and national economic trends
- competition in the area
- skills shortages and excesses
- age distribution in the travel-to-work area
- availability of training grants or regional funding
- local rates of pay.

In other words, the organisation needs to know whether there are sufficient numbers of people with relevant skills looking for the type of employment that is being offered, or looking for employment at all. Some areas, for example, have a high 'retired' population which does not wish to join the job market, and this will affect the ability of an organisation to attract new employees.

Developing the manpower plan

Manpower planning aims to ensure an optimum supply of staff to meet demand. The plan itself encompasses recruitment, selection and training of staff, redundancies and redeployment (the move from one type of job to another). The creation of the plan involves consideration of the statistical information available and, on the basis of this analysis, designing labour plans sufficient to meet organisational demands.

ACTIVITY 4

Ian and Amy, the owners of Freestyle, are considering the need to develop a human resource function, particularly in the light of their planned expansion. They think that they have been 'successful' to date by recruiting staff as and when they need them without any forward planning. Identify some benefits that they could gain by adopting a manpower plan.

Planning leads to employing the correct number of staff so that costs of over-employment can be avoided; the level of staffing will meet production and sales demands, thus enabling profit opportunities to be taken. Effective planning should mean that Freestyle employs people suited to the job, which could lead to a reduction of labour turnover. Manpower planning includes making training plans, so the development of individuals for higher positions or for training in different skills can be undertaken, and this will create a more highly skilled and flexible workforce.

HUMAN RESOURCE PLANNING

Human resource planning is a development which could be described as one stage further from manpower planning. In fact, it builds on the process of manpower planning and is a continuous process in organisations. It is not simply about skills in the workplace but also uses the concept of competence, the sets of behaviour that enable people to carry out a job. Human resource planning sees people as a source of competitive advantage. It is part of corporate strategic planning.

There is, however, a debate about the differences between manpower planning and human resource planning similar to that about the differences between personnel management and human resource management. To some, the difference between the two terms is in name only. It is difficult to determine which organisations carry out human resource planning and which a manpower planning process. Some organisations consider human resource planning to be a vital part of HRM. In an absolute sense, human resource planning can only be carried out in those organisations where HRM exists – where human resource managers are involved in strategic decision making.

Features of human resource planning are that it:

- makes a greater use of more qualitative techniques for assessing future requirements – it does not simply analyse statistics but poses the question 'what if?'
- is concerned with people in the longer term
- is concerned with business strategy.

2.2 Recruitment and selection

Recruitment is the process by which organisations contact and interest potential workers, through advertisements in newspapers or trade journals, through the Internet, and through specialist recruitment agencies. Then, using application forms, interviews, tests or other means, it **selects** those applicants it thinks might be suitable for appointment.

The recruitment procedure itself is one of the keys to organisational success. There are several reasons why it should be well planned and well executed.

- **Optimum profitability** – an organisation must make the best use of its resources. Poor recruitment can lead to high labour turnover which in turn reduces profits. Staff are an expensive resource and organisations wish to achieve optimum return on the money invested. The cost of interviewing job applicants and the associated administration and training costs are high, creating a drain.
- **Organisation image** – staff project the image of an organisation. This influences the outsiders' view of the organisation, determining whether they wish to do business with the organisation or whether or not they would like to work for it. The recruitment process is two way. It is not simply about the employer's judgements of the acceptability of applicants, but it is also a judgement by the applicant about the organisation, which is then often transmitted to others.
- **Efficiency** – the employees provide the service that can either make or break an organisation. Poor service will inevitably reduce the number of customers and clients, therefore reducing profits.
- **Legal implications** – the legislation involved in the recruitment of staff has to be taken into consideration. When an organisation recruits the wrong person, it may need to consider dismissal at a later stage. This process is costly in terms of time and money, and is unproductive in terms of company image.
- **Attitudes within the organisation** – where there are high levels of labour turnover, staff tend not to receive adequate training as both staff and managers expect new members of staff to remain with the organisation for a relatively short time. As a result, staff are never able to achieve the standards required and may leave due to lack of training. The process also creates departmental and organisational unrest.

We have considered the reasons why it is important to recruit the right staff. However, many of us can think of times when we, or friends and family, have applied for jobs and interviews and found that recruitment procedures have not been carried out well. Examples include organisations failing to reply to the applicant's letter or application form, interviewees kept waiting unnecessarily, and interviewers asking sexist or racist questions.

ACTIVITY 5

Think back to an interview you have had or an application for a job that you have made (even, perhaps, your application for university or college). Analyse both the good and bad features about your dealings with the organisation and write down at least two reasons why you think that the recruitment process is not always carried out effectively.

Although managers are often aware that recruitment and selection should be carried out effectively, it is often not the case in practice. New businesses are sometimes successful in spite of the staff they employ because the product itself is successful. This, however, is a short-term benefit. In the longer term as competition intensifies, there is a pressing need to employ the right staff. In answering the activity, you might have identified some of the following points.

- Effective recruitment takes time and there are few immediate benefits to the process.
- Often people do not enjoy playing the interviewer role as they do not like to judge others in a formal situation.
- Pressures of the business create situations where a manager is desperate for staff but does not want to take up valuable time to interview. As a result, the short-term problems take priority and the manager fails to take account of the implications of employing the wrong person for the job.
- Interviewers are poorly trained in interviewing techniques.
- The impact on potential applicants is not fully thought through.

The recruitment procedure should be logical. It should proceed by following through a number of stages:

- Stage 1 – **Job analysis**
- Stage 2 – **Defining the post**
- Stage 3 – **Attracting the applicant**
- Stage 4 – **Selection**
- Stage 5 – **Evaluation**

We now consider each stage in more detail.

JOB ANALYSIS

Decisions on recruitment need to 'fit' with the human resource plan. Organisations must make the optimum use of their limited salary budgets. Consequently, no organisation should take it for granted that any vacancy that arises should automatically be filled in the same way as before, or even at all. Job analysis is the first stage in the process, when information is collated about the job itself. The analysis can be complex or straightforward, depending upon the situation. In some cases, the analysis can be carried out by the formulation of a number of questions.

- What does the job actually involve?
- Is the job necessary in its current form?
- Is it necessary at all?
- Has it arisen due to increased workload and, if so, has rescheduling been considered?
- Has the vacancy arisen due to a backlog of work? Is the need likely to be long term or short term – is it a temporary or permanent appointment? Should there be a review of hours worked?

- Should the post be open to applications from existing staff or is it an external appointment?
- Should it be part time or full time?

In other cases, such as a large-scale recruitment programme, more complex methods are needed. Four basic methods can be used to carry out job analysis:

- observation of employees in the workplace
- work diaries that record the time an individual spends on daily activities
- individual interviews with staff doing the same or similar jobs
- questionnaires (these are useful when a large number of people are doing the same job, but the questions need to be carefully constructed otherwise information may go undetected).

Job analysis collects and analyses all the features of a particular job and considers the reward structure that might be used. It might result, for example, in replacing a full-time post with part time, or a full-time salaried position with a full-time partly commission-based post. The job analysis results in the job description and the person specification.

ACTIVITY 6

In commenting on the scenario described in Activity 3, we described how the supermarket considered introducing part-time rather than full-time positions on the main checkouts. Many more organisations are now employing staff to work non-standard hours (*IRS Employment Trends 570*). What reasons might an organisation have for replacing full-time positions with a number of part-time appointments? List some disadvantages of this practice.

Part-time working has been adopted by organisations for a number of reasons. It is a more flexible use of the hours, and organisations, particularly those in the service sector, can cover all hours to match fluctuating trading patterns. Organisations employing solely full-time staff have encountered times when they are overstaffed and others where staff levels have not been sufficient to meet customer demand.

Part-time hours might be convenient to both the member of staff and the organisation. Some potential leavers could be retained if offered work on a part-time basis. Part-time staff are able to cover a wider range of hours particularly the 'unsociable' hours, such as evenings and weekends. Some organisations are now using part-time staff specifically to retain particular skilled labour.

One problem with part-time staff concerns the continuity in the workplace. If a job is split between two or three staff, it can be more difficult to manage. However, many organisations, particularly in the retail and service sector have successfully developed this work practice. There are some drawbacks: by employing part-time staff, organisations employ larger numbers of staff which increases their administration and training costs.

There are many different ways in which staff can be employed by organisations in addition to the standard weekly hours contracts. Examples include annual hours contracts (where the hours worked are averaged over the year), no hours contracts (staff do no have set hours but are on call to work as and when required), and home working (staff work from their homes). These are all being used by a variety of organisations as a means of obtaining the most flexible use of the resource.

DEFINING THE POST

Job descriptions and person specifications are vital to the recruitment process. **Job descriptions** define the job to be carried out. Job descriptions are the output from the job analysis. They are the basis for the design of the person specification. **Person specifications** outline the skills and attributes needed by the postholder to carry out the job efficiently. Well-constructed descriptions and specifications form profiles of the job and of the person best suited to fill the position. They enable the recruiter to find the best match between the applicants with the job.

There are a number of different formats used to set out job descriptions. But, typically, they include information on:

- **the job title** – as used by the organisation
- **location** – the base for day-to-day work
- **responsible to** – who the post holder reports to
- **responsible for** – which people the post holder takes responsibility for
- **aim** – a statement as to why the job exists and its purpose
- **duties and responsibilities** – a description of all the tasks that the post holder must perform; this may be divided up into topic areas covering, for example, staff, production, health and safety, customers, sales and administration.

The duties and responsibilities can be classified under any range of headings, depending upon the actual job involved. A simple example of a job description is shown in Figure 1.

The job description is not only useful in the recruitment process, but it is also used when staff are being assessed in the workplace to determine the standard of work being produced, to discuss promotion and careers prospects and to identify and agree a programme of staff development for the employee. This process is known as **staff appraisal** and we discuss it later in the unit.

Job descriptions alone do not provide sufficient information for interviewers involved in staff selection. A statement about the skills and attributes needed by the post holder has to be designed – the person specification. This can be done in a number of ways, from an in-depth profile identifying the knowledge, skills and attitude required for every task on the job description to a simple overall profile specifying the general needs for the job and the organisation.

JOB TITLE:	Store Manager
Responsible to:	Trading Director
Responsible for:	All department staff
Aim:	To operate the department to optimum profitability, according to the organisation's rules and regulations
Duties:	
Staff	To recruit staff within the wage budgets
	To train, appraise and manage all staff
	To ensure effective workforce planning
	To ensure effective discipline is maintained
	To communicate all relevant information to staff and ensure that instructions are carried out
Health and safety	To ensure safe working practices and hygiene standards within area of control
Security	To carry out procedures necessary to protect stock and equipment
Administration	To ensure accurate completion of all stock, orders, delivery, price and credit administration
	To maintain a level of administration so that stock can be accurately calculated, and to assist with stock take
	To ensure returns are made correctly as requested
Communication	To organise unit meetings
	To communicate all relevant information to staff
	To communicate with outside agencies in the promotion of company image and reputation.
Stock	To ensure that stock is ordered, warehoused and sold according to turnover levels and organisation instructions
	To ensure that stock levels maintained to produce optimum profitability
Customer relations	To ensure the highest standard of customer relations at all times and to ensure that the store contributes positively to company image
Legislation	To ensure that store adheres to relevant legal requirements
General	To carry out any other duties as designated by the Trading Director

Figure 1: Job description for a store manager

Although both over 30 years old, the best known and most widely used schemes developed as guidance in this process are the seven-point plan (Table 1) and the five-fold grading system (Table 2). Both systems are designed to assist in the recruitment process and, when used effectively, they help to identify the type of person required, together with the traits, skills and abilities that are expected by that organisation for any job.

Attribute	**Indicators**
Physical make-up	Health, physique, appearance, bearing, speech
Attainments	Education, qualifications, experience
General intelligence	Fundamental intellectual capacity, problem solving ability, initiative
Special aptitudes	Mechanical and/or manual dexterity, facility in use of words and figures
Interests	Intellectual, practical, constructional, physically active, social, artistic
Disposition	Acceptability, influence over others, steadiness, dependability, self-reliance
Circumstances	Domestic, occupations of family

Table 1: Seven point plan (Rodger, 1952)

Attribute	**Indicators**
Impact on others	Physical make-up, appearance, speech and manner
Acquired qualifications	Education, vocational training, work experience
Innate abilities	Quickness of comprehension, aptitude for learning
Motivation	Individual goals, consistency and determination, success in achieving goals
Adjustment	Emotional stability, ability to deal with stress, ability to get on with people

Table 2: Five-fold grading system (Fraser, 1966)

Although these two systems are still widely used, they have some problems and they should be used with care. It is discriminatory, unethical and unacceptable to refer to an individual's personal circumstances. The use of age as a descriptor is currently under enormous criticism and efforts are being made to bring in legislation which will prevent 'ageism'.

ACTIVITY 7

The do-it-yourself chains, Do It All and B&Q, have policies to recruit older staff in some of their stores. Give some reasons that they might give for this recruitment policy? Remember the concept of competitive advantage.

The new policy has proved to be successful, not only in terms of acquiring the staff, but also in terms of profitability and, in the case of Do it All, on labour turnover. For Do It All, the policy stemmed from the strategic decision to recruit 1,000 customer service staff. New recruits had to possess good communication skills. It recruited a large number of people for the posts who had previous professional management experience and the proportion of people the company employed in the 40–65 age group grew from 17 per cent to 21.6 per cent.

Do It All based this decision on the identified need for added value in its product offer and felt that older workers possessed the desired skills for the organisation. Labour turnover decreased as older workers tend to stay in jobs longer and this has reduced employment costs. For example, W H Smith found that the older employees (late 40s to early 50s) stayed in employment five times as long as those in their twenties. For B&Q, the decision was made to employ older staff on the premise that people who shopped at its stores needed advice on the products it sold and the company felt that this could be done more effectively by people who have carried out DIY themselves.

Profiles

Profiles are also useful in the recruitment process. A profile is an outline description of the job or of the individual who would be suitable for the job. Consider the following position:

- **job title**: receptionist
- **responsible to:** customer services manager
- **responsibilities:** to deal effectively with all guests and visitors.

If you think about what the job entails, you can draw a profile of suitable post holders. To do the job, applicants would need to possess the attributes of politeness, courtesy, good communication skills, a good working knowledge of the systems and procedures that exist in the organisation, and knowledge of the organisational structure and who is responsible for different areas of the business. Recruiters would therefore be seeking evidence of these qualities during the selection process.

Some qualities are **essential** on appointment, so, for example, Do It All would expect applicants for customer service posts to possess communication skills. On the other hand, some qualities may simply be **desirable;** the organisation would be pleased if the applicant possessed them, but training could be given to develop them at a later stage.

The use of profiles can assist in the prevention of discriminatory practices on the grounds of gender, racial background, disability and age. The design of both the job description and the person specification must take relevant legislation into account such as the Sex Discrimination Act 1975, Race Relations Act 1976, and the Disability Discrimination Act 1995.

Once the job profile has been created, a general statement of the terms and conditions of employment for the post need to be agreed. The terms and conditions should be realistic, while also meeting the organisation's objectives in terms of profitability. They should be of an appropriate level to attract the type of candidate that the organisation requires, taking into account labour market conditions.

The stages of recruitment considered so far have been concerned with the authorisation of the vacancy, how (if at all) it is to be filled, the design of the job description and the personnel specification and consideration of reward for the post.

ATTRACTING THE APPLICANTS

Prior to advertising a post or going to a recruitment agency, an organisation should find out whether anyone currently employed is suitable for the post especially if it has a policy of internal promotion and personal development. This provides very suitable candidates as they are already committed to the organisation, are part of its culture, know what they are taking on, and it pursues a policy of promotion from within.

ACTIVITY 8

As a result of analysing the information given in exit interviews, Freestyle has found out that a number of staff are leaving due to lack of opportunity. As a result, the company is considering whether to adopt a policy of only filling 'promotion' posts with internal candidates. Write down some advantages and disadvantages of this practice.

If opportunities are open to existing staff, they provide an incentive and a development opportunity for employees. Additionally, this policy enables the organisation to make use of existing experience and gain greater benefit from training that has already been carried out. The advantage of recruiting from outside the organisation is that new ideas can be introduced. It is generally accepted that a balance of the two is ideal. Freestyle is currently developing and growing and it could therefore be argued that the organisation might benefit from the wider experience of some staff and managers with other organisations.

Advertising

Organisations need to decide how the appropriate target groups can be attracted. Jobs can be advertised:

- in the national and local press
- in specialist trade journals
- at job centres and careers offices
- on vacancy boards on the premises
- through management selection consultants or employment agencies
- by using the milk round – some organisations visit a number of universities each year and interview prospective students for graduate recruitment
- on the Internet.

The most appropriate method should be chosen for each vacancy. For example, if a organisation wished to recruit graduates, it might do the milk round. If an organisation wished to recruit temporary administration staff, it could use an employment agency. Factors such as the cost, the expertise of agency in a particular field of work, the speed of the recruitment agency or method and urgency for a replacement will influence the choice of method.

The media should be relevant to the target group. The use of some media can also discriminate against certain groups of individuals, if, for example, organisations only advertised in journals and media which are rarely read by certain ethnic groups. The costs of the advertisement have to be considered. Should national or local press be used? By analysing the response, success rate and the cost of previous advertisements, decisions can be made about the most effective media for any vacancy.

Advertisements should be clear and state briefly:

- requirements of the job
- necessary and desirable criteria for job applicants
- job location
- reward package
- job tenure
- application procedure.

SELECTION

The aim of the selection process is to identify whether the applicant has the skills and expertise as specified in the person specification or has the potential to develop those skills in the workplace. Selecting the right person is obviously important both to the organisation and to the applicant. It is important not to select anyone who is either unable to do the job at one extreme or is overqualified to do so at the other. Poor selection decisions can also be damaging to departmental and organisational morale.

There are various selection methods available to organisations, ranging from the one-to-one interview through to more complex and lengthy processes such as three-day assessment centres. The vacancy, the speed at which it needs to be filled, the administrative arrangements needed, the acceptability to the candidates, and the costs of the various methods will affect the method used. Staff involved in the process have to be trained and suitably qualified (for example, in the use of testing if required). The process should appear open from the selector's side and the prospective employee's side.

The selection methods that organisations can choose include:

- application forms
- interviews
- assessment centres
- testing.

Application forms

These provide a standardised format for information gathering on applicants. They are mostly used in conjunction with other methods and as a pre-screening process so that the number of applicants can be reduced by comparing the information given on the form with the criteria specified for the job. This pre-screening process can be carried out by computer.

Interviews

These can take the form of either one-to-one or panel interviews, where there are a number of interviewers. Interviewing is one of the most popular methods used although it can be unreliable. They are, however, one of the easiest methods to administer and are relatively cheap to operate, particularly in the one-to-one format. They rely on the skill and expertise of the interviewer(s) to be totally objective.

Assessment centres

Assessment centres are often used for management and graduate recruitment. They require candidates to spend one or more days at a centre. At the centre, candidates work together on a series of tasks and will be assessed on their ability to carry them out. The tasks include group or individual problem-solving exercises, in-tray exercises, presentations and role plays. Assessment centres are expensive to set up and operate, due to the assessor's interviewing time, the training involved, accommodation and travel costs.

Testing

There has been an enormous growth in the use of testing in the UK. It requires a measuring instrument – standardised, reliable and valid – so that the results can be used as a predictor of performance. They can be used:

- for measuring such factors as intelligence – giving an indication of overall mental capacity
- to test aptitude – as a means of predicting future potential; special aptitudes for specific abilities can be measured although some tests do not allow for differences in culture and ethnic approach

- to test response to training
- to test attainment – measuring skills already acquired
- to test how the individual reacts in certain situations – in effect, to test personality.

The final category here, personality testing, is very contentious. As there are many views about the determinants of personality, testing may be open to criticism. If it is used in the selection process, it must be carried out by personnel qualified to administer the test. It also depends on the honesty of the answers given by the candidate as a socially acceptable answer may be given not an honest one. Some tests are also seen to be biased against women.

Validity, **reliability** and **appropriateness** of the selection method is essential. The method should be valid, that is it should measure what it sets out to measure, and there is a correlation between the test scores and the future performance. For example, if a hand-eye co-ordination test is used for a particular machine operator, but a high test result is ultimately shown to be unrelated to future performance in the workplace, then the test is invalid.

Interviewing can be unreliable as it is subject to the behaviour and skills of the interviewer and the interaction between the interviewer and the candidate. Unreliable means that the method cannot be repeated in a consistent way, each candidate will get a different reaction from the same interviewer. In addition, an interview may have poor validity if carried out by untrained interviewers – the future performance of candidates is unrelated to the interview criteria and the way they came across in the interview. Interviewing may be supplemented with tests that are more valid, more reliable, but more expensive.

It is of little value to spend time and money on a three-day assessment centre for a typist or a machine operator when a one-to-one interview would be appropriate for the job, combined with say an additional typing test. On the other hand, some organisations such as Asda have decided that testing is appropriate for all their staff from sales floor level through to managerial appointments, even though the costs of this policy are high.

EVALUATION

Evaluation is the final stage of the process. As with all other tasks in an organisation, the effectiveness of the procedures used should be evaluated. This can be done by evaluating:

- the frequency of response to the advertisement
- the percentage of rejections from pre-screening
- the number of successfully presented candidates
- the number of successful candidates who turn down the post
- labour turnover figures both in the short term (six months) and in the long term.

The recruitment and selection process is expensive, but high labour turnover will increase costs. If labour turnover is high amongst those staff with less than six months service, it could be argued that the recruitment methods need to be reviewed. The induction process and initial training would also need to be assessed.

The recruitment and selection process is an important part of human resource management. It is a process which cannot be carried out in isolation but which must take into account corporate aims, objectives and strategy, corporate image and the organisation's target market. People are a key resource in an organisation and a means of competitive advantage. An effective recruitment and selection strategy as part of HRM is essential for organisational success.

REVIEW ACTIVITY 2

Freestyle has used the one-to-one interview for all appointments so far. This has been fairly successful in some areas but, in others, the company has encountered situations where staff have left after a few months expressing the view that they 'didn't realise what the job involved'. Freestyle has also had to spend more time than it expected on training as the staff recruited did not really have the skills or attributes that are needed.

Ian and Amy have decided that a different approach to recruitment and selection is needed. They will shortly be recruiting a store manager for their new retail outlet: The job description is given in Section 2.2 (see Figure 1). An overall requirement is additionally that the staff that they appoint for the new store should demonstrate good product knowledge and customer care skills.

Consider the stages of the process of recruitment and selection. Write brief notes for Ian and Amy to remind them what has to be done at each stage.

Summary

Manpower planning and human resource planning are important elements in the management of people. Organisations need to employ staff in sufficient numbers at appropriate times to meet productive and customer demand. Those staff need to demonstrate the skills and attributes for the job for which they are employed. Additionally, the organisation needs to plan ahead and consider the implications of factors such as the impact of competition and the economic environment on the staffing needs.

Effective recruitment and selection policies and procedures are needed to ensure that the 'right' person is recruited to meet both current and future needs.

SECTION 3

Employee Training and Development

Introduction

Success in organisations is not simply achieved by recruiting the right people, employees also need to be trained and developed to enable them to fulfil the functions and reach the standards required to meet organisational objectives. Today, training and development has a crucial role in organisational culture, change and development and the adaptation for particular activities. It is a two-way process – of benefit to the organisation for productivity, motivation and adaptation to change and of benefit to the individual for personal achievement, job satisfaction and career development. As you saw in the earlier units, we are living in a fast-changing environment and to achieve organisational success employees have to be flexible and multiskilled. There has to be an ongoing programme to develop and train internal staff to meet the current and future needs of the organisation. In addition, new government employment and education initiatives provide opportunities and threats in an organisation's environment that need to be addressed. It can start to do this through its training and development programme.

Trends indicate an increased demand for higher level, better, broader and more flexible skills to cope with environmental, organisational and workplace changes. The roles of employees in relation to the employer have changed, they are seen as part of an organisation's means of coping with these changes, rather than just resources to be used up and discarded. Equally, employees have to be flexible and adaptable if they are to be able to meet organisational objectives on a continuous basis. The nature of careers has changed, there are no more 'jobs for life' and individuals increasingly have to take responsibility for their own direction rather than rely on their employer. In doing this, training and development are important for acquiring the necessary skills and flexibility. For example, technology has obviously changed the way that many people work and, to keep pace, individuals have to learn new skills and change their attitudes to existing job functions.

Staff can be developed by a variety of means and organisations should choose those training and development methods which are the most appropriate. Factors which influence the choice include cost, individuals' preferred learning styles, and organisational restrictions such as ability to release staff for any period of time. A number of government-led initiatives have been introduced over the years to encourage employers to train their staff, such as training levies and training credits. Recent research suggests, however, that most employers do not need to be convinced of the overall benefit of training but need to be persuaded that specific training will offer tangible benefits (Labour Force Survey, 1995/6, p. 10). As with other areas of HRM, the benefits accrued from training are often long term and not easily measured.

3.1 The training process

The key terms we discuss are training, learning and development. We outline the rationale for training in organisations and explain the training cycle. The ways in which people learn impacts on training decisions. We describe the various methods of assessment and appraisal and their possible uses.

We can define **learning** as the acquisition of new knowledge, skills or attitudes by an individual. It results in relatively permanent changes in behaviour. We need to have some idea of how individuals learn and the different learning styles that might be adopted and that affect how training and development can be delivered most effectively. We can define training and development as processes that help the individual to learn. We can further differentiate between training and development.

- **Training** is the transmission to the learner of a specific body of knowledge or skill by a trainer using a set of objectives and controlling the process – the result is to achieve effective performance in a particular workplace activity and in an individual's ability.
- **Development** is the process of a learner using fundamental knowledge and skills to build and extend expertise in cognitive, personality, skills, moral areas – the learner is controlling the process, the result is not likely to be measurable in terms of a specific job task but in the general 'wellbeing' of the individual, the organisation and its culture. Individuals can take responsibility for managing their own development through a continuous professional development (CPD) process.

The difficulty with using such definitions is that they are very broad and sometimes miss salient points. And where does education fit in with these definitions? Education is often regarded as 'for life' and training as 'for work.' If this is the case, where does a programme such as the GNVQ (General National Vocational Qualification) in retail and distribution fit in? Do we educate people in work or do we train them? Or both? Is this programme education, training or development?

Training is more specific and typically takes a shorter time to complete than education. Training tends to be workplace based and pursues more mechanistic behavioural objectives. However, there are some grey areas. For example, NVQs are claimed to be workplace oriented, but it is possible to obtain this qualification while a student at school or college, by carrying out exercises which simulate the workplace. More in-depth analysis can be found in Reid and Barrington (1994).

ACTIVITY 9

Identify four circumstances which might bring about a need for training.

You might have included any of the following:

- the introduction of new staff to the organisation and to the job itself
- the training needed by staff who have been promoted or who have the potential for promotion
- the introduction of new technology and/or equipment or new tasks
- changes in organisational structure, policy or strategy
- as a result of the action plan agreed through staff assessment
- legislative changes.

We can breakdown training needs into four main levels:

- **organisational** – strategic change, structural change, cultural change, new procedures, technology, competitive effects
- **departmental** – management skills and other requirements for internal functional activities, such as customer services
- **job function** – skills required for new or changed tasks within individual functions
- **individual** – individual requirements for training for a specific task, say, working a new machine or some new software.

We can break the process of training into a number of steps (see Figure 2). We start with the identification of the need at any of the four levels identified above. The need is also identified in terms of a gap between the attitudes, knowledge and skills of the employees and the skill requirements of the organisation for those employees.

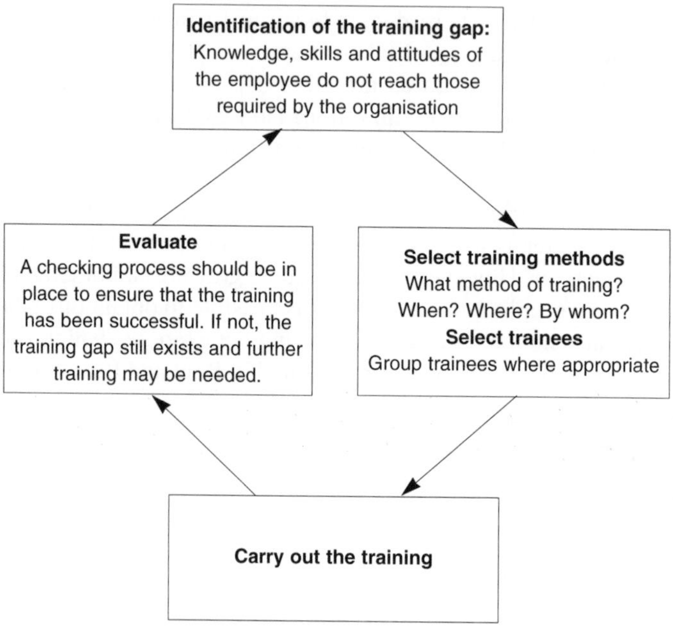

Figure 2: The training cycle

Once a need is identified and the training objectives formulated then training methods and trainees need to be selected, and the training needs to carried out and then evaluated. We look at each of these stages.

TRAINING METHODS

When the need for training has been established, the method of training should be determined. Training should:

- improve the performance of the employee
- be perceived by the employee as being effective in improving performance
- be pitched at the appropriate level for the job
- be efficient and cost effective so that training costs are exceeded or matched by improvement in performance (Riding, 1993, p.8).

The method chosen to bring the staff to the desired standard should be the one which is most appropriate for the task itself. It should be suitable for the level of staff, appropriate to the organisation, and it should be efficient. The objectives of the training will affect the choice of training method. Is it to develop manual skills? Leadership styles? Problem solving? Strategic thinking ability?

Training methods include:

- **on-the-job training** – learning by just doing the job, by following an experienced worker ('sitting with Nellie') or by mentoring where guidance is given by an experienced worker
- **job rotation, traineeships and field training** – trainees get experience in all areas of the organisation, this is useful for training graduates to be managers and to give them a broad understanding of what goes on throughout the organisation
- **simulation** – pilots train on air-flight simulators, in business managers can learn using management games, case studies and role plays where they must decide on a particular course of action given a scenario
- **lectures and demonstrations** – where basic information is imparted or a basic skill shown
- **group methods** – including group discussion, role playing, seminars, teamworking and outdoor activities, group methods can be used to develop team building, and performance in stressful and unusual situations
- **self-paced learning** – through printed materials, videos and computer-based packages.

Training in the workplace can be on a one-to-one basis on the premises or it can involve leaving the workplace for periods of time. Computer-assisted learning (CAL) is now used in some universities to teach specific modules and by some organisations (such as British Aerospace and British Gas) for training purposes.

Training methods should also be appropriate to the learning styles of the trainee, which differ from one individual to another. The way that we learn is likely to impact upon the effectiveness of the training method chosen.

LEARNING

We start by looking at some of your own learning experiences in the next activity.

> ## ACTIVITY 10
>
> Identify some of your own learning experiences over the past two weeks, both as part of your studies and outside them. Think about the learning process for each one. Was it the same in each case? Or did you learn in different ways.

It is likely that you identified a number of different learning experiences. Some of them will (hopefully) have been as a result of working through this module in which you have learnt by reading through information and have had the information reinforced by doing various activities. Other learning may have been as the result of a particular experience - good or bad! If you are careless and crash your car, you learn that cars are expensive to repair and that parts can take days to arrive. You learn through instruction from others, a colleague comments that a particular feature on his or her computer has saved a lot of time, you try it and learn that it does the same for you. These are all different forms of learning. Some we find easier than others.

There are many learning theories, most can be divided into two main schools of thought.

- The **stimulus response** or **behaviourist** school includes the work by Pavlov (1941) and Skinner (1953). This is learning by association, the response is linked to the stimulus, and can then be reinforced by some other action. In a training situation, reinforcement might be through praise from the trainer.
- The **cognitive school** includes the work of Piaget and the Gestalt psychologists and concerns the functioning of the brain, the role of perception, and the development of understanding.

Social learning theory is another area that is useful to trainers. This takes the view that social interaction has a role to play in the learning process and that we can learn from observation as well as direct experience and people model themselves on others. A form of training that is based on the same observation is 'sitting by Nellie' where training is carried out simply by observing or working with another, more experienced individual.

An individual is likely to build up a variety of different ways of learning depending on personal experiences, abilities and what is to be learnt. An individual's style of learning will impact on the way in which we perceive information and deal with it.

It will affect the way that we think, manage others and relate to people in general. This has obvious consequences for the design and choice of training methods. It is possible to choose training programmes which suit individual learning styles. The choice of a programme which the trainee actually dislikes might also open up a development opportunity. Training can be designed to enable the learner to experience different learning methods, which he or she previously would not have considered.

The work of Honey and Mumford (1981) proposed four basic learning styles: activist, reflector, theorist and pragmatist.

- **Activists** wish to be totally involved in the learning process. They tend to be prepared to attempt to do anything and are not at all sceptical. They have a need to be constantly active and will seek out the next learning experience.
- **Reflectors** take a more cautious approach by gathering all relevant information and considering this before acting. They tend to stand back from events and observe others in action.
- **Theorists** have a need to rationalise and prefer things to be logical and make sense. Problems are thought through in a totally logical way and they have a dislike of the subjective analysis of problems.
- **Pragmatists** are practical people who are ready to take concepts and try them out. They have a need to 'do' the job and look upon opportunities offered as challenges to tackle, preferably without too much discussion.

ACTIVITY 11

Suggest what might be the most appropriate method for carrying out:

- training in till operation for a checkout operator in a multiple retail organisation
- training in disciplinary procedures for a personnel officer
- training in team-building skills for a production manager.

The basic skills required by a checkout operator could be learnt through demonstration with written instructions and procedures, followed by on-the-job training or with a more experienced operator. Mini case studies could be used to identify particular customer-related problems and as a basis for role play in a specific training environment.

For the personnel officer, you might consider using lectures, group discussions and role play. Planned reading could be given beforehand to develop background knowledge of relevant legislation. Outdoor training, management games and role play would be suitable to develop team-building skills for the production manager.

One last factor in the choice of training concerns the question of who should carry it out. In some cases, this is not negotiable. Certain qualifications can only be acquired through specified educational establishments which are approved by the awarding body. The Institute of Personnel and Development qualifications, for example, can only be obtained through agreed establishments.

In many organisations, training managers or training officers are appointed to organise and/or carry out training. Often, within the organisation, specific staff are identified who will carry out skills training for all new staff. For management and supervisory training, consideration might be given to the use of external consultants. This is also the case for cultural or organisational behavioural change programmes which involve a training programme for all staff. This has occurred in a number of local authorities when, through local government reorganisation and funding changes, decisions were made to focus on the customer, and customer care programmes were implemented.

So far in the training cycle, we have considered the identification of the training gap and the process of deciding the appropriate method. Selecting the trainees is, to all intents and purposes, an administrative role. Decisions have to be made as to the best times for training to take place and staff need to be chosen to attend the training.

Training itself is a skilled area which is covered in more detail in specialist human resource modules. There are, however, some features of training design which you should consider. Whatever training method is chosen, it should:

- state measurable and achievable objectives
- be organised in a logical order
- be structured in small enough blocks of information to give the trainee the opportunity to understand
- be well timed, both in terms of the amount of time spent on it and when it is carried out
- give the opportunity to the trainee to put theory into practice
- maximise the use of the senses.

There should be a statement of objectives for any training package stating what the trainee will achieve by the end of the training period. The objectives should be both measurable and achievable and should reflect the individual's training needs to ensure that the training is appropriate. Carrying out training which does not meet the needs of the individual or the organisation can act as a demotivator and will influence employee willingness to attend further sessions.

One form of training – that everyone who is employed in an organisation should experience – is the **induction programme**, which introduces an employee to the organisation. This strongly influences an individual's perception of the organisation and ultimately, their performance within it. You may have experienced an induction programme for your studies, when you were informed of the overall programme, who was responsible for you and for each element of the programme. You will, hopefully, have been informed of methods of assessment and the consequences of failing to submit a piece of work. Induction is designed to introduce you to the programme itself, but also to inform you of anything which is relevant to you and your progress. In the workplace, induction programmes broadly fall into two areas; an introduction to the organisation itself, particularly structural, cultural, strategic and employment issues and training to carry out the specific job.

ACTIVITY 12

When its labour turnover figures were analysed, Freestyle noticed that a large number of staff were leaving within six months of joining the organisation. Ian and Amy discussed the reasons for this with some of the staff. Many said that they felt at a loss when they first joined, they were 'just thrown in at the deep end' on the first day and 'had to find things out for themselves' and, as a result, often made frustrating mistakes. Ian and Amy decide that some form of introduction to the organisation is needed but are unsure what this involves. Note down a list of suggestions that Ian and Amy could use within an induction programme.

Induction training differs from organisation to organisation, according to individual needs. However, the overall aim is to give the new employee information which will be relevant, particularly during the first few weeks of employment. You might have suggested that Ian and Amy's programme should cover:

- Organisational background, history, structure, reporting procedures, aims and objectives. Specific rules and regulations that are relevant to the wellbeing of the employee, such as health and safety, disciplinary and grievance procedures, hygiene regulations and assessment and appraisal systems, and information on reward and benefits.
- Training. Employees have to be shown how to do the job and should receive, as a minimum, some on-the-job training. The new employee will be shown how to carry out specific tasks in the department by the supervisor, manager or by an experienced member of staff. At this stage, the employee should be closely supervised while carrying out the job and given feedback where required. In addition, a new member of staff should be given a tour of the work unit and be introduced to members of staff. The training programme should be issued together with information on a probationary period.

The final stage of the training cycle is the evaluation. Evaluation can take two forms: evaluation of the actual training itself and assessment of the value of the training to the organisation. There are a number of ways of evaluating the training itself from simple feedback forms from the participants through to measurement of performance before and after the training event to see if there has been any improvement. Training objectives should be checked to see that they have been met.

In the wide view, the organisation, HRM and the individual are interested in the effectiveness of training. If the training department is separate from the strategic decision making of the business, there is a tendency to make an evaluation simply on the basis of the immediate pay back for the investment in training. However, an organisation should consider training as an investment which will reap benefits in the future. The pay back might be in improvements in organisational performance, in efficiency of achieving organisational objectives, in competitive advantage, and in a flexible multiskilled workforce that can easily adapt to change.

ACTIVITY 13

Identify some benefits to both the organisation and the individual of successful training and development policies and procedures. Make a separate list of benefits to the organisation and benefits to the individual. Perhaps, you could consider what benefits that you have gained from your current programme of study.

Organisations can benefit from effective training and development by:

- competitive advantage from a skilled and motivated workforce
- reduced absenteeism and labour turnover
- improved productivity levels
- enhanced organisational image from better trained staff which attracts the best staff
- improved service and customer care
- easier succession planning
- flexibility, a multiskilled workforce better able to adapt and change.

The individual can gain by:

- enhanced performance, which may be directly related to pay
- increased job satisfaction
- more confidence through the ability to do the job efficiently
- better chances for promotion
- improved knowledge, skills, attributes and peer perception
- greater job security within the organisation and more marketability outside.

You have also seen that government and society have an interest in the benefits of training and development. Britain needs to continue to update and upgrade skills and knowledge in the workforce so that British companies can compete internationally not just nationally or in Europe. Now that there is a global marketplace in terms of organisational inputs and outputs, one key factor in competitive advantage is the efficiency and effectiveness of people.

3.2 Staff assessment and appraisal

Assessment is something that we all do from time to time, either subjectively or objectively. As you work through this unit, you should be assessing whether you are meeting the objectives we set out at the beginning. In addition, you will probably be making some kind of appraisal of whether you found it useful or interesting. Appraisal systems in organisations are a means of formalising assessment which are already made in an informal way through examination of the current performance in a job. Generally they are used to:

- improve current performance
- provide feedback
- increase motivation
- identify training needs
- identify potential and staff for promotion
- assist in workforce planning
- monitor individuals and set them job objectives
- award salary increases
- identify succession and career paths
- assess the effectiveness of selection processes.

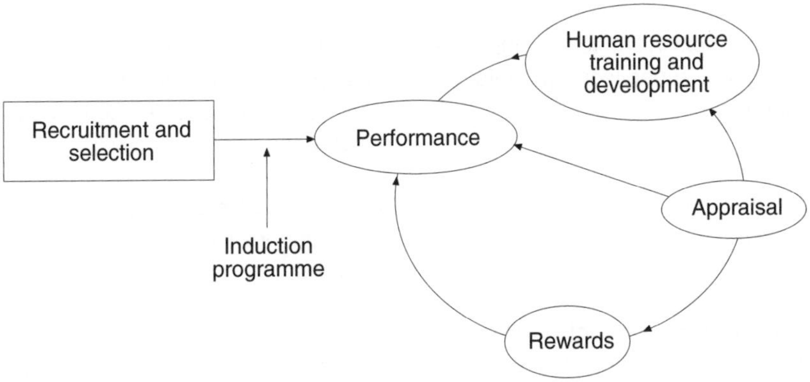

Figure 3: Appraisal as part of the human resource cycle
Source: Adapted from Devanna et al. in Bratton and Gold (1994, p. 28)

Figure 3 illustrates how appraisal fits as part of the human resource cycle. You can see the interlinking of appraisals with development, performance and reward. The most effective use can be made of appraisal systems by tying them into a more complete system of performance management. This links the appraisal to precise job descriptions, individual objectives, individual development plans and the reward system.

Assessment of performance can take a variety of forms, ranging from assessing the way a specific task is carried out as in NVQ assessment to complex appraisal systems which might involve overall assessment of performance by all people who come into contact with an employee. For NVQs, an employee's performance is measured against performance standards. The assessor must hold the appropriate qualifications, or be in the process of obtaining them. The employee is either assessed as 'competent' or 'not yet competent' and, in the latter case, would be given the opportunity to have further training and be assessed again at a later date. This assessment considers specific criteria. Overall performance is considered in the appraisal.

In the appraisal system, interviews take place on a regular basis, perhaps once or twice a year. At this time, an employee would be interviewed to discuss his or her performance since the last appraisal, to identify strengths and weaknesses, and to formulate an action plan about how weaknesses can be improved and how strengths could be developed and used. Appraisals can be carried out by different personnel (see Table 3).

Appraisal by	**Comment**
Immediate manager or supervisor	Most often used as the immediate manager should have greatest knowledge of the employee and should formalise feedback given during the year
Manager next in line to the employee's manager or supervisor - 'grandfather' approach	Sometimes used in conjunction with the appraisal by the immediate manager or as a counter signature to endorse the appraisal
Staff that directly report to the employee – 'subordinate appraisal'	Normally used in conjunction with other methods such as 360 degree appraisal
All parties who come into contact with the employee – '360 degree appraisal'	Recently this approach has received more publicity and is being used by a number of organisations such as Tesco to provide a total view of an employee's performance
Personnel manager	Used where there is no immediate line manager as in matrix management structures – can be used in conjunction with appraisals from project managers

Appraisal by	Comment
Employee's colleagues – 'peer appraisal'	Not often used on its own due to concerns about criticising staff at own level in the organisation
Employee – 'self appraisal'	Often used in conjunction with appraisals carried out by others – can be used as an interim report to be formalised with the manager's appraisal
Assessment centres	The employee's potential is assessed as in a recruitment and selection type of situation with various tests

Table 3: Methods of appraisal

ACTIVITY 14

Consider these jobs in organisations:

- senior manager working in store in retail organisation
- personnel manager of manufacturing company
- cashier in high street bank
- customer care manager for local council.

For each position, suggest which type of appraisal might be the most appropriate.

It is possible to use any of the appraisal methods for any job. The aim is to choose the most appropriate method for the organisation and for the level of staff. Carrying out 360 degree appraisals would be costly and time consuming because of the need to contact all the relevant people for comment, therefore to use it for large numbers of employees such as cashiers might be considered inappropriate due to costs. Similarly, assessment centre appraisals are expensive. If, however, the organisation considers this to be a worthwhile investment, the cost may be worth bearing.

Here are our possible choices for each of the jobs.

- Senior manager – assessment centres could be used to identify potential store managers, appraisal by their immediate manager and perhaps the regional or head office manager (the grandfather approach) might also be used to identify potential.

- Personnel manager – for a single unit organisation, the appraisal would probably be carried out by the immediate manager. Self appraisal could also be used to provide additional information. Peer appraisal could be used to assess how well the manager works with other managers within the organisation.
- Cashier in high street bank – appraisal by immediate manager or supervisor.
- Customer care manager – this might be the ideal opportunity to use 360 degree appraisal particularly where the role is an all-embracing customer care role for both internal and external people.

Whichever method is adopted by an organisation, the appraisal can be classified into three basic stages:

- **assessment of performance** – assessing the standards achieved by the employee against those expected and those previously agreed
- **identification of potential** – as a result of the performance assessment, identifying what the employee is capable of achieving
- **action plan** – an agreement between the appraiser and the appraisee about what is to be done to achieve the standards required by the organisation and the employee him or herself.

Within the performance management system, the process is also linked to reward, which can cause problems as the appraiser becomes both a helper, discussing and helping with performance improvements, and as a judge, deciding about reward as a result of performance.

Assessment and appraisals are obviously important to the organisation but they are also an essential part of an individual's development process. They provide the opportunity for an individual to get precise feedback on performance, guidance and help on performing better and achieving competence. They also allow any training needs to be identified and some guidance to be given on future career possibilities.

REVIEW ACTIVITY 3

Freestyle has recruited employees for its new retail outlet, but at present it has no formal induction programme. Few of the new entrants have any retail experience, nor have they previously worked for the organisation. They are predominantly female staff who have been recruited to work on a part-time basis and, for many, this is their first job on returning to work after staying at home to look after their children. They are all familiar with Freestyle products and have bought them for their children.

Staff in the retail outlets have very broad job descriptions and are expected to be able to carry out any non-management task as required. The induction programme should not include any on-the-job training but should consider the implications of the job on general skills that would be required by the employees.

1 Identify the information that should be included in the induction programme. Suggest the content of a seven session, one-day induction programme for the new employees. Suggest what method of instruction might be suitable for each session.

2 Suggest what frequency and type of assessment and appraisal would be most appropriate.

Summary

Training and development of staff is essential if competitive advantage is to be achieved. Efficient, valid training and development procedures enhance both the organisation and the individual. Individual development requires staff to take responsibility for their own development in organisations. Staff assessment and appraisal are tools which can be used to assist in training needs analysis, to assist in personal development, and to enhance an individual's competence in the workplace.

SECTION 4

Employee Relations

Introduction

Employee relations include all forms of relationships between employer and employee in organisations, whether through a direct relationship or through a trade union or staff council. Historically, the relationship has been largely based on conflict and confrontation and often has been be viewed negatively. The needs of employers and employees are different and, as such, are likely to create differences in opinion and approaches. However, it is possible to work towards common goals and to aim to satisfy all parties. In this section, we consider a number of factors that affect employee relations and look at the different approaches to trade union involvement.

You will become aware of the factors influencing the employer/employee relationship and recognise the role of unions in the process and the different forms it can take. We discuss the various reasons for union membership and investigate the use of and practical implications of employee relations procedures in organisations.

4.1 Historical aspects

The way in which the relationship between the employer and the employee develops will differ from one organisation to another, one employment sector to another and perhaps even vary within an organisation. The size, structure, history and culture of the business are influencing factors. Changes to production methods, technology and market conditions, together with the growing need for adaptability, customised products and services, and quality, have impacted upon demands made of the workforce. Legislative change and government policies in the last 30 years in particular have helped to shape the relationships seen in organisations today. The Consequently the roles of management and of the unions have changed over this time.

During the 1970s, there was an increase in union membership as a result of recognition for non-manual ('white collar') workers and support for the 'closed shop' which means that individuals would not be hired unless they were a member of the union. 1979 saw the election of a Conservative government that had pledged to reduce union influence, which they did both through legislation and the impact of other government policies. The recession in the early 1980s resulted in large scale job losses and a subsequent reduction in union membership. There was a decline in trade union membership from 13 million in 1979 (55 per cent density of unionisation) to 8 million in 1995 (33 per cent density).

In the 1990s, with organisations needing to maintain flexibility and adaptability to survive, unions recognise that unsuccessful companies cannot afford to pay hefty pay increases and that they need to work with, rather than against, management to achieve success. Equally, management has recognised that the workforce is an integral part of its success, and that a reciprocal relationship needs to be worked out such that the organisation delivers what employees want and the employees, in return, help to meet organisational objectives in the most efficient and effective way. As you have seen recruitment, selection, training and development are important in this process. The area of pay rewards and benefits is obviously crucial to the relationship between employer and employee and has changed markedly as organisations are now treating staff as key stakeholders and offering reward packages based on performance, profit-sharing bonuses and share options to increase the employee's involvement and stake in the organisation.

Generally, unions have been more of a force in the public sector than the private. However, now there is a move away from national pay bargaining to the use of pay review bodies in the public sector. Privatisation itself has fragmented national agreements, so large utilities such as British Gas have been divided up into a number of much smaller units. Moreover, industry-wide bargaining agreements in the private sector such as that with the Employer's Engineering Federation (EEF) have been terminated, thus ending collective bargaining on a national level.

We look at the relationship between the employer, employee and unions by examining the perspectives of each party. As you can see, there are some conflicts in the interests of the different parties. These can be resolved through negotiation and by recognising that the workforce is an organisation's chief asset and should be treated as such, and that the workforce has to work towards achieving competitive advantage and meeting organisational objectives. An unsuccessful organisation is of no value to any of the parties.

MANAGEMENT

Management wants, through its workforce, to:

- meet organisational objectives
- increase productivity
- avoid any conflict or disruption
- follow agreed procedures for any grievances
- control and monitor staff performance and reward
- foster employee commitment and co-operation
- reinforce organisational values through the organisational structure and culture.

How particular managers or management teams achieve these will vary. We can identify four different management styles that affect employee relations and, specifically, the attitude towards unions in organisations.

- **Traditionalist** – managers feel that they have a right to manage without interference from what they see as an outside party. Employee relations procedures are undeveloped and open hostility to trade unions exists. This type of situation still exists in some small, owner-managed businesses.
- **Paternalist** – extensive benefits are provided for the workforce, and unions are regarded as unnecessary and some opposition still exists. The intention is that the benefits will remove the need for collective bargaining. The workforce is encouraged to identify with organisational objectives. Many relatively new businesses would fit here.
- **Sophisticated moderns** – accept the development of trade union power, recognise unions and the inevitability of collective bargaining, and operate mainly through consultation though some take a more extreme adversarial approach, and have formal arrangements with unions. This type of approach is found in many public sector organisations.
- **Standard modern** – the pragmatists who adapt their approach to trade unions according to internal and external pressures. These include many large companies that rely on their subsidiaries to deal with employees, and don't mind what they do as long as they make profits (Sisson, 1994; Purcell and Sisson, 1983).

The employer/employee relationship is important to organisational success. Organisations have a choice of ways that this can develop from total recognition of trade unions through to non recognition and outright opposition. The approach which is most likely to enable the organisation to implement strategic policy is likely to be the most appropriate.

UNIONS

A union is concerned with the employees' terms and conditions, hiring and firing, allocation of work, and matters of discipline. It acts on behalf of the employees that are members by collective bargaining with management. Because of this collective nature, its bargaining power can be substantial. In unionised organisations, management may consult on major changes that it wishes to implement including changes in new products, new markets, new technology, opening and closing of establishments, investment in new equipment. In addition, the union will push for better conditions and pay increases. The union representative can also represent staff in grievance and disciplinary procedures. The role of a union is to protect its members' terms of pay and conditions of employment, and to represent the best interests of employees in the employee relations process. It should also provide advice and guidance to members where required.

When a trade union has recruited a number of members in an organisation, it seeks to be recognised by the organisation to represent these individuals. There is currently no legislation on the percentage of employees that need to be members before an organisation must grant recognition; the employer may refuse and try to create some other way of worker representation. A smaller bargaining unit within an organisation may be recognised, such as operators on the shop floor, even when the workforce as a whole is not represented.

There are a number of different types of management/union relationships. In recent years, a number of organisations have reached specific agreements with a single union for negotiating purposes. An organisation might wish to implement a particular set of personnel policies based on teamwork and employee flexibility. Pirelli, for example, decided that it wanted to choose the most appropriate union to deal with. It sent details of its philosophy to a small number of unions and asked them to make a presentation to the organisation and put their case forward for being the recognised union.

A similar approach was taken by Bosch at its Cardiff plant. The human resources director suggested that the nature of the site and its location meant that recognition of a union would be inevitable in the long run and there would be some disruption in the interim period. Additionally, if the resultant situation involved recognition of more than one union, this would provide greater choice for the employees, but would increase the amount of time spent on negotiation. By putting forward the organisation's philosophy at the outset, one union which was the most appropriate could be chosen. In this case, it was EETPU (now AEEU).

At the other end of the spectrum of employee relations lie non-recognition, derecognition and marginalisation of trade unions. Organisations may decide not to recognise unions as they feel that union involvement will inhibit the achievement of organisational objectives.

Derecognition is increasing as:

- union membership is diminishing and the act of derecognition is not contested by the staff
- partial derecognition is in place with a view to moving towards single union agreements
- collectivism becomes less appropriate in many modern businesses, particularly in the move towards individual contracts
- individuals are taking more responsibility for their working life and changes that require more flexibility not the constraints of a collective situation
- redundancy is regarded as a fact of life and more an issue between the employer and the employee than a union issue.

Some organisations simply work without any union involvement. In the UK, organisations such as Marks and Spencer are well known for non-recognition of unions. Marks and Spencer has adopted the paternalistic approach and provides a substantial range of benefits for staff at all levels in the organisation. Other examples of organisations that do not recognise unions are IBM, Safeway and J Sainsbury. They tend to be organisations which adopt a full package of human resource strategies and practices, so that the benefits offered are perceived to be strong enough to negate the need for union involvement.

The other side of the coin however, shows the organisation, traditionally classed as the 'sweatshop' type of business, in which employees are ruled by fear rather than by rational employment strategies. In new companies, staff often accept that pay will depend on the initial success of the business and will continue in this way for some time, and there will usually be no union involved.

Marginalisation occurs in organisations where management attempts to minimise the role of the unions and the shop stewards (workers' representatives). In this situation, the union may still be involved in collective bargaining, but it is not always involved in other developments, and agreements for time off for union activities might be curtailed. In some instances, organisations reduce the numbers of shop stewards.

There are a number of reasons why organisations benefit from working with unions:

- there may be a certain inevitability of union involvement that has to acknowledged
- agreement by a staff representative or support from the union can legitimise decision making and allow for strategies and change to be implemented effectively
- staff representatives can help in communication and feedback important information from the shop floor
- the staff as a collective whole are in agreement – if, for example, the organisation is paying agreed union rates then individuals will have to

accept this pay and are not in a position to renegotiate their own individual package.

Where they are recognised by the organisation, unions are active in the process of **collective bargaining**. If these negotiations are free from government restrictions, such as pay constraints, this is known as **free collective bargaining**. Collective bargaining can take place at three levels:

- **national advisory level** – where discussion of the economic environment takes place between groups such as the TUC (Trades Union Congress), CBI (Confederation of British Industry) and government representatives
- **national participative level** – involves individual unions, employers' associations and individual employers to conclude agreements made at advisory level
- **local participative level** – where individual unions negotiate with specific employers.

As an alternative to (or in parallel with) trade unions, organisations can create advisory groups such as works or staff committees. These consist of representatives from the staff and management in the organisation. They can also include specific relevant individuals such as safety representatives or quality assurance managers. Works and staff committees can operate in both union and non unionised organisations. Where unions are recognised, representatives from the union tend to automatically be members of the committee.

ACTIVITY 15

Imagine that you have just joined an organisation as a shop floor worker and have been approached by the shop steward and asked to join the union. Give reasons for and against joining.

You would probably want to know the answers to a few questions. What is the union's relationship with management? Is the union recognised? What is the history of industrial relations in the company? Are all other workers members? What other unions are involved in the organisation? What do they do? What have they achieved? What is it going to cost you? Is there any other staff representation? What are the future expectations of the organisation? Is it likely to be bringing about major changes through restructuring or downsizing? Is it profitable? How do terms and conditions and rates of pay compare with competitors? How secure is the job? What are the career prospects?

You might join the union for a number of reasons. In organisations that recognise unions for collective bargaining, you might consider that joining the union will enable your views to be heard, or that you will get the best pay deal that is possible. The union provides protection for employees in disciplinary and grievance situations. Employees might see membership as a means of protection against arbitrary judgements by managers. Peer group pressure 'encourages' many people to join, you won't want to be the only person in your department who hasn't joined. In other cases, employees join due to a belief in collectivism and because of what the union stands for. Where pay and conditions are recognised by the employees as above average, and there is minimal risk of redundancy, you are probably less likely to join a union. If you are not prepared to strike in an extreme situation, then again perhaps you wouldn't join.

EMPLOYEES

Employees have a wide range of views about their work, their employer and the union and what they want or are prepared to accept in terms of employee participation in management decisions that concern them. We can identify seven categories that characterise different types of employee involvement:

- **normative** – individuals have a high sense of moral obligation and shared norms and they would not wish to challenge management, this would be the case, for example, in religious bodies
- **disorganised** – no employee organisation regardless of any collective views
- **organised** – usually through trade unions with more emphasis on grievance procedures than on participation
- **consultative** – employees are asked for opinions about management proposals before they are implemented
- **negotiated** - both parties hold some power so agreement has to be mutual and by bargaining
- **participative** – employees actively participate in management and strategic issues, remember John Lewis's committee system and involvement of its partners in Unit 1
- **controlling** – employees have control of the organisation through, for example, a workers' co-operative.

Employees will have a range of concerns about their work that is very individual to them, their experience, the work, the organisation, and their personal circumstances. Here we have been more concerned about employees as a collective workforce than individuals, but one key skill for HRM is to balance the needs of the individuals with the workforce requirements of the organisation. This has to be carried out with and without union involvement, depending on the organisation. It is helped in this balance by a number of procedures that guide its action with employees, management and the unions, and also by the legislation that cover many factors of an employee's terms and conditions. We look at some procedures and policies next.

4.2 Procedures

Organisations develop and publicise procedures that explain the way in which 'things are done' in the organisation and that clarify the roles of the management, employees and the unions. There has been an increase in the number of procedure agreements over the last 25 years mainly as a result of legislation such as the Industrial Relations Act 1971. Up until this time, for example, it had been possible to dismiss an employee without giving a reason. A procedure is a set of rules for any given situation. Some procedures are required to enact legislation.

Procedural agreements are required to inform staff and managers of actions to take in a variety of circumstances. The procedures have to be flexible and able to change with changing circumstances. New legislation and changing organisational strategies will also bring about the need for procedural review. The procedures should not be an imposition on the way that managers work, but should enable work to be carried out more effectively. The aim of procedures is to attempt to ensure equity and consistency. The procedures should also provide a guide to managers about the aims of the organisation and values in relation to staff, for example, in relation to fairness of treatment.

Organisations might set up procedures covering any or all of the following:

- **grievance** – to specify who is the first point of contact in the case of a complaint from any employee and how the complaint will be handled
- **disciplinary** – to clearly lay out the process in the case where an employee fails to reach specified standards of conduct and work levels
- **equal opportunities** – explains the organisation's policy regarding equality of opportunity and diversity
- **recognition** – the extent of any agreement with unions which might include a definition of the shop steward's role
- **redundancy** – explanation of the organisation's approach to redundancy, means of selection, compensation and employee assistance agreements
- **health and safety** – to define the management and staff roles and to demonstrate an organisation's commitment to looking after its staff
- **new technology** – information on agreements for introduction and implementation of new practices and machinery
- **promotion** – how internal promotion might be achieved, the criteria to be used
- **training and development** – management outlines its policies, what they are designed to achieve for the individual and for the organisation, what opportunities the individual has, how the organisation is responding to government initiatives
- **recruitment and selection** – how recruitment decisions will be made, the composition of selection panels, standard requirements such as probationary periods.

Employees are informed of these procedures, either through the induction process or in writing as part of the contract of employment. In some cases, organisations will issue the procedures in written form as part of an information pack for reference. Procedures are designed primarily by human resource departments. However, they are implemented by line managers with human resource advice and guidance where necessary. The human resource role is to demonstrate to line managers that such procedures have use and value to the organisation and that they can assist in achieving organisational objectives.

It is not appropriate for us to cover all of the procedures in detail. However, we consider some aspects of procedures which impact on all managers and staff in organisations that relate to the legislation on equal opportunities and health and safety. We do not cover the vast range of employment legislation that covers the employer's, the union's and the employee's rights and obligations here.

4.3 Legislation and policies

There are several important Acts within UK legislation that impact on human resource issues.

- **Equal Pay Act 1970** – pay and contractual conditions should be the same for males and females where work is classed as the same through job evaluation or is deemed to be of equal value in decision making, skills and effort.
- **Race Relations Act 1976** – prohibits direct and indirect discrimination on the grounds of colour, race, or ethnic origins. Direct discrimination is where an applicant or employee is treated less favourably than others and indirect is where conditions are imposed which open more opportunities to one group only.
- **Sex Discrimination Act 1976 and 1986** – prohibits direct and indirect discrimination on the grounds of gender or marital status. Where gender is a specific qualification for the job for reasons of decency, authenticity or personal privacy, the act does not apply.
- **Social Security Act 1989** – provides for equality in benefits.
- **Employment Protection (Consolidation) Act 1978** (amended) – gives the right to time off for antenatal care, to maternity leave and to return to work.
- **Disability Discrimination Act 1995** – unlawful for employers with more than 20 employees to treat people with disabilities less favourably than they do other people, unless they can justify the treatment.

Where individuals feel that they have been discriminated against, they can take their case to a tribunal. The publicity from such tribunals is detrimental to organisational image and, if the case is lost, it is financially damaging.

EQUAL OPPORTUNITIES

The legislation we listed above provides the framework for an organisation's equal opportunities policy. In addition, competition for labour market supply means that organisations who do discriminate against certain groups unwittingly, such as women, ethnic minority groups and the disabled, restrict their choice of possibly limited resources. Organisations may actually discriminate in their selection procedures, for example, by their choice of advertising media, but may internally have excellent policies regarding equal pay, creche facilities to support the female workforce with children or special training programmes for mothers returning to work. Organisations which adopt and publicise sound equal opportunities practices develop an enhanced image. These practices result in improved employee relations. In terms of recruitment, selection and internal promotion, image is enhanced as applicants are seen to be treated fairly, regardless of gender, race or disability.

ACTIVITY 16

Consider the responsibilities within the human resources function such as recruitment and selection, appraisals and staff development and describe how Freestyle might use these to foster a culture of equal opportunities or 'diversity management'.

Freestyle can approach the problem in two particular ways: by putting in policies and procedures which ensure that it is 'seen' to comply with the legislation or by taking the approach that the organisation will benefit from a diverse workforce and set about encouraging this view in the employees. The selection process can be used to recruit staff who themselves believe in equal opportunities, particularly at management level. The recruitment and selection process would need to be reviewed to ensure that no discriminatory practice is involved either in the advertising or selection methods, checking for example, whether tests used in recruitment discriminate against women and ethnic groups. If organisations want to encourage equal opportunities, then equal opportunities should be part of the assessment criteria for managers.

So far we have talked about the general benefits of adopting an equal opportunities or diversity policy. One of the criticisms of equal opportunities has been that it is based on a principle of defence – procedures are put in place to prevent the occurrence of industrial tribunals.

HEALTH AND SAFETY

The human resource function has a role to play in the health and safety of the employees. This has developed from the original welfare role we discussed in Section 1. Operating in a safe and healthy environment can only help to improve the effectiveness of the workforce. And if workers are suffering from work-related illnesses or injury then the costs of sickness to organisations are high – both directly in terms of sick pay and lost working hours, and indirectly in terms of organisational image. 'Illness' or absenteeism may also be a symptom of other problems within the organisation as you see later, but the first step the organisation must make is to have a safe working environment. Industrial injury and illness accounts for millions of lost working days every year.

The benefits of a safe working environment are:

- increased productivity
- reduction of costs – in sick pay and staff coverage for absent colleagues
- facilitates employee commitment
- improvement in employee relations as employer either meets or exceeds responsibility
- improvement in quality of product and service.

In the past, little emphasis has been placed on health and safety. It was generally accepted in some industries that 'there are risks in the job'. In the 1970s, the Robens committee was set up to scrutinise occupational health and its recommendations formed the basis of the 1974 Health and Safety at Work Act (HASAWA). This placed responsibility on both the employer and employee (see Table 4). The general aims of HASAWA were to:

- streamline and simplify existing legislation
- cover all categories of people in the workplace
- centralise and co-ordinate the system of enforcement
- strengthen the powers of the inspectors.

The employer should:	**The employee should:**
provide safe systems of work	take reasonable care for own and others' safety
ensure safety and absence of risk to health	co-operate with the employers as far as necessary to execute statutory duties
provide education and training	not intentionally misuse or damage equipment
maintain the workplace to make it free from risk	
ensure safe access and entry	
set up safety committees with representatives from management, staff and unions	

Table 4: Responsibilities of employers and employees under the Health and Safety at Work Act

In addition to those issues identified in Table 4, under the Act employers are required to ensure that:

- an effective health and safety policy exists
- responsibilities are clearly defined
- the policy is known by all.

In 1988, the Control of Substances Hazardous to Health (COSHH) regulations were introduced. There are five main features of these regulations which impact on the workplace. Employers become responsible for assessing the risks and identifying what precautions are needed to limit risk, and for introducing measures which control or prevent risk in the workplace. They have to ensure that control measures are used, procedures are followed and equipment is regularly maintained. Health surveillance has to be carried out and there has to be provision of information to employees and training given.

In the 1990s, European Union directives under article 189 of the Treaty of Rome provided a framework for action. These are binding but the member states can decide how to give them legal and administrative effect. In the UK, they are normally expressed in the form of regulations which are published with codes of practice. Examples include directives on manual handling and use of VDUs.

Risk assessment in the COSHH regulations was expanded into a general requirement by the 1992 Code of Practice for the Management of Health and Safety at Work. As a result, some organisations introduced risk assessment managers to be responsible for implementation of risk management, thus taking a proactive approach to health and safety. Organisations should be aware of possible risks to employees and determine the action required to reduce those risks, in order to prevent accidents and occupational dangers to health.

Our comments here just give you a brief introduction to the legislation that exists to ensure that employers and employees work in such a way that there is minimal risk to health in the workplace. Other issues, such as absenteeism, which are in the domain of human resource specialists and line managers also concern the overall sense of well being in an organisation.

ABSENTEEISM

Millions of pounds are lost by industry each year by absence, both directly and in lost production. Absence for any reason is a cost to the organisation. Responsibility for its control lies with both human resource departments and with line managers. Risk assessment is a means of identifying some of the problems within an organisation and implementing procedures to prevent accidents and absenteeism.

Occupational stress has been the focus of research in organisations for some time and although this was assumed to be a feature of managerial work, it has been identified as a problem at a number of levels in organisations. American research identified the most stressful jobs as secretary and manual labourer (Bratton and Gold, 1994). According to the Royal College of Nursing, stress is responsible for nearly half of all sickness absence among nurses – 45 per cent of absence is stress related *(People Management*, 21 December 1995, p. 6). The case of *Walker vs. Northumberland County Council* demonstrated that stress was the factor which forced an individual from the job, and it reinforced the view that organisations could no longer simply accept stress as 'normal'. There obviously are some stressful elements in all jobs, but in some cases these reach unacceptable levels.

The COSHH regulations, extended by the 1992 Code of Practice for the Management of Health and Safety at Work, concern risk assessment and require organisations to recognise the causes of stress. Factors such as role ambiguity, work overload, inequity, frustration including mechanical failures, job design, harassment, 'dual-role syndrome' where staff have conflicting roles at work and home are all recognised as potential stress inducers. Stress traditionally was regarded as the individual's problem, but now organisations are taking more responsibility for reducing stress in the workplace. This change has happened through the legislation and also through the recognition that it costs the organisation so much money and the change in attitude is to the value of the workforce.

One option offered by Cable Midlands in 1995 was to offer stress management workshops. In addition, the company chose a range of different approaches ranging from alternative health treatments such as aromatherapy through to confidential counselling. It has seen significant developments that include reduction in absence and turnover and evidence of a positive attitude towards the organisation. Although Cable Midlands decided against telephone counselling, other organisations have found this to be useful. The Employment Service introduced an Employee Assistance Programme (EAP) which includes both face-to-face and telephone counselling.

Practical solutions concern the actual design of jobs and task allocation. The introduction of 'family friendly' policies has been encouraged during the last few years to try to alleviate some of the stresses caused by the dual role, but also to enable groups such as women with children back into the workplace. The government welfare-to-work programme announced in 1997, should provide additional childcare resources in the marketplace through training of single mothers.

REVIEW ACTIVITY 4

Read this letter of resignation that has been received from one of Freestyle's part-time retail sales assistants.

Dear Mr Green

I wish you to accept this letter of resignation as from today. I feel that I have to write to you as I have finally had enough, but nobody seems to be prepared to listen. I have worked for you for four years and during that time have never taken any time off – even though I have sometimes had to pay extra to childminders when my children have been ill and I have been due to work. I accepted when I took the job that this might happen, but I believed that I should be able to resolve these problems if I took on the hours. I have often done extra hours if there has been a crisis and there have been plenty of those during the last 4 years!

I asked for some time off in two weeks time as my husband was made redundant six months ago and has been lucky to get another job. However, it is in Scotland and he will have to be away from home for periods of time when he takes up the appointment. I was told that there were too many people off work at that time and so I cannot take the holiday, even if I take it unpaid. I was told that only two people were allowed to be on holiday at any time and two were already booked for the dates that I wanted. I did not know anything about this rule, which my supervisor now tells me has always existed and that 'you should know that by now!'. None of the other staff that I work with are aware of this. I have also been told that my hours will change again next week and will include Saturdays. I have had my days and hours changed four times since I joined and I have always tried to fit in with them, but I told the lady who interviewed me for the job that I could not work weekends because of the children and I took the job on this basis.

I am the only person in the branch with more than two year's service and am often left on my own when staff are off sick. I have sometimes had the store keys and have had to lock up at night and arrive early the next day to open up for the cleaners. I have received no extra pay for this – however I am not complaining about that but about the lack of any recognition for any of this. I have also now found out that I am paid less per hour that the new full-time lad who has joined us and he has also been told he will be made up to supervisor if he works well, as they really need a male member of staff with the store keys for security reasons. There have been a number of accidents in the store, particularly after a delivery when there is always a lot of stock left around the rear entrance to the store for days. We have complained to the manager, but he claimed that there is nothing that can be done about it. If we had a union, none of this would happen!

Jane Smith

Jane Smith
Newtown branch

Obviously an unhappy member of staff! What problems are identified within the letter? Set out what action you think that Ian and Amy should take.

Summary

In this section, we have investigated some aspects of the relationship between the employer and employees. This may or may not be through the intervention of unions. We looked at some of the issues that unionisation affects. Legislation has been drawn up that affects many of the interactions between the employer and the employee and, if the company is unionised, the union. This legislation needs to inform the set of procedures drawn up by human resources to guide the action of all parties. Some areas where the organisation and the individual may have particular concerns include equal opportunities, and health and safety. Although legislation covers many aspects, the organisation needs to have a policy that fosters both the individuals' and the organisation's wellbeing.

Unit Review Activity

You have just taken up an appointment as personnel manager in Bailey's department store. The previous manager left the store a year ago after 30 years of service having started as a sales assistant. Over the years, she had been promoted and had spent her last five years before retiring as the personnel manager. Any 'personnel' issues have been dealt with by either the deputy store manager or the personnel clerk during the last year.

During the last few weeks you have been made aware of a number of complaints from customers about the service that they have received while in the store. The last complaint was made by a customer who was extremely unhappy with the level of service. She wanted a particular brand of iron and electric toaster for her niece who was getting married in two weeks. She had visited the store twice in the last two weeks but had found that the items were not available, even though they had been promoted in the local and national press. She had seen the department manager, who, although very polite and pleasant, started his conversation by telling her that the item was in fact on sale, as he had taken delivery of it the previous week. He pointed her in the direction of electrical goods, telling her exactly where the items could be found. Not surprisingly, when the customer went back to check 'that my eyes had not deceived me' and found that the neither the iron nor the toaster were on display, she tried to find the manager – but he had disappeared. The customer angrily approached a member of staff and demanded to speak to the store manager, but by now he was at a head office meeting. You have been called to deal with her and receive a litany of complaint.

> 'This store is appalling. The staff cannot be expected to know anything about the stock, which is fortunate, because they have absolutely no idea of what stock you carry; the managers do not even know what stock is on sale or what deliveries they have taken in. You are always putting adverts into the papers just to get us poor customers into the store, when in fact the stock has never been here in the first place.
>
> 'Last time I came to the store, it took me ten minutes to find a member of staff, and when I did she was too busy talking to her friend to take any notice of me. Fortunately another member of staff came onto the department, but she told me that she was new that day and had no idea what stock was in as she had started work at 9 o'clock. This was at 10 o'clock! I am not surprised that she didn't know anything, but that didn't excuse her rudeness, and are they allowed to

chew gum when they are serving? When I finally did find out that one of the items I wanted was not in stock, I then couldn't get served at the tills. They were all full of customers, but only two out of the ten were open. It is like this all the time. There are never enough tills open for the customers, and the staff are so slow – that day the customer in front of me wanted to pay by credit card and the boy on the till didn't know what to do with it. In the end she left the item as he asked her to pay by cash, and she said she was going elsewhere and would not shop in the store again.

'The store is filthy; last week one of my friends slipped in the store on some face cream that a member of your staff had spilt on the floor and hadn't bothered to clean up. I know that because the girl was standing there when Jane slipped, and she actually said that she was sorry, she meant to clear it up but she was busy. Not only that, but there was no one around to see to Jane, to check that she was all right. Fortunately her husband came in to find her and took her home. She sprained her ankle you know.

'Every time I come in here there are different staff. I don't suppose that you can keep them – they are paid less than everyone else for a start, but they never know anything when you ask them for help. When Sherwood's opens at the other end of town, we will all be going there. One thing's for certain, you shouldn't lose any staff to them, I doubt if they would have them. I have been shopping in this store for the past ten years, and the standards have just simply gone downhill'.

Apparently this is not the only customer who has been complaining. When you and the store manager talk to the staff, you find that these complaints are commonplace and that the staff believe that it is inevitable that they will lose business to Sherwood's when it opens and many are planning to apply there for jobs! You discuss the problems with the store manager, who is also newly appointed. You have agreed to make some recommendations as to how these problems could be resolved.

List the HR related problems identified in the case study. It might help to consider why you as a customer would be frustrated by the situation.

Produce a report containing your recommendations for action. At this stage, you cannot make any assumptions about the causes, therefore you will need to consider the areas covered in HRM and decide which of those will need to be reviewed and why.

Unit Summary

Effective people management in organisations is essential, as it impacts strongly upon the organisation's ability to achieve its objectives. In this unit, we have studied the human resource management function in organisations and become aware of the debate which exists within people management about personnel management and HRM. Organisational success requires not only the recognition that people are the source of competitive advantage but it needs effective people management.

We have examined some of the roles and responsibilities within the function, all of which are carried out in organisations either by the human resource and/or personnel specialists or by line managers where no specialist role exists.

We have investigated the reasons why effective human resource planning is needed by organisations. We have examined the process and procedures for recruitment and selection of staff, highlighting the impact of inadequate planning, execution and evaluation of those procedures. We have studied the different selection methods available, and have demonstrated their possible uses and noted some of the problems inherent in them.

We have considered why training is needed in organisations and have studied the various forms that training and development can take. How people learn should be taken into account in setting up training programmes and there are other factors involved in the choice of training method. We have studied the various forms of staff assessment and appraisal and again considered their possible uses for specific groups of staff.

Employee relations is a vital role in organisations for effective HRM. We have considered the role of unions in this process. Employment legislation including health and safety legislation provide a framework for relations and a basis for procedures developed by HRM.

References

Armstrong, M (1989) 'Personnel director's view from the bridge' *Personnel Management*, October

Armstrong, M (1991) *A Handbook of Personnel Management Practice*, Kogan Page

Bratton, J and Gold, J (1994), *Human Resource Management Theory and Practice*, Macmillan.

Fraser, M J (1966) *Employment Interviewing*, McDonald & Evans

Honey, P and Mumford, A (1981) *A Manual of Learning Styles*, Honey

Hutchinson, S (1995) 'Variations on the partnership model' *People Management*, November 1995

IRS *Employment Trends 570*, October 1994

Purcell, J and Sisson, K (1983) 'Strategies and practices in the management of industrial relations' in Bain, G S (ed.) *Industrial Relations in Britain*, Basil Blackwell

Reid, M A and Barrington, H (1994) *Training Interventions*, Institute of Personnel Development

Riding, R (1993) *A Trainer's Guide to Learning Design*, Learning Methods Project Report OL201, Employment Department

Rodger, A (1952) *The Seven Point Plan*, National Institute for Industrial Psychology

Sisson, K (1994) *Personnel Management: A Comprehensive Guide to Theory and Practice in Britain*, Blackwell.

Storey, J (1992) *Developments in the Management of Human Resources*, Blackwell

Torrington, D and Hall, L (1995) *Personnel Management: A New Approach*, Prentice Hall.

Recommended Reading

Allen, K R (1991) 'Personnel management on the line: How middle managers view the function' *Personnel Management*, June 1991

Beardwell, I and Holden, L (1995) *Human Resource Management: A Contemporary Approach*, Pitman

Butler, S (1996) 'Alternative ways to take out stress' *People Management*, 16 May

Clements, A (1996) 'Probing into recruitment' *Retail Week*, 11 October

Fair, H (1992) *Personnel and Profit*, Institute of Personnel Management

Ford, V (1996) 'Partnership is the secret of progress' *People Management*, 8 February

Fowler, A (1994) 'The way we were 1969–1994' *Personnel Management*, December

Fowler, A (1996) 'How to pick a job evaluation system' *People Management*, 8 February

Guest, D (1989) 'Personnel and HRM: can you tell the difference?' *Personnel Management*, January

Hendry, C (1995) *Human Resource Management: A Strategic Approach to Employment*, Butterworth Heinemann

IRS *Employment Trends 568*, September 1994

Institute of Personnel and Development (1997) *Key Facts: Recruitment,* Institute of Personnel Development

Irving, I (1997) 'Seasoned campaigners' *People Management*, 20 March

Lee, R (1996) 'The pay forward view of training' *People Management*, 8 February

McHenry, R (1997) 'Tried and tested' *People Management*, 23 January

Manpower Services Commission (1981) *Glossary of Training Terms*

Marchington, M and Wilkinson, A (1996) *Core Personnel and Development*, Institute of Personnel Development

Purcell, J and Sisson, K (1983) 'Strategies and practices in the management of industrial relations' in Bain, G S (ed.) *Industrial Relations in Britain*, Basil Blackwell

Rees, T (1992) *Women and the Labour Market*, Routledge

Rothwell, S (1995) 'Does human resource management make a difference' *Labour Force Survey* 1995, HMSO

Schuler, H, Farr, JL and Smith, M (1993) *Personnel Selection and Assessment: Individual and Organisational Perspectives*, Lawrence Erlbaum

Sisson, K (1994) *Personnel Management: A Comprehensive Guide to Theory and Practice in Britain*, Blackwell.

Storey, J and Sisson, K (1994) *Managing Human Resources and Industrial Relations*, OUP

Storey, J (1996) 'Is HRM catching on?' *International Journal of Manpower*, vol. 16 no. 4

Thatcher, M (1996) 'Bouncing back from the scrapheap at 41' *People Management*, 11 January

Torrington, D, Hall, L, Haylor, I and Briggs, J (1992) *Employee Resourcing*, IPM

Uncle, M (1995) 'Viewpoint: securing competitive advantage through progressive staffing policies' *International Journal of Retail and Distribution Management,* vol. 23 no. 7

Answers to Review Activities

Review Activity 1

HRM might include any, or all, of these tasks:

- recruitment and selection
- workforce planning
- budgeting
- welfare
- personnel administration and documentation
- training and development
- industrial relations – dealing and negotiating with trade unions
- performance appraisals
- disciplinary procedures
- staff counselling
- employee development
- team development
- quality control
- employee records
- public relations
- reward management
- productivity agreements

- developing organisational culture
- drawing up policies and procedures and matching them with the organisation's values and beliefs.

Review Activity 2

Job description: since you already have a job description, you need only check that nothing has changed since it was drawn up.

Person specification: draw up a list of the skills, knowledge and attributes of an individual who could do the job described in the job description. Specify which of these are essential at appointment and which could be acquired later.

Attracting the applicant: advertise in the local press and in a trade journal.

Selection: you will have to decide what selection method you think is best. Choose one, or a combination, of application forms, interviews, an assessment centre and tests.

Evaluation: you should evaluate the recruitment process by analysing the number of responses to each advertisement, the number of applicants shortlisted and invited to the interview, the number who attended the interview, whether the offer was accepted, whether the appointee is still in post in six months, and quality of the appointee's performance at that time.

Review Activity 3

The induction programme should be an introduction to the organisation's aims, objectives and strategy. It should include information on:

- the payroll
- training and development opportunities
- details on assessment and probationary period
- absence procedure
- organisation structure – who's who, what to do if a problem arises
- grievance and disciplinary procedures
- health and safety introductory training setting out the employee's responsibilities.

It could, depending upon the jobs that the new staff have been recruited to carry out, include any team building, interpersonal skills training and customer care training.

The one-day programme could be divided up into blocks which could be interspersed with on-the-job training. An important factor to remember is that new staff are apprehensive and that the trainer's role in the first instance is to try to alleviate fears and worries. Table 5 contains a suggested programme.

Session	**Topic**	**Method**
1	Introductory session aims and objectives	Informal discussion and presentation to group by trainer
2	Background to the organisation	Presentation by trainer
3	Customer service	Video and group discussion
4	Teamwork	Group exercise to identify the skills required
5	Health and safety in the organisation	Case study on an organisation, video and hazard spotting exercise
6	What to do if?	Question and answer session covering new entrants' problems, general enquiries
7	Summary, feedback and evaluation	Led by trainer – a summary of the day's work.

Table 5: Suggested induction training programme

The appraisal used at this level could involve appraisal by the immediate manager together with self assessment. The timescales involved should be determined for the organisation as a whole but assessment during and at the end of the probationary period is essential. Once this period has been successfully completed either an annual or biannual appraisal would be useful. In terms of performance assessment, this should be regularly carried out during the probationary period. Each task involved should be assessed against the expected standards and a record made of the employee's competence or non competence. Obviously, retraining should take place as required.

Review Activity 4

Hopefully, you have identified some or all of the following points:

- there seem to be no holiday rotas
- there are no written procedures that staff can refer to
- staff are not informed of any procedures that relate to their terms and conditions
- inadequate planning in terms of rotas and hours worked
- staff are operating at a different level to that which they are paid for or employed to do
- staff are not paid for taking on extra responsibility
- opportunities for promotion arise on an *ad hoc* basis
- lack of fair treatment in pay
- obvious discriminatory practice and attitudes both regarding pay and gender
- no grievance procedures
- lack of awareness of health and safety procedures.

In general, there is poor people management being practised in the branch. There appears to be a communication problem. Recruitment and selection procedures should be reviewed to check that records are made of specific agreements made on interview, although these circumstances might change in the future, one week's notice of such a change is inadequate. The induction must include information on procedures for time off. Those procedures should be recorded either in a staff handbook or displayed on a notice board for staff. Staff should also be aware of the grievance procedures. If staff are aware of the rules and regulations, they are probably less likely to be aggrieved by them.

Ian and Amy will need to investigate the jobs being carried out in the units and perhaps carry out some form of job evaluation exercise to identify exactly what staff are expected to do in each job role. A review of pay also needs to be carried out to ensure equity of payment within the organisation. A union could undoubtedly work for employees to try to resolve these issues. The organisation can, however, take the necessary steps to improve communication and work practices and procedures. Freestyle is about to lose a skilled and experienced member of staff who apparently has been loyal to the organisation – it seems to be a loss that it cannot afford to take considering its current labour turnover figures and planned expansion.

The health and safety training of the manager needs to be reviewed and a check carried out to identify the problem and to implement better procedures within the branch. It is likely that the problem is not isolated to this branch alone and Ian and Amy will need to check all units.

Answer to Unit Review Activity

Identified problems:

- stock not available although advertised
- stock delivered but not on sale
- staff 'telling' customers that stock is on sale without checking
- no follow up by managers of customer problems
- perceived image of staff and managers is poor
- assumption by customers that advertisements are misleading
- inappropriate staff levels for customer demand
- new staff on departments with no training
- perceived high labour turnover
- perceived low rates of pay for staff
- image and behaviour of staff does not match customer expectations
- insufficient customer service points open, staff are slow and do not know the payment procedures
- store is filthy
- no responsibility taken by staff for safety.

You might assume that this has very little to do with the personnel department but there are a number of issues which can be resolved with its help. There is no doubt that a competitor in the town will impact on sales. If the staff are the source of competitive advantage, the current problems will encourage customers to change allegiance.

The personnel manager will have to take a number of actions.

- Review human resource planning. Go through the stages of human resource and manpower planning to analyse the current staffing skills and expertise. An analysis of staffing levels against sales will be needed. In this case, it will be essential that the personnel manager works with line managers to obtain appropriate information. In addition, an analysis of labour turnover and absenteeism would provide invaluable information – the current perceived shortages of staff might not be as a result of poor planning but as a result of absenteeism.
- Review the skills in the store and carry out a training needs analysis to highlight training gaps that might currently exist and to highlight skills needs to enable the store to stave off competition.
- Consider the current situation regarding induction. What does it consist of? Is it compulsory? Who should and does carry it out?
- Review recruitment and selection criteria and review against organisational aims and objectives. Do the selection criteria match skills, knowledge and attributes requirements to achieve those objectives?

Remember Do It All's approach to recruitment of customer service staff. This review will need to include recruitment and selection procedures for all employees as it seems that managers present a poor image to both staff and customers.

- Review health and safety procedures and how these are explained to staff. Training needs might have been highlighted by the training review. On the other hand, it might be that the concern for health and safety, as with concern for customer care, is a criterion that should be brought into the recruitment and selection procedures.

UNIT 8

BUSINESS STRATEGY

Introduction

Every year in Britain thousands of new businesses are created. A few will grow to become global companies employing thousands of people, others will never make the world stage; in fact, the majority will cease trading within two or three years.

To survive, managers need a good understanding of the business environment, the opportunities and threats it offers, a realistic appreciation of the abilities and limitations of the business, knowledge of what they want to achieve, and a fairly clear idea of the direction in which the business should go. The route the business takes to achieve its objectives is often known as the **corporate** or **business strategy**. In this unit, we look at some of the tools that we can use to decide on the strategy. As you will see, the tools we describe are those which link the various functions of the business and are to do with operating the business as a complete organisation rather than as a collection of functions or departments. The business strategy concerns the overall direction of the organisation. Here, we consider the operational or functional strategies that contribute to the business strategy.

We start by looking at key issues involved in setting strategy and at a process for choosing the strategy. Then, in Unit 9, we examine how to convert the broad strategy into a business plan and, finally, we will explore some of the project planning techniques which can be used to help implement strategy.

Objectives

By the end of this unit, you will be able to:

- explain how businesses need to align their objectives and capabilities with the needs of their customers and with the environment
- give examples of business objectives, mission and value statements
- understand how the business environment provides opportunities for the business but also limit its freedom of action
- explain how the resources and behaviour of the organisation constrain the choice of strategy
- describe a range of business strategies and explain the circumstances in which they might be appropriate for a business
- describe how an organisation copes with an uncertain future and responds to complex environmental change.

SECTION 1

Environment, Values and Resources

Introduction

In this module, we have covered two broad areas: the main features of an organisation and the nature and effects of its environment, and the functions and processes of the organisation and how they add value. In this section, we link the two areas by examining the need for the business to ensure continually that it has the ability to:

- meet the needs of its customers by offering products and services that people want to buy
- achieve the objectives required by its stakeholders (owners, staff, shareholders, etc.) in an appropriate way
- use its resources and capabilities well.

This process is sometimes referred to as achieving E-V-R congruence, that is aligning the demands of environment with the values and resources of the business (Thompson, 1993). In this section, we describe how:

- the **environment** determines the opportunities, constraints and threats that face the business, for example, the level of competition, the technology that can be used, the wage rates, the expected dividend on shares, etc.
- the **values** identify the objectives of the key stakeholders, the approach they want the business to take and the scope of the business activities
- the **resources** (staff, finances, equipment, systems, etc.) determine the capability of the business, its strengths and weaknesses.

In re-examining these issues, we will go back over the material in previous units, but here we will be specifically looking at them from the perspective of the organisation as a whole not as a number of parts, and from the perspective of achieving competitive advantage and maintaining the continuing success. If a business is going to survive for long, it must have a balance between what its stakeholders want to happen, the **values**, what it is actually capable of making happen through the effective and efficient use of its **resources**, and what is feasible within the prevailing **environment**.

Say, for example, you wanted to run an enterprise making and selling televisions from your garage (the values). But, if the local council will not give you planning permission (the environment) and you have not got the manufacturing equipment (the resources) to produce them as cheaply as, say, Sony, you will not succeed. It is only when the environment, values and resources overlap, and we have E-V-R congruence, that the business will be able to operate successfully (see Figure 1). Overlap will not happen by accident, somebody must make it happen and ensure that overlap is maintained.

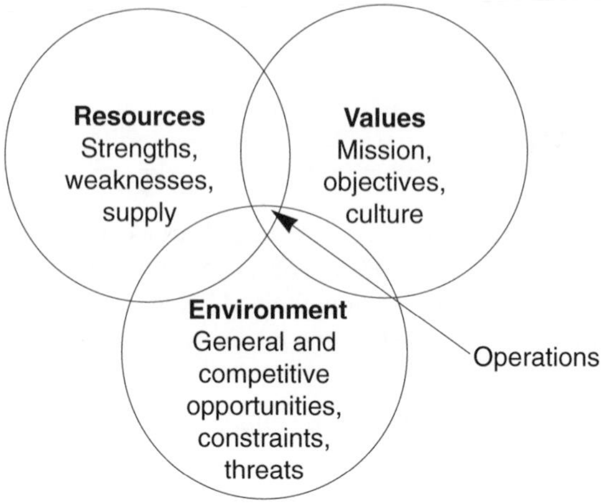

Figure 1: E-V-R congruence

It is a mistake to think that it is possible to forecast the future in any detail. In the short term, the business manager can only strive to make the best use of the existing resources. In the long term, the manager should set out to orientate the business values to maximise the overlap with the expected future environmental conditions and to develop strong, flexible resources capable of exploiting successfully a range of possible future opportunities. With any luck, at least one of the opportunities will come about.

1.1 Values

Values identify the objectives of the key stakeholders, and how the business goes about achieving the objectives. The business mission defines the nature of the business it is in and the markets it serves, while the values statement identifies the core beliefs and policies of the business. In Unit 1, we identified the crucial role that the organisation's objectives and mission have as the basis for mapping out its future success. We also identified the role that the stakeholders play both in the mission and in the overall organisational culture that enable and encourage these objectives to be met. In our context here, we can bring these issues together and describe values as encompassing:

- the objectives the business is trying to achieve
- the overall way that the business attempts to achieve these objectives.

We look at this in more detail here in the context of the business's strategy as without recognising what an organisation wants to do in an overall sense and at a more detailed objective level, it is pointless investigating and detailing a precise and very directed strategy. As the saying goes, if you don't know where you are going, then any road will take you there. We need to understand and clarify what the objectives and the mission actually mean for a particular organisation. The mission defines the overall **corporate strategy** of an organisation; the business objectives define the **competitive strategy**; which leads finally to the **functional strategy** of each function.

We start by looking at some examples of objectives and mission statements. In many organisations, the values are unwritten, they have just developed over time and everybody knows (more or less) what the business is trying to achieve and how its going to do it. However, more businesses are now publishing their values as they find it helps to reduce ambiguity, helps staff to understand their role and other stakeholders to understand how the organisation will behave.

MISSION, BUSINESS OBJECTIVES AND VALUES

Organisations have a range of terms that describe what they hope to achieve. These include mission, aims, objectives, business objective statement, value statement, promise, vision, commitment, and goals. These vary enormously in complexity, detail and measurability; they may indicate a broad feeling about what the organisation values or specific details about what it hopes to achieve and when. You met a number of these different ideas in Unit 1 when we looked at some mission statements.

Generally speaking, the statement of business objectives identifies what the key stakeholders want to derive from the organisation, the mission and value statements identify how it will go about it. The mission defines the nature of the business it is in and the markets it serves. For example, the mission statement of BT is:

> 'BT's mission, our central purpose, is to provide world-class telecommunications and information products and services, and to develop and exploit our networks, at home and overseas...'

This mission statement tells us the product areas BT wants to exploit (telecommunications and information products and services), the target markets (home and overseas) and the focus of the operations (the networks). In its 1996 annual report, BT stated that its aim was 'to become the most successful worldwide telecommunications group'. This suggests that BT is concerned about market share and customer perceptions. It is unlikely to get involved in some other business, say, the hotel industry, but it will concentrate on its core business, and possibly take over other companies that perform similar functions. In 1997, BT was trying to buy MCI, America's second biggest long distance telephone operator; this obviously fits in with its 'worldwide' aim.

Some organisations also include a value statement with the mission. The **value statement** identifies the core beliefs and policies of the business, and indicates how it intends to behave towards its stakeholders. Marks and Spencer in its 1996 annual report stated it was committed to:

> '... putting the customer first at all times. To this end we are determined to sell only merchandise of the highest quality at outstanding values. We are determined to offer the highest standard of customer care in an attractive shopping environment and aim to improve standards continually throughout our operations using the latest technology. We establish mutually rewarding, long-term partnerships with our suppliers, developing overseas sources to serve our expanding international business, at the same time maintaining support for our British supplier base. We aim to minimise the environmental impact of our activities. We nurture good human relations with staff, customers and the community, and ensure staff and shareholders share in our success.'

Marks and Spencer's motto is 'quality, value and service worldwide'. In 1997, the company bought 19 high street stores from Littlewoods giving 600,000 sq. ft. of extra selling space in prime locations throughout Britain, providing the customer with more convenience and opportunity to purchase. Clearly business development such as this would need to be consistant with the mission statement.

The mission and value statement can be particularly useful to staff and other stakeholders as they clearly identify the range of activities the organisation is prepared to consider and the way it wants to do business. However, developing mission and value statements can be a long and complex process as it involves a great deal of consultation within the organisation. In fact, many organisations choose not to develop them, preferring to allow an unwritten 'way of doing things' to emerge. The mission and value statement can be a useful starting point for developing strategy, or something that might be put together after developing strategy.

Publishing the business objectives helps staff to understand what is required of them and helps other stakeholders to predict the way the business is likely to act. For example, Hanson plc, a manufacturing conglomerate, said in its 1990 annual report:

> 'We aim to enhance shareholder value by increased earnings per share and dividends, generated through profitable internal growth, selective acquisitions and control of positive cash flow from our companies.'

Hanson's objective is clearly to make money for the shareholders, consequently the company will be very concerned about levels of profitability. It has been through a phase of mergers and takeovers. In the late 1990s, Hanson 'demerged' and sold parts of the business as it sought to get rid of unprofitable companies.

A business objective should state what the organisation is trying to achieve and why it is trying to achieve it. The BT mission and aim and the Hanson objective statement give a fairly clear idea of what the organisations are trying to achieve. BT's aim is rather vague and not measurable so it would be fairly difficult to say if it is actually making progress towards its objective, even with knowledge of all its acquisitions and the company's performance. It all depends upon how 'success' and 'telecommunications' are defined. These objectives are called **open** objectives. Conversely, if an objective is expressed in terms of achieving a **measurable** result in a particular **timescale**, it is called a **closed** objective. Is the Hanson objective open or closed? There's no timescale, so it's open, even though shareholders' dividends would be easy to measure.

Closed business objectives usually refer to the achievement, within a given timescale, of a target level of one of the following:

- profit
- return on investment
- growth of turnover
- market share
- value added per employee.

ACTIVITY 1

It is common for published objectives to be open, and for those used within the business to be closed. Note down at least three reasons why businesses tend to adopt this practice.

It is generally thought that when organisations set clear, closed objectives it motivates staff in their work. What you measure is what you get, so this is a good reason for writing closed objectives for internal use. Because closed objectives are measurable and are set within a timescale, they can be used by management as trigger points. For example, if the actual production falls below 90 per cent of the objective (target) level then productivity increases must be triggered to get back to the required level.

However, most businesses have competitors that are only too keen to find out what they are planning to do. Publishing closed objectives could give competitors vital information. Also, as most business activities are only partially successful, objectives are often changed before they can be fully achieved. So publicising closed objectives could easily lay management open to criticism, especially by the shareholders. As a result, objectives for public consumption are usually open – nobody can tell whether they have been achieved!

CASE STUDY

George Stares and Reg Pearce

Poor health kept George Stares and Reg Pearce out of the armed forces during the Second World War. George Stares had found a job as a salesman and Reg Pearce spent the war years as a tool-maker. At the end of the war they formed a company, Pyramid Toys Limited, to make and sell die-cast toys. Both men had young families and saw the business as a way of making a living, with the possibility of making a fortune. One of their early products was a clockwork scale model train set; by die-casting (a technique used to mould metal) aluminium components they were able to create a level of detail that was previously unknown. As a result, the train set found a ready market with both children and collectors and the company grew rapidly.

In 1952, the fortunes of the company took a reverse. The Korean War started and all supplies of aluminium were allocated to the manufacture of military equipment, bringing the production of the toy trains to a halt. Determined to keep the business going, George and Reg searched around for new products and through their existing links with Woolworth's came up with a card and paper product known as the Mickey Mouse Playpad. This was an instant success and over the next few years the company again grew steadily.

However, by the late 1950s, sales of the playpad started to decline and the search was on for new products. A range of new plastics was coming on to the market and Reg Pearce started experimenting with products made from PVC sheet. By the early 1960s, he had developed a range of PVC office products: pen holders, desk tidies, folders, coasters and telephone indexes. Initially these were a great success, especially the telephone index. The company changed its name to Cayse Limited as it felt the old name, Pyramid Toys, was no longer appropriate, and set about increasing its range of PVC products. Despite many attempts, it was unable to find a product as successful as the telephone index and the Cayse Limited traded through the 1960s with a stable turnover and a workforce of about 25 people.

In the early 1970s, with their children grown-up, George Stares and Reg Pearce decided to sell up and retire. However, inflation soon eroded their savings, and by the early 1980s Reg Pearce was back in business making automatic assembly machines. During his 'retirement', an old business colleague had asked him to produce a device that would fix the sticky pads on to the backs of self-adhesive mirror tiles. The machine Reg Pearce designed proved so successful that he ended up making over a dozen similar machines in his garage at home. The reputation of these machines spread and orders followed for a wide variety of automation equipment. Eventually, lack of garage space forced Reg Pearce to put the business on a proper footing and acquire factory premises. The new business flourished and by the time of his death in 1989, Reg Pearce was providing equipment to many of the world's multinational engineering companies.

Source: Prepared by the authors based on information kindly provided by Mrs N M Pearce

ACTIVITY 2

Read the case study about the business careers of George Stares and Reg Pearce.

1 Describe and compare Reg Pearce's business objectives in 1948, 1968 and 1988.

2 List the events which brought about the changes in objectives.

In 1948, the company had just got going. The directors' personal objectives were to 'earn a living and perhaps make a fortune' so the business objective was one of 'maintaining rapid growth and maximising the benefit to the shareholders'. By 1968, the objective had changed to 'maintain current turnover and profitability in order to preserve the standard of living of the shareholders and staff'. In 1988, the business objective for Reg Pearce had become something like 'make a profit by producing sophisticated machines and enjoy myself while doing it'.

By 1968, Reg Pearce and George Stares were making a comfortable living from the company, their children had left home and the business had become, to some extent, routine. There was no longer the desire to make a fortune so the objective became 'stability'. By 1988, spurred on by his recent success, Reg Pearce was enjoying himself using his skills as an engineer and seeing how far he could take his new business.

This short case study highlights how it is not just customers and competitors that make businesses change direction. The values of the key stakeholders, Reg Pearce and George Stares in this case, can change over time. As we saw in Figure 1, if the values change then the business will probably have to find a new target area of operation involving new skills and resources. The case study also illustrates how businesses can develop, not through detailed forward planning, but by taking advantage of opportunities that present themselves. The skills of Reg and George were in spotting the good opportunities.

ACTIVITY 3

In our area there were very few play facilities for children in the local parks. With some friends we decided to do something about it. The local council agreed that if we could raise £50,000 it would purchase, install and maintain suitable play equipment (swings, slides, etc.).

One of our group was on an arts and design course and had designed a novel table lamp. We thought we could probably produce these lamps and sell them at a profit of £2 a time. In fact, things went better than we had hoped. The council provided us with a small factory unit, the local college helped us set up the production equipment, a retired businessman agreed to man the phone and do the administration, and we found a wholesaler that was willing to market the lamp. We called ourselves Playlight. Over time, we designed a range of lamps and every evening, with the help of a growing band of enthusiastic helpers, we assembled and packed them. By the end of the 18 months we had raised the £50,000 and 3 months later the play equipment was installed.

Write down an open business objective for the Playlight organisation for external publication and a closed business objective for internal use, and set out mission and value statements. (Take no longer than 30 minutes.)

The open objective would be something like 'through the efforts of local people, to raise money to provide play equipment in the local parks'. The closed objective could be 'to create and run a business which will generate £50,000 in 18 months which will be used to place specified play equipment in the parks by month 21'. The mission of the business could be 'to provide playground equipment for local parks by running a successful business producing lighting equipment for sale in the UK'.

The value statement would indicate how the needs of the different key stakeholders will be satisfied:

- staff – by working together and respecting each others' abilities, they are able to satisfy their common desire to create a better environment for local children
- customers – by providing high quality products and services
- local community – by demonstrating that local initiatives can bring local benefits.

The value statement might also indicate how the business will be run, for example 'with honesty, openness and respect for the individual'.

1.2 Resources

We have already seen how business objectives, mission and value statements enable stakeholders to identify:

- why the business exists
- what it is trying to achieve
- which markets it serves
- how it intends to behave.

The objectives, mission and value statements can be so much hot air if they do not reflect the resources of the organisation. There is no point in having objectives, mission and value statements if there is no way that they can be delivered.

In this context, resources include not only the financial and physical resources, but also the systems and methods, the speed of decision making and the attitude to risk. In a changing environment, it is very unlikely that the resources we have now will be exactly those we require in the future. The business will have to change to meet the new opportunities and threats. Making the resources fit the business values and environment would not be a problem if resources were cheap and easily changed. But this is far from the case. Resources have 'inertia': deciding to change takes time, people react differently to change and some will resist it, recruitment and training of staff is costly and it is expensive making people redundant. Plant is expensive, time consuming to install and often has little resale value. Products, services and systems take time and money to develop and are usually worthless when no longer required. We look at this 'inertia' and consider two approaches to categorising the overall behaviour of a business, and then look at some of the issues to be considered when trying to change resources.

ORGANISATIONAL BEHAVIOUR AND STRUCTURE

The business needs to use its resources to meet the needs of the environment and the values of the organisation. We start by looking at the overall behaviour of the business and examine the organisational classification systems developed by Miles and Snow and by Mintzberg. We then look at how businesses develop: in terms of their processes, they move from periods of stability through periods of significant change back to stability. Processes, tasks and internal structures need to be appropriate for existing market and environmental conditions; as the market and environment changes, there must be corresponding internal changes within the organisation.

Although individual staff and equipment will have a direct bearing on the capability of an organisation, it is recognised that the overall performance will also be a reflection of:

- organisational history – the skills, knowledge, systems and methods developed over a number of years and also the past experiences and beliefs about how the market and the industry operate
- the market and the industry – the stability and complexity, the level of competition, the rate of environmental change, etc.
- organisational culture – the pace of work, the expected quality standards, the level of delegation and trust, the split between formal and informal communication, the level of risk that is deemed appropriate, the willingness to change, etc.

Miles and Snow (1978) have developed a useful way of categorising the behaviour of organisations. They define four types of organisations.

- **Defenders**. These organisations operate in secure, fairly stable markets, and they are inclined to adopt low-risk strategies, focus on narrow segments and strive to improve their present methods rather than go for new products, markets or processes. An example of a 'defender' organisation would be a small town solicitors' partnership. While their markets remain stable, defenders can perform very well. However, if the environment or markets change, for example, a new competitor moves in next door, defenders struggle to survive as they do not have the resources to find new markets and develop new products.

- **Prospectors**. Prospectors unlike defenders are always looking for new opportunities. They are prepared to adopt high-risk strategies and to break new ground. Prospectors are often found in markets with low entry barriers where it is easy for new competitors to set up, such as double glazing or Internet service providers, or in markets where product life cycles are short, such as consumer electronics. The focus in such organisations will be on product innovation, identifying customer needs (marketing) and speed of reaction in satisfying those needs (speed of new product development).
- **Analysers**. These organisations want to optimise internal effectiveness, through continuous improvement of their systems and processes. They also closely monitor their marketplace, following competitors that develop promising new products and services. The staff in analyser companies are encouraged to evaluate what they are doing and find ways of doing it more effectively.
- **Reactors.** These organisations fail to be proactive in developing either internal effectiveness or market opportunities. In such organisations, there is likely to be large resistance to change. As a result, they find it difficult to satisfy customers and other stakeholders, and they spend their efforts trying to avoid one crisis after another.

Many people would say that:

- Amstrad, with its high rate of new product introduction, is a prospector organisation
- Marks and Spencer, with its emphasis on staff training and operational excellence, is an analyser
- the public library service, with its limited funding and constrained range of activities, is a defender
- some companies prior to privatisation (such as BT, British Coal) gave the impression of being reactors – they often failed to recognise fully the changes in their environment and the need to deliver value to their customers.

ACTIVITY 4

Based on your own experience, identify four companies, one for each of Miles and Snow's organisational types.

As you probably found, this exercise can be a more difficult task than it first seems. Many organisations exhibit characteristics of more than one type. For instance, their accounts department is likely to be a 'defender', the marketing department could be a 'prospector' and the manufacturing department an 'analyser'.

Another approach to categorising organisations is that of Mintzberg (Mintzberg, Quinn and Ghoshal, 1995). He links the business context and the structure of the organisation with its behaviour and identifies five types of organisation.

- **The entrepreneurial organisation**. This form of organisation is dominated by its leader, for instance the owner manager in a small company. The leader takes most of the key decisions and usually enthusiastically drives forward the strategy of the company. The organisation structure is very flat, often with everybody reporting to the leader. The entrepreneurial organisation is flexible and can react quickly to changes in the environment. However, staff can find it very restricting when the leader refuses to delegate and very stressful when the leader becomes obsessed with an idea.
- **The machine organisation**. This sort of organisation is typified by the mass-market, traditional car assembly plants. In order to ensure a high volume of quality products, the car plants have to break down the assembly process into a number of relatively simple activities, then apply rigid systems for planning and control. The organisation is, therefore, split into a number of specialist functions handling activities such as purchasing, design, quality control, machining, assembly, etc. Each function is expert in its own area, but only the top managers can see the full picture and it is they who are able to set strategy. While the business environment is stable, the machine organisation is great at delivering a standard product in a very effective way. The only problem is co-ordination: everything must happen in the right way at the right time and the job of the managers becomes one of solving the problems caused by disruptions to the processes. When the business environment is changing, the machine organisation really struggles. The inertia created by the carefully crafted systems prevents rapid response to new circumstances.
- **The diversified organisation**. Siebe is one of the world's largest engineering companies. Within Siebe, there are several groups of companies, each run as an almost independent unit. By being within the Siebe organisation, each company gains access to technical and management expertise and to funds for investment. In return, Siebe expects the companies to achieve demanding financial targets. Within the subsidiary companies of the diversified organisation various types of culture can exist, but the demands imposed by the group headquarters often leads them to adopt the machine organisation described above. As one manager of such a company commented 'we have two key stakeholders, the customers and the group HQ. You can get away with poor delivery [of products] to a customer, but you will not get away with poor delivery [failing to hit financial targets] to the HQ.' The HQ will have its own objectives and will buy and sell companies in order to maintain a

portfolio of businesses which will minimise risk (that is, the chances of an unexpected overall drop in business) and maximise profit.

- **The professional organisation**. Organisations like universities, hospitals and consultancies contain within them two subgroups: administrative staff and professional staff. The behaviour, structure and culture of the professional subgroup is quite unlike that of the administrative subgroup. The professional subgroup is a collection of professionals who provide complex services to customers, often on a one-to-one basis. The professionals are usually organised into loose groups according to their specialisms, and the level of management imposed is normally relatively low. In these organisations, the demands of the customers vary widely and the organisation has to assume the professionals know what to do. The training required to deliver these services makes the professionals expensive to employ. As a result, these organisations have administrative functions to carry out the routine tasks, enabling the professionals to focus on their areas of expertise. The administrative side of the business often has the characteristics of a machine organisation. The professional organisation gives a high level of independence to its staff who are often dedicated to their profession and highly motivated. Problems arise when the organisation needs to respond to changes in the environment because the professionals are extremely hard to co-ordinate and decision making can be a long and drawn out process.
- **The innovation organisation**. Some organisations rarely do the same thing twice, they are in business to generate new ideas, new ways of doing, making and selling things. Examples include advertising agencies, R&D laboratories and software houses. In such organisations, it makes no sense to have rigid organisation structures, people are grouped together depending on the task to be tackled. There is obviously a high rate of change and a high level of risk associated with this sort of business. The manager's job is one of trying to ensure that there is always a new project for the staff to work on and that the best resources are allocated to each task. In such an organisation, it is difficult to plan strategy as new ideas and opportunities are springing up all the time. The manager tries to select those opportunities that need the skills available and which have the greatest number of spin-off possibilities. It is very difficult for a business with an entrepreneurial or innovation organisation to develop without changing its behaviour and culture.

Many small businesses fail to grow beyond a certain size (often at a point where they employ about 20 staff), because what has to be done (**behaviour**) and the way things are done (**culture**) has to change so radically. At this critical point two things can happen:

- the business needs to find new markets and encounters new forms of competition
- the owner manager finds it hard to know everything that is going on and finds it increasingly difficult to make all the decisions – the entrepreneurial organisation fails to be effective.

If the company is to grow, there must be a greater awareness of market requirements, more delegation of tasks and the adoption of effective, standardised systems of working – it must move towards a machine organisation. These problems are illustrated in the Chemwelder case study.

CASE STUDY

Chemwelder

Hugh Collins had been a skilled welder on North Sea oil rigs. When his first child was born he decided to look for work which would enable him to spend more time with his family. He soon got a contract to weld pipes in a chemical plant. Because he was quick, reliable and prepared to work at any time of the day or night, he soon gained a good reputation and work came flooding in. In fact, so much came in that he persuaded a number of other North Sea welders to join him. Business flourished. Hugh organised the contracts and planned the work while the others did the welding. At one point a customer offered Hugh a job as their plant engineer, but Hugh turned it down preferring to remain independent. The team tackled any type of job and occasionally they had to fabricate quite large components. To cope with this type of work Hugh rented a small factory unit and decided to call the business 'Chemwelder'.

Within a few years, Hugh had a team of 20 welders and fabricators working for him. He was still trying to manage Chemwelder on his own, but it was getting beyond a joke. He was finding it difficult to remember the status of all the jobs and with 20 staff to support he was spending most of his time seeing new clients or troubleshooting on existing projects. More or less by accident Hugh contacted the local branch of the DTI and it advised him to seek the help of a business consultant. The consultant suggested Hugh should make some changes to the business, develop some formal systems and delegate some of the management activities to other staff. Hugh could see this was the only option if the firm was continue to grow, but the decision to trust somebody else with key decisions and to spend time thinking about administration systems was a very hard one to make.

However, over a two-year period, the business changed dramatically. Jim Hooper was appointed as business manager to run the accounts, marketing, quotations and order processing. Three welders were promoted to run the factory and the on-site activities and most of the systems (accounts, materials control and design) were computerised. The biggest change was that Hugh found time to take his first holiday in eight years.

Growth continued to be the major objective. Driven by Jim Hooper, the business was marketed as 'a one-stop shop for the design, manufacture and installation of chemical processing equipment'. The business was now based in purpose-built premises, with fully integrated computer-based systems and nearly 200 staff. Hugh retained overall control of the company, but he now had five directors reporting to him (finance, marketing, materials, operations and human resources) and they in turn had managers and supervisors reporting to them. On the fifteenth anniversary of Hugh giving up his job as North Sea welder, the company's turnover hit £10 million. This coincided with an approach by its largest competitor (a US multinational), which suggested a merger. Unlike previous approaches, Hugh did not dismiss it out of hand; the contracts Chemwelder was handling were getting larger and the cash needed to finance them was increasing as well. He saw that the merger would bring an injection of cash and it was a way to enable growth to continue. Within six months, the merger was completed. Chemwelder now formed part of the chemicals technology division of the multinational, with responsibility for manufacture of stainless steel products and marketing in Europe and the Middle East. However, this meant Hugh had to refer many decisions to the New York HQ. Hugh found working within the new company extremely difficult, and within a year he had sold his remaining shares and left the business. Jim Hooper was made general manager of Chemwelder and within three years he had taken the turnover to £25 million.

approach by its largest competitor (a US multinational), which suggested a merger. Unlike previous approaches, Hugh did not dismiss it out of hand; the contracts Chemwelder was handling were getting larger and the cash needed to finance them was increasing as well. He saw that the merger would bring an injection of cash and it was a way to enable growth to continue. Within six months, the merger was completed. Chemwelder now formed part of the chemicals technology division of the multinational, with responsibility for manufacture of stainless steel products and marketing in Europe and the Middle East. However, this meant Hugh had to refer many decisions to the New York HQ. Hugh found working within the new company extremely difficult, and within a year he had sold his remaining shares and left the business. Jim Hooper was made general manager of Chemwelder and within three years he had taken the turnover to £25 million.

ACTIVITY 5

Read the Chemwelder case study carefully. Identify the different types of organisation according to Mintzberg that are present. What do you think were the main tasks that Hugh had to carry out in each type of organisation? Why do you think Hugh found working within the group so difficult?

Early in the life of the organisation Hugh had to do everything, the organisation was 'entrepreneurial'. As the organisation grew he delegated more and more, leaving himself time to focus on longer-term issues (identifying new processes, product and markets), and the organisation gradually became more 'machine' like. Once the organisation had been taken over, Hugh's role became one of satisfying group requirements, ensuring turnover, profit and cash targets were met. The overall organisation was 'diversified', with Hugh's area becoming even more of a 'machine organisation'. Given Hugh's background, it is probably not surprising that he found his final role at Chemwelder far from satisfying, his own values were no longer congruent with those of the organisation.

ACTIVITY 6

Earlier we described the Playlight organisation that was set up to raise money to get better play facilities for children. Describe the Playlight business using the classification systems of Miles & Snow and Mintzberg.

Once the target £50,000 had been raised, two of the founders decided to continue to make lamps and run Playlight as a limited company (that is, as a normal small private business). In the first year or two of running as a limited company, what type of organisation (as defined by Mintzberg) do you think would exist ?

The Playlight business was set up by an number of enthusiastic individuals who had a clear objective of raising £50,000 by any means possible. It is probable that the organisation would have been an 'innovation organisation' (Mintzberg) and a 'prospector' (Miles and Snow). With the change to a private limited company, it is likely that one or two individuals started to dominate the organisation and it would move towards being an 'entrepreneurial organisation'.

ORGANISATIONS AND GROWTH

When a business is first set up, it will try to acquire the people, equipment and systems which are ideally suited to producing its products and services. The problem comes as the business needs change, for example:

- customers start to want more choice, so more products have to be introduced and although the total sales may increase each product is made in smaller quantities
- new technology is introduced, this may reduce the staff skill requirement leading to loss of job satisfaction and higher absenteeism
- the growth of the company may demand much more effective communication and planning systems.

We saw in the Chemwelder case study how growth led to changes in organisational structure and management style and also the loss of job satisfaction for Hugh Collins. This sort of change is not at all uncommon, as businesses grow they periodically find that the present way of doing things is no longer appropriate.

If we consider how organisations grow in size as they age and progress through their life cycle, we can identify various phases that they go through as they expand and have to make structural changes. As with all descriptive models, not all organisations will follow this precise pattern, but it does give us some key developments to watch for. Greiner (1976) identified five phases of evolutionary growth which most businesses go through. At the end of each evolutionary phase, he identified a dominant management problem that must be solved – a crisis – before the organisation can continue to grow (Figure 2).

In **phase 1**, the dominant management task is **creativity**: trying to identify products and markets which will get the company established. In this phase there is little formal management, as staff do whatever is required to get the business going. The crisis comes as the company becomes established and formal systems and techniques are required to cope with the growing complexity of the business. The existing managers lack the skills to develop and implement these systems, in fact many of them probably enjoy jumping from one problem to the next with little planning or thought about priorities. If the business is to grow, these managers have to change and start showing **leadership** and giving direction.

In **phase 2**, the dominant management activity is **direction**: formalising tasks and creating functional specialists. Initially this works well, but in the end the top management are no longer able to make all the decisions, there are just too many. The top managers must delegate responsibility and give autonomy to junior management (trust them to make the right decisions). This is something which is initially very hard to do, hence a crisis of **autonomy**.

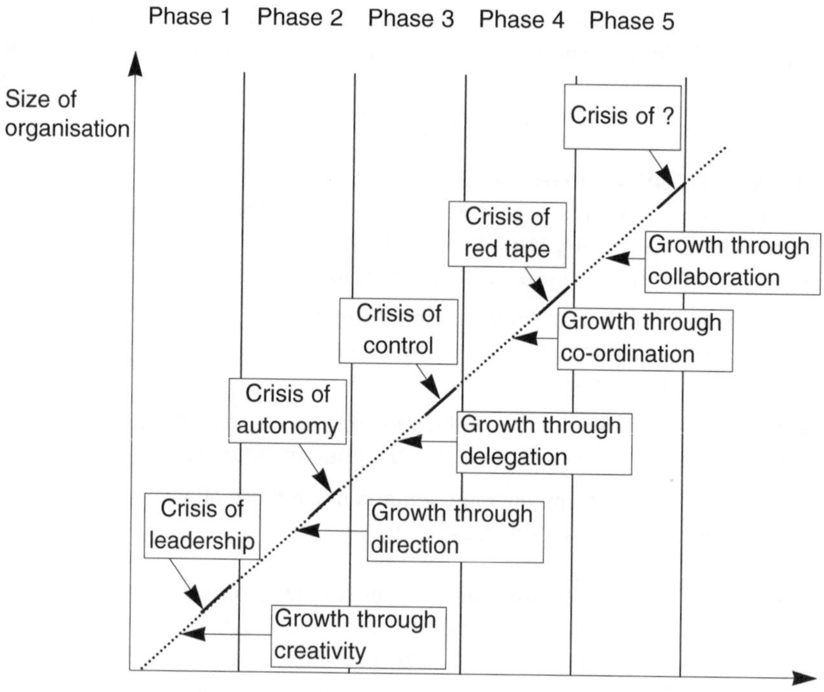

Figure 2: Five phases of evolutionary growth

In **phase 3**, the dominant management task is **delegation**: getting junior managers to run the existing business. This allows the top managers more time to develop plans for expansion into new products and markets and rapid growth can often occur. The problem comes when top managers feel they are getting out of touch and losing control of what is becoming a highly diversified organisation, a crisis of **control**.

In **phase 4**, the crisis of control has been solved by greater **co-ordination** between the various parts of the business. Often a corporate headquarters is created to plan and control investment, cash flow, marketing and operational strategies, etc. Although this works to a point, the heavy hand of the headquarters staff can breed resentment with other managers, who feel they are getting swamped with **red tape**.

Finally, in **phase 5, collaboration** enables the business to grow: a focus on cross-functional and cross-divisional team work and problem solving is adopted. This keeps staff involved in the decision-making process. When Greiner formulated his model in the 1970s, few organisations had reached the crisis which he predicted would strike some time in phase 5. He was, therefore, unable to identify what it was. A possible crisis is one of **size**: many large global organisations such as ICI have found no benefit in being very large and have split themselves in to smaller, more focused units.

As we have seen, the structure and processes of the organisation change as it grows. But what structure is appropriate to what market conditions? What features should management build into the organisation for different market conditions? We can consider the appropriateness of the organisational structure, particularly in terms of centralisation or decentralisation of decision-making, by examining certain features of the market and the business process. Remember from Unit 5, how we characterised different operations (or business processes) and how these change particularly with volume of production. In Table 1 (Hill, 1995), we identify the 'business position' for all the market and process characteristics. This is the position that the organisation holds on the continuum of high-to-low product range, customer emphasis on service or price, low-volume demand to high-volume demand, etc. We have indicated three positions on the continuum – A, B and C – indicating roughly the two extremes and the middle position. If, for example, a company is in a low-demand market (A), with emphasis on customer services (A), and with a highly individual process (A), then a more decentralised structure (A) is appropriate, and a key task will be developing new products (A). However, if a company is in a high-demand market (C), with a rigid specialised process (C), then a more centralised structure (C) is required. As you can see, there is the potential for many variations. If a company's position in the market and process characteristics is all 'A', all 'B' or all 'C', then the company is probably fairly easy to manage; if the company is a mixture of As, Bs and Cs, more sophisticated management practices are required.

Consider Cartew Limited, a company making special purpose manipulation equipment for microelectronic components. In the early 1990s, demand for its equipment was low as customers experimented with alternative manipulation techniques. To get business, Cartew had to react quickly, making special products to match the individual requirements of each customer. Often price was relatively unimportant to the customers, delivery lead time and product quality were the two most important factors. Cartew hired highly skilled engineers and developed multipurpose machines to meet the needs of a market in which no two products were the same. Cartew was in business position 'A' all the way down Table 1.

			Business position	
Market	**Demand**	low	◄——► A B C	high
	Product range	large	◄——► A B C	small
	Order size	small	◄——► A B C	high
	Customer emphasis	on service	◄——► A B C	on price
Process	**Flexibility**	high	◄——► A B C	low
	Labour skill	high	◄——► A B C	low
	Management emphasis	service	◄——► A B C	low cost
	Facilities	multipurpose	◄——► A B C	special purpose
Organisation	**Structure**	decentralised	◄——► A B C	centralised
	Key tasks	new products	◄——► A B C	process improvement

Table 1: Links between market, process and organisational structure

In 1996, the market changed. The way microelectronic components were manipulated was more or less standardised and Cartew started to receive orders for much larger quantities of a small range of products. Price started to be much more important to the customers. The market had moved to business position 'B'. The problem that then faced Cartew was how to match the change in the market. The need for flexibility and highly skilled production staff reduced. It needed people to operate special-purpose equipment capable of manufacturing components very much more cheaply than the old multipurpose machines. The focus of attention for management moved away from the design of new products, to improving the effectiveness of the production processes as they tried to satisfy demand and keep costs under control. The processes and organisation gradually moved to business position 'B'.

ACTIVITY 7

Using Table 1, identify the business position of:

- a 'cash and carry' supermarket
- a supermarket like Sainsbury or Safeway.

The cash and carry supermarket is in business position 'C' in all areas on Table 1. It is using low price to encourage customers to buy large quantities of a relatively small range of groceries. The cash and carry must, therefore, design its processes and organisational structure to match this with centralised decision-making and a fairly rigid bureaucracy with attention to process improvement, that is efficiencies in its operations such as deliveries, links with suppliers, shop layout and storage facilities.

Safeway and Sainsbury, on the other hand, are trying to compete with the cash and carry and the corner shop by giving low prices, product quality and service. This means they are trying to be in markets in both business position 'A' and 'C'. This results in complex processes and organisation. They must hold a large range of products, which requires sophisticated purchasing and logistics management. They must also have knowledgeable staff, which demands a low labour turnover and an emphasis on staff training and development.

1.3 Environment

A business has to meet the needs of its customers, generate the benefits required by its stakeholders and do it in a way which those stakeholders find acceptable. If the business is successful in this process, it has achieved E-V-R congruence; that is, it has aligned the demands of environment with the values and resources of the business. Here, we examine how the business can cope with changes in the environment.

The environment determines the opportunities, constraints and threats that face the business; these might include the level of competition, the technology that can be used, the wage rates, the expected dividend on shares. What is considered as a threat or a constraint by one organisation may offer another an opportunity.

It is rare for the environment of a business to remain stable for long. Something is almost bound to happen which will have a significant impact on an important aspect of the business. It may be a change in interest rates, a new competitor entering the market or new laws affecting the way machinery can be used. The business must quickly find ways of reacting effectively to these kind of changes. If it can cope well, then the change may give an advantage over less effective competitors; if it copes badly, it will probably fail to meet its objectives. A business that can spot the imminent arrival of environmental changes obviously has an advantage, it will have a chance to plan how to react and make sure the necessary resources are in place. We focus on how the environment creates pressure for change.

ENVIRONMENTAL PRESSURES FOR CHANGE

An organisation which has failed to keep pace with environmental change has a major task trying to catch up. A good example is IBM. For years, IBM based its business around large- and medium-sized computer systems, but in the 1980s it began to realise that the customers wanted PCs and networks. However, IBM had become a huge and unwieldy business and appeared to be unwilling to change at the rate demanded by the market. In 1992, IBM reported a loss of $2.8 billion. After several more years of huge losses, accompanied by revolutionary change within the company, IBM eventually returned to profit (Heller, 1994).

There is no doubt that implementing change before it is forced on the organisation is a preferable strategy. This means managers have to recognise opportunities for change.

As you saw in Units 2 and 3, there are a range of factors that cause change:

- customers could stop buying or develop new requirements
- suppliers could put up their prices
- staff could demand higher wages
- banks could withdraw loans
- shareholders could want a higher return on their investment
- competitors could bring out new or cheaper products
- legislation could force different employment or environmental practices
- political changes could mean new markets opening up or closing down
- new technology could become available making new products possible or reducing process times making others obsolete.

These changes, and those like them, will create the opportunities and threats to the organisation. The organisation's strengths in responding to these changes might include a skilled and flexible workforce, better access to raw materials than its competitors, an inspired leader, access to capital for development, good supply chain management, accurate knowledge of the market; weaknesses might include poor information and, therefore, a poor decision-making system, an out-of-date manufacturing process, problems with customer service. Analysis of these strengths and weaknesses against the opportunities and threats that the environment offers is known as a **SWOT analysis**. The SWOT analysis provides a first step in determining future strategies, and continuing the best fit of values, resources and environment. To investigate the environmental threats and opportunities we need to go back to our environmental analysis in Units 2 and 3, using PEST and Porter's five forces as a framework.

CASE STUDY

North Bank Co-operative Farmers Limited

North Bank Co-operative Farmers Limited (NBCF) is a co-operative set up in 1923 by farmers to supply them with animal feed, fertiliser, equipment (tractors, etc.) and other farm supplies (boots, nails, buckets, etc., known in the business as sundries). At present, NBCF has over 4,500 members and shareholders, nearly all farmers. NBCF operates from ten depots around its area. It has a turnover of over £40 million, of which the majority is from feed and fertiliser sales. Each depot has a 'Town & Country' retail store which sells sundries. These stores are open to the general public, but over 70 per cent of sales are to NBCF's shareholders. The headquarters and main depot are located in Truro in modern premises, but most of the other depots are older and less well appointed. Pay rates in the area are generally low compared with the rest of Britain and NBCF has difficulty attracting new staff from outside the county. However, the company has a loyal and experienced workforce and excellent links with the local community.

In recent years market conditions have changed considerably:

- the influence of the European Union has increased causing swings in farming profitability and some farmers have diversified into other activities such as golf courses, camping and theme parks
- many farmers have become more demanding, requiring faster service and more competitive prices often due to the pressure put on them by the large supermarkets
- a number of other co-operatives – Mole Valley Farmers and Avon Farmers – have moved into to the locality creating additional competition in all areas
- many of the national retail DIY chains now offer the sundries and this has increased competition in this sector of the business
- some of the larger farmers are buying feed and fertiliser direct from the manufacturers
- business has also been disrupted by a number of food scares – BSE, for example
- regulations in the handling of fertiliser and some other products have been tightened considerably.

NBCF has responded by:

- installing modern computer systems linking all its depots
- increasing the emphasis on sales and marketing
- installing facilities to cope with the new regulations
- creating close links with its main suppliers, who provide not only products but help and advice.

The future for NBCF has many uncertainties. Agriculture is generally declining in Europe and the range of farming outputs is changing, consumers are demanding better quality produce at low prices and the power of buyers is steadily increasing. The European Union is committed to reforming the Common Agricultural Policy (CAP), cutting subsidies but making direct aid payments. This is likely to make the environment more competitive, with smaller farmers being hardest hit. A SWOT analysis of NBCF is shown in Figure 3.

Strengths from their:

- Experience of the business
- Range of products
- Customer links
- Geographical spread in Cornwall
- Modern HQ and computer system
- Low labour costs
- Loyal and experienced work force
- Links with local community

Opportunities to:

- Expand into other parts of Britain
- Attract general public into their Town & Country stores
- Set up sole agency agreements with suppliers (i.e the supplier will only supply NBFC in the area)
- Offer information services to farmers and gardeners
- Expand their product range

Weaknesses as they**:**

- Operate in only one locality
- Are not often used by general public
- Occupy some old premises
- Find it difficult to attract good staff

Threats from:

- Farmers diversifying away from agriculture (to golf courses, etc.)
- Farmers demanding better service
- New competition threatening profit margins
- Farmers buying direct from NBCF suppliers
- Reduced sale of animal feed resulting from food scares (e.g. BSE)
- New regulations on the storage and use of products

Figure 3: SWOT analysis of North Bank Co-operative Farmers Limited

ACTIVITY 8

Study Figure 3 and the NBCF case study carefully. Using the SWOT analysis, note down what you consider to be North Bank Co-operative Farmers' most significant strength, weakness, opportunity and threat from those listed.

Are there any items which you think have been entered in the wrong box? For example, is the fact that farmers are diversifying into say golf courses a *threat*, or is there a real *opportunity* for North Bank Co-operative Farmers to start selling golfing equipment?

North Bank Co-operative Farmers sees the greatest threats to be loss of market share from increased competition and reduction in farmers' spending power resulting from BSE and changes in the Common Agricultural Policy. The greatest opportunities are in attracting the general public to its Town & Country stores; the greatest weakness is the difficulty to attract new staff to the company; the greatest strength is NBCF's vast experience of the business and its close relationship with its customer base.

A strength in one situation may be a weaknesses in another: a company in a booming market will see high labour turnover as a weakness (because of the high recruitment and training costs it brings); in a slump, high labour turnover will be a strength (because it means staff numbers can be reduced quickly with low redundancy costs).

Table 2 reveals the main causes of change in NBCF's environment. It is based on an environmental analysis using PEST factors and Porter's five forces at market or industry level and identifies opportunities and threats in the environment. We introduced PEST analysis and Porter's five forces in Units 2 and 3. To recap, PEST involves an analysis of the general environment in terms of:

- **P**olitical change
- **E**conomic change
- **S**ocial change
- **T**echnological change.

It also takes into account other changes such as environmental awareness or social responsibility. Porter's five forces used in an analysis of the competitive environment are:

- customer power
- supplier power
- threat of new entrants
- threat of substitutes
- competitive rivalry.

Opportunity	**Cause of opportunity**	**Category of cause**
Expand into other parts of Britain	Staff becoming more experienced and management systems able to cope with remote locations	New internal strengths
Attract general public into the Town & Country stores	Public are more mobile and prepared to travel greater distances for convenience shopping	Social
Set up sole agency agreements with suppliers (so that the supplier will only supply NBCF in the area)	Suppliers realise the benefits of collaborative agreements	Supplier power
Offer information services to farmers and gardeners	Customers' needs change as a result of economic conditions and the power of their customers	Economic and customer power
Expand the product range	Improved IT systems enable NBCF to satisfy a greater range of customers' needs, reducing reliance on a narrow range of products and markets	Technology and the threat of new market entrants
Threat	**Cause of threat**	**Category of cause**
Farmers diversifying away from agriculture (to golf courses, etc.)	The Common Agricultural Policy has caused swings in farming profitability	Politics and economics
Farmers demanding better service	Farmers are under pressure from customers to react quickly, and people have come to expect high quality products and service	Customer power, social change and competitive rivalry
New competition threatening profit margins	Without market growth, new competition means lower sales for NBCF	Threat of new entrants
Farmers buying direct from NBCF's suppliers	NBCF's suppliers have realised they can afford to service large farmers without going through NBCF	New entrants
Reduced sale of animal feed resulting from food scares (such as BSE)	The outbreaks of animal diseases reduces demand for animal products	Environment
New regulations on the storage and use of products	People are more aware of the danger of chemicals to the environment and they want better storage and operating methods; as technology becomes available to give extra protection, politicians create laws to enforce its use	Environment, politics and technology

Table 2: Causes of change in NBCF's environment

We looked in detail at Porter's model in Unit 3. Although we are covering some of the same ground, we are taking a slightly different perspective. Here, we look at how the forces affect the organisation to different degrees according to its strengths. For example, if customer power is great and supplier power is low, then the situation clearly favours the customer. We now consider the underlying factors themselves that determine the strength and timing of each of Porter's five forces (Table 3).

Porter's force	**Underlying factors** (which determine the size of Porter's forces)
Supplier power Customer power	Relative size of organisations Significance of each transaction Switching costs (cost of changing supplier)
Threat of new entrants Threat of substitutes	Product differentiation Switching costs Entry barriers Profitability
Competitive rivalry	Product differentiation Entry and exit barriers Capacity of the industry

Table 3: Factors which underlie Porter's five forces (Porter, 1979)

We can see that there are usually several factors, which might pull in opposing directions, influencing the resultant strength of each factor. We can also see that some of these underlying factors can be within the control of the organisation. For instance, the organisation can minimise the impact of changes in customer power by:

- ensuring that it limits the percentage of its trade with any one customer
- differentiating its products and services from those of the competition
- making it difficult for customers to change to a competitor or substitute product by, for example, designing products that are not interchangeable or negotiating long-term contracts.

Failing to take this kind of action to minimise customer power can have severe consequences. Take as an example Lock Components Limited (LCL). The company made garden toys, swings and slides and decided to concentrate its sales on two large national retail chains. This strategy reduced its manufacturing and administration costs. However, when one of the retailers went bankrupt, the other retailer, realising how desperate LCL was for orders, demanded lower prices. As a result, LCL was soon forced out of business. If LCL had traded with garden centres and small toy shops, it may have had higher costs, but it would not have been forced to close down by the bankruptcy of one customer and the power of the other.

We now look specifically at each underlying factor.

RELATIVE SIZE OF ORGANISATIONS

Companies that supply the large retailers like Burton's and Marks and Spencer are usually considerably smaller organisations. For these small organisations, orders from their large customer represent a significant part of their turnover. Having set up to supply the large retailers – a task often involving considerable cost and time – it would be a significant blow to the business if they were to lose these orders. The large retailers know that many of their suppliers cannot afford to lose their custom and can use this **power** to 'encourage' the small suppliers to adopt business practices which benefit the retailers.

Small suppliers can reduce the power of their larger customers by increasing switching costs and product differentiation or reducing the significance of each transaction. Suppliers must be on the look out for events that will impact on the importance (or power) of individual customers. This can happen when customers merge or form purchasing groups.

ACTIVITY 9

When you buy petrol for your car, who holds the power: you or the oil company?

In this case, neither you or the petrol company normally have much power. It is easy for you to go to another garage, but on the other hand, the petrol company is not going to be that worried about losing one customer. The power arises when either the supplier or customer has limited options. So, if your car was out of petrol and the petrol station was the only one for miles, the petrol station would have the power and you would probably be prepared to pay any price for the petrol.

SIGNIFICANCE OF EACH TRANSACTION

As we have just described, a small supplier can be at a disadvantage to a large customer because of the importance the supplier attaches to retaining the business of the customer. A similar shift of power occurs when the turnover of the supplier is made up of relatively few transactions.

If you go into Marks and Spencer to buy five pairs of socks but decide you don't like its range, the loss of your business (transaction) is not going to significantly alter the profitability of M&S. However, if British Airways decides not to buy five aircraft from Boeing, the loss of this transaction could be very serious for Boeing. An aircraft company may have an annual turnover of billions of pounds, but only sell a few hundred aircraft each year. Since 1958, Boeing has produced less than 9,000 jet airliners (Boeing web page). In such circumstances, it becomes extremely important to win a high proportion of all orders placed for aircraft, particularly if the organisation is below target on sales. Win an order and the company may have work which will last for years, lose an order and it may have to close down factories and lay off staff. The airlines obviously realise the power they hold in these circumstances and use it to get very favourable terms for any transactions they make with the aircraft manufacturers.

Suppliers must be aware of changes that could make individual orders large when compared with the total turnover. This can happen as customers demand 'packages' – rather than buy components from a large number of suppliers, they approach one supplier and ask them to supply all the components. This has been a trend in the oil and motor industry over recent years.

Changes to the products themselves can alter the balance of power. For example, as the technology used in products becomes more sophisticated a supplier can offer a more expensive product with many additional features. This has happened in some areas of instrumentation: a few years ago a basic instrument to measure the speed of ocean currents cost a few hundred pounds; now, because of computer technology, the instrument costs several thousand pounds but has many additional features, for example, it can automatically control its depth and transmit data by radio removing the need to recover the device to obtain readings.

Suppliers can minimise the power of buyers through product differentiation.

ACTIVITY 10

A government decides to build a new railway system. Who holds the power, the government or one of four design and construction consortia bidding for the business?

Suppose the government has appointed a consortium and work has started. If it then decides to change the route of the railway, who now holds the power – the government or the consortium?

In the first instance, the power will lie with the government. There are relatively few railway systems ordered each decade, so each consortium will be very keen to get the business and would be quoting low prices for the contract.

Once the contract is underway, the power will shift towards the consortium. It would be difficult for the government to change supplier mid-contract, so the consortium will feel able to demand a reasonable price for any additional work they have to do.

SWITCHING COSTS

Switching costs relate to the cost associated with changing from one supplier's product to another. An example of a situation in which switching costs are frequently encountered in business is the decision to upgrade software. If staff are already familiar with a particular brand of software and it is difficult to transfer data to other software, then a business will often stay with its existing brand even though other software packages may be better. The switching costs are just too high to make the change worthwhile.

Switching costs rise fast whenever a customer needs special (once-only) products and services. If a customer requires special software to run the business, then when that software needs changing, the customer will probably have no choice but to use the original supplier to carry out the changes as nobody else understands how it works!

Customers can keep switching costs low by encouraging suppliers to provide standard products. At one time, every manufacturer of pipe fittings for central heating systems had its own screw thread design. This meant that if you wanted to replace a component you had to use the original supplier or the parts would just not fit together. Through customer pressure, things have changed and there is now an international standard for the threads on these products; this almost totally eliminates switching costs.

ACTIVITY 11

Your bank provides poor service, but to change to another bank involves a great deal of paperwork, especially in changing standing orders and direct debit instructions. Who holds the power, you or your present bank?

Sainsbury, where you shop every week, starts offering a banking service. Who holds the power, you or your unhelpful bank?

Your present bank holds the power because of the high switching costs in terms of paperwork. However, the power derived from high switching costs can be lost if:

- the costs of switching are reduced – in this case, somebody else could complete the paperwork involved in changing bank
- the benefits of switching increase – if Sainsbury, which you like and trust, offers a banking service which promises to be much better than your present bank, you will hold the power.

PRODUCT DIFFERENTIATION

For a supplier working in a market in which switching costs are low, product differentiation offers a way of reducing customer power. Until the early 1980s, all sportswear looked very much the same; the power lay with the customer, and the suppliers made low margins. Since then, the suppliers have concentrated on differentiating their products by convincing customers there is a real difference – in kudos, if not performance – to be gained from using their products and they have reinforced this message by using sports stars for promotion and advertising. The strategy has worked; many customers now ask for specific brands of sportswear, such as Nike or Adidas. This gives power to the suppliers, increasing market size as well as margins.

If a customer perceives there is a difference between one supplier's product and the next, then, whether or not these differences are real, product differentiation exists. If the customer thinks a differentiated product is what he or she wants, then the supplier has gained power. BMW has convinced many people that there is no other car quite like a BMW. In reality, there is very little difference between the engine performance, reliability and comfort of all the cars in the class, but try telling that to a BMW owner!

Customers can reduce the power of suppliers by claiming that the benefits of product differentiation are of no value to them. If all you want is to get about as cheaply as possible, then a BMW has no advantages over a Lada and, in fact, has one disadvantage – its cost.

ACTIVITY 12

In most supermarkets there are large numbers of branded products such as Kellogg's cornflakes and Heinz beans. However, there is little branding on fruit, vegetables and milk. In less than 100 words, explain why.

There is a limit to what you can do with advertising and packaging. In the end, there must be some discernible difference between the products of different suppliers but there will be little difference in fruit from different suppliers or farms, for example. In fact, consumers actually want the product to be consistent regardless of the supplier. Petrol companies have the same problem as fruit or milk producers. There is little difference in the performance of different brands of petrol. So petrol companies try to differentiate the services they offer with the product by offering free gifts, issuing loyalty cards, providing 'mini-supermarket' facilities at the petrol station, etc.

ENTRY BARRIERS

Entry barriers are factors which deter new companies from entering a business sector. They can be created at a number of points in the supply chain. Table 4 lists some of the most common entry barriers. Changes in legislation and technology can easily reduce some of these barriers, allowing new companies to enter the market, thereby increasing competition and reducing profit margins. British Gas was once a comfortable public sector monopoly, but it is now facing a highly competitive environment after privatisation and the lowering of entry barriers to the industrial and domestic gas markets.

Often, the changes to entry barriers can be spotted well in advance. Organisations must be aware of how entry barriers protect their existing business and should plan how to maintain the barriers and how to cope should they disappear.

Entry barrier	Example	Comment
Geography	Road-stone companies only face limited competition from far distant competitors because of the cost of transport.	Geographical barriers come about when transport is difficult because the product is fragile, perishable or dangerous; an example is radioactive waste disposal.
Legislation	British Airways was able to survive and offer poor value for money until privatisation subjected the organisation to market forces and the threat of takeover.	Many public sector organisations have legal barriers to protect them from competition. An example is the Inland Revenue.
Costs and risks	The aero-engine business can be extremely profitable but, despite the high rewards, potential new entrants are put off entering the market by the high capital investment needed and the costs and risks of product development.	Industries, such as oil exploration, with technologically complex products and processes generally have high capital costs and high risks.
Experience	In the 1950s, Metal Box dominated the UK container market. Its experience in producing tin cans deterred competitors from entering the market. In the 1970s, with the growing market for plastic and aluminium containers, the entry barriers disappeared.	A company with considerable experience of operating within a market will have significantly lower costs than a company new to that market. This cost gap will act as a real barrier to entry.
Patents and rights	Pharmaceutical companies are prepared to invest colossal sums in the development of new drugs because they know that for several years they will have a legal monopoly over their manufacture and sale.	Patents and copyright are powerful deterrents to new entrants, especially if it is known that the patent or right holders will defend any infringements through the courts.
Retaliation by the competition	As Richard Branson found when he started transatlantic air services, competitors do not allow market share to be taken away without putting up a fight.	Retaliation by the competition is fairly rare, as in most markets it is difficult to carry out.
Technology	The Royal Mail is protected by legislation on its national letters delivery services. However, this entry barrier is being breached, not by competing letter services, but by fax and e-mail.	Technology is unlikely to be a entry barrier in its own right for long. It is more effective when associated with patent and experience barriers.
Market size	If markets are small, they often fail to attract interest and remain very profitable. Once they start to grow, new entrants flood in and competition forces down margins.	Companies can give the appearance of operating in small markets by clearly differentiating their products. For example, Morgan operates in the huge car market but, by producing open sports tourers to a traditional 1930s design, sells in a small niche market.

Table 4: Typical entry barriers

EXIT BARRIERS

Exit barriers are factors that deter companies from leaving a business sector. They include considerations about the investment of time and money that will have to be thrown away if the company leaves a sector, the cost of redundancies and the need to continue to service existing customers.

It is important for a business to monitor carefully the attractiveness of the sectors it is in. As the attractiveness starts to decline, then the business can gradually 'lower' the exit barriers by reducing its investment in the sector, for example, by selling off plant, by not replacing staff who leave and by subcontracting.

PROFITABILITY

As profits increase within a business sector, it will become more attractive to other companies. They will try to enter the sector, particularly if the entry barriers are low. Companies entering the sector increase the total sector capacity; this will increase the level of competition and profits will tend to fall.

As profits fall, companies will try to leave the sector, especially if the exit barriers are low. This reduces capacity and competition, and profits will tend to increase.

It is obviously to the benefit of companies that want to stay in a sector both to try to increase the entry barriers to stop new competitors from coming in and to lower the exit barriers to encourage existing competitors to leave.

ACTIVITY 13

In recent years, home shopping through catalogues or the television has become increasingly popular. This is obviously having some impact on high street stores. Identify at least three entry barriers that the existing high street retailers can erect to protect their business.

Entry barriers can be created at a number of points in the supply chain, for example:

- in the provision of resources, through exclusivity deals with suppliers
- in the technology of processes and products, through patents and economies derived from years of experience
- in the organisation of processes, through economies of scale and quality of service
- in the supplier/customer relationships, through reputation, branding, personal contacts.

High street chains such as Boots, Next and W H Smith could build entry barriers in any of these areas. However, note the other approach is to compete in the same market. Next also offers catalogue shopping and W H Smith has a mail-order division for books, videos and CDs, so they are competing in the home shopping market as well as retailing through their high street stores.

SECTOR CAPACITY

In periods of undercapacity, demand exceeds the ability to supply and prices tend to rise. Higher prices should lead to higher profits, but the urgent need to satisfy customer demand and maintain market share can inflate costs and overload the production staff. When there is overcapacity and capacity exceeds demand, prices fall and marketing costs rise as companies try to maintain market share through increased advertising, etc.; this reduces profits and overloads the sales staff.

If entry and exit barriers are low and capacity is easy to gain and lose, such as in a consultancy business, overcapacity or undercapacity is not a problem. Resources can be easily adjusted to meet the new market requirement and the imbalance soon disappears. However, if capacity is expensive to create, such as in a car plant, it is also usually expensive to shed; in these circumstances, suppliers can easily find that they have too much capacity.

Organisations must recognise the inertia of their capacity and the ease with which it can be changed, and strive to avoid the harmful impact of overcapacity or undercapacity. Many manufacturing organisations maintain their own capacity below peak demand and use subcontractors to top-up capacity when the need arises. In this way, they avoid costs of capacity problems as the level of demand varies – the costs are borne by the subcontractor!

ACTIVITY 14

Hotels have a capacity balancing problem. They are expensive to build and have a fixed number of bedrooms. However, demand varies wildly, often depending on the time of year. What action can a hotel take to overcome the problem that in winter customers are difficult to find and in summer there are too many of them.

Hotels could obviously close down all or part of their operation during quiet periods. But the problem is not just the number of rooms available, a key issue is the availability of trained staff. Many hotels try to maintain a core of highly trained staff, who in quiet times will carry out all of the duties in the hotel. In busy times, they take on temporary staff to do jobs like cleaning rooms and washing up, while the core staff do key customer service and management tasks. Hotels also offer special breaks at discounted prices, hold other functions such as conferences and seminars at special rates. You find that hotels in seaside resorts, such as Eastbourne, utilise spare capacity by hosting business conferences and meetings out of season.

We have examined the factors which underlie environmental causes for change. This understanding of the pressure for change may enable us to remove the cause, to anticipate change and to minimise the negative impact – or, at least, to know what's going on when it does happen.

REVIEW ACTIVITY 1

Supermarkets understand Porter's five forces probably better than any business and they exploit this knowledge to the full. Identify how they do this, considering each of the underlying factors that we identified in Table 3. One or two sentences on each factor is fine.

Summary

We have examined the need of a business to ensure continually that it has the ability to:

- meet the needs of its customers by offering products and services that people want to buy
- generate the benefits required by its stakeholders – owners, shareholders, employees, etc. – according to their values
- use its resources and capabilities.

This process achieves E-V-R congruence, aligning the demands of environment with the values and resources of the business.

- The **values** identify the objectives of the key stakeholders, the approach they want the business to take and the scope of the business activities.
- The **resources** – staff, finances, equipment, systems, etc. – determine the capability of the business, its strengths and weaknesses.
- The **environment** determines the opportunities, constraints and threats that face the business, for example, the level of competition, the technology that can be used, the wages rates, the expected dividend on shares, etc.

The organisation's mission directs the organisational objectives and the values. The mission statement may identify open or closed objectives and include a value statement.

There are problems in matching business resources to the changing environment. We looked at ways of classifying business behaviour and organisations. We then analysed how mismatch could arise between an organisation's processes and the needs of the market.

We investigated Porter's five market forces and the underlying factors – customer size, transaction size, switching costs, product differentiation, entry and exit barriers, profitability and sector capacity – that could influence these forces.

SECTION 2

Strategic Planning

Introduction

Understanding the need for this E-V-R congruence is the first fundamental of business management, skill in its achievement is the second. We now look at the different strategies an organisation can use to achieve its objectives. Then, we identify some of the processes that we can use to choose and implement a strategy.

2.1 Types of business strategies

When it comes to choosing the best strategies, it is important that managers are aware of the alternatives open to them. First, we examine some of the more common strategies used in business. Table 5 shows how strategic plans are designed to answer a number of different strategic questions and how they form a hierarchy of strategies.

Hierarchy of strategies	Strategic questions
1 Product/market strategy	Which products should we make and which markets should we sell them in?
2 Market sector strategy	Which market sectors should we be in?
3 Business integration strategy	Should we change the range of activities in which we are involved?
4 Competitive strategy	How should we compete?
5 Organisation strategy	What must we be good at?

Table 5: Hierarchy of strategies

If the pressures on a company are very great, then the managers may feel that they ought to move into another business altogether. In these circumstances, they would be trying to identify a new **product/market strategy**.

In the case study described in Section 1.1 (see Activity 2), we saw how declining sales in the toy business forced Reg Pearce to develop a product/market strategy which moved the company into the office accessory market. Having made the decision to enter this new market, Reg Pearce then had to choose the sectors of the office accessory market in which he wanted to compete – he had to set the **market sector strategy.** He chose a strategy of supplying desktop products made from PVC plastic (pen holders, folders, etc.). This market sector could have been supplied in a number of ways. For example, Reg's company could have:

- operated as import agents for foreign manufacturers of office equipment
- designed the products and had them made by subcontractors
- designed and manufactured the products and sold direct to the end user.

In the event, it decided to design and manufacture the products and sell through agents and wholesalers. In making this choice, it set its **business integration strategy**. As you can see, as you work down the hierarchy of strategies, they become more short term; a company will not change its product/market strategy as nearly as often as its business integration strategy. The **competitive strategy** looks at how the company is going to gain competitive advantage – persuade customers to choose its products rather than those of the competition. You met Porter's three generic competitive strategies in Unit 3. Reg Pearce decided to offer a range of unique products manufactured to very high-quality standards; a competitive strategy based on quality and innovation. This competitive strategy meant that the company had to adopt an **organisation strategy** focused on design and manufacturing excellence.

ACTIVITY 15

State which level of strategy is involved if Reg Pearce decided to:

(a) market office desks aimed at the top managers of large companies

(b) focus on marketing and distribution and sell off the production facilities

(c) offer very large discounts to customers that purchased over £300,000 worth of products a year

(d) offer a next-day delivery service.

The move into the office desk market represents a complete change of product and market and, therefore, is part of the product/market strategy. The decision to target top managers has set the market niche in which it will operate, and is, therefore, part of the market sector strategy. By focusing on marketing and distribution, he has changed the business integration strategy.

By offering large discounts and next-day delivery, Reg is setting the competitive strategy. This change will have big implications on the operational strategy: he will have to find ways of reducing costs and speeding up the time taken to despatch orders.

We now examine each level of the strategy hierarchy in turn.

PRODUCT/MARKET STRATEGY

Some business organisations use their financial resources to move into new products and markets, not because they are uncomfortable in the present arena but because they see the new one as a good investment. Some large organisations use this form of product/market strategy, frequently buying and selling businesses. For most organisations, however, a change of product/market occurs either when it is forced upon them or, more gradually, when they use their existing skills in new ways. So, for example, many former defence contractors have been forced to move into civilian markets following the ending of the Cold War. DML, which runs the naval dockyard in Plymouth, has created a new division which maintains the diesel engines of Intercity 125 railway locomotives. Marks and Spencer has expanded its range of business activities by building on its retailing strength to move into food, furniture and financial services.

Organisations need to operate in those product markets in which they can do well, and to get out of those in which they are struggling. A number of matrices help clarify this decision. The Boston Consulting Group matrix uses measures of relative market share and the market growth rate to balance products, product lines and SBUs, that use up cash or supply cash within the business (Hedley, 1976). This matrix was used widely in the 1970s and 1980s. The Shell directional policy matrix, shown in Figure 4, compares the attractiveness of the product or market and the organisation's competitive position. It gives an idea of when an organisation should stay in a particular arena and when it should get out.

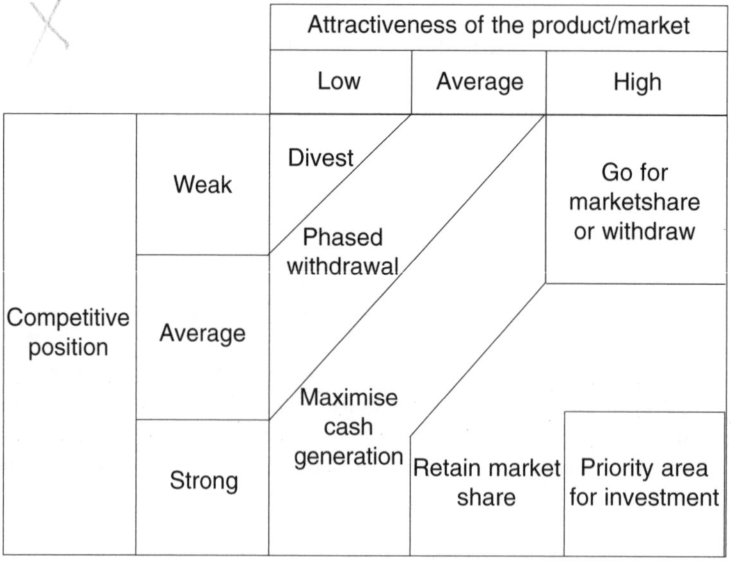

Figure 4: The Shell directional policy matrix

This matrix is based upon the idea that businesses should be in markets which are growing and in which they can perform really well. The key thing is to be able to gain high market share and as a result sell large quantities of product or service. This often leads to economies of scale – the more you make the cheaper they become – and higher profits.

Many other models have been developed that measure elements of the market against the organisation's performance in the market using various criteria. Some identify where the market/industry is in its life cycle, and the competitiveness of the organisation's products. You will investigate these models further in other modules.

ACTIVITY 16

Tanktop Products is the leader in the market for large water tanks used in hotels, hospitals, etc. Over recent years, sales have started to decline as the water companies improve their supply systems. Tanktop is still making a healthy profit, but it can see that it won't last for ever. What does the Shell directional policy matrix say it should do? Why does it say this?

Tanktop is still making a good profit so it must be in the 'average to strong' area on competitive position, but the attractiveness of the product/market is sinking into the 'low' area. This means Tanktop is in the 'maximise cash generation' area of the matrix and is likely to move into the 'phased withdrawal' area in the near future. It should seek to generate as much cash as possible in the short term, which should be invested in a new product/market into which it can move when ready. Hopefully, this will be before the water tank business starts to become unprofitable.

When organisations need to divest themselves of some of their business activities – that is, by closing them down (internal divestment) or selling them off (external divestment) – they are usually faced with the problem of what to do next. Two strategies are open to them:

- **internal development strategy** – moving into the new arena by using the existing staff and resources to generate new products or services
- **external acquisition strategy** – taking over an existing company in the desired product/market.

ACTIVITY 17

For two of the issues listed in Table 6, identify one risk that managers face if they adopt an internal development strategy and one risk if they choose to adopt an external acquisition strategy. Overall, which strategy do you think has the greater risk of failure?

Table 6 shows the advantages and disadvantages of these alternatives.

Issue	**Internal development strategy**	**External acquisition strategy**
Speed of entry	Slow – developing new resources, knowledge and skills is a slow process	Fast – a company already in the market can be purchased in a matter of months
Cost	Can be expensive, as there is a great deal of experience to be gained and many mistakes can be made	More often than not external acquisition is the cheapest option
Management effort	Relatively easy – managers learn to cope as they go	Managers can get overloaded as they try to cope with both the old and the new businesses
Impact on competition	This strategy is seen as a threat, as it increases the total capacity of the sector; overcapacity leads to higher competition, lower prices and profits	Seen as less threatening as sector capacity does not increase

Table 6: Entering a new product/market

Research has shown that product/market strategies are fairly risky (Kay, 1993). The greatest risk of failure appears to be with the external acquisition strategy, where failure is most often due to overloading the management and the inability to cope with the cultural differences between the two organisations. Table 7 shows some of the risks of internal and external development strategies.

An alternative to internal development or external acquisition is the 'joint venture' strategy, in which two or more organisations get together to exploit a new idea or enter a new market. On the face of it, a joint venture has all the advantages and none of the disadvantages of the other strategies; but, in practice, they can be difficult to run and a high percentage end in failure, often due to disagreements between the partners.

Issue	Risks of an internal development strategy	Risks of an external acquisition strategy
Speed of entry	Market opportunity may have passed if slower internal strategy is used	External strategies are often taken because of the need for speed – but may lead to a poor acquisition being made
Cost	Through lack of experience in the new area, expensive mistakes can be made	External strategies have a high risk of failure – so although the purchase price may be low, it may be expensive in the long run
Management effort	Because of the longer timescale allowed for internal development, the strategy may not be given the priority and resources it needs	The management of the acquired company could leave before managers understand the business
Impact on competition	Time taken to implement an internal strategy may give competitors an opportunity to take retaliatory action	Disenchanted staff from the acquired company could move to the competition

Table 7: Risk associated with entering a new product/market

MARKET SECTOR STRATEGY

Within markets, there are often sectors or niches which are more attractive than others. Many organisations would find that a strategy of serving the whole market beyond their capabilities and serving a niche may be more viable. In creating a market sector strategy, we are trying to identify groups of customers who we are able to serve particularly well. These customers may be identified by a number of criteria such as:

- location
- age, sex
- lifestyle
- nationality
- their use of the product or service
- their need for back-up service
- their customer power.

For any supplier trying to set the market sector strategy, the key thing is that these customers should be easy to identify, should find the advantages of the supplier's product/services to be significant and should generate enough demand to make the sector worthwhile.

ACTIVITY 18

Identify two ways that supermarkets are able to attract specific customer sectors.

Supermarkets attract specific types of customer in a number of ways:

- through the location of the stores (if you are trying to attract prosperous customers, there is little point in locating the store in an area of high unemployment)
- through the range of goods offered, their quality and price (in the City of London many supermarkets cater for single people who work long hours, they therefore open early, close late and offer a good range of convenience food in one-person portions)
- through the car parking and free bus services they provide.

In setting the market sector, the organisation is trying to choose the customers with whom it wants to trade. Customers are, of course, not the only stakeholders with which the organisation will trade, for example, employees trade their labour, financial institutions trade money, suppliers trade materials and components, landlords trade premises, etc. The organisation must have a sector strategy for each stakeholder type (not just one for customers). For instance, the supplier sector strategy should identify the types of supplier that best meets the needs of the organisation. Several issues will be important in determining a supplier sector strategy.

- **Location of suppliers** – it may be important that they are close to the organisation.
- The **relationship** which can be built up with the supplier – car companies want to work with suppliers which produce very high-quality products, deliver on schedule, with costs which go down each year. The only way that this can be achieved is for the car companies to help their suppliers find better methods, and this demands a very close relationship.
- The **additional services** provided by the supplier – some organisations want the suppliers of computer equipment to provide a comprehensive back-up service, others will provide this service in-house.

- The **package of products** and services supplied – many organisations are now looking to their suppliers to provide packages of products rather than a limited range. For instance, an oil rig requires several sources of power including electricity, compressed air and hydraulic power. When considering suppliers, an oil company will be looking for a company that can supply all these power sources. The supplier may only produce one source, say compressed air, but the oil company will expect the supplier to put together the whole power package.

ACTIVITY 19

List three issues that you think could be important when an organisation is setting its employee sector strategy for its future managers.

The sorts of issues an organisation might consider include age range, work experience, educational background and special skills, personality type and ambitions.

BUSINESS INTEGRATION STRATEGIES

If you think about the processes that even quite simple products undergo before they are ready for use, you will soon realise that most manufactured items pass through the hands of a large number of people and organisations. If we go back to our transformation model of an organisation, at each stage inputs are transformed into outputs with added value. Take for example wooden furniture, the wood used will go through the stages shown in Figure 5.

As we know from Unit 1, the group of activities involved in getting from raw materials and other resources through to the final customer is called the **value system** – as each step in the system adds value to the product. The set of activities carried out by a particular company within the value system defines that company's **value chain**. The collection of organisations involved in the activities required to produce a product or service is known as the **supply chain**. Those activities close to the end user (the customer) are known as **downstream** activities, those nearer the source of raw material are known as **upstream** activities. Companies that are involved in many parts of the value system or that have taken on other functions in the supply chain are said to have high **vertical integration**.

The **business integration strategy** determines which activities in the supply chain the company is going to undertake. Many organisations change their activities in the value system as a way of gaining competitive advantage. For example, MFI changed the traditional supply chain for furniture. In return for low prices, MFI expects customers to collect products from its warehouses and to carry out assembly of the furniture at home.

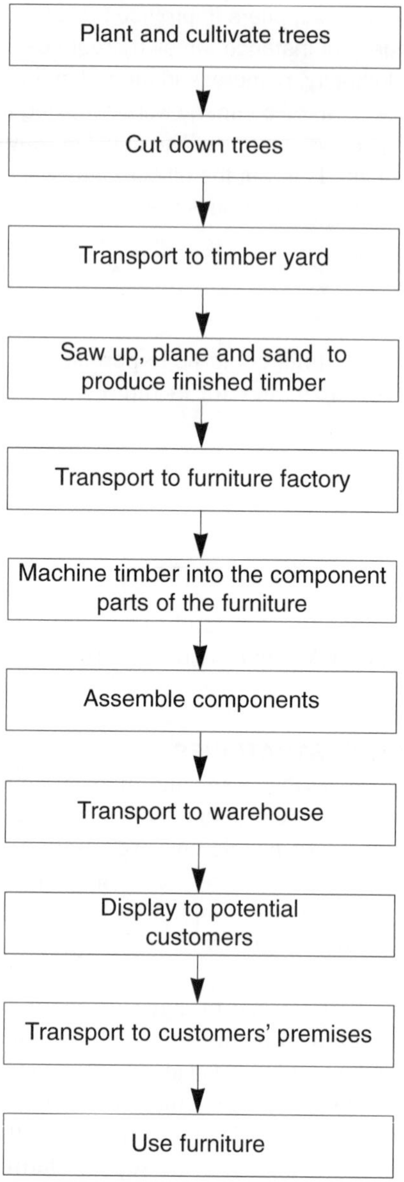

Figure 5: Stages in making furniture

Many supermarkets have blurred the interface between food producers and retailers by becoming involved in food production, thereby increasing their level of vertical integration. They have also changed their value chain activities, for example, by asking customers to use bar-code readers to total up the price of goods purchased.

In recent years, many companies and public sector organisations have reduced the activities they carry out by contracting them out to independent organisations. For instance, in the 1960s many motor companies manufactured the vast majority of components used in their vehicles, today nearly all car manufactures buy in most of the less important parts. In doing so, they have reduced their level of vertical integration.

Highly vertically integrated companies seek to gain control over a larger part of the value system. Purchasing items from another company always carries the risks that the items may be delivered late, to a poor quality or the price may be increased. By taking over the supplier – a strategy called **backward vertical integration** – the company reduces these risks. However, by doing so, they are reducing the supplier's exposure to competition and in the long term there is a danger that the supplier will become complacent and fail to maintain high levels of performance.

ACTIVITY 20

Suppose you are the managing director of a paint manufacturer that sells 23 colours of your gloss paint, nine coloured undercoats and two white priming paints. You sell to five wholesalers which supply some 15,000 outlets. Annual production of gloss paint is 2,500,000 litres.

You have decided that, from next year, instead of supplying different coloured paints you will introduce a new system. DIY retailers with special machines will be able to produce virtually any colour of paint on their premises using a base of white paint and small quantities of colouring which you will supply.

Describe the change in terms of vertical integration. Outline the advantages of the new system to the manufacturer, retailers and customers. State who, if anyone, might be disadvantaged?

The mixing process to make different coloured paints has been passed from the manufacturer to the retailer, moving a stage in the value system from one supplier to another. This has made the manufacturer less vertically integrated; control of the paint-mixing process passes to the retailer so that consistency and reliability of the product is now controlled by the retailer not the manufacturer. Before the paint-mixing machines were developed, paint manufacturers had to forecast demand for each colour of paint. Based on these forecasts, they produced paint in bulk and stored it in large warehouses. The retailers also held stock of a large range of colours. When the stock got down to a few tins – as a result of sales to the end users – the retailer would order some more from the manufacturer or a wholesaler.

With the old system the manufacturer was constantly cleaning out the production system to mix up different colour batches of paint and manufacturers, wholesalers and retailers all had large amounts of stock. With the new system all this has gone: the paint manufacturer only makes and stocks the base paint in bulk, the only other things that need to be stored are the small quantities of colouring. The new system means less stock, less cleaning, lower risk for retailers who are able to give the customers the colours they want, and fewer purchase orders to be handled. So by transferring the mixing operation to the retailer, benefits have been created for the manufacturer, the retailer and the customer. The disadvantages are that the manufacturer now does not have control of the final colours so the customer may end up with an unreliable product. Customers are dependent on the retailer for the consistency of performance, they cannot buy the product from any retailer and be assured that the shade matches the colour they want as they would have been able to previously.

COMPETITIVE STRATEGY

When customers trade with an organisation, they are looking for a mix of benefits in return for their money. They want products that:

- meet their requirements
- are at a price which they can afford
- operate effectively and do not go wrong etc.

They also want the transaction to go smoothly, which means that:

- they can easily find out about the products and how to acquire them
- the products are available when they want them
- there is no problem with the exchange of goods for money
- they are helped with the selection of the product when there is a choice
- they are able to minimise their time and effort
- they are left feeling that they have got value for money
- their friends will admire the product they have purchased
- things are sorted out efficiently if they go wrong.

Hill (1995) suggests that businesses must divide the customer benefits into three types: **winners**, **qualifiers** and **losers**. In a brand new market, each of these product and transaction benefits represents an opportunity for competitive advantage for the organisation, so every benefit is a **winner**. In a mature market, however, many organisations will be offering the same benefits to the consumer. For example, in most towns there are several pubs supplying a similar range of drinks and snacks at similar prices – so price and range are not winners. However, one or two will gain most of the customers, because of their atmosphere, service, location, etc. It is these factors that are the winners in this market.

In all markets, there will be some benefits which are offered by all the suppliers. The customers will come to see these benefits as an essential part of the product offering; for example, everybody expects wide choice and low prices in supermarkets. These benefits are known as **qualifiers**. If an organisation wants to start trading in a market, it must offer the qualifier benefits to get any business at all. For example, a petrol station that charges 10p per litre more than its competitor half a mile away is not going to gain much business. Until it can reduce the price by 9p or 10p, it will not reach the qualifying level.

Losers are those activities that can reduce the level of business by significant amounts. However, a corrected loser does not mean business will flow again. For example, a company is likely to lose business if there isn't a prominent sign outside its premises because customers will not be able to find the organisation. But, putting a sign up is unlikely, in itself, to create business. Another example could be the way the receptionist answers the phone: a speedy and efficient receptionist is unlikely to be the direct cause of new business; but, if telephone calls are not answered promptly and politely, then the receptionist can easily lose business for the organisation.

The impact of winners, qualifiers and losers on the level of business is illustrated in Figure 6. Winners don't always stay winners for long. As the winners are copied by the competition, they tend over time to become qualifiers.

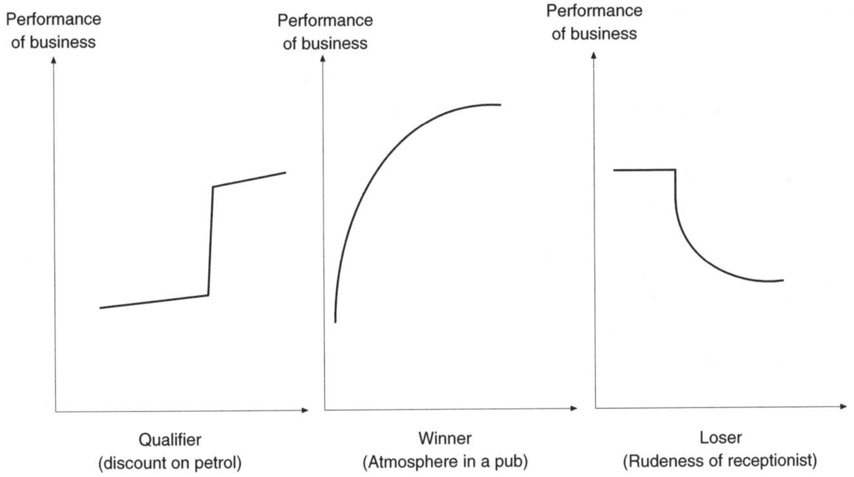

Figure 6: The impact of qualifiers, winners and losers
Source: Based on the ideas of Hill (1995, pp. 60–105)

ACTIVITY 21

Consider two high street retailers. Identify the winners used by each retailer and list one qualifier and one loser found in its particular market.

You could have picked, say

- Body Shop – its winner is its image of being environmentally friendly
- Argos – its winner is its catalogue shopping at very low prices
- Virgin Records – its winner is its image of mastery of the popular music business, the staff are knowledgeable and the range of music and related goods is complete.

In nearly all high street retailers, price is a qualifier. If a retailer is known to be expensive, it will get little or no business. Another qualifier is location: if the shop is at the wrong end of the high street or away from the car park, trade will be much reduced. Losers include poorly trained staff, shabby premises and an unwillingness to exchange goods or give refunds.

It is unlikely that organisations can be good at everything and generally they focus on offering one or two winners. Some companies like Ford focus on product-related winners. Ford designs its products to be made in high volume, giving excellent value for money, and it places great emphasis on the control of product costs and on maintaining quality standards. Rigibore Tools, which produces and markets small special drills and boring bars (for making large holes in metal), manufactures in very small quantities and focuses on quality of design and speed of response.

Other companies focus on the transaction-related benefits, trying to maximise the added value delivered with each sale, by associating additional benefits with the product such as status, image, advice, speed and reliability of delivery. Blacks, which retails camping, climbing and leisure equipment, not only offers competitively priced products but attracts many customers because of the expertise of its staff. Ferrari cars provide their owners with not only a superb sports car, but also an almost unique image.

ACTIVITY 22

Consider these organisations:

- Harrods
- Tesco
- Nike.

Which has a transaction focus and which a product focus?

Although Harrods do sell some products in large quantities and very competitively, much of its business is low volume, large range and its competitive focus is transaction related – people like the high quality of service and, for some customers, the important thing is to be seen shopping at Harrods (transaction focus).

Tesco sells many of the same products as Harrods but its focus is quite different. It goes for high-volume products, and gains competitive advantage from the product attributes, low prices and high quality (product focus).

Nike sports shoes are made in very high volumes and in a relatively small range. Nike's competitive strategy is to provide advanced products (product focus) and market them in such a way that its customers feel good about being seen wearing

Nike shoes (transaction focus).

There is a another way which companies can gain competitive advantage and that is through the control they are able to exert over the customers. This **external control** allows organisations to increase prices or reduce costs without losing business. The company can exert some external control:

- if it is the sole supplier of the product required by the customer
- if a customer is on very friendly terms with a particular supplier
- if the customer finds it too much hassle to change to another supplier.

ORGANISATIONAL STRATEGY

The organisation must decide how it is going to provide the benefits to the customer. It must also make sure it is able to satisfy the other key stakeholders. For example, it must make a profit, pay suppliers, protect the environment, pay employees and pay shareholder dividends. The organisational strategy describes how this is going to be done. It determines the organisational structure, operating policies, rules of behaviour and the performance measures. The organisational strategy must focus on those activities which are essential for the organisation's success.

Organisations do not have to be world class at everything they do, but for long-term survival they must be exceptional in some aspects of its operations. These are known as the **critical success factors** (CSFs) (Boynton and Zmud, 1984).

Look at Table 8, the second column shows some of the many ways of encouraging a customer to trade with the organisation. These are product and transaction benefits that we identified earlier. The third column identifies the key qualities the organisation must possess if it is to deliver these benefits to the customer. The fourth column identifies the critical success factors it must undertake to develop the key qualities. As you can see from the table, the CSFs include:

- market research and product promotion
- product and process innovation
- processes which are low cost, responsive and customer focused
- products and processes of high quality
- products and processes with high customer switching costs
- high market entry barriers.

Critical success factors (CSFs) can be divided in four types:

- industry dictated CSFs
- customer dictated CSFs
- environmentally dictated CSFs
- organisation dictated CSFs.

Dimension	**Customer benefit**	**Key qualities**	**Key activities (critical success factors)**
Product	Good match to customer's requirements	A high level of customer understanding	Market research and product innovation
	Affordable price	Low costs	Low cost processes and overheads
	The product operates effectively and does not go wrong	Quality products	Total quality management
Transaction	Customer can easily find out about the product and how to acquire it	An excellent knowledge of who the customers are and how to contact them	Product promotion
	Products are readily available	Delivery speed and reliability	Responsive processes
	No problems with the exchange of money for goods or services	Quality transactions	Total quality management
	Reliable information available about the product and its use	An excellent appreciation of how the customer will use the product	Customer-focused processes
	There is no hassle involved with the transaction	An excellent interface between the company and the customer	Customer-focused processes
	The customers feel they have got good value for money	An excellent appreciation of what the customer values	Market research
	The customer's friends admire the product purchased	An excellent appreciation of customer and public taste	Market research
	Things are sorted out effectively if they go wrong	Quality after-sales service	Customer-focused processes
External control	Customer unable to purchase elsewhere	Market control	Maintenance of market entry barriers

Dimension	Customer benefit	Key qualities	Key activities (critical success factors)
	The supplier is local and the customer has high transport costs	Geographic control	Maintenance of local market entry barriers
	The customer is tied into supplier perhaps via purchasing system	Process control	Specialised processes for carrying out transactions
	The supplier offers a unique product or service	Product control	Product and process innovation (patents)
	The customer likes dealing with the supplier	Personal control	Customer focused processes
	It is too much hassle for the customer to change supplier	Perceived control	High product switching costs

Table 8: Customer requirements, competitive advantage and organisational capability

Industry dictated CSFs

These are the activities at which an organisation must excel if it is to survive in its chosen marketplace. They generate the 'qualifiers' we described earlier.

- In the hotel sector, the process of selecting the location (geographical control, see Table 8) of the hotel is probably the most important CSF. A hotel far away from the amenities the customers want to visit is unlikely to attract much business.
- In the personal computer market, product innovation is a key CSF. A PC manufacturer will find business hard to generate without state-of-the-art products.

Customer dictated CSFs

These are the activities which generate the competitive advantage (the 'winners'). The unique tastes of Coca Cola and Kentucky Fried Chicken are winners for their organisations. The product innovation which created the distinctive taste has enabled the organisations to develop product control (see Table 8) and prevents customers from being able to purchase identical products elsewhere. In these organisations, product innovation and protection are going to be CSFs.

Environmentally dictated CSFs

These are activities that organisations must carry out to prevent loss of trade or even closure of the business (an extreme form of 'losers').

- Failure to maintain extremely high standards of cleanliness at McDonald's could result in the poisoning of customers and the closure of restaurants by environmental health officers. Cleanliness and hygiene is therefore a CSF for McDonald's.
- Customer and workforce safety is another obvious CSF, particularly for an organisation such as Alton Towers that runs a theme park.

Organisationally dictated CSFs

Organisations themselves can demand that certain activities are treated as CSFs.

- The Siebe group – one of the world's major engineering companies – sees the shareholder as the key stakeholder and every attempt is made to maintain good dividends and a high share price. The group demands that its subsidiary companies hit rigorous financial performance targets, so activities such as excellent cash management become CSFs.
- One of the key objectives of Parker Hannifin – a market leader in the hydraulic equipment market – is achieving high market share. In Parker Hannifin, market research and product promotion are key CSFs.

ACTIVITY 23

1 Identify one 'winner' customer benefit that Cadbury's, the confectionery manufacturer, is trying to achieve.

2 Based on these benefits, what are the customer dictated CSFs for the organisation?

3 Identify two environmentally dictated CSFs that Cadbury's is likely to have.

The winners include the unique taste and texture of chocolate bars and other products. Product quality and price are probably qualifiers in today's marketplace. The customer dictated CSF will be product innovation and protection. The marketing of the chocolate will obviously stress the unique taste and texture (the eating experience). Environmental CSFs are concerned with preventing damage to the environment and the stakeholders. For Cadbury's, these will include cleanliness, quality control of raw materials and safe disposal of waste products.

2.2 Choosing a strategy and setting targets

Here we explain three techniques which help managers overcome three important problems encountered in strategic planning.

- How to cope with an uncertain future? The technique discussed is scenario planning which you briefly met in Unit 3.

- How to respond to complex environmental changes? The technique discussed is quality function deployment.
- Just how good should an organisation try to be? The technique considered is benchmarking, which you briefly met in Unit 7.

COPING WITH AN UNCERTAIN FUTURE

One of the problems that organisations face is that they need to plan some way ahead: some decisions take years if not decades to come to fruition. These long-term decisions are inherently risky; they rely on being able to forecast the future and, as we all know, the future can easily be very different from the one we expected. **Scenario planning** helps managers to understand the future and to reduce the risks (Schoemaker, 1995). This technique has three stages.

- Stage 1 – Identify the facts, trends and uncertainties which underlie any future strategy. Almost by definition, the facts and trends are relatively easy to handle, we know what we are going to be dealing with. The uncertainties are more difficult, as we are unable to forecast what might happen and, again by definition, there will be more than one possible outcome. However, the uncertainties are unlikely to have hundreds of possible outcomes, normally there are only a few.
- Stage 2 – Create a small number of scenarios based on the facts, trends and a small range of possible values of the uncertainties. Each scenario is a 'story' or 'rich picture', describing a possible version of the future.
- Stage 3 – Identify a range of strategies to cope with the scenarios.

The strategies required to cope with each scenario are then identified and compared. The strategies will fall into four categories (Clemons, 1995):

- **no brainers** – those strategies that must be undertaken in all scenarios
- **no regrets** – those actions which could be undertaken in all scenarios, as they are unlikely to have a detrimental effect
- **contingent possibilities** – those strategies which are only appropriate in a few circumstances
- **no ways!** – there will be some scenarios which the business would find hard to cope with and strategies need to be developed to prevent or minimise the chances of these scenarios occurring.

CASE STUDY

Church Vale Bakeries

Church Vale Bakeries (CVB) employs 100 staff. Based in Birmingham, CVB produces meat pies, savoury and sweet slices for schools and small retail outlets across the Midlands. Some decisions at Church Vale can be left to the last minute, but others must be made over a year ahead. Table 9 shows how long it takes to implement some of the decisions that have to be taken at CVB.

When it comes to taking decisions, managers will have a few facts to go on (like how many meat pies they can make a day and their average cost), but they will have to make a range of assumptions. The decision to change production from, say, meat pies to cheese slices is based upon the assumption that CVB has made enough meat pies (assuming demand will not be extraordinarily high tomorrow) and it needs to make some cheese slices (assuming customers will place some orders for them).

When decisions are quick to implement, then CVB can easily rectify a mistake if the assumptions prove to be wrong: it can make another batch of meat pies early tomorrow. When decisions take a long time to implement, it's another problem. For example, the long-term decision to enter a new market requires managers at Church Vale to make assumptions about what life will be like some years into the future: they need to estimate demand for products, consider how eating habits might alter, how people will do their shopping, etc.

Consider the situation if market research has shown that cheese slices should sell well in Germany. Based on the assumptions that this research is correct and demand will remain high for a few years at least, the decision is taken to market cheese slices in Germany. As Table 9 indicates, it will take 12–18 months to get sales started in Germany and at least two or three years before managers find out if there really is a sustainable, high demand for cheese slices. If demand proves to be weak, CVB will probably have lost a great deal of money and meanwhile missed a number of other opportunities.

Note: Church Vale Bakery is a fictitious company, this case study and the commentary that follows is based on information kindly supplied by Peter Nathan of Abbey Vale Bakery Limited, a bakery that has some resemblance to this case study.

Decision	**Action required**	**Time to implement**	**Time before you can tell if the decision was correct**
Change the product being produced	Clean and reset machines	Few hours	Days
Increase output by 5%	Overtime and change in shift patterns	1 or 2 days	Weeks
Increase output by 10%	Recruit and train new staff	Few weeks	Few months
Increase output by 25%	Purchase new production and freezing equipment	1 or 2 months	6 months

Decision	Action required	Time to implement	Time before you can tell if the decision was correct
Increase output by 50%	Acquire new factory premises	Few months	A year
Increase output by 100%	Develop new production and management systems	A year	A year or two
Develop a new range of products	Design and test new products, produce sales literature	6 to 12 months	A year or two
Enter new export markets	Identify new agents and outlets and set up distribution system	12 to 18 months	Two or three years

Table 9: Time to implement a decision at Church Vale Bakeries Limited

The problem for managers is how to minimise the risk of the decision, given the uncertainty of the forecasts they have to make. Scenario planning helps managers by, first of all, categorising the types of forecast that are being made, then identifying the impact of the different possible outcomes.

Identify the facts, trends and uncertainties which underlie any future strategy

Some forecasts can be considered to be concrete facts. For example, in the year 2005 people will need to eat, and most food will still be bought in shops and not by television shopping. But most forecasts have some degree of risk. For example, the forecast that in the year 2005 the number of vegetarians in Britain will be below 50 per cent of the population has a fairly low risk of being wrong; the forecast that in three years time more than 35 per cent of people in Britain will eat breakfast away from home has a fairly high chance of being wrong; the forecast that our competitors will not copy our best selling product has a very high risk of being wrong.

For Church Vale Bakeries. a number of changes in the environment must be taken into account when planning its future strategy.

- Changes in government policy mean that, over the next two years, the purchase of food for school meals is to be moved out of local authority control and into the hands of contract caterers or the schools themselves. If this happens, Church Vale will have to change its method of marketing. It is difficult to see what could stop these changes – so treat it as a **fact** (a **known result** happening at a **known time**).

- Over the last few years, small retail bakeries have gradually been forced out of business by the supermarkets. If this continues to happen, Church Vale will need to find alternative outlets. It is difficult to see what could stop this decline in small bakeries – so treat this as a **trend** (a known result expected over a **known time**).
- The average age of the population is increasing and older people prefer to eat light slices rather than meat pies. If this continues, Church Vale will need to introduce a new range of products. It is difficult to see that changes in the age profile will be halted or reversed – so treat this as a **trend**. Old people are unlikely to suddenly develop bigger appetites, so treat their preference for light slices as a **fact**.
- The business occupying the premises adjacent to the Church Vale factory is aiming to relocate to new premises within the next three years. When this happens, Church Vale could expand on that site. This is a forecast change with **known result** but **uncertain timing**.
- An agreement is to be signed next year with a chain of small supermarkets in the north of England and Scandinavia. Depending on the effectiveness of the supermarket chain, this could result in an increase in sales. This is a forecast change with **known timing** but **uncertain result**.
- Earlier we looked at the forecast of the percentage of people who, in three years time, do not eat breakfast at home, (**known timing,** in three years, **uncertain result**, the percentage). For Church Vale, this is quite an important matter. Demand for its 'Brekky' (breakfast pastry with bacon and egg) will be determined largely by the number of people who eat breakfast away from home and grab a bite to eat on the way to work.
- BSE will eventually be eradicated in the UK. But it is not known when, or whether demand for steak meat pies will return to their old levels. So, any forecasts of demand changes based on the eradication of BSE will be of **uncertain timing** and **uncertain result**.

ACTIVITY 24

Church Vale Bakeries produces a range of pastries. Identify two changes in the business environment which could affect the sale of pastries. Categorise these changes in terms of the timing and result.

All sorts of events could affect the sale of pastries. For instance, you may think that the public will increasingly resist food with a high fat content (pastries are 30–40 per cent fat), this change in eating habits has both uncertain timing and result. As the disposable income of people in Britain increases, the expenditure on cakes and snacks will probably continue to increase. Consider this increase in demand as a trend.

Create scenarios

When Church Vale looks at the facts, trends and uncertainties, it can see that the facts and trends are pretty clear. It will need to make a definite response to the fact that:

- there will be a change of purchaser for school food
- demand from local bakers will diminish
- new products are required to meet the needs of working women and older people.

The total impact of the 'uncertainties' is not so easy to identify. It appears that there are three key issues:

- when will the BSE scare be over and will meat pie sales recover
- the percentage of non-breakfast eaters and their impact on the sales of Brekkys
- the success of the new supermarket chain and the increase in sales this will generate.

In three years time:

- BSE could still be an issue, depressing the sales of meat pies
- BSE could be forgotten about and sales of meat pies have returned to their old levels (meaning that total sales will increase by 20 per cent).

In three years time, the percentage of people who eat breakfast away from home could be:

- less than 10 per cent -– meaning no increase in overall sales
- between 10 and 25 per cent – meaning about a 10 per cent increase in overall sales
- over 25 per cent – meaning sales could be up 20 per cent.

In three years time, the new supermarket chain could be:

- a flop with no increase in sales
- a partial success, increasing overall sales by 10 per cent
- a great success, increasing sales by 20 per cent.

These alternative outcomes can be put together in a matrix to give an idea of the possible total impact on sales (Table 10).

We still don't know which of these outcomes will actually happen, but this table will give us the basis for making some decisions, as you can see when we look at Stage 3 of the scenario planning process, which is to identify a range of strategies.

Identify a range of strategies

Stages 1 and 2 have enabled us to identify the facts, trends and range of sales outcomes (the scenarios). The final stage is to decide what action to take.

	BSE forgotten (sales up 20%)			BSE still depressing sales (no change in sales)		
Increase in sales from new supermarket chain	Percentage away-breakfast eaters			Percentage away-breakfast eaters		
	<10% (no extra sales)	10-25% (sales up 10%)	25% + (sales up 20%)	<10% (no extra sales)	10-25% (sales up 10%)	25% + (sales up 20%)
0	120	130	140	100	110	120
10%	130	140	150	110	120	130
20%	140	150	160	120	130	140

Table 10: Matrix of Church Vale Bakeries sales levels in three years time (present sales level = 100)

The facts and trends tell Church Vale that to maintain existing sales levels it must:

- develop new approaches to selling food products for use in schools
- find replacement outlets to make up for the loss of sales to local bakers
- develop new ranges of products for working women and older people.

The range of sales outcomes is harder to analyse. However, it is often the case that there is only a limited number of possible outcomes which need to be considered. When Church Vale is considering future investment in plant and machinery, it is the overall level of future sales which is the determining factor – different sales levels require different action. For example:

- if overall demand remains static, then there will be no need to increase production or distribution facilities
- if overall demand is up by over 20 per cent, then it will be worth setting up a new production line
- if overall demand is up by over 35 per cent, then it will be worth setting up a new factory
- if overall demand is up by over 55 per cent, then it will be worth setting up a new distribution system.

In doing this, we have identified the **decision points**. The projections in Stage 2 (Table 10) show that in only three cases do sales rise by less than 20 per cent, so it is probably worth taking the risk and installing a new production line.

However, in only one case do sales increase more than 55 per cent, so the decision to develop a new distribution system should be put on hold. In just less than half the cases, there is sufficient demand to justify setting up a new factory. In light of this, the management think it is worth going for a new factory. If sales actually increase by less than the 35 per cent required, they think they would be able to either increase sales by increasing their marketing efforts or sublet the old factory on a short-term lease.

We can now consider strategies for Church Vale Bakeries under the four categories identified by Clemons (1995).

No brainers

These actions must be undertaken no matter what happens:

- changing the approach to selling to schools
- finding new outlets to replace the reduced sales to local bakeries
- finding new ranges of products to suit working women and old people.

No regrets

These actions should be taken, no matter what happens, as they are unlikely to have a detrimental effect:

- installing a new production line
- acquisition of the new factory premises.

Contingent possibilities

These actions are only likely to be appropriate in a few circumstances:

- increasing the marketing effort
- subletting the old factory
- developing a new distribution system.

No ways!

Church Vale wants to avoid the scenario at all costs in which it had the new factory, but sales were low and it was unable to sublet the old factory. Church Vale must think how it is going to avoid this situation. One possibility would be to invest in new refrigeration facilities within the old factory. This would help solve some of Church Vale's storage problems, but more importantly it would be very much easier to sublet the factory should the need arise. Although this is an expensive solution, it lowers the risk of a much more expensive event occurring (paying rent on an empty factory), and makes the investment worthwhile.

ACTIVITY 25

Earlier we looked at North Bank Co-operative Farmers and developed a SWOT analysis (see Figure 3). Table 11 shows the opportunities and threats we identified and also lists some of the changes which created them. Fill in the three gaps in third column of the table.

Which of the uncertainties could be investigated further in an attempt to convert them into facts or trends? Identify two actions that NBCF could take to address these opportunities and threats. Categorise your chosen actions into 'no brainers', 'no regrets', 'contingent possibilities' and 'no ways!'.

Opportunity	**Cause of opportunity**	**Fact, trend or uncertainty**
Expand into other parts of Britain	Staff becoming more experienced and management systems able to cope with remote locations	Largely happened already, so **fact** and **trend**
Attract general public into the Town & Country stores	Public are more mobile and prepared to travel greater distances for convenience shopping	
Set up sole agency agreements with suppliers (so that the supplier will only supply NBCF in the area)	Suppliers realise the benefits of collaborative agreements	**Uncertainty** (unknown timing)
Offer information services to farmers and gardeners	Customers' needs change as a result of economic conditions and the power of their customers	**Uncertainty** (unknown timing and result)
Expand the product range	Improved IT systems enable NBCF to satisfy a greater range of customers' needs, reducing reliance on a narrow range of products and markets	Improved IT systems are a **fact**, but impact on customers' needs is an **uncertainty** (unknown result)
Threat	**Cause of threat**	**Fact, trend or uncertainty**
Farmers diversifying away from agriculture (to golf courses, etc.)	The Common Agricultural Policy has caused swings in farming profitability	
Farmers demanding better service	Farmers are under pressure from customers to react quickly, and people have come to expect high quality products and service	Happened so **fact**, but customers will want even better service, so **trend**
New competition threatening profit margins	Without market growth, new competition means lower sales for NBCF	
Farmers buying direct from NBCF's suppliers	NBCF's suppliers have realised they can afford to service large farmers without going through NBCF	Happened so **fact**, but large customers may want to leave NBCF, so **uncertainty**
Reduced sale of animal feed resulting from food scares (such as BSE)	The outbreaks of animal diseases reduces demand for animal products	**Uncertainty** (unknown timing and result)
New regulations on the storage and use of products	People are more aware of the danger of chemicals to the environment and they want better storage and operating methods; as technology becomes available to give extra protection, politicians create laws to enforce its use	Bound to happen, so **trend**

Table 11: Opportunities and threats faced by North Bank Co-operative Farmers

In thinking that there is an opportunity to attract the general public to the 'Town & Country' stores, NBCF is assuming that the public is willing to drive to the stores rather than go to other retailers. Market research would soon test this assumption, probably well enough to categorise the result as a fact. NBCF thinks that there is a risk that farmers will move out of farming into other activities. Again this can easily be tested by market research, which will probably reveal a trend. The SWOT analysis has revealed a threat from competition. Already some competitors have moved into the area and the loss of business is known. So this is already a fact. There is a risk that more competitors could move in, but the timing and impact on sales are unknown.

NBCF must strive to continually improve its service (a 'no brainer' strategy). The idea of diversifying into other products could be attractive for NBCF as a 'no regrets' strategy: it would overcome any drop in sales as farmers move away from farming and reduce the impact of another scare like BSE. NBCF needs to identify a 'no way!' strategy which will prevent large farms buying direct from the suppliers. It also needs to consider how to react if new competitors enter the market. 'Contingent possibilities' such as reducing prices and loyalty discounts could be triggered as soon as NBCF is aware that a company is considering entering the market.

RESPONDING TO COMPLEX ENVIRONMENTAL CHANGES

Changes in the business environment often demand a complex response from the organisation. For example, if a company is finding it hard to recruit new staff – perhaps some new businesses have started up nearby and taken all the good people in the labour market – it is unlikely that just increasing wages will be the answer. An increase in wages would push up costs and it may then be necessary to acquire more sophisticated technology to keep the costs down, and this in turn will have knock on implications, for example, on raw material, suppliers, planning systems, etc. **Quality function deployment** (QFD) (Hofmeister, 1992) is an easy way to link environmental changes to internal processes. To see how QFD works, consider the following case study.

CASE STUDY

Ctools Limited

Ctools Limited manufactures air compressors. These are the machines which produce the compressed air to drive tools like rock-drills for use in quarries or for pumping up car tyres in petrol stations. Figure 7 shows how the main components of an air compressor are arranged.

There are four main components in an air compressor. The motor (usually diesel or electric) drives the compressor unit which pumps air into an air receiver. The air is held in the air receiver under high pressure and is drawn off when required. The controller governs the speed of the motor in an attempt to ensure that the rate at which air is being used is equal to the rate at which it is being compressed. In that way, the controller keeps the pressure of the air in the receiver at a constant value.

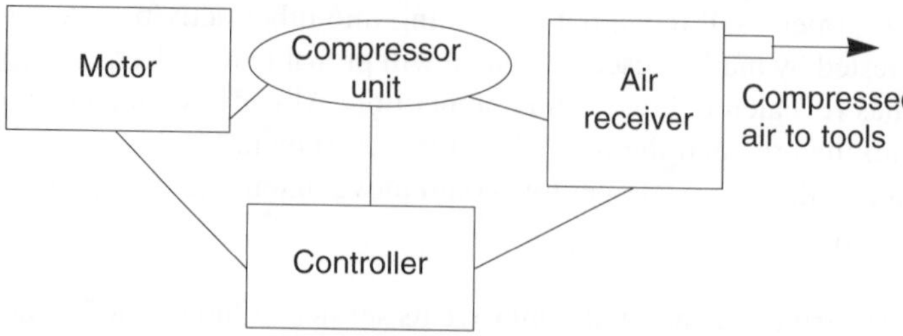

Figure 7: Air compressor components

In recent months, Ctools have been losing business to its main competitor and it is very keen to determine what action should be taken to reverse this trend. As a result of some market research, Ctools has been able to compare the performance of its compressors with those of the main competitor. Ctools has a small range of compressors, based on a patented principle which leads to improved performance and reliability. Ctools is good at product promotion and is generally cheaper. The competition has a wider range of lower efficiency products, and it does have a very good delivery performance (a very short time between customer order being received and the compressor installed on customer's premises) and a good repair service (it can quickly repair compressors which have broken down). This analysis prompts the question: are Ctools' products underpriced? But more importantly it shows that Ctools has got to put effort into improving its delivery performance and service.

Table 12 is designed to show how the marketplace performance of the product is linked to Ctools' internal performance. This sort of matrix is a form of QFD table (Hofmeister, 1992). Table 12 compares the market performance with the internal performance. The first column identifies the key characteristics that the customer is seeking and the final two columns compare Ctools' performance with that of its competitor in terms of an 'X' score (5 = excellent, 1 = bad). The middle columns identify the internal processes that impact on the market performance. Here, we cannot show all the relevant internal activities, obviously in reality other activities such as staff training would be included. Within the body of the matrix, the strength of the link between market performance and each internal process is indicated by a 'Y' score (3 = strong, 2 = medium, 0 = none). By multiplying each 'Y' score by its corresponding 'X' score we get the 'Z' scores (the numbers shown in brackets) – Ctools first, the competitor second. Adding all the 'Z' scores shown in a column gives a process performance score (PPS) for Ctools and the competitor (see the bottom two rows). Comparison of 'Z' scores and PPSs gives a clear idea of the internal processes which need improvement. In this case, Ctools must improve the operations management significantly (Ctools scored only a PPS of 26 compared with the competition's 40). Ctools also needs to look at the machining and assembly processes, and the low 'Z' scores on delivery and repair service mean Ctools must improve in these areas.

Link between market performance and process – the 'Y' score

Product characteristics	Quality of processes used: Marketing management	Operations management	Controller design	Compressor design	Machining	Assembly	Performance: The 'X' score: Ctools	Competitor
Product promotion	3 (15,6)	0 (0,0)	2 (10,4)	2 (10,4)	0 (0,0)	0 (0,0)	5	2
Price	3 (12,6)	2 (8,4)	2 (8,4)	3 (12,6)	2 (8,4)	2 (8,4)	4	2
Range of products	3 (9,15)	0 (0,0)	0 (0,0)	3 (9,15)	0 (0,0)	0 (0,0)	3	5
Delivery speed	0 (0,0)	3 (3,12)	0 (0,0)	2 (2,8)	3 (3,12)	3 (3,12)	1	4
Delivery reliability	0 (0,0)	3 (6,9)	0 (0,0)	2 (4,6)	3 (6,9)	3 (6,9)	2	3
Product reliability	0 (0,0)	0 (0,0)	3 (12,9)	3 (12,9)	2 (8,6)	3 (12,9)	4	3
Repair service	0 (0,0)	3 (9,15)	3 (9,15)	3 (9,15)	2 (6,10)	2 (6,10)	3	5
Product efficiency	0 (0,0)	0 (0,0)	3 (15,3)	3 (15,3)	2 (10,2)	0 (0,0)	5	1
Ctools	36	26	54	73	41	35		
Competitor	27	40	35	66	43	44		

Table 12: Link between market performance and internal processes for two companies producing air compressors

HOW GOOD SHOULD WE BE?

The QFD matrix (Table 12) identified a number of processes that Ctools needs to improve in order to be better than its main competitor. Ideally, it would want to be not only better than its immediate competitor but world class, that is, up with the best in the world.

Although the higher target of being world class is probably more difficult to achieve than just beating the competition, it makes the job of determining the target somewhat easier. The reason for this is it is unlikely that the competition is going to allow Ctools to examine its processes in detail as, quite rightly, it will be worried that it might copy its best ideas and steal its business. However, a non-competing organisation may well give Ctools the opportunity to examine its methods.

Ctools has discovered that it needed to improve the quality of its operations management in order to compete in the area of the repair service. As we have said, it is unlikely to be able to get in to see how its competitors managed this function, in fact Ctools probably wouldn't want to as its competitors aren't world class anyway! But it may well be possible to visit an aero-engine servicing company and examine its processes to get an idea of the level of service that is attainable. The company is bound to be very good (if not world class) because minimising the time aircraft are not flying is of paramount importance in its market. This process for establishing world-class targets is known as **benchmarking** (Zairi, 1996). You met this concept in Unit 6.

2.3 Implementing strategy

Both the analysis of the business environment and the generation of strategic plans is relatively easy. The hard bit is the implementation as you saw briefly in Unit 3. Implementation of strategy involves **change**. Management of the change process is almost a discipline in its own right and you will study it in more detail in further modules. Here, we just look at a few aspects that concern people. Basically change will occur in the following areas:

- developing new products and markets
- creating new trading relationships
- installing new equipment and processes
- giving staff new jobs, knowledge and skills.

It is that last of these which is usually the hardest! In modern business, the level of change is such that managers cannot do it alone, all staff must be involved in helping to bring it about. Phillippe de Woot (1997) has identified four prerequisites for getting staff to bring about change.

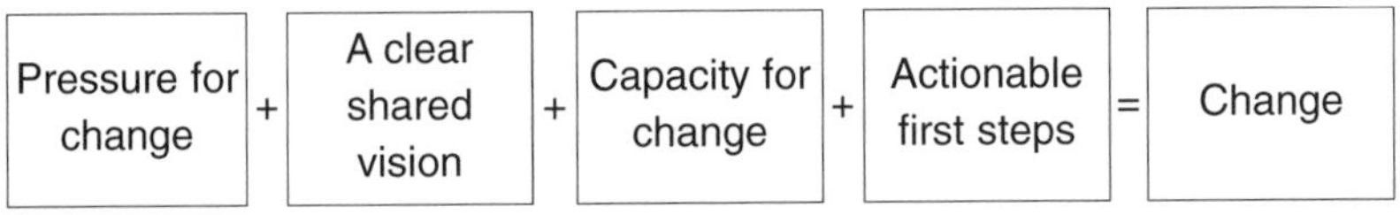

Figure 8: Model of change

The **pressure for change** will come from an awareness of opportunities and threats. It is essential that everybody within the organisation is aware of the pressure for change and appreciates that if the organisation is to prosper things must change. A key part of making staff aware of the pressure for change is showing them how their efforts will help the organisation succeed.

The quality manager of a large US engineering company had the job of vetting potential suppliers. This involved visiting potential suppliers and carrying out a detailed examination of their resources and systems. If the supplier passed, it could do business with the US engineering company; if it failed, it was unlikely ever to get an order. This process took a long time and often resulted in the supplier being rejected. After many such vettings, the quality manager realised that there was a good correlation between the state of the toilets used by a factory workforce and the quality of the systems and products: if the toilets were clean and tidy then the same approach was applied to all the company's activities. So, in future, the quality manager made a point of visiting the factory toilets before starting the full vetting process; if they were untidy, he failed the supplier and left immediately saving himself a great deal of time.

The point of this story was that although they probably didn't know it, the toilet cleaners were in fact extremely important in helping their organisation gain business. The quality manager had stumbled across the rule of business which says 'if you want to provide quality products and services, you must have quality systems and processes throughout your organisation'. If the failing suppliers had realised this, the toilet cleaners would have been consulted on how to make the toilets more presentable, and they would have been better trained, better respected and probably better paid.

A **clear shared vision** sets the direction the company wants to go. A vision statement is more than the mission statement, it describes a 'holy grail' that the organisation is trying to reach. Cable and Wireless plc (1990), a large telecommunications company, set its vision as 'creating a global digital highway'. It wanted to create a fibreoptic network which circled the world, enabling it to offer one of the world's most comprehensive telecommunications services.

Collins and Porras (1996) suggest that to be effective vision statements must be 'Big, Hairy, Audacious Goals' (BHAGs). They say: 'A true BHAG is clear and compelling, serves as a unifying focal point of effort, and acts as a catalyst for team spirit. It has a clear finishing line, so the organisation can know when it has achieved the goal... It is tangible, energising, highly focused. People get it right away; it takes little or no explanation.'

One of the best known BHAGs was set by President Kennedy when he charged NASA with landing a man on the moon by 1970. During the 1960s, everybody in NASA saw the moon mission as the BHAG. At its best, this shared vision is exciting, challenging and energising. In an organisation, it stimulates people to give of their best, to work tirelessly for the common goal – it is motivating.

Without a shared vision, change may happen, but is unlikely to create an organisation which performs to its full potential.

The **capacity for change** includes enabling the staff with the necessary time, training, motivation and resources to bring about the change. This means staff must be involved in the planning of change, and allowed and encouraged to use their abilities to the full when bringing it about. Without the capacity to make change happen, staff will just become frustrated.

It is only when the **actionable first steps** are taken that staff will really believe that change is going to occur. If the actionable first steps happen quickly, staff motivation is likely to rise, the organisation will quickly learn what works and what doesn't, new ways of doing things will be developed and the change process will gain momentum. Failure to quickly turn plans into action leads to demotivation and haphazard implementation.

Many managers make two mistakes when they try to bring about change.

- They spend too much time planning. In most organisations change is an iterative process: a small change is tried, if it works then a bigger change is implemented, if it doesn't another small change is tried, and so on. So, it is important to take the first steps and start learning what works.
- They try to do it on their own. In modern business, there is so much pressure to change that no single person can identify everything that needs to be done and put it into practice. An organisation can only get the full benefits of change when it utilises the full capability and energy of all its staff.

REVIEW ACTIVITY 2

Consider the supply chain of organisations involved in producing the bedding plants that you can buy from a garden centre.

- Stage 1. For many varieties of plant, it starts with a nursery which maintains a range of 'stock' from which small cuttings are taken. These cuttings are propagated (persuaded to grow roots); this usually takes a few weeks.

Stage 2. The plants are then grown to the point at which they can be sold to the public; this can take as little as a week or two, to over a year.

Stage 3. Once they are ready, the plants are labelled and priced and

- Stage 2. The plants are then grown to the point at which they can be sold to the public; this can take as little as a week or two, to over a year.
- Stage 3. Once they are ready, the plants are labelled and priced and put on sale to the public.

These three stages can be done by one organisation, but often there are separate businesses handling each stage of the process.

Running a nursery handling stage 1 of this process involves a number of tasks:

- propagating plants (growing 'stock' plants, taking cuttings and getting them to root) – note, a typical flower nursery may sell tens or even hundreds of different varieties of plant
- taking orders from garden centres, local authorities or other organisations that want large quantities of plants
- sorting the rooted cuttings into batches and despatching them to customers
- invoicing customers and chasing payment
- planning and controlling these activities.

Suppose you want to benchmark these five tasks. Which sort of organisations would you benchmark the nursery against?

Summary

We have examined alternative business strategies and shown how they formed a hierarchy. The product/market strategy looks at the present markets and products and considers if a change is required. The Shell directional policy matrix guides this decision. We then examined internal development or external acquisition strategies. The market sector strategy looks at the requirements of different market sectors and introduces the concept of product and transaction related benefits. The business integration strategy examines the value system and looks at the advantages and disadvantages of vertical integration. The competitive strategy introduced Terry Hill's idea of winners, qualifiers and losers. We looked at critical success factors and saw how they related to winners and competitive advantage.

We have looked at three techniques that help managers overcome problems encountered in strategic planning. **Scenario planning** gives us a way of coping with the fact that it is very difficult to forecast the future. We showed that businesses need to generate four types of strategy to cope with the different futures (scenarios). **Quality function deployment** gives us a way of relating the demands of the external environment to those activities carried out within the organisation. **Benchmarking** helps us set targets for improvement of internal activities.

Finally, we examined some of the fundamental problems of implementation of strategies that involve change and identified the need to:

- develop pressure for change
- have a clear shared vision (BHAG)
- create the capacity for change
- take actionable first steps.

Unit Review Activity

In Activity 3, we described the success of Playlight, a small business which had been created to raise money to provide play equipment for local parks. In Activity 6, two founders of Playlight decided to continue running the business as a normal private limited company as a way of making a living.

1 List two problems that the founders may have with the original stakeholders of the business.

2 In no more than 50 words, write an objective and mission statement for the new business.

3 List two or three decision areas related to the business and its environment that you think the new company must examine. Consider this question under the headings: customers; suppliers; staff.

4 List some of the problems that could come about and that you think the new company must take into account when setting its strategy. Again, consider this question under the headings: customers; suppliers; staff. List at least one fact, one trend and one uncertainty for each.

5 List no more than four ways that the new company should try to gain competitive advantage.

6 List three critical success factors (CSFs) for the organisation.

Unit Summary

In this unit, we have shown how businesses must attempt to align their objectives and abilities with the ever-changing needs of their customers and the pressures of their markets. This process is known as E-V-R congruence. The V is the values of the organisation and these are communicated as the business objectives, mission and value statements. The R is the organisation's resources. In this area, we looked at how the resources, culture and structure of the organisation affect its behaviour and performance. We showed how, as the environment changes, the resources must change as well. The E is business environment and we examined how companies could identify changes in their environment using the factors underlying Porter's five market forces.

We looked at alternative strategies and examined ways of deciding which strategies should be adopted, identifying which internal processes need improvement and how to set targets. The section finished with a brief examination of some of the fundamental issues involved in the implementation of strategy.

We have focused on those business activities which cross the boundaries of functions and departments. It has shown methods that can be employed to help managers decide on the overall direction of the business and determine the action that needs to be taken within the business to make sure it really starts to head in the desired direction.

References

Boeing web page, http://www.boeing.com/quick.facts.htm#2

Boynton, A C and Zmud, R W (1984) 'An assessment of critical success factors' *The Sloan Management Review*, Summer

BT (1996) *Annual Report and Accounts*, BT

Cable and Wireless (1990) *Strategy in Action 1: Strategic Intent*, video, Hawkshead Production

Collins, J C and Porras, J I (1996) 'Building your company's vision' *Harvard Business Review*, September-October

Clemons, E K (1995) 'Using scenario analysis to manage the strategic risks of re-engineering' *Sloan Management Review*, Summer

Greiner, L. (1972) 'Evolution and revolution as organisations grow' *Harvard Business Review*, July-August

Hanson plc (1990) *Annual Report and Accounts*, Hanson plc

Hedley, B (1976) 'A fundamental approach to strategy development' *Long Range Planning*, 9 (6), 2–11 December

Heller, R (1994) *The Fate of IBM*, Warner Books

Hill, T (1995) *Manufacturing Strategy: Text and Cases*, Macmillan Business

Hofmeister, K (1992) *Quality Function Deployment*, ASI Quality Systems

Kay, J A (1993) *Foundations of Corporate Success*, Oxford University Press

Marks and Spencer (1996) *Annual Report and Financial Statement*, Marks and Spencer

Miles, R E and Snow, C C (1978) *Organisation Strategy, Structure and Process*, McGraw-Hill

Mintzberg, H, Quinn, J B and Ghoshal, S (1995) *The Strategy Process* (European Edition), Prentice Hall

Porter, M E (1979) 'How competitive forces shape strategy' *Harvard Business Review*, March-April

Schoemaker, P J H (1995) 'Scenario planning: a tool for strategic thinking' *Sloan Management Review*, Winter

Thompson, J L (1993) *Strategic Management: Awareness and Change*, Chapman Hall

Zairi, M (1996) *Benchmarking for Best Practice*, Butterworth Heinemann

de Woot, P (1997) 'Managing change at university', unpublished paper

Recommended Reading

Mintzberg, H, Quinn, J B and Ghoshal, S (1995) *The Strategy Process* (European Edition), Prentice Hall

Rockart, J F (1979) 'Chief executives define their own data needs' *Harvard Business Review*, March-April

Answers to Review Activities

Review Activity 1

Relative size and entry barriers – the supermarkets recognise the benefits that size can bring: it gives them power when dealing with small suppliers; it creates entry barriers, for example, local councils will only allow a small number of large supermarkets in a given area; it has enabled them to force suppliers to standardise many of their products.

Significance of each transaction – each supermarket turns over thousands of pounds each week, each customer makes up only a small proportion of this turnover, so the customers have little power. The supermarkets, however, buy in large volumes and, for their suppliers, each order often represents a significant percentage of the total business, giving the supermarket a great deal of negotiating power.

Switching costs and product differentiation – the suppliers of supermarkets try to increase their power by creating product differentiation in the mind of the ultimate consumer. The supermarkets counter this strategy by promoting own-brand products – which gives them an alternative source of supply. At the same time, supermarkets have increased their own differentiation and their customers switching costs by introducing loyalty cards and bonuses and other services such as banking.

Capacity of the industry – supermarkets try to limit competitive rivalry by acquiring the best sites in each locality, preventing competitors from moving into a market. They are not always successful in this strategy and in many parts of the country there is fierce competition.

The self-service system that supermarkets use gives them limited control over capacity costs: the number of tills operated and the amount of stock held on the shelves can be changed to match demand. However, the overhead costs of a supermarket are fairly high and when demand falls, profits quickly follow.

Review Activity 2

Propagating plants is a process which is almost unique to the plant business and it will be very difficult to find an organisation that isn't in the same business to benchmark against. The best approach would be to identify a large nursery which serves a different geographic market, say in Holland, where plant propagation is a very well-developed process.

Handling customer orders is a very common business task and many organisations are extremely good at it. Home shopping companies such as Next have perfected the art of processing telephone orders and could provide a very good benchmark.

Sorting and despatching is another very common business activity. What makes the nursery slightly unusual is the delicate nature of the products. A large egg-packing plant might be worth examination as would an organisation like RS Components that runs a large business supplying thousands of customers with very small quantities of mainly electrical and electronic components.

Again there is nothing unusual about invoicing and chasing payments. The public utilities (water, gas, etc.) handle vast numbers of invoices and there would be much a nursery could learn from them.

The planning and control activity is unusual, as the uncertainties associated with working with living raw material make it very complex: plants can get diseased, they grow faster when it's sunny and slower when it's cold, the number of cuttings which can be taken from a stock plant varies considerably, etc. For benchmarking, it will be necessary to find another company handling living raw material in a non-competing sector such as wine or cheese making.

Answer to Unit Review Activity

1 The change to a private limited company would probably affect most of the stakeholder relationships: the local council would want rent for the premises, the staff would want a realistic wage. It is also likely that as the objectives changed from 'providing play equipment' to 'making money' many of those initially involved would drift away from the business as it no longer satisfied their personal objectives such as helping the community. These changes would put up costs and this, in turn, would force the business to develop effective management and operating systems.

2 The original open objective would have been something like 'through the efforts of local people, to raise money to provide play equipment in the local parks'. The new open objective might be 'to run a successful business providing employment for the directors and local people'. The closed objective could be 'to create and run a business which will generate £50,000 gross profit in year 1 and will grow at least 20 per cent per annum'. The mission of the business could be 'to run a successful business producing lighting equipment for sale in the UK, providing well-paid employment for local people'.

3 In relation to customers, the company must decide which sectors it is trying to serve, the range of products it wants to market, whether it will do special commissions or stick to standard products, how it is going to promote the products, etc.

In relation to suppliers, the company must decide what items it wants to produce within the business and which components it wants to buy, whether to stick to local suppliers or buy nationally or globally, what sort of relationship it needs to build up with suppliers, how many suppliers to have for each component, etc.

In relation to staff, it needs to consider what conditions of service to set (wages, hours, holidays, etc.), how to involve staff in decision making, the training to be given, etc.

4 In relation to customers, change may come from cheap imports that might swamp the market, from new forms of lighting (very effective LEDs are being developed which may take over from light bulbs) may change the need for lamps, from the larger customers may want improved quality and reduced prices. In relation to suppliers, key suppliers could go out of business, prices could go up, components could be of poor quality or not delivered on time. In relation to staff, key staff could leave, motivation levels (and therefore output) could fall, wages in the locality could rise (resulting from, say, a new large employer moving into the area).

For answers to tasks 5 and 6 see Table 8 for the possible ways competitive advantage can be gained and the CSFs associated with them.

UNIT 9
BUSINESS PLANNING AND PROJECT MANAGEMENT

Introduction

In this unit, we build on Unit 8 and look at how to turn the strategic plan into reality. We consider two activities. First, creating the business plan. This is an essential communication document identifying the key issues, costs and benefits of what the organisation is trying to do. Second, project management. This is the management of one-off tasks and requires special techniques.

This will give you some ideas about specific aspects of the implementation of strategy that you will address in detail in further modules on strategy and change. It will also introduce you to some useful techniques. In drawing up a business plan, we develop ideas that have practical application in achieving the strategic direction of the organisation and, in doing this, we highlight key features of the strategy itself.

In the section on project management, we look at an overall technique that can be used in implementing major change, but we also consider a number of other significant techniques that are used in operations management and can be used in other business functions to great effect. We take a very practical approach to some of the concepts that we have discussed from a more theoretical perspective elsewhere in this module.

Objectives

By the end of this unit, you will be able to:

- explain what business plans are and their use in different situations
- identify the main features of a business plan
- draw up a simple plan
- explain the roles of the people involved in project management and the information they require
- produce a one-page project specification
- produce a project work breakdown structure, milestone plan, activity chart and Gantt chart
- explain the meaning of baseline, scheduled and actual costs, and earned value
- understand how to construct and read project 'S' curves
- identify the main source of risks in projects and which risks require action.

SECTION 1

Drawing up a Business Plan

Introduction

A few companies grow and prosper with very little planning, while some companies with thorough, well-laid plans disappear. So, although good planning is not vital for success, what good planning will do is increase the chance of success and reduce **risk**. By planning the future of a business, from money to staffing, from products to ownership, the chance of success is multiplied and the risk of failure is drastically reduced.

The aim of planning, then, is not to predict the future precisely, but to improve the chances of achieving future objectives by encouraging:

- realism among managers
- a coherent view of the whole business
- the business to face up to unpleasant risks or threats
- investigation into competitors, the market and the business's position
- the business to plan finances rationally
- people to make mistakes on paper rather than in reality.

The end result of the business planning process is the business plan. This may have a number of uses within and outside of the organisation. In this section, we identify the features of a business plan and what it should achieve. You learn how to draw one up.

1.1 What is a business plan?

A good business plan is a description of **what the business intends to achieve and how**, setting out where the business is going, the steps along the way and the route it is going to take. It incorporates results from investigation of markets, production, finance, the organisation itself and, of course, the potential risks. In essence, the business plan explains how the business strategy (see Unit 8) is going to be put into practice through functional strategies.

Frequently, a business plan outlines a competitive strategy proposal for making a new product or starting a new business. It may be drawn up to persuade investors to put money into the strategy. However, a business plan is just as useful for an existing business which is carrying out internal strategic changes such as reducing staff or restructuring. Whatever the objective, the planning process is valuable, giving the best chance of success and ultimately survival; it is an essential follow-on from the strategic planning process.

Whatever the strategy, a business plan will have much the same content and structure, although different parts of the plan will be emphasised depending on the company strategy and the precise purpose of the plan.

- A plan for **setting up a new business** that seeks to obtain investment will firstly need to attract the attention of potential investors. It will need to explain what the return on the investment will be – how much money the business will make. If this is too low, nobody will invest of course; but if it is too high, the plan may look unrealistically optimistic. Investors will also need to know whether they will get their money back if the business fails.
- A plan for a **new product within a business** probably needs less detail on financing, although a return on investment will be expected. The company will often be interested in how the new product fits in with existing products and strategy and will look for detail on how it will be manufactured.
- A general plan for a **small business for the next five years** may aim to clarify and set down the thinking of the company management. The overall objectives and implementation issues will be given the most emphasis. The plan will act as a reference document, so that as the plan is brought into reality, managers can compare their actions and performance against the planned target.

The plan should aim to answer five fundamental questions.

- What is the company trying to do? Is it planning a new product, entering a new market, starting a new business, reshaping or reducing the business or making a general plan for the next few years?
- What will the proposal do for the company, both strategically and financially?
- How much will it cost and who will pay?
- What is involved in implementing the plan, and when and how will it be done?
- What will happen if things don't go as planned?

There are many ideas on what should be included in a business plan (Crowner, 1991, chapter 5; Hyypia, 1992). However, a common approach is to structure a business plan along the following lines:

- executive summary
- description of the business and the industry
- explanation of the company strategy
- analysis of the market
- description of the marketing strategy and how it is to be put into operation
- description of the operations strategy and how the products and services are going to be produced

- description of the resource implications, particularly the financial aspects
- an action plan, what is going to be done and when
- a risk assessment.

We now develop a typical business plan, illustrating the key features and demonstrating how it links with the company strategy.

1.2 Creating the business plan

To illustrate the different parts of a business plan, we look at a real plan for a small manufacturing company. All the names have been fictionalised, the market details have been changed and some of the details have been omitted. This plan is not an 'ideal', it has many flaws and limitations, but so do many companies' plans.

Lombard Ltd specialise in supplying large castings for other manufacturing firms. The company was set up six years ago by two friends who were made redundant by British Steel. They started small and carried out very little planning, but they knew their market and by working hard the company has grown to employ 15 people. Recently, it has landed a very large contract from London Transport. This triggered the management to re-examine its business strategy. As a result, a new strategy has been formulated, which requires some major changes and additional finance. We describe the business plan which was drawn up to convince Lombard's bank manager that further investment in the business would be a good thing.

After we have discussed a section of the plan in the text, you will have the chance to put what you have learned into practice by writing sections of a plan for Playlight. So, as you read the examples remember to ask yourself 'How does this apply to Playlight?'. Playlight you will recall was a case study that you investigated in Unit 8; it featured in Activities 3 and 6, and again in the Unit Review Activity.

EXECUTIVE SUMMARY

The executive summary condenses the whole plan into one page. Often, this is where readers decide whether or not they are interested in reading further to gain more detailed information. This page needs to sell the plan. It needs all the basic information – what the plan is about, what the company is trying to achieve and how much money is involved – but it also needs to make sure the reader wants to read the rest of the plan.

First, set out the basics.

```
Company name and address:
Lombard Ltd
Smokepot Industrial Estate
Ebbw Afon
Gwent NG37 2LG
Tel: 01367 242367
Fax: 01367 247291
```

`Contact name` [generally the plan's author]

```
Herbert Lom

Managing Director
Lombard Ltd

Lombard Ltd is a small foundry specialising in the supply of
castings for the heavy transport and plant industry. For the
past six years, Lombard has enjoyed steady growth. It now
employs 15 people.
```

Next, create the interest. Explain what the plan is about in very simple terms.

```
This growth has led to expansion of the production area,
which is located on two sites. Lombard needs to expand
further to cater for a large new contract with London
Transport. A larger production area is needed and some of
the older machinery will be replaced, increasing capacity
and efficiency.
```

What sort of growth is expected?

```
This and other new contracts are expected to lead to a 60
per cent increase in turnover.
```

What is the timescale?

```
This growth is expected to happen over the next five years.
Relocation is planned to take place in the next six months.
```

What work has been carried out?

```
The London Transport contract requires the first delivery to
be made in nine months. New premises have already been
located and the required machinery has been sourced.
```

What money is involved? What investment is required and what is the likely return?

```
The total cost of the move and expansion will be £243,000

Financed through: Welsh Development Agency grant      £90,000
                  British Steel employment loan       £75,000
                  Bank loan                           £78,000

It is anticipated that all loans will be repaid within four
years.
```

THE BUSINESS AND THE INDUSTRY

This section of the plan must include the basic details of the business itself, the nature of the industry and the competition. This is where it starts to be necessary to provide some proof to substantiate the information you are using.

In this section, you would include information about the company: its legal set-up (charity, limited company, plc, partnership, etc.), owners, number of employees, company structure, age (of the business) and how it has been performing recently. Very brief financial details such as turnover should be included here.

> In the six years since its creation, Lombard has grown by 400 per cent. Net profits were low for the first three years, as all available finance was reinvested, but have stabilised over the last two years at around £80,000 from a turnover last year of £600,000.

Describe the product range.

> Lombard supplies large cast components, machined and ready to use, to the transport and plant industry. Most products are specially designed, with one-off or small batch parts developed using Lombard's design service.

Describe the customers – who and where are they, and how many of them are there?

> Lombard currently supplies 45 customers. Five main customers are responsible for 80 per cent of orders by value. These include Fumpingret Machinery (Holland) and Metro Camell Weighbridge (Coventry).

Summarise the industry outlook, picking out size, trends, growth, recent developments.

> ... the specialist casting industry in Britain suffered a sharp decline from 1989 to 1994 with the general decline in manufacturing, falling from £104 million to £68 million annually (Component Suppliers Guild estimate 1995). Over the past two years, an increase in demand from British companies has been noted by Lombard, with UK sales increasing by 32 per cent ...

List key competitors, explaining who are they and what are they doing. What is the spread of other companies: large or small, growing or shrinking, merging or fragmenting?

> Since the closure of the British Steel plant at Aberfanwy in 1990, there has been no dominant company in this area of specialist casting. Lombard's four direct competitors are:
>
> - Pressurecast Ltd, Coventry
> - Slimins (part of Triplex plc), Linwood

- `Nordex-Amplewad, Derby`
- `G&N Tucker, Birmingham.`

Note that Lombard has no information on the size or plans of these companies and it does not seem to have any competitors outside Britain.

ACTIVITY 1

In Unit 8, we described an organisation called Playlight (see Activities 3 and 6). Later, in the Unit Review Activity, you examined some of the issues involved in turning the Playlight business into a private limited company. Remind yourself of the details of this company.

Playlight now needs to find some financial support, say £100,000, to develop the business. A business plan is required by the bank before it is prepared to consider making a loan. In the five activities in this section, you will be asked to create some of this business plan. You will need to use your imagination as you will not have all the details of Playlight's industry and market. However, you should be able to identify the headings that you would want to include, and add some ideas if you can.

In this activity, use the model provided earlier to outline the information required for the 'business and industry' section.

- List the main headings you would use for this section.
- For each heading, write a few (no more than ten) short sentences of description.

Obviously, you do not have all the information to produce this section in full. Where you lack data, just identify the type of information you would want to include.

Playlight's 'business and industry' section could be organised under six headings.

- **The company** – Playlight is a private limited company created as a result of a local co-operative venture.
- **The track record** – Over the last 18 months, Playlight has raised £50,000 for local playground equipment. The company's resources are now refocused on developing a successful business.
- **The product** – Playlight has created a range of novel table lamps.
- **The customers** – It sells through wholesalers to independent retailers.
- **The outlook** – The industry has come out of the recession of the early 1990s and is now showing strong evidence of prolonged, steady growth.
- **The competition** – The competition is mainly from cheap imports that generally have uninspiring designs.

THE COMPANY STRATEGY

The next stage is to explain in some detail the company strategy and give reasons for why funding is required. Some **background** on how the strategy has developed will help set the scene.

> The past success of Lombard Ltd has led to rapid expansion of the company, leading to the use of two sites 400 metres apart. The split location has caused transport and co-ordination problems. A single new location is needed because future planned growth will require further space and machinery.

This should be followed by enough **description** to allow the reader to understand what the plan is all about. If it is to do with developing a product, a clear description, perhaps with pictures will help the reader.

> Premises, with 400 sq. m. floor space, have been found two miles from the current location (see picture). Previously used by a company producing trailers, the site has all necessary services but will require some refurbishment and conversion. Two mufflegrinders and an automated tindler are also to be purchased.

This is a good place for a brief outline of the **target market** if the plan is for a new product.

Finally, this section should explain what the project will do for the company. Is it a huge step towards massive expansion, will it revolutionise the marketplace? Perhaps it's just a small part of a long-term programme of new product development. This section should also include the company's objective, mission and value statements (see Unit 8)

> These expansion plans form part of Lombard's strategy of continuous sustainable growth through customer satisfaction.
>
> The current and planned new contracts will provide an annual growth rate of just under 10 per cent for the company, leading to 60 per cent growth over five years.

ACTIVITY 2

Produce a brief outline of the 'company strategy' section of the Playlight business plan. List the main headings, followed by a few short sentences (no more than ten, see Activity 1).

The strategy section should concentrate on three areas.

- Background – Playlight was formed to raise money for playground equipment... This proved so successful that the organisation has been turned into a limited company.
- Description of the plan – This business plan is to convert local premises into offices and a production area and to produce sales literature to assist the sales effort.
- How this plan fits in with the company's objectives and overall strategy – The company's objective is to 'run a successful business providing employment for the directors and local people.' The target is to generate a profit of £50,000 in year 1 and to grow at a rate of 20 per cent per annum for the first five years. The intention is to build upon the business already established in the domestic light-fitting market.

THE MARKET

The market section is an important part of the plan, proving that there is a market for the products and forecasting possible sales. In this section, therefore, you should identify the main opportunities and threats in the marketplace (see Units 3 and 8).

> The overall market for castings in the UK is £480 million (DTI report on UK productivity, 1994), of which £68 million is specialist casting of the type Lombard produces (finished parts for heavy machinery). Of this, it is estimated that 17 per cent is associated with rail transport, 22 per cent with other transportation (cranes, forklifts, etc.) and 61 per cent with production machinery (see Figure 1).

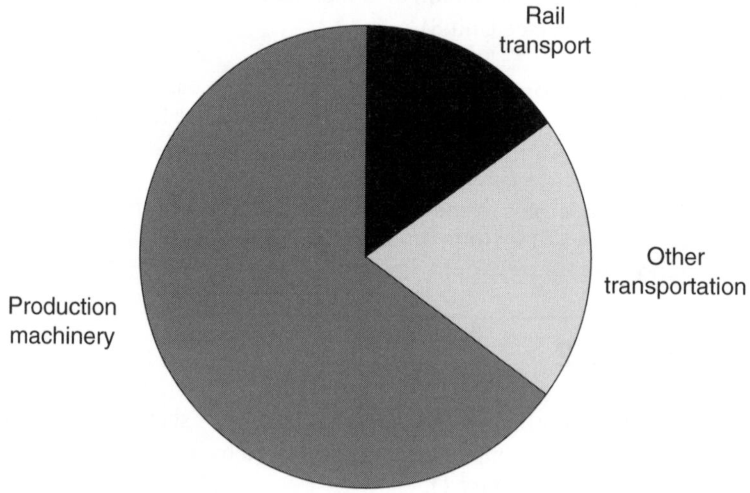

Figure 1: Industrial market for specialist castings

> Over the past 10 years, customers have moved away from competitive tendering to using one preferred supplier, that not only manufactures products but carries out the design activities as well. In addition, few castings are supplied 'rough', most are now delivered machined and ready to use. Price is still a vital factor, of course, and Lombard has won many new customers by beating the competition on price, but the company's design skills are becoming increasingly important in the battle to win business. In a survey of 30 customers, 90 per cent expected to be ordering more over the next 12 months and three had only recently started using castings. This suggests growth within a previously declining market.

So, customers are demanding more services with the goods, but are still very price sensitive. Note that this (very useful) information appears to be purely from experience and Lombard's justification for growth is rather limited.

ACTIVITY 3

Produce a brief outline of the 'market' section of the Playlight business plan. Lack of information in the Playlight case study means you will have to limit your answer to broad headings.

In the market section of the Playlight business plan you should cover:

- the overall market size in the UK and Europe (at this stage in the company's development it is probably not necessary to look beyond Europe)
- the structure of the market – sales through large retail chains, sales through independent retailers, sales through wholesalers
- the market breakdown – sales of light fittings, sales of table lamps
- the purchasing policies and practices used by the major customers
- the market changes and the consequent opportunities and threats.

MARKETING STRATEGY

In the marketing strategy section, you identify what the company is going to sell, when, and how. In effect, it explains:

- the company's strategies – product/market, market sector, business integration and competitive strategies (see Unit 8)
- the method of promotion and selling.

If the business plan involves changes to the marketing function, then these changes must be explained at this point.

Lombard supplies large cast components, machined and ready for use, to the transport and plant industry. Most products are specially designed one-off or small batch parts developed using Lombard's design service.

Lombard currently operates in the rail transport and production machinery sectors, but is looking to expand into supply of castings for forklift manufacturers.

This would be a good place to set out any results of market research on customers, suppliers, retailers and competitors.

Lombard has successfully expanded over the last six years by offering a good service at the best price. This winning formula will be continued into the future.

Lombard promotes its products through:

- word of mouth, approximately 40 per cent of all new customer enquiries are as a result of recommendations from existing customers
- direct approaches, particularly to local companies and former customers of British Steel; this has generated 60 per cent of new business, but it is very time consuming.

London Transport has recently placed an order worth £5 million over four years and other new orders have meant that the order book is 12 per cent bigger than last year. The forecast over the next five years is for 60 per cent growth overall.

Lombard has a very simple marketing strategy that has developed little since the start up six years ago. It is not suggesting any major changes. Bearing in mind its growth to date, and provided it is not relying too heavily on the London Transport contract (which runs out in five years), this simple plan may be enough.

For a new product it would be worth including details about which market sectors will be targeted and when. Explain how customers will get to know about the product. Is it the intention to use advertising (where), retailers, direct mail, and/or a sales team? Try to provide some proof that the customers are likely to be attracted to buy in this way.

ACTIVITY 4

Produce a brief outline of the 'marketing strategy' section of the Playlight business plan. Carry out the activity by listing the main headings followed by a few short sentences.

In this section, you must cover six issues.

- **The product/market strategy** – Playlight focuses on the supply of table lamps to the UK and European market.
- **The market sector strategy** – Playlight supplies the independent retail sector, by working through a small number of local and national wholesalers.
- **The business integration strategy** – Playlight designs, manufactures and markets.
- **The competitive strategy** – Playlight gains competitive advantage by supplying table lamps of high quality and novel design at reasonable prices.
- **The selling operation** – New business is obtained through direct contact with wholesalers. In year 2, it is planned to start dealing direct with the major retail chains.
- **The requirements of the business plan** – To help promote the products, Playlight needs to develop a comprehensive range of high-quality literature. Details should be provided on the cost of artwork and the initial production run.

OPERATIONS STRATEGY

The marketing section has shown that the product can sell, but the plan needs to show the company can produce a competitive product. This section not only needs to explain the operating processes, but it must also identify those activities which are vital to the organisation's future success, the critical success factors (CSFs). Obviously, if the business plan involves changes to the operations function, then they must be explained at this stage.

At Lombard, there are six stages to the casting process:

- pattern making
- mould filling
- melt and pour
- cooling
- shakeout
- machining.

Pattern making is a skilled and labour-intensive process. The main constraints on production at the present time are space for cooling, machining and the sand removal and recycling process.

The market for castings is quite competitive and all suppliers offer low prices and high quality [the qualifiers]. The company wins orders by offering very short lead times and a comprehensive design service [the winners]. In this business, the ability to respond quickly to customer requirements with high-quality, well-designed products is critical to future success.

> The new factory, combined with reorganisation and rationalisation, will more than double the space of the cooling area. It will improve quality and enable a further reduction in lead times. Two mufflegrinders will be purchased (second-hand cost £24,000 each). These are used to machine non-planar components. An automated tindler will be purchased (cost £15,000). This will assist in sand removal. In addition to the capacity benefits, it is estimated that 25 per cent of the cost of sand and 55 per cent of rework could be eliminated, a saving of £31,000 per year through the use of more up-to-date machinery.

This is the area where an existing business like Lombard should have plenty of knowledge, given its experience. There is a risk of putting in too much technical detail, confusing and boring the reader. The emphasis here should be to show there will be few problems in the areas of supply, production processes, staff, space and delivery.

ACTIVITY 5

Produce a brief outline of the 'operations strategy' section of the Playlight business plan. You probably have little knowledge of how table lamps are made, so just list the main headings (no more than 10) you think should be included.

This section could be broken into four areas.

- A brief description of the operating processes.
- More detail on the processes which generate competitive advantage (the winners). In the case of Playlight, the winners will be created by the product design and quality management processes.
- Details of other important processes (those that create the qualifiers).
- The nature of the refurbishment and the new equipment to be installed as part of the business plan.

RESOURCE IMPLICATIONS

The Lombard business plan is aimed at persuading the three funders, particularly the bank, to invest in the company, so the finance section is crucial. The plan will need to identify the new resources and show that they will be managed effectively. This is particularly important if the company is planning to grow rapidly (see Unit 8). The plan will need to prove that any money on loan is safe and that the activities described in the plan will allow the company to survive or grow and to repay the loan.

Previous years' accounts should be included to show the financial health of the company, along with predicted outline accounts for the next five years, based on the expected growth. In Lombard's case, it will be particularly important to show details of the planned investment and the savings that are expected to accrue from its plans.

Costs of the project:		
New premises:	£85,000	
Refurbishment and adapting premises	£57,000	
Relocation costs	£38,000	
New machinery	£63,000	
Total		**£243,000**
Annual savings		
Rework and sand	£31,000	
Transport between sites	£4,700	
Total		**£35,700**

Annual loan repayments £27,600

Growth in sales of 60 per cent and in profits of 70 per cent are expected.

Lombard's figures suggest that the loans could be repaid both by expected savings and by sales growth, suggesting the money is reasonably safe. However, the bank will want to see some proof that these figures are accurate, not just wild guesses. It will also expect to see some evidence that Lombard has thought through the management implications of the planned expansion.

The management recognises that growth will necessitate changes in the way the company is planned and controlled. To this end, a materials manager will be appointed with responsibility for purchasing, inventory and sales order processing.

ASSESSING THE RISKS

One of the main aims of a business plan is to reduce risk wherever possible. There will always be some element of risk remaining, of course, but identifying, reducing and planning for risk will greatly reduce its impact.

THE ACTION PLAN

The action plan needs to show the timescale covered by the project, emphasising enough time has been allowed to implement each stage of the business plan. You could centre this section around a bar chart. You should identify when each activity starts and finishes and give a concise explanation of the most important steps. The bar chart in Figure 2 shows the activities for part of Lombard's expansion project.

The planning process should:

- identify the risks involved, noting where the plan could fail, what could cause failure and what the impact would be
- reduce or eliminate these risks through better product development and testing, marketing research, and supply and distribution planning
- develop plans to reduce the effect of the risks.

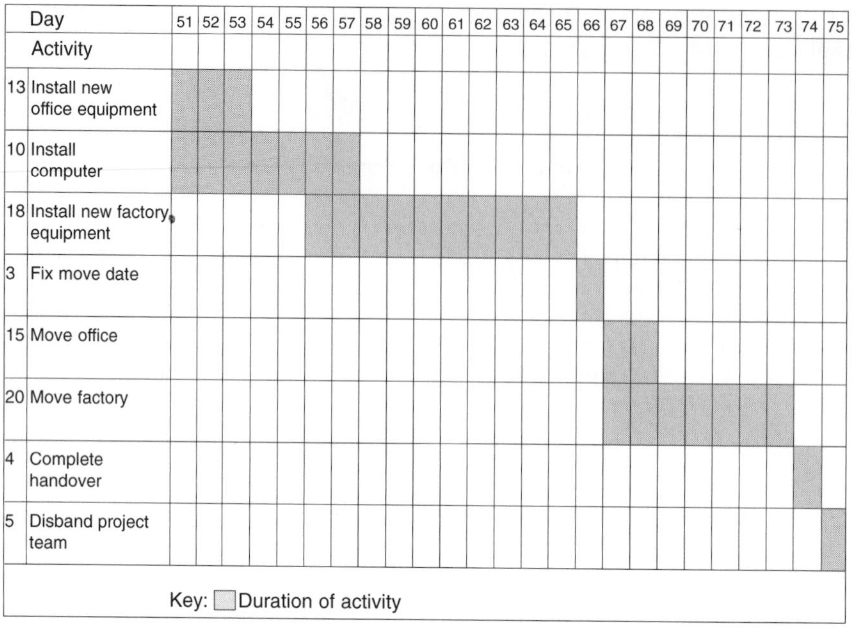

Day
Activity
51 52 53 54 55 56 57 58 59 60 61 62 63 64 65 66 67 68 69 70 71 72 73 74 75
13 Install new office equipment
10 Install computer
18 Install new factory equipment
3 Fix move date
15 Move office
20 Move factory
4 Complete handover
5 Disband project team
Key: Duration of activity

Figure 2: Lombard's expansion project

In order to identify risks, it is worth looking at the way the plan could fail. Businesses find new and interesting ways to fail every week but, for a new business, the risks generally come from four external sources:

- lack of sales – this is the major cause (NatWest, 1995)
- the cost of borrowing money – profits don't cover interest payments
- product failure or technical difficulties.
- problems with suppliers or customers – suppliers don't deliver to requirements or customers fail to pay.

Every business plan must convince the reader that these four risks have been considered and reasonable precautions have been taken. It isn't necessary to show the full risk analysis in the business plan itself, this would probably give the impression the plan was doomed to failure. Instead, a few highlights should be included. For example, a cafe next to a busy main road would experience a drastic drop in trade if the road is bypassed. Any plans for investment in such a cafe must identify if there are any plans to build a bypass and what would be the exit costs if this did happen. For Lombard, an important risk would be the cancellation of the London Transport contract or other large orders. In this case, some 'what if' scenarios and sensitivity analysis should be included. These would show how much sales could drop before the business plan or the business itself is no longer viable.

The business plan should also make clear what would happen if the strategy fails: what can be recovered, what will be lost. In Lombard's case, the bank will want to know the resale value of the newly purchased machinery and the ease with which the new premises could be sold.

REVIEW ACTIVITY 1

Produce a one-page executive summary of the Playlight business plan.

Summary

In this section, we have described the main purposes and features of a business plan using Lombard Ltd as an example. In completing the activities, you have begun the process of drawing up a business plan for Playlight to use as a basis for an application for a bank loan to support new investment. A plan has to start with a strategy. Competitive, operational or functional strategies form part of the overall corporate strategy.

SECTION 2

Implementing the Business Plan

Introduction

As you have seen in Units 3 and 8, implementing a strategy involves change within the organisation and success depends on good management of the change process. There are many strategies for managing change, that you will investigate in future modules. Here we take a look at one technique – project management – that can be used to implement some types of business plan. In the business context, a project is defined by Turner (1993, p. 8) as: 'an endeavour in which human, material and financial resources are organised in a novel way, to undertake a unique scope of work, of given specification, within constraints of cost and time so as to achieve beneficial change defined by quantitative and qualitative objectives'.

The key issues in this definition are that a project is:

- a one-off activity
- with a planned start and end date
- that will achieve a result worth having.

Note also that usually a project will not been tackled before, it involves a high level of risk and will draw in a number of people from inside and outside the organisation.

For many organisations, the implementation of the business plan will involve carrying out a number of interrelated projects. Managing projects requires different management techniques and skills to managing everyday business functions within the organisation. What makes projects different from processes is that you only have one chance to get it right. With a process, say making roofing tiles, the manufacturing activities can be refined over time and the risky elements reduced or removed; everybody who works in a roofing tile factory soon gets to understand their role and how to put things right if they go wrong. With a project, however, there will be many situations of which staff have had no previous experience. Projects are, therefore, much harder to manage than processes; more often than not they are a constant battle against time, rising costs and unexpected problems. Don't forget that the project also has to be put into the context of the organisational structure and culture as these are key elements of the change process. The project will be even harder to implement if the organisational structure or culture also needs to be changed. Remember, too, that even though a project may focus on a change to a project or a process, it will almost inevitably require change for the people affected.

In this section, we look at the project management process from a very practical perspective. We illustrate the process by following what goes on at Lombard Ltd (the company we described in Section 1) as it moves into its new factory following the business plan drafted earlier. At the end of the unit, you will be asked in the Unit Review Activity to follow the project management process using the Playlight case study.

2.1 Initial planning

We first consider project organisation and project definition. Who should be responsible for what? If we get the project organisation and definition right, then the project stands a good chance of success; if we get them wrong or they are poorly specified, then the project will probably fail.

Some people in the organisation might find the idea of carrying out a major project exciting, but for many others it will represent a large, additional workload. Although the managers might want to be involved in detail, they have very limited time. As the staff involved in the project are going to be pressed for time, we need to clarify:

- **the project organisation** – who is going to be responsible for each aspect of the project
- **the project definition** – what needs to be achieved.

PROJECT ORGANISATION

A typical project organisational structure is shown in Figure 3. This is the structure used in our case study at Lombard. It has been found to work well in practice and is part of the PRINCE (Duhig Berry) approach to project management. There are other organisational structures which have also been found to work well in practice and these are discussed fully by Turner (1993, pp. 63–73) and Meredith and Mantel (1995, chapters 3 and 4). Note that in very large projects, members of the project board would not be given the role of guarding the user and business interests. This task would be given to the **project assurance team (PAT)**. There would normally be a project assurance team member looking after the interests of the project manager and his or her team, making sure the board was not placing unreasonable burdens on the project staff.

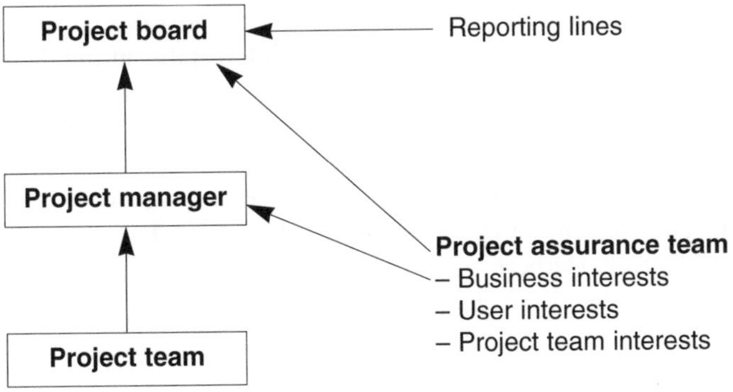

Figure 3: A typical project organisational structure

CASE STUDY

Lombard's project organisation

At Lombard, the move to new premises was seen as the biggest step the company had taken since it started business. However, day-to-day pressures (keeping the orders coming in and the castings going out) meant that neither Herbert Lom (the managing director) nor Frank Bard (the production director) felt able to manage the move themselves. They decided to ask Elizabeth Louisa to manage the project. Elizabeth was a recent graduate who had joined Lombard some months earlier.

Herbert Lom decided that the best way to handle the project would be to set up a clear reporting and responsibility structure. Elizabeth would be responsible for the planning of the move and its day-to-day management, and would take charge of managing resources – people, money and equipment – and schedules. This is the role of a **project manager**.

On a weekly basis, Elizabeth was to report verbally to Herbert on general progress. Every month, Elizabeth was to report formally to Herbert and Frank, giving a detailed breakdown of progress, expenditure, problems encountered and any risks that might occur. Herbert and Frank, as owners of the company and the instigators of the project, have the final say over:

- whether or not the project goes ahead
- key decisions such as when to start the move of equipment
- whether to replace Elizabeth or change her responsibilities, if they think she is not doing a good job.

In this role, they are acting as a **project board.**

Frank would make sure that Elizabeth drew up a plan that met the needs of the production department. Frank needs to check that Elizabeth's plans ensure that the new factory is going to be a safe and easy place to work in, and that the supply of goods to customers is not going to be interrupted during the move. In this role, Frank is guarding the interests of the ultimate users of the factory, the production staff.

Herbert would make sure that the needs of the office staff are catered for in the new factory and that the new factory meets the longer-term needs of the business. In this role, Herbert is guarding the interests of the office staff and the long-term interests of the business.

PROJECT DEFINITION

There needs to be a clear and consistent view of what a project is all about, a clear statement of the priorities, and a definition of what is to be included in the project and also what is not included in the project. This information is usually written down in the **project definition statement**. This includes the project purpose and project objective statements as well as setting out the project scope.

- The **project purpose statement** defines how the project contributes to the company's strategy and business plan.
- The **project objective statement** defines what the project is trying to achieve or, to put this in a more useful form, what will have been achieved when the project is completed.

Without the project objective statements, it is easy for projects to drift and never deliver the benefits. Without the project purpose statement, it is possible for the project to deliver unwanted benefits. Consider, for example, the bank that installed cash-dispensing machines in 3,000 branches in year 1 and closed down 1,000 of these branches in year 2: it achieved its project objective to 'install machines', but failed in its purpose to 'maximise revenues'. If the project **purpose** is no longer being met, then the project should be stopped or changed regardless of whether the project **objectives** are being achieved.

The **project scope statement** identifies what is to be achieved. It sets out the project benefits, how they are to be delivered and measured, the means of communication and control, the assumptions and risks (see Table 1).

CASE STUDY

Defining the project at Lombard

Elizabeth realised that her first step was to get a clear statement of what she was trying to achieve **(project definition)**. In discussions with Herbert and Frank, Elizabeth identified the **project objectives** and its **scope** (limit to the range of activities carried out as part of the project).

- The idea was to get the new factory up and running within six months.
- The point of the new factory is to get all the activities under one roof, introduce some new production equipment and streamline the way material flowed around the shop floor. It is hoped that these changes would reduce annual production costs by £35,000 and give the company the ability to grow by 60 per cent over five years.
- The new factory had already been purchased, but it required considerable modification to make it suitable for the London Transport order. It also had to meet the longer-term requirements of the business, which is seeking 10 per cent annual growth and a wider range of customers and castings.
- It was recognised that staff would require training in the use of the new equipment and that some employees would not want to move – as the new factory is on the other side of town. But it was decided that these issues were not to be included in the project management tasks but were to remain the responsibility of the HRM function.
- Whatever else happened, the supply of castings to customers was not to be disrupted and the budget could not be overspent. If necessary, the project could be delayed slightly to ensure the constraints of cost and quality of customer service are met.

Elizabeth decided to get the project definition formalised and give copies to the Lombard management. A written statement would help clarify issues in her own mind and ensure that she was carrying out exactly what Herbert and Frank wanted. Table 1 shows a project definition produced for a project carried out at Rigibore Limited, Elizabeth decided to copy this format.

The University of Plymouth undertook a project with Rigibore Limited of Hayle in Cornwall. Rigibore manufactures special cutting tools for engineering companies such as Ford, Boeing, and Toyota. The project's four key statements are given in Table 1.

Project purpose	To enable Rigibore Limited to maintain its competitive position in the marketplace by reducing the time taken to respond to customer enquiries and to fulfil customer orders.
Project objective	An automated product design process based on an intelligent software system.
Project scope	
To be achieved	To develop software to: ● enable the customer's requirements to be recorded on a computer ● design special purpose tools by computer ● produce the CNC code (the instructions which drive automated machines) to enable the tools to be manufactured without further human intervention.
The benefits	Reducing lead time from receipt of order to ready for machining, from three weeks to one week.
The measure	Lead time achieved.
To be delivered	Fully working software, full documentation, at least two Rigibore staff trained in the use of the software.
Monitoring and communication	Weekly progress meetings will be held with the project team, and a weekly progress sheet will be circulated. Monthly project meetings will be held with the Rigibore management.
Assumptions	It is assumed that it will be possible to 'capture' the knowledge of the Rigibore engineers and to develop software that will mimic their thought processes. The project team will inform Rigibore management by week 15 of the programme, if this proves not to be the case.
Constraints and risks maximum	The major constraints are time and cost. A limit of two years has been placed on the project as well as cost of £100,000. The major risks are: ● Rigibore might lose the need for the project ● university personnel may not be sufficiently skilled or motivated.
Outside scope of project	Interfacing with Rigibore's other computer-based business systems.
Priorities	Most important is quality, followed by scope, then time and cost.

Table 1: Project definition for a software project at Rigibore Limited.

PROJECT DIMENSIONS

Notice that Table 1 contains a statement about project priorities. When setting priorities it is important to realise that all projects have four dimensions (see Figure 4). They must achieve their objectives:

- within a defined scope
- for a certain cost
- in a set time
- to an appropriate quality standard.

Projects can be high-risk activities and it is unlikely that everything will go precisely to plan. When things go wrong, it is important to know which of the dimensions will be sacrificed. For example, if an activity gets delayed, project managers could:

- sacrifice cost, by hiring extra staff to bring the project back on schedule
- sacrifice scope, by dropping aspects of the project
- sacrifice quality, by lowering the standard of the work to enable it to be done more quickly
- sacrifice time, by extending the duration of the project.

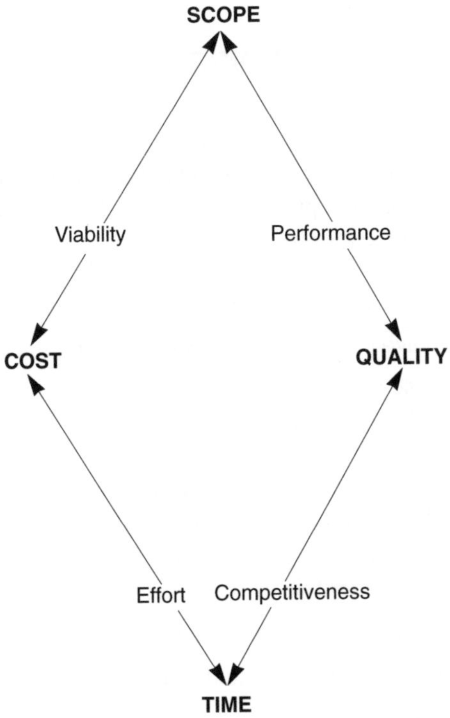

Figure 4: Project dimensions

Figure 4 shows the relationship between scope, cost, time and quality. Scope and cost represent the viability of the project and define the costs and benefits. Cost and time together represent the main inputs from the organisation. Scope and quality define what is to be achieved. Quality and time will be the main determinants of the level of competitive advantage that the organisation gains from the project. Studies have shown that a small cost overrun has only a minor impact on the success of the project, but late delivery and poor quality have a major impact on the overall result (Turner, 1993, p. 12).

ACTIVITY 6

Based on the information that you have been given so far about the Lombard project, produce a project definition in the same format as Table 1. You may need to draw on information about the project contained in Section 1.

Hopefully you've managed to get the project specification on one piece of paper. In projects, there is a tremendous amount of information flowing around and if you want other people to read your reports it is essential that they are kept short – **single-sheet** reporting should always be the target. Table 2 sets out a specification for the Lombard project.

2.2 Creating a project plan

The project definition gives a clear idea of what has to be achieved and the major issues involved in the project. The project plan breaks this down into more detail. The project planning stage will produce a number of key documents which will be essential for the management of the project.

Project planning starts by working out what needs to be done:

- the project objective has told us what we are trying to achieve
- the project purpose has told us why we are doing it
- the project plan will tell us what we have got to do.

With any project of a reasonable size, there will usually be a large number of small tasks to be carried out, each contributing towards the achievement of the project objective. The first step of project planning is to clearly identify these tasks. If we don't do this, it will be impossible to:

- calculate the resources required to implement the project
- set responsibilities (who is going to do what)
- estimate the project cost
- establish the project duration.

Project purpose	To provide Lombard Limited with the manufacturing capacity to enable it to achieve a 60% increase in
turnover	within the next five years.
Project objective single	The manufacturing facilities to be relocated on to a
	site, new production equipment installed and the flow of work around the factory enhanced. Completed within six months.
Project scope To be achieved	Key tasks: ● to relocate manufacturing activities on the new site ● to acquire and install new production equipment ● to lay out the new factory premises to improve work flow.
The benefits	Main benefits: ● 10% reduction in production costs ● 75% increase in production capacity.
The measure	Performance measures: ● production costs (excluding raw materials) ● manufacturing (excluding overtime working).
To be delivered	The new factory, ready to operate – all plant and equipment installed, staffed trained in its operation and fully documented.
Monitoring and communication	Weekly progress meetings will be held with the project team, and a weekly progress sheet will be circulated. Monthly project meetings will be held with the Lombard management.
Assumptions	That the purchase of the new premises and new plant will be available on time and that the new plant will operate satisfactorily.
Constraints and risks	Primary constraints are quality (of customer service) and cost. The supply of products to customers must not be adversely affected and the cost must not exceed £158,000. The major risks within the project are: ● the new plant could be delivered late ● production might be unable to restart on time in the new factory.
Outside scope of project	The purchase of the new factory (already underway) and the involvement in the day-to-day management of the production processes.
Priorities	Most important is quality, followed by cost, then scope and time.

Table 2: Project definition for the factory relocation and reorganisation at Lombard Limited.

This is where the project starts in earnest. The project manager must let people affected by the project know what's going on and get the project team together. It is very important that the people who will be affected by the project feel they are involved in the decisions which will affect their lives. As you know from our earlier discussions, failure to do this can lead to tremendous resistance to change, ranging from non co-operation through to sabotage. The project manager must identify all the stakeholders to the change process and decide how they are to be involved and kept informed. These will generally be the stakeholders (that we identified earlier in Unit 3) that affect an organisation's operation. Table 3 identifies the stakeholders in the case of Lombard, describes their involvement in planning and decision making, and considers the means and timing of communication. Note that this is a specific case; the involvement of different stakeholders will depend on the changes being planned and the organisation. In other circumstances, different involvement at various stages could be more appropriate.

Consider this example. In the mid 1980s, Alpark Engineering (name changed) decided to build a new factory. The company had three factories, all of which were old and very cramped and many staff worked in unpleasant conditions. The management thought that by moving to a new factory it could cut costs and, more importantly, provide a very pleasant working environment for the staff. Because the management thought that the move was so obviously a 'good thing', it didn't bother to sell the idea to the workforce. What managers didn't realise was that most of the staff lived close to the old factories and were prepared to put up with poor working conditions in return for being able to 'pop home' at lunch time and avoid struggling through traffic every day. The new factory was located on a very pleasant industrial estate about two miles from the old factories, but the journey involved crossing a narrow bridge, which was always jammed with traffic. When the new factory was finally completed, the management was very surprised when most of the workforce resigned to take up jobs with a new company which had set up in the old factory premises.

CASE STUDY

Lombard: project communication

Elizabeth decided to hold a brief meeting with all the factory and office staff to tell them about:

- the proposed move, timing and cost
- the benefits to Lombard
- what it would mean to the staff in terms of the working conditions and job tasks
- how they would be involved in the planning and decision making process.

The matrix shown in Table 3 indicates the way she planned to communicate with each stakeholder group.

Stakeholders	Involvement in planning and decision making				Communication			Presentations	
	Purpose and objectives	Project plan	Factory and office layout	Milestone decisions	Weekly	Monthly	Key dates and changes	Project plan	New office and factory layouts
Company management	x	x	x	x	x	x			
Project team		x	x			x			
Factory and office staff	x		x				x	x	x
Project suppliers, subcontractors	x						x		
Other staff (salesforce, etc.)	x							x	x
Suppliers	x						x		
Customers	x						x		

Table 3: Analysis of Lombard's stakeholders and means of communication

ACTIVITY 7

Imagine that you have been asked by the headteacher of your old school to help organise a fête to raise funds for new computer equipment. The fête will include produce and games stalls (staffed by parents and teachers), and entertainment provided by the school children and some parents. Make a list of five or more stakeholders of the fête project.

You will need to communicate with some or all of these stakeholders. List at least five planning, decision and other topics that you will need to discuss with different groups. List five or more ways in which you could communicate with the various groups. Using Table 3 as a template, match stakeholder, topics of communication, frequency of communication and method of communication.

The stakeholders in the fête project will include:

- the school's headteacher, as owner of the project
- teachers, as members of the project team responsible for organising the entertainment provided by the school children
- teachers and parents, as project team members running stalls
- parents and friends, as potential customers of the fête
- school children, as project team members and potential customers
- local businesses, as potential sponsors of the fête
- other schools, as potential competitors or supporters
- the school's maintenance staff, as project team members involved in the physical organisation of stalls, etc.

You will want to arrange a number of meetings with some of these stakeholders to:

- clarify objectives
- generate ideas for stalls and entertainment
- identify the team members to take responsibility for activities
- raise sponsorship
- report on progress
- finalise details.

You will also want to communicate with some of the stakeholders by other means, for example, by advertising in the local press to make potential customers aware of the fête and sending letters to parents informing them of the children's involvement in the fête.

CREATING THE WORK BREAKDOWN STRUCTURE

A key reason for project planning is to make it easier to monitor and control the project once it really gets underway. If you don't know what is supposed to be happening, it is very difficult to tell if progress is being made or if more resources are required. One of the problems of managing a project is finding out how particular tasks are going. Suppose, for example, a team member is writing a software program as part of the project. The task is supposed to take three weeks. If in the second week you ask the team member how the task is getting along, the chances are that you will get an answer like 'oh, fine there's not much more to do'. If you try to get a more specific answer, you'll probably get 'oh, I'm 90 per cent there'. The problem is that most people are optimistic and they forget how hard it is to finish off a task (error checking, tidying up the software code, writing the manual); when they say 'I'm 90 per cent there', they often mean 'I've done most of the interesting bits and I'm probably half way through'. There are two 'rough' rules of thumb which highlight this problem.

- In computing, there is the 90 per cent rule: 10% of your time is spent writing the software code and the other 90% is spent in error correction.
- In project management, there is the 99 per cent rule: 99% of the time, 99% of tasks are 99% completed (Reiss, 1995, p. 101).

This may seem a trivial problem, but failure to estimate progress correctly can have serious implications. To overcome this optimism the project manager needs to do two things.

- Never allow team members to say they are '90 per cent or 99 per cent complete'. Turner (1993, p. 199) recommends that you allow only three answers to 'how are you getting along': not started (0%), half way (50%) finished (100%).
- Clearly define what it means when a particular task is completed.

So, in our software example, the task may be seen as being 'write software to carry out function 6'. The definition of the completed task must be more than 'software for function 6 completed', you must define it in terms like: 'the task is completed when the code is written, error checking has been carried out, the manual is written and approved, and the end users of function 6 have agreed that the software meets their requirements.'

If you can get the project team members to think in terms of 'what result needs to be delivered before a task can be called complete', the role of the project manager becomes considerably easier. But, first of all you must identify what needs to be completed. The first step in the process is the **work breakdown structure** (Turner, 1993, chapter 6).

Imagine you are constructing a house, a project with a large number of tasks. It is easy to see that if you don't think carefully about what needs to be done a great deal of time and effort could easily be wasted. For ease of purchasing of materials and, perhaps, to make best use of skilled labour, you will probably want to group the tasks. For example, foundations, bricklaying and plastering could be grouped as 'building' activities; mains water, boiler and radiators could be grouped as 'plumbing' activities; there will be other groups of activities such as 'electrical' and 'decorating'. Some of these activity groups may have subgroups, so 'electrical' might be split into '13 amp ring main' and 'lighting'. Figure 5 illustrates this process; obviously there are other tasks involved, but this should give you an idea of how a hierarchy of tasks can be created.

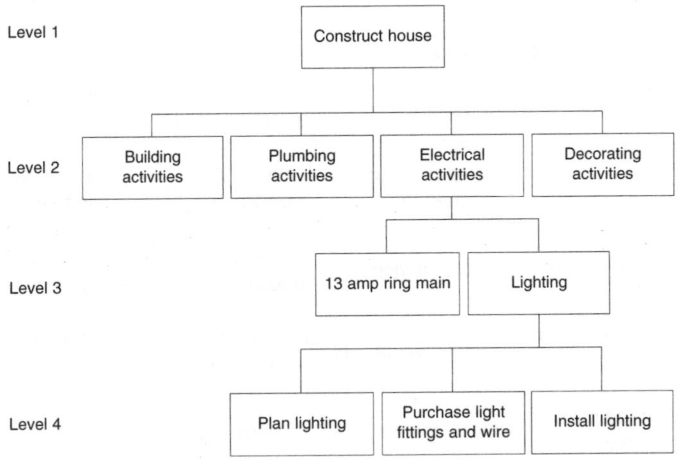

Figure 5: Grouping tasks in constructing a house

A work breakdown structure shows how the tasks which form the project come together. It is drawn as a pyramid, usually of four to six levels. Using Figure 5, we can see that the top level represents the total **project**; on level 2, there are the divisions into **major areas** of activity (electrical, etc.); on level 3, the key **groups of tasks** within each area (lighting, etc.). For each group of tasks, there is a further level (level 4), which identifies the individual **tasks** (plan lighting, install lighting, etc.). In a large project, it may be necessary to break the tasks into smaller steps. The work breakdown structure will be the basis of our plan of action. When we are trying to manage a project it is important to think in terms of the results that have to be delivered. To keep this focus on results, the work breakdown structure is created in two stages.

- The first stage considers **actions**. At each level, you identify what needs to be done to complete the higher level. For the Lombard project, this is illustrated in Figure 6 (for levels 1, 2 and 3) and Figure 7 (for one task in level 4).
- The second stage considers the **results** of the actions. At each level, you identify the result of the actions of stage 1. Again, for the Lombard project, Figures 8 and 9 set out the results that have to be delivered.

In developing work breakdown structures, brainstorming techniques can be used to generate creative ideas. (In brainstorming sessions, criticism is not allowed and participants are encouraged to think laterally.) At Lombard, for example, Elizabeth Louisa could hold a brainstorming session with managers and supervisors to identify all the tasks that need to be done. The tasks can then be grouped into categories and presented as work breakdown structures (see Figures 6, 7, 8 and 9).

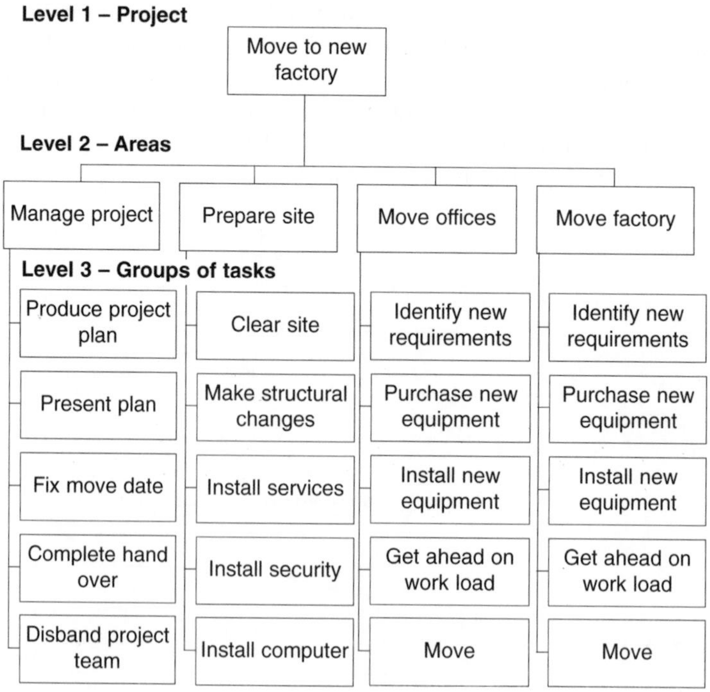

Figure 6: Stage 1 (action) work breakdown structure for the Lombard project

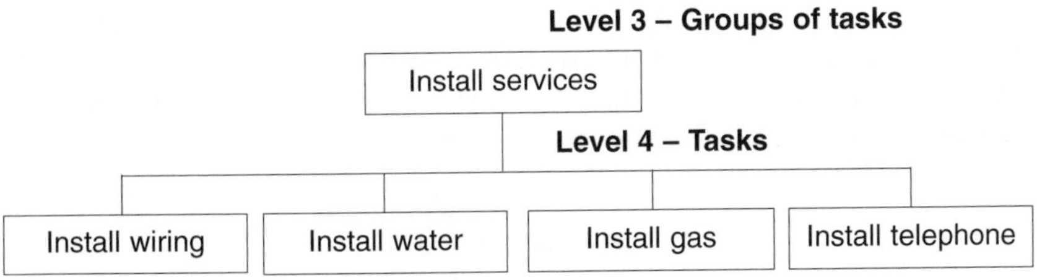

Figure 7: Actions needed in the 'install services' group of tasks

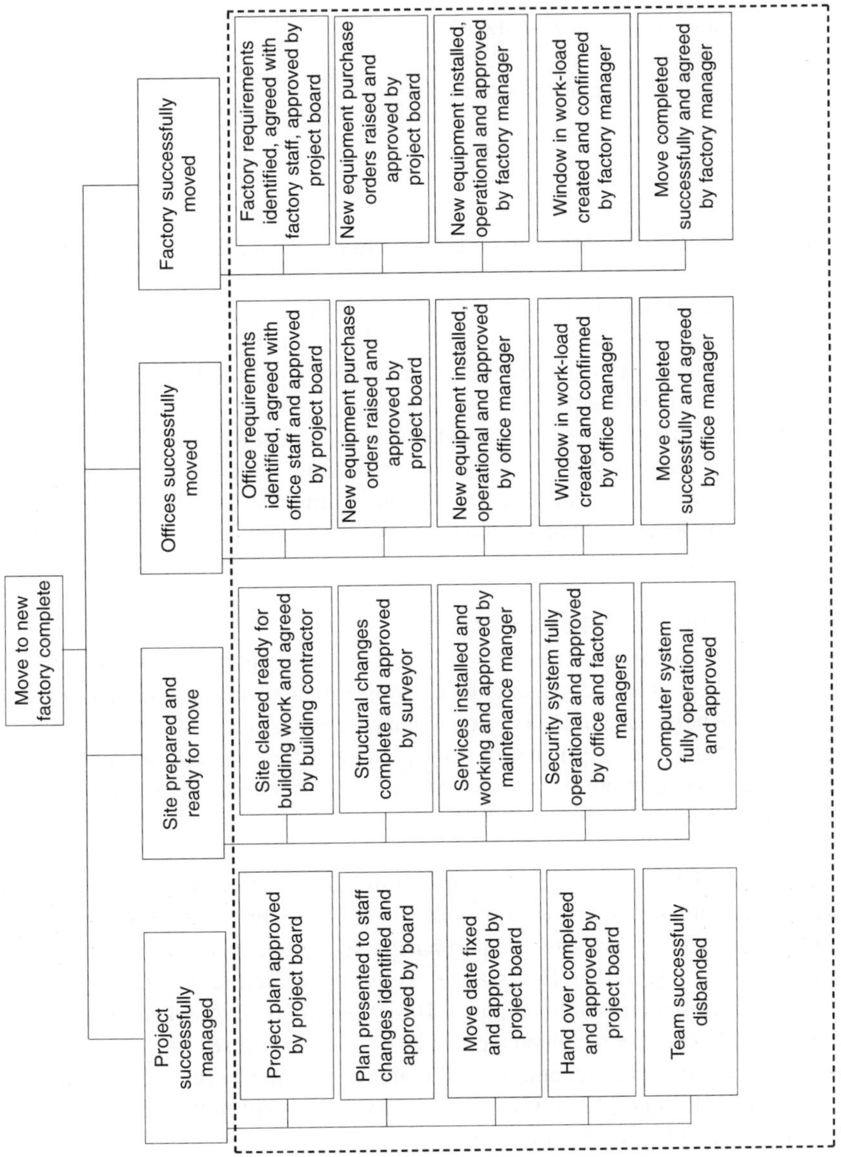

Figure 8: Stage 2 (results) work breakdown structure for the Lombard project

The differences between Figures 6 and 8 and Figures 7 and 9 may appear to be small. But, as we have already discussed, looking at results rather than actions simplifies project management. We shall also see that having the stage 2 (results) work breakdown structure diagrams makes the creation of the **milestone plan** – the plan which shows the key decision points – considerably easier.

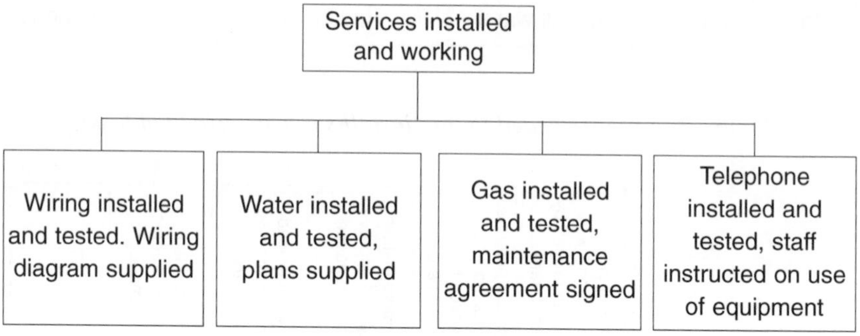

Figure 9: Results needed to reach the 'services installed and working' milestone

It can be quite a tricky job sorting out the work breakdown structure. It is most easily done by writing each task on a 'Post-it' note then sticking them on a wipe board. You should keep rearranging the notes on the wipe board until you are happy with the work breakdown structure. The four levels of the work breakdown structure hierarchy will normally be sufficient for all but a million pound project. It is easy to get carried away with detail at this stage, but remember, projects are risky ventures and rarely go exactly to plan, so the level of detail of the work breakdown structure should be kept to the minimum required to make decisions and monitor progress.

CREATING THE MILESTONE PLAN

Milestones are major points in the project. They are usually events or points at which the project board needs to make a major decision, such as whether or not to proceed to the next stage of the project, to approve a large expenditure, to authorise the start of production, etc. The milestone plan identifies, and reminds everybody, when these important points will be reached. It is, therefore, the main working document for the project board.

The milestone plan can be derived from the third layer of the stage 2 (results) work breakdown structure. Figure 10 shows the stage 2 work breakdown structure for a project to design and implement a purchasing and inventory control system. The project has two stages. The first stage develops an effective manual system, the second stage computerises this manual. Based on this work breakdown structure, a milestone plan has been created (see Table 4). As you will see, the milestones are listed in chronological order and the major area to which they relate is indicated by an **'O'**. The milestone plan forms a list of key points within the project – points where the project board ought to be involved.

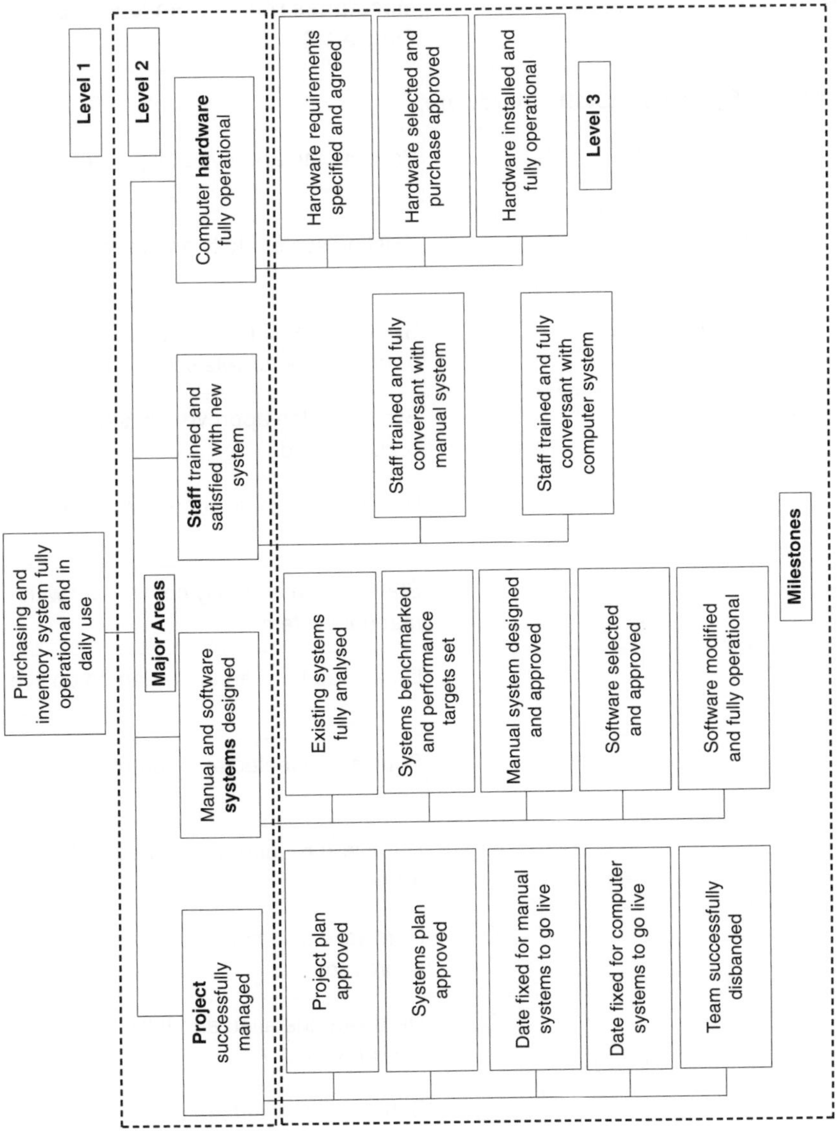

Figure 10: Stage 2 (results) work breakdown structure for a project to design and implement a purchasing and inventory control system (levels 1 to 3 only)

Major areas				Milestones (taken from level 3 of Figure 10)
Project	Systems	Staff	Hardware	
O				Project plan approved by project board
	O			Existing system fully analysed
	O			Systems benchmarked and performance targets set
O				Systems plan approved by staff and project board
	O			Manual system designed and approved
		O		Staff trained and fully conversant with manual system
O				Date fixed for manual system to go live
	O			Software selected and approved
			O	Hardware requirements specified and agreed
			O	Hardware selected and purchase approved
			O	Hardware installed and fully operational
	O			Software modified and fully operational
		O		Staff trained and fully conversant with computer system
O				Date fixed for computer system to go live
O	O	O	O	Purchasing and inventory system fully operational and in daily use
O				Project team disbanded

Table 4: Milestone plan for a project to design and implement a purchasing and inventory control system

ACTIVITY 8

Using the same methods described in the purchasing and inventory control system case study in Figure 10 and Table 4, create a milestone plan for Lombard. You will need to refer to Figure 8.

Your milestone plan should look like Table 5, although you may have some of the milestones in a slightly different order.

Major areas				Milestones
Project	Site	Offices	Factory	
O				Project plan approved by project board
O				Plan presented to staff, changes identified and approved by project board
	O			Site cleared and ready for building, and approved by building contractor
		O		Office requirements identified and agreed with office staff and approved by project board
		O		Factory requirements identified and agreed with factory staff and approved by project board
		O		New office equipment purchase orders raised and approved by project board
			O	New factory equipment purchase orders raised and approved by project board
	O			Structural changes made and approved by surveyor
	O			Services installed and working, and approved by maintenance manager
		O	O	Security system fully operational and approved by office and factory managers

Major areas				Milestones
Project	**Site**	**Offices**	**Factory**	
			O	New equipment installed and operational and approved by factory manager
		O		New equipment installed and operational and approved by office manager
	O			Computer system fully operational and approved
			O	Window in work load created and confirmed by factory manager
		O		Window in work load created and confirmed by office manager
O				Move date fixed and approved by project board
		O		Move successfully completed and agreed by office manager
			O	Move successfully completed and agreed by factory manager
O				Handover completed and approved by project board
O				Project team disbanded

Table 5: Milestone plan for the Lombard project

SCHEDULING OF TASKS

Projects are often very complex, with large numbers of tasks needing to be undertaken simultaneously. Without a systematic approach, it is very easy to do things in the wrong sequence and to allocate resources to non-priority work. Here, we look at how the scheduling of tasks – getting them in the right sequence – is made easier using a technique known as **critical path analysis**. This technique identifies which activities are most important and when they need to be carried out. It is also known as the **programme evaluation and review technique** (PERT). These techniques are used extensively in operations management and logistics to break down jobs and tasks in the best way for efficient scheduling. To help you understand critical path analysis, consider a simple project – making and having breakfast. The activities in this project are shown in Table 6.

	Activities	**Time taken** (minutes)
1	Get out of bed and find kitchen	0.5
2	Cut the bread and put in toaster	0.5
3	Toast bread	2
4	Put plate, knife, milk, butter and marmalade on table	1.5
5	Fill kettle	0.5
6	Boil water	3
7	Put coffee and boiling water in cup	0.5
8	Take cup and toast to table	0.5
9	Eat breakfast	5

Table 6: The breakfast project

The total time of these activities is 14 minutes, but obviously some of the tasks can be done in parallel (simultaneously) so the actual project time should be less than 14 minutes. The activity chart shown in Figure 11 indicates the basic sequence of activities which must be followed. In Figure 11, each box represents an activity –within the box is recorded the time the activity takes and the description of the activity. At this stage don't worry about what else goes in the boxes, we explain that later. The arrows show the relationship between activities.

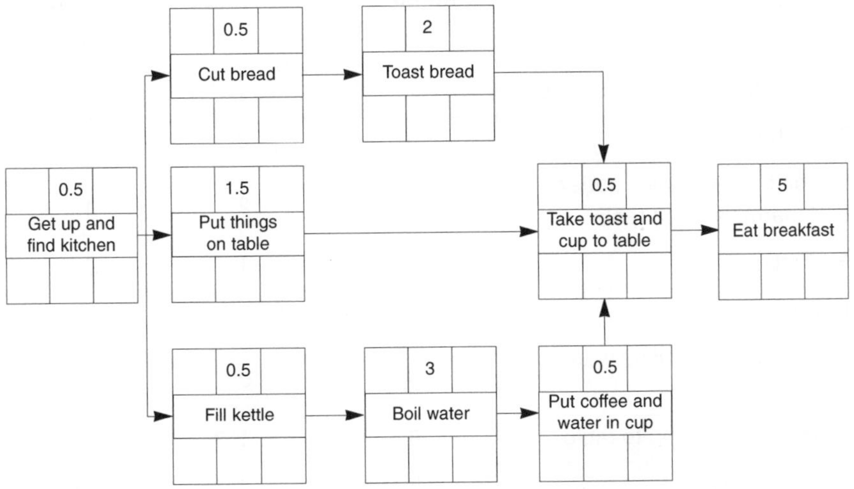

Figure 11: Activity chart – sequence of activities in making breakfast

The problem with Figure 11 is that it assumes that three things can be done at once – cutting the bread, putting things on the table and filling the kettle. As there is only one person making breakfast, these activities have to be sequenced so that only one manual activity is being done at a time. Figure 12 shows how this can be achieved.

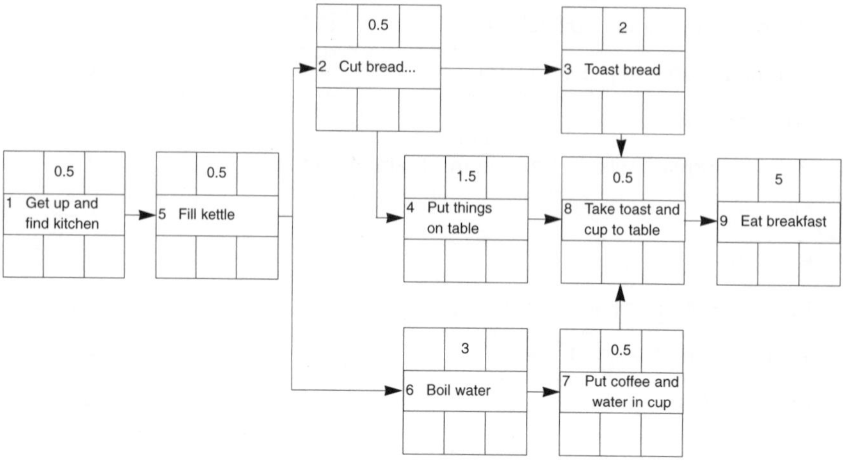

Figure 12: Activity chart – rearranged sequence of activities in making breakfast

The information shown in Figure 12 can be put in the tabular form of a precedence chart (see Table 7). 'Preceding activities' means those activities which must come before the activity under consideration.

Activity	**Activity number**	**Preceding activities**	**Time taken (minutes)**
Get out of bed and find kitchen	1		0.5
Cut the bread and put in toaster	2	1	0.5
Toast bread	3	2	2
Put plate, knife, milk, butter, and marmalade on table	4	2	1.5
Fill kettle	5	1	0.5
Boil water	6	5	3
Put coffee and boiling water in cup	7	6	0.5
Take toast and cup to table	8	3, 4, 7	0.5
Eat breakfast	9	8	5

Table 7: Precedence chart for making breakfast project

Examine Figure 12 and you will see there are three activity paths leading from activity 1 (get up) to activity 9 (eat breakfast). Add up the total time taken to complete each.

Path 1 consists of activities 1, 5, 2, 3, 8 and 9, and takes 9 minutes:

1	Get up, find the kitchen	0.5
5	Fill kettle	0.5
2	Cut bread	0.5
3	Toast bread	2.0
8	Take toast and cup to table	0.5
9	Eat breakfast	5.0
	Total	9.0

Path 2 consists of activities 1, 5, 2, 4, 8 and 9, and takes 8.5 minutes:

1	Get up, find the kitchen	0.5
5	Fill kettle	0.5
2	Cut bread	0.5
4	Put things on table	1.5
8	Take toast and cup to table	0.5
9	Eat breakfast	5.0
	Total	8.5

Path 3 consists of activities 1, 5, 6, 7, 8 and 9, and takes 10 minutes:

1	Get up, find the kitchen	0.5
5	Fill kettle	0.5
6	Boil water	3.0
7	Put coffee, water into cup	0.5
8	Take toast and cup to table	0.5
9	Eat breakfast	5.0
	Total	10

As all activities have to be completed before the project can be completed, the minimum time to finish to the project is 10 minutes. **The minimum time to complete a project is always determined by the longest path**.

In project management, the longest path is known as the **critical** path; the activities that make up the critical path are known as **critical activities**; and the process of finding the critical path is called **critical path analysis**. In this example, the critical activities are those in path 3:

1 get up, find the kitchen
5 fill kettle
6 boil water
7 put coffee and water in cup

8 take toast and cup to table
9 eat breakfast.

If any of these critical activities takes longer than expected, then the total project time will be extended. Obviously, if a non-critical activity, say, toasting the bread took 10 minutes (instead of 2) the project would be extended, but not necessarily by the additional time (8 minutes). Up to a limit, non-critical activities can be extended or delayed without affecting the total duration of the project. The amount of extension or delay is known as the **slack** or **float**. Critical activities have zero slack as they cannot be extended without extending the total project duration. Slack is a useful thing to know, because it tells the project manager to what extent he or she is able to let a non-critical activity drift.

ACTIVITY 9

How long can toasting take without extending the project beyond the minimum 10 minutes? If toasting the bread takes 10 minutes, how much longer would the project take ?

The 'toasting path', path 1, takes 9 minutes. As long as this path takes less than 10 minutes (the duration of the critical path, path 3), the activities in path 1 will remain non-critical. So toasting can take up to 3 minutes without extending the project. Toasting only takes 2 minutes, so the slack on the toasting activity is 1 minute.

If toasting takes 10 minutes, then the 'toasting path' would take 8 minutes longer. In total, it would take 17 minutes (8 + 9 = 17). So path 1 would become the longest and, therefore, the critical path and the project would take 17 minutes, 7 minutes longer than the minimum.

ACTIVITY 10

At Lombard, Elizabeth has analysed the level 3 activities shown in Figure 6 and created the precedence chart shown in Table 8. Using this precedence chart, produce an activity chart along the lines shown in Figure 12. Use the box structure in Figure 12, as you will need to use your chart again in activity 11.

This is a difficult activity. It is unlikely that you will get this chart correct at your first attempt – but it is well worth trying. You will need a large sheet of paper, a pencil and a rubber, and you must double check everything you do. Good luck!

Activity	**Activity number**	**Preceding activities**	**Time taken** (days)
Produce project plan	1		5
Present plan	2	1	1
Fix move date	3	10,13,18	1
Complete handover	4	15,20	1
Disband project team	5	4	1
Clear site	6	2	10
Make structural changes	7	6	15
Install services	8	7	15
Install security	9	8	5
Install computer	10	9	7
Identify office requirements	11	2	10
Purchase new office equipment	12	11	15
Install new office equipment	13	9,12	3
Get ahead on office workload	14	2	25
Move office	15	3,14	2
Identify factory requirements	16	2	15
Purchase new factory equipment	17	16	35
Install new factory equipment	18	9,17	10
Get ahead on factory workload	19	2	25
Move factory	20	3,19	7

Table 8: Precedence chart for the Lombard project

Your Lombard activity chart should look something like Figure 13.

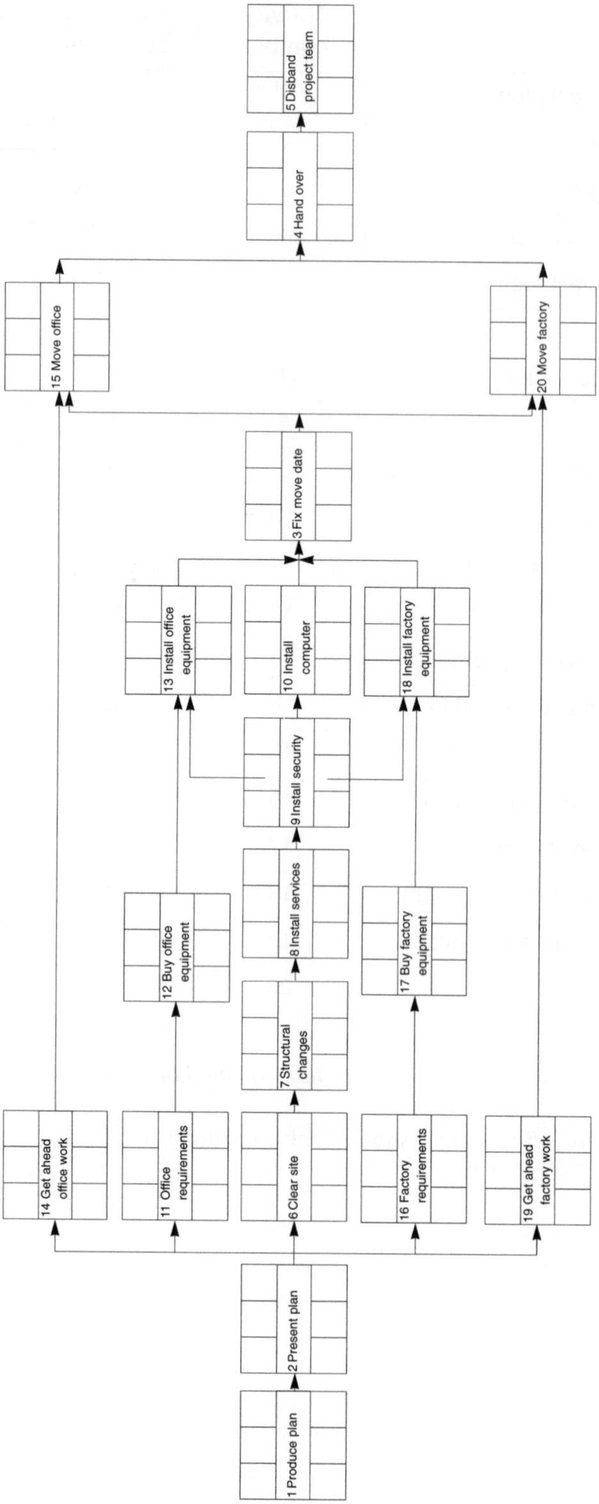

Figure 13: Activity chart for the Lombard project

With simple projects, it is fairly easy to see which is the critical path and to calculate the amount of slack associated with non-critical activities. However, as projects grow in size, a systematic approach is required. To do this, we need to develop our activity charts. Figure 14 shows the 'getting breakfast' project with numbers entered in all the activity boxes.

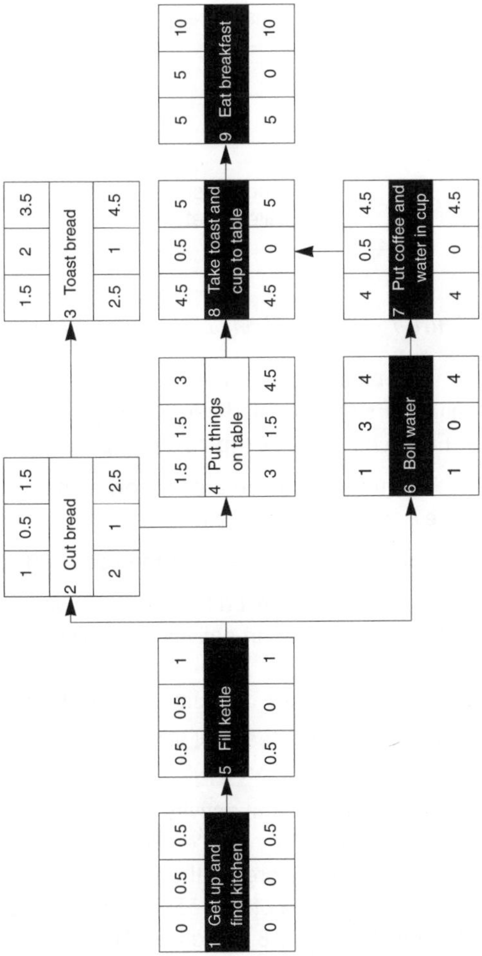

Figure 14: Completed activity chart for the breakfast project

In Figure 14, the critical activities are shaded. As we mentioned earlier, these are easy to spot because they have zero slack. Note the 'zero' in the middle of the bottom numbers in each activity. In Figure 14, the middle number of the top row of numbers is the time required for each activity. The other values in the boxes relate to when the activity starts and finishes. The boxes on the top row concern the earliest start and finish times, and the boxes underneath concern the latest start and finish times. This is shown in more detail for one activity in Figure 15. Note that if it is a critical activity, then there is no slack and the next activity must take place immediately.

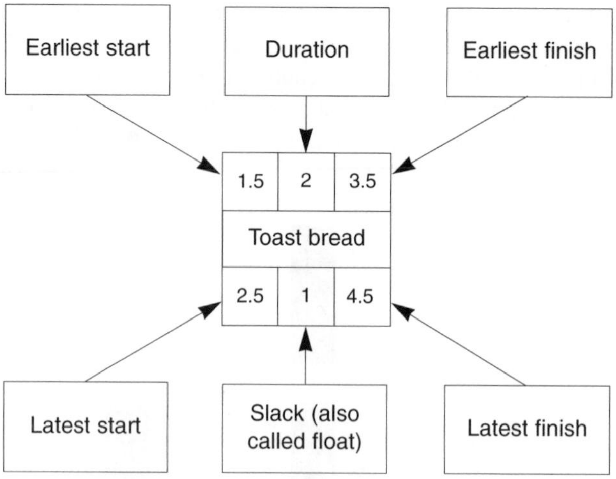

Figure 15: Detail of one activity from Figure 14

We now explain how to calculate the numbers in the boxes. Read through this section slowly to make sure that you understand the process, and keep referring to Figures 14 and 15. First, consider the **top row** of figures against each activity:

- the number in the left-hand box on the top row signifies the **'earliest start time'** – the earliest time the activity can start
- the middle number of the top row is the **time required** for the activity
- the number in the right-hand box on the top row signifies the **'earliest finish time'** – the earliest time an activity can finish.

The earliest start and finish times are calculated by starting at the first activity.

- The 'earliest finish time' is the 'earliest start time' plus 'the time required for the activity' (the middle box on top).
- The 'earliest start time' of the first activity is zero. For all other activities, the 'earliest start time' is equal to the 'earliest finish time' of the preceding activity (the one before). If there is more than one preceding activity, it is equal to the latest of the 'earliest finish times'. Look at 'take toast and cup to table' (activity 8 in Figure 14), it can only start after the preceding activity 4, 'put things on table'.

Now consider the **bottom row** of figures against each activity:

- the number in the left-hand box on the bottom row signifies the **'latest start time'** – the latest time the activity can start without changing the duration of the project
- the middle number of the bottom row is the **slack** associated with the activity
- the number in the right-hand box on the bottom row signifies the **'latest finish time'** – the latest time an activity can finish without changing the duration of the project.

The latest start and finish times are found by starting at the last activity.

- The 'latest start time' is the 'latest finish time' minus (less) the 'time required for the activity' (the middle box on the top)
- The 'latest finish time' of the last activity is equal to its 'earliest finish time'. For all other activities, the 'latest finish time' is equal to the 'latest start time' of the subsequent activity (the one after). If there is more than one subsequent activity, then it is equal to the earliest of the 'latest finish times'. Look at the 'cut bread' (activity 2 in Figure 14), it has to supply the bread for 'toast bread' (activity 3).
- The 'slack' of an activity is its 'latest finish time' minus its 'earliest finish time'.

Activity charts are important tools for the project manager. As projects rarely go as expected – some activities are done faster or slower than planned – it is important to frequently recalculate the critical path, to make sure resources are put where they are most urgently needed.

ACTIVITY 11

Complete the activity chart you created for the Lombard project in Activity 10 and identify the critical path. You will probably find this very difficult, but don't worry if you cannot do it and don't take too long puzzling over it. It is still a useful exercise if you can recognise what you have to do and the importance of identifying the critical path which has no slack in the activities.

Figure 16 shows the completed activity chart for the Lombard project. As you can see (and we hope you got the same answer), the minimum project duration is 76 days. The critical activities are 1, 2, 16, 17, 18, 3, 20, 4 and 5. They are shaded grey – and note the zero slack times in each case, this is the number in the middle box on the bottom row.

If you have not got the same answer, there are a couple of areas where it is easy to make a mistake:

- **activity 13** – the 'earliest start time' is the *later* of the 'earliest finish times' of activities 9 and 12 (you can't start activity 13 until both 9 and 12 are finished)
- **activity 18** – the 'earliest start time' is the *later* of the 'earliest finish times' of activities 9 and 17
- **activity 3** – the 'latest finish time' is the *earlier* of the 'latest start times' of activities 15 and 20 (you must finish activity 3 before the latest start time of activities 15 and 20).

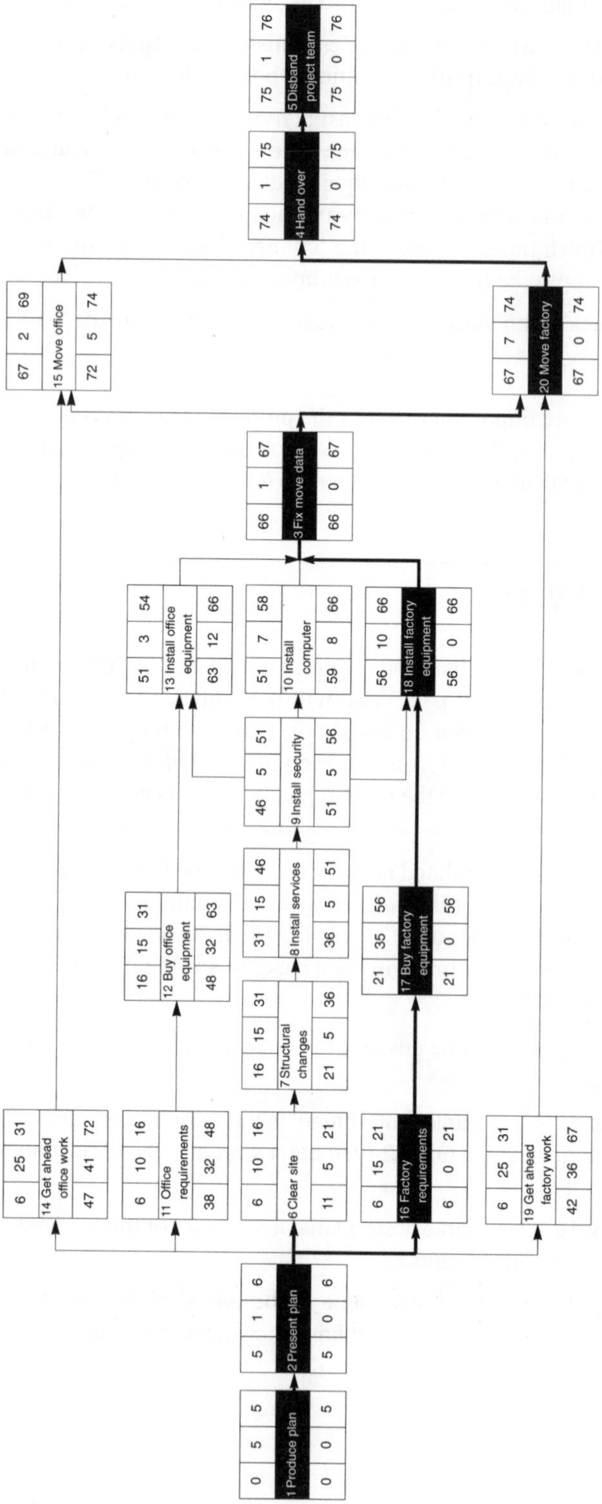

Figure 16: Completed activity chart for the Lombard project

CREATING A GANTT CHART

We now go back to our 'getting breakfast' project. Although all the start and finish times are shown on the activity chart (see Figure 14), it is pretty difficult to see at a glance what should be happening at any point in time. This problem is overcome by creating a **Gantt chart**. These are widely used to present sequenced events and are used in the operations of many manufacturing processes, for example.

The Gantt chart shows clearly the steps that have to be undertaken in each time period of the project. The scale used for time should be based on the duration of the shortest activity and cover a useful period of the project. If the project extends over several days or weeks, then it is easy to show actual progress on the chart and identify where steps are falling behind.

A Gantt chart is produced by:

- listing the activities of the project down the left-hand side with a grid alongside
- then from the completed activity chart mark the 'earliest start times' and 'latest finish times' on the grid for each activity
- shade in the grid using different colours to indicate the duration of the activity and the slack.

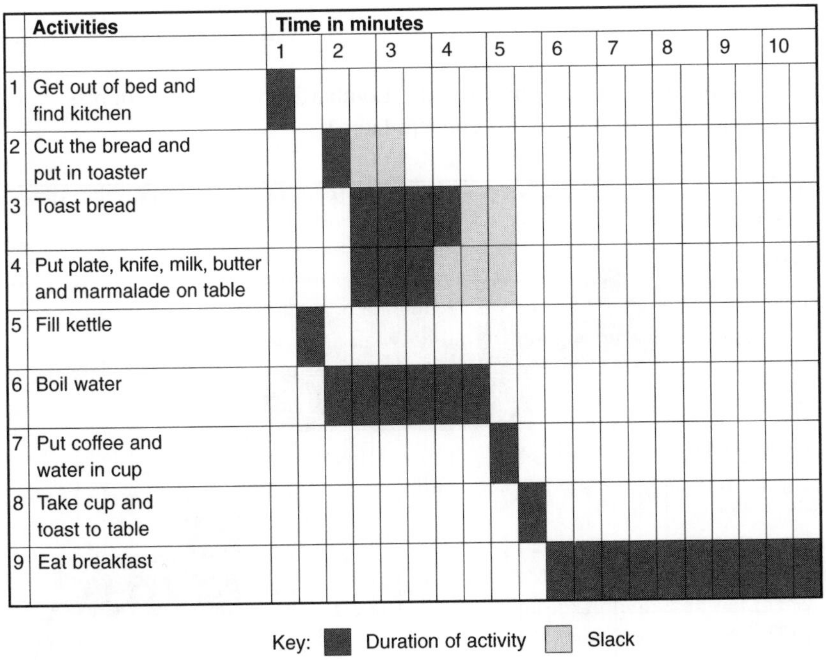

Figure 17 Gantt chart for the breakfast project

Figure 17 shows the Gantt chart for the breakfast project. It is based on the completed activity chart for the project (Figure 14). The slack areas indicate how long the activities can be delayed or extended without extending the duration of the whole project. As you will have realised, the Gantt chart turns the information of the activity chart into a really useful form, that can easily be communicated to all members of the project team and to all staff affected by the project.

For a project the size of the breakfast project, the critical path analysis and the Gantt chart can be produced by hand in a few minutes. With larger projects, it can take a great deal of time to produce the charts. There are relatively inexpensive computer packages, such as Microsoft Project and CA-SuperProject, which enable the critical path analysis and Gantt chart to be produced directly from a list of activities.

ACTIVITY 12

Produce a Gantt chart for those activities in the Lombard project with an 'earliest start date' greater than day 50. This includes activities 13, 10, 18, 3, 15, 20, 4 and 5. You will need to draw on the information in Figure 16.

Figure 18 shows the Gantt chart for the Lombard project. (A progress wave is shown at day 56, we come to this concept later.)

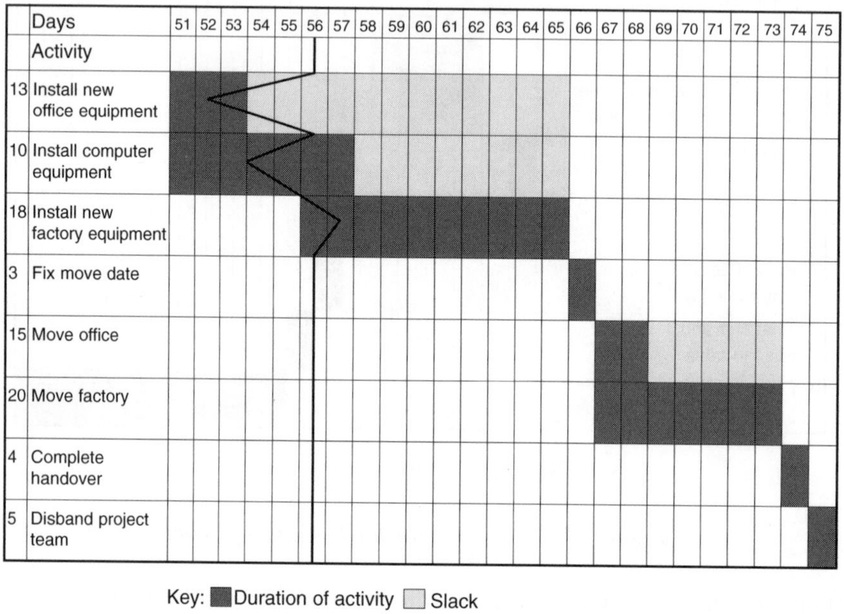

Figure 18: Gantt chart for the Lombard project from day 50

Hopefully, you will find your Gantt chart looks similar. The Gantt chart is very much easier to 'read' than the activity chart. For this reason, it is used as the main communication document for any project. At a glance, you can see what should be happening at any point in time. Note that **time 51** is the start of work of **day 51** or the end of work on **day 50**. So, **time '0'** is the start of work on **day 1**, and **time 76** – the end of the project – is the end of work on **day 75**.

ALLOCATION OF TASKS TO INDIVIDUALS

The work breakdown structure identified the tasks that have to be undertaken to complete the project. The next step in the project management process is to agree who has the responsibility for carrying out each of the activities and who is going to do the work. Staff often work on the projects in a part-time capacity, joining the project for a few days when required, then returning to their normal work. Because of the pressures of normal work, it can be difficult to get staff released when they are needed on the project. This problem is overcome by agreeing 'who is going to do what' at the planning stage of the project, and then putting it in writing as a form of contract. By carrying out this stage thoroughly, many potential problems and arguments can be avoided.

The vehicle used to hold this 'who does what' information is known as the **responsibility chart** (Turner, 1993, pp. 142–153). Figure 19 shows the responsibility chart for a project concerned with producing a computer database. There are five activities and the chart shows the responsibilities involved with the achievement of those tasks.

The responsibility chart contains a large amount of information on one piece of paper. Once it has been produced, it should be agreed and signed by those involved. It then becomes a contract between the project manager and those involved with the project.

You should note that there are other symbols that could be used in responsibility charts. These include:

D	has responsibility for taking the decision
d	is involved in taking the decision
I	must be informed
T	carry out training
t	to be trained

Milestone	Task	Step	Description	Managing director	Sales manager	Marketing manager	Marketing staff	Sales staff	Data entry clerk	Computer manager	Systems analysts	Programmers	Systems operator
■			Create customer data base										
	■		**Identify requirements of staff**										
		■	Interview MD and managers	x	x	x					X		
		■	Interview marketing and sales staff				x	x			X		
		■	Discuss with programmer								X	x	
		■	Produce requirements specification								X		
		■	Approve requirements specification	a	a	A					a		
	■		**Design structure of database**										
		■	Produce flow chart								X		
		■	Discuss with the programmer								X	x	
		■	Finalise database structure								X		
	■		**Design input and output screens**										
		■	Rough out format		c	c					X		
		■	Discuss with marketing and sales staff				x	x			X		
		■	Discuss with data entry clerk						x		X		
		■	Finalise input and output screens								X		
	■		**Write and test software**										
		■	Discuss specification with systems analyst								x	X	
		■	Write and debug software								x	X	x
		■	Test with users				x	x	x			X	
		■	Sign off software	a	a	a					A	a	
	■		**Implement**										
		■	Load software onto user system				x	x	x				X
		■	Train users				x	x	x		X		x
		■	Monitor performance								X		
		■	Carry out final changes								X	X	
■			Sign off database	a	a	A					a		

Key to symbols

- X has the major responsibility for executing the step
- x is involved in executing the step
- A has the responsibility for approval (or signing off)
- a is involved in the approval
- c must be consulted

Figure 19: Responsibility chart for a computer database project

2.3 Management of progress, costs and risks

The tools and techniques we have described build the project plan. This section looks at the management of the project once it is underway.

MANAGEMENT OF TIME

Figures 18 and 20 show the Gantt charts for the Lombard project activities in the period day 50 to day 76. The 'progress wave' on Figure 18 shows the situation on day 56. For each activity, the progress so far has been marked on the chart and the progress wave connects up the marks. As you can see, activities 13 and 10 are running behind schedule, activity 18 is a little ahead and the remaining activities have yet to start.

Figure 20 shows the situation on day 60; the day 56 progress wave is still shown and the new progress wave for day 60 has been added. From this diagram, you can see that activity 13 is now complete, but activities 10 and 18 have made little progress since day 56. A Gantt chart with progress waves is an excellent tool for the project manager, at a glance he or she can see where problems are arising and where things are going all right.

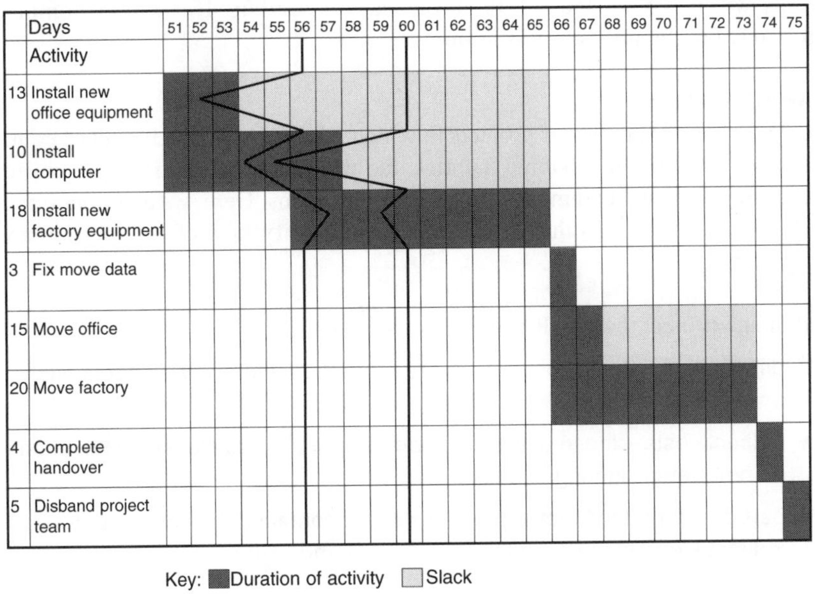

Figure 20: Gantt chart for the Lombard project showing progress on days 56 and 60

If activities take longer to complete than planned, there is a danger that the project will fail to meet its target completion date. If delays are occurring on the critical path, then the project will definitely be delayed. To prevent this from happening, the project manager will usually put more resources into the critical path activities to reduce their duration. However, in reducing the duration of critical activities, there is a danger that the critical path may change. For instance in the breakfast project, if the time taken to boil the water is reduced to one minute, then the critical path would change to the path containing the toasting activity. Check this on the Gantt chart in Figure 17. To determine whether or not this will happen, it is important for the project manager to update the critical path analysis and Gantt charts.

ACTIVITY 13

Examine the Gantt chart shown in Figure 20. Determine:

- which activities are running late
- which activities require more resources to be devoted to them.

Only two activities need to be considered, activities 10 and 18. Activity 18 is a critical activity (no slack) and is starting to run behind schedule. The project manager should be concerned about this and see what can be done to catch up. Activity 10 is taking longer than expected to complete, but this activity has eight days slack. The project manager should find out if, with present resources, the activity will be completed before all the slack is used up. If it will be completed before day 66, then no action is required.

MANAGING COSTS

There are many examples of projects in which costs have got badly out of control. Examples include the Channel Tunnel, the new British Library, most military aircraft development and many computer installations. Here, we examine some of the techniques that help the project manager identify how effectively money is being spent.

Within any project there will be three sorts of costs:

- direct costs – those costs which are proportional to the work done, such as labour and materials
- indirect costs – those costs which are proportional to elapsed time, such as rent, rates, lighting of offices
- part direct, part indirect – those costs that contain both a direct and indirect element, such as the hire of plant and equipment.

The cost of a project is determined not only by the amount of work to be done, but also by how long the project takes to complete. Figure 21 shows how the total cost of a project varies with its duration. The total cost is made of indirect and direct costs. The indirect costs are proportional to the time taken for the project; so, the longer the project, the greater the indirect costs. For example, the longer the project goes on the more rent you have to pay for the project manager's office. The direct costs should remain constant. But, if you try to complete a project in a very short time, the use of resources can become inefficient due to interference – you have so many people working on the project at any one time, that they get in each other's way. Similarly, with a very extended project, direct costs tend to rise. For example, it is more expensive to hire a skilled engineer for one hour a day for 21 days, than to hire one for seven hours a day for three days. The lowest costs, therefore, are to be found when the maximum amount of direct resource is being used compatible with avoiding inefficiencies of interference.

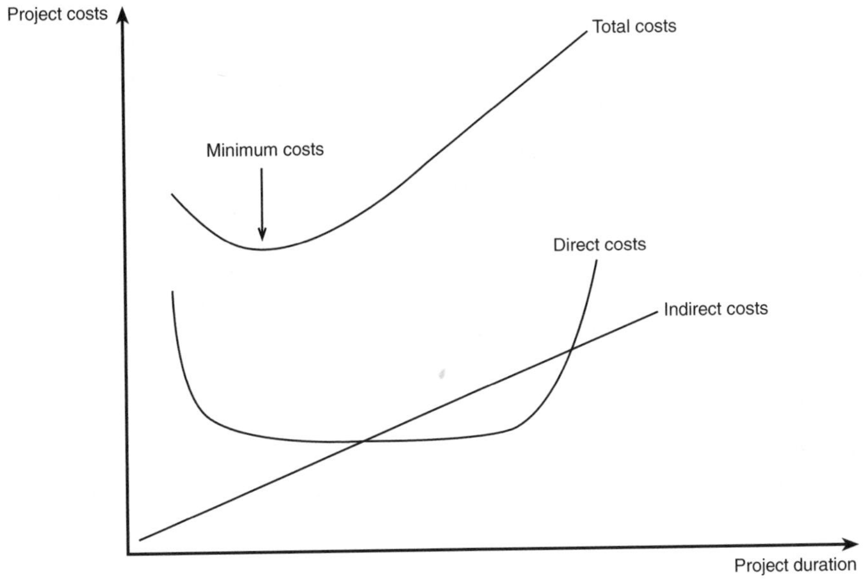

Figure 21: Project costs
Source: Dilworth (1996, pp. 714–715)

For each activity of the project, there will be an estimated or **budget cost** for each direct and indirect element. The initial estimate of each cost – made when the project was first planned in detail – is known as the **baseline cost**. The latest estimate of an activity's cost is known as the **scheduled cost**. The amount of money that the activity actually used is known as the **actual cost**.

It is easy to spend a lot of money and not achieve anything. For example, £1,000 could be spent digging a trench only for it to collapse due to a flash flood. Money has been spent but nothing has been achieved or, in project terminology, nothing has been earned. There are, therefore, four types of cost that are of interest to the project management:

- **baseline cost** – the original planned cost for the completion of an activity
- **scheduled cost** – the present expected cost for the completion of the activity
- **actual cost** – the money spent on the activity to date
- **earned value** – the baseline cost of what has been achieved to date, what we expected to pay for the work completed so far.

CASE STUDY

Lombard's project costs

On completion of the project plan, Elizabeth was able to estimate the baseline cost of each activity. These are shown in Table 9 along with the expected date that the cost would be incurred. The total cost comes to £156,500. As the business plan allows £158,000 for the project, this gives Elizabeth a small **contingency reserve** (money that can be spent on unexpected requirements) of £1,500.

Activity	Activity number	Baseline cost £	Week in which work is expected to be completed	Cumulative baseline cost £
Produce project plan	1	500	1	500
Present plan	2	500	2	1000
Clear site	6	12,500	4	13,500
Identify factory requirements	16	500	5	14,000
Make structural changes	7	22500	7	36,500
Identify office requirements	11	1000	8	37,500
Install services	8	15,000	9	52,500
Install security	9	6000	11	58,500
Purchase new office equipment	12	13,000	11	71,500
Get ahead on office workload	14	1500	11	73,000
Get ahead on factory workload	19	4500	12	77,500
Install computer equipment	10	8000	12	85,500
Purchase new factory equipment	17	63,000	12	148,500
Install new office equipment	13	1000	13	149,500
Fix move date	3	0	14	149,500
Install new factory equipment	18	2000	14	151,500
Complete handover	4	500	15	152,000
Move office	15	1000	15	153,000
Move factory	20	3000	15	156,000
Disband project team	5	500	16	156,500
Total = SUM (ABOVE)		**156,500**		

Table 9: Lombard's project baseline costs

Figure 22 shows how the cost of the Lombard project rises week by week, using the cumulative baseline costs information contained in Table 9. As you can see, the cumulative baseline costs form an 'S curve'. This is the expected shape for most projects, in the early stages of the project spending is usually slow, once the project gets underway spending accelerates only to slow down again as the finishing touches are made.

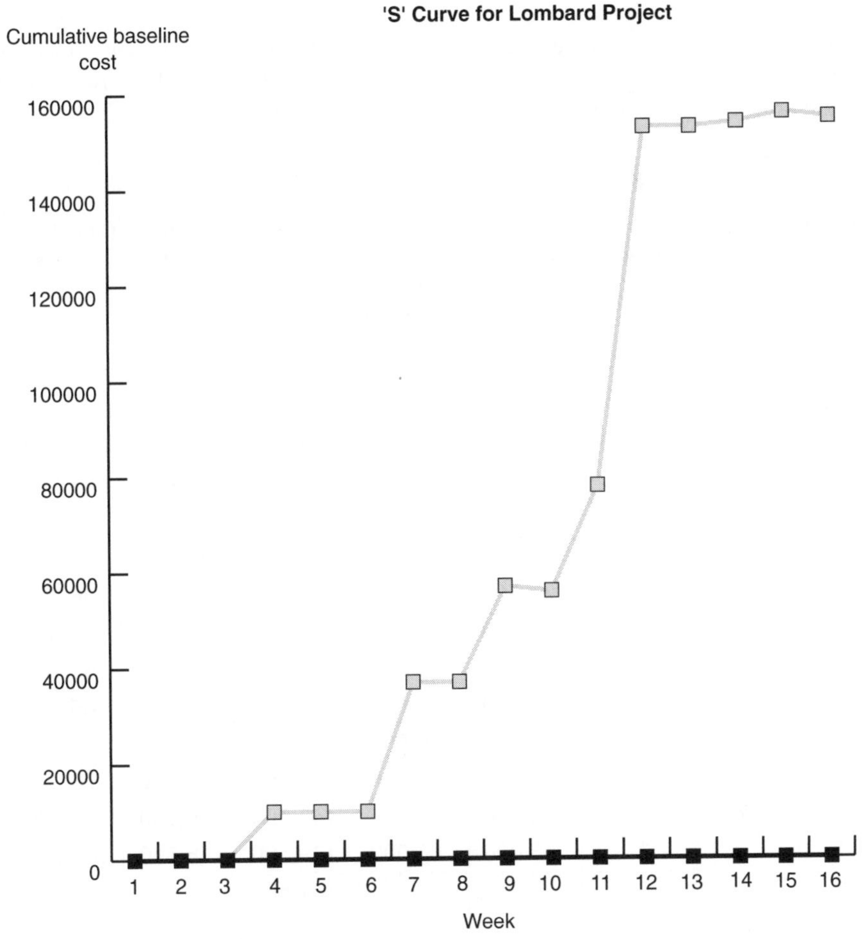

Figure 22: 'S' curve for the Lombard project

Table 10 reports the financial situation of the Lombard project in week 13. It shows:

- the activities that are planned to be completed each week (column A)
- the activities that were actually completed (column B)
- the baseline cost of the activities that were actually completed (column C) – this is the earned value

- the actual cost of the activities completed so far (column D)
- the cumulative baseline cost (column E), this is what we expected to have spent by a particular week and is the same information as contained in Table 9
- the cumulative earned value (column F)
- the cumulative actual cost (column G).

In week 13, the earned value is £1,000 below the baseline cost, so the project is running very slightly behind plan. The actual cost is £600 below the earned value so the project is turning out a little cheaper than expected.

	A	B	C	D	E	F	G
Week	**Planned activities**	**Activities completed**	**Baseline cost of completed activities (earned value)**	**Actual cost of completed activities**	**Cumulative costs**	**Cumulative costs**	**Cumulative costs**
1	1	1	500	400	500	500	400
2	2	2	500	300	1,000	1,000	700
3		11	1,000	1,100	1,000	2,000	1,800
4	6	6, 16	13,000	12,300	13,500	15,000	14,100
5	16		0	0	14,000	15,000	14,100
6		7	22,500	22,600	14,000	37,500	36,700
7	7	8	15,000	13,800	36,500	52,500	50,500
8	11	12	13,000	13,200	37,500	65,500	63,700
9	8	14	1,500	1,600	52,500	67,000	65,300
10		9	6,000	6,600	52,500	73,000	71,900
11	9, 12, 14	19	4,500	4,100	73,000	77,500	76,000
12	10, 17, 19	10	8,000	7,900	148,500	85,500	83,900
13	13	17	63,000	63,000	149,500	148,500	147,900
14	3,18				151,500		
15	4, 15, 20				156,000		
16	5				156,500		
Total	**=SUM (ABOVE)**		**148,500**	**146,900**			

Table 10: Lombard project costs at week 13

CASE STUDY

Estimating Lombard's final project costs

Elizabeth was asked to estimate the final cost of the project. She used the formula:

$$\text{forecast cost} = \frac{\text{total baseline cost} \times \text{actual cost (to date)}}{\text{earned value (to date)}}$$

In words, the forecast cost is what you expected to pay (the total baseline cost) multiplied by your efficiency. Efficiency is measured by how much each pound of earned value is actually costing; this is the actual cost divided by the earned value.

The original estimate of the total cost for the project was £156,500 (total baseline cost) and, by the end of week 13, the amount spent is £147,900 (actual cost) and the earned value is £148,500, So the forecast cost for the project is:

$$\frac{156{,}500 \times 147{,}900}{148{,}500} = £155{,}868$$

So, with luck, the project will come in about £600 under budget.

MANAGING RISKS

Because projects are generally one-off affairs, many activities will be carried out for the first time. There is, therefore, a good chance that things will not go to plan: materials will cost more than expected, tasks will take longer than expected, etc. An important task for the project manager is to look at each activity and to work out what could go wrong and plan what to do if it does go wrong. This is known as **risk management**. The risks of most projects originate from six sources:

- **the natural environment** – for example, it snows before the slates can be put on the roof of a house, soaking all the timbers
- **the stakeholders** – for example, the suppliers are late delivering critical materials or a project team leader is ineffective
- **technology** – for example, a hard disc crashes as data are being updated on a computer
- **the organisation** – for example, wage packets are late and the project team goes on strike
- **the law** – for example, a team member is injured and the project is stopped while the accident is investigated by the Health and Safety Executive
- **the public** – Friends of the Earth picket the project site, attracting the national press and holding up work.

Note, there are various ways of identifying the source of risk, see Turner (1993, pp. 235–259) and Reiss (1995, pp. 187–204).

ACTIVITY 14

Imagine you are planning to cycle from Land's End to John O'Groats. Identify six risks which could delay the project, one originating from each source. Also think how you would cope if the risk actually occurred.

There are obviously plenty of risks originating from each source, here are some of our thoughts:

- natural environment – it is very hot (need to take a water bottle), it is very cold weather (need to take some warm clothes), it snows (replan project for summer months)
- stakeholders – you are busy at work and the boss wants you to cancel your holiday (tell the boss about the trip well in advance)
- technology – the bike breaks down (take spares and tools)
- organisation – you fail to save up enough money to pay for bed and breakfast (be prepared to camp)
- law – you get prosecuted for poor cycling or having the wrong lights (read and follow the Highway Code)
- public – you fail to make it to John O'Groats with a consequent loss of face (don't tell anybody about the trip).

If these risks actually occur, they will impact on the time, cost, quality and scope of the project, the motivation of the project team and the image of the organisation. In projects, the risk can be measured using a formula. Risk is the:

likelihood of something untoward happening × consequences
of it happening × a 'perception' factor

The perception factor is important. Often, project stakeholders may consider a risk to be particularly great even though, in reality, the risk may be slight. For example, nuclear installations in the UK are made to withstand severe earthquakes. The risk of a severe earthquake in the UK is virtually nil, but the action is taken to provide reassurance to the public about the safety of the installation. For some events – particularly where safety is involved – it doesn't matter how low the risks are in reality, people will always want to err on the safe side.

It is very difficult to put accurate quantitative values on likelihood, consequences and perception. So a simple scoring system is usually used:

- likelihood is usually scored out of 3, with 3 for very likely to happen, 1 for unlikely

- consequences are measured out of 5, with 5 for very severe, 1 for very minor
- perception is given a score of 1 or 2, perception scores 2 if the people involved in the project are particularly worried about this risk, 1 if they are not.

The greatest risks will probably arise with activities on the critical path, as there is no slack time here. Risks are also high when an activity involves communication with a large number of different stakeholders. The identification of possible risks should be seen as a formal part of project management and it is often well worth paying experts for advice in this area. With all but the smallest of projects, there will be a large number of risks identified. It will probably be too time consuming to address them all. The usual policy is to rank the risks and then address the worst 20 per cent.

There are four basic types of action that can be taken to 'cover' the high risks (Turner, 1993, pp. 251–255):

- **avoidance** – work around the risk so, for example, rather than risk the problems of snow in winter, schedule the work to take place in spring
- **deflection** – let another party take the risk, so avoid the costs arising from the theft of a key piece of plant by taking out of insurance
- **reduction** – reduce the risk by using more or better resources, for example reduce the likelihood of a component breaking by using a higher specification material
- **contingency** – plan an alternative course of action to be taken should the risk occur, for example in the event of computer failure arrange for an alternative machine to be used.

The size of a risk changes throughout the life of the project, so risks should be regularly reassessed. Take, for example, a risk that relates to the weather; as weather forecasts are more accurate in the short term, we can be more certain of the action to be taken as the time nears to carry out the activity.

It is an almost golden rule that the sooner the risk is addressed, the easier and cheaper it will be to handle. It is usually a lot easier to get extra equipment, say, if you have plenty of time to arrange it rather than having to do it at the last moment. So identifying, measuring and planning for risks is a task which should be addressed in the project planning phase and repeated regularly until the project is complete.

At Lombard, for example, Elizabeth listed the 20 milestone activities. For each of these milestones, she identified what she considered to be the main risk. Table 11 shows the likelihood score, the consequences, the perception and the risk value for each milestone activity.

Activity	Risk	Likelihood	Consequence	Perception	Risk Value
Produce project plan	Fail to understand the objectives	1	5	1	5
Present plan	Fail to get backing for plan	1	5	2	10
Identify office requirements	Miss a key requirement	1	4	1	4
Clear site	Knock down a supporting wall	1	4	1	4
Identify factory requirements	Fail to allow enough space for storage	2	3	1	6
Make structural changes	Sub contractors take longer than expected	2	4	1	8
Purchase new office equipment	Requirements exceed baseline (planned) costs	2	3	1	6
Install services	Delay laying water pipes	1	2	1	2
Get ahead on office workload	High orders stops office from getting ahead	2	4	1	8
Get ahead on factory workload	As office	2	5	2	20
Install security	Security system fails to work	1	4	2	8
Install computer	Computer delivered late	1	3	1	3
Install new office equipment	Equipment comes in the wrong colour	1	1	2	2
Purchase new factory equipment	Equipment costs more than expected	1	4	1	4
Complete handover	Managers not happy with small details	1	4	2	8
Install new factory equipment	Unable to get equipment through factory door	1	3	1	3
Move office	Telephone system fails to work	1	4	2	8
Move factory	Key piece of equipment falls off removal lorry	1	4	2	8

Table 11: Lombard's project risks

REVIEW ACTIVITY 2

Note down what action would you take to cover the risks identified in Table 11.

Summary

In this section, we looked at some techniques for project management illustrated by the situation at Lombard. These techniques are useful in the implementation of the business plan and business strategies in general. They are also relevant in other functions, particularly operations and logistics. Throughout, in discussing these very practical approaches, we have generally ignored one crucial factor in implementation, which is the people. However, project management does give a starting point for many of the practical planning considerations in organisational strategy and change.

Unit Review Activity

In Section 1, you created a business plan for the Playlight project. Assume that you have been successful in getting funding from the bank. You now want to plan in some detail the launch of the business. You have identified these major activities (with the time necessary to complete each activity).

First, premises:

- produce detailed plan of factory and offices (2 weeks)
- make structural changes and decorate (5 weeks)
- install security system (2 weeks)
- install telephone and fax (1 week).

Second, sales and administration functions:

- recruit and train staff (6 weeks)
- set up office and equipment (8 weeks)
- design and produce sales literature (5 weeks)
- start selling.

Third, factory:

- recruit and train staff (4 weeks)
- set up factory and equipment (10 weeks)
- start production.
- Develop a project plan. You will need to do this in stages. Prepare:
  - a project definition with a purpose and objective statement, scope and priorities
  - a work breakdown structure
  - a milestone chart
  - a precedence chart
  - an activity chart
  - an assessment of the risks
  - a table of possible risk reduction activities.

You will need to use your imagination in this activity, so there is not going to be a right answer. Make sure you don't try to carry out the activities; for example, don't produce a plan of the factory and offices. You are only trying to plan the management of the work, when it should be done and by whom. And don't be too frightened by the apparent complexity of this activity, you have covered all these issues already with Lombard, and have the necessary frameworks for all the tables and charts that you will need. Don't try to be too creative, just follow the outlines that you used in Lombard.

Unit Summary

In this unit, we have examined the value of the business planning process and identified when it is important. Using the Lombard case study, we have identified the main features of a business plan and drawn up a plan for Playlight.

Using the Lombard case study and others, we have shown how to produce the main planning documents used in project management and what underlies the basic information in these documents. The techniques we have introduced are also used in other functions for scheduling, progress chasing and work design. We have shown how the project manager can use the Gantt chart for monitoring the progress of the project. We examined the costs of projects and looked at the use of cumulative cost curves in monitoring project progress and cost performance. Finally, we looked at the sources of risks in projects and showed how to identify and manage risks.

References

Crowner, R P (1991) *Developing a Strategic Business Plan with Cases: An Entrepreneuer's Advantage*, Irwin

Dilworth, J B (1996) *Operations Management*, McGraw-Hill

Duhig Berry, *An introduction to PRINCE*

Hyypia, E (1992) *Crafting the Successful Business Plan*, Prentice Hall

Meredith, J R and Mantel, S J (1995) *Project Management: A Managerial Approach*, John Wiley & Sons

NatWest Bank (1995) *New Technologies Appraisals Service for Small Businesses*

Reiss, G (1995) *Project Management Demystified*, E & F Spon

Turner, J R (1993) *The Handbook of Project-Based Management*, McGraw-Hill

Recommended Reading

Harrison, F L (1995) *Advanced Project Management*, Gower

Kleim, R L and Ludkin, I S (1994) *The People Side of Project Management*, Gower

Lock, D (1996) *Project Management*, Gower

Meredith, J R and Mantel, S J (1995) *Project Management: A Managerial Approach*, John Wiley & Sons

Naylor, J (1996) *Operations Management*, Pitman

Turner, J R (1993) *The Handbook of Project-Based Management*, McGraw-Hill

Also look at *Managing product creation: a management overview* (1991). Prepared for the Department of Trade and Industry by the Design Council, this free booklet examines the issues surrounding the product creation process and gives many good examples and handy tips. Note also that free copies of *An introduction to PRINCE* are available from Duhig Berry Ltd, Templars House, Templars Way, Chandlers Ford, Eastleigh SO5 5ZU.

Answers to Review Activities

Review Activity 1

Company: Playlight Limited
12 Eastern Road
Newbridges
WE3 6TY

Tel: 01382 556
Fax: 01382 557

Contact: Jim Borthwick
Joint Managing Director

Playlight is a newly formed business, manufacturing and marketing table lamps to the independent retail sector. Set up initially as a co-operative, trading during the first 18 months of business generated profits of £50,000. The financial projections show that profit margins will be maintained and annual growth of 20 per cent will be possible over the next five years.

In order to achieve the projected profit and growth, Playlight needs to refurbish and re-equip its offices and factory and to produce a new range of sales literature.

The breakdown of the costs of this work is as follows:

Refurbishment of premises	£25,000
Re-equipment of offices	£36,000
Re-equipment of factory	£40,000
Sales literature	£5,000
Total	£100,000

Preliminary contracts have already been drawn up for the premises, and the refurbishment work will be carried out over a period of six months, at which point production and selling will commence.

The refurbishment and sales literature is to be financed by a local authority grant of £50,000 (this has already been agreed) and a bank loan of £50,000. The anticipated pay back period for the bank loan is five years.

Review Activity 2

With most of the risks outlined in Table 11, the solution is fairly simple and, with a little preparation, the risk can be managed. For example, to minimise the risk of equipment being damaged during the 'move factory' activity, it should be possible to find another company which uses the same equipment that in the event of a mishap would allow you to use its equipment until a replacement could be obtained. Organise this in advance and the risk is covered.

Answer to Unit Review Activity

Tables 12, 13, 14, 15 and 16 and Figures 23, 24 and 25 provide a possible solution to this activity.

Project purpose	To set up successful business providing employment for the directors and local people.
Project objective	Operational factory, sales and administration functions.
Project Scope	
To be achieved	Operational factory, sales and administration functions with: ● fully working equipment ● staff recruited and trained ● systems implemented.
The benefits	Cost-effective manufacturing and profitable product sales.
The measure	Performance measures: ● costs, margins and turnover ● product and service quality.
To be delivered	A fully operational company.
Monitoring and communication	Weekly progress meetings will be held with the project team, and a weekly progress sheet will be circulated. Monthly project meetings will be held with the project board.
Assumptions	It is assumed that there will be a continuing market for Playlight's products.
Constraints and risks	The major constraints are time and cost. A limit of six months has been placed on the project as well as a maximum cost of £100,000. The major risks are that the market for Playlight shrinks and that it runs out of money before the company gets going.
Outside scope of project	The ongoing management of the company.
Priorities	Most important is cost, followed by quality, then time and scope.

Table 12: Project definition of the Playlight project

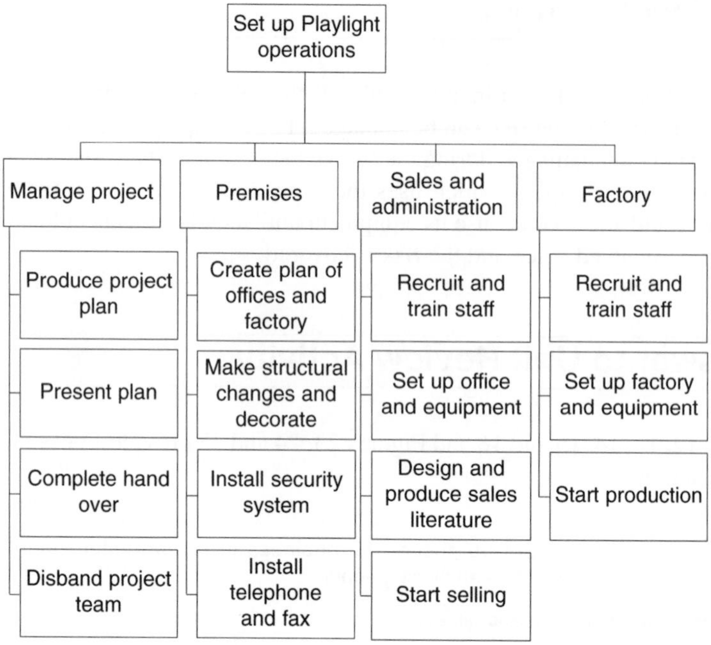

Figure 23: Stage 1 (action) work breakdown structure for the Playlight project

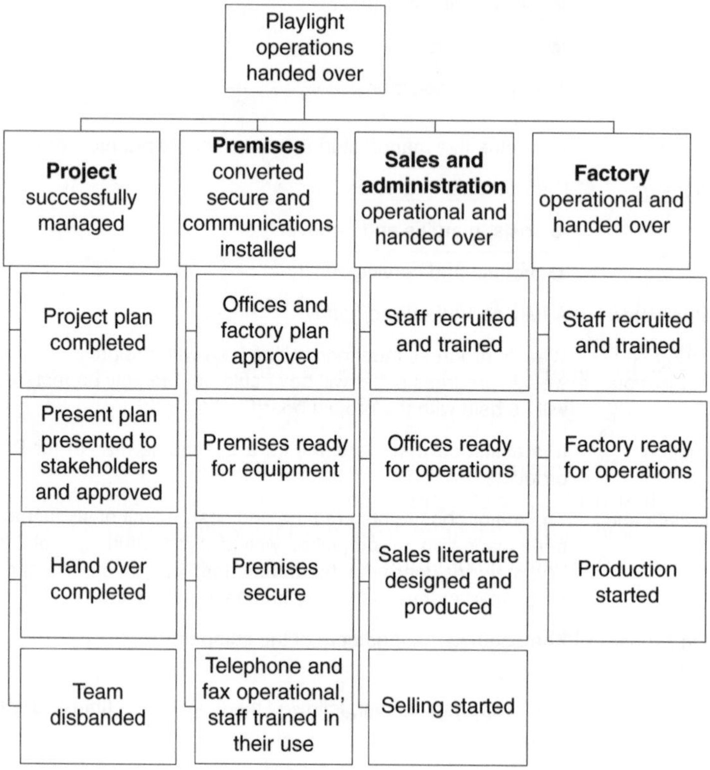

Figure 24: Stage 2 (results) work breakdown structure for the Playlight project

Major areas				Milestones
Project	**Premises**	**Sales administration**	**Factory**	
O				Project plan completed
O				Plan presented to key stakeholders and approved
	O			Offices and factory plan approved by project board
O	O			Structural changes and decorating complete and premises ready for equipment
	O			Security system installed and premises secure
	O			Telephone and fax installed and staff trained in their use
			O	Office staff recruited and trained
			O	Factory staff recruited and trained
			O	Factory operational and signed off
		O		Offices ready for operations and signed off
		O		Sales literature designed and produced
O				Factory and offices handed over to operational management
			O	Production started
		O		Selling started
O				Project team disbanded

Table 13: Milestone plan for the Playlight project

Activity	**Activity number**	**Preceding activities**	**Time taken (weeks)**
Produce project plan	1		1
Present plan to key stakeholders	2	1	1
Produce factory and office plan	3	2	2
Make structural changes to premises and decorate	4	3	5
Install security system	5	4	2
Install telephone and fax	6	4	1
Recruit and train sales and office staff	7	3	6
Recruit and train factory staff	8	3	4
Set up factory and equipment	9	5	10
Set up offices and equipment	10	5,6	8
Design and produce sales literature	11	2	5
Hand over factory and offices	12	9, 10	1
Start production	13	8, 12	1
Start selling	14	7, 11, 13	1
Disband project team	15	14	1

Table 14: Precedence chart for Playlight project

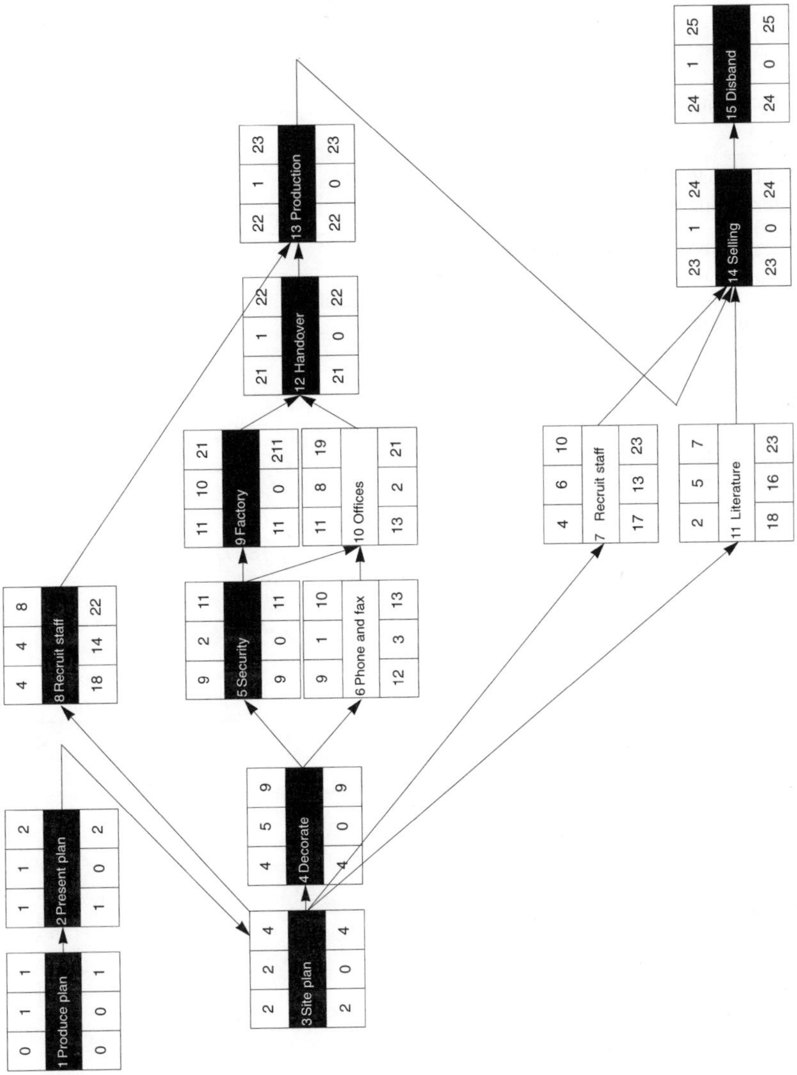

Figure 25: Completed activity chart for the Playlight project

Activity	Risk	Likelihood A (max = 3)	Consequence B (max = 5)	Perception C (max = 2)	Risk value A x B x C (max = 30)
Produce project plan	Fail to include all the tasks	1	4	1	4
Present plan to key stakeholders	Fail to gain approval	1	5	2	10
Produce factory and office plan	Fail to include some key details	2	4	2	16
Make structural changes to premises and decorate	Builders take longer than planned	2	3	2	12
Install security system	Security system fails to operate effectively	1	2	1	2
Install telephone and fax	Installation delayed	1	3	1	3
Recruit and train sales and office staff	Some of the recruits prove unsuitable	2	4	1	8
Recruit and train factory staff	Unable to recruit sufficient staff	1	4	1	4
Set-up factory and equipment	Some of the equipment fails to operate	2	4	2	16
Set up offices and equipment	Computer system delayed	1	4	2	8
Design and produce sales literature	Mistakes found in finished literature	1	4	2	8
Hand over factory and offices	Hand over delayed at last minute	1	4	2	8
Start production	Production delayed	1	4	1	4
Start selling	Selling delayed	1	4	1	4
Disband project team	Team unhappy with way project has been managed	1	2	2	4

Table 15: Project risks

The risks which score more than four have been included in Table 16.

Activity	Risk	Risk value	Action required to reduce risk
Present plan to key stakeholders	Fail to gain approval	10	Consult widely with key stakeholders during preparation of plan
Produce factory and office plan	Fail to include some key details	16	Consult widely during preparation of plan. Visit other companies for ideas
Make structural changes to premises and decorate	Builders take longer than planned	12	Include a late finish penalty clause in contract with builder
Recruit and train sales and office staff	Some of the recruits prove unsuitable	8	Identify an employment agency which could provide suitable temporary staff
Set factory and equipment	Some of the equipment fails to operate	16	Engage some temporary maintenance engineers to be present during this activity
Set up offices and equipment	Computer system delayed	8	Develop alternative manual systems to be used until computer system ready
Design and produce sales literature	Mistakes found in finished literature	8	Ask all staff to check the proofs
Hand over factory and offices	Hand over delayed at last minute	8	Warn people of a possible delay a few days in advance

Table 16: Risks management